Shyness

Perspectives on Research and Treatment

Edited by

Warren H. Jones
University of Tulsa
Tulsa, Oklahoma

Jonathan M. Cheek
Wellesley College
Wellesley, Massachusetts

and

Stephen R. Briggs
University of Tulsa
Tulsa, Oklahoma

PLENUM PRESS • NEW YORK AND LONDON

Library of Congress Cataloging in Publication Data

Main entry under title:

Shyness: perspectives on research and treatment.

(Emotions, personality, and psychotherapy)
Includes bibliographies and index.
1. Bashfulness. I. Jones, Warren H. II. Cheek, Jonathan M. III. Briggs, Stephen R. IV.
Series. [DNLM: 1. Anxiety—psychology. 2. Emotions. 3. Interpersonal Relations. 4. Per-
sonality. 5. Social Behavior. BF 575.B3 S562]
BF575.B3S58   1985   155.2′32   85-25889
ISBN 0-306-42033-3

© 1986 Plenum Press, New York
A Division of Plenum Publishing Corporation
233 Spring Street, New York, N.Y. 10013

Printed in the United States of America

Contributors

Lynn Alden, *Department of Psychology, University of British Columbia, Vancouver, British Columbia, Canada*

Robert M. Arkin, *Department of Psychology, University of Missouri at Columbia, Columbia, Missouri*

Jens Asendorpf, *Max-Planck-Institute for Psychological Research, Munich, Federal Republic of Germany*

Ann H. Baumgardner, *Department of Psychology, Virginia Polytechnic Institute and State University, Blacksburg, Virginia*

Michael J. Beatty, *Department of Speech Communication, West Virginia University, Morgantown, West Virginia*

Stephen R. Briggs, *Department of Psychology, University of Tulsa, Tulsa, Oklahoma*

Arnold H. Buss, *Department of Psychology, University of Texas at Austin, Austin, Texas*

Robin Cappe, *Department of Psychology, University of British Columbia, Vancouver, British Columbia, Canada*

Bruce N. Carpenter, *Department of Psychology, University of Tulsa, Tulsa, Oklahoma*

Andrea M. Carpentieri, *Department of Psychology, University of Michigan, Ann Arbor, Michigan*

Charles S. Carver, *Department of Psychology, University of Miami, Coral Gables, Florida*

Jonathan M. Cheek, *Department of Psychology, Wellesley College, Wellesley, Massachusetts*

W. Ray Crozier, *School of Psychology, Lancashire Polytechnic, Preston, England*

Carolyn E. Cutrona, *Department of Psychology, University of Iowa, Iowa City, Iowa*

Denise Daniels, *Institute for Behavioral Genetics, University of Colorado, Boulder, Colorado*

Russell G. Geen, *Department of Psychology, University of Missouri at Columbia, Columbia, Missouri*

Carol R. Glass, *Department of Psychology, Catholic University, Washington, DC*

Harrison G. Gough, *Institute of Personality Assessment and Research, University of California, Berkeley, California*

Frances M. Haemmerlie, *Department of Psychology, University of Missouri at Rolla, Rolla, Missouri*

Robert O. Hansson, *Department of Psychology, University of Tulsa, Tulsa, Oklahoma*

Marion C. Hyson, *Department of Individual and Family Studies, University of Delaware, Newark, Delaware*

Carroll E. Izard, *Department of Psychology, University of Delaware, Newark, Delaware*

Warren H. Jones, *Department of Psychology, University of Tulsa, Tulsa, Oklahoma*

v

Jerome Kagan, *Department of Psychology and Social Relations, Harvard University, Cambridge, Massachusetts*

Elissa Koff, *Department of Psychology, Wellesley College, Wellesley, Massachusetts*

Elizabeth A. Lake, *Department of Psychology, University of Missouri at Columbia, Columbia, Missouri*

Mark R. Leary, *Department of Psychology, Wake Forest University, Winston-Salem, North Carolina*

James C. McCroskey, *Department of Speech Communication, West Virginia University, Morgantown, West Virginia*

Rowland S. Miller, *Department of Psychology, Sam Houston State University, Huntsville, Texas*

Robert L. Montgomery, *Department of Psychology, University of Missouri at Rolla, Rolla, Missouri*

Gerald M. Phillips, *Department of Speech Communication, Pennsylvania State University, University Park, Pennsylvania*

Paul A. Pilkonis, *Department of Psychiatry, University of Pittsburgh School of Medicine, Pittsburgh, Pennsylvania*

Robert Plomin, *Institute for Behavioral Genetics, University of Colorado, Boulder, Colorado*

J. Steven Reznick, *Department of Psychology and Social Relations, Harvard University, Cambridge, Massachusetts*

Jill Rierdan, *Department of Psychology, Wellesley College, Wellesley, Massachusetts*

Dan Russell, *Graduate Program in Hospital and Health Administration, College of Medicine, University of Iowa, Iowa City, Iowa*

Barbara R. Sarason, *Department of Psychology, University of Washington, Seattle, Washington*

Irwin G. Sarason, *Department of Psychology, University of Washington, Seattle, Washington*

Michael F. Scheier, *Department of Psychology, Carnegie-Mellon University, Pittsburgh, Pennsylvania*

Cheryl A. Shea, *Department of Psychology, Catholic University, Washington, DC*

Thomas G. Smith, *late of the Department of Behavioral Statistics, Baylor University, Waco, Texas*

Timothy W. Smith, *Department of Psychology, University of Utah, Salt Lake City, Utah*

C. R. Snyder, *Department of Psychology, University of Kansas, Lawrence, Kansas*

Avril Thorne, *Department of Psychology, Wellesley College, Wellesley, Massachusetts*

Philip G. Zimbardo, *Department of Psychology, Stanford University, Stanford, California*

Preface

This volume is about shyness: its definitions and conceptualization as a psychological construct, research on its causes and consequences, methods for measuring shyness, strategies for alleviating the unpleasant experiences associated with shyness, and its connection to other forms of social anxiety and inhibition. The principal goal in putting the book together was to provide a resource for psychologists from several subdisciplines, most notably social, personality, clinical, and developmental psychology, in addition to social scientists from other disciplines. We do not assume that these chapters, considered collectively or individually, provide answers to every conceivable issue with respect to shyness. Rather, we hope that the book will serve to integrate what is known about shyness on the basis of current research and theorizing and to provide both directions and impetus for continued research, theoretical evolution, and improved techniques of assessment and intervention.

But one might ask, why another book on shyness? In particular, why a book at this time given the recent appearance of other books on the topic and in view of the extensive literature on related topics such as introversion and anxiety—topics that would seem to compete with shyness for the same conceptual space? Our decision to edit this volume was prompted by several considerations, some practical, others more substantive in nature.

On the practical side, no single volume contains the scope and variety of perspectives that we have included. For example, in the chapters that follow, shyness is treated as a personality trait, a situational variable, an emotional state, a self-handicapping strategy, a style of self-presentation, and a personal problem in need of remediation. Furthermore, shyness is examined in terms of cognitive, physiological, genetic, developmental, and experiential processes. Most previous books have been based on a single theoretical viewpoint drawing on a particular program of studies, whereas this volume describes numerous models and data sources. A second practical consideration that led to the initiation of this volume was the recent growth of the research literature on shyness and the corresponding need to summarize major empirical trends and issues in need of additional research.

Perhaps more important were reasons based on conceptual and empirical considerations. For example, although the interplay between the individual and the social context has been a major interest for psychology from the inception of the discipline, never before has this nexus received such widespread attention as that evidenced by the recent growth of research into such topics as social support, loneliness, public self-consciousness, interpersonal attraction, social anxiety, personal relationships, and so on. In our judgment, these trends in the collective research agenda represent more than just the periodic ebb and flow of popular topics of research. Instead, they represent the recognition, or more precisely, the rediscovery of the most fundamental and undeniable features of human nature: human beings are by nature social animals and human existence is both taken up with and calibrated by interpersonal exchanges and emotional commitments to other people. The literature on shyness is particularly interesting in this regard, as it provides a window through which to examine the reciprocal influence of internal subjective experience and external social consensus.

Moreover, the evidence has become increasingly strong that shyness is neither synonymous with nor subsumed by the conceptual terms with which it is associated (e.g., introversion, speech anxiety, evaluation apprehension, low sociability, etc.). Also, available evidence has begun to suggest that shyness is not just another trait term elevated to the status of a construct by virtue of the existence of a widely used scale and scores of willing researchers eager to pick up the shyness banner. On the contrary, although shyness has proven to be a fruitful if unlikely topic of research, several of the authors of these chapters confess to having "stumbled into it" while exploring some other psychological issue, such as interpersonal problems or the structure of personality. Authors have remarked at being surprised to have learned about the existence of a shyness literature beyond their own immediate interests. Nevertheless, research demonstrates that shyness is both common and problematic, that it is implicated in a variety of cognitive, affective, behavioral and physiological processes, and that it is a useful and possibly necessary ingredient in the recipe for models of human experience at the molar level of analysis.

One final point regarding our motives and intentions. Shyness is rich in what might be called phenomenological validity; that is, you do not have to be a psychologist to know what it means, to use the term in conversation, or to think that it is important. It is not often the case that the social scientist, the mental health practitioner, and the lay person can understand one another, much less engage in a useful exchange of ideas and opinions. Shyness is an exception in this regard and we see nothing wrong in that. In fact, our experience has been that shyness is of enormous interest to practitioners, educators, teenagers, college students, parents, journalists, and the general public. Thus we hope that in addition to its scientific impact, others would find the volume interesting and useful as well.

It is customary to acknowledge indebtedness to many other people in the pursuit of a project of this magnitude and complexity. We are grateful to Lucy Mylar, Vicki Booth, Melina Morton, and Debra Stephens for their typing and clerical assistance and to Robin Snider for her help with references and other editoral details. We very much appreciate the promptness as well as the good-natured cooperation of the many authors in this volume without whose ideas and research this book would have been impossible and unnecessary. We are also thankful for the patience of our families, friends, and colleagues. We are particularly grateful to Eliot Werner, our editor at Plenum, and to Cal Izard and Jerome Singer (Series Editors) for their encouragement, support, and advice.

Regrettably, we must also acknowledge the untimely death of our friend and former colleague Thomas G. Smith of Baylor University, who died during the preparation of this volume. It is fitting, therefore, that we dedicate this book to his memory.

Contents

1

Introduction

Stephen R. Briggs, Jonathan M. Cheek, and Warren H. Jones

We are by nature social animals and virtually everything we do, say, and think about is either focused directly on our social interactions and relationships or is shaped profoundly by them. Our lives are played out in an arena of social affairs; we are confronted with a continuing flow of ongoing and one-time-only interactions—some intimate and some casual, some pleasant and some distasteful, some routine and some unexpected—but all social nonetheless. Consequently, personal attributes or experiences that either facilitate or hinder interpersonal functioning stand out as conspicuous features of our social lives and are likely to be noticed. Shyness is a case in point. Most everyone knows what it means to experience shyness and almost everyone has acted or felt shy at one time or another in their lives or has used the label to describe the feelings or actions of others. Widespread usage of the word *shyness* in ordinary language is indicative of its importance as a way of describing, interpreting, and explaining our actions and the actions of others; it is also indicative of its utility as a psychological construct.

The purposes of this volume are as follows: (a) to summarize what is known about the phenomenon of shyness, including information from a number of new studies and ongoing projects; (b) to present recently developed models and theories of shyness; and (c) to point to the relevant questions and issues that are most in need of additional research. We begin our introductory chapter with a brief look at the development of interest in shyness among social scientists and mental health practitioners. Next, we survey the recent—but rapidly growing—body of literature on shyness. Finally, we will discuss the organization of this volume.

Ironically, issues regarding the origins, consequences, and treatment of shyness have gained substantial research attention only recently. Perhaps shyness, like the common cold in medicine, has been neglected over the years

---

STEPHEN R. BRIGGS • Department of Psychology, University of Tulsa, Tulsa, OK 74104. JONATHAN M. CHEEK • Department of Psychology, Wellesley College, Wellesley, MA 02181. WARREN H. JONES • Department of Psychology, University of Tulsa, Tulsa, OK 74104.

because it lacks the exotic symptomatology and gross pathology associated with psychological conditions that have been studied more extensively (e.g., schizophrenia). Perhaps shyness—like the shy person—is easy to ignore because its manifestations are quiet and unobtrusive. Perhaps also, in part, shyness has been subsumed by larger, more complex constructs, such as introversion and neuroticism. Despite this apparent neglect, the study of shyness can be traced back almost a century to its origins in psychiatry.

DEVELOPMENT OF SHYNESS RESEARCH

The development of shyness research can be described generally in terms of three phases that overlap somewhat in time but that are conceptually and methodologically distinct. First, there was what we call the descriptive phase, in which shyness was analyzed on the basis of casual and clinical observation. As is often the case with psychosocial problems, the earliest accounts originated from medical and psychological practitioners. In one such example, Harry Campbell, a British physician, delivered a detailed report on "morbid shyness" to the British Medical Society in 1896. His analysis was remarkably prescient in that it considered as causes and consequences a number of factors that are similarly treated in the chapters of this volume, including the influence of heredity, the excessive self-consciousness of the shy person, and the ways in which shyness can disrupt social encounters and impair the development of relationships. Campbell described the shy person as follows:

> His soul is full of love and longing, but the world knows it not; the iron mask of shyness is riveted before his face, and the man beneath is never seen. Genial words and greetings are ever rising to his lips, but they die away in unheard whispers before the steel clamps. (p. 807)

Campbell also noted inconsistencies in the way shyness is expressed. For instance, the shy person usually seems to have a meek, unpretentious, diffident demeanor, but sometimes may also come across as ill-tempered, irascible, and suspicious. Similarly, the shy individual often seems to be particularly compliant and easily persuaded, yet views that the same individual puts forward with quiet modesty sometimes turn out to be deeply rooted and unchangeable. Furthermore, although shy individuals are often quiet, shyness also seems occasionally to lead, in Campbell's account, to excessive and nervous conversation. Contradictory patterns of behavior were also described in Litwinski's (1950) discussion of active versus passive forms of shyness. Thus, as was recognized very early, shyness may not manifest itself in the intuitively obvious ways that one would expect.

Another descriptive approach to understanding shyness is exemplified by psychoanalytic writers such as Hampton (1927) and Lewinsky (1941). Lewinsky, for instance, concluded that shyness represents unconsciously blocked aggression among narcissistic and rigid personality types. A more recent interpretation of neurotic shyness in the psychoanalytic tradition has been offerred by Kaplan (1972).

The second phase in the study of shyness might be called simply its popularization. In recent years, long-term relationships have become more problematic as once secure social bonds are routinely broken by geographic mobility, high divorce rates, and the dissolution of family support groups. More than ever, individuals are required to initiate and nurture new friendships and alliances on their own, outside of traditional group and family ties, and here shyness seems to play an important role. Perhaps because of these trends, in the middle and late 1970s, several popular books on shyness were written for the general public. Some were written by academics and contained empirical evidence regarding the nature of prevalence of shyness; others took a more speculative and commonsensical approach. All, however, attempted to explain shyness to the layperson, and most important, to offer advice and techniques for overcoming shyness to shy persons and parents with shy children.

By far the best known, most widely read, and most often cited book of this type is Zimbardo's *Shyness: What It Is and What To Do about It* (1977). Zimbardo describes the symptoms of shyness, its origins and consequences, the self-image problems with which it is related, the use of the term as a label, and the societal causes of shyness. Similar to earlier writers, he uses case histories, interview material, and quotations to illustrate and underscore his main points: that shyness is a serious personal liability of epidemic proportions caused by a highly competitive society but which, nevertheless can be alleviated. In addition, Zimbardo presents data using the Stanford Shyness Survey regarding the extent of shyness self-labeling among young adults. For example, he reports that 42% of the American college students sampled described themselves as shy and that the proportion increased to 73% when respondents were asked about previous as well as current shyness. Zimbardo concludes further that shyness is a universal experience with a variety of unpleasant and dysfunctional consequences (e.g., preoccupation with one's own reactions, cognitive and communicative interference, negative emotions, interpersonal inhibition, and conformity). On the other hand, Zimbardo was among the first to argue that not all shy people are unhappy social misfits and that shyness is sometimes viewed as an endearing quality by others.

Zimbardo has authored two subsequent books on shyness with Shirley Radl, *The Shy Child* (1981) and *The Shyness Workbook* (1983). Other popular books on shyness include Girodo's *Shy? You Don't Have To Be* (1978), *Help for Shy People and Anyone Else Who Ever Felt Ill at Ease on Entering a Room Full of Strangers* (Phillips, 1981), *Overcoming Shyness* (Powell, 1979), *Conquer Shyness* (Teear, 1977) and *Shy Person's Guide to a Happier Love Life* (Weber & Miller, 1979).

The third phase in the study of shyness is distinguished by more traditional empirical analyses of the construct and has been marked by an increase in the number of reports published in research journals. During the last decade, shyness was defined more carefully and in ways that lend themselves to empirical verification. Thus, the domain of shyness was conceptualized more clearly (e.g., Buss, 1980; Crozier, 1979; Harris, 1984; Leary, 1982; Schlenker & Leary, 1982) and its relationship to other constructs and theoretical models was explained (Asendorpf, 1984; Hansson, Jones & Carpenter, 1984; Schlenker & Leary, 1982).

New scale measures were developed, starting with Watson and Friend's questionnaire in 1969, and efforts were directed toward producing scales that were conceptually pure, behaviorally valid, and psychometrically sound (Cheek & Buss, 1981; Glass, Merluzzi, Biever, & Larsen, 1982; Jones & Russell, 1982; Leary, 1982, 1983; Maroldo, Eisenreich, & Hall, 1979; Patterson & Strauss, 1972). As we will discuss shortly, however, most research has examined the causes, correlates, and consequences of shyness among diverse groups of subjects.

In addition to these direct attempts to understand shyness, concurrently—and in many cases predating the current research on shyness as a separate construct—other research traditions have contributed to an interest in shyness. There has been work on shyness as a dimension of emotion—and as related to other emotions, such as shame—as is exemplified by the work of Izard (1972, 1977) and other emotion theorists (e.g., Lynd, 1958; Mosher & White, 1981; Tomkins, 1963). Similarly, much of the earliest empirical information regarding shyness came from various studies involving multifactorial personality inventories that include shyness as a dimension of personality. Examples here include the work of Guilford and Guilford (1936), Cattell (1946, 1973), and Comrey (1965). Interestingly, although much of this research confounded the measurement of shyness with other dimensions of personality, recent factor analytic studies strongly indicate that shyness is a fundamental component of the structure of personality regardless of the manifest content of scale items and the original purpose of the scale (Howarth, 1980).

Finally, it should also be noted that recent research on shyness has been stimulated by previous and ongoing investigations into related topics from several areas of psychology and other disciplines. A complete listing is beyond the scope of the present discussion, but it is clear that shyness research has benefited from studies in the related areas of introversion (e.g., Eysenck, 1956; Morris, 1979), assertiveness (e.g., Linehan, Goldfriend, & Goldfriend, 1979, McFall & Twentyman, 1973), minimal dating (Melnick, 1973), and social skill (Curran, 1977), as well as the variety of topics that fall under the general heading of social anxiety, such as shame, embarrassment, evaluation apprehension, and so on (e.g., Modigliani, 1971; Sarason, 1975). In short, the study of shyness has taken hold over the last decade. The domain has been fairly well charted, the boundaries drawn, and the issues identified.

SURVEY OF RESEARCH ON SHYNESS

Shyness may be described as excessive and nervous attention to the self in social settings resulting in timid and often inappropriate overt behaviors (e.g., silence) as well as emotional and cognitive distress (e.g., anxiety, poor self-regard, etc.). More specifically, Zimbardo and his colleagues (Zimbardo, Pilkonis, & Norwood, 1975; Zimbardo, this volume) found that self-identified shy persons report experiencing seven types of interpersonal problems: (1) problems in meeting people, making new friends, enjoying new and different experiences; (2) negative affective states such as anxiety, depression, and loneliness; (3) lack of assertiveness and difficulty in expressing opinions; (4) excessive reticence making it difficult for others to appreciate the shy person's true qualities and assets; (5) poor self-projection, including the tendency of others to stereotype the shy and reticent person as unfriendly, snobbish, disinterested in relating to others, etc.; (6) difficulties in communicating and thinking in the presence of others, particularly strangers and groups; and (7) excessive self-consciousness.

Theoretical Issues

These personal accounts clearly suggest that shyness is typically an important and disruptive condition, but questions remain with respect to the exact nature of shyness and thus how it should be conceptualized, examined, and, if necessary, treated. Several such theoretical issues have been the focus of recent publications on shyness.

Definition of Shyness. One issue of fundamental importance is illustrated by the disagreement regarding how shyness should be defined, particularly in relation to other forms of social anxiety. For example, Buss (1980) conceptualizes shyness as one form of social anxiety along with audience anxiety, embarrassment, and shame, with shyness and audience anxiety being most similar in terms of determinants and reactions. Other approaches define shyness as a global, unitary construct without regard to its relation to other forms of social anxiety (e.g., Jones & Russell, 1982). A related issue has to do with whether shyness is conceptualized as the basic unit of analysis, as is typically the case, versus dividing shyness into components or types. For example, Eysenck (1956) distinguished between two types of shyness: introverted shyness and neurotic shyness. The former refers to people who are low in sociability and prefer solitude but who are capable of effective interaction, whereas the latter denotes those who experience anxiety in interacting with others and who are inept at doing so even when they would like to or need to socialize.

Buss (1984; this volume) has also recently distinguished between what is called early developing or fearful shyness (i.e., shyness based on a genetic predisposition) and late developing or self-consciousness shyness associated with the transition through adolescence. By contrast, Leary (1982, 1984) has defined social anxiety generally in terms of its subjective, internal manifestations, thereby distinguishing it from any overt behavioral manifestations with which it may be associated.

Measurement. Alternative definitions and conceptualizations of shyness have also been expressed in varying strategies of measurement. Although shyness is most often assessed through some form of self-report, physiological and behavioral measures have also been used (e.g., Garcia-Coll, Kagan, & Reznick, 1984) as have ratings by others (Jones, Cavert, & Indart, 1983). Even among self-report measures, however, there has been considerable diversity. For example, the well-known studies of Zimbardo (1977) and his colleagues were based on a single-item, self-labeling measure of shyness. By contrast, several recent scales assessing shyness specifically or social anxiety more generally have also been developed. Of these, some measure shyness broadly conceived (e.g., Jones

& Russell, 1982) whereas others have been designed as more narrowly defined measures (e.g., Cheek & Buss, 1981), and yet others were constructed to measure putative components of shyness or social anxiety (Leary, 1983; Watson & Friend, 1969). Recent evidence (Briggs & Smith, this volume; Jones, Briggs, & Smith, 1985) strongly suggests that the various measures of shyness and social anxiety have remarkably similar psychometric properties and correlates, with the one exception of their ability to predict the behavioral characteristics of shyness.

State versus Trait. Shyness may be conceptualized as either an emotional response to certain social situations or as a relatively enduring personality disposition, and there is evidence to support the utility of both conceptualizations. As an emotional state, shyness is transitory, situation bound, and may be experienced from time to time by virtually anyone. For example, Izard and his colleagues (Izard & Hyson, this volume) have argued that the emotion of shyness, although disruptive, is nevertheless functional as it signals the potential for social loss. As a personality disposition, shyness influences behavior across situations and time (Briggs, 1985). Research has shown that shyness occupies an important position in the universe of trait-descriptive terms, and also that shyness or social anxiety is a major component of the pattern of responses to most multifactor personality inventories, often subsuming the largest proportion of the common variance in item responses (Howarth, 1980).

Stability of Shyness. An important issue that emerges from the conceptualization of shyness as a dimension of personality concerns its stability from one situation to the next and over time. Although this issue has not been extensively investigated, there is evidence of the stability of shyness across the life span. For example, one group of researchers reported on the psychological adjustment of 24 individuals who had been classified as shy and withdrawn children from 16 to 27 years earlier, finding substantial consistency in shyness (Morris, Soroker, & Burruss, 1954). In a more recent study involving over 800 Swedish school children, Backteman and Magnusson (1981) found considerable agreement between informed observers who rated children independently and three years apart. Also, there is preliminary evidence of situational stability in the experiences associated with shyness; shy persons apparently experience greater distress than do not shy persons regardless of the situation, although the situation appears to be associated with the overall level of distress reported (Jones & Russell, 1985; Russell, Cutrona, & Jones, this volume).

Research Topics

Researchers have begun to identify potential causes and consequences of shyness. Because a review of recent and ongoing research on shyness is one purpose of this volume, we will only briefly present the issues that have received the greatest attention. Also, some researchers treat shyness and social anxiety as synonymous. Consequently, where appropriate, we will also touch on the literature on social anxiety.

Development of Shyness. Several developmental issues have been addressed in recent research. For example, shyness appears to have a genetic component (Plomin & Rowe, 1979; Plomin & Daniels, this volume) and there is evidence also of an underlying physiological mechanism (Garcia-Coll, Kagan & Reznick, 1984; Kagan & Reznick, this volume). As indicated previously, shyness during childhood apparently predicts the experience of shyness in later life (Backteman & Magnusson, 1981; Morris *et al.*, 1955). Furthermore, measures of shyness are significant predictors of intellectual and social functioning among various age groups including, for example, children (Asendorpf, this volume; Lazarus, 1982; Ludwig & Lazarus, 1983), adolescents (Cheek, Carpentieri, Smith, Rierdan, & Koff, this volume), and the elderly (Hansson, this volume).

Affective and Cognitive Correlates. Shyness has been frequently linked to a variety of unpleasant and disruptive affective and cognitive dimensions. For example, shyness appears to be related to depression, hostility, neurosis, fear, communication apprehension, shame, alienation, and self-consciousness (e.g., Jones, Briggs, & Smith, 1985; Izard, 1972; Jones & Russell, 1982). Shyness is also inversely correlated with empathy (Davis, 1983). Several studies (e.g., Brodt & Zimbardo, 1981; Zimbardo, 1977) have found that the immediate experience of shyness is associated with physiological arousal (e.g., blushing, butterflies in the stomach, pounding heart, dry mouth, etc.), unpleasant thoughts (e.g., thoughts about escaping, how poorly one is doing in the situation, etc.), and excessive self-consciousness. On the other hand, despite these generally strong and consistent patterns of correlations, there is evidence that shyness is not synonymous with general anxiety or fearfulness. For example, studies indicate that shyness measures are significantly more strongly related to measures of social fears, such as meeting strangers, than nonsocial fears and phobias, such as those related to high places or sharp objects (Jones & Russell, 1982; Jones, Briggs, & Smith, 1985).

Several studies have examined the connections between shyness and attributional processes, finding, for example, that shy as compared to not shy persons are more likely to make self-protective, internal, and stable attributions for their social distress (e.g., Arkin, Appelman, & Berger, 1980; Girodo, Dotzenroth, & Stein, 1981). Other studies have examined the potential effectiveness of attributional therapies in alleviating some of the symptoms associated with shyness and related states (Brodt & Zimbardo, 1981; Hoffman & Teglasi, 1982; Slivken & Buss, 1984). Similarly, shyness and social anxiety appear to be associated with constricted cognitive control (Ludwig & Lazarus, 1983) and irrational beliefs (Gormally, Sipps, Edwin, Raphael, & Varvil-Weld, 1981).

Self-Attention and Self-Concept. A number of studies have compared shyness and measures of self-attention, such as public and private self-consciousness and self-monitoring (Franzoi, 1983; Jones & Briggs, 1984; see also Carver & Scheier, this volume). As predicted by Buss (1980), the correlations between public self-consciousness (i.e., the tendency to attend to oneself as a social object) and shyness are stronger and more consistent than the correlations between private self-consciousness (i.e., attention to one's mood, thoughts, etc.) and shyness. Shyness scores are only modestly related to total scores on the Self-Monitoring Scale, but this occurs because the factors that underlie the Self-Monitoring Scale are related to shyness in different directions, thereby suppressing any overall relationship (Briggs & Cheek, in press; Briggs, Cheek, & Buss, 1980). For example, in one study the correlation between shyness and total self-monitoring was not significant, whereas the correlation between shyness and the sum of the extraversion items of the Self-Monitoring Scale was significant but negative, and the correlation between shyness and the other directedness items was significant and positive (Jones & Briggs, 1984).

Shyness appears to be even more strongly related to negative self-evaluation and anxious self-preoccupation (Crozier, 1979; Jones & Briggs, 1984; Smith, Ingram, & Brehm, 1983) as well as to self-derogating judgments of one's own interpersonal performances (e.g., Clark & Arkowitz, 1975; Cacioppo, Glass, & Merluzzi, 1979). Similarly, global measures of self-esteem consistently correlate with shyness scores in excess of $-.50$ (Briggs, Snider, & Smith, 1983; Cheek & Buss, 1981; Jones & Russell, 1982), although this relationship is stronger when social as opposed to nonsocial aspects of the self are assessed (Cheek, 1982; Crozier, 1981).

Behavioral Correlates of Shyness. Previous research also suggests that shyness involves differences in actual conversational and nonverbal behaviors. In particular, shyness has been linked to less effective and less responsive conversational styles. For example, several researchers have reported that high shy as compared to low shy college students talk and smile less, give less eye contact, show fewer facial expressions, and have slower speech latencies in conversations with dyadic partners (Cheek & Buss, 1981; Daly, 1978; Mandel & Shrauger, 1980; Pilkonis, 1977). High as compared to low socially anxious persons also show differences in the use of utterances that express objective information (Leary, Johnson, & Knight, 1984). Moreover, shy persons are typically rated as less friendly, less assertive, less relaxed, less talented, less poised, and more shy in unstructured dyadic conversations and monologues (Cheek & Buss 1981; Jones *et al.*, 1983; Pilkonis, 1977; Jones & Carpenter, this volume). Not surprisingly then, shyness and social anxiety are related to both self-reported and objectively assessed indicators of social and interpersonal skill (Holford & Foddy, 1982).

Laboratory studies have demonstrated the implications of shyness and social anxiety for various social-psychological processes. For example, shyness and social anxiety have been associated with greater interpersonal distances (Carducci & Webber, 1979), conformity (Santee & Maslach, 1982), and reduced helping (McGovern, 1976). One group of researchers has suggested that shyness may be used also as a form of self-handicapping (Snyder, Smith, Augelli, & Ingram, 1985; Snyder & Smith, this volume).

Shyness and Relationships. Recently, a number of studies have investigated the consequences of shyness for social and intimate relationships. For example, among college students, shyness has been found to be inversely correlated with number of dating partners, number of friends, dating frequency, and dating satisfaction (e.g., Jones & Russell, 1982). In addition, shyness has been found to be related to more subjectively assessed indexes of relationships, such as measures of love and jealousy (e.g., Maroldo, 1982) and perceptions within marital couples (Gough & Thorne, this volume). One study that investigated shyness and interpersonal relationships found that the correlations were generally stronger for male as compared to female respondents, suggesting that the inhibitory effects of shyness on the development of relationships may be greater for men (Jones & Briggs, 1984). Another study found that social anxiety is related to various aspects of sexual behavior, including, for example, less sexual experience and fewer sexual partners, and greater apprehension about sex and sexual dysfunction (Leary & Dobbins, 1983).

Substantial correlations between shyness and loneliness have been reported by several investigators (e.g., Cheek & Busch, 1981; Jones, Freemon, & Goswick, 1981; Maroldo, 1981). It has also been found that shyness is most strongly related to loneliness regarding one's community relationships and friendships and less so for romantic and family relationships (Jones & Briggs, 1984). Similarly, studies have indicated modest—but significant—inverse correlations between shyness and quantitative measures of social support (e.g., number of persons in one's social network, network density, etc.) and qualitative measures of social support (e.g., satisfaction with the degree of support received). Typically, however, shyness is more strongly related to the qualitative than to the quantitative measures of social support (Jones, 1984).

Shyness Situations. Buss (1980) has argued that the situations leading to shyness may be categorized as involving (a) novelty (b) the presence of others, and (c) certain actions of others (e.g., excessive or insufficient attention). These speculations have received some empirical verification especially with respect to novelty and the presence of others (Jones & Russell, 1984; Russell *et al.*, this volume). Situations in which one is the focus of attention (e.g., giving a speech) and is among strangers have been found to be particularly powerful elicitors of shyness among both college students and elementary school children (Zimbardo, 1977; Zimbardo & Radl, 1981). Also Izard and his colleagues (Izard, 1972; Izard & Hyson, this volume) have found that situations that elicit shyness as opposed to other emotions also elicit higher tension and, paradoxically, higher pleasantness. In fact, the pleasantness associated with shyness situations is greater than that of any of the other negative emotions.

Treatment. Clinically oriented investigators have recently begun to introduce and evaluate treatment strategies designed to alleviate the problematic aspects of shyness (e.g., Kanter & Goldfried, 1979; Lazarus, 1976; Loxley, 1979; Pilkonis, Heape, & Klein, 1980). Although the treatment strategy deemed appropriate to shyness clearly depends on how individual researchers conceptualize shyness as a personal problem, most of the clinically relevant research has focused on behavioral and cognitive-behavioral approaches to teaching social skills (e.g., Alden & Cappe, this volume; Glass & Shea, this volume). Other researchers (e.g., Brodt & Zimbardo, 1981; Haemmerlie & Montgomery, 1982, this volume) have developed techniques that require inducing the shy person to attribute interpersonal anxiety to external distractors and effective performances to oneself. By contrast, Slivken and Buss (1984) conducted a partial replication of Brodt and Zimbardo's experiment with contradictory results.

Available evidence on shyness generally suggests, therefore, that it is a relatively common feature of personality and experience that is associated with a variety of unpleasant cognitive and affective responses to social stimuli, including negative self-evaluations, internal attributions for distress, constrained cognitive control, and anxiety. It would also appear that shyness involves certain behavioral inadequacies. Furthermore, these differences are detectable by observers and correctly labeled as shyness. On the other hand, consistent with the beliefs of many shy people, the reticence of shyness appears to elicit gratuitous attributions from others and specifically the assumption on the part of observers that shy people are disinterested in social interaction, which at any given moment may or may not be true. Consequently, shyness is associated with smaller social networks, fewer friends, and especially with dissatisfaction with one's available relationships. Predictably, situations that elicit shyness involve novelty and other people; surprisingly they are also associated with pleasantness, and social interest.

ORGANIZATION OF THE BOOK

As is often the case, previous research has raised a variety of questions regarding the causes, consequences, and treatment of shyness. The present volume organizes these questions into six parts as follows: (I) Issues in the study of shyness; (II) The development of shyness; (III) The experience of shyness: Personal aspects; (IV) The experience of shyness: Social aspects; (V) Related constructs; and (VI) Therapeutic interventions.

To begin, Part I includes a discussion of the Stanford Shyness Project, which stimulated much of the popular and research attention directed toward shyness, as well as several of the basic issues confronted in the study of shyness, such as how shyness should be defined and conceptualized, and the related questions of how shyness should be measured and the relative merits of available instruments and techniques. Part II examines shyness from a developmental perspective, focusing on genetic and physiological determinants along with experiential and developmental causes of shyness. This section also provides the perspective from which to compare variations in the experience of shyness at different stages in the developmental process including childhood, adolescence, and maturity. Although focused on other issues as well, subsequent chapters serve to fill out the developmental picture, particularly the essays in Parts III and IV.

Part III examines the correlates and consequences of shyness, largely from the point of view of the individual, that is, the personal processes with which shyness is associated, including shyness as a dimension of personality, a discrete emotion, a self-handicapping strategy, and as a consequence of broader self-regulatory processes. The section also describes the experience of shyness and suggests mechanisms that may account for the development of dispositional shyness or the momentary feeling of being shy. By contrast, Part IV attempts to place shyness within the social context of interpersonal behavior, perceptions, and relationships, as well as external social events and situations. Included here are examinations of shyness as a form of self-presentation, the influence of shyness on the perceptions of self and others (e.g., spouse), and as well as the connections between shyness and interpersonal behavior as well as the quality and quantity of various types of relationships. Part IV also contains an analysis of the relative contributions of dispositional as contrasted with situational determinants of shyness.

Understanding shyness, however, also requires understanding the inhibiting processes of social anxiety more broadly considered. For this reason, Part V includes discussions of recent research on related constructs and in some cases the connections between these constructs and shyness, including general anxiety, extraversion–introversion, communication apprehension, and embarrassment. Finally, although shyness may well have positive and functional consequences, it nevertheless is most often experienced as an unpleasant state, and dispositionally shy persons often wish that they could somehow be different or that they could at least overcome their shyness when it is of great importance for them to do so. Consequently, the final section of the volume surveys various approaches to the treatment of shyness, including cognitive, self-perception, rhetorical, interpersonal, and group interventions.

REFERENCES

Arkin, R. M., Appelman, A. J., & Burger, J. M. (1980). Social anxiety, self-presentation, and the self-serving bias in causal attribution. *Journal of Personality and Social Psychology, 38*, 23–35.

Asendorpf, J. (1984). *Shyness and sociability revisited.* Paper presented at the Second European Conference on Personality, Bielefeld, Federal Republic of Germany.

Backteman, G., & Magnusson, D. (1981). Longitudinal stability of personality characteristics. *Journal of Personality, 49*, 148–160.

Briggs, S. R. (1985). A trait account of social shyness. In P. Shaver (Ed.), *Review of personality and social psychology* (Vol. 6). Beverly Hills, CA: Sage.

Briggs, S. R., & Cheek, J. M. (in press). The role of factor analysis in the development and evaluation of personality scales. *Journal of Personality.*

Briggs, S. R., Cheek, J. M., & Buss, A. H. (1980). An analysis of the Self-Monitoring Scale. *Journal of Personality and Social Psychology, 38*, 679–686.

Briggs, S. R., Snider, R., & Smith, T. G. (1983). *The assessment of shyness: A comparison of measures.* Paper presented at the meeting of the American Psychological Association, Anaheim, CA.

Brodt, S. E., & Zimbardo, P. G. (1981). Modifying shyness-related social behavior through symptom misattribution. *Journal of Personality and Social Psychology, 41*, 437–449.

Buss, A. H. (1980). *Self-consciousness and social anxiety.* San Francisco: Freeman.

Buss, A. H. (1984). Two kinds of shyness. In R. Schwarzer (Ed.), *Self-related cognitions in anxiety and motivation.* Hillsdale, NJ: Erlbaum.

Cacioppo, J. T., Glass, C. R., & Merluzzi, T. V. (1979). Self-statements and self-evaluations: A cognitive-response analysis of social anxiety. *Cognitive Therapy and Research, 3*, 249–262.

Campbell, H. (1896). Morbid shyness. *The British Medical Journal, 2*, 805–807.

Carducci, B. J., & Webber, A. W. (1979). Shyness as a determinant of interpersonal distance. *Psychological Reports, 44*, 1075–1078.

Cattell, R. B. (1946). *Description and measurement of personality.* New York: World Book.

Cattell, R. B. (1973). *Personality and mood by questionnaire.* San Francisco: Jossey-Bass.

Cheek, J. M. (1982). *Shyness and self-esteem: A personological perspective.* Paper presented at the meeting of the American Psychological Association, Washington, DC.

Cheek, J. M., & Busch, C. M. (1981). The influence of shyness and loneliness in a new situation. *Personality and Social Psychology Bulletin, 7,* 572–577.

Cheek, J.M., & Buss, A. H. (1981). Shyness and sociability. *Journal of Personality and Social Psychology, 41,* 330–339.

Clark, J. V., & Arkowitz, H. (1975). Social anxiety and self-evaluation of interpersonal performance. *Psychological Reports, 36,* 211–221.

Comrey, A. L. (1965). Scales for measuring compulsion, hostility, neuroticism, and shyness. *Psychological Reports, 16,* 697–700.

Crozier, W. R. (1979). Shyness as a dimension of personality. *British Journal of Social and Clinical Psychology, 18,* 121–128.

Crozier, W. R. (1981). Shyness and self-esteem. *British Journal of Social Psychology, 20,* 220–222.

Curran, J. P. (1977). Skills training as an approach to the treatment of heterosexual-social anxiety: A review. *Psychological Bulletin, 84,* 140–157.

Daly, S. (1978). Behavioral correlates of social anxiety. *British Journal of Social and Clinical Psychology, 18,* 121–128.

Davis, M. H. (1983). Measuring individual differences in empathy: Evidence for a multidimensional approach. *Journal of Personality and Social Psychology, 44,* 113–126.

Eysenck, H. J. (1956). The questionnaire measurement of neuroticism and extraversion. *Revista de Psicologia, 50,* 113–140.

Franzoi, S. L. (1983). Self-concept differences as a function of private self-consciousness and social anxiety. *Journal of Research in Personality, 17,* 275–287.

Garcia-Coll, C., Kagan, J., & Rezneck, J.S. (1984). Behavioral inhibition in young children. *Child Development, 55,* 1005–1019.

Girodo, M. (1978). *Shy? You don't have to be!* New York: Pocket Books.

Girodo, M., Dotzenroth, S. E., & Stein, S. J. (1981). Causal attribution bias in shy males: Implications for self-esteem and self-confidence. *Cognitive Therapy and Research, 5,* 325–338.

Glass, C. R., Merluzzi, T. V., Biever, J. L., & Larsen, K. H. (1982). Cognitive assessment of social anxiety: Development and validation of a self-statement questionnaire. *Cognitive Therapy and Research, 6,* 37–55.

Gormally, J., Sipps, G., Raphael, R., Edwin, D., & Varvil-Weld, D. (1981). The relationship between maladaptive cognitions and social anxiety. *Journal of Consulting and Clinical Psychology, 49,* 300–301.

Guilford, J. P., & Guilford, R. B. (1936). Personality factors S, E and M and their measurement. *Journal of Psychology, 2,* 109–127.

Haemmerlie, F. M., & Montgomery, R. L. (1982). Self-perception theory and unobtrusively biased interactions: A treatment for heterosocial anxiety. *Journal of Counseling Psychology, 29,* 362–370.

Hampton, F. A. (1927). Shyness. *Journal of Neurology and Psychopathology, 8,* 124–131.

Hansson, R. O., Jones, W. H., & Carpenter, B. N. (1984). Relational competence and social support. In P. Shaver (Ed.). *Review of personality and social psychology; 5, Emotions, relationships and health.* Beverly Hills, CA: Sage.

Harris, P. R. (1984). Shyness and psychological imperialism: On the dangers of ignoring the ordinary language roots of the terms we deal with. *European Journal of Social Psychology, 14,* 169–181.

Hoffman, M. A., & Teglasi, H. (1982). The role of causal attribution in counseling shy subjects. *Journal of Counseling Psychology, 29,* 132–139.

Halford, K., & Foddy, M. (1982). Cognitive and social skills correlates of social anxiety. *British Journal of Clinical Psychology, 21,* 17–28.

Howarth, E. (1980). Major factors of personality. *Journal of Psychology, 104,* 171–183.

Izard, C. E. (1972). *Patterns of emotions: A new analysis of anxiety and depression.* New York: Academic Press.

Izard, C. E. (1977). *Human emotions.* New York: Plenum Press.

Jones, W. H. (1984). *Social anxiety in interpersonal behavior, relationships and social support.* Paper presented at the Second International Conference on Personal Relationships, Madison, WI.

Jones, W. H., & Briggs, S. R. (1984). The self-other discrepancy in social shyness. In R. Schwarzer (Ed.). *The self in anxiety, stress and depression* (pp. 93–107). Amsterdam: North Holland.

Jones, W. H., & Russell, D. (1982). The social reticence scale: An objective instrument to measure shyness. *Journal of Personality Assessment, 46,* 629–631.

Jones, W. H., Freemon, J. E., & Goswick, R. A. (1981). The persistence of loneliness: Self and other determinants. *Journal of Personality, 49,* 27–48.

Jones, W. H., Cavert, C. W., & Indart, M. (1983). *Impressions of shyness.* Paper presented at the meeting of the American Psychological Association, Anaheim, CA.

Jones, W. H., Briggs, S. R., & Smith, T.G. (1985). *Shyness: Conceptualization and measurement.* Unpublished manuscript, University of Tulsa.

Jones, W. H., Russell, D., & Cutrona, C. E. (1985). *A personality congruent analysis of situations.* Unpublished manuscript, University of Tulsa.

Kanter, N. J. & Goldfried, M. R. (1979). Relative effectiveness of rotational restructuring and self-control desensitization in the reduction of interpersonal anxiety, *Behavior Therapy, 10,* 472–490.

Kaplan, D. M. (1972). On shyness. *International Journal of Psychoanalysis, 3,* 439–453.

Lazarus, P. J. (1976). *An experimental treatment program for the amelioration of shyness in children.* Unpublished doctoral dissertation. University of Florida.

Lazarus, P. J. (1982). Incidence of shyness in elementary-school age children. *Psychological Reports, 51,* 904–906.

Leary, M. R. (1982). Social anxiety. In L. Wheeler (Ed.). *Review of personality and social psychology* (Vol. 3, pp. 97–120). Beverly Hills, CA: Sage.

Leary, M. R. (1983). Social anxiousness: The construct and its measurement. *Journal of Personality Assessment, 47,* 66–75.

Leary, M. R. (1984). *Understanding social anxiety: Social, personality, and clinical perspectives.* Beverly Hills, CA: Sage.

Leary, M. R., & Dobbins, S. E. (1983). Social anxiety, sexual behavior and contraceptive use. *Journal of Personality and Social Psychology, 43,* 1347–1354.

Leary, M. R., Johnson, K.A., & Knight, P. D. (1984, August). *Social anxiety and dyadic conversation.* Paper presented at the annual meeting of the American Psychological Association, Toronto.

Lewinsky, H. H. (1941). The nature of shyness. *British Journal of Psychology, 32,* 105–113.

Linehan, M., Goldfried, M., & Goldfried, A. (1979). Assertion therapy: Skill training or cognitive restructuring. *Behavior Therapy, 10,* 372–388.

Litwinski, L. (1950). Constitutional shyness: Its active and passive forms. *Journal of General Psychology, 42,* 299–311.

Loxley, J. C. (1979). Understanding and overcoming shyness. In S. Eisenberg & L. E. Patterson (Eds.), *Helping clients with special concerns.* Boston: Houghton-Mifflin.

Ludwig, R. P., & Lazarus, P. J. (1983). Relationship between shyness in children and constricted cognitive control as measured by the Stroop color-word test. *Journal of Consulting and Clinical Psychology, 51,* 386–389.

Lynd, H. M. (1958). *On shame and the search for identity.* New York: Harcourt, Brace.

Mandel, N. M., & Shrauger, J. S. (1980). The effects of self-evaluation statements on heterosocial approach in shy and nonshy males. *Cognitive Therapy and Research, 4,* 369–381.

Maroldo, G. K. (1981). Shyness and loneliness among college men and women. *Psychological Reports, 48,* 485–486.

Maroldo, G. K. (1982). Shyness and love on the college campus. *Perceptual and Motor Skills, 55,* 819–824.

Maroldo, G. K., Eisenreich, B. H., & Hall, P. (1979). Reliability of a modified Stanford Shyness Survey. *Psychological Reports, 44,* 706.

McFall, R. M., & Twentyman, C. T. (1973). Four experiments on the relative contributions of rehearsal, modeling and coaching to assertion training. *Journal of Abnormal Psychology, 81,* 199–218.

McGovern, L. P. (1976). Dispositional social anxiety and helping under three conditions of threat. *Journal of Personality, 44,* 84–97.

Melnick, J. (1973). A comparison of replication techniques in the modification of minimal dating behavior. *Journal of Abnormal Psychology, 81,* 51–59.

Modigliani, A. (1971). Embarrassment, facework and eye contact: Testing a theory of embarrassment. *Journal of Personality and Social Psychology, 17,* 15–24.

Morris, D. P., Soroker, E., & Burruss, G. (1954). Follow-up studies of shy, withdrawn children. I. Evaluation of later adjustment. *American Journal of Orthopsychiatry, 24,* 743–754.

Morris, L. W. (1979). *Extraversion and introversion: An interactional perspective.* Washington, DC: Hemisphere.

Mosher, D. L., & White, B. B. (1981). On differentiating shame and shyness. *Motivation and Emotion, 5,* 61–74.

Patterson, M. L., & Strauss, M. E. (1972). An examination of the discriminant validity of the social avoidance and distress scale. *Journal of Consulting and Clinical Psychology, 39,* 169.

Phillips, G. M. (1981). *Help for shy people.* Englewood Cliffs: Prentice-Hall.

Pilkonis, P. A. (1977). The behavioral consequences of shyness. *Journal of Personality, 45,* 566–611.

Pilkonis, P. A., Heape, C. & Klein, R. H. (1980). Treating shyness and other relationship difficulties in psychiatric outpatients. *Communication Education, 29,* 250–255.

Plomin, R., & Rowe, D. C. (1979). Genetic and environmental etiology of social behavior in infancy. *Developmental Psychology, 15,* 62–72.

Powell, B. (1979). *Overcoming shyness.* New York: McGraw-Hill.

Santee, R. T., & Maslach, C. (1982). To agree or not to agree: Personal dissent amid social pressure to conform. *Journal of Personality and Social Psychology, 42,* 690–700.

Sarason, I. G. (1975). Text anxiety and the self-disclosing coping model. *Journal of Consulting and Clinical Psychology, 48,* 148–153.

Schlenker, B. R., & Leary, M. R. (1982). Social anxiety and self-presentation: A conceptualization and model. *Psychological Bulletin, 92,* 641–669.

Slivken, K. E., & Buss, A. H. (1984). Misattribution and speech anxiety. *Journal of Personality and Social Psychology, 47,* 396–402.

Smith, T. W., Ingram, R. E., & Brehm, S. S. (1983). Social anxiety, anxious self-preoccupation, and recall of self-relevant information. *Journal of Personality and Social Psychology, 44,* 1276–1283.

Snyder, C. R., Smith, T. W., Augelli, R. W., & Ingram, R. E. (1985). On the self-serving function of social anxiety: Shyness as a self-handicapping strategy. *Journal of Personality and Social Psychology, 48,* 970–980.

Teear, C. H. (1977). *Conquer shyness.* Wellingborough, England: Thomas & Co.

Tomkins, S. S. (1963). *Affect, imagery, consciousness, Vol. 2. The negative affects.* New York: Springer.

Watson, D., & Friend, R. (1969). Measurement of social-evaluative anxiety. *Journal of Consulting and Clinical Psychology, 33,* 448–457.

Weber, E., & Miller, J. (1979). *Shy person's guide to a happier love life.* New York: Symphony Press.

Zimbardo, P. G. (1977). *Shyness: What it is and what to do about it.* New York: Addison-Wesley.

Zimbardo, P. G., & Radl, S. L. (1981). *The shy child.* New York: McGraw-Hill.

Zimbardo, P. G., & Radl, S. L. (1983). *The shyness workbook.* New York: McGraw-Hill.

Zimbardo, P. G., Pilkonis, P. A., & Norwood, R. M. (1975). The social disease called shyness. *Psychology Today, 8,* 68–72.

I
Issues in the Study of Shyness

The chapters in Part I consider some fundamental issues in the conceptualization and measurement of shyness. Many of these issues are treated and elaborated on throughout the volume and thus they serve as both an introduction to and a conspectus of the study of shyness.

Much of the current interest in shyness can be traced to the work of Zimbardo and his colleagues. It seems appropriate, therefore, to begin Part I with Zimbardo's account of the Stanford Shyness Project. In addition to providing a comprehensive view of shyness as it affects the individual and society, Zimbardo discusses his own attraction to the topic and describes the inception of the research and treatment program at Stanford University. Furthermore, he brings the description of his research program up-to-date by reporting on a current series of investigations that examine the relationship between shyness and performance on group problem-solving tasks.

In the second chapter, Leary focuses on what we mean when we use the word shyness. He points out that shyness can be (and has been) defined in many different ways, and argues that disagreement as to the meaning of the construct can result only in confusion and controversy. Leary goes on to suggest that the affective components of shyness should be distinguished conceptually and operationally from the behavioral components of shyness. He then provides a definition of shyness that distinguishes between the affective and behavioral components and discusses the ways in which these two aspects of shyness might be related.

The third chapter in this part provides another conceptual analysis of shyness. Buss examines the etiology of shyness and differentiates between shyness that begins early in childhood and that which originates in adolescence. Early shyness is seen as linked to fearfulness, possibly having a genetic basis, whereas later developing shyness is explained in terms of self-consciousness. Buss compares and contrasts the two types of shyness, discusses the implications of the distinction, and suggests a research agenda for examining the genetic and acquired aspects of shyness. Several of the chapters in the second section of the book also make use of this distinction as it relates to the development of shyness.

The final chapter in Part I discusses the strategies and measures that have been used in research on shyness. Although a wide range of measures are available to researchers, Briggs and Smith note that most of the available research uses self-report scales. In their review, they describe the instruments and procedures designed to measure shyness, discuss the advantages and disadvantages of different types of measurement, and argue for the importance of multimethod investigations. In addition, they review the evidence for the reliability and validity of the most widely used self-report inventories, and draw some broad conclusions as to the comparability of the scales and the status of shyness as a personality construct.

2

The Stanford Shyness Project

Philip G. Zimbardo

INTRODUCTION

Shyness offers a fascinating realm for psychological study because it reveals many issues central to understanding human nature. The shy person is the prototype of individual vulnerability, not from physical weakness or disability, or impaired mental functioning, but from the very essence of the human condition—the desperate need for acceptance, approval, and affiliation.

Other people can fulfill or frustrate these desires by establishing and enforcing criteria for acceptable public performance. Because these assessment criteria may be ambiguous, shifting, and unrealistic, or misinterpreted and exaggerated by the shy person, they function as barriers to feeling comfortable in the presence of anyone who might conceivably be one's judge. Construing the world as a stage in which one's behavior and appearance are subject to this critical evaluation sets the shy person—as actor—apart from those designated as critics in the audience.

In this way, shyness becomes a state of heightened individuation in which there is a perceived isomorphism between one's ego and one's performance. They both are perceived to be interchangeable objects of evaluation whose worth is established by others. A dominant defensive strategy that emerges then involves giving minimal performances that entail little initiation, volition, or spontaneity. By inhibiting such self-directed action, the ego is spared the ever-threatening rejection presumed to follow adverse performance ratings. Such a view recasts shyness from its traditional conception as a passive personality trait into a dynamic social construct in which self-attentional and attribution processes direct interpersonal relations. This new conception likewise forces us to acknowledge certain social forces that create and perpetuate shyness as a fragile interface between individual and society. Subtle cultural programming, mediated through socialization practices and institutions, may become apparent and may warrant investigation using shyness as an index variable.

The universal experience of shyness is, in its broadest conception, an internal

---

PHILIP G. ZIMBARDO • Department of Psychology, Stanford University, Stanford, CA 94305.

force that prevents people from making and maintaining the human connection. At the same time, it also alienates the individual from an acceptance and full appreciation of self. The shy person is voluntarily surrendering basic freedoms of action, opinion, and association in exchange for an illusion of security that shields the ego from the anticipated greater loss of respect and love.

Among the paradoxes of human nature that come to the surface when we study shyness are the publicly outgoing person who is privately shy, or the timid exterior that belies rage that has been festering from years of perceived injustice, or the self-handicapping that makes an intelligent, knowledgeable, caring person seem dull, insensitive, and aloof. The presence of unrecognized shyness likewise leads us as observers to misperceive unresponsiveness as a symptom of deficiency in ability, emotion, or motivation.

Shyness becomes implicated in a host of negative outcomes, some obvious, such as lowered self-esteem, failure to act in appropriately assertive ways, sexual problems, and chronic loneliness. But less obvious consequences can be equally destructive for the shy person and for society. Shyness may lead to alcoholism or drug use in order to mellow social anxiety and public discomfort. It can reduce the pool of leadership talent, limit individual initiative and ambition, or lead to support of an undesirable but familiar status quo (as in abusive relationships, or unjust dictatorial governments).

Awareness of the cognitive, affective, and motivational complexity involved in shyness is stimulating researchers to explore these dynamics. But shyness can also mean suffering. Because it can be so debilitating and impose such constraints on the human spirit, clinicians are starting to recognize the need for programs to treat and prevent shyness.

Curiously, this age-old human phenomenon has not been investigated in a systematic fashion until the past decade. Previously, interest in shyness had been limited to psychometricians concerned with assessing its trait structure, or developmental psychologists attempting to correlate its presence with processes at different stages in childhood.

In another sense, "shyness" did not even exist as a psychologically valid concept until quite recently. It is not a term readily found in the indexes of any psychology textbooks, even those in the areas of personality, developmental, or introductory psychology. Instead, one finds a host of academically more respectable synonyms such as timidity, reticence, social phobia, social anxiety, behavioral inhibition, introversion, or communication apprehension. But despite its origins in lay psychology, and its overlap with the above constructs, shyness remains a distinctive concept worthy of academic respectability (see Crozier, 1982; Kelly, 1982). Indeed, the present volume may represent the most significant conferral of academic legitimacy that "shyness" has ever received.

THE SHYNESS RENAISSANCE

Forsaking intellectual modesty, I claim that the current interest among research psychologists in the topic of shyness can be traced circuitously to an unlikely source—a simulated prison experiment conducted at Stanford University in 1971 (see Zimbardo, Haney, Banks, & Jaffee, 1973). In this section, I would like to outline the thinking that led to the creation of the Stanford Shyness Project, the range of research it has generated, and our attempts at "consciousness raising" among colleagues to take shyness seriously. In the final section, some of our more recent, unpublished research will be briefly detailed.

While observing the impact of a prison-like setting on the behavior of normal, average individuals acting in the roles of mock prisoners and guards, we were struck by the dramatic contrasts that emerged between young men in these two categories. A central task of the guards was to limit the freedom of the prisoners, doing so primarily through coercive, often arbitrary rules. The prisoners either rebelled at the loss of liberty (for which they were punished) or complied (eventually). Compliance meant inaction, restraining oneself from doing things the prisoner had the ability and desire to do. It also meant agreeing to acts not congruent with one's motives or values. In the process of accepting these externally imposed constraints on one's basic behavioral freedom, the prisoners began to internalize a negative self-conception that comes with the trade-off of autonomy—with its attendant risks and uncertainty—for the security associated with being "a good prisoner." This exchange seemed comparable to that observed in neurotic individuals or the shy. One difference, of course, is the embodiment of the dual mentalities of prisoner and guard within a single neurotic or shy person.

After elaborating on this metaphor in a class discussion the following year, several shy students requested a tutorial on shyness. A literature search of the topic came up with relatively few references, most dealing with shyness personality scales, clinical case studies, or armchair speculation on how to cure timidity. For the next three years we conducted a shyness seminar at Stanford University for both shy and not shy students. Because there was apparently no expert on shyness nor an authoritative reference, the students generated a set of questions for which they wanted answers—and then proceeded to get the answers themselves.

First we developed an open-ended survey questionnaire that was given to about 400 students. Amazed at the unexpectedly high percentage of students who reported being shy, we persisted in refining the survey into a more efficient checklist and then administered it to a larger sample of students at different schools. The data convinced us that shyness was not only an interesting concept, it was much more pervasive than any of us had imagined. Over and over, the figure of 40% ± 3 emerged as a reliable index of current, dispositional shyness. Approximately the same percentage was found for those who reported being in the formerly shy category. When we added the 15 or so percent who regarded themselves as only "situationally shy," that left but a small minority for whom shyness did not fit at all.

These data on the prevalence of shyness were supplemented by additional self-reported input on the causes, correlates, and consequences of shyness. Because we were sensitive to the variety of possible definitions of shyness, our survey instrument did not provide a standard definition. Rather, each respondent provided a personal portrait by first classifying him or herself into one of the shyness categories, then filling in the details of its personal meaning. Such a procedure enabled us to use this survey with a wide range of respondents, thereby making it readily adaptable for cross-cultural research (see Zimbardo & Zoppel, 1984).

After surveying several thousand respondents, we were able to dispel some of the myths about shyness that may have been implicated in the previous lack of research interest on shyness. Traditionally, shyness was assumed to be a natural stage through which most children passed and grew out of, although it was typically seen as a female problem. There was also a myth concerning the extreme heritability and nonmodifiability of the trait of shyness (perpetuated by Cattell, 1965, and others).

We found no sex differences in reported shyness, except for the relatively greater increase among adolescent females than males. Shyness was also less likely among elementary school children than teenagers or young adults. Whereas many people stopped being shy over time, just as many continued to be shy all their lives as first became shy after childhood.

We discovered that shyness can be conceptualized as a response continuum, with verbal and nonverbal components, manifested at physiological, cognitive, affective, and behavioral levels (independently validated by Fatis, 1983). There was also much evidence of the distressful nature of shyness, along with the contrasts of publicly extroverted individuals who were nevertheless privately, often painfully, shy.

When we first reported these findings (Zimbardo, Pilkonis, & Norwood, 1974, 1975), reactions to it fell into three general classes. Some colleagues refused to accept self-report survey data without behavioral validation. Others refused to consider the study of shyness as scientifically worthwhile. But the general public was generally delighted at seeing the subject treated seriously, and wanted to know how to overcome the inhibiting effects of shyness.

With the aid of funds from the National Institute of Mental Health and the Office of Naval Research, we addressed these concerns. Paul Pilkonis (1977a) conducted a rigorous laboratory study that revealed clear behavioral differences between individuals identified on our survey as shy and others identified as not shy. He also demonstrated several different forms that shyness takes, as well as its relationship to other aspects of social behavior (Pilkonis, 1977b).

Our research team then used the survey instrument to select groups who would be exposed to different experimental treatments. Memory deficits were found for intelligent shy males whose shyness was aroused (by the presence of an attractive female)—but only when they believed they were the object of evaluation (Hatvany & Zimbardo, 1977). In another experiment, shy subjects were more easily persuaded than not shy peers to change their attitudes to agree with the views expressed by a speaker—when they anticipated public evaluation of their speech (Souza e Silva, 1977). In a correlational study we found felons convicted of homicide to be shy, nonmasculine in sex role orientation, and overcontrolled in their impulses—if they were "sudden murderers" who had never previously broken the law. In contrast, habitual criminal offenders were characterized as not shy, masculine, and undercontrolled (Lee, Zimbardo, & Bertholf, 1977). We also found that West Point cadets who defined themselves as shy on our survey received significantly lower leadership effectiveness scores than not shy cadets, when evaluated by a host of independent military raters. These and other findings from our multimethod, multiresponse approach to studying shyness are reported in Zimbardo (1977), Pilkonis & Zimbardo (1979), and Zimbardo (1982).

In response to numerous requests for therapeutic assistance, we started a shyness clinic at Stanford in 1975. With Meg Marnell and Rochelle Kramer, I explored various treatment strategies for specific aspects of shyness. Using a social-psychological approach, we decided to use small group therapy with dual therapists who could act as process facilitators and models for social interaction. We focused our time-limited efforts at changing inadequate social skills, improving low self-esteem, and initiating cognitive restructuring that altered how clients viewed their shyness and their relevant attributions.

We have varied these treatments and other procedural aspects of the therapy across different groups. Currently our shyness clinic has moved into the community (as the Institute for Social Competence, Co-director, Carlo Piccione). We are preparing an evaluation report to document the effectiveness of such a treatment approach in reducing social anxiety and distress, in improving the client's self-image, and in attaining a variety of behavioral objectives set by the clients.

Perhaps the major contribution of the Stanford Shyness Project was less in any of these particular studies than in its function as a polymorphous consciousness-raiser. The popular interest in shyness shown by readers of our early *Psychology Today* article encouraged me to write a popular summary of our views and findings in the trade book, *Shyness: What It Is, What to Do about It* (1977). Promotion of this book entailed cross-country media presentations on a host of national network TV and radio shows, as well as interviews in newspapers and magazines. During this period, that bellwether of "hot topics," *The National Enquirer*, went as far as to state in a banner headline, "Shyness: America's Number One Problem." Despite this hyperbole, our reasonable message was getting out to the public, and to some professionals, albeit more slowly. The latter were more likely to be persuaded by our shyness workshops, convention addresses, and university colloquia than by appearances on the *Phil Donohue* or *Today* shows.

And what is that message? Simply put, shyness is a significant social and personal problem of major and increasing proportions. It is largely a learned experience that can be prevented (by changing social structures and socialization practices) or treated (by a variety of therapies). But it is also an exciting domain for the curious psychological investigator—not only for developmental researchers, but for those with interests in social, cognitive, and personality psychology.

We began our research with adults in part to show the extent to which shyness is a problem for grown-ups and not just for kids. Because it is, colleagues beyond those with a traditional interest in developmental processes have been able to take their "piece of the action."

Our more recent book, *The Shy Child* (Zimbardo & Radl, 1981), reports observational and interview studies of children, parents, and teachers. Its goal is to encourage greater awareness of the causes of shyness, the forms it takes, and the ways that the home and school environments may contribute to the problem or to its solution.

RECENT STUDIES OF SHYNESS AND GROUP PROBLEM-SOLVING

Our most recent systematic investigation into the social dynamics of shyness has involved a series of laboratory experiments designed to increase the participation level of shy members of problem-solving groups. With the collaboration of David Stodolsky and Joan Linsenmeier, a computer-controlled message system was developed to investigate communication processes in four-person problem-solving teams. Several variables that bias the extent of an individual's verbal participation on group tasks were identified. Equitable (or democratic) participation in task-centered work teams is affected by dispositional factors, such as shyness or communication apprehension, by social-situational factors such as gender (sexual) composition of teams, and by leadership roles.

Intervention in the communication process during team problem-solving activities was achieved by using computer-mediated turn-taking algorithms, computer displays of feedback (informational prompts) regarding each member's on-going amount of participation, and assignment of leadership roles. Outcome measures included quality of team decisions, extent of individual verbal participation, social-emotional reactions, and group dynamics (see Zimbardo & Linsenmeier, 1983). Our concern centered on several of the dispositional and situational variables that contribute to the social-psychological nature of a team's composition and its operational dynamics.

We have been guided by the assumption that optimal team performance usually requires sharing the available resources among members. Sharing information-based knowledge and social-emotional support are vital to small group effectiveness. For many types of team tasks, markedly unequal levels of team member participation should generate an adverse effect on the quality of the primary task outcome—the solution to the team's problem. When some members of the team withhold potential contributions, the team cannot fully benefit from their wisdom and skills. In addition, when participation rates differ to an obvious extent, the social climate of the team suffers as well. Those not contributing fully are likely to become more bored and to feel less competent. Their self-esteem will be lowered, whereas their dependence on those to whom they defer is increased. The high contributors, on the other hand, should enjoy their superior status. Over time, though, they may come to resent the inequity of a situation that forces them to carry a heavier burden of responsibility for the team's success. Thus, the reactions of both low and high contributors combine to lower group morale and reduce feelings of group cohesiveness.

When a team needs to work together over an extended time period, such reactions will threaten its stability. Attempts may be made to reorganize the team. If more balanced participation is achieved, it should be accompanied by enhanced attitudes toward the group process, its products, and its unique identity.

With fuller participation and more positive team attitudes, the probability of attaining the team's goals—of effective problem solving—should be increased.

Our primary experimental situation is characterized by the following features: (a) four individuals, previously unknown to each other, are assembled as a problem-solving team; (b) they are physically separated and can communicate orally by means of an intercom system and in writing by typing responses on computer terminals (selected responses are shown on the CRT display screens of other subjects); (c) to request the opportunity to talk, a team member presses a talk-request button and keeps it activated until displayed instructions announce that he or she has the floor (e.g., "subject X, you may talk now"); (d) the subject who is granted the opportunity to talk then presses a talk button that activates a microphone, allowing the other team members to hear what the subject says through their earphones; (e) subjects are told how long each discussion period will be, allowed one minute maximum of uninterrupted talk time per turn, and, through the use of computer displays, kept informed of the elapsed time during each discussion period and each speaking turn; (f) during group discussions, the primary data that the computer files sequentially is information on when and by whom request buttons and talk buttons are pressed or released, along with information on when requests to speak are granted; (g) instructions, information, and rating scales related to the experimental tasks are presented on each participant's screen. Each person first works alone and makes some individual judgments about the team tasks, and after group discussion, a common team solution has to be proposed; (h) the quality of the final solution generated by the team is assessed by comparing it to expert judgments (this constituted the major outcome measure of the effectiveness of team problem-solving efforts); (i) aspects of the dynamics operating within each group are measured on self-report questionnaires following the consensus decision. In our later studies this was supplemented by ratings of interaction profiles obtained from observations of taped discussions.

Unknown to the subjects, the computerized message-handling system interposed algorithms that determined speaker selection by either: (a) *autocratic rules* that give priority to those who request to talk first and thus initially control the domain of the interaction; these individuals seek opportunities to participate more actively and quickly than their teammates, and do, in fact, obtain the floor more often (FIFO—First In—First Out); or (b) *democratic rules* that attempt to equalize speaker opportunities over the entire course of the interaction (EQTS—Equal Time Sharing).

The body of results generated from this three-year program of research is summarized in our ONR Final Report (Zimbardo & Linsenmeier, 1983). A brief summary of the major findings will offer a sense of the way shyness functions in such a setting, how it can be studied in relation to important social and cognitive processes, and how new technology can be utilized for treatment interventions. We found that: (a) initially the total amount of time spent requesting a talking turn was directly and negatively related to shyness level; (b) the EQTS rule exerted a significant effect on those who were moderately shy. Over time, they substantially increased their requests to talk until they were doing so more than even the most assertive participants; however, it had little effect on the extremely shy; (c) teams of assertive participants made better decisions than those composed of only shy individuals; (d) the highest team effectiveness was found in groups that performed under computer-mediated conditions of EQTS with prompts; (e) prompts proved to have a range of effects on participation and perception measures. The shys talked more, while the not-shys talked less when they got objective feedback on the extent of each member's participation. The usual dominance of not-shys over shys was reduced, as reflected in both request time and talk time. Prompts made the shys feel more influential and the not-shys feel less so; (f) not-shys were more likely to be perceived by others and by themselves as leaders—but only in the FIFO condition, and not under EQTS; (g) shys were more likely than not-shys to perceive their main contribution to the team as the passive one of "listening." However, prompts eliminated this difference by leading shys to perceive themselves as more active participators; (h) prompts changed the perceptions of team members, making them more likely to perceive the shys as leaders; (i) within mixed-sex teams, females felt less tension than males without prompts, but more tension when prompts were present; (j) prompts increased the average length of requests among all subjects, significantly so for the shys; (k) as expected, shys of both sexes offered task solutions in a less assertive manner than did not-shys, and they expressed fewer emotions, either positive or negative—findings that held across task settings of face-to-face interaction or teleconferencing; (l) teams working in the telecommunication setting made better decisions than those that were face to face (their rankings of the value of survival items were closer to expert rankings). In addition, members perceived their teams' decisions to be better in the telecommunication setting.

The deference of the shy to the not-shy and of females to males found in our baseline conditions can be modified by designing social situations in which the usual autocratic participation norms are changed to be more democratic, by providing informational feedback of differential participation levels, and of arbitrary assignment of these low participation, low influence subjects to leadership roles.

Over the past dozen years that the Stanford Shyness Project has been in operation, we have come to believe that in studying shyness we are exploring an essential attribute of human existence. Those researchers and theorists represented in this book on shyness are peering into and beyond the mirror of the human condition to discover how individuals can live more enriched lives as part of, rather than apart from, the human condition.

REFERENCES

Cattell, R. B. (1965). *The scientific analysis of personality*. Baltimore: Penguin.
Crozier, W. R. (1982). Explanations of shyness. *Current Psychological Reviews*. 2, 47–60.
Fatis, M. (1983). Degree of shyness and self-reported physiological, behavioral, and cognitive reactions. *Psychological Reports, 52*, 351–354.

Hatvany, N., & Zimbardo, P. G. (1977). *Shyness, arousal and memory: The path from discomfort to distraction to recall deficits.* Unpublished manuscript, Stanford University.

Kelly, L. (1982). A rose by any other name is still a rose: A comparative analysis of reticence, communication apprehension, unwillingness to communicate, and shyness. *Human Communication Research, 8,* 99–113.

Lee, M., Zimbardo, P. G., & Bertholf, M. J. (1977, November). Shy murderers. *Psychology Today,* 68–70, 76, 148.

Pilkonis, P. A. (1977a). The behavioral consequences of shyness. *Journal of Personality, 45,* 596–611.

Pilkonis, P. A. (1977b). Shyness, public and private, and its relationship to other measures of social behavior. *Journal of Personality, 45,* 585–595.

Pilkonis, P. A., & Zimbardo, P. G. (1979). The personal and social dynamics of shyness. In C. E. Izard (Ed.), *Emotions in personality and psychopathology* (pp. 133–160). New York: Plenum Press.

Souza e Silva, M. C. (1977). *Social and cognitive dynamics of shyness.* Unpublished master's thesis. Stanford University.

Zimbardo, P. G. (1977). *Shyness: What it is, what to do about it.* Reading, MA: Addison-Wesley.

Zimbardo, P. G. (1982). Shyness and the stresses of the human connection. In L. Goldberger & S. Breznitz (Eds.), *Handbook of stress: Theoretical and clinical aspects* (pp. 466–481). New York: Free Press.

Zimbardo, P. G., & Radl, S. (1981). *The shy child.* New York: McGraw-Hill.

Zimbardo, P. G., & Zoppel, C. (1984, August). *The emic and etic of shyness.* Paper presented at the International Association of Cross-Cultural Psychology, Acapulco, Mexico.

Zimbardo, P. G., Haney, C., Banks, W. C., Jaffe, D. (1973, April 8). The mind is a formidable jailer: A Pirandellian prison. *The New York Times Magazine,* Section 6, 38–60.

Zimbardo, P. G., Pilkonis, P. A., & Norwood, R. (1974). *The silent prison of shyness* (ONR Tech. Rep. Z-17). Stanford, CA: Stanford University.

Zimbardo, P. G., Pilkonis, P. A., & Norwood, R. (1975). The social disease called shyness. *Psychology Today, 8,* 68–72.

Zimbardo, P. G., & Linsenmeier, J. A. W. (1983). *The influence of personal, social and system factors on team problem solving* (Z-83-0l). Office of Naval Research, Final Technical Report, Stanford University.

3

Affective and Behavioral Components of Shyness

Implications for Theory, Measurement, and Research

Mark R. Leary

With much of their research focused on mundane behavior, social and personality psychologists often borrow terms from everyday language, such as attitude, trait, aggression, and consciousness. Unfortunately, we are often remiss in explicitly defining our specialized uses of these ordinary sorts of words, especially in the early stages of research on a topic. And, even when writers clearly define their terms, they often adopt different connotations of the everyday definitions. Only after realizing that the multiplicity of implicit and explicit definitions has led to confusion and miscommunication have researchers typically paused to address conceptual issues.

The central theme of this chapter is that shyness research has reached a stage where conceptual self-examination is essential if we are to make sense out of our research efforts thus far and are to further our understanding of this fascinating and important phenomenon. Leafing through a short pile of reprints dealing with shyness, I am able to identify no fewer than *14 different definitions* of shyness (Buss, 1980; Cheek & Buss, 1981; Crozier, 1979; Girodo, 1978; Jones & Russell, 1982; Kaplan, 1972; Kelly, Phillips, & McKinney, 1982; Leary & Schlenker, 1981; Lewinsky, 1941; Phillips, 1980; Pilkonis, 1977a; Twentyman & McFall, 1975; Zimbardo, 1977; Zimbardo, Pilkonis, & Norwood, 1974). No doubt, there are more. In addition, there are several papers in this stack in which no definition of shyness is provided, although the authors' implicit meanings are clear in some cases. Many of the explicit and implicit definitions of shyness in these reprints share certain characteristics, but a high proportion have little in common. In fact, from my perusal of the various conceptualizations, I am forced

MARK R. LEARY • Department of Psychology, Wake Forest University, Winston-Salem, NC 27109.

to conclude that the term *shyness* has been used in the literature to refer to different psychological phenomena. Put another way, we have used a single term—shyness—to refer to what I believe are distinctly different constructs.

The implications of this are disconcerting: any two studies that purport to deal with shyness may, in fact, have little or nothing to do with one another. Thus, my first goal in this chapter will be to disentangle these various conceptualizations and to suggest ways of resolving the conceptual ambiguities in the area.* Having done that, I will examine the implications of the conceptualization of shyness one adopts for the kinds of theoretical issues that are raised and for the research and measurement strategies adopted in answering them.

SORTING THROUGH THE DEFINITIONS

With some exceptions, most existing conceptualizations of shyness can be classified, roughly, into three categories. Although the definitions in each category are not identical, they share common characteristics that distinguish them from definitions in other categories.

First, several writers have viewed shyness as a *subjective experience* characterized by apprehension and nervousness in interpersonal encounters (e.g., Buss, 1980; Leary & Schlenker, 1981; Zimbardo, 1977). This conceptualization is reflected in everyday language when someone speaks of "*feeling* shy." Defined in this way, shyness may be regarded as a particular form of social anxiety (Buss, 1980; Leary, 1983a).

A second class of definitions takes an exclusively behavioral perspective, defining shyness in terms of inhibition, reticence, or social avoidance. For example, Pilkonis (1977b, p. 596) defines shyness as "a tendency to avoid social interactions and to fail to participate appropriately" in them. In common usage, people sometimes describe themselves or others as "*acting* shy" when they behave in an inhibited or hesitant manner.

Strictly speaking, there is absolutely nothing wrong with either of these ways of conceptualizing shyness. Most dictionaries offer at least two definitions of shyness, one referring to subjective anxiety and the other to behavioral inhibition or "bashfulness." My objection to these two classes of definitions arises not from linguistic concerns, but from the conceptual confusion created by using the same term to refer to both an affective experience and overt behavior (Leary, 1983b). Although anxiety and behavior are correlated (a point to which I will return below), they are clearly not the same thing, and using the same term to refer to both is quite confusing. This confusion has led several researchers (including myself) to erroneously conclude that all studies dealing with "shyness" are examining the same psychological phenomenon.

---

*Having just bemoaned the large number of existing definitions and having already contributed one such definition to the literature (Leary & Schlenker, 1981), I am abashed to admit that I am about to add another.

For clarity, I recommend that we use other, more precise terms to capture the affective and behavioral experiences that are sometimes called shyness. For instance, the term *social anxiety* and its various forms (e.g., dating anxiety, speech anxiety, communication apprehension) more precisely characterize the affective definition of shyness (Leary, 1983a). Saying that a client or research subject is "socially anxious" is considerably more precise and less ambiguous than saying she is "shy" if we are referring to the fact that she becomes apprehensive and nervous in certain social settings. Likewise, there are several adjectives that more accurately capture the behavioral definitions of shy, such as inhibited, reticent, introverted, and avoidant. Using one of these terms is more descriptive than simply speaking of shyness. In short, whether speaking of shy anxiety or shy behavior, using more precise terms serves to reduce ambiguity and confusion.

Does all of this mean that we have no need for the construct of shyness? Not at all. A third class of definitions suggests what may be the optimal con-ceptualization of shyness. These identify shyness as a psychological *syndrome* that includes both subjective social anxiety and inhibited social behavior (e.g., Cheek & Buss, 1981; Crozier, 1979; Jones & Russell, 1982). Although social anxiety and interpersonal inhibition can occur independently, there is a low to moderate positive correlation between them (Leary, 1983a). The concurrent experience of nervousness and inhibition/hesitancy/awkwardness appears to constitute an identifiable psychological syndrome in its own right, and it is this syndrome that I would like to call *shyness*.

However, even if we agree to define shyness as the simultaneous occurance of social inhibition and anxiety, we still face the difficulty of identifying a definition that precisely characterizes the construct and that distinguishes it from other instances of anxious inhibition that most people would not call shyness. None of the existing definitions of shyness are much help in this respect; they generally fail to distinguish shyness from nonsocial discomfort and lack of responsivity that may occur in social settings. (One of my colleagues commented that one existing definition of shyness could double as a definition of constipation.) In developing a more precise and useful conceptualization of shyness, I found it necessary to make a few basic assumptions.

The first assumption I make is that shyness is truly a *social* phenomenon, as opposed to a phenomenon that may occur in social settings. In other words, there are many instances of anxiety and inhibition experienced in social situations that I think we would want to exclude as instances of shyness. Being held at gunpoint results in anxiety and inhibition (i.e., "Don't move or I'll shoot"), but I would not label the hostage's reaction as "shyness" even though he is in a social encounter of sorts with the gunman. Thus, I assume that we want to exclude from our conceptualization of shyness instances of anxiety and inhibition that occur for nonsocial reasons. But how can we distinguish shyness from other forms of anxiety and inhibition in social settings?

My second assumption is that the threat that produces shyness is inherently interpersonal, involving people's concerns with how they are being perceived and evaluated by other people. Put another way, shy anxiety and inhibition seem to occur when people are concerned about the impressions others are forming of them (Leary, 1983a; Leary & Schlenker, 1981; Schlenker & Leary, 1982). Because others' perceptions and evaluations have important implications for people's outcomes in life (Goffman, 1959; Schlenker, 1980), real or imagined evaluation by others can, under certain circumstances, elicit social anxiety and interpersonal inhibition (Leary, 1983a). Thus, we can distinguish shyness from other instances of anxious inhibition in terms of its proximal cause—the prospect or presence of interpersonal evaluation.

I can anticipate a major objection to this assumption. Fearfulness and inhibition in response to other people are often observed in infants and young children who are presumably incapable of worrying about how they are perceived by others (Buss, 1980; Stroufe, 1977). Do we want to include this phenomenon, often called wariness or stranger anxiety, under our conceptualization of shyness? There is honest disagreement on this question. Buss (1980, this volume) refers to this phenomenon as "early developing" or "fearful shyness," which he distinguishes from "late developing shyness" brought about by high self-consciousness. According to Buss, fearful shyness in infancy is precipitated by social novelty and intrusiveness (as when a person approaches the infant too quickly or closely). I have three reasons for preferring to exclude wariness from my conceptualization of shyness. First, it is not clear to me that the infant reaction is to inherently *social* factors. Stranger anxiety or wariness in infants seems to be more akin to children's reactions to strange dogs, scary toys and masks, Santa Claus, and other frightening stimuli than it is to adult shyness. Even though other people cause the reaction, infants seem to react to physical rather than social characteristics of others. Second, the behavioral effects observed in infants are only marginally similar to the behavioral components of shyness in older children and adults. True, infants confronted by strangers and shy adults appear to be anxious and, often, inhibited, but the similarity ends there. Few shy adults cry, scream, physically hide, or cover their faces when socially anxious, although these reactions might be observed in adults confronted by *physically* frightening stimuli (watch any horror movie for potential victims' reactions). Third, most evidence suggests that adult shyness is precipitated by social-evaluative concerns (Crozier, 1979; Leary, 1983a; Leary & Schlenker, 1981; Zimbardo, 1977), whereas we know that infants are incapable of worrying about such things, suggesting that the two reactions are functionally different. Given that the immediate causes and behavioral manifestations of adult and infant "shyness" are markedly different, my preference is to regard them as conceptually different psychological phenomena. Calling both reactions "shyness" seems to mix apples and oranges.

My third and final assumption has already been mentioned in passing: shyness is best characterized as a syndrome defined in terms of social anxiety and inhibition. I have already discussed conceptual and pragmatic reasons for using the term shyness to refer to the syndrome, and other terms to refer to its individual components when they occur separately.

Operating on these three assumptions, I offer the following definition of shyness: *shyness* is an affective-behavioral syndrome characterized by social anxiety and interpersonal inhibition that results from the prospect or presence of interpersonal evaluation.

For clarity, I should note that writers have used the term shy to refer to both a state of social anxiety and inhibition and to the trait associated with the predisposition to become anxious and inhibited across social situations. These two uses of the term are equally acceptable and compatible; there are many dispositional analogues of psychological states. However, it is important for researchers to make their uses of the term perfectly clear in order to avoid confusion.

SOCIAL ANXIETY AND INTERPERSONAL INHIBITION

Having defined shyness as social anxiety plus inhibition, I would now like to discuss the affective and behavioral components of shyness in a bit more detail. When anxious, people experience sympathetic nervous system arousal and its concomitants, as well as cognitive apprehension regarding the possibility of receiving negative outcomes (such as physical harm, bad grades, rejection, financial loss). In the case of social anxiety, the individual's apprehension revolves around how he or she is being perceived and evaluated by other people (Leary, 1983a; Zimbardo, 1977). More specifically, people appear to become socially anxious when they are motivated to make particular impressions on other individuals, but doubt they will successfully do so (Schlenker & Leary, 1982). Virtually all situational and dispositional antecedents of adult social anxiety appear to have their effects by heightening people's desire to create certain impressions and/or by lowering the subjective probability of doing so (see Leary, 1983a).

The second component of shyness—inhibition—is more difficult to define. Strictly speaking, inhibition is not the same as simple inactivity. If you do not interact with me because I am painfully boring, your lack of personal involvement would not be called inhibition. Nor is a failure to "participate appropriately" or to "interact as expected" necessarily indicative of shy inhibition, as some definitions suggest. People often behave inappropriately and in unexpected ways for reasons that have nothing to do with shyness. Rather, the term inhibition implies that a behavioral plan has been restrained or checked before execution. The inhibited interactant desires to respond in a particular fashion but, for one reason or another, does not do so. When shy, people report that they wish they could be more talkative, assertive, and outgoing, but can not bring themselves to participate more fully in interactions (Zimbardo, 1977).

Characterizing shyness in terms of both anxiety and inhibition raises a number of theoretical and methodological issues that do not arise if other views of shyness are adopted. The most obvious questions involve the nature of the relationship between social anxiety and interpersonal inhibition. When do anxiety and inhibition occur together? When do they not? Are social anxiety and inhibition caused by the same factors? If not, what are their different antecedents? Is there a direct causal relationship between social anxiety and inhibition? In short, how are the components of the syndrome related?

A full discussion of the relationship between anxiety and behavior requires a great deal more space than I can devote to the topic here. However, let me suggest a few avenues by which we might approach this question. The first thing to keep in mind is that there is not a direct causal relationship between anxiety *per se* and inhibition. After all, when anxiety arises for nonsocial reasons, such as the threat of electric shock, people prefer to affiliate with others (Schachter, 1959). Thus, anxiety does not appear to cause social inhibition in any general sense.

There are at least four plausible explanations of the relationship between social anxiety and behavior. These alternative hypotheses should not be regarded as mutually exclusive; it seems likely that all of these processes may operate at one time or another. First, subjective anxiety can be viewed as punishment for behaviors that increase it. Anxiety is an inherently aversive experience that people try to avoid when possible and reduce once it occurs. To the degree that social anxiety is precipitated by encounters with others, the tendency to affiliate will be punished by the experience of anxiety. Presumably, the punishing effects of social anxiety affect inhibition only in regards to those who are the source of the anxiety. The individual who is socially anxious, like the one expecting to receive an electric shock, may actually prefer to interact with other individuals who are not socially threatening. For example, a man waiting for a job interview may feel very socially anxious, yet interact fully with other applicants in the waiting room. Only when dealing with the interviewer will the man experience the tendency to be inhibited. This hypothesis deserves future attention.

A second approach to the anxiety–behavior link suggests that the self-preoccupation that accompanies episodes of social anxiety interferes with complex social responses (cf. Sarason, 1975). It is difficult to devote one's full attention to the ongoing encounter and to lose oneself in it when preoccupied by one's social concerns, thereby resulting in less than full participation. Unfortunately for the shy individual, failure to devote full attention to the encounter and to participate fully in it can create additional social difficulties. In many cases, others will notice that the person is not appropriately involved in the conversation, resulting in annoyance, negative evaluations, and unease among the participants (Goffman, 1957). In addition, the self-preoccupied interactant may realize that his or her interpersonal behavior is awkward, stilted, and uninvolved and purposefully refrain from complete involvement in an attempt to conceal his or her self-preoccupation, anxiety, and awkwardness. Although the role of self-preoccupation has been examined in the context of test anxiety (Sarason, 1975; Wine, 1971), its role in shyness and social anxiety has not been adequately examined (see Smith, Ingram, & Brehm, 1983).

Third, inhibition may be viewed as an interpersonal strategy designed to minimize one's self-presentational difficulties in certain social situations (Leary, 1983a). Given that social anxiety appears to occur when people are concerned with the impressions others are forming of them, socially anxious individuals may think that full participation in a difficult encounter will further erode their public image (Schlenker & Leary, 1982). Thus, inhibition may serve as a way of not revealing too much when one fears he or she will be judged as lacking in some respect or wants to conceal the fact that he or she is having difficulty responding in a poised and skillful manner.

The fourth possibility is that, in some cases, inhibition may *precede* social anxiety. People are often uncertain about how to respond in a social encounter because cues regarding appropriate behavior are absent, ambiguous, or contradictory. When this is the case, people are understandably reluctant to interact fully. Instead, they tend to hold back, participating as minimally as possible, while they attempt to ascertain the most efficacious manner of responding. The motto of shy people seems to be, "When in doubt, don't." Although inhibition is often the "safest" tactic, it may raise concerns that others will draw unfavorable inferences about the individual's lack of involvement, thereby elliciting social anxiety. The individual whose inhibition arises from uncertainty about how to respond is in a double bind; full participation under conditions of uncertainty carries interpersonal risks, but so does inhibition. Pilkonis (1977b) suggested that individuals can be taught to create their own interaction agendas in encounters in which they are uncertain of how to respond, thereby reducing shyness.

The existing literature is strangely silent regarding the relationship between social anxiety and interpersonal behavior. Partly, this is due to our incomplete understanding of the relationship between affect and behavior in general. In addition, research shows that the relationship between social anxiety and its behavioral concomitants is very complex. Although studies have demonstrated a low to moderate positive correlation between social anxiety and inhibition, it is clear that there is no necessary relationship between them and that they can occur and vary independently (Leary, 1983a, c). In addition to the fact that the anxiety–behavior link may be mediated by a number of different processes (see preceding), many people are able to hide overt indices of their inner distress from others and participate fully in encounters in which they feel very socially anxious. These individuals, whom Zimbardo (1977) calls "shy extraverts," are poised and outgoing in spite of their subjectively experienced anxiety.* To use an analogy, confronting a bear at close range in the woods is likely to arouse a certain degree of fear in almost everyone. However, individuals' reactions will differ. Some will run away, some will throw rocks, others will be paralyzed with fear, whereas still others will try to appear calm for the benefit of onlookers. In each instance, the subjective reaction is similar, but the behavioral reactions differ, resulting in only a weak relationship between anxiety and any particular behavior.

Along the same lines, Pilkonis (1977a) found that people differ in the degree to which they are troubled by affective versus behavioral aspects of shyness. Based on a cluster analysis of respondents' ratings of five manifestations of shyness, Pilkonis classified respondents as either publicly or privately shy. Privately shy people were bothered primarily by their inner discomfort and apprehension regarding others' evaluations, whereas publicly shy respondents were bothered more by their failure to participate appropriately in social encounters. Although all dispositionally shy people experience affective and behavioral

---

*Using the definition of shyness proposed here, the individuals whom Zimbardo (1977) calls "shy extraverts" are, in fact, not shy. In my terminology, they are socially anxious, but not inhibited. Not manifesting both the affective and behavioral components, they would not be labeled "shy."

components of shyness to some degree, they differ in the extent to which each is a problem. Interestingly, whether a subject was classified as privately or publicly shy was only weakly related to their behavior in a laboratory interaction (Pilkonis, 1977b). Identifying factors that predispose people to be publicly versus privately shy or to experience social anxiety without being inhibited may be one route to understanding the relationship between social anxiety and interpersonal inhibition.

THE ANXIETY–INHIBITION CYCLE

To complicate matters even further, each component of the shyness syndrome can, directly or indirectly, elicit or exacerbate the other, creating a spiraling anxiety–inhibition cycle. For example, Cheek and Busch (1981) obtained a moderately strong positive correlation between scores on the Shyness Scale (Cheek & Buss, 1981) and the Revised UCLA Loneliness Scale. Two plausible explanations of this finding come to mind. The most obvious is that shy individuals tend to avoid social encounters and participate less in them, thereby making fewer friends and having fewer social activities. In addition, because shy people are judged to be less friendly and likeable by others (Jones & Russell, 1982; Zimbardo, 1977)—presumably because they are less open and outgoing—others may seek out their company less often. Either way, inhibition-induced loneliness may heighten social anxiety and inhibition even further. When people feel lonely, they are unusually sensitive to others' evaluations of them, viewing every social contact in terms of its opportunities for friendship, companionship, or romantic involvement (Peplau & Perlman, 1982). As a result, lonely people may become increasingly concerned with others' perceptions and evaluations of them, thereby increasing shyness further (Leary, 1983a). Added anxiety and inhibition may then result in greater loneliness, and so on.

In another domain, people who become anxious and inhibited in cross-sexed interactions are less sexually experienced than their less shy peers (Leary & Dobbins, 1983d; Zimbardo, 1977). Not only are shy individuals less likely to date and get to know people of the other sex well, they are more reluctant to initiate and respond to sexual overtures. Over time, people who perceive their romantic and sexual experience to be low, compared to their peers, may come to doubt their desirability as a romantic or sexual partner. In turn, these doubts promote anxiety and inhibition in real or contemplated interactions with the other sex and decrease even further opportunities for heterosexual relationships. Many individuals find that shyness stands in the way of pursuing satisfying romantic and sexual relationships and precludes having the experiences necessary to build confidence (Leary & Dobbins, 1983d; Solomon & Solomon, 1971; Zimbardo, 1977).

These sorts of anxiety–inhibition cycles are quite devastating for individuals who fall into them. However, we have only a meager understanding of the processes involved and how to break them. How can the link between the anxiety and inhibition components of shyness be broken to shortcircuit these endless loops? The theoretical and practical benefits of addressing this and related questions are substantial.

IMPLICATIONS FOR MEASUREMENT AND RESEARCH

In addition to the theoretical issues raised, conceptualizing shyness as composed of distinct anxiety and behavioral components has implications for how psychologists measure and study shyness. Elsewhere, I have discussed the methodological implications of failing to distinguish between the affective and behavioral components, so I will not do so here (Leary, 1982, 1983a,b,c). Rather, the point I wish to make is that, if we define shyness in terms of both social anxiety and inhibition, it is most informative to assess both components in our research and practice. This is not to say that studies may not focus on either anxiety or behavior if researchers are interested in only social anxiety or in inhibition. But studies dealing with shyness should generally be interested in both anxiety and behavior.

If one is interested in individual differences in shyness, one can take one of two routes. The first is to use an instrument that taps both the affective and behavior components of shyness within a single scale (Cheek & Buss, 1981; Jones & Russell, 1982). If a researcher is interested in only the overall level of shyness and not in the relative degree of each component, this is a reasonable approach. The second option is to utilize separate measures of social anxiousness and inhibition. My interest in disentangling the two components of shyness led me to construct and validate a self-report measure that assesses only the self-reported tendency to experience social anxiety, while eliminating items that refer specifically to inhibition and other behaviors (Leary, 1983a, b).

To my knowledge, no pure self-report measures of the tendency to be inhibited in social encounters exist that measure inhibition independently of sociability, introversion, assertion, anxiety, and general social avoidance. Such a scale would make a welcome addition to the literature. (Elsewhere in this volume, Briggs and Smith examine measures of dispositional shyness and related constructs in greater detail.)

For researchers interested in situationally based (i.e., "state") shyness, the anxiety component may be assessed through self-reports and/or physiological measures, such as heartrate and GSR (see Brodt & Zimbardo, 1981; Leary, in press; Martin, 1961). Self-reports are more problematic in this regard than they appear on the surface because it is not clear how questionnaire items should be phrased. Specifically, what adjective should be inserted in the following question to elicit what we want to know: "How ——— did you feel during your conversation with the other subject in this study?" Anxious? Nervous? Relaxed? Shy? Aroused? Worried? Apprehensive? Distressed? From my experience it seems that using different words elicits somewhat different answers. One solution is to use Zuckerman's (1960) Affect Adjective Checklist, which asks subjects which terms in a list of 21 anxiety-related adjectives describe the way they currently nervous, tense, calm, afraid). This measure has been widely used in counseling research and is sensitive to treatments designed to decrease subjective anxiety.

From all I have said so far, it should come as no surprise that I discourage researchers from measuring the anxiety component of shyness via observed behaviors, an approach that has been particularly common in treatment research. Not only does using behavioral indexes of an affective state create conceptual confusion, but, as we have discussed, there is no necessary relationship between social anxiety and interpersonal behavior. Behavioral measures may be used to buttress self-reports and physiological measures of anxiety only to the degree that the relationship between subjective anxiety and the target behavior is straightforward. I have fewer objections to using measures of fidgeting than measures of social participation as indicators of anxious arousal, for example. Even so, it must be recognized that people may be anxious without showing it in overt behavior and behavioral data should be regarded only as suggestive of subjectively experienced anxiety.

Behavioral measures can, of course, be used for assessing the behavioral component of shyness. A difficulty arises, however, in the identification of target behaviors that constitute inhibition. By definition, inhibition involves the absence of certain behaviors, so how are we to know whether an individual is inhibited? This question can be answered in two ways. One is through between-group comparisons of behaviors that are known to decrease in frequency when people are shy, specifically verbal participation and certain nonverbal measures, such as eye contact. We badly need a small set of clearly delineated behaviors that are widely accepted as measures of shy inhibition. A second, less direct approach is to ask respondents the degree to which they refrained from doing and saying the things they wished to do and say during an interaction. To my knowledge, this tactic has not been used, but I can imagine several creative ways of asking people about their degree of inhibition. One possibility is to ask subjects to rate their perceived level of involvement in a conversation on several behavioral dimensions, as well as their ideal or preferred level of involvement if they had acted precisely as they would have liked to. The discrepancy between these two measures could be used as a rough index of inhibition.

SUMMARY

Shyness might best be conceptualized as a psychological syndrome char-acterized by social anxiety and interpersonal inhibition that results from the prospect or presence of interpersonal evaluation. Conceptualizing shyness as composed of two separate, yet interrelated components raises a number of theoretical, empirical, and methodological questions. Perhaps of central impor-tance is the nature of the relationship between anxiety and inhibition; our current understanding of why socially anxious people are often, but not always inhibited is quite meager. The anxiety–behavior link is very complex, mediated by a number of variables, and often involving an interplay between the anxiety and behavioral components themselves. One thing is clear: there is no necessary relationship between social anxiety and interpersonal behavior. A two-component view of shyness also raises issues regarding the measurement of shyness in research and clinical settings. Distinct measures of subjective social anxiety and behavioral inhibition are required to capture both components of the shyness syndrome.

REFERENCES

Brodt, S. E., & Zimbardo, P. G. (1981). Modifying shyness-related social behavior through symptom misattribution. *Journal of Personality and Social Psychology, 41,* 437–449.

Buss, A. H. (1980). *Self-consciousness and social anxiety.* San Francisco: Freeman.

Cheek, J. M., & Busch, C. M. (1981). The influence of shyness on loneliness in a new situation. *Personality and Social Psychology Bulletin, 7,* 572–577.

Cheek, J. M., & Buss, A. H. (1981). Shyness and sociability. *Journal of Personality and Social Psychology, 41,* 330–339.

Crozier, W. R. (1979). Shyness as a dimension of personality. *British Journal of Social and Clinical Psychology, 18,* 121–128.

Girodo, M. (1978). *Shy?* New York: Pocket Books.

Goffman, E. (1957). Alienation from interaction. *Human Relations, 10,* 47–59.

Goffman, E. (1959). *The presentation of self in everyday life.* New York: Doubleday.

Jones, W. H., & Russell, D. (1982). The social reticence scale: An objective instrument to measure shyness. *Journal of Personality Assessment, 46,* 629–631.

Kaplan, D. M. (1972). On shyness. *International Journal of Psychoanalysis, 53,* 439–453.

Kelly, L., Phillips, G. M., & McKinney, B. (1982). Reprise: Farewell reticence, good-by apprehension. *Communication Education, 31,* 211–219.

Leary, M. R. (1982). Social anxiety. In L. Wheeler (Ed.), *Review of personality and social psychology* (Vol. 3, pp. 97–120). Beverly Hills: Sage.

Leary, M. R. (1983a). *Understanding social anxiety: Social, personality, and clinical perspectives.* Beverly Hills, CA: Sage.

Leary, M. R. (1983b). Social anxiousness: The construct and its measurement. *Journal of Personality Assessment, 47,* 66–75.

Leary, M. R. (1983c). The conceptual distinctions *are* important: Another look at communication apprehension and related constructs. *Human Communication Research, 10,* 305–312.

Leary, M. R. (in press). The impact of interactional impediments on social anxiety and self-presentation. *Journal of Experimental Social Psychology.*

Leary, M. R., & Dobbins, S.E. (1983d). Social anxiety, sexual behavior, and contraceptive use. *Journal of Personality and Social Psychology, 45,* 1347–1354.

Leary, M. R., & Schlenker, B. R. (1981). The social psychology of shyness: A self-presentational model. In J. T. Tedeschi (Ed.), *Impression management theory and social psychological research* (pp. 335–358). New York: Academic Press.

Lewinsky, H. (1941). The nature of shyness. *British Journal of Psychology, 32,* 105–113.

Martin, B. (1961). The assessment of anxiety by physiological behavioral measures. *Psychological Bulletin, 58,* 234–255.

Peplau, L. A., & Perlman, D. (Eds.) (1982). *Loneliness: A sourcebook of current theory, research, and therapy.* New York: Wiley.

Phillips, G. (1980). *Help for shy people.* Englewood Cliffs, NJ: Spectrum.

Pilkonis, P. A. (1977a). Shyness, public and private, and its relationship to other measures of social behavior. *Journal of Personality, 45,* 585–595.

Pilkonis, P. A. (1977b). The behavioral consequences of shyness. *Journal of Personality, 45,* 596–611.

Sarason, I. G. (1975). Anxiety and self-preoccupation. In I. G. Sarason & C. D. Spielberger (Eds.), *Stress and anxiety* (Vol. 2). New York: Wiley.

Schachter, S. (1959). *The psychology of affiliation.* Stanford: Stanford University Press.

Schlenker, B. R. (1980). *Impression managment: The self-concept, social identity, and interpersonal relations.* Monterey: Brooks/Cole.

Schlenker, B. R., & Leary, M. R. (1982). Social anxiety and self-presentation: A conceptualization and model. *Psychological Bulletin, 92,* 641–669.

Smith, T. W., Ingram, R. E., & Brehm, S. S. (1983). Social anxiety, anxious self-preoccipation, and recall of self-relevant information. *Journal of Personality and Social Psychology, 44,* 1276–1283.

Solomon, G. V., & Solomon, J. C. (1971). Shyness and sex. *Medical Aspects of Human Sexuality, 5,* 10–19.

Stroufe, L. A. (1977). Wariness of strangers and the study of infant development. *Child Development, 48,* 731–746.

Twentyman, C. T., & McFall, R. M. (1975). Behavioral training of social skills in shy males. *Journal of Consulting and Clinical Psychology, 43,* 384–395.

Wine, J. (1971). Test anxiety and direction of attention. *Psychological Bulletin, 76,* 92–104.

Zimbardo, P. G. (1977). *Shyness: What it is, what to do about it.* New York: Jove.

Zimbardo, P. G., Pilkonis, P. A., & Norwood, R. M. (1974). *The silent prison of shyness* (ONR Tech. Rep. Z-17). Stanford, CA: Stanford University.

Zuckerman, M. (1960). The development of an Affect Anxiety Check List for the measurement of anxiety. *Journal of Consulting Psychology, 24,* 457–462.

4

A Theory of Shyness

Arnold H. Buss

This chapter presents a theory that is an elaboration of a conception first developed in my book, *Self-Consciousness and Social Anxiety* (1980) and in a recent paper
(Buss, 1985). Though there is empirical support for several of my assumptions,
in the interests of brevity and clarity, I shall not include such data. The interested
reader is likely to find such evidence in the more empirical chapters in this
volume. In any event, the novel features of my approach are speculations that
are stated as hypotheses. Some of these may be difficult to test because they
involve statements about the development of shyness and therefore might require
a longitudinal study. Others should be relatively easy to test.

FEARFUL SHYNESS

Fearful shyness starts during the first year of life, usually during the latter
half of the year. Sometimes called *stranger anxiety*, the reaction occurs mainly
when unfamiliar people, usually adults, confront the infant. The typical response
is wariness, retreat, and the seeking of comfort in the security of mother's arms;
more intense reactions include a cry-face or the crying and shrinking back that
characterize fear.

Fearful shyness occurs not only among human infants but also among the
young of most mammalian species. Its adaptive value, if there is any, is that
the presence of strangers (especially adults), even members of one's own species,
may be associated with danger.

Fearful shyness tends to wane as children mature. After many repetitions,
nonthreatening strangers are no longer unfamiliar and therefore do not evoke
fear. Also, children gradually develop the instrumental means for coping with
potential threats. For a minority of children, however, fearful shyness persists.
It is characterized less by the crying and escape attempts of children and more

ARNOLD H. BUSS • Department of Psychology, University of Texas at Austin, Austin, TX 78712.

by the inhibition of speech and behavior interactions that are typical of adult shyness.

Fearful shyness is different from other fear reactions in its being a social anxiety. Thus it involves being upset about social interactions or being frightened when being with others. It is different from such nonsocial fears as the fear of flying, of snakes, or of heights. The distinction lies not in the reaction—which in physiological terms involves activation of the sympathetic division of the autonomic nervous system—but in the immediate cause of the reaction. Thus we can distinguish two kinds of evaluation anxiety. The first kind occurs in a testing situation, in which one's competence in a particular subject matter or skill is assessed, usually by the paper-and-pencil format. If there is worry and disorganization in this context, it is nonsocial evaluation anxiety. The second kind of evaluation anxiety occurs on a first date, when one first meets prospective in-laws, or when one is giving a public speech. In these contexts, whether general competence is being assessed, one's self or person is being evaluated; this is social evaluation anxiety. In brief, fearful shyness is construed as a social anxiety, in contrast to the majority of nonsocial anxieties.

Immediate Causes

The major cause of fearful shyness is the social novelty just discussed. Fearful shyness is not merely stranger anxiety, for it may be caused by two other conditions. The first is intrusiveness. Even when the other person is moderately familiar, if he or she approaches too quickly or moves in too close, the infant may be frightened. A similar reaction may occur in older children and adults, for each of us has a personal spatial zone that we prefer not to be penetrated by most people (Hall, 1966). Intrusiveness can be not only spatial but also psychological. The other person may disclose intensely personal information or ask for a similar disclosure. Either way, most older children and adults find this excessive intimacy aversive and perhaps even threatening, and they react by becoming inhibited and seeking to escape from the situation.

Once past infancy, children are subjected to social evaluation, the third immediate cause of fearful shyness. There are various personal and social criteria used in this evaluation, the major ones being attractiveness, friendliness, social skills, and conformity to the standards and requirements of the particular sub-culture. When people are rejected by others or recognize that they have failed or will fail a social test, they become concerned and socially cautious. The worry and social inhibition—that is, fearful shyness—occur only in older adults and children, who have been socialized sufficiently to be aware of the appropriate standards and the negative consequences of failing a social evaluation.

SELF-CONSCIOUS SHYNESS

This kind of shyness involves the self as a social object. The term *self-conscious* will be limited here to a sense of oneself as a social object. When such self-awareness is acute, most people feel excessively exposed to the scrutiny of others, almost as if they were found naked on a public street. When this feeling is especially intense—a private act is suddenly made public, for example—the outcome is often embarrassment, the extreme endpoint of shyness.

Embarrassment is usually characterized by blushing, though at times people report feeling embarrassed when they are not blushing. Nevertheless, blushing may be regarded as the hallmark of embarrassment, and we are the only animal that blushes. Why? I have suggested elsewhere that we are the only animals to be aware of ourselves as social objects—that is, to possess a social self. Such public self-awareness appears to be a universal feature of socialization training. Children are taught that others are observing them, scrutinizing their appearance, manners, and other social behavior. After several years of such training, children develop the requisite social awareness and may be as aware of their own observable aspects as are those around them. This tendency to focus on oneself as a social object is not present in infants because they lack not only socialization training but also the necessary cognitive ability, which is present only in older children and adults.

We know that infants possess certain cognitive capabilities and that they can, for example, recognize their mirror image before two years of age (Amsterdam, 1972). The higher apes can also recognize their own image in a mirror (Gallup, 1970), which is evidence for self-awareness. Animals and human infants are also aware of their body boundaries and of the difference between being touched by another and being touched by oneself. These capabilities are evidence for a primitive, sensory sense of self, which is present in both animals and humans.

Animals and human infants, however, do not have self-esteem, do not understand the distinction between shared and unshared feelings (the inner experiential aspects of anger or affection versus their observable expressions), and do not know that others have a different perspective. These advanced cognitions seem to develop by the fourth or fifth year of life. They enable children to have a sense of themselves as social objects and to understand that certain feelings or tendencies should not be exposed to observation. Once they possess this sense of a social self, they have something to blush about and are susceptible to embarrassment and self-conscious shyness.

I am aware of only one study of the development of a social self (Buss, Iscoe, & Buss, 1979). We reasoned that a sure sign of the social self would be embarrassment, for if there were no sense of oneself as a social object, there would be no need to blush. Several hundred parents were asked to report if their children had displayed embarrassment during the past six months and if so, what the occasion was. Then we divided the replies according to the age of the children. A small percentage of three year olds blushed or showed other signs of embarrassment. The percentage jumped in four year olds and peaked in five years olds, thereafter to remain a steady majority of children. We therefore concluded that the norm for the appearance of a social self is the fourth or fifth year of life.

Notice that embarrassment represents an extreme of self-conscious shyness, but not all of this kind of shyness is embarrassment. One may be aware of one's public self or be inhibited or disorganized in social behavior (that is, shy) without being embarrassed. Thus, the tendency to become embarrassed easily is only one member of the class of responses that constitute the trait of shyness. In other words, self-conscious shyness is closely linked to embarrassment, but the two are not identical.

Self-conscious shyness is even more distinct from shame, which involves the more serious, moral derivative of public self-awareness. And this kind of shyness is different from the audience anxiety of public speakers. When on stage, the speaker is the focus of the entire audience and is responsible for the social event. In dyadic interactions, in which shyness occurs, the focus of attention and the responsibility for speaking shift back and forth. It is possible to speak without being closely scrutinized, and one can refrain from speaking without censure.

Immediate Causes

The most important cause of self-conscious shyness is conspicuousness. Few people like to be stared at, for such close observation makes them feel naked and vulnerable. Presumably, when children are taught to become aware of themselves as social objects, their parents and other caretakers tend mainly to correct mistakes. Thus public self-awareness can easily become associated with criticism. When people stare at us, we wonder what we have done wrong to become so conspicuous. Such discomfort is intensified when some aspect of oneself (clothes, manners, or a secret crush) is held up to ridicule. Teasing often leads to embarrassment and shyness.

Another source of conspicuousness is being demonstrably different from others. On some college campuses, blacks stand out among whites when they represent one or two percent of the student population. Aside from such chronic conspicuousness, there are many brief occasions during which people become sharply aware of their uniqueness: a small boy in a men's locker room, a man at a club meeting of the National Organization for Women, or a man waiting for his wife in the lingerie section of a department store.

Conspicuousness also derives from breaches of privacy, in which private functions or body parts are made public. Virtually all societies teach their children bodily modesty, and in many societies (certainly our own), eliminative functions and sexual behavior are supposed to be unseen and unheard. In addition, there are thoughts, feelings, and ambitions that are personal and private; when they are disclosed inadvertently or suggested by teasing, most people become self-consciously shy, often to the extent of embarrassment.

Thus we are likely to feel conspicuous when the social context is public and therefore when one is open to scrutiny or made aware of how uniquely different he or she is. Both characteristics mark formal situations, which are not only public but emphasize the status of the participants; the person of subordinate status is often acutely reminded of his or her lesser status, and many people are inhibited and disorganized when they are in the presence of Nobel Prize winners, governors, and others of great status. Formal contexts also involve more social rules, more specific rules, and more inflexible rules. Thus a man is likely to feel conspicuous and embarrassed when wearing a business suit to a dinner at which all the other men are wearing tuxedos. Similarly, if one is the only person in a small group who does not know and therefore cannot sing the words to the national anthem, the usual reaction is acute self-conscious shyness.

COMPARISON

The two kinds of shyness are compared in Table 1. Fearful shyness differs from other fears in its source, which is other people. It is similar to other fears in the nature of the reaction to the frightening stimulus. The reaction involves one or more of three components: (a) a motor component, which consists of attempts to shrink back, to escape, or to avoid the situation; (b) a physiological component, which involves activation of the sympathetic division of the autonomic nervous system and therefore a potentially intense state of bodily arousal; and (c) a cognitive component, which consists of concern over past fearful situations and apprehension about future social situations.

Self-conscious shyness does not involve fearfulness but feelings of being awkward, foolish, and vulnerable. The three possible components of the reaction are: (a) a motor component, which consists mainly of fumbling, disorganization, and inhibition of social behavior; (b) a physiological component, which is present only in embarrassment and then only when the parasympathetic division is activated in blushing; and (c) a cognitive component, which is acute awareness of oneself as a social object.

Fearful shyness requires no special, advanced sense of self and therefore can occur when there is only a primitive, sensory self: in mammals and in human infants. Self-conscious shyness involves public self-awareness, which requires an advanced, cognitive self, and it is therefore present only in older human children and adults.

Though fearful shyness may start during the first year of life, it may not begin until later. Two of its immediate causes, novelty and intrusion, may occur any time in life, starting in infancy. Social evaluation, however, does not commence until the child is several years old.

TABLE 1. Fearful versus Self-Conscious Shyness

	Fearful	Self-conscious
Affective reaction	fear, distress	public self-awareness
Kind of self involved	sensory	cognitive
Present in	mammals, human infants	humans: older children and adults
First appearance	first year	fourth–fifth year
Immediate causes	novelty	being scrutinized
	intrusion	being uniquely different
		breach of privacy
		formal situations

The causes of self-conscious shyness have no impact until the fourth or fifth year of life, by definition. Thereafter, they begin to have an impact in the developmental sequence listed in Table 1. The earliest cause is being the focus of attention, but it may take a few more years before children become sensitive to being uniquely different from others. Breaches of privacy become important later in childhood, when teasing is most important and reaches a peak in adolescence, when teenagers develop an acute sense of privacy. The impact of formal situations awaits the completion of socialization and is ordinarily an important cause of self-conscious shyness starting in adolescence.

PERSONALITY TRAITS

One need not be a psychologist to discern marked individual differences in shyness, which is a personality trait of considerable importance in social behavior. There are several extant self-report measures of the trait of shyness, including one that I helped develop (Cheek & Buss, 1981). None of these measures, however, distinguishes between fearful shyness and self-conscious shyness. If my theoretical conception has any substance, all these measures represent a combination of two different shyness traits. A practical question remains, though: How important is it to separate shyness into two traits, one for each kind of shyness?

One answer to this question may be found in the immediate causes of transient shyness (see Table 1). Those who are high in the trait of fearful shyness are expected to be especially sensitive to novelty, intrusion, and social evaluation but not to the four causes of self-conscious shyness. Those who are high in the trait of self-conscious shyness are expected to be especially reactive to being scrutinized, being uniquely different, breaches of privacy, and formal situations. Thus, separating shyness into two traits offers a more precise prediction of the stimuli that will have the greatest impact.

Another reason for distinguishing between two kinds of shyness traits may be their different origins. Once source of the trait of fearful shyness may be intense and frequent classical conditioning of fear during childhood. Some children, though properly nurtured by their parents, are bullied, threatened, or rejected when turned over to other caretakers. Smaller, weaker children may be the target of aggression by older children, adolescents, or adults. After years of such conditioning, they may associate strangers or casual acquaintances with being harmed or threatened.

One class of children would be especially susceptible to such fear conditioning and therefore prime candidates for the trait of fearful shyness: those high in the temperament of fearfulness. The tendency to be fearful, part of the more general trait of emotionality, has been found to have a strong inherited component (Buss & Plomin, 1975, 1984).

Another potential cause of the trait of fearful shyness is the relative isolation of children so that they rarely encounter strangers and have few acquaintances. Such an upbringing fails to allow children the opportunity to habituate to the novelty of strangers or unfamiliar social contexts, and the initial fear response simply does not wane. The importance of this variable may be seen in its opposite: when children are exposed repeatedly to strangers and strange places. This experience is common to the children of members of the Army or the Air Force, whose parents move from one base to the next, sometimes overseas, every three or four years. As adolescents or adults, they have virtually no fearful shyness, for they have habituated completely to social novelty.

The origin of self-conscious shyness tends to be different. The principal cause is likely to be excessive socialization training in the importance of the social self. Some parents are continually reminding their children of how others are examining them, of how important are proper appearance and manners. After many such admonitions, the child is likely to develop so strong and negative a sense of himself or herself as a social object as to be self-consciously shy. Notice that the child is not frightened but made to feel conspicuous and vulnerable.

Another origin of self-conscious shyness is the failure to develop social skills, so that one might cope with being conspicuous or different, or with breaches of privacy and formal contexts. Lack of social skills is also a likely cause of fearful shyness, however, and therefore cannot be used as a rationale for distinguishing between the two traits of shyness.

If the assumptions about the diverse origins of the two shyness traits are correct, each trait should be related to different personality traits. Fearful shyness should correlate with the temperaments of fearfulness and general emotionality. Self-conscious shyness should be closely related to the trait of public self-consciousness.

These hypotheses suggest a way of separating people into those who are either high in one shyness trait or the other. The method would involve administering a standard shyness scale that is unconfounded by sociability (Cheek & Buss, 1981), a fearfulness scale (Buss & Plomin, 1984), and a public self-consciousness scale (Fenigstein, Scheier, & Buss, 1975). Subjects who scored in say, the upper 40% of the shyness distribution might be higher in either shyness trait or both. These subjects would then be divided into three groups: (a) those in the top 40% of the fearfulness distribution but in the bottom 40% of the public self-consciousness distribution; (b) those in the top 40% of the public self-consciousness distribution but in the bottom 40% of the fearfulness distribution; and (c) the remaining subjects. The first two groups would consist, respectively, of fearful shy people who are not self-consciously shy and self-conscious shy people who are not fearfully shy.

Once these two groups were identified, it would be possible to determine whether each is differentially sensitive to a class of immediate causes of each kind of shyness. It would also be possible to test another hypothesis that derives from splitting the trait of shyness into two different kinds. This hypothesis deals with remediation of the discomfort of those who suffer from excessive shyness. For fearful shyness, the treatment of choice would seem to be systematic desensitization, in which the client would be introduced slowly to successively more threatening social contexts. For self-conscious shyness, remediation is more problematic, for it would be directed at reducing public self-consciousness. One technique might be to teach people ways of diverting attention from themselves and to demonstrate that they are not being examined as closely as they might think. The point here is that fearful shyness and self-consciousness shyness have not only different origins but different consequences for treatment.

REFERENCES

Amsterdam, B. (1972) Mirror self-image reactions before the age of two. *Developmental Psychology, 5*, 297–305.

Buss, A. H. (1980) *Self-consciousness and social anxiety*. San Francisco: Freeman.

Buss, A. H. (1985) Two kinds of shyness. In R. Schwarzer (Ed.) *Anxiety and cognitions*. Hillsdale, NJ: Erlbaum.

Buss, A. H., & Plomin, R. (1975) *A temperment theory of personality development*. New York: Wiley-Interscience.

Buss, A. H., & Plomin R. (1984) *Temperment: early developing personality traits*. Hillsdale, NJ: Erlbaum.

Buss, A. H., Iscoe, I., & Buss, E. H. (1979) The development of embarrassment. *Journal of Psychology, 103*, 227–230.

Cheek, J., & Buss, A. H. (1981) Shyness and sociability. *Journal of Personality and Social Psychology, 41*, 330–339.

Fenigstein, A., Scheier, M. F., & Buss, A. H. (1975) Public and private self-consciousness: Assessment and theory. *Journal of Personality and Social Psychology, 43* 522–527.

Gallup, G. G., Jr. (1970). Chimpanzees: Self-recognition. *Science, 167*, 86–87.

Hall, E. T. (1966) *The hidden dimension*. New York: Doubleday.

5

The Measurement of Shyness

Stephen R. Briggs and Thomas G. Smith

Shyness is not unlike many psychological constructs in that it connotes a rich cluster of behaviors, cognitions, feelings, and bodily reactions. It reduces to no single, concrete object or referent; rather, it represents a convenient abstraction of characteristics we observe in others and in ourselves. The breadth of the construct explains in part its popularity as a label in everyday discourse, but this breadth also creates some confusion among those who wish to understand the nature, origins, and consequences of shyness. Everyone is familiar with the common usage and general meaning of the term, and thus there is substantial overlap in the definitions and measures used in shyness research. At the same time, however, there are areas of fundamental disagreement. Those who study shyness differ in their emphasis and level of specificity, and these differences are reflected in the various ways in which shyness is conceptualized and operationalized as well as in the type of questions that are researched.

In this chapter we will examine a number of the measures that have been developed and used in studies of shyness. The bulk of the chapter will focus on self-report measures because they dominate the extant literature. The measurement of shyness is in no way limited to the questionnaire format, however, and other modes of measurement will also be discussed. The first section considers a variety of measures that have been used in shyness research, and the second section focuses specifically on shyness inventories.

MODES OF MEASUREMENT

Psychological measures exhibit enormous diversity but can be grouped nonetheless into a limited number of categories. Although different classification systems have been developed (e.g., Cattell, 1973; McClelland, 1951), the present

STEPHEN R. BRIGGS • Department of Psychology, University of Tulsa, Tulsa, OK 74104. THOMAS G. SMITH • Late of the Department of Behavioral Statistics, Baylor University, Waco, TX 76704.

discussion will follow the system proposed by Fiske (1971). His scheme emphasizes the mode by which information is gathered and group measures into one
of six categories: self-description (e.g., questionnaires and biographical inventories); current experiencing (preferences and judgments); capabilities (ability or
achievement tests); prior behavior (peer ratings and ratings based on records);
observation of behavior (interviews, laboratory recordings, and projective tests);
and psychophysiology (heart rate, galvanic skin response, and blood chemistry).
Several of these modes have been used widely in shyness research and several
have not, but each of the modes provides a distinct type of information. It would
be misleading, therefore, to focus on one or two modes of measurement to the
exclusion of the others. A comprehensive understanding of shyness requires a
comprehensive set of methods and measures.

Space limitations prevent us from exhaustively describing and evaluating
each of the measurement modes, but we will review briefly the issues that arise
and the measures that are available for the various measurement modes, and
we will also point to the work currently being done in these areas (much of
which is represented elsewhere in this volume).

Current Experiencing

Included in this category are measures that ask participants to make judgments, indicate preferences, and report on current feelings. These measures
differ from traditional personality inventories in that they ask about one's present
condition and experience, rather than about one's typical manner of responding;
these measures focus, therefore, on an immediate situation or state rather than
an enduring trait.

In his investigations of human emotion, Izard (1977, this volume) has
developed a Differential Emotions Scale (Form I), which employs 30 adjectives
to assess 10 fundamental emotions. One of the fundamental emotions is labelled
shame/shyness and consists of the adjectives sheepish, bashful, and shy.
Respondents are asked to describe the way they feel at the present time using
a 5-point Likert format. The same adjectives can also be used as a trait measure
by simply rewording the instructions (Izard's Form II).

A second example of this mode of measurement can be found in the Stanford Shyness Survey (Zimbardo, 1977). One part of the survey (Items 37 to 40)
asks individuals about the symptoms they experience when they feel shy. These
symptoms can be grouped into physical reactions, thoughts and feelings, and
actions (see Briggs & Metz, 1985; Fattis, 1983).

Finally, several investigations have asked individuals to make decisions
that carry some behavioral obligation. These questions—which are sometimes
labelled "behavioroid measures"—include whether participants would rather
participate in an experiment alone or with someone else (McGovern, 1976),
whether they would return for the second session of an experiment (Watson &
Friend, 1969), and whether they would enroll for a treatment program (Leary,
1983).

Capabilities

The capabilities category includes measures that span a wide range of skills and activities, from intelligence and achievement tests to perceptual-motor and athletic tasks. At first glance, this category might seem irrelevant to the domain of shyness, but competency in social interaction requires as much in the way of knowledge and skill as does any other form of competency.

Social skills and social knowledge can be assessed in two basic ways. First, the actual behavior of individuals can be compared with some standard. Skilled individuals should approximate the standard more closely than their unskilled counterparts. Second, individuals can be tested for their knowledge of appropriate acts and responses. Notice that both methods require a comparison to some yardstick. Neither method has been used much in research on shyness, perhaps because it is difficult to specify and quantify excellence in the realm of social skills and social knowledge. Asendorpf (this volume) reviews two studies that relate social problem solving to shy, isolated behavior in children, but by and large this topic remains unexplored.

Prior Behavior

Studies that examine an individual's prior behavior generally rely on the personal recollections and experiences of someone who has known the target well for an extended period of time. That person will typically be a relative, friend, colleague, teacher, or supervisor. Such individuals are privy to information that might otherwise be unobtainable, and they can therefore be called knowledgeable observers. At the same time, however, they may also be unable to provide impartial ratings for in most cases they are not disinterested onlookers.

Regardless of the source, recollections of prior behavior must somehow be collected and recorded. In applied settings, a variety of formats have been developed ranging from unstructured methods such as letters of reference and lists of critical incidents to psychometrically sophisticated methods such as behaviorally-anchored rating scales (BARS). Research in the area of shyness, however, has generally used fixed response formats and broad trait labels, a rather simple approach.

One standard type of rating instrument employs a group of adjectives. For example, the chapter by Gough and Thorne (this volume) uses groups of positive and negative adjectives from the Adjective Check List, and the chapter by Jones and Carpenter (this volume) reports ratings by friends using a list of descriptive adjectives called the Dimensions of Friendship Rating Scale. Another approach, less widely used, is to rewrite a personality inventory in the third person for use as a rating instrument. McCroskey, Anderson, Richmond, and Wheeless (1982) present such a revision of their shyness scale, and the Shyness Situations measure (Russell, Cutrona, and Jones, this volume) can be used this way as well.

Observation of Behavior

Whereas studies of prior behavior generally rely on raters who know the target well, a second type of rating study emphasizes objectivity. Raters observe the targets in a standard setting (e.g., a laboratory paradigm or a structured interview) or have available to them some permanent record of information (e.g., written files or videorecordings). The ratings can be called objective for three reasons: the raters are typically trained, they are generally unacquainted with the target participants, and they usually see all (or a large number) of the targets and can therefore judge each target relative to the rest of the sample. At the same time, however, the external validity of such ratings is often limited by the artificiality of the setting. Ratings based on a single period of observation in a specific setting can hardly reflect the richness of an individual's behavior, nor can this limited opportunity provide substantial insight into behavioral regularities.

In attempting to observe the behavioral consequences of shyness, researchers necessarily make decisions which will color and constrain their findings. These fundamental decisions can be grouped into two categories: the setting for data collection and the level of measurement.

Setting. Behavior is influenced by the context in which it occurs. When shy behavior is studied, therefore, it matters whether the data are collected in a laboratory or natural setting, whether the participants are aware of recording apparatus or observers, whether the interaction is staged or spontaneous, and whether it involves a dyad, a group, or a person alone. Spontaneous interactions involving a group or dyad in a natural setting where subjects are unaware of being observed may reflect the ideal setting, but ethical and practical considerations generally compel researchers to settle for something less than ideal. Thus, most research is conducted in the laboratory, although Asendorpf (this volume) reports some observational studies conducted on a playground, and most studies inform subjects of recording apparatus and hidden observers prior to participation, although Cheek and Buss (1981) used a procedure that side-stepped this practice (see Ickes, 1982, for a review of such procedures).

Several studies have examined the impact of shyness on dyadic interactions (e.g., Cheek & Buss, 1981; Leary, Knight, & Johnson, 1984), but such studies must contend with the problem of dyadic dependency, which is the tendency for the behavior of a participant to be related to (and presumably determined in part by) the behavior of the partner. This problem is handled sometimes by analyzing the behavior of dyads rather than that of individuals (e.g., Cheek & Buss, 1981). Another approach—particularly apt for opposite-sex pairs—is to analyze one member of each pair initially (e.g., the women) and then to use the partners as a replication sample (Jones, Sansone, & Helm, 1983).

Other researchers choose to circumvent the problem altogether by employing a confederate as one member of the dyad (Pilkonis, 1977) or by opting for a role-playing or monologue task that an individual can perform alone (Daly, 1978; Jones, Briggs, & Smith, 1985). Although these methods avoid some of the statistical problems associated with dyadic dependency, they have their own shortcomings. The use of confederates does not completely avoid the problem of dyadic dependency because the confederates still have an impact on the interaction and, insofar as the confederates are trained to follow a script, the interaction loses spontaneity and becomes a product of the scripted questions and answers. Although solitary tasks avoid the problem of dependency, they are probably more appropriate as measures of stage fright or acting ability than as measures of social shyness.

Levels of Measures. Many recent studies of social interaction have used videorecording to obtain permanent records of interactions. Such records are clearly advantageous, but they are also disconcerting because they can be analyzed in so many ways. Two basic strategies for analyzing taped interactions can be identified: global observations and behavioral measures.

Global observations capitalize on the ability of observers (trained or untrained) to process, analyze, and integrate various sources of information. Observers, in fact, are flawed in these abilities and their observations often are biased and subjective. Nevertheless, they provide the only realistic way to synthesize a complex set of data, and presumably the process by which they form impressions is similar to the process of person perception as it occurs in daily life. Global observations often show substantial correlations with behavioral and self-report measures of shyness (e.g., Cheek & Buss, 1981; Jones, Briggs, & Smith, 1985; and Pilknois, 1977).

Behavioral measures would appear to provide more objective assessments of a data record. A number of behavioral indexes have been used in previous research on shyness, including measures of frequency (number of gestures, head nods, smiles, utterances, and questions), measures of duration (amount of time spent talking to and looking at one's partner and time spent touching self), and measures of latency (amount of time needed to initiate conversation initially and after a period of silence); for example, see Cavert, 1982; Cheek & Buss, 1981; Daly, 1978; Mandel & Shrauger, 1980; Orchard, Schallow, & Perlman, 1984; and Pilkonis, 1977. Interrater reliability for these behavioral indexes tends to be noticably larger than for global observations, but correlations with self-reported shyness are often smaller. The lower correlations may be due in part to the specificity of the measures; it is often the pattern of behaviors that betrays an individual's anxiety, not the presence or absence of any one behavior. In fact, shyness may manifest itself in seemingly contradictory ways (Campbell, 1896; Litwinski, 1950). For instance, smiling may indicate the shy person's anxious desire to fit in (Pilkonis, 1977), but the absence of smiling can also signify anxiety (Mandel & Shrauger, 1980). The proper interpretation can only be made in light of the complete pattern of responses.

Psychophysiology

Izard and Hyson (this volume) argue that shyness is a dimension of emotion that involves (like other emotions) three basic components—the neurophysiological, the motor-expressive, and the subjective-experiential—and that an understanding of shyness requires an understanding of its physiology along with an understanding of its characteristic feelings and behaviors. They list several measures relevant to the study of shyness: heart rate measures, electroencephalography (EEG), and electromyography (EMG). These measures are consistent with Buss' (1980, this volume) suggestion that shyness is characterized by activation of the sympathetic branch of the autonomic nervous system. Kagan and Reznick (this volume) have used measures of heart rate variability and pupil dilation in their studies of behavioral inhibition and psychological uncertainty in young children.

Previous research has not always found a straightforward relationship between self-report measures of shyness or social anxiety and physiological measures of arousal, such as heart rate (e.g., Miller & Arkowitz, 1977). The absence of a relationship probably reflects both complexity in the psychophysiology of the responses and inconsistencies in the way that individuals interpret such responses. Rather than detract from the importance of psychophysiological measures, however, these findings suggest that it is important to examine shyness from all available angles and to integrate these complementary sources in our models of shyness.

SELF-DESCRIPTIVE MEASURES OF SHYNESS

A number of measures have been developed and used wherein participants describe the extent to which they see themselves as shy or socially anxious. This section focuses on seven of these self-report measures although in so doing it ignores several measures of social anxiety (e.g., see Dixon, de Monchaux, & Sandler, 1957; Fenigstein, Scheier, & Buss, 1975; Sears, 1967), measures of related constructs (sociability, audience anxiety, shame, communication apprehension, social self-esteem, etc.), and shyness measures that are part of larger omnibus inventories (including Cattell's threctia, and shyness scales by Comrey and Guilford). Each of the seven measures is described briefly below along with some of the relevant reliability and validity information.

In reviewing and evaluating these measures, we emphasize the *behavioral validity* of these scales. By doing so, we do not mean to claim that behavioral measures provide the only appropriate criteria by which self-report scales can be judged. With a rich construct such as shyness, no one mode of measurement can serve as the sole standard. Mapping out the relationships which establish the validity of a construct necessitates diverse approaches. Often, however, it is the relationships between self-description and behavior which critics find particularly compelling and which prove particularly difficult to demonstrate (cf., Mischel, 1968). Thus, the review of validity data focuses specifically on behavioral and observational studies although this emphasis admittedly neglects other important sources of information.

Social Avoidance and Distress Scale

An often used measure of shyness is the Social Avoidance and Distress Scale developed by Watson & Friend (1969). It was designed to measure social-evaluative anxiety in conjunction with the Fear of Negative Evaluation Scale.

Items were written to measure social avoidance—defined as "avoiding being with, talking to, or escaping from others for any reason" (p. 449)—and social distress—defined as being tense, upset, distressed, or anxious in social interactions. Items referring to impaired performance or physiological manifestations were excluded deliberately.

The Social Avoidance and Distress Scale consists of 28 true-false items that also can be grouped into two factors identified as social approach-avoidance and social anxiety (Patterson & Strauss, 1972). The original article recorded a one-month test–retest reliability of .68 for the full scale and a KR-20 of .94. A one-month test–retest correlation of .86 was obtained by independent investigators (Girodo, Dotzenroth, & Stein, 1981).

The Social Avoidance and Distress Scale has been used in a number of behavioral studies. The original article reported that individuals scoring high on the scale—compared to those scoring low—showed less interest in and were more worried about returning for a follow-up experiment, particularly if the session involved a group discussion. High scorers also reported talking less in a dyadic conversation but were more likely to keep scheduled appointments.

In a videotaped interview where participants answered open-ended questions and acted out a role-playing task, scores on Social Avoidance and Distress correlated $-.47$ with the amount of unsolicited talking and $-.28$ with the amount of eye contact maintained while talking (Daly, 1978). Recent research has also demonstrated that the length of time talking in a dyadic interaction is related to both the Anxiety ($r = -.30$) and Avoidance ($r = -.40$) subscales of the Social Avoidance and Distress Scale (Leary, Knight, & Johnson, 1984). Correlations between the number of utterances spoken and the two subscales also approached statistical significance ($rs = -.24$ and $-.20$, respectively). Leary *et al.* also analyzed the content of these conversations using a coding scheme devised by Stiles (1978). Although there were a number of significant correlations, the results are enigmatic in that they differed by gender and by subscale for each of the verbal response categories. In general, the relationships appeared to be stronger for women than for men, for the Anxiety subscale than for the Avoidance subscale, and for acknowledgments ("uh-huh") and confirmations ("I agree") than for questions.

Stanford Shyness Survey

Although widely cited, the Stanford Shyness Survey (Zimbardo, 1977) is not actually a scale at all. Rather, it consists of 44 questions that can be grouped roughly into the following categories: self-labelling; causal attributions; others' perceptions; situational and interpersonal elicitors; physical, cognitive/affective, and behavioral reactions; and positive and negative consequences. The questions are not meant to be summed into a total score and the response format varies across the survey. The structure of the Stanford Shyness Survey is consistent with Zimbardo's emphasis on societal causes of shyness and shyness as a label rather than as a trait.

Because the survey has not been used as a scale, its psychometric properties have generally been ignored (but see Maroldo, Eisenreich, & Hall, 1979). In practice, shy individuals are identified by their answers to the first question alone—"Do you consider yourself to be a shy person? 1 = Yes; 2 = No"—or in conjunction with self-report ratings of the degree of their shyness, the variability of their shyness across situations, and how their shyness compares to that of others. Shy individuals identified in this way talked less frequently and tended to speak for a smaller percentage of time during a 5-minute interaction with a trained confederate than did nonshy participants (Pilkonis, 1977). Shy individuals also tended to wait longer before initiating the conversation, allowed more periods of silence to develop during the interaction, and interrupted less frequently the periods of silence that did occur. Shy males exhibited greater gaze aversion (e.g., number of glances and percentage of time looking) than their nonshy counterparts, whereas, perhaps surprisingly, females scoring high on shyness smiled and nodded toward their partners more often than nonshy females. Finally, judges' ratings of shyness (averaged across several raters) correlated substantially ($r = .58$) with self-ratings of shyness. In another study that also used items from the Stanford Shyness Survey to identify shy individuals, those scoring high opted to sit farther away from their partners than did those scoring low, particularly if the partner was of the opposite sex (Carducci & Webber, 1979).

Since the publication of Zimbardo's (1977) book, a number of investigators have developed scale measures of shyness. These measures evolved independently and can be ordered along a dimension ranging from broad to narrow. Two broader measures (by Morris, 1982, and by Jones and Russell, 1982, and Jones, Briggs, & Smith, 1984) will be introduced first, followed by three more focused scales (Cheek & Buss, 1981; Leary, 1983; McCroskey, Anderson, Richmond, & Wheeless, 1982).

Shyness Scale. Morris (1982) introduced a 14-item measure for assessing discomfort in the presence of others. The items on the scale were selected from a larger pool of items primarily on the basis of the item–total relationship. The original item pool included items assessing feelings and behaviors associated with shyness along with items that were related indirectly to shyness. Some of the indirect items were deliberately retained on the final scale, including items that appear to assess loneliness, self-esteem, and audience anxiety. Thus, this scale defines shyness loosely rather than rigorously. No studies examining the behavioral validity of the scale have been reported.

Social Reticence Scale. Jones and Russell (1982) developed a 21-item instrument designed to measure 7 components of dispositional shyness (e.g., difficulties in meeting people or expressing opinions, feelings of isolation). A coefficient alpha of .91 was reported in the original scale article along with test–retest correlations of .78 for 12 weeks and .88 for 8 weeks. In addition, scores on the Social Reticence Scale were shown to correlate negatively with frequency of dating and number of close friends.

Subsequent research with the scale has focused in part on the characteristics attributed to shy persons by others in a variety of situations (Jones, Cavert, & Indart, 1983; Jones & Briggs, 1984). In a study of dyadic interaction between opposite-sex strangers, women scoring high on the Social Reticence Scale were rated by their male partners as being less open and less warm than those scoring low, whereas men scoring high on the scale were rated as less attractive by their female partners. In a second study, participants interacted in small groups of 9 to 12 people for 3, 1-hour discussions over a period of 3 days. Scores on the Social Reticence Scale were inversely correlated with the average rating of friendliness made by other group members. Individuals scoring high on the Social Reticence Scale were also less likely than those scoring low to be nominated as group leader, to be able to name fellow group members, or to be identified correctly by name by other group members.

Recently, the Social Reticence Scale was revised in order to replace a few items of marginal quality and to reword half of the items in the reverse direction so that endorsement indicated a lack of shyness (Jones, Briggs, & Smith, 1984). The mean interitem correlation for the revised scale was .33 with an alpha of .91. The new scale had a test–retest correlation of .87 over an 8-week period.

Behavioral validity was evaluated by correlating scores on Social Reticence Scale II with judges' ratings of 2-minute videotaped monologues in which participants talked about themselves informally. Shyness scores correlated positively with judges' ratings of shyness ($r = .50$) and anxiety ($r = .36$), and negatively with 4-item measures of poise ($r = -.44$) and talent ($r = -.38$).

Shyness Scale. Cheek and Buss (1981) suggested that shyness and sociability are not merely the opposing extremes of a bipolar dimension and proceeded to clarify this distinction by developing independent measures of shyness and sociability. By differentiating these two constructs, they of course restricted the domain of each. They defined sociability as a "need to be with people" and shyness as "the discomfort and inhibition that may occur in the presence of others" (p. 330). The measures of shyness and sociability correlated .30 in their study, suggesting that the two constructs are related, but only moderately so.

Cheek and Buss reported a mean interitem correlation of .30, an alpha coefficient of .79, and a 90-day test–retest correlation of .74 for their 9-item shyness cale. In a dyadic-interaction study where pairs of women interacted for five minutes, participants scoring high on shyness talked less, engaged in more self-manipulations (i.e., touching the body or face with one's hands), and were rated by observers as more tense, inhibited, and unfriendly than those scoring low on shyness. Finally, the case for separate measures of shyness and sociability was bolstered in that it was individuals scoring high on *both* shyness and sociability who were rated by observers as being most interpersonally impaired. Apparently, the behavioral problems associated with shyness are accentuated when the shy person also wants or needs to be with other people.

Interaction Anxiety. For many, shyness connotes a cluster of behaviors, cognitions, feelings, and physiological reactions. Leary (1983), however, has argued that items measuring subjectively experienced anxiety should not be confused with items measuring patterns of behavior that sometimes accompany such anxiety, because "there is not a strong relationship between social anxiety and its concomitant behaviors nor any reason to expect one" (p. 67). Leary's measure of interaction anxiety, therefore, focuses solely on the cognitive and affective components of shyness or social anxiety.

The Interaction Anxiousness Scale consists of 15 items that were developed simultaneously with a 14-item measure of Audience Anxiousness. The two measures correlated .44 in Leary's original article, and Interaction Anxiousness had an alpha coefficient of .89 and an 8-week test–retest reliability of .80. Individuals who had sought professional help for interpersonal problems scored higher on Interaction Anxiousness than a control group, and similarly, individuals scoring high on Interaction Anxiousness showed more interest in participating in a treatment program than low anxious individuals.

Shyness Scale. McCroskey and his colleagues have also emphasized the distinction between subjectively experienced anxiety, which they call communication apprehension, and behavioral manifestations for which they reserve the term shyness. The Personal Report of Communication Apprehension (McCroskey, 1981) is a 25-item scale measuring anxiety in four interpersonal contexts: dyadic, group, meetings, and public speaking. This measure is analogous to—though perhaps slightly broader than—Leary's Interaction and Audience Anxiousness Scales. Unlike Leary, however, McCroskey, Anderson, Richmond, & Wheeless (1982) also developed a scale to measure the behavioral aspects of shyness specifically. Their 14-item shyness scale consists of items that assess talkativeness or that ask about shyness directly. McCroskey and Richmond (1982) compared scores on their Shyness Scale with ratings made by friends using a third-person version of the same scale. Observer reports correlated .53 with the self-reports in a large sample of elementary and secondary school teachers.

Comparing Self-Report Measures of Shyness

Clearly, all of the self-report measures of shyness overlap to some extent. But to what extent? To answer this question and to compare the various measures, we examined five of the measures presented above in a single study (Jones, Briggs, & Smith, 1985). The results of our research can be summarized in three points.

Point one is that all five scales appear to exceed conventional standards for internal consistency. We administered the five shyness scales—along with numerous other measures of personality, emotionality, and relationships—to 1,213 (718 women, 495 men) high school and college students from five different institutions. Alpha coefficients ranged from .82 to .92, and interitem correlation means varied from a low of .25 for the Social Avoidance and Distress Scale to a high of .36 for the Social Reticence Scale II. (The mean interitem correlation coefficient is the average correlation of all possible pairs of items. It provides a relatively pure index of scale homogeneity. Unlike Cronbach's alpha coefficient, it is not affected by the number of items on a test and therefore can be used to compare homogeneity across tests of different lengths.)

The second point is that despite differences in conceptual orientation and scale development, all five scales appear to measure more or less the same construct. Evidence for this conclusion comes from three sources. As one might expect, the five shyness scales correlated highly with one another; the pair-wise correlations varied from a low of .70 to a high of .86, with a mean of .77. In addition, the five measures showed a remarkably similar pattern of correlations with other self-report measures. All five scales were inversely related to measures of self-esteem ($\bar{r}$ = −.55), assertiveness ($\bar{r}$ = −.55), extraversion ($\bar{r}$ = −.38), and social desirability ($\bar{r}$ = −.24), whereas they were positively correlated with loneliness ($\bar{r}$ = .51), fearfulness ($\bar{r}$ = .47), neuroticism ($\bar{r}$ = .35), other-directedness ($\bar{r}$ = .38), resentment ($\bar{r}$ = .23), and suspicion ($\bar{r}$ = .27). Finally, all of the measures yielded roughly the same pattern of correlations with peer ratings on a set of adjectives. All five measures were inversely correlated with ratings on outgoing ($\bar{r}$ = −.44), talkative ($\bar{r}$ = −.34), likes people ($\bar{r}$ = −.26), flirtatious ($\bar{r}$ = −.27), and leadership ($\bar{r}$ = −.23), but were positively correlated with shy ($\bar{r}$ = .35), conscientious ($\bar{r}$ = .18), rule abiding ($\bar{r}$ = .17), and dependable ($\bar{r}$ = .16).

The only evidence we found that contradicted the notion that all of the scales measure essentially the same thing was in correlations between the scales and ratings of a videotaped monologue. A sample of 39 participants who had completed the 5 shyness measures also were videotaped while talking about themselves for 2 minutes. Eight observers rated the participants on shyness. Judges' ratings were averaged for each participant and then correlated with the five shyness scores. Although the average ratings of shyness were positively correlated with scores on all five measures, the correlations for the Social Reticence Scale (r = .39), the Morris Shyness Inventory (r = .34), and the Social Avoidance and Distress Scale (r = .31) were statistically significant (two-tailed tests), whereas those for the Cheek & Buss Shyness Scale (r = .25) and the Interaction Anxiousness Scale (r = .11) were not.

The third and final point from our comparison of the five shyness measures involves types of shyness items. Both Leary and McCroskey distinguish between internal, affective experiences and behavioral consequences on the grounds that they are conceptually distinct and that the relationship between the two can only be assessed empirically if they are measured independently. One way to test this notion is to examine the factor structure of a pool of items that includes both types. We factor analyzed the 88 items that comprise the 5 shyness measures on the assumption that they would provide a representative sample of items. It is important to note that items asking about behavior are not isomorphic with behavior itself. The relationship between behavioral items and items measuring social anxiety is probably independent of the extent to which either set of items correlates with actual measures of behavior.

Although the items tended to cluster into three factors, these factors did not reflect a simple distinction between measuring anxiety versus behavior. The first factor consisted largely of items from the Social Avoidance and Distress Scale; the early emergence of these items is not surprising because the scale accounted for 34% of the total item pool. The second factor included items that described competent and effective communication and social initiative (i.e., items worded in the opposite direction of shyness). Interestingly, this factor also contained the four items that asked explicitly about shyness. The last factor consisted of items describing feelings of nervousness in the presence of someone in authority. The four items loading highest on this factor were all worded similarly, and this factor probably reflects item redundancy rather than revealing any important component of shyness.

Items loading .4 or higher on the factors were summed to produce a total score for each factor. Factors 1 and 2 correlated .63; they also correlated similarly with other self-report measures although Factor 1 tended to be more highly related to pejorative dimensions (e.g., loneliness and neuroticism), whereas Factor 2 was more closely related to the self-ascribed adjectives of shy and outgoing. Factor 2 was also significantly related to judges' ratings of shyness from videotaped monologues, but Factors 1 and 3 were not.

Point three, therefore, can be summarized as follows: there is little reason to differentiate between types of items, the distinction between anxiety and behavior notwithstanding (see also Briggs, 1984). To the extent that such a distinction exists, it is the items involving social facility or effectiveness (Factor 2) that provide the best evidence for behavioral validity and that also appear to be the opposite of self-labelled shyness.

CONCLUSION

Our analysis of the current state of shyness measures leads us to the following points of conclusion.

1. As a group, the self-report measures of shyness display exceptional psychometric characteristics. They show excellent stability over time as measured by test–retest correlations, and the homogeneity of their items is striking. They relate consistently to measures of social behavior and relational satisfaction and to ratings by peers, and thus they provide an important perspective for the study of the construct of shyness.

2. The quality of the self-report measures can be attributed in part to careful analyses and systematic development by the scale authors, but this quality must also be in part a function of the construct itself. Shyness appears to involve a fundamental dimension of personality. In a major factor analytic study testing 20 putative dimensions of personality, the first factor to emerge was labelled *social shyness* (Browne & Howarth, 1977). Evidence for an inherited component to shyness (Plomin & Daniels, this volume) also supports the notion that shyness is a basic dimension of personality. In addition, shyness appears to be defined at the appropriate level of specificity. Shyness is not one of the superfactors of personality (such as extraversion or adjustment), but neither is it so specific that it suffers from a lack of applicability. Shyness measures seem to be well balanced in terms of internal consistency and validity; their level of specificity leads to fidelity on the one hand without sacrificing bandwidth on the other.

3. In practical terms, the overall quality of the shyness measures and their considerable overlap implies that the various scales are for the most part inter-changeable. Thus, findings from studies using different scales can be compared and generalized justifiably. The decision to use a particular scale may well depend on the exact nature of one's project. Investigators wanting to maximize predictive

validity might want to use a scale that defines shyness more broadly (e.g., The Social Reticence Scale; Jones, Briggs, & Smith, 1984). Researchers interested in measuring a specific component of shyness, however, might want to choose one of the scales with a more focused item pool (e.g., the Shyness Scale by Cheek & Buss, 1981 or Leary's Interaction Anxiety Scale, 1983).

4. Future research should begin to employ different modes of measurement simultaneously in order to map out the relationships between these complementary approaches (e.g., behavioral, physiological, peer ratings, and self-descriptions). Multimethod studies of this sort will provide the foundation necessary for a systematic understanding of the construct of shyness. Future research should also attend closely to those individuals who violate the typical pattern of results—the exceptions, outliers, and off-diagonal cases. Qualitative researchers have long recognized the importance of negative case analysis. Individuals who defy our predicted relationships provide us with a unique opportunity to reexamine and refine our theories, and they enable us to generate and test new hypotheses. In our efforts to understand the general nature of shyness, we must not forget that shyness always occurs in the context of and is complicated by an individual's life history.

REFERENCES

Browne, J. A., & Howarth, E. (1977). A comprehensive factor analysis of personality questionnaire items: A test of twenty putative factor hypotheses. *Multivariate Behavioral Research, 12,* 399–427.

Briggs, S. R. (1984, August). *Components of shyness.* Paper presented at the meetings of the American Psychological Association, Anaheim, CA.

Briggs, S. R., & Metz, D. M. (1985, August). *The factor structure of shyness reactions.* Paper presented at the meetings of the American Psychological Association, Toronto, Canada.

Buss, A. H. (1980). *Self-consciousness and social anxiety.* New York: W. H. Freeman.

Campbell, H. (1896). Morbid shyness. *The British Medical Journal, 2,* 805–807.

Carducci, B. J., & Webber, A. W. (1979). Shyness as a determinant of interpersonal distance. *Psychological Reports, 44,* 1075–1078.

Cattell, R. B. (1973). *Personality and mood by questionnaire.* San Francisco: Jossey-Bass.

Cavert, C. W. (1982). *A trait-situation analysis of shyness.* Unpublished M.A. thesis, University of Tulsa, OK.

Cheek, J. M., & Buss, A. H. (1981). Shyness and sociability. *Journal of Personality and Social Psychology, 41,* 330–339.

Daly, S. (1978). Behavioral correlates of social anxiety. *British Journal of Social and Clinical Psychology, 17,* 117–120.

Dixon, J. J., deMonchaux, C., & Sandler, J. (1957). Patterns of anxiety: An analysis of social anxieties. *British Journal of Medical Psychology, 30,* 102–112.

Fatis, M. (1983). Degree of shyness and self-reported physiological, behavioral, and cognitive reactions. *Psychological Reports, 52,* 351–354.

Fenigstein,A., Scheier, M. F., & Buss, A. H. (1975). Public and private self-consciousness: Assessment and theory. *Journal of Consulting and Clinical Psychology, 43,* 522–527.

Fiske, D. W. (1971). *Measuring the concepts of personality.* Chicago: Aldine.

Girodo, M., Dotzenroth, S. E., & Stein, S. J. (1981). Causal attribution bias in shy males: Implications for self-esteem and self-confidence. *Cognitive Therapy and Research, 5*(4), 325–338.

Ickes, W. J. (1982). A basic paradigm for the study of personality, roles, and social behavior. In W. J. Ickes & E. S. Knowles (Eds.), *Personality, roles, and social behavior* (pp. 305–341). New York: Springer-Verlag.

Izard, C. E. (1977). *Human emotions*. New York: Plenum Press.

Jones, W. H., & Briggs, S. R. (1984). The self-other discrepancy in social shyness. In R. Schwarzer (Ed.). *The self in anxiety, stress and depression*. Amsterdam: North Holland.

Jones, W. H., & Russell, D. (1982). The Social Reticence Scale: An objective measure of shyness. *Journal of Personality Assessment, 46*, 629–631.

Jones, W. H., Cavert, C., & Indart, M. (1983, August). *Impressions of shyness*. Paper presented at the annual meeting of the American Psychological Association, Anaheim, CA.

Jones, W. H., Sansone, C., & Helm, B. (1983). Loneliness and interpersonal judgments. *Personality and Social Psychology Bulletin, 9*, 431–441.

Jones, W. H., Briggs, S. R., & Smith, T. G. (1984). *Shyness: Conceptualization and measurement*. Unpublished manuscript, University of Tulsa.

Leary, M. R. (1983). Social anxiousness: The construct and its measurement. *Journal of Personality Assessment, 47*, 66–75.

Leary, M. R., Knight, P. D., & Johnson, K. A. (1984). *Social anxiety and dyadic conversation: A verbal response analysis*. Unpublished manuscript, University of Texas at Austin.

Litwinski, Leon. (1950). Constitutional shyness; its active and passive forms. *The Journal of General Psychology, 42*, 299–311.

Mandel, N. M., & Shrauger, J. S. (1980). The effects of self-evaluative statements on heterosocial approach in shy and nonshy males. *Cognitive Therapy and Research, 4*, 369–381.

Maroldo, G. K., Eisenreich, B. H., & Hall, P. (1979). Reliability of a modified Stanford Shyness Survey. *Psychological Reports, 44*, 706.

McClelland, D. C. (1951). *Personality*. New York: Holt, Rinehart & Winston.

McCroskey, J. C., Andersen, J. F., Richmond, V. P., & Wheeless, L. R. (1981). Communication apprehension of elementary and secondary students and teachers. *Communication Education, 30*, 122–132.

McCroskey, J. C. (1981). Oral communication apprehension: Reconceptualization and a new look at measurement. In M. Burgoon (Ed.), *Communication Yearbook 6*. Beverly Hills, CA: Sage.

McCroskey, J. C., & Richmond, V. P. (1982). Communication apprehension and shyness: Conceptual and operational distinctions. *Central States Speech Journal, 33*, 458–468.

McGovern, L. P. (1976). Dispositional social anxiety and helping behavior under three conditions of threat. *Journal of Personality, 44*, 84–97.

Miller, W. R., & Arkowitz, H. (1977). Anxiety and perceived causation in social success and failure experiences: Disconfirmation of an attribution hypothesis in two experiments. *Journal of Abnormal Psychology, 36*, 665–668.

Mischel, W. (1968). *Personality and assessment*. New York: Wiley.

Morris, C. G. (1982). *Assessment of shyness*. Unpublished manuscript, University of Michigan.

Orchard, J., Schallow, J., & Perlman, D. (1984). *The behavioral consequences of shyness and the responses of others to the shy*. Unpublished manuscript, University of Manitoba.

Patterson, M. L., & Strauss, M. E. (1972). An examination of the discriminant validity of the social avoidance and distress scale. *Journal of Consulting and Clinical Psychology, 39*, 169.

Pilkonis, P. A. (1977). The behavioral consequences of shyness. *Journal of Personality, 45*, 596–611.

Sears, D. O. (1967). Social anxiety, opinion structure and opinion change. *Journal of Personality and Social Psychology, 7*, 142–151.

Stiles, W. B. (1973). *Manual for a taxonomy of verbal response modes*. Chapel Hill: Institute for Research in Social Science, University of North Carolina.

Watson, D., & Friend, R. (1969). Measurement of social-evaluative anxiety. *Journal of Consulting and Clinical Psychology, 33*, 448–457.

Zimbardo, P. G. (1977). *Shyness: What it is and what to do about it*. Reading, MA: Addison-Wesley.

II

Development of Shyness

Part II examines shyness from a developmental perspective. The five chapters explore the distinctive ways in which shyness is manifested at different ages, and they provide insight into the complicated processes that underlie the acquisition of shyness.

Plomin and Daniels (Chapter 6) begin the section with a comprehensive review of the behavior genetics literature on shyness. Most of the relevant research assesses the role of genetic factors by studying the relative similarity of monozygotic versus dizygotic twins. Plomin and Daniels review 17 twin studies that, as a whole, comprise a persuasive case for the heretability of shyness. In addition, they summarize the results of a recent study examining adoptees, their adoptive parents, and their biological mothers. This full adoption design permits the authors to assess independently the effects of genes, environment, and the gene–environment interaction. Plomin and Daniels conclude their chapter with a careful discussion of what heretability does and does not mean for understanding shyness.

Kagan and Reznick (Chapter 7) report on a program of research in which physiological and behavioral indexes are measured longitudinally. Their research grew out of earlier observations that linked behavioral inhibition in unfamiliar situations to heart rate variability. Their current research shows not only that behavioral inhibition is related to measures of sympathetic arousal (pupil dilation, voice stress, and heart rate variability), but also that these behavioral and physiological measures are stable from early to middle childhood. This chapter complements and extends the behavior genetics research reported by Plomin and Daniels, and both chapters are consistent with Buss' account (see Chapter 4) of early developing shyness. Taken together, these two chapters provide empirical support for Buss' hypotheses, and they fill in a number of important details in the etiology of early developing shyness. Kagan and Reznick are careful to point out, however, that these mechanisms probably account for only a small percentage (perhaps 10%–20%) of those who label themselves as shy.

In Chapter 8, Asendorpf reviews the empirical literature on shyness in middle and late childhood. Although common experience and survey data suggest that shyness is an important problem among preadolescent children, Asendorpf argues that shyness as a distinct construct has largely been ignored by researchers. A reasonably large literature exists on social interaction and social competence in grade school children, but the constructs employed in these studies often are vague and cannot be interpreted specifically as shyness. Asendorpf also reviews recent studies of peer group status, social withdrawal, social skills, and social knowledge and pinpoints the ways in which shyness is related to these behavioral domains. He draws some tentative conclusions, but more importantly, indicates issues warranting clarification through further research. He concludes his paper with a brief discussion of the possible causes of shyness.

Adolescents often become preoccupied with their identities and social lives. In the chapter on adolescent shyness (Chapter 9) Cheek, Carpentieri, Smith, Rierdan, and Koff present evidence regarding the increase in the incidence of self-reported shyness during this developmental transition. They also examine the evidence for the stability of shyness from childhood to adolescence and for gender differences in the incidence and expression of shyness. In addition, they consider adolescent shyness in the context of Buss' concept regarding early versus late developing shyness. Whereas early developing shyness can be traced to the genetic and physiological factors outlined in the first two chapters in this part, late developing or adolescent shyness presumably reflects an awareness of and an uncertainty about one's social identity. Cheek et al. examine this hypothesis using self-report data of the onset of shyness. Finally, they speculate about how the early-late shyness distinction might be applied in treatment settings.

The final chapter in Part II focuses on the consequences of shyness among the elderly. By skipping from adolescence to old age, we do not mean to imply that shyness is unimportant during adulthood. In fact, this period of development is covered in depth in Part III and Part IV of this volume. Hansson considers the psychological issues and problems that characterize the later years in life. At the end of the life span many individuals must cope with chronic stressors, such as economic and interpersonal loss, deterioration of health and physical functioning, and the demise of previously important role functions. Hansson presents evidence indicating that when an older individual needs assistance, shyness can inhibit the initiation of appropriate and effective coping responses and can limit access to available networks of social support. Fortunately, shy individuals seem to be particularly responsive to the assistance they do receive. Also, Hansson argues that as individuals disengage from the roles and institutions with which they have been affiliated, interactions with others become less evaluative and less demanding, thereby eliminating many of the occasions that elicit shyness. On the other hand, Hansson's presentation clearly demonstrates the limitations of considering shyness a factor in the adjustment of children and adolescents only.

6

Genetics and Shyness

Robert Plomin and Denise Daniels

Heredity plays a larger role in shyness than in other personality traits in infancy (Plomin & Rowe, 1979), early childhood (Plomin & Rowe, 1977), middle childhood (O'Connor, Foch, Sherry, & Plomin, 1980), adolescence (Cheek & Zonderman, 1983), and adulthood (Horn, Plomin, & Rosenman, 1976). The purpose of this chapter is to review evidence concerning the etiology of individual differences in shyness and to consider conceptual and clinical implications of findings that indicate genetic influence.

BEHAVIORAL GENETIC STUDIES OF SHYNESS

Although traits related to shyness—sociability, extraversion, emotionality—have received considerable attention in behavioral genetic research, there are surprisingly few studies of shyness *per se*. The questionnaire and laboratory research of Cheek and Buss (1981) makes it clear that shyness (social responding to unfamiliar persons) and sociability (gregariousness) can be differentiated at a phenotypic level. Extraversion is primarily a measure of sociability: the correlation between extraversion and sociability is about 0.80 (Buss & Plomin, 1984), whereas that between extraversion and shyness is only about 0.40 (Briggs, Snider, & Smith, 1983). Although emotionality or general fearfulness has been suggested as a component of shyness (Buss & Plomin, 1984), correlations between emotionality and shyness are moderate to low—typically about 0.45 for general fearfulness (which includes fearfulness in social contexts), 0.35 for neuroticism, and 0.15 for fearfulness in nonsocial contexts (Briggs *et al.*, 1983). Other traits, such as self-esteem (Briggs *et al.*, 1983) and physical attractiveness (Liebman & Cheek, 1983), may be related to shyness.

ROBERT PLOMIN and DENISE DANIELS • Institute for Behavioral Genetics, University of Colorado, Boulder, CO 80309. Analyses involving the Colorado Adoption Project data set were supported by grants from the National Institute of Child Health and Human Development (HD-10333) and from the National Science Foundation (BNS-7826204 and BNS-8200310).

Our review will focus on shyness considered as separately as possible from these other traits because it could be etiologically distinct, despite the observed phenotypic correlations with other traits. Recent reviews of behavioral genetic data relevant to other personality traits are available (Buss & Plomin, 1984; Goldsmith, 1983).

The results of 18 relevant twin studies, one family study, and one adoption study are described in Table 1. The studies cover the life span from the first year of life through middle age and include diverse methods of measurement, such as observations, parental ratings and interviews, and self-report questionnaires. Without exception, the data from these studies converge on the conclusion that heredity is involved in the etiology of individual differences in shyness. A discussion of general issues relevant to behavioral genetic analyses—including twin, family, and adoption designs—can be found in Plomin, DeFries, and McClearn (1980).

The twin study of middle-aged twins (Horn et al., 1976) is particularly interesting because it suggests that shyness may be more heritable than other personality traits. The items of the California Psychological Inventory (CPI) were winnowed for reliable items that showed the greatest difference between identical and fraternal twin correlations using a cross-validation procedure. A rotated factor accounting for 28% of the variance of the 41 most heritable items involved shyness. The highest loading items on this factor all had two facets: social responding, and the involvement of strangers. More specifically, the items all seemed to involve talking to strangers. For example, the two highest loading heritable items on this factor were "It is hard for me to find anything to talk about when I meet a new person" and "It is hard for me to start a conversation with strangers."

In another twin study, which also employed the items of the CPI, Cheek and Zonderman (1983) reanalyzed data from Loehlin and Nichols' (1976) adolescent sample of 839 pairs of twins. A shyness scale extracted from the CPI items correlated 0.84 with another measure of shyness. The twin correlations suggested substantial heritability for shyness.

These two twin studies are most pertinent because they used item analyses to guide the construction of shyness scales independent of the numerous correlates of shyness. The dozens of other twin studies that used self-report questionnaires do not provide data relevant specifically to shyness because typical personality questionnaires do not distinguish shyness from other traits. A typical situation can be seen in Thurstone's temperament survey, based on Guilford's work, which spawned many of the modern personality questionnaires (Thurstone, 1951). The Thurstone measure includes a social introversion scale that consists of shyness items on the high end of the scale and sociability items on the low end. Other personality questionnaires also mix shyness with other traits. A possible exception is Cattell's Sixteen Personality Factor Questionnaire (16 PF) described by Cattell, Eber, & Tatsuoka (1970). Cattell's 16 PF Factor H (threctia-parmia) seems to distinguish shyness from other factors such as outgoingness (Factor A), dominance (Factor E), surgency (Factor F), and dependence (Factor Q_2). The 16 PF Factor H has as its characteristic description in the 16 PF manual:

TABLE 1. Behavioral Genetic Studies of Shyness

Reference	Sample (age; N)[a]	Measure	Results[b]
		A. Twin studies	
Torgerson & Kringlen (1978); Torgerson (1982)	2 and 9 months; 34 MZ, 16 DZ	Parental interview data on approach/withdrawal to strangers based on the New York Longitudinal Study (Thomas & Chess, 1977)	Twin correlations not reported; MZ significantly more similar than DZ at 9 months
Plomin & Rowe (1979)	22 months average; 21 MZ, 22 DZ	Time-sampled observations of social responding during initial interactions with a stranger: approach proximity positive vocalizations smiling looking	0.50 vs. −0.05 0.40 vs. −0.03 0.58 vs. 0.34 0.08 vs. 0.25 0.67 vs. 0.08
Plomin & Rowe (1977)	43 months average; 36 MZ, 31 DZ	Colorado Childhood Temperament Inventory (CCTI) (Rowe & Plomin, 1977) maternal ratings on shyness scale	0.48 vs. −0.16
Plomin (1974)	54 months average; 60 MZ, 51 DZ	EASI-III (Buss & Plomin, 1975) midparent ratings on shyness scale	0.47 vs. −0.12
	29 MZ, 30 DZ	EASI-III midparent ratings of "parents in agreement" subsample	0.55 vs. −0.13
Buss, Plomin, & Willerman	55 months average; 78 MZ, 50 DZ	EASI (Buss & Plomin, 1975) midparent ratings on shyness scale	0.58 vs. 0.23
Buss & Plomin (1975)	55 months average; 81 MZ, 57 DZ (sample overlaps Buss et al., 1973)	EASI maternal ratings of shyness	0.62 vs. 0.13
Cohen, Dribble, & Grawe (1977)	1–5 years; 181 MZ, 84 DZ	Childhood Personality Scale (Dibble & Cohen, 1974) maternal ratings of shyness	0.69 vs. 0.24
Plomin (unpublished; see Plomin & Foch, 1980)	7.6 years average; 51 MZ, 33 DZ	CCTI maternal ratings of shyness	0.56 vs. 0.05

Continued

TABLE 1. (Continued)

Reference	Sample (age; N)[a]	Measure	Results[b]
O'Connor et al. (1980)	7.6 years average; 51 MZ, 33 DZ	Conners (1970) Parent Symptom Rating Shyness factor	0.69 vs. 0.27
Scarr (1969)	6–10 years; 24 MZ, 28 DZ	Fels Behavior Scales (Richards & Simons, 1941) social apprehension rating by tester	0.88 vs. 0.28
Vandenberg (1967)	high school students; 137 MZ, 102 DZ (combined samples from Cattell, Blewett, & Beloff, 1955; Vandenberg, 1962; Gottesman, 1963)	Cattell's 16 PF (high school version) Factor H	Twin correlations not reported; significant F ratio of DZ within-pair variance to MZ within-pair variance
Osborne (1980)	high school students; 82 MZ, 61 DZ	Cattell's 16 PF (high school version) Factor H	0.17 vs. −0.08
Klein & Cattell (unpublished; reported by Cattell, 1982)	high school students; 43 MZ, 55 DZ	Cattell's 16 PF (high school version (Factor H)	Twin correlations not reported; heritability of 0.33
Canter (1973)	adolescents and adults; 40 MZ, 45 DZ	Cattell's 16 PF Factor H	0.58 vs. 0.30
Cheek & Zonderman (1983)	high school juniors; 514 MZ, 236 DZ	Shyness scale composed of items from the California Psychological Inventory (based on reanalysis of data reported by Loehlin & Nichols, 1976)	0.53 vs. 0.24
Horn et al. (1976)	55 years average; 99 MZ, 99 DZ	Most heritable items from the California Psychological Inventory	Of the 41 reliable items that yielded the largest differences between MZ and DZ correlations, one rotated factor that accounted for 28% of the variance primarily involved shyness.

Table 1. (*Continued*)

Reference	Sample (age; N)[a]	Measure	Results[b]
	B. Parent–offspring studies		
Plomin (1974)	54 months average; 137 nonadoptive families	Midparent ratings on the EASI-III shyness scale for the children and:	
		Mothers' self-rating of EASI-III sociability	0.26
		Fathers' self-rating of EASI-III sociability	0.11
		Fathers' rating of mothers' EASI-III sociability	0.23
		Mothers' rating of fathers' EASI-III sociability	0.16
Colorado Adoption Project (Plomin & DeFries, 1985)	12 and 24 months; 182 adoptive and 164 nonadoptive families	Midparent ratings on CCTI shyness scale for infants; parents' 16 PF shyness, EASI sociability, and 16 PF extraversion	See Table 2

[a]MZ refers to monozygotic (identical) twins and DZ refers to dizygotic (fraternal) twins; the N denotes number of pairs.
[b]With the exceptions described in the table, results are presented as twin correlations in Part A (MZ vs. DZ) and as parent–offspring correlations in Part B.

"shy, timid, restrained, threat-sensitive versus adventurous, 'thick-skinned,' socially bold" (Cattell *et al.*, 1970, p. 91). Because of the possible relevance of the 16 PF Factor H to our review of shyness, Table 1 includes the results of six twin studies that employed Cattell's measure. In addition to Canter's (1973) study of adolescent and adult twins and the studies of high school twins by Osborne (1980) and by Klein and Cattell (Cattell, 1982), Vandenberg (1967) summarized the results of three other small twin studies that used the high school version of Cattell's measure. In all of these studies, identical twins were found to be more similar than fraternal twins on the 16 PF Factor H. The 16 PF manual states that "present evidence indicates [Factor H] to be one of the two or three most highly inherited of personality factors" (Cattell *et al.*, 1970, p. 92).

These are the only twin studies relevant to shyness that have used self-report questionnaires, which is noteworthy because such questionnaires usually are much more commonly used than are other measures of personality. As mentioned earlier, one reason for the scarcity of behavioral genetic research on shyness is that few self-report questionnaires assess shyness as distinct from other traits, such as sociability and extraversion. Another reason is that there only recently has been a surge of interest in temperament in infancy and childhood and in shyness as a focal issue (Plomin, 1983a). Especially for infants, sociability and extraversion are rarely measured because infants do not often have an opportunity to express their preference for being with other people.

Finally, even though shyness is a conspicuous dimension of individual differences among infants and young children, measurement has been difficult because studies of shyness in infancy and early childhood cannot rely on the ubiquitous self-report questionnaire that provides all the data in behavioral genetic studies of personality in adolescents and adults.

Nearly all of the other studies in Table 1 involve parental ratings. Six of the parental rating studies employed a shyness scale that was developed as part of the temperament theory of Buss and Plomin that focuses on emotionality, activity, sociability, and impulsivity (EASI) (1975, 1984). Although the scale has been referred to as a "Sociability" scale, the items in fact primarily involve shyness. For example, the Sociability scale of the Colorado Childhood Temperament Inventory (CCTI) (Rowe & Plomin, 1977), which is an amalgamation of EASI items and items based on the temperament theory of Thomas and Chess (1977), has "Child tends to be shy" and "Child takes a long time to warm up to strangers" as its highest loading items. The twin studies that have used these EASI and CCTI shyness scales have consistently yielded identical twin correlations that are substantially greater than fraternal twin correlations—in fact, the differences between the identical and fraternal twin correlations are too great to be explained by a simple twin model. For a discussion of this issue, see Buss and Plomin (1984) and Plomin (1981).

In addition to parental ratings, temperament research has begun to use observational ratings of children in structured settings (Plomin, 1983a). The most widely used instrument is Bayley's Infant Behavior Record (IBR) (Bayley, 1969), which is used by testers to rate an infant's temperament after administration of the Bayley mental and motor scales of development. Two recent twin studies in which the IBR has been used (Goldsmith & Gottesman, 1981; Matheny, 1980) have found evidence of genetic influence. However, although the IBR yields an extraversion-like factor (Matheny, 1980), shyness is at most a small part of this factor because the factor includes items related to social responsiveness, cooperativeness, endurance, and happiness. It makes some sense that shyness is not well represented among the IBR items because the infant is supposed to have warmed up to the tester prior to the administration of the Bayley tests.

One twin study (Scarr, 1969) employed ratings other than the IBR. In a study of 24 identical and 28 fraternal pairs of twins (girls from 6 to 10 years of age), the Fels Behavior Scales (Richards & Simons, 1941), which include a rating scale of "social apprehension," were used. The identical twin correlation was 0.88 for this scale, and the fraternal twin correlation was 0.28.

Specific behaviors related to shyness were observed by Plomin and Rowe (1979) in their study of infant twins. Members of 21 identical twin pairs and 25 same-sex fraternal twin pairs with an average age of 22 months were observed in their homes using time-sampled observations of specific behaviors in seven situations. Each twin partner was rated by a different observer who took an unobtrusive position in the home, kept a neutral facial expression, and did not return overtures for attention from the children. An important feature of the study was that social responding to the stranger and to the mother was recorded in alternating 15-second intervals. The first situation, *warm-up*, included measures of the infants' social responding to the mother and to the stranger while they were engaged in discussing the project and attempting to avoid interaction with the children. The measures included infants' approaches, proximity, touches, positive vocalizations, smiles, and looks. In the second episode, *stranger approach*, the stranger enticed the children to play with him using a standard protocol. The third situation involved play with the stranger using an interactive toy. The other situations were play with the mother, cuddling with the stranger and mother, and separation from the mother. In the first three situations (when the stranger was strangest), social responding towards the stranger suggested genetic influence. The same social responses directed towards the mother showed no genetic influences. This observational study adds considerably to the confidence of our conclusion, based primarily on self-report and parental rating data, that heredity affects individual differences in shyness.

It is ironic that far more behavioral genetic data on personality are available for twins than for more common family relationships such as those between parent and offspring and between nontwin siblings. For shyness, no nontwin sibling correlations have been reported. There is a need for converging data from methods other than the classical twin method because twin studies can overestimate genetic influence. For example, family studies (Ahern, Johnson, Wilson, McClearn, & Vandenberg, 1982) and adoption studies (Loehlin, Horn, & Willerman, 1981; Scarr, Webber, Weinberg, & Wittig, 1981) that have used self-report personality questionnaires suggest less genetic influence for extraversion than do twin studies.

Only one family study with data relevant to shyness has been reported (Plomin, 1974). In 137 families with children of the average age of $4\frac{1}{2}$ years, parents rated their children on shyness and also rated themselves and their spouses on sociability using EASI measures. Table 1 lists parent–offspring correlations based on midparent ratings of the children and parents' self-reports and spouse ratings. Although there are no comparable data for young children, these correlations are substantial even when compared to parent–offspring personality correlations for older children (e.g., Loehlin *et al.*, 1981). The results suggest a maternal effect in that mothers' sociability was more highly correlated than fathers' sociability with infants' shyness, even when mothers' sociability was rated by fathers. These parent–offspring correlations suggest a correlation of about 0.20 for first-degree relatives. Substituting this value for the often low and sometimes negative correlations for fraternal twins' EASI shyness in Table 1 yields more reasonable estimates of heritability. However, even these "corrected" twin estimates of heritability imply that all of the similarity between parents and their offspring is due to heredity rather than family environment. Such family studies cannot disentangle nature and nurture because the parents share heredity as well as family environment with their offspring.

The most powerful behavioral genetic design is a full adoption design in which nature and nurture are separated: biological parents who share heredity but not family environment with their offspring are compared to adoptive parents who share family environment but not heredity with their adopted children. The Colorado Adoption Project (CAP) is a longitudinal, prospective adoption study of adopted infants and matched nonadopted infants who have been studied yearly in their homes (Plomin & DeFries, 1983, 1985). The parents of these infants—the biological mothers who relinquish the adoptees at birth, the adoptive parents of the adoptees, and the parents of the nonadopted infants—complete a 3-hour battery of behavioral tests that includes several measures of personality. Nonadoptive parents and their infants share both heredity and family environment; in the absence of selective placement, biological parents share only heredity with their adopted-away infants and adoptive parents share only family environment with their adopted children. Thus, the full adoption design of the CAP provides a powerful tool to disentangle genetic and environmental sources of familial resemblance. Although some analyses of shyness using the CAP data set have been reported previously by Daniels and Plomin (1985), the current analyses involve a 20% larger sample.

The sample consists of 182 adoptive families and 164 nonadoptive families in which infants have been tested at 12 and 24 months of age. It has been shown to be representative of metropolitan middle-class Caucasian families, and selective placement is negligible (Plomin & DeFries, 1983, 1985). Midparent ratings on the CCTI (Rowe & Plomin, 1977) Sociability (shyness) scale are used as a measure of infant shyness. Measures of parents' personality include Cattell's 16 PF (Cattell et al., 1970) and the EASI temperament survey of Buss and Plomin (1975). From the 16 PF, we shall report data for the Shyness factor (Factor H) and second-order Extraversion factor; the EASI Sociability scale will also be considered.

Table 2 presents parent–offspring correlations between infants' CCTI shyness at 12 and 24 months of age and parents' 16 PF shyness, EASI sociability, and the second-order 16 PF Extraversion factor. Data for boys and girls have been combined because no significant mean or variance differences were observed. The parent-offspring correlations for the nonadoptive families replicate those reported by Plomin (1974) and suggest that infant shyness is negatively related to parental sociability as well as positively related to parental shyness. In nonadoptive families, parent–offspring relationships could be mediated either genetically or environmentally. However, the correlations between the biological mothers and their adopted-away offspring at 24 months hint at the influence of heredity. The significant negative correlation between infant shyness and biological mothers' sociability is particularly noteworthy because this correlation involves the biological mothers' self-report of sociability and the adoptive parents' midparent rating of the adoptees' shyness more than a year later. In the nonadoptive families, infant shyness is related to adult extraversion and to sociability and shyness; however, no evidence of a replicated relationship between infant shyness and adult extraversion emerged for biological mothers and their adopted-away offspring.

The presence of genetic influence suggested by the correlations between biological mothers' shyness/sociability and their adopted-away infants' shyness

TABLE 2. Parent-Offspring Correlations from the Colorado Adoption Project: Comparisons between Midparental Ratings of Infant Shyness at 12 and 24 Months and Parental Shyness, Sociability, and Extraversion

| | CCTI Shyness | | | |
| | 12 Months | | 24 Months | |
Parent measures	Correlation	N	Correlation	N
Nonadoptive mothers				
16 PF shyness	−0.17*	135	0.16*	130
EASI sociability	−0.23*	154	−0.22*	149
16 PF extraversion	−0.24*	126	−0.22*	121
Nonadoptive fathers				
16 PF shyness	−0.02	126	0.18*	121
EASI sociability	−0.09	154	−0.13	148
16 PF extraversion	−0.05	111	−0.17*	107
Biological mothers				
16 PF shyness	0.08	147	0.10	156
EASI sociability	−0.02	156	−0.15*	165
16 PF extraversion	0.03	135	−0.02	145
Adoptive mothers				
16 PF shyness	0.11	126	0.04	129
EASI sociability	−0.19*	156	−0.24*	164
16 PF extraversion	−0.02	119	0.08	121
Adoptive fathers				
16 PF shyness	0.07	127	0.19*	130
EASI sociability	−0.15*	158	−0.25*	165
16 PF extraversion	−0.07	121	−0.14	124

*$p < 0.05$.

at 24 months is exciting because the CAP parent–offspring design is not a particularly powerful method for detecting genetic influence in infancy. Significant resemblance between biological parents and their adopted-away infants requires that both the infant and the adult measures be influenced by heredity and that the genes that affect the infant measure overlap with the genes that affect the adult measure. When resemblance does emerge between biological parents and their adopted-away infants, it suggests that these three conditions have been met and thus implies the existence of a genetically mediated continuity between infancy and adulthood. For a detailed discussion of this topic, see Plomin and DeFries (1985).

The correlations between adoptive parents and their adopted infants shown in Table 2 suggest a major role for family environmental influences as indexed by parents' personality. Adoptive parents' shyness and sociability, but not their extraversion, are related to adopted infants' shyness.

In summary, this first adoption study of shyness suggests parent–offspring similarity even in infancy. This resemblance possibly involves heredity and certainly involves family environmental influences.

OTHER BEHAVIORAL GENETIC ANALYSES

We have seen that behavioral genetic studies point to a significant and perhaps substantial genetic influence on differences in shyness among individuals. However, behavioral genetic analyses can provide considerably more information than merely to indicate the presence of significant genetic influence. In this section, we shall consider three examples of further explorations of the interface between genetics, environment, and shyness: multivariate analyses, analyses of specific environmental influences, and analyses of genotype–environment interaction.

Multivariate Behavioral Genetic Analyses

Multivariate behavioral genetic techniques can be applied to study the etiology of the relationship between shyness and other characteristics, such as sociability and extraversion. Any behavioral genetic method that can be used to partition the variance of a single character into genetic and environmental components can also be used to study the etiology of the covariance among traits (Plomin & DeFries, 1979). The genetic contribution to the phenotypic correlation between two traits is a function of the heritability of each trait and the genetic correlation between them. A genetic correlation can be thought of as a measure of the extent to which the genes that affect one trait overlap with the genes that affect the other trait. Just as phenotypic variance of a trait can be largely due to genetic variability among individuals or to experiential differences among them, so can the phenotypic covariance between two traits be genetically or environmentally mediated. Multivariate techniques can be extended to longitudinal behavioral genetic data (Plomin & DeFries, 1981) to permit us to ask the key question of developmental behavioral genetics (Plomin, 1983b): To what extent are genetic factors responsible for change and continuity in development?

A combination of these two approaches—multivariate and longitudinal—was used to analyze data from the Colorado Adoption Project. In fact, we view any comparison between infant and adult characteristics in this way because isomorphism between infancy and adulthood cannot be assumed for any trait—not even for shyness, even though there seems to be some evidence of phenotypic similarity in shyness from infancy to adulthood. Although we did not state the fact explicitly, our interpretation of the CAP data reported in Table 2 did not assume isomorphism between infant shyness and the adult personality traits. We indicated that infant shyness appears to be related genetically to adult sociability as much as it is to adult shyness. These results imply that shyness is heritable in infancy and in adulthood and that the genes that affect infant shyness are substantially correlated with those that affect adult shyness and sociability.

We can explore further the etiological nexus surrounding shyness by asking whether infant shyness is related genetically to adult emotionality or neuroticism. Table 3 presents correlations of infant shyness with parental 16 PF neuroticism and EASI emotionality-fear. The median correlation between nonadoptive parents and their children is approximately zero, as is the correlation between

TABLE 3. Parent–Offspring Correlations from the Colorado Adoption Project:
Comparisons between Midparental Ratings of Infant Shyness at 12 and 24 Months
and Parental Neuroticism and Emotionality-Fear

| | CCTI Shyness | | | |
| | 12 months | | 24 months | |
Parent measures	Correlation	N	Correlation	N
Nonadoptive mothers				
16 PF neuroticism	0.07	131	0.05	126
EASI emotionality-fear	−0.04	152	−0.15*	146
Nonadoptive fathers				
16 PF neuroticism	0.08	122	0.17*	117
EASI emotionality-fear	0.10	152	0.15*	147
Biological mothers				
16 PF neuroticism	−0.08	138	0.03	148
EASI emotionality-fear	−0.07	154	0.07	163
Adoptive mothers				
16 PF neuroticism	−0.05	117	0.08	119
EASI emotionality-fear	0.00	157	0.04	164
Adoptive fathers				
16 PF neuroticism	0.02	125	0.08	128
EASI emotionality-fear	0.03	156	0.07	163

$*p < 0.05$.

biological mothers and their adopted-away children. Thus, there appears to be
no genetic relationship between shyness in infancy and adult general emotionality or neuroticism.

Specific Environmental Influences

Another example of the usefulness of behavioral genetic analyses in going
beyond the usual partitioning of observed variance into its genetic and environmental components is the analysis of specific environmental influences in
adoptive families. Nearly all investigators of specific environmental factors have
studied nonadoptive families in which heredity and family environment is shared
by family members. Because heredity and environment are confounded in nonadoptive families, relationships between ostensibly environmental influences
and children's development could be mediated genetically and environmentally.
In adoptive families, in which family environment is shared but heredity is not,
relationships between environmental factors and children's development must
be purely environmental. Moreover, comparing environmental–development
relationships in nonadoptive families to those in adoptive families provides an
estimate of the extent to which purported environmental relationships are in
fact mediated genetically. A recent review suggests that many environmental
relationships—particularly in the area of personality and behavior problems—
are in fact influenced by heredity (Plomin, Loehlin, & DeFries, 1985).

Although most discussions of the etiology of shyness implicitly assume that its origins are environmental, there are surprisingly few relevant data. One example from the literature is the suggestion that shyness may be related to lack of exposure to social situations (Kagan, Kearsley, & Zelazo, 1978; Schaffer, 1966). However, it cannot be assumed that a relationship of this type is truly environmental in origin because of an alternate hypothesis: exposure to social situations might be a covariate of the fact that shy parents who avoid social encounters have shy children for genetic rather than for environmental reasons. An adoption study is needed to disentangle these genetic and environmental possibilities. Data from the Colorado Adoption Project are interesting for this reason and several others: the inclusion of adoptive and nonadoptive families in the CAP permits environmental analyses of the kind just described; the CAP includes standard measures of family environment; and the availability of personality data on biological parents as well as adoptive parents permits analyses of genotype–environment interaction, as described in the following section.

The CAP environmental measures include the Family Environment Scale (FES) (Moos, 1974), a 90-item questionnaire that assesses family relationships and the organizational structure in the family. Mothers and fathers completed this questionnaire when their infants were 12 months of age, and their ratings were averaged to increase reliability. The usual 10 FES scale scores were analyzed, although we will focus on two second-order factors that we extracted in factor analyses of the 10 scales: Personal Growth, which includes cultural, recreational, and expressive aspects of the home, and Traditional Organization, which involves high organization, strong moral-religious emphasis, and low conflict.

The Home Observation for Measurement of the Environment (HOME) (Caldwell & Bradley, 1978), a 45-minute observational/interview measure of parent–infant interaction, was employed at both 12 and 24 months of age during the visit to the homes of the CAP adopted and nonadopted infants. In order to expand the ability of the HOME to assess environmental variability in middle-class homes, we modified its dichotomous format to a quantitative scoring scheme. Also, rather than using the traditional scales of the HOME, we focused on factorially derived dimensions. For details concerning the FES and HOME measures as used in the CAP, see Plomin and DeFries (1985).

Correlations between infant shyness and the environmental measures are presented in Table 4. The HOME general factor (an unrotated first principal component) is negatively correlated with shyness at 12 months, suggesting that warmer, more responsive parents have infants who are less shy. However, the correlations between shyness and the general factor are lower at 24 months, and the other HOME factors are only slightly correlated with shyness, although consistently in the same direction.

The most interesting results involve the FES Personal Growth factor. The significant negative correlation between Personal Growth and infant shyness in the adoptive homes implies that family environmental influences are important. However, the significantly greater negative correlation in the nonadoptive families indicates that genetic factors mediate the relationship between FES Personal

TABLE 4. Correlations of Infant Shyness at 12 and 24 Months with Environmental Measures in Adoptive Families (N = 159–164) and in Nonadoptive Families (N = 151–158)

	CCTI Shyness			
	12 months		24 months	
	Adoptive	Nonadoptive	Adoptive	Nonadoptive
FES second-order factors[a]				
Personal growth	−0.16*	−0.34*	—	—
Traditional organization	−0.12	−0.01	—	—
HOME factors				
General	−0.16	−0.17*	−0.07	−0.13
Toys	−0.01	−0.04	−0.08	−0.01
Maternal involvement	−0.01	−0.13*	−0.03	−0.06
Encouraging advance	−0.07	−0.07	−0.07	−0.13
Restrictiveness	0.04	−0.03	−0.03	−0.09

[a]The FES was administered only when the infants were 12 months old.
*$P < 0.05$.

Growth and infant shyness. This finding demonstrates the possibility that genetic factors are involved in the relationship between parental perceptions of the family's social climate and their perceptions of their children. Genetic involvement in this apparently environmental relationship is not simply mediated by parental personality or IQ—partialing out these parental traits had little effect on the pattern of correlations in the adoptive and nonadoptive families. A model and discussion of genetic correlates of environmental relationships can be found in Plomin *et al.*, 1985.

Genotype–Environment Interaction

A final example of additional uses of behavioral genetic methodology is the analysis of genotype–environment interaction, which refers to the possibility that environmental factors affect children differentially as a function of their genetic predispositions. In the temperament field, the word *interaction* is frequently used and has become paramount to some theorists, such as Thomas and Chess (1980), who propose an "interactionist view that behavioral attributes must at all times be considered . . . in their interaction with environmental opportunities, demands, and expectations" (p. 86). Thus, "interaction" is sometimes used to refer to the truism that both an organism and an environment are prerequisites for behavior. In order to understand differences among individuals in traits such as shyness, however, the important question is the extent to which individual differences in the trait can be explained by differences in environments, by differences in genotype, and by genotype–environment interactions (Plomin & Daniels, 1984).

In previous sections, environmental measures including adoptive parents' personality have been related to infant shyness; similarly, genetic effects have been discussed in terms of correlations between biological parents and their adopted-away offspring. Genotype–environment interaction, like any statistical interaction, is the extent to which joint information about these environmental and genetic factors predicts infant temperament once the "main effects" of environment and genotype have been removed (Plomin, DeFries, & Loehlin, 1977).

We used the hierarchical multiple regression procedure described by Plomin and Daniels (1984) to search for genotype–environment interaction using various combinations of biological mothers' personality (as a measure of genetic disposition of the infant), adoptive parents' personality and home environment (as a measure of the environment), and the dependent measure of infant shyness. None of the genotype–environment interactions was significant, and the usual amount of adjusted variance explained by the interaction was zero. For example, although main effects emerged for biological mothers' sociability and adoptive parents' FES Personal Growth as they affect infant shyness, the interaction between them accounted for only 1.7% of the variance in infant shyness at 12 months and 0.1% of the variance in shyness at 24 months. The power of our analyses to detect major genotype–environment interactions if they were present was reasonable: given our sample size and total variance explained of 10% to 20%, we have approximately 80% power to detect interactions that account for 5% of the total variance (i.e., 25% to 50% of the total explained variance) as described by Cohen and Cohen (1975, pp. 117–120). Thus, if such interactions between genotype and environment account for 5% of the variance of infant shyness, we should have been able to detect them. However, if the interactions account for as little as 1% of the variance, one would need a sample size of over 600 to detect a significant interaction with 80% power given an R^2 of 10% to 20%.

CONCEPTUAL AND CLINICAL IMPLICATIONS

Behavioral-genetic data on shyness reviewed in this chapter indicate genetic influence, perhaps beginning as early as infancy. Data from the Colorado Adoption Project also suggest that genetic factors may be involved in the relationship between infant shyness and ostensibly environmental measures, such as the FES. What follows from these conclusions? First, what does *not* follow is that individual differences in shyness are immutable to the extent that heredity plays a part in the etiology of the trait. Behavioral genetic data describe the mix of genetic variance and environmental variance as it relates to observed differences in shyness among individuals in a particular population at a particular time. Because these data describe population averages, it is certainly possible for a shy individual to change. The finding of genetic effects implies hereditary propensities, not predestination.

Looking outside the field of shyness for an example, consider the accumulating evidence that alcoholism has a genetic component (Cloninger, Bohman, & Sigvardsson, 1981). This does not imply that genes act as puppeteers, forcing people repeatedly to pick up drinks containing alcohol. Genetic influence in this case means that, given the normal exposure of people in our society to alcohol, some individuals are more likely to become dependent on the drug for genetic reasons than others. There are no genes *for* alcoholism; rather, evidence suggests that a genetic tendency toward greater sensitivity to alcohol's effects may protect some individuals from the likelihood of consuming large amounts of alcohol. In a similar way, there is no "shyness gene," but rather a host of genetically induced differences among individuals that, given the social interactions typically experienced by individuals in our society, lead to enhanced uneasiness in interactions with strangers. Shy individuals on the average are likely to experience strain as they rub against the grain of their genetic proclivities, but it can be done. We all experience fears and often manage to overcome them without traumatic consequences.

Nonetheless, because we see no reason to uphold the stereotypic notion of the American as extravert, we suggest that there is room for greater recognition of and respect for individual differences in shyness. Part of understanding our children and ourselves lies in recognizing genetic predispositions that distinguish us from other people. A nice feature of heredity in relation to childrearing is that like begets like—shy parents are likely to have shy children on the average, and shy parents also are likely to be accepting of their children's propensity towards shyness. We can accept these differences in ourselves and in our children rather than assume that deviations from the norm are necessarily aberrant. Again using childrearing as an example, parents of a shy child could attempt to ameliorate the child's shyness although, as we just indicated, shy children might not appear terribly shy to their equally shy parents. Another possibility is to recognize the child's shyness and respect the child's need to take his time in warming up to strangers. As another example, consider occupational choices. A shy woman could choose to overcome her shyness so that interactions with strangers need not be a factor in her choice of jobs. However, another possibility is to throw the fact of her shyness into the equation of interests and abilities as she thinks about selecting an occupation. Other things being equal, a job that requires constant interaction with strangers may not be her wisest choice.

In addition to leading to greater recognition of and respect for individuality in shyness, the likelihood of genetic influence suggests a tool for possible differential diagnosis: individuals with a family history of shyness could represent an etiologically distinct subtype of shy persons. The CAP data suggest that it might be profitable to consider individual history in addition to family history. Persons who have been shy since infancy and who have a family history of shyness might represent a genetic subtype of shyness. Other areas of research, such as the study of cognition and psychopathology, have profited from a differential diagnostic approach at the level of etiology rather than symptomatology, and it is not too soon to think about applying differential diagnosis to the study of shyness. Even though causes are not necessarily related to cures, identification of etiologically distinct subtypes of shyness is likely to lead to rational intervention and perhaps primary prevention tailored to the specific needs of individuals who choose to seek treatment.

SUMMARY

We have reviewed behavioral-genetic data that suggest that heredity influences individual differences in shyness perhaps more than in any other personality trait, beginning as early as infancy. Data from a longitudinal adoption study, the Colorado Adoption Project, were used to illustrate three possibilities for behavioral genetic analyses beyond the demonstration of significant genetic influence. First, multivariate analyses suggest that infant shyness may be related genetically to adult sociability (gregariousness) as much as it is to adult shyness (social responding to unfamiliar persons); however, infant shyness does not appear to be related genetically to adult general emotionality or neuroticism. Second, analyses of specific environmental influences in adoptive families, as measured by the HOME and the FES, indicate that variability in family environments accounts for some of the variance in infant shyness independent of heredity; however, the finding that the correlation between infant shyness and the FES second-order factor of personal growth was significantly higher in nonadoptive homes than in adoptive homes implicates genetic factors in this ostensibly environmental relationship. The third example is genotype–environment interaction, although no significant interactions were identified for shyness in infancy. A discussion of the conceptual and clinical implications of finding genetic influence on shyness led to the exhortation to recognize and respect individual differences in shyness.

ACKNOWLEDGMENTS

We gratefully acknowledge the editorial advice of Rebecca Miles and the expert typing of Dianne Johnson, both of the Institute for Behavioral Genetics.

REFERENCES

Ahern, F. M., Johnson, R. C., Wilson, J. R., McClearn, G. E., and Vandenberg, S. G. (1982). Family resemblances in personality. *Behavior Genetics, 12,* 261–280.

Bayley, N. (1969). *Manual for the Bayley Scales of Infant Development.* New York: Psychological Corporation.

Briggs, S. R., Snider, R., & Smith, T. G. (1983). *Assessment of shyness: A comparison of measures.* Paper presented at the 91st annual meeting of the American Psychological Association, August 30, 1983, Anaheim, CA.

Buss, A. H., & Plomin, R. (1975). *A temperament theory of personality development.* New York: Wiley-Interscience.

Buss, A. H., & Plomin, R. (1984). *Temperament: Early developing personality traits.* San Francisco: Freeman.

Buss, A. H., Plomin, R., & Willerman, L. (1973). The inheritance of personality traits. *Journal of Personality, 41,* 513–524.

Caldwell, B. M., & Bradley, R. H. (1978). *Home observation for measurement of the environment.* Little Rock, AR: University of Arkansas.

Canter, S. (1973). Personality traits in twins. In G. Claridge, S. Canter, & W. I. Hume (eds.), *Personality differences and biological variations: A study of twins* (pp. 21–51). New York: Pergamon Press.

Cattell, R. B. (1982). *The inheritance of personality and ability.* New York: Academic Press.

Cattell, R. B., Blewett, D. B., & Beloff, J. R. (1955). The inheritance of personality: A multiple-variance analysis of approximate nature-nurture ratios for primary personality factors in Q-data. *American Journal of Human Genetics, 7,* 122–146.

Cattell, R. B., Eber, H.W., & Tatsuoka, M. M. (1970). *Handbook for the Sixteen Personality Factor Questionnaire (16 PF).* Champaign, Il: Institute for Personality and Ability Testing.

Cheek, J. M., & Buss, A. H. (1981). Shyness and sociability. *Journal of Personality and Social Psychology, 41,* 330–339.

Cheek, J. M., & Zonderman, A. B. (1983). *Shyness as a personality temperament.* Paper presented at the 91st annual meeting of the American Psychological Association, August 30, 1983, Anaheim, CA.

Cloninger, C. R., Bohman, M., & Sigvardsson, S. (1981). Inheritance of alcohol abuse. *Archives of General Psychiatry, 38,* 861–868.

Cohen, D. J., Dibble, E., & Grawe, J. M. (1977). Fathers' and mothers' perceptions of children's personality. *Archives of General Psychiatry, 34,* 480–487.

Cohen, J., & Cohen, P. (1975). *Applied multiple regression/correlation analysis for the behavioral sciences.* Hillsdale, NJ: Erlbaum.

Conners, C. K. (1970). Symptom patterns in hyperkinetic, neurotic and normal children. *Child Development, 41,* 667–682.

Daniels, D., & Plomin, R. (1985). Origins of individual differences in infant shyness. *Developmental Psychology, 21,* 118–121.

Dibble, E., & Cohen, D. J. (1974). Companion instruments for measuring children's competence and parental style. *Archives of General Psychiatry, 30,* 805–815.

Goldsmith, H. H. (1983). Genetic influences on personality from infancy to adulthood. *Child Development, 54,* 331–355.

Goldsmith, H. H., & Gottesman, I. I. (1981). Origins of variation in behavioral style: A longitudinal study of temperament in young twins. *Child Development, 52,* 91–103.

Gottesman, I. I. (1963). Heritability of personality: A demonstration. *Psychological Monographs, 77* (Whole No. 572), 1–21.

Horn, J. M., Plomin, R., & Rosenman, R. (1976). Heritability of personality traits in adult male twins. *Behavior Genetics, 6,* 17–30.

Kagan, J., Kearsley, R. B., & Zelazo, P. R. (1978). *Infancy: Its place in human development.* Cambridge, MA: Harvard University Press.

Liebman, W. E., & Cheek, J. M. (1983). *Shyness and body image.* Paper presented at the 91st annual meeting of the American Psychological Association, August 30, 1983, Anaheim, CA.

Loehlin, J. C., & Nichols, R. C. (1976). *Heredity, environment and personality.* Austin, TX: University of Texas Press.

Loehlin, J. C., Horn, J. M., & Willerman, L. (1981). Personality resemblance in adoptive homes. *Behavior Genetics, 11,* 309–330.

Matheny, A. P. (1980). Bayley's Infant Behavior Record: Behavioral components and twin analyses. *Child Development, 51,* 1157–1167.

Moos, R. H. (1974). *Preliminary manual for Family Environment Scale, Work Environment Scale, and Group Environment Scale.* Palo Alto, CA: Consulting Psychologists Press.

O'Connor, M., Foch, T., Sherry, T., & Plomin, R. (1980). A twin study of specific behavioral problems of socialization as viewed by parents. *Journal of Abnormal Child Psychology, 8,* 189–199.

Osborne, R. T. (1980). *Twins: Black and white.* Athens, GA: Foundation for Human Understanding.

Plomin, R. (1974). *A temperament theory of personality development: Parent–child interactions,* unpublished Ph.D. dissertation, University of Texas.

Plomin, R. (1981). Heredity and temperament: A comparison of twin data for self-report questionnaires, parental ratings, and objectively assessed behavior. In L. Gedda, P. Parisi, & W. E. Nance (eds.), *Progress in clinical and biological research, vol. 69B, twin research 3: Part B. Intelligence, personality, and development* (pp. 269–278). New York: Alan R. Liss.

Plomin, R. (1983a). Childhood temperament. In B. Lahey, & A. Kazdin (eds.), *Advances in clinical child psychology, vol. 6* (pp. 45–92). New York: Plenum Press.

Plomin, R. (1983b). Developmental behavioral genetics. *Child Development. 54,* 253–259.

Plomin, R., & Daniels, D. (1984). The interaction between temperament and environment: Methodological considerations. *Merrill-Palmer Quarterly, 30,* 149–162.

Plomin, R., & DeFries, J. C. (1979). Multivariate behavioral genetic analysis of twin data on scholastic abilities. *Behavior Genetics, 9,* 505–517.

Plomin, R., & DeFries, J. C. (1981). Multivariate behavioral genetics and development: Twin studies. In L. Gedda, P. Parisi, & W. E. Nance (eds.), *Progress in clinical and biological research, vol. 69B, Twin research 3: Part B. Intelligence, personality, and development* (pp. 25–33). New York: Alan R. Liss.

Plomin, R., & DeFries, J. C. (1983). The Colorado Adoption Project. *Child Development, 54,* 276–289.

Plomin, R., & DeFries, J. C. (1985). *Origins of individual differences in infancy: The Colorado Adoption Project.* New York: Academic Press.

Plomin, R., & Foch, T. T. (1980). A twin study of objectively assessed personality in childhood. *Journal of Personality and Social Psychology, 39,* 680–688.

Plomin, R., & Rowe, D. C. (1977). A twin study of temperament in young children. *Journal of Psychology, 97,* 107–113.

Plomin, R., & Rowe, D. C. (1979). Genetic and environmental etiology of social behavior in infancy. *Developmental Psychology, 15,* 62–72.

Plomin, R., DeFries, J. C., & Loehlin, J. C. (1977). Genotype-environment interaction and correlation in the analysis of human behavior. *Psychological Bulletin, 84,* 309–322.

Plomin, R., DeFries, J. C., & McClearn, G. E. (1980). *Behavioral genetics: A primer.* San Francisco: Freeman.

Plomin, R., Loehlin, J. C., & DeFries, J. C. (1985). Genetic and environmental components of "environmental" influences. *Developmental Psychology, 21,* 391–402.

Richards, T. W., & Simons, M. P. (1941). The Fels Child Behavior Scales. *Genetic Psychology Monographs, 24,* 259–309.

Rowe, D. C., & Plomin, R. (1977). Temperament in early childhood. *Journal of Personality Assessment, 41,* 150–156.

Scarr, S. (1969). Social introversion-extraversion as a heritable response. *Child Development, 40,* 823–832.

Scarr, S., Webber, P. L., Weinberg, R. A., & Wittig, M. A. (1981). Personality resemblance among adolescents and their parents in biologically related and adoptive families, *Journal of Personality and Social Psychology, 40,* 885–898.

Schaffer, H. R. (1966). The onset of fear of strangers and the incongruity hypothesis. *Journal of Child Psychology and Psychiatry, 1,* 95–106.

Thomas, A., & Chess, S. (1977). *Temperament and development.* New York: Brunner/Mazel.

Thomas, A., & Chess, S. (1980). *The dynamics of psychological development.* New York: Brunner/Mazel.

Thurstone, L. L. (1951). The dimensions of temperament. *Psychometrika, 16,* 11–20.

Torgerson, A. M. (1982). Influence of genetic factors on temperament development in early childhood. In R. Porter & G. M. Collins (eds.), *Temperamental differences in infants and young children* (pp. 141–154). London: Pitman.

Torgerson, A. M., & Kringlen, E. (1978). Genetic aspects of temperamental differences in infants: A study of same-sexed twins. *Journal of the American Academy of Child Psychiatry, 17,* 433–444.

Vandenberg, S. G. (1962). The hereditary abilities study: Hereditary components in a psychological test battery. *American Journal of Human Genetics, 14,* 220–237.

Vandenberg, S. G. (1967). Hereditary factors in normal personality traits (as measured by inventories). In J. Wortis (ed.), *Recent Advances in Biological Psychiatry, vol. IX* (pp. 65–104). New York: Plenum Press.

7

Shyness and Temperament

Jerome Kagan and J. Steven Reznick

One of the profound principles of the sciences that study life processes is that the inherent properties of the unit under study, whether it be cell, organ, or individual, make a contribution to its development through successive encounters with varied surroundings. History tells us that whenever an investigator overemphasizes the influence of the surroundings to the exclusion of the unit, or the unit to the exclusion of the environment, a correction will occur. In the decades immediately following publication of *On the Origin of Species*, many biologists translated Darwin's work to mean that the individual organism's contribution was minimal and natural selection was the important determinant of evolution. This supposition made evolutionary theory vulnerable to a wave of Lamarckianism that reached a crest at the turn of the century. When this perspective was defeated by discoveries in the new field of genetics, the modern synthesis that acknowledged the complementary role of both genes and environment became possible (Bowler, 1983).

Psychological explanations of development since the First World War, especially explanations of individual differences among young children, have emphasized environmental forces and ignored those biologically based qualities of the child that some investigators classify as temperamental. Fortunately, this state of affairs is being repaired as a result of the research on temperament by Thomas and Chess (1977), Buss and Plomin (1975), Plomin and Rowe (1979), Rothbart and Derryberry (1981), Carey and McDevitt (1978), Garcia-Coll, Kagan, and Reznick (1984), Kagan, Reznick, Clarke, Snidman, and Garcia-Coll (1984), as well as many others. These investigations imply that some psychological characteristics of infants influence the older child's future psychological profile, as well as monitor interactions with the family. It is too early to know how many

JEROME KAGAN and J. STEVEN REZNICK • Department of Psychology and Social Relations, Harvard University, Cambridge, MA 02138. This research was supported in part by a grant from the John D. and Catherine T. MacArthur Foundation.

fundamental temperamental dispositions will be discovered, but it appears that at least two qualities, which we call inhibition and lack of inhibition to the unfamiliar, are moderately stable over the first 5 years of life and have a pattern of physiological correlates that imply the role of genetics and/or prenatal influences.

A DEFINITION OF THE QUALITIES

Encounter with an unfamiliar person, object, or situation is a pervasive feature of human experience. During the initial period of encounter, while the child tries to assimilate the event and to cope with it, he or she is in a special psychological state we might call uncertainty. Children react in different ways to the state of uncertainty. A small group of young children become quiet, cease the activity in which they are engaged, retreat to a familiar person, or withdraw from the field in which the unfamiliar event occurred. Other children of similar intellectual ability and social background show no obvious change in their ongoing behavior and often approach the unfamiliar event quickly and with no hesitation. We call the former group inhibited, the latter uninhibited (Garcia-Coll *et al.* 1984). Parents often name the former class of child watchful, shy, timid, or vigilant, and the latter exploratory, outgoing, bold, or fearless. Although we suspect that the more fundamental bases for this difference among young children rests with variation in the ease with which the stress syndrome that involves hypothalamus, pituitary, and the sympathetic nervous system is provoked, we have chosen constructs that name the phenotypic outcome in behavior in order to communicate the forms this deep disposition takes in young children.

The constructs *inhibited* and *uninhibited* are not popular in everyday language because parents or psychologists usually choose terms that have some implicit reference to the event that caused the inhibition. Thus, if the unfamiliar event is dangerous to the child's physical integrity, the inhibited child is called cautious and the uninhibited one is called bold. If the unfamiliar event is a new food, the inhibited child is likely to be called sensitive and the uninhibited child adaptable. But, if a person or a social group is the source of the unfamiliar, the inhibited child is called shy and the uninhibited one social. We are not suggesting that all children who are labeled shy, or social, acquired this quality as a result of temperamental predispositions, only that some children are born with a vulnerability to one or the other of these dispositions. We believe that there is a small group of children who will apear shy with unfamiliar people, timid in situations that contain risk or harm, and cautious in situations with risk of failure. The initial reaction typically runs its course in a short period and when the uncertainty has passed these children often behave in a way that is similar to others. But the tendency to be inhibited or uninhibited is consistent across situations. Although the purpose of this chapter is to summarize our recent work on these two qualities, some historical introduction is useful.

HISTORY OF THE CURRENT RESEARCH EFFORT

In the longitudinal evaluation summarized in *Birth to Maturity* (Kagan & Moss, 1962/1983), a sample of 71 Caucasian children from the Fels Research Institute's longitudinal population was studied from infancy thorough adolescence and evaluated as young adults when they were between 19 and 29 years of age. Only one of the many variables quantified during the first three years of life revealed preservation of individual differences across childhood, adolescence, and young adulthood. We called this quality "passivity" in the original research, but, upon reflection, now realize it referred to inhibition to the unfamiliar. Individual differences in this quality were preserved from the first three years of life to the early school years ($r = 0.6$). The children who were inhibited during the first three years of life showed a coherent cluster of behaviors during the early school years. They avoided dangerous activities, were minimally aggressive, conformed to parental demands, and avoided social situations. The young boys who were rated as inhibited avoided sports and other traditional masculine activities during the adolescent years, and the four boys rated as most inhibited during the first six years of life chose intellectual careers as adults (music, physics, biology, and psychology). The four least inhibited boys chose more traditional masculine vocations (football coach, salesman, and two engineers). Further, the adults who had been extremely inhibited during the first three years of life showed more dependency on their love objects, either sweetheart or spouse, than did those who were uninhibited, and the former reported feelings of anxiety in social situations (Kagan & Moss, 1962/1983).

A replication study with 45 girls and 45 boys from the Fels sample revealed that extreme inhibition during the first three years was associated with low dominance with other children and high dependency on adults during the second three years of life (Kagan & Moss, 1983).

These results are in accord with the research of Bronson (1970) who found that fearful 1-year-old boys remained fearful when assessed from 6 to 8 years of age. Further, two independent teams of investigators studying laboratory reared macaque monkeys have reported that a behavioral variable that resembles inhibition to the unfamiliar is stable from infancy to reproductive maturity (Stevenson-Hinde, Stillwell-Barnes, & Zunz, 1980; Suomi, Kraemer, Baysinger, & DeLizio, 1981).

The Day Care Experiment

Fifteen years after publication of the Fels longitudinal project, one of us was involved in a second longitudinal evaluation of the effect of continuous day care on Chinese-American and Caucasian infants growing up in the Boston area (Kagan, Kearsley, & Zelazo, 1978). Perhaps the most significant result was that the Chinese children were more inhibited across the period from 3 to 29 months of age than were the Caucasians, whether the children were raised only at home or attended a day care center 5 days a week. (See Weissbluth, 1982, for a similar result). Further, more of the Chinese than Caucasian children had a minimally variable heart rate when processing unfamiliar visual and auditory information, and variability of heart rate was the best preserved quality across the 26 months of the investigation, better preserved than differences in attentiveness, irritability, vocalization, or smiling. This result is important because an intriguing finding from the original Fels study was the association, among adult men, between extreme inhibition during the first three years of life and a minimally variable heart rate during a baseline period before a set of stressful tasks was to be administered. The inverse relation between behavioral inhibition and heart rate variability in both the day care study and the earlier Fels investigation was the main incentive for the current research.

Current Research

Our research group has been following two cohorts of children, each containing from 40 to 50 children. Cohort 1 was assessed at 21 months, 48 months, and is currently being evaluated at 5½ years of age. Cohort 2 was assessed initially at 31 months and subsequently at 43 months of age. The children in both cohorts were selected from much larger groups of 200 to 300 children with a procedure that began with telephone interviews with mothers who replied to questions about their child's tendency to be inhibited or uninhibited in unfamiliar situations. On the basis of the answers to these telephone interviews, children were brought to our laboratory where their behavior to unfamiliar situations was recorded on videotape. If a child was consistent in his or her tendency to be inhibited or uninhibited, the child was retained for the longitudinal study. The initial situations used for classification of the children in Cohort 1 included encounters with unfamiliar women, unfamiliar toys, a model displaying a trio of acts that was difficult to remember, exposure to a large metal robot, and temporary separation from the mother. The screening situation for Cohort 2 involved primarily a play situation with an unfamiliar child of the same age and sex, with the mothers of both children present in the playroom. The behavioral signs of inhibition emphasized long latencies to interact with the unfamiliar persons, physical retreat from the unfamiliar persons or the robot, cessation of play or vocalization, occurrence of fretting or crying, and long periods of proximity to the mother, especially while not playing with any toy. Children who did or did not display these behavioral signs of inhibition consistently were selected to form groups of extremely inhibited and extremely uninhibited children. Each group comprised about 10% of the original samples and contained equal numbers of boys and girls.

Cohort 1. The procedures administered to the children in each of the cohorts at their respective follow-up evaluations were not identical; hence, we summarize the findings separately for the two groups. Each 4-year-old in Cohort 1 was observed twice in a laboratory playroom with an unfamiliar peer of the same age and sex in order to evaluate each child's tendency to be inhibited or uninhibited with an unfamiliar child while both parents were present. We regard the behavior with an unfamiliar peer as an unusually sensitive index of these two temperamental qualities during the third and fourth years of life because cognitive maturation has permitted the 3-year-old to generate forms of uncertainty that the 1-year-old cannot produce. However, by 5 and 6 years of age, the child has learned coping strategies for social situations that make a play situation with an unfamiliar child a less sensitive index of these dispositions. Each child was also assessed twice in a testing situation, once with a female examiner and once with a male, in order to evaluate the child's heart rate pattern to cognitive tasks and characteristic behavior with the examiner. Details of this evaluation can be found in Kagan *et al.* (1984).

The child's behavior in the two play sessions with the unfamiliar peer, the primary indexes of behavioral inhibition and lack of inhibition, was related to individual variation in inhibition and lack of inhibition at 21 months of age (correlations averaged 0.5, $p < .01$). The 4-year-old children who had been inhibited at 21 months were reluctant to approach the unfamiliar peer, showed frequent staring at the other child, remained close to their mother for long periods, and spoke infrequently and very late in the session. Additionally, during the testing situation with a female examiner, the inhibited children glanced more often at the examiner ($r = 0.3$, $p < .05$), showed very few restless trunk movements ($r = -0.3$, $p < .05$), and occasionally refused to offer an answer to difficult problems ($r = 0.4$, $p < .01$). As expected, the mothers of inhibited children described their child as more fearful than did the mothers of uninhibited children ($r = 0.6$ for the relation between behavior at 21 months and the mother's Q-sort at age 4).

A change in behavior from inhibition to lack of inhibition was more likely than the reverse change. Five inhibited children became much less inhibited behaviorally by their fourth birthday, whereas only one uninhibited child changed a bit toward the inhibited classification. Because the mothers of inhibited children were more distressed by their child's personality they consciously made a more sustained effort to change this aspect of their child's behavior.

Relation to Heart Rate. The expected relation between behavioral inhibition and a higher and less variable heart rate to cognitive tasks occurred at both 21 months and 4 years of age (for details, see Garcia-Coll *et al.*, 1984; and Kagan *et al.*, 1984). This association is in accord with the earlier data on the Fels adults and the Chinese children in the day care study and, moreover, is theoretically reasonable. Cardiac rate and variability are regulated by both the sympathetic and parasympathetic branches of the autonomic nervous system. At rest, there is a phasic alternation in the parasympathetic and sympathetic influences on the heart. The most prominent influence is associated with the respiratory cycle and is called respiratory sinus arrhythmia. Heart rate, blood pressure, and sympathetic activity typically increase during inspiration as vagal tone is inhibited and decrease with expiration as the vagus is disinhibited (Grossmann, 1983). As a result, a person's heart rate at rest usually displays a regular cycle and is moderately variable over epochs of 10 to 20 seconds. However, when the vagus is restrained, the cardiac deceleration that normally accompanies expiration is muted and heart rate becomes much less variable (Bunnell, 1982). The mental effort associated with cognitive tasks is one of the conditions usually associated with a loss of respiratory sinus arrhythmia, and a rise and stabilization of heart rate.

Not only did the inhibited children have higher and less variable heart rates than the uninhibited children during cognitive tasks, but, in addition, individual differences in heart rate variability were preserved from 21 months to 4 years of age at a magnitude that matched the stability coefficients for the behavioral indexes of inhibition and lack of inhibition ($r = 0.5$). (Although individual differences in absolute heart rate were not preserved from 21 to 48 months, there were significant levels of stability for both heart rate and heart rate variability from age 4 to 5½ years of age). Further, the children who had been behaviorally inhibited at 21 months had higher and less variable heart rates at 4 years of age ($r = 0.4$, $p < .01$), and the inhibited children who had the most stable heart rates at 21 months were more likely to remain inhibited than were the inhibited children who showed a variable heart rate.

We are currently assessing the children in Cohort 1, who are now 5-years-7-months old, in procedures that are similar to those administered at age 4. Individual differences in behavior as well as heart rate and variability are preserved to a significant degree from age 4 to 5½. Additionally, the inhibited children continue to be less active and quieter during the testing sessions. One of the striking differences between the two groups during the individual testing session is that most of the inhibited children sit with a rather stiff posture, but show frequent, small movements of the fingers and hands. Many of the uninhibited children show either an unusually relaxed posture, or gross motor restlessness of the limbs and trunk. Further, as we observed at age 4, the inhibited children show a rise in heart rate over succeeding trials of a particular cognitive procedure, whereas the uninhibited children show no change or a steady decrease in heart rate over the trials of a test.

Each child was also observed on his or her first day at kindergarten in a procedure that required the training of large numbers of graduate students, each one blind as to the child's classification, in observational methodology. This effort is part of Michelle Gersten's doctoral research. The children who had been classified as inhibited at 21 months were often isolated from their peers and frequently stared at the other children. Indeed, the behavior that best differentiated the inhibited from the uninhibited children was the frequency with which the former group stared at a classmate from a position of isolation.

Cohort 2. The second cohort of 54 children was selected at 31 months of age based on a half hour of behavior with an unfamiliar peer and a brief interaction with an unfamiliar woman and the robot toy. The children were classified as inhibited or uninhibited based on the consistency of their behavior across these situations and were observed one year later, at 43 months of age, in situations that were similar to, but not identical with, those used with Cohort 1 at age 4. These data are part of Nancy Snidman's doctoral research.

As we found with Cohort 1, no uninhibited child became inhibited over the 12-month interval. About one-half of the inhibited children remained extremely inhibited, whereas the remaining half changed toward a less inhibited style. However, as we found with Cohort 1, the inhibited children who had very stable heart rates at 31 months were more likely to remain inhibited than were those inhibited youngsters who had variable heart rates at the earlier age.

Two procedures that were not administered to Cohort 1 provide information suggesting that the inhibited children have a lower threshold for physiological arousal and/or sympathetic discharge to cognitive stress. Each child was first asked to repeat a set of familiar words one at a time and subsequently asked to recall the same words in groups of three, four, and five, in a procedure that placed mild stress on the child. The taped vocal utterances were analyzed for changes in the variablity of the vocal signal from the prestress repetition of single words to the more stressful recall memory procedure. Philip Lieberman of Brown University has developed a computer program that permits quantification of the variability of the pitch periods of single vocal utterances, a construct he calls "jitter." Decreases in jitter are associated with increased tension in the vocal cords and the surrounding laryngeal muscles. The children who had been classified as inhibited at 31 months of age showed a greater decrease in jitter from prestress recitation of single words to the more stressful repetition of several words in the recall procedure. The uninhibited children showed either no change or an increase in jitter from the prestress to the stressful condition.

Because pupillary dilation is a moderately sensitive index of sympathetic activity to the stress accompanying cognitive effort (Stanners, Coulter, Sweet, & Murphy, 1979) we measured each child's pupillary dilation during a baseline interval and during a series of cognitive procedures. The children who had been inhibited at 31 months displayed larger pupillary dilations during the initial baseline period, and, additionally, showed larger increases in pupillary dilation from baseline to cognitive tasks than did the uninhibited children. These results are in accord with the earlier suggestion that the inhibited children experience greater sympathetic arousal to cognitive stress.

Finally, interview data provided by the mothers of children in both cohorts revealed that the incidence of symptoms suggestive of higher physiological arousal was more frequent for the inhibited than for the uninhibited children, especially the symptoms of chronic constipation and allergy during the first two years of life and, during the second and third years, many fears and frequent nightmares. From 25% to 50% of the inhibited children showed one or more of the above symptoms, compared with less than 10% of the uninhibited children.

DISCUSSION

The total corpus of data implies that shyness in young children can be influenced by the temperamental quality we call inhibition to the unfamiliar. We do not believe that all shy children are born with this temperamental disposition, only that this disposition makes it more probable that a particular child will become shy. The tendency to be unusually shy or social during the childhood years can be reliably detected during the 3rd year of life from a 30- to 40-minute play session with an unfamiliar child.

More important, the correlates of these two behavioral profiles imply genetic and/or prenatal influences. The strongest support for this claim comes from the heart rate and pupil reactions to mild cognitive stress. The fact that a larger proportion of inhibited than uninhibited children showed a higher and more stable heart rate and a larger pupillary dilation to cognitive problems implies an inherently lower threshold for sympathetic discharge to psychological uncertainty. Readers who are familiar with the adult literature on personality may detect a relation between Eysenck's (1967) constructs of introversion and extraversion and our terms inhibition and lack of inhibition. Adult introverts display higher heart rates and larger pupillary dilations to stress (Gange, Geen, & Harkins, 1979; Hinton & Craske, 1977; Orlebeke, 1973; Stelmack & Mandelzys, 1975; Thackray, Jones, & Touchstone, 1974). Indeed, it is even possible that Pavlov's bold suggestion of weak versus strong nervous systems has some validity, for the children we call inhibited behave in ways that are somewhat congruent with Pavlov's hypothesis of a weak nervous system.

Our current view is that a small group of children, perhaps 15% of the normal population, are born with either a very high or low threshold for physiological arousal and an accompanying state of uncertainty following encounter with the unfamiliar (see Asendorpf in this volume for a similar estimate based on a survey of teachers of over 1,000 preschool children living in Munich). But environmental conditions, especially chronic ones, determine the degree to which this biological tendency is actualized. It is possible that actualization of this biological potential requires some continuous stressful experience—an older sibling, marital quarreling—but that an unusually benevolent environment that gently promotes an uninhibited coping style could create a socially outgoing manner in a child who was born with an inhibited temperament. Further, a chronically stressful environment might create behavioral inhibition in a child who was born with a temperamental disposition that favored lack of inhibition.

It is not clear how long these two qualities are preserved. The data from the original Fels study suggested that individual differences in these qualities persist into adulthood for some children. Moreover, there is an association between a childhood history of anxiety over separation from parents and a fear of school, on the one hand, and a predisposition to panic reaction and agoraphobia in adulthood (Gittelman & Klein, 1984). However, some inhibited children do learn to control their initial disposition to withdraw to the unfamiliar and the unexpected. One of the most inhibited children in the Fels sample decided, during adolescence, to cope with his fears, and did so successfully. When this boy was 2½ years of age he was described as an unusually cautious child.

> He spent an unhappy week at nursery school. He cried a great deal and looked
> ready to cry even when he was not actually doing it. He drew away when other children

approached him and he seemed afraid of them. Usually he stood around and looked lost.

Inhibition was still a salient characteristic of this child when he was 4 years old.

> He was one of the group's most isolated members. He was noncompetitive, unassertive, and sedentary. He shrank from actual physical contact with others and his relationships with peers were mild, long distance, verbal ones. He was petrified at rough handling. When he was verbally rebuffed or teased he smiled weakly and put his hands behind his back. He was the most eclipsed member of the group because of his apprehension, shyness, and inhibition.

However, this boy's anxiety and apprehensiveness to challenge became a source of conflict during adolescence, for his private standards did not permit withdrawal from potential failure situations. When he was 16 years old he realized that he was afraid of dating girls and decided that the best way to conquer this fear was to invite the most popular girl to a school dance, even though he had never dated her before. When interviewed as an adult, he derogated men who were overly cautious, dependent on others, and easily frightened. When asked if he ever went to his family for advice he replied,

> My father was not approachable and I didn't go to him for advice—in fact—he used to tell me to solve my own problems by myself, and I felt uneasy about going to him for help, my mother, she wouldn't know what to tell me anyway. (Kagan & Moss, 1962/1983, pp. 72–73)

It is important that this boy graduated from high school as valedictorian in a small class and chose physical science as a career. His extraordinary success in high school and college helped mute the anxiety he experienced in social situations and facilitated his self-consciously directed attempts to control his tendency to withdraw from unfamiliar social situations.

The selection of constructs to describe these data poses a problem. Individual differences in behavioral inhibition or lack of inhibition are best described with a construct like *vulnerability to psychological uncertainty to the unfamiliar*. However, psychological uncertainty is not the most appropriate term for individual differences in the rise and stabilization of heart rate to cognitive demands. The cardiac reactions seem best attributable to *vagal restraint* or to *increases in sympathetic tone*. Neither of these two phrases is synonymous with vulnerability to psychological uncertainty. Thus, we do not regard the two phenomena, which are related under some conditions, as indexing the same construct.

Research is needed to resolve several important problems. We have not yet proven that either genetic variables or prenatal events are partially responsible for the behavioral differences between inhibited and uninhibited children. Second, it is not clear that the behavioral differences between the two groups at age 4 and 5 will persist into adolescence or early adulthood. Finally, we must determine if the inhibited children who show the high and stable heart rate do so because they have a lower threshold for sympathetic discharge to psychological uncertainty. Current work in our laboratory is addressed to these three critical issues.

REFERENCES

Bowler, P. J. (1983). *The eclipse of Darwinism*. Baltimore, MD: The Johns Hopkins University Press.

Bronson, G. W. (1970). Fear of visual novelty. *Developmental Psychology, 2*, 33–40.

Bunnell, D. E. (1982). Autonomic myocardial influences as a factor determining intertask consistency of heart rate reactivity. *Psychophysiology, 19*, 442–448.

Buss, A. H., & Plomin, R. A. (1975). *A temperamental theory of personality development*. New York: Wiley.

Carey, W. B., & McDevitt, S. C. (1978). Stability and change in individual temperament diagnoses from infancy to early childhood. *Journal of the American Academy of Child Psychiatry, 17*, 331–337.

Eysenck, H. J. (1967). *The biological basis for personality*. Springfield, IL: Charles C Thomas.

Gange, J. J., Geen, R. G., & Harkins, S. G. (1979). Autonomic differences between extraverts and introverts during vigilance. *Psychophysiology, 16*, 392–397.

Garcia-Coll, C., Kagan, J., & Reznick, J. S. (1984). Behavioral inhibition in young children. *Child Development, 55*, 1005–1019.

Gittelman, R. & Klein, D. F. (1984). Relationship between separation anxiety and panic and agoraphobic disorders. *Psychopathology*, Suppl. 1, *17*, 56–65.

Grossman, P. (1983). Respiration, stress, and cardiovascular function. *Psychophysiology, 20*, 284–300.

Hinton, J. W. & Craske, B. (1977). Differential effects of test stress on the heart rates of extraverts and introverts. *Biological Psychology, 5*, 23–28.

Kagan, J. & Moss, H. A. (1983). *Birth to maturity*. New Haven: Yale University Press (Original work published 1962).

Kagan, J., Kearsley, R. B., & Zelazo, P. R. (1978). *Infancy: Its place in human development*. Cambridge, MA: Harvard University Press.

Kagan, J., Reznick, J. S., Clarke, C., Snidman, N., & Garcia-Coll, C. (1984). Behavioral inhibition to the unfamiliar. *Child Development, 55*, 2212–2225.

Orlebeke, J. F. (1973). Electrodermal vasomotor and heart rate correlates of extraversion and neuroticism. *Psychophysiology, 10*, 211. (Abstract)

Plomin, R. A. & Rowe, D. C. (1979). Genetic and environmental etiology of social behavior in infancy. *Developmental Psychology, 15*, 62–72.

Rothbart, M. K. & Derryberry, D. (1981). Development of individual differences in temperament. In M. E. Lamb & A. L. Brown (Eds.), *Advances in Developmental Psychology, Vol. 1*. Hillsdale, NJ: Erlbaum.

Stanners, R. F., Coulter, M., Sweet, A. W., & Murphy, P. (1979). The pupillary response as an indicator of arousal and cognition. *Motivation and Emotion, 3*, 319–340.

Stelmack, R. M., & Mandelzys, N. (1975). Extraversion and pupillary response to affective and taboo words. *Psychophysiology, 12*, 536–540.

Stevenson-Hinde, J., Stillwell-Barnes, R., & Zunz, M. (1980). Subjective assessment of rhesus monkeys over four successive years. *Primates, 21*, 66–82.

Suomi, S. J., Kraemer, G. W., Baysinger, C. M., & DeLizio, R. D. (1981). Inherited and experiential factors associated with individual differences in anxious behavior displayed by rhesus monkeys. In D. F. Kline & J. Rabkin (Eds.), *Anxiety: New research and changing concepts* (pp. 179–199). New York: Raven Press.

Thackray, R. I., Jones, K. N., & Touchstone, R. M. (1974). Personality and physiological correlates of performance decrement on a monotonous task requiring sustained attention. *British Journal of Psychology, 65*, 351–358.

Thomas, A. & Chess, S. (1977). *Temperament and development*. New York: Brunner/Mazel.

Weissbluth, M. (1982). Chinese-American infant temperament and sleep duration: An ethnic comparison. *Developmental and Behavioral Pediatrics, 3*, 99–102.

8

Shyness in Middle and Late Childhood

Jens Asendorpf

INTRODUCTION

John and Ann are both quiet children. In kindergarten they have no friends, and they relate better to adults than to their peers. John does not seem to be unhappy with children in general but he shows little interest in them and apparently prefers to play alone. Ann always acts in the background and never volunteers for a task where she is the focus of attention. She does seem interested in other children, but she acts very coy, sometimes anxiously, toward them.

Most of us would agree that Ann is shy. But some of us would also regard John as shy whereas others would call him introverted. The greatest problem in reviewing the (rather sparse) literature on shyness in childhood is that shyness is a label that is used rather loosely both by laypersons and by psychologists concerned with shyness. Shyness is a fuzzy concept. There is no agreement in the literature as to how we should define shyness, particularly in childhood. Even within one psychodiagnostic system, such as the *Diagnostic and Statistical Manual of Mental Disorders* (DSM-III) of the American Psychiatric Association (1979), shyness and introversion are treated as different diagnostic categories but cannot be clearly distinguished from each other (cf. Wanlass & Prinz, 1982).

This vagueness of the concept seems to be one of the reasons why shyness in general has received little attention so far in the empirically oriented literature. As we will see, this is all the more true for shyness in middle and late childhood. Zimbardo and Radl (1981) have written a relatively comprehensive book entitled *The Shy Child*, but this book is based predominantly on clinical evidence and the convictions of the authors, not on empirical research.

A second reason for the neglect of research on childhood shyness undoubtedly is that shy children do not seem to present as obvious a problem for parents

JENS ASENDORPF • Max-Planck-Institute for Psychological Research, 8000 Munich 40, Federal Republic of Germany.

and teachers as do aggressive children, at least in school. People often simply fail to notice shy children; this oversight applies to psychologists as well.

But shyness is a real problem—not only in adolescence and adulthood but also in childhood. In a study by Cranach, Huffner, Marte, and Pelka (1976), teachers of 1,115 preschool children in Munich classified 16.8% of these children as "shy-inhibited"; additional interviews showed that 59% of the children the teachers held to be in need of therapy manifested shy-inhibited behavior. Thus, by childhood shyness already appears to be a quite common problem that calls for a better understanding of its nature. But given the fuzziness of the present conceptualizations of shyness, how can we approach this problem in empirical research?

Here, shyness is regarded to be both an affective *state* and an affective *trait* (see, Asendorpf, 1983, for a more detailed discussion of these concepts). *Situational shyness* is conceived to be a transient, situation-bound affective state encompassing experiential, motor-expressive, and physiological components; *dispositional shyness* is conceived of as a temporally stable tendency of a person to react with situational shyness in a broad class of social situations. By these definitions, we can trace dispositional shyness back to situational shyness.

Accordingly, we will begin our review of shyness in middle and late childhood with situational shyness. A definition of situational shyness will be proposed that provides a basis for the following discussion of the ecology of shyness, dispositional shyness, and its development.

SITUATIONAL SHYNESS

Most of us do experience some degree of shyness in certain situations. Thus, it is quite misleading to regard shyness as only a pathological phenomenon. As Zimbardo and Radl (1981) put it, "normal shyness" functions as a protective device—a sensible reserve that allows people to size up new experiences before rushing in. Because most children lack many of the self-presentation tactics used by adults to overcome their shyness, they express their shyness more directly in their nonverbal behavior. Although this more direct expression offers special opportunities for observational studies of shyness, only a few studies have provided information about shyness in childhood as a normal state.

The most interesting data in this respect come from a study of Greenberg and Marvin (1982) who were concerned with the development of wariness toward strangers (cf. Kagan & Reznick, this volume) beyond the second year of life. They observed the responses of 2-, 3-, and 4-year-olds to an approaching adult stranger when their mother was present. About half of the 2-year-olds showed the characteristic wariness behavior in this situation. But the 3- and 4-year olds did not display this wariness pattern. They either approached the stranger or continued exploring the room, or they showed a highly ambivalent behavior toward the stranger consisting of a low-intensity mixture of wary and sociable behavior that usually took the form of lengthy coy expressions. About half of the children who continued exploring the room also displayed these coy expressions, but of much shorter duration. Altogether, a majority of the 3- and 4-year-olds acted shy at least for a short time.

This study bears on several important issues in the study of childhood shyness. First, it provides an instance where shyness seems to be the normal reaction. Second, it shows some continuity between infant wariness and childhood shyness regarding the situational elicitors and the behavioral reactions. And last but not least, it calls attention to an important difference between infant wariness and childhood shyness: a clearly expressed *ambivalence* between tendencies to approach and at the same time to avoid the stranger. Perhaps this ambivalence can be observed so clearly only in middle childhood. Later, it may be obscured by self-presentation tactics. But it may still endure into adulthood as a conflict more hidden to the observer.

Besides this study, little has been written about situational shyness in childhood. Do children experience shyness in a similar manner as adults do—as a mixed feeling of negative and positive emotions with a particularly large proportion of interest and enjoyment (cf. Izard, 1972)? The behavioral ambivalence observed by Greenberg and Marvin (1982) points to such a similarity. Self-reports of emotions in real and imagined shyness situations for older children and a detailed analysis of children's facial expressions in such situations could help to answer these questions.

Taken together, the few data available for situational shyness in childhood suggest the following definition:

> *Situational shyness* is an ambivalent affective state during social encounters. The acutely shy child tries both to approach and to avoid interaction partners at the same time. Behaviorally, this approach–avoidance conflict leads to a mixture of wary and sociable behavior. Experientially, this conflict gives rise to mixed feelings of anxiety and interest.

This definition helps us to overcome the common confusion of shy and introverted behavior: conflict-free disinterest in peers should not be regarded as an indicator of shyness.

THE ECOLOGY OF SHYNESS

Further evidence for the nature of situational shyness comes from studies concerned with the ecology of shyness. What are the situations that are likely to make children shy? How frequent are they in the lives of our children? Are there common features of these situations, or should we distinguish between different types of shyness corresponding to different types of shyness elicitors?

Presently we know very little about these issues. Zimbardo and Radl (1981, p. 121) report the results of teachers' and parents' ratings of shyness elicitors for preschool children. Teachers and parents rate "meeting strangers" and "being the focus of attention" to be among the three most powerful inducers of shyness. Besides that, however, the ratings by the two groups differed substantially. For example, teachers rated "being with peers" to be of third importance whereas parents ranked this situation as last among the eight rated elicitors. These differences obviously reflect the fact that teachers observe children more in situations that involve peer interaction than do parents.

Apart from this rater bias the different ratings also appear to reflect important differences between shyness elicitors at home and in school: parents and teachers are often surprised to learn that the same child who appears to be not shy at all in one setting acts shy in the other setting (cf. Zimbardo & Radl, 1981, p. 121). A longitudinal study by Chamberlin (1977) supports this view. Shy-withdrawn behavior that was observed with the same methodology in kindergarten and at home showed some stability over a 1-year period in the same setting (test–retest correlations between .25 and .61) but did not significantly correlate between settings. Thus, shyness appears to be relatively context specific in the sense that it may be stable across situations within a particular setting but it may also vary considerably across different settings.

A second important distinction must be made regarding the interaction partners of the child. Children who often react shy toward adults are not necessarily shy toward peers or younger children, and vice versa. Adult shyness and peer shyness may be quite different phenomena, and shyness toward younger children seems to occur infrequently. Surprisingly, no systematic study of these differences seems to exist. A recent observational study by Hinde, Easton, Meller, and Tamplin (1983), however, provides some indirect evidence for these differences. Preschool children directed their behavior to peers and adults quite differently; no evidence for a general sociability factor was found in these observations. It seems likely that a similar study focusing on shy behavior toward adults and peers would come to a similar conclusion.

DISPOSITIONAL SHYNESS

Few studies have been directly concerned with dispositional shyness in childhood. In some studies of social-emotional phenomena related to dispositional shyness, such as peer group status, social withdrawal, social skills, or social knowledge, shy behavior has been included as a minor variable among others. ·

Shyness and Peer Group Status

In a study reported in Zimbardo and Radl (1981, p. 119), teachers' ratings of preschoolers indicated that shy children had fewer friends than their nonshy peers. A more direct way to determine the number of children's friends in a peer group or, more generally, the degree to which children are liked or disliked by the members of a particular peer group is to ask each child in such a group to nominate children the child likes most and children the child likes least. In this way the peer group status of each group member can be defined by the number of positive or negative choices received; we can distinguish between *rejected* children (i.e., highly disliked), *neglected* children (i.e., neither disliked nor liked), *popular* children (i.e., highly liked and not disliked), and *controversial* children (i.e., both highly liked and disliked; cf. Newcomb & Bukowski, 1983). We can also introduce two hypothetical dimensions called social preference and social impact to describe differences between popular versus rejected and controversial versus neglected children. Are any of these dimensions related to shyness?

In two studies with third- and fifth-grade children done by Coie, Dodge, and Coppotelli (1982), peer ratings of shy behavior correlated neither with social preference nor with liking or disliking, but did correlate with social impact. Among the four types of peer group status, the controversial children were perceived by their peers as the least shy and the neglected children as the most shy whereas popular and rejected children fell in between and did not differ in shyness. Furthermore, observational analyses of the behavior of third- and fifth-grade children in the classroom and on a playground revealed that in both situations the neglected children did not approach their peers as often as did other children, but their peers did not differ in the number of social approaches toward them. In addition, teachers judged that the neglected children made fewer social approaches toward peers than did children in the other groups (Dodge, Coie, & Brakke, 1982).

Although these studies show that peer perception of shy behavior is related to low social impact, this relationship is nevertheless not a very strong one. In the Coie *et al.* (1982) study, the mean shyness score of the neglected children did not differ significantly from the mean shyness score of an average group consisting of children with medium values on both social preference and social impact. The authors speculate that this may be due to the low "social visibility" of the neglected children: it is difficult for their peers to evaluate any of their personal characteristics, including shyness.

Furthermore, in both studies the relationship between shyness and social impact was investigated in well established, large groups of peers. Coie and Kupersmidt (1983) created new groups of fourth-grade boys who differed in peer group status and were unfamiliar with each other. Within 3 weeks, the rejected children were also rejected in the new, small group of peers. The neglected children, however, achieved a satisfactory social position in the new group and were perceived to be less shy by their new group members than by their classmates. Thus, the neglected children were able to make a fresh start in the new group.

Further evidence for the relative temporal instability of peer neglect comes from a longitudinal study by Coie and Dodge (1983). They retested the sample of Coie *et al.* (1982) (2 cohorts of 3rd- and 5th-grade children) each year for the next 4 years. Whereas the rejected group was relatively stable (45% remained rejected after one year) only 25% of the neglected children were again classified as neglected after one year. Interestingly, children who had neglected status at the beginning of testing almost never became rejected (1%) or controversial (0%) at the end of the 5-year testing period; instead, they spread themselves across the average (45%), neglected (24%), and popular (24%) status categories. Thus, neglected elementary school children continued to be socially inoffensive and had a good chance to improve their peer group status. Peer ratings of shy behavior in one year predicted neglected status in the subsequent year, but only to a marginal degree.

Taken together, these studies demonstrate that there may exist some link between peer perceptions of shyness and peer group neglect, but this link is not a very strong one. Perceived shyness predicts subsequent neglected status only to a marginal degree, and low social impact in one group is not highly predictive of low social impact or shyness in another group of peers.

Last, but not least, the very definition of shyness in these studies does not allow us to draw a distinction between shy and introverted children: "acts shy" was qualified by "seems always to play or work by themselves. It's hard to get to know this person." Thus, we have to be very cautious in generalizing from these peer-perception data to real shyness.

Shyness and Social Withdrawal

In the last decade there has been a growing interest in methods to assess social withdrawal in children and to improve their peer relations (see, Wanlass & Prinz, 1982, for a review). At the first glance, social withdrawal seems to be closely connected with shyness. A closer look shows, however, that this is not necessarily the case.

Social withdrawal is defined either as low peer group status (which we have already discussed separately) or as a low rate of peer interaction—alone or in combination with additional criteria of the quality of interaction.

Quantity of Peer Interaction. Total rate of peer interaction as a measure of social withdrawal has come under heavy criticism in recent years (Asher, Markell, & Hymel, 1981; Wanlass & Prinz, 1982). It is not predictive of peer group status, and there seem to be quite different subgroups of "low interactors": autistic children, depressed children, children stigmatized for physical, racial, or socioeconomic reasons, children who lack certain social skills, shy children, and simply introverted children. Thus, there is some evidence that shy children are low interactors, but low interactors are by no means necessarily shy.

Quality of Peer Interaction. Rubin (1982) analyzed the behavior of kindergarten children during indoor free play and related the frequency of different play qualities to peer group status and various measures of social competence. An analysis of different types of nonsocial and quasi-social activities revealed that there are important differences in their impact on social-emotional development. Some activities such as solitary-constructive play and onlooking were positively related to social competence. The quasi-social activity of parallel-constructive play that often is misconceived as nonsocial in nature was positively correlated with peer popularity, teacher ratings of social competence, and tests of impersonal and social problem solving.

This study clearly shows that it may be quite misleading to pool all kinds of nonsocial behavior together in studies of social withdrawal. And more importantly, this study suggests that global ratings of shy behavior made by teachers, parents, or peers suffer from the same problem: when asked to rate shyness, naive observers are very likely to lump constructive and nonconstructive non-social activities together. What is called for, therefore, are observational studies of children's behavior that carefully distinguish between different types of social and nonsocial activity and that link these types to shyness.

The behavioral observations reported in Zimbardo and Radl (1981) are not very informative in this respect. Children regarded as shy appear to play more alone, to look more than to act, and to show less social initiative (e.g., asking questions or asking for help). But it remains unclear which type of play they prefer. By combining measures of peer group status and observational codings, Gottman (1977) identified five different groups of preschool children. One group, called "tuned out," was characterized by a high amount of time spent alone and off task (daydreaming, staring out in space, tuned out), a high percentage of shy, anxious, and fearful behaviors called "hovering," and peer neglect. This characterization comes close to shyness, but the small number of children in the groups (only four "tuned outs") prevents any generalization. As of now, apparently no study has directly focused on the quality of the social interaction of shy children.

To summarize, the relationship between shyness and social withdrawal heavily depends on our conception of withdrawal. If we equate social withdrawal with a mere lack of peer interaction we will simply conclude that social withdrawal is a necessary, but not sufficient condition of shyness. On the other hand, if we want to look more closely at the quality of shy children's behavior in peer groups, we are confronted with a lack of knowledge; we know very little about the quality of social behavior of shy children.

Shyness and Social Skills

Do shy children lack certain social skills? If we define social skills merely by criteria of *performance* (occurrence of particular behaviors) there is some evidence that shy children indeed lack certain social skills. In a study by Dodge, Schlundt, Schocken, and Delugach (1983), neglected children showed more "wait and hover" behavior during entry into a new group of peers. The observations reported in Zimbardo and Radl (1981) suggest that these may be typical characteristics of shy children in general.

If we define social skills in terms of the general *availability* of particular behaviors, however, it is less clear whether shy children lack such social skills. The studies of neglected children have shown that peer neglect is a fairly unstable, group-specific phenomenon in middle childhood; this speaks against a general social-skills deficit of neglected children. Unfortunately, no studies have followed this line of investigation for shyness. We simply do not know about the stability of the observed social-skills deficit in shy children. If the deficit were quite stable, this would suggest that these children do not have certain skills available in general. However, if the observed skills deficit occurred only under specific situational circumstances—for example, only in a specific group of peers—it is more likely that there are other reasons for the observed lack of performed skills, such as an anxious inhibition of skills.

Shyness and Social Knowledge

One way to study the availability of social skills in children is to ask them how they would act in hypothetical social situations. Social skills are tested indirectly by testing social knowledge. Richard and Dodge (1982) pursued this approach. They asked popular, aggressive, and isolated elementary school boys to generate alternative solutions to interpersonal situations. The isolated group was defined by multiple criteria among which were neglected peer group status, teacher ratings of low peer interaction frequency, and peer ratings of high shyness. The popular group generated more solutions than either the aggressive or isolated groups, which did not differ. Ratings of the effectiveness of the solutions revealed that the three groups did not differ in the effectiveness of the first solution generated. The effectiveness of the subsequent solutions, however, was different between the groups: the popular group continued to propose effective solutions, whereas both the aggressive and the isolated groups generated less effective solutions.

Rubin, Daniels-Beirness, and Bream (1984) found similar differences when they compared the frequency of preschoolers' isolated behavior with their solutions generated in a social-problem-solving test. Isolated behavior was defined by the frequency of solitary, unoccupied, and onlooking behavior. It correlated negatively with the number of solutions generated and with a measure of the flexibility of problem solving, and it was positively related to the proportion of adult intervention strategies suggested by the children as appropriate for solving the problem presented. Thus, socially withdrawn children were deficient in social problem solving. A retest one year later showed that social withdrawal in preschool predicted both social withdrawal and deficient problem solving in elementary school.

Thus, both peer neglect and social withdrawal have been found to be associated with deficient social problem solving. But it is yet unclear whether shy children are also deficient in social problem solving.

Taken together, we know very little about the social skills and the social knowledge of shy children. We can only speculate that there may be an important difference between children who are shy because they lack certain social skills or social knowledge, and children who have sufficient skills and knowledge available but who often cannot apply their skills and knowledge in social situations because of an anxious inhibition of their behavior.

THE DEVELOPMENT OF DISPOSITIONAL SHYNESS

Early and Late Developing Shyness

Buss (this volume) proposes that we should distinguish between early developing shyness and late developing shyness. He assumes that late developing shyness is a consequence of the emergence of the psychological state of public self-awareness: around the age of 5 years children learn to become aware of themselves as "social objects." Also, individual differences in the degree of this awareness emerge (the trait of public self-consciousness). Children high in public self-consciousness are, according to Buss, more sensitive to the impact of their own behavior and personality on others; this sensitivity makes them prone to shyness.

This is an important and plausible hypothesis because shyness in adolescence and adulthood is associated with public self-consciousness (cf. the chapters of Cheek, Carpentieri, Smith, Rierdan, & Koff and Carver & Scheier in this volume). Unfortunately, this hypothesis as yet has no empirical basis. There are few studies of self-awareness in childhood, and apparently no single study exists that is concerned with the development of the state of public self-awareness or the trait of public self-consciousness. Buss cites as evidence for the onset of late developing shyness around the age of 5 years the finding of Buss, Iscoe, and Buss (1979) that this is the earliest age at which a majority of children shows embarrassment reactions (according to their mothers' report). But shyness and embarrassment seem to be only two aspects of the same phenomenon (cf. Asendorpf, 1984; Leary & Schlenker, 1981). What we need are longitudinal studies that operationalize public self-awareness *independently* of shyness or embarrassment reactions and then compare the development of public self-awareness with the development of shyness and embarrassment. Such studies could answer the question as to whether and in which way the emergence of public self-awareness influences the development of shyness both as a trait and as a state.

Stability of Shyness

The Coie and Dodge longitudinal study mentioned before sheds some light on the stability of shyness during late childhood and the transition into adolescence. The stability of the peer ratings of shy behavior (determined by the test–retest correlation between subsequent years) showed a clear increase over time. Between grades three and four, stability was lowest ($r = .35$), and then it increased fairly monotonically up to a quite high stability between grades eight and nine ($r = .85$). Grade-three ratings were not significantly related to ratings in grade five through seven, whereas grade-five ratings were significantly related to all ratings in the following four years. Because grade five just about marks the onset of puberty, these data suggest that childhood shyness is a relatively unstable phenomenon that does not predict shyness in adolescence, although adolescent shyness is a stable personality trait. But this interpretation may be misleading. The observed increase of the stability of the shyness ratings could be attributed to an increased detection of shyness by their peers as children grow older. Only a longitudinal study that applies more objective measures of shyness, such as behavioral ratings of trained observers, can determine the extent to which the observed instability of peer ratings of shyness in middle childhood can be attributed to an instability of the trait itself. No such study appears to exist.

Possible Causes of Shyness

Three factors often have been discussed as possible causes of childhood shyness: genetic dispositions, relations with peers and siblings, and parenting styles. Plomin and Daniels (this volume) provide rather strong evidence for genetic influences on shyness in middle and late childhood. Our discussion of peer group status has shown that a (rather weak) relationship exists between peer group neglect and shyness. Presently, no data exist on the direction of influence between these two variables. That is, we do not know whether shyness leads to peer group neglect, or peer neglect increases shyness.

Children's birth-order position in their family appears to have some influence on their shyness toward other children. In a yet unpublished study we found a significant relationship between mothers' reports of their children's shyness toward peers and the children's birth order. Single children were perceived as most shy, followed by firstborns, and then children with younger and older siblings; lastborns were perceived to be the least shy of all four groups. Because the shyness ratings were not significantly related to age, social status, or the mere number of siblings, this pattern suggests that shyness is related to the amount of interaction with older siblings: the more opportunity children have to interact with older siblings, the less shy they are. It is not clear yet, however, which features of these interactions are responsible for this effect.

Although a vast number of investigators have attempted to relate children's social behavior to the childrearing behavior of their parents, there is no clear evidence that shyness is associated with particular parenting styles. Early studies seemed to indicate that a restrictive-hostile, or a less nurturant and less involved style, were associated with shyness and social withdrawal (cf. Baumrind, 1967; Becker, 1964). But later studies, reviewed by Maccoby and Martin (1983), did not corroborate these results. An adequate description of the present state of research seems to be the summary of Koch and Butollo (1983), who concluded that childhood aggression is related either to neglecting-permissive or to highly restrictive childrearing, but that no clear relations can be established between shy, withdrawn behavior and parenting styles. The (too often overlooked) fact that not only parents influence their children's personality, but that children's early temperament also influences their parents behavior toward them, further weakens the causal role of parenting styles on childhood shyness.

CONCLUSION

Presently, the greatest problem seems to be that there is no consensual definition of shyness. Only very few studies allow us to distinguish between shyness and introversion. Peers, parents, teachers, and psychologists not primarily interested in shyness appear to use the shyness label in a very sloppy sense, including introversion and other kinds of social withdrawal.

The definition of shyness proposed here distinguishes between shy children who try to approach and to avoid interaction partners at the same time and introverted children who are simply not interested in interaction and display no signs of a conflict. Although this conception of shyness can be considered to be an important step toward a better understanding of shyness, presently little research exists on childhood shyness in this more restricted sense.

Most of all, this view applies to normal situational shyness and its ecology. Nearly nothing is known about the different situations that elicit shyness in childhood, their frequency, and the possible subclasses that induce different types of shyness. There is only some indirect evidence that shyness at home and at school are quite different phenomena, and that shyness toward adults is fairly independent of shyness toward peers.

Shy behavior toward adults has not been studied at all except for shyness toward an adult stranger. Here, some continuity seems to exist between infant wariness and childhood shyness although in childhood a strong ambivalence toward the stranger emerges as a new quality.

Shy behavior in a group of peers appears to be associated with neglected peer group status, lack of friends, withdrawal behavior, and lack of certain social skills, such as entering a new group of peers or approaching a peer in a well-known group, but these relationships are not very strong ones. On the other hand, we do not know whether shy children generally lack these skills because they do not have sufficient social knowledge or social practice, or whether they often cannot apply their skill and knowledge because of an anxious inhibition of their behavior.

The latter interpretation calls attention to the motivational basis of shyness. If it makes sense, indeed, to conceive of shyness as an approach–avoidance conflict in social encounters, we need to know more about the needs, interests, and fears of shy children compared with introverted or sociable children. Why do shy children try both to socialize with others and try to avoid them? What do they fear in social situations, and where does this fear come from? Why do they not resolve their conflict by giving up their wish to socialize and becoming introverts?

Answers to these questions would also further our understanding of the developmental causes of shyness. There seems to exist some genetic disposition to become shy. What are the environmental contributions to shyness? The studies on the influence of parenting styles on shyness do not allow a conclusion. Peer neglect (but not peer rejection) may play some role in increasing children's shyness but the evidence for it is not very strong. The opportunity for interaction with older siblings seems to counteract the development of shyness but we do not know yet which particular features of these interactions are responsible for this effect.

Perhaps we have to distinguish between different types of shyness when we try to settle these questions: early developing shyness closely associated with infant wariness may be quite different from late developing shyness closely associated with public self-awareness and fear of negative evaluation, and shyness toward peers may be quite different from shyness toward adults. A longitudinal study comparing the development of these "shynesses," the development of shyness-related emotions, such as social anxiety and embarrassment, and the development of self-awareness could help to answer these questions. Such a study is now underway at the Max-Planck-Institute for Psychological Research.

REFERENCES

American Psychiatric Association (1979). *Diagnostic and statistical manual of mental disorders—III.* Washington, D.C.: Author.

Asendorpf, J. (1983). *Development of shyness* (Paper 5/1983). Munich: Max-Planck-Institute for Psychological Research.

Asendorpf, J. (1984). Shyness, embarrassment, and self-presentation: A control theory approach. In R. Schwarzer (Ed.), *The self in anxiety, stress, and depression* (pp. 109–114). Amsterdam: North Holland.

Asher, S. R., Markell, R. A., & Hymel, S. (1981). Identifying children at risk in peer relations: A critique of the rate-of-interaction approach to assessment. *Child Development, 52,* 1239–1245.

Baumrind, D. (1967). Child care practices anteceding three patterns of preschool behavior. *Genetic Psychology Monographs, 75,* 43–88.

Becker, W. C. (1964). Consequences of different kinds of parental discipline. In M. L. Hoffman & L. W. Hoffman (Eds.), *Review of child development research* (Vol. 1, pp. 169–208). New York: Russell Sage Foundation.

Buss, A. H., Iscoe, I., & Buss, E. H. (1979). The development of embarrassment. *Journal of Psychology, 103,* 227–230.

Chamberlin, R. W. (1977). Can we identify a group of children at age 2 who are at high risk for the development of behavior or emotional problems in kindergarten and first grade? *Pediatrics, 59,* 971–981.

Coie, J. D., & Dodge, K. A. (1983). Continuities and changes in children's social status: A five-year longitudinal study. *Merrill-Palmer Quarterly, 29,* 261–282.

Coie, J. D., & Kupersmidt, J. B. (1983). A behavioral analysis of emerging social status in boy's groups. *Child Development, 54,* 1400–1416.

Coie, J. D., Dodge, K. A., & Coppotelli, H. (1982). Dimensions and types of social status: A cross-age perspective. *Developmental Psychology, 18,* 557–570.

Cranach, B. V., Huffner, U., Marte F., & Pelka, R. (1976). Einschatzskala zur Erfassung gehemmter Kinder im Kindergarten. *Praxis der Kinderpsychologie und Kinderpsychiatrie, 25,* 146–155.

Dodge, K. A., Coie, J. D., & Brakke, N. P. (1982). Behavior patterns of socially rejected and neglected preadolescents: The roles of social approach and aggression. *Journal of Abnormal Child Psychology, 10,* 389–410.

Dodge, K. A., Schlundt, D. C., Schocken, I., & Delugach, I. D. (1983). Social competence and children's sociometric status: The role of peer group entry strategies. *Merrill-Palmer Quarterly, 29,* 309–336.

Gottmann, J. M. (1977). Toward a definition of social isolation in children. *Child Development, 48,* 513–517.

Greenberg, M. T., & Marvin, R. S. (1982). Reactions of preschool children to an adult stranger: A behavioral systems approach. *Child Development, 53,* 481–490.

Hinde, R. A., Easton, F., Meller, R. E., & Tamplin, A. (1983). Nature and determinants of pre-schoolers' differential behaviour to adults and peers. *British Journal of Developmental Psychology, 1,* 3–19.

Izard, C. E. (1972). *Patterns of emotion.* New York: Academic Press.

Koch, H. J., & Butollo, W. (1983). *The course and causes of behaviour disorders in early childhood.* Paper presented at the Seventh Biennial Meeting of the International Society for the Study of Behavioural Development, Munich, FRG.

Leary, M. R., & Schlenker, B. R. (1981). The social psychology of shyness: A self-presentation model. In J. T. Tedeschi (Ed.), *Impression management: Theory and social psychology research* (pp. 335–358). New York: Academic Press.

Maccoby, E. E., & Martin, J. A. (1983). Socialization in the context of the family: Parent-child interaction. In P. H. Mussen (Ed.), *Handbook of child psychology* (4th ed., Vol. 4, pp. 1–101). New York: Wiley.

Newcomb, A. F., & Bukowski, W. M. (1983). Social impact and social preference as determinants of children's peer group status. *Developmental Psychology, 19,* 856–867.

Richard, B. A., & Dodge, K. A. (1982). Social maladjustment and problem solving in school-aged children. *Journal of Consulting and Clinical Psychology, 50,* 226–233.

Rubin, K. H. (1982). Nonsocial play in preschoolers: Necessarily evil? *Child Development, 53,* 651–657.

Rubin, K. H., Daniels-Beirness, T., & Bream, L. (1984). Social isolation and social problem-solving: A longitudinal study. *Journal of Consulting and Clinical Psychology, 52,* 17–25.

Wanlass, R. L., & Prinz, R. J. (1982). Methodological issues in conceptualizing and treating childhood social isolation. *Psychological Bulletin, 92,* 39–55.

Zimbardo, P. G., & Radl, S. L. (1981).*The shy child.* New York: McGraw-Hill.

9

Adolescent Shyness

Jonathan M. Cheek, Andrea M. Carpentieri, Thomas G. Smith, Jill Rierdan, and Elissa Koff

INTRODUCTION

The transition from childhood to adolescence involves many dramatic changes. Adolescents must contend with three major sources of novelty: the bodily changes of puberty, the new cognitive abilities of formal operations, and new demands and opportunities caused by changing social roles and relationships (e.g., Damon, 1983). As Buss (1980) has noted, the most prominent cause of shyness is novelty. Thus, it is not surprising that early adolescence is the time of greatest shyness in the course of personality and social development (Zimbardo, 1977). In this chapter we review research findings and theoretical formulations on adolescent shyness and also present some of our own data. We begin by examining studies on the prevalence of shyness; then we will consider the issues of the stability of shyness, gender differences, and implications for treatment.

A major problem in reviewing the literature on shyness concerns the degree of equivalence among different measures of the construct. We decided to focus on studies that either employed a global shyness label for self-reports and observer ratings or used a measurement scale that approximates the operational definitions of contemporary shyness scales (see Briggs & Smith, this volume). In agreement with the conceptualization of Cheek and Buss (1981), we eliminated research that confounded introverted social withdrawal with shyness and we defined shyness as the tendency to be tense, worried, and awkward during social interactions with strangers, casual acquaintances, and persons in positions of authority.

JONATHAN M. CHEEK, JILL RIERDAN, and ELISSA KOFF • Department of Psychology, Wellesley College, Wellesley, MA 02181. ANDREA M. CARPENTIERI • Department of Psychology, University of Michigan, Ann Arbor, MI 48109. THOMAS G. SMITH • Late of the Department of Behavioral Statistics, Baylor University, Waco, TX 76704.

AGE TRENDS FOR SHYNESS

The percentage of people who label themselves as being currently shy shows one important age difference. Lazarus (1982a) reported that 38% of a sample of 396 fifth-grade children labeled themselves shy, and he noted that this finding is highly similar to the approximately 40% of young adults who said they were shy on the Stanford Shyness Survey (Zimbardo, Pilkonis, & Norwood, 1975). Older adults also report the presence of shyness at about the 40% level, but 54% of seventh and eighth grade students label themselves as shy (Zimbardo, 1977). Because these surveys were conducted with relatively large samples, the age trend in labelling oneself shy appears to be well established. There is, however, one difficulty in applying these data to a developmental theory of shyness. The use of a global self-label prevents the testing of Buss's (this volume) conceptualization of two qualitatively different types of shyness: fearful shyness and self-conscious shyness. Buss argues that self-conscious shyness first appears in late childhood and adolescence. The increased prevalence of the shyness label in early adolescence does not tell us whether or not it is the appearance of the self-conscious type of shyness that accounts for this finding.

Two other studies, however, provide some provocative evidence bearing on Buss's theory. He defines self-conscious shyness in terms of acute awareness of oneself as a social object, which involves feeling excessively exposed to the scrutiny of others. As such, it is a cognitive reaction or a psychic form of anxiety, whereas fearful shyness is more of a physiological reaction or a somatic form of anxiety (Buss, 1962; Schalling, 1975). A personality scale that closely approximates Buss's definition of the self-conscious type of shyness is the Self-Consciousness Scale (Rosenberg, 1979). Two sample items are, "If you were to wear the wrong kind of clothes to a party, would that bother you?" and "When I'm with people I get nervous because I worry how much they like me." Other items concern wondering what others are thinking about oneself and disliking being looked at by peers or teachers. This scale and a modified version of it have been administered to two large cross-sectional samples of students ranging in age from 8 to 18.

The first study compared three age groups on the original 7-item Guttman Scale version of the Self-Consciousness Scale (Simmons, Rosenberg, & Rosenberg, 1973). With a low score indicating high self-consciousness, the survey results showed that 8- to 11-year-olds were significantly less self-conscious than 12- to 14-year-olds and that high school students aged 15 and over fell between the other two groups (medians of 3.8, 3.0, and 3.2, respectively, in a total sample of 1,984 students). A closer examination of these findings revealed that a major part of the change in self-consciousness was accounted for by the difference between 12-year-olds still in elementary school (22% classified as highly self-conscious) and those who had started junior high school (41% highly self-conscious). The authors conclude that the intensification of age trends due to changing schools is a vivid illustration of the way social context can affect individual personality in addition to the physical impact of puberty (Simmons *et al.*,

1973). This reasoning is consistent with Buss's (1980) conceptualization of novelty as the most powerful situational cause of shyness.

The second study was conducted as part of Elkind's research and theoretical work on the imaginary audience phenomenon in adolescence. Due to the onset of formal operations in early adolescence, young people become able to think about other people's thoughts, yet they are often unable to distinguish between what is of interest to the self and what is of interest to others (Elkind, 1978). Adolescents begin to understand that many of their own hypotheses are wrong, thus acquiring a new respect for data but also experiencing decreased self-confidence. In addition, the young adolescent's egocentrism involves becoming concerned with the reactions of others to oneself and imagining that one is the constant focus of everyone's evaluative attention. One outcome of these cognitive changes may be a type of shyness characterized by anxious self-preoccupation (Crozier, 1979).

Age trends in this self-conscious type of shyness were examined in a survey of 697 4th-, 6th-, 8th-, and 12th-grade students (Elkind & Bowen, 1979). The 6-item Abiding Self Scale used in this study is a modified version of the Simmons *et al.* (1973) Self-Consciousness Scale. It employs a Likert-type response scale with a higher score indicating greater self-consciousness. Eighth grade students had significantly higher scores on the Abiding Self Scale than did students in the other three grades. For girls, the means were 5.9 in 4th grade, 6.5 in 6th grade, 7.5 in 8th grade, and 5.7 in 12th grade. The comparable means for boys were 5.5, 5.6, 6.3, and 5.5, respectively. The gender differences will be discussed below, but the age trends for girls and boys are similar. Elkind and Bowen's (1979) results, in agreement with the findings of Simmons *et al.* (1973), show that this type of self-conscious shyness peaks in early adolescence around ages 12 to 14, and declines somewhat thereafter. Taken together, these two studies suggest that the temporary increase in the percentage of people who label themselves as shy in junior high school (Zimbardo, 1977) may be accounted for by the appearance of self-conscious shyness as defined by Buss (this volume).

THE STABILITY OF SHYNESS

A related question concerns whether the decrease in the prevalence of shyness after age 14 is due to the waning of the acute self-conscious shyness of adolescence specifically or to some more general combination of factors. A longitudinal study that included measures of both the fearful or early developing type of shyness and late developing self-conscious shyness would be the ideal way to answer this question. Because fearful shyness is believed to have a genetic component and a strong basis in physiological correlates of social anxiety (Kagan & Reznick, this volume; Plomin & Daniels, this volume), it should be more stable and enduring as a type of shyness than the self-conscious type. No such longitudinal data exist at present, so we conducted a small retrospective survey to provide some preliminary evidence on this issue. We reasoned that college students who say that they were once shy but no longer label themselves as being shy would tend to identify the onset of their shyness predominantly in the age ranges Buss suggests for self-conscious shyness. We expected that currently shy college students would show no differences in early versus late onset of shyness.

One hundred and eighteen women undergraduates at Wellesley College completed a survey asking them whether they considered themselves currently shy, and, if not, whether there had been some previous period in their life during which they considered themselves to be a shy person. Forty-three percent said they were currently shy, 41% reported previous but not current shyness, and 16% said they had never been shy. These percentages are almost identical to findings from thousands of male and female college students reported by Zimbardo (1977), which suggests that our sample is representative of American college students. The currently shy and previously shy respondents identified the age range in which they first remember feeling shy, and their answers are presented in Table 1.

Forty-five percent of the currently shy students said they were first shy before age 6, which is the age range Buss (this volume) specifies for the early developing fearful type of shyness, and 55% answered in the later age range for the self-conscious type of shyness. In contrast, 79% of the previously shy students identified the age range of self-conscious shyness as their time of first feeling shy whereas only 21% said they had been shy in early childhood. A chi-square analysis of the frequency data reported as subtotals in Table 1 was significant [χ^2 (1, $N = 118$) = 6.56, $p < .03$]. Although we have only retrospective reports here, these data are consistent with Buss's conceptualization of two types

TABLE 1. Frequency Distribution for Self-Reports of the Time of First Feeling Shy

	Currently shy respondents	Previously but not currently shy respondents
Years of late developing self-conscious shyness		
On entering college	1	1
On entering high school	1	7
On entering junior high school	3	1
During later elementary school years	15	19
On entering elementary school	8	10
Subtotal	28	38
Years of early developing fearful shyness		
Before starting elementary school	9	2
As long as I can remember	14	8
Subtotal	23	10
Totals	51	48

of shyness. Therefore, we suggest that a complete longitudinal study would be a worthwhile undertaking.

There are three longitudinal studies on the stability of shyness that are worth noting even though they do not address the distinction between the fearful and self-conscious types of shyness. Unlike the surveys discussed earlier, these studies employed observer ratings rather than self-reports. In the first study, social workers made annual clinical judgments of the degree of shyness among a sample of about 100 children from ages 7 through 14 (Macfarlane, Allen, & Honzik, 1954). Correlations across the various age spans tended to be moderately strong, typically in the .35 to .60 range. The most noticeable difference was between the age 7 to 12 period (r = .22) and the 11 to 14 period (r = .73), leading the authors to conclude that the degree of shyness generally becomes increasingly stable over the years within the time span investigated.

A second longitudinal study obtained peer ratings of shyness over a 5-year span from 2 cohorts totalling 220 students, one cohort starting in the third grade and the other in fifth grade (Coie & Dodge, 1983). The stability coefficients across the years were substantially lower for the cohort followed from the third-grade (mean r = .21) than for the fifth-grade cohort (mean r = .57). The annual retest correlations generally increased over time, with the r of grades 3 to 4 being .35 and the r of grades 8 to 9 being .85. Even though they used different types of observer ratings, these two studies converge in reaching the conclusion that shyness is not highly stable over the time span beginning in middle childhood and ending in adolescence; however, within the early adolescent age range shyness shows a high level of stability.

The third longitudinal study obtained teacher's ratings on 858 students at age 10 and again at age 13 (Backteman & Magnusson, 1981). These ratings were based on one teacher's observation at each occasion and employed a single 7-point shyness item, but each teacher had taught the student for 3 years prior to making the rating. The stability coefficient was .44 for boys and .42 for girls (.55 and .52, respectively, after correction for attenuation). The shyness ratings showed convincing evidence of discriminant validity from other traits measured in the study, and Backteman and Magnusson (1981) concluded that shyness is a distinct personality characteristic that has considerable longitudinal stability in the period from ages 10 to 13. Although Backteman and Magnusson (1981) did not find gender differences in their study, several research findings discussed thus far have revealed differences between boys and girls. Therefore, we now turn our attention to the issue of gender differences in adolescent shyness.

GENDER DIFFERENCES

Zimbardo (1977) reported that the increased prevalence of labelling oneself shy in junior high school—54% compared to about 40% in elementary school children and young adults—was accounted for by the teenage girls in his sample. Similarly, the results we described from Elkind and Bowen's (1979) cross-sectional study of students revealed that eighth-grade girls had the highest peak on their measure of self-conscious shyness (7.5 versus 6.3 for boys). The original version of this Self-Consciousness Scale also shows significant gender differences, with girls reporting greater increases in self-consciousness after age 11 than do boys (Simmons & Rosenberg, 1975). All of these findings are consistent with the general conclusion that the decline in overall self-concept occurring in adolescence is more pronounced in girls than in boys (Petersen, 1981).

The gender differences in the prevalence of adolescent shyness, especially on scales that approximate the definition of self-conscious shyness, suggest a qualification to Buss's (1980; this volume) conceptualization of the late developing, self-conscious type of shyness. That is, it seems that the appearance of self-conscious shyness in adolescence may occur primarily among girls. In order to examine this implication from previous survey results, we administered a set of personality questionnaires to a sample of 100 ninth-grade students. Because Buss has linked the self-conscious type of shyness to the trait public self-consciousness (i.e., the tendency to be aware of oneself as a social object), we wanted to examine the correlation between shyness and the Public Self-Consciousness Scale (Fenigstein, Scheier, & Buss, 1975) in this group of 14 and 15 year old girls and boys. Our sample was drawn from a longitudinal study on adolescent personality development, and the questionnaire packet included Cheek's (1983) 13-item revision of the Cheek and Buss (1981) Shyness Scale, the Public Self-Consciousness Scale (Fenigstein *et al.*, 1975), the short form of the Beck Depression Inventory (Beck & Beck, 1972), and Rosenberg's (1979) Self-Esteem Scale.

The correlations among these scales are reported separately for girls and boys in Table 2. There were no significant gender differences for the mean scores on any of the scales. The absence of a difference for shyness may be due to the fact that the Cheek and Buss (1981) Shyness Scale assesses the affective and behavioral, but not the cognitive, self-conscious aspects of shyness. Note, however, that shyness is significantly correlated with public self-consciousness for girls but not for boys. Among college students, the correlation between these two scales typically falls in the .20 to .29 range for both sexes (Cheek & Buss, 1981), suggesting that adolescent girls may be somewhat distinct in terms of the relationship between shyness and public self-consciousness. Even though this finding must be considered tentative, it is consistent with the gender differences

TABLE 2. Correlations among Personality Scales for Ninth-Grade Students

	Shyness	Public self-consciousness	Depression	Self-esteem
Shyness		.35*	.39**	− .40**
Public self-consciousness	.23		.21	− .22
Depression	− .30*	− .11	− .61***	
Self-esteem	− .46**	− .14	− .60	

Note: The correlations for the 50 girls are presented above the diagonal, and those for the 50 boys appear below the diagonal.
*p < .05, **p < .01, ***p < .001.

in self-conscious adolescent shyness described above. Self-esteem had a substantial negative correlation with shyness in both genders at a level comparable to findings from all age groups (Cheek & Buss, 1981; Lazarus, 1982b). The relationship between depression and shyness is stronger in the present sample than among college students (Traub, 1983), which may reflect the general increase in self-concept disturbance typically found in early adolescence.

A recent reviewer has argued that the existing data on gender differences in shyness across all ages are inconsistent and inconclusive (Leary, 1983). We believe that the differences found among adolescents should be viewed both in light of sex roles and with regard to the different types or components of shyness. As Bronson (1966) has pointed out, in terms of social stereotypes it is more appropriate for girls to be seen as shy than for boys; in fact, the self-descriptive adjective "shy" is scored on the Femininity Scale of the Bem (1981) Sex Role Inventory. Not surprisingly, elementary school teachers nominate girls twice as frequently as boys for being among the five most shy youngsters in their class (Lazarus, 1982a).

But the situation is not entirely straightforward. In a survey of 15-year-olds, Porteus (1979) found that although boys and girls were equally concerned about attracting members of the opposite sex, girls were more worried about physical attractiveness whereas boys reported that shyness was more of a problem for them. Thus the higher level of self-conscious shyness in adolescent girls may be masking a more severe sex role related problem for the boys. Because the traditional male role requires initiative in social contacts to a much greater degree than the more passive feminine stereotype, the burden of shyness as a behavioral problem, if not as a disturbance in self-concept, appears to be especially severe for adolescent boys (see also Snyder & Smith, this volume). To fully understand these gender differences, we need further research that not only includes separate measures of the self-conscious and fearful types of shyness defined by Buss, but that also involves behavioral assessments of social skills. The finding that students high in communication apprehension date half as frequently and with fewer partners than those low in apprehensiveness (Richmond, 1984) suggests that adolescent dating relationships should be a particularly important focus for such research.

The timing of puberty may complicate the sex role issues involved in adolescent shyness. Several longitudinal studies reviewed by Burns (1979) indicate that late maturing boys and early maturing girls tend to suffer the greatest social adjustment problems, but these studies were not specifically focused on shyness. Bronson's (1966) suggestion that the age of menarche might influence the degree of shyness among girls is one example of the possible hypotheses about adolescent shyness, body-image, and physical attractiveness that merit empirical testing. There is, however, a problem in extending this type of research to the topic of teenage sexuality. Zimbardo and Radl (1981) report that they were unable to include questions about sexual activities in their shyness survey of adolescents due to restrictions in state laws. They do provide anecdotal evidence that some shy girls may become promiscuous as a way of finding acceptance in their peer group, but there may be no reliable way to test such hypotheses.

IMPLICATIONS FOR TREATMENT

We have reported that adolescent shyness is strongly associated with low self-esteem and depression. In another high school sample, we found that shyness correlates in the .50s with self-reports of loneliness for boys and girls, which is slightly higher than the typical finding for college students (e.g., Cheek & Busch, 1981). The loneliness of shy students is consistent with their reluctance to get involved in dating relationships (Richmond, 1984). Beyond these personal and social adjustment problems, shy adolescents seem to experience specific educational problems. In a recent review, Friedman (1980) concluded that shy students avoid contributing to classroom discussion, do not seek help from teachers and advisors even when they are having trouble, and have a more negative attitude toward school than do nonshy students.

Shyness may even contribute to delinquency among adolescents. Zimbardo and Radl (1981) found that twice as many shy adolescents felt that peers put pressure on them to drink or use drugs compared to those who were not shy. Moreover, shy teenagers in their survey said that drugs or alcohol helped them feel less self-conscious and more a part of the group in social situations. Other research suggests that the relationship between shyness and delinquent behavior may be somewhat more complex than Zimbardo and Radl (1981) imply; shy teenagers who are not aggressive or impulsive may be particularly well behaved, whereas those who are both shy and aggressive tend to be especially prone to alcohol and drug abuse (for reviews, see Capuzzi & LeCoq, 1983, and Mervis, 1984).

All of the adjustment problems just described point to the need for successful treatment approaches to adolescent shyness. The most popular approach has been social-skills training, which is designed to improve social competence with peers, parents, and authority figures through the behavioral therapy methods of role playing, modeling, and reinforcing appropriate behavior (e.g., Sarason, 1981). Such techniques have been applied to the treatment of shy adolescents with some degree of success (Franco, Christoff, Cummins, & Kelly, 1983; Trower, 1978). A second treatment approach focuses on the somatic distress component of shyness by employing relaxation training and systematic desensitization, whereas the third major approach concentrates on the cognitive component of shyness by means of rational-emotive therapy and cognitive restructuring techniques (see the Therapeutic Interventions section of the present volume for details). As Reid (1983) has argued, this range of treatment approaches raises a critical question: How does a therapist or a parent decide which treatment is appropriate for a particular shy child or adolescent?

We believe that research and theory on adolescent shyness identify some ways to look for answers to this question. Buss's (this volume) distinction between the fearful and self-conscious types of shyness implies that adolescents who have been shy since early childhood should be particularly in need of relaxation training and systematic desensitization techniques that focus on the emotional arousal of the temperamentally shy. Adolescents who recently became shy for the first time, on the other hand, should benefit most from a cognitive approach that lessens self-preoccupation and increases empathic concern for others (e.g., Alden & Cappe, this volume). The cognitive approach is consistent with theory and research on adolescent egocentrism (Elkind, 1978; Elkind & Bowen, 1979).

The gender differences we described in self-conscious shyness indicate that early adolescent girls may have a greater need for this cognitive type of therapy than do boys. The discussion of general sex role issues, and particularly of Porteus's (1979) finding that adolescent boys report more behavioral problems with shyness, suggests that boys may be in greater need of social-skills training than girls. Finally, Furnham and Gunter (1983) have argued that the presence or absence of other personality traits, such as neuroticism or extraversion, might provide useful guidelines for deciding what type of treatment is best for a particular shy adolescent. Clearly, the important question of which treatment or combination of treatments will be most efficient for which shy people requires further research among all age groups.

CONCLUSION

Our review of the existing literature and presentations of new data on adolescent shyness have been focused on theoretical issues relating to Buss's (1980, this volume) distinction between early developing, fearful shyness and later developing, self-conscious shyness. We have discussed the prevalence of shyness, its stability during childhood and adolescence, the existence of gender and sex role related differences, and the implications of research findings for treatment strategies. At this time we can conclude only that Buss's conceptualization provides a promising framework for understanding the development of shyness because past research has been mostly descriptive rather than guided by theory.

We have noted the need for new research that simultaneously yet separately assesses both the somatic anxiety of fearful shyness and the psychic anxiety of self-conscious shyness, in terms of the distinction between these two types of anxiety proposed by Buss (1962) and Schalling (1975). In addition, we need to measure separately the behavioral or social-skills component of shyness, which may be viewed as the potential overt or instrumental consequence of these two types of internally experienced social anxiety. The complete conceptualization of shyness as a psychological phenomenon involving three relatively distinct components—somatic, cognitive, and behavioral—is a new development (Buss, 1984; Hartman, 1983); it is certainly true that a great deal of progress has been made since Zimbardo (1977) stated that "shyness is a fuzzy concept" (p. 13). It is to be hoped that a new wave of research on the three components of shyness will advance our understanding to a new level both empirically and theoretically.

The task of understanding adolescent shyness requires more than just new empirical research using specific operational definitions of the three components described above. In order to understand the role of shyness in personality and social development as a whole, researchers need to consider broader theoretical issues involving the structure, dynamics, and function of various personality characteristics. One way to do this is to study shyness within an organized framework of personality dimensions such as the "central orientations" proposed by Bronson (1966) or the general psychological constructs ego-control and ego-resiliency introduced by Block and Block (1980).

A new personality theory of developmental phases or stages also seems to be required, especially since Erikson's focus on late rather than early adolescent self-concept disturbance and his assumption of universal adolescent storm and stress have not been supported empirically (Burns, 1979; Petersen, 1981). There are, for example, distinct cultural differences in the extent to which both students and adults experience problems with shyness (Klopf, 1984; Zimbardo, 1977), and differences involving ethnicity or socioeconomic status within any one culture may also be important. One potentially useful new personality theory is Hogan's (1982) socioanalytic theory, which specifies three broad phases of personality development—character structure, role structure, and life style—that may be used to organize the understanding of a specific trait such as shyness (cf. Hogan, Jones, & Cheek, 1985). We conclude, therefore, by suggesting that future research on adolescent shyness should progress in two directions by becoming more empirically specific and more theoretically general.

REFERENCES

Backteman, G., & Magnusson, D. (1981). Longitudinal stability of personality characteristics. *Journal of Personality, 49,* 148–160.

Beck, A. T., & Beck, R. W. (1972). Screening depressed patients in family practice: A rapid technique. *Postgraduate Medicine, 52,* 81–85.

Bem, S. L. (1981). *Bem sex-role inventory professional manual.* Palo Alto, CA: Consulting Psychologists Press.

Block, J. H., & Block, J. (1980). The role of ego-control and ego-resiliency in the organization of behavior. In W. A. Collins (Ed.), *Development of cognition, affect, and social relations* (Minnesota Symposium on Child Psychology, Volume 13, pp. 39–101). Hillsdale, NJ: Erlbaum.

Bronson, W. C. (1966). Central orientations: A study of behavior organization from childhood to adolescence. *Child Development, 37,* 125–155.

Burns, R. B. (1979). *The self concept.* London: Longman.

Buss, A. H. (1962). Two anxiety factors in psychiatric patients. *Journal of Abnormal and Social Psychology, 65,* 426–427.

Buss, A. H. (1980). *Self-consciousness and social anxiety.* San Francisco: Freeman.

Buss, A. H. (1984). A conception of shyness. In J. A. Daly & J. C. McCroskey (Eds.) *Avoiding communication* (39–49). Beverly Hills, CA: Sage.

Capuzzi, D., & LeCoq, L. L. (1983). Social and personal determinants of adolescent use and abuse of alcohol and marijuana. *Personnel and Guidance Journal, 62,* 199–205.

Cheek, J. M. (1983). *The revised Cheek and Buss Shyness Scale.* Unpublished manuscript, Wellesley College.

Cheek, J. M., & Busch, C. M. (1981). The influence of shyness on loneliness in a new situation. *Personality and Social Psychology Bulletin, 7,* 572–577.

Cheek, J. M., & Buss, A. H. (1981). Shyness and sociability. *Journal of Personality and Social Psychology, 41,* 330–339.

Coie, J. D., & Dodge, K. A. (1983). Continuities and changes in children's social status: A 5 year longitudinal study. *Merrill-Palmer Quarterly, 29,* 261–282.

Crozier, R. (1979). Shyness as anxious self-preoccupation. *Psychological Reports, 44,* 959–962.

Damon, W. (1983). *Social and personality development.* New York: Norton.

Elkind, D. (1978). Understanding the young adolescent. *Adolescence, 13,* 127–134.

Elkind, D. & Bowen, R. (1979). Imaginary audience behavior in children and adolescents. *Developmental Psychology, 15*, 38–44.

Fenigstein, A., Scheier, M. F., & Buss, A. H. (1975). Public and private self-consciousness: Assessment and theory. *Journal of Consulting and Clinical Psychology, 43*, 522–527.

Franco, D. P., Christoff, K. A., Cummins, D. B., & Kelly, J. A. (1983). Social skills training for an extremely shy young adolescent: An empirical case study. *Behavior Therapy, 14*, 568–575.

Friedman, P. G. (1980). *Shyness and reticence in students.* Washington, DC: National Education Association.

Furnham, A., & Gunter, B. (1983). Sex and personality differences in self-reported social skills among British adolescents. *Journal of Adolescence, 6*, 57–69.

Hartman, L. M. (1983). A metacognitive model of social anxiety: Implications for treatment. *Clinical Psychology Review, 3*, 435–456.

Hogan, R. (1982). A socioanalytic theory of personality. In M. M. Page & R. A. Dienstbier, (Eds.) *Nebraska symposium on motivation 1982* (55–89). Lincoln, NE: University of Nebraska Press.

Hogan, R., Jones, W. H., & Cheek, J. M. (1985). Socioanalytic theory: An alternative to armadillo psychology. In B. Schlenker, (Ed.) *The self and social life.* New York: McGraw-Hill.

Klopf, D. W. (1984). Cross-cultural apprehension research: A summary of Pacific Basin studies. In J. A. Daly & J. C. McCroskey (Eds.) *Avoiding communication* (157–169). Beverly Hills, CA: Sage.

Lazarus, P. J. (1982a). Incidence of shyness in elementary-school age children. *Psychological Reports, 51*, 904–906.

Lazarus, P. J. (1982b). Correlations of shyness and self-esteem for elementary school children. *Perceptual and Motor Skills, 55*, 8–10.

Leary, M. R. (1983) *Understanding social anxiety: social, personality, and clinical perspectives.* Beverly Hills: Sage.

Macfarlane, J. W., Allen, L., & Honzik, M. D. (1954). A developmental study of the behavior problems of normal children between 21 months and 14 years. *University of California studies in child development, 2*, 1–221.

Mervis, J. (1984). Adolescent behavior: What we think we know. *APA Monitor, 15*(4), 24–25.

Petersen, A. C. (1981). The development of self-concept in adolescence. In M. D. Lynch, A. A. Norem-Hebeisen, K. J. Gergen (Eds.). *Self-concept: Advances in theory and research* (191–202). Cambridge, MA: Ballinger.

Porteus, M. A. (1979). Survey of the problems of normal 15 year olds. *Journal of Adolescence, 2*, 307–323.

Reid, J. B. (1983). A description and theory of shyness. [Review of *The shy child. Contemporary Psychology, 27*, 809–810.

Richmond, V. P. (1984). Implications of quietness: Some facts and speculations. In J. A. Daly & J. C. McCroskey, (Eds.) *Avoiding communication* (145–155). Beverly Hills, CA: Sage.

Rosenberg, M. (1979). *Conceiving the self.* New York: Basic Books.

Sarason, B. R. (1981). The dimensions of social competence: Contributions from a variety of research areas. In J. D. Wine & M. D. Smye, (Eds.) *Social competence* (100–122). New York: Guilford.

Schalling, D. S. (1975). Types of anxiety and types of stressors as related to personality. In C. D. Speilberger & I. G. Sarason, (Eds). *Stress and anxiety* (279–283). Washington, DC: Hemisphere Corporation.

Simmons, R. G., & Rosenberg, F. (1975). Sex, sex roles, and self-image. *Journal of Youth and Adolescence, 4*, 229–258.

Simmons, R., Rosenberg, R., & Rosenberg, M. (1973). Disturbance in the self-image at adolescence. *American Sociological Review, 38*, 553–568.

Traub, G. S. (1983). Correlations of shyness with depression, anxiety, and academic performance. *Psychological Reports, 52*, 849–850.

Trower, P. (1978). Skills training for adolescent social problems: A viable treatment alternative? *Journal of Adolescence, 1*, 319–329.

Zimbardo, P. G. (1977). *Shyness: What it is, what to do about it.* Reading, MA: Addison-Wesley.

Zimbardo, P. G., & Radl, S. (1981). *The shy child.* New York: McGraw-Hill.

Zimbardo, P. G., Pilkonis, P., & Norwood, R. (1975). The social disease called shyness. *Psychology Today, 8*, 69–72.

10

Shyness and the Elderly

Robert O. Hansson

INTRODUCTION

The purpose of this paper is to explore the implications of shyness for older adults. Shy people are inhibited, anxious, and preoccupied with the self in social and evaluative situations (Jones & Russell, 1982). Consequently,they approach such situations with hesitation, and with less adequate social skills. For younger adults the implications of shyness seem straightforward. Inhibited and less skilled social behaviors may constrain the formation of a variety of personal relationships essential to friendship development, romantic involvement, social exchange, social support, and so on. From a role-theoretical perspective (cf., Hogan, Jones, & Cheek, 1985), such characteristics also would interfere with effective role performances within one's important social and reference groups, threatening one's acceptance and status in society.

Among the elderly, however, the implications of shyness are potentially more complex. Role theorists (e.g., Athay & Darley, 1982; Hogan et al., 1985) have suggested that personality characteristics take on meaning only as they influence important interpersonal consequences. Shyness from that perspective is only important to the extent that it influences valued interpersonal outcomes. Yet, in old age interpersonal needs may change, opportunities for social interaction may change, and relationships may become more problematic in nature. So the assumptions that underlie current theory on shyness may need to be reconsidered when applied to the elderly. In this essay those assumptions will be integrated into current theory regarding the social environment of older adults.

The situations in which shyness may be important to the elderly might be divided into two categories: (a) those that affect only one's instrumental-survival needs, and (b) those that more broadly affect psychological adjustment and well-being. The first section of this paper will focus on the potential vulnerability of

ROBERT O. HANSSON • Department of Psychology, University of Tulsa, Tulsa, OK 74104.

shy older persons in instrumental situations, with particular emphasis on the need to successfully interact with other people who may control needed coping resources. This section of the paper will draw from recent work on the construct of *relational competence*, which focuses on personality variables that influence one's ability to adaptively construe, construct, access, and maintain needed social support relationships (Hansson, Jones, & Carpenter, 1984). The second section of the paper explores issues of shyness in adjustment and well-being. In this area, theory regarding patterns of social integration, emotional responsiveness more generally, and the tasks of adaptation in later life will be considered in relation to shyness.

INSTRUMENTAL ISSUES

Two very practical issues illustrate the importance of older adults being able to competently and assertively interact with others who may control coping resources.

Social Support

Although there is great individual variability, old age is a time of physical and sensory decline, and for many it involves a threat to independence. Under these circumstances the most important factor in deferring institutionalization appears to be the existence of a supportive family network (Lawton, 1981). Complementing the family unit, and one's secondary personal relationships are the outreach service programs in many communities that make it possible for marginally independent elderly persons to remain in their homes for as long as possible. The provision of interpersonal and logistical services of this type by informal and semiprofessional networks has been widely studied under the rubric of social support (Gottlieb, 1983).

Hansson *et al.* (1984) have suggested, however, that a number of structural and dispositional barriers may exist to effectively accessing or maintaining one's social support networks in general. Many of these barriers seem particularly applicable to the elderly. For example, in later life such events as widowhood or the death of one's siblings (or even one's children) are more likely to disrupt the support network quite broadly, eroding its ability to support the most immediately affected member. Also, economic constraints and the physical and sensory declines attending old age may limit one's mobility and ability to actively seek support from community resources. In addition, social support for the elderly often involves the problem of long-term care, and caregiver strain. More than half of the caregivers of older persons are age peers, with health problems and limitations of their own (Johnson, 1983). In such cases the provisions of constant support may be quite stressful, and eventually result in burnout or failure of the support system. Moreover, caregiver responsibility (among one's family) is generally passed from person to person in serial order, rather than being assumed by an integrated, concurrently functioning support network

(Johnson, 1983). Thus, the older parent or patient will likely experience periodic, involuntary changes of residence, and will be required to adjust to the rules and routine of a new household, and to refocus interpersonal efforts and involvements to another part of the family network.

Supportive efforts from family, but also from within the community may also be influenced by stereotyped assumptions regarding old age. For example, any cognitive decline or disorientation in an older person may quickly be interpreted as the beginning of senility. Such symptoms may actually be the result of infection, improper medication, heart problems, or malnutrition (Butler & Lewis, 1982), and might be reversible if promptly treated. Yet a substantial proportion of such persons are simply placed in nursing homes with a diagnosis of senile dementia.

Stereotypes of the aged may also have broader effects on support. Older victims of street crime, for example, particularly if they exhibit infirmities of vision or hearing, are likely to receive less attention from authorities, and may be discounted as witnesses in any investigation (Herrington, 1983). Also, in the case of physical disability, the elderly may find that much of the community is uncomfortable dealing with them; not knowing what to say or how to to help. In such cases the older individual may have to be the one to put the others at ease, before any supportive interactions can begin (Trieschmann, 1978).

Thus, older adults appear to face a variety of potential difficulties with respect to accessing and maintaining social and caregiver support networks. Their support needs are likely to be long term. Yet their available networks are more likely to be stressed, discontinuous, and unpredictable. Under such circumstances, individual difference variables should influence one's ability to rise to the occasion, to construct where possible, and to maintain supportive interactions. Research on younger populations suggests that shy persons may be least able to effectively do such things.

Older Unemployed Adults

Jones and Russell (1982) have noted that a potentially important area of inquiry concerns the vulnerability of shy individuals in situations that are either threatening or ambiguous. In such situations, especially, other people often control needed information and access to available coping resources or opportunities. Thus, a critical element of the coping process also involves the ability to engage in competent and assertive social interaction. The inhibited and unskilled social behavior characteristic of shy persons would be expected to disrupt such interactions, frustrating independent efforts to cope. Conversely, shy individuals should be particularly benefitted by reassurance and social support from important others as they try to cope with a threatening or ambiguous situation. My colleagues and I have been investigating the role of shyness in older adults (age 50 and over) coping with such a situation—chronic unemployment (Hansson, Rule, Briggs, & Thompson, 1984). Unemployment constitutes an important life stressor among all age groups (Buss & Redburn, 1983; Hayes & Nutman, 1981). The severity of health and psychological consequences, however, appears to be related to the meaning of one's work, and the importance of what a person loses when one loses a job. For many people, work is more than simply a source of income. It provides structure and predictability, it can be a source of status and identity, and it provides for many a critical network for structural and supportive social interaction. Thus, becoming unemployed may threaten one's identity, self-esteem, and level of integration into supportive social networks, as well as one's economic status. We would therefore expect eventual adjustment to unemployment to be affected as much by dispositional factors (which render persons psychologically vulnerable to such events) as by the length of time unemployed. For example, shy or less assertive people might find it harder to initiate contact with potential new employers or support networks.

Recessionary unemployment is particularly threatening. Over time, personal and financial resources are likely to be consumed, and benefits run out. With increasing length of unemployment and with repeated experiences of unsuccessful job interviews, unemployed persons should come to experience decreased feelings of personal control, and decreased perceptions that important personal outcomes are contingent on their own efforts (i.e., learned helplessness; Seligman, 1975). To the extent that the job search involves difficult social interactions at every turn, shy persons should experience particular difficulties in this regard.

Older adults constitute one of the most critical unemployed populations (see review by Sheppard, 1976). In a plant closing, their earned seniority often cannot protect them. They must therefore compete for scarce jobs with younger and better educated workers. They are more likely to expect a recall, and delay longer beginning to search for work. Their job hunt skills also have atrophied over time, and they may exhibit naive job hunting tactics, such as applying to fewer companies, hesitating to try new industries, and avoiding companies they expect to discriminate on the basis of age. Understandably, then, older unemployed workers are more likely to become discouraged and to simply drop out of the workforce.

In our research, older, chronically unemployed adults were surveyed to assess the relationships between shyness, former job success, perceptions of barriers to reemployment (some of which may be social), emotional adjustment to their economic situation, and perceptions of personal control (or helplessness) in their situation. Finally, because shyness is construed to inhibit effective, independent social performances in such threatening circumstances, the role of social support as a mediating factor also was assessed.

Shyness was assessed using a form of the Social Reticence Scale (Jones & Russell, 1982). Preliminary results from the study suggest that shy persons may enjoy less occupational success generally, as shyness scores were inversely and significantly related to the prestige rating of the title of one's last job. Moreover, the unemployment experience appeared to have been generally more troublesome and uncontrollable for shy persons. For example, these older subjects were asked to compare themselves to the average worker they knew *under* the age of 50 on 11 dimensions important to productivity and employability (ability to learn, dependability, energy level, attitudes toward work, pride in a job well done, and current skill level, etc.). Shy individuals compared themselves less favorably. Similarly, subjects indicated the extent to which they expected such factors as their health, educational level, or skill obsolescence to constitute a barrier to reemployment. Again, shy individuals anticipated more tangible barriers to finding work. Consistent with such findings, shyness was also found to be generally associated with decreased self-esteem and with increased reports of depression, using standard scales of these phenomena (Beck, 1967; Rosenberg, 1965).

Perhaps most interesting, however, were the comparisons of high-shy and low-shy subjects with respect to two critical variables in the unemployment situation. The first of those variables is the length of time one had been unemployed. Subjects in this study had been unemployed for a mean of 22 weeks. There is some consensus in the literature that reaction to job loss progresses through a sequence of stages, ranging from disbelief and denial to anxiety and panic, to serious coping efforts, which if unsuccessful result in self-doubt, resignation, and depression (cf., Buss & Redburn, 1983; Hayes & Nutman, 1981). As a function, perhaps, of demographic circumstances and dispositions, the timing and strength of such reactions would be expected to vary. Shyness, for example, was expected to increase one's vulnerability to emotional reactions to length of time unemployed, and to any resulting, counterproductive cognitive restructuring or self-defeating attributions, as social inhibition and poor social skills frustrated efforts to effectively interact with people who controlled job opportunity or who might at least help in the job-hunt process. Consistent with expectations, among high-shy respondents (only), length of time unemployed was associated with less favorable comparisons of self—to younger workers, with reduced estimates of one's chances for finding a job soon, and with higher depression scores. An interesting adjustment also seems to have taken place among shy respondents with respect to their personal standards for the kind of job considered to be acceptable. Subjects had indicated the extent to which they felt such aspects of the job as interesting work, safe and comfortable working conditions, insurance benefits, or a considerate boss were important criteria for accepting a job. For shy subjects, the importance of these criteria diminished as the length of time unemployed increased. Finally, subjects had completed an index of relevant social support, indicating the extent to which family, friends, employment agency personnel, and employers had been supportive in the job hunt. Once again, among shy subjects, as the length of time unemployed became longer, the experience of social support from important others appeared to deteriorate. None of the above relationships approached significance among low-shy subjects.

The second variable that appeared to affect shy and nonshy persons differently was social support. Shy subjects appeared to be particularly responsive to the supportive efforts of important others (when available). Under conditions of high social support, shy persons retained high standards regarding the kind of job they would find acceptable (e.g., interesting, safe, insurance benefits, fair pay, a considerate boss). Similarly, when supported by important others, shy persons were more likely to prepare properly for their job interviews (e.g., looking their best for the interview, trying to learn about the company beforehand, and arriving early for the interview). Finally, subjects had completed an index of their feelings of personal control (or helplessness) when going for an interview (the critical social interaction in the job search). Items from this index included, "How much does the outcome of the interview seem to depend upon how hard you have tried?"; "How easily can you tell the circumstances under which you have a chance for the job from those when you don't?"; and "How well are you usually able to predict whether an employer will like you and want to hire you?" The index then, reflected the kinds of emotional and cognitive elements that comprise what Seligman (1975) has termed learned helplessness. In the job-hunt situation, the relationship between one's efforts and one's outcomes are socially mediated by a series of people with whom the applicant must skillfully and assertively interact. It was theoretically consistent, then, that among shy persons, under conditions of high support from important others (including agency and employer personnel) the experience of helplessness decreased. Again, among nonshy subjects, none of these relationships even approached significance.

PSYCHOLOGICAL ADJUSTMENT AND WELL-BEING

The role of shyness in adjustment and well-being, like other emotional responses, cannot be assessed out of context. Averill (1980), for example, has suggested that emotions be viewed as transitory social role enactments. To express an emotion toward another person (e.g., anger, lust, or shyness) is thus to enter into a temporary and predictable social relationship with that individual. Similarly, Izard (cf. 1978) has proposed that emotional patterns evolve as they become adaptive within a person's social context, subsequently stimulating and focusing appropriate cognitive and behavioral responses. The importance of a social context, governed by rules and expectations, suggests additional questions about shyness generally, and about its role in adjustment to old age. In some cases, for example, shyness simply may be a self-presentational device (an emotional portrayal for instrumental purposes). For the unskilled or anxious person, a public portrayal of shyness could provide secondary gains, relieving one of the responsibility for having to work on relationships. In another sense, it could become a useful social-handicapping strategy, lowering others' expectations for one's performance, or placing the burden of social interaction on the shoulders of others. These examples illustrate the point that shyness is only relevant to the extent that one is dependent on the social environment for status or acceptance. We might thus expect shyness to drop from one's emotional repertoire with decreasing demands that one work on social relationships to acquire status and acceptance.

Role Changes in Old Age

Rosow (1976) has proposed a useful model for conceptualizing social role involvement and change across the life span. His model includes two substantive role types (institutional, and tenuous) relevant to the present analysis. For the purposes of his model, Rosow distinguishes between a status and a role; a status is "a position in a social structure," and a role is "the pattern of activity intrinsic to that position," or the expectations the group holds for a person in that status

(1976, p. 458). In Rosow's model, the role types vary with respect to their associated status and roles. An institutional role type has a clearly defined status or position in the social group, and quite well defined expectations for a person occupying that position. Tenuous role types, however, have clearly delineated status positions for which there may be no clear roles. These positions may thus be only symbolic or token, as they involve no actual functions or responsibilities. Tenuous role types (for example, that of a parent) may also be vulnerable to "role emptying," in which a position loses over time its rights and functions. In other instances in old age the status position itself is often lost, as in the case of widowhood, disability, or retirement. Subsequently, associated roles (expectations and psychological links to the social network) also would be lost. Rosow notes that such losses represent substantial reductions in the older person's opportunities for social participation. Moreover, in old age there are also fewer opportunities for role replacement or role succession. Older persons thus come to have fewer responsibilities for self or others. Rosow suggests that as one's roles contract and lose their function and status, subsequent role behavior has "relatively little effect on other persons and is thereby socially inconsequential" (p. 465). Thus, social interactions may become less evaluative and less threatening. Under such circumstances, the power of the social context to elicit shyness, and the extent to which shyness could interfere with important interpersonal consequences would be considerably reduced.

Finally, Rosow proposes a normative model of involvement in the two role types over the life span. Institutional role involvement increases from childhood through late middle age, after which it declines dramatically. Tenuous role involvement is most intense during childhood and old age.

Tasks of Adapting to Old Age

Pfeiffer (1977) has suggested that successful aging involves adapting to continually changing circumstances: finding ways to meet one's basic needs without undue suffering. He further notes the utility of a variety of physical, cognitive, and emotional skills in the process of adapting. For example, it is important in old age to be able to replace lost social relationships, to retain (or to retrain) threatened capacities, and to begin to learn to make do with less. Broader tasks involve accepting one's limitations, and finding new ways for one's life to have purpose and meaning as former responsibilities and opportunities appear to decline. Clearly, a portion of the tasks of adjusting to old age involves social interaction, such as maintaining stressed or disrupted relationships where possible, constructing new ones where necessary, and accommodating loss.

Easing the Transition

The practical circumstances of advanced old age suggest a number of factors that may help in adapting to loss and changing social status. Role transitions and most declines are less traumatic, for example, if they are perceived as having happened "on time" with respect to normative social timetables across the life span (Neugarten & Hagestad, 1976). Also, in advanced old age one's age peers and friends who may serve as social models are more likely already to have undergone similar losses, thus providing opportunities for adaptive social comparison. In addition, in one's old age, such events as widowhood are less unexpected, so there will have been opportunity to rehearse and prepare to cope with significant changes to come. Finally, there is some evidence that older persons receive less pressure from family and friends to make immediate changes or to actively cope with a stressful life event like widowhood (Lopata, 1979).

Again, the implications for shyness in old age involve the way in which the social environment becomes less threatening and evaluative. With reduced group demands that one continue to demonstrate competence and socially valued characteristics, the conditions that elicit shyness, and the social consequences of shyness should be reduced.

Preliminary Investigations of Shyness in Elderly Populations

My colleagues and I have begun to investigate the implications of shyness among noninstitutionalized persons between the ages of 60 and 90 years, assessing shyness either with the Social Reticence Scale (Jones & Russell, 1982) or the Shyness Scale (Cheek & Buss, 1981). The two scales are highly correlated ($r = .78$). We have now surveyed approximately 200 such individuals.

The predominant finding is that shyness among our older samples appears to operate in a manner similar to younger populations. For example, shy subjects generally report seeing fewer people every day, and they report more loneliness (on the UCLA Loneliness Scale: Russell, Peplau, & Cutrona, 1980) and lower morale (using the Revised Philadelphia Geriatric Morale Scale: Lawton, 1975). In addition, in one study, subjects were asked to indicate the extent to which the major events of later life (e.g., retirement, widowhood, change of residence, reduction of income) had seriously disrupted the quality of their personal relationships and networks generally. Shy subjects reported having experienced more such disruption. It is theoretically consistent with previous research that shy persons would be less effective in reconstructing their social networks after such events or in finding ways to subsequently develop available secondary relationships into primary relationships.

A related, practical issue among the vast majority of elderly persons who continue to live independently, but often in older urban neighborhoods, concerns fear for personal safety. Although older adults appear not to be at greater statistical risk of victimization, they do exhibit more intense fear of crime (Yin, 1980). Social support has been viewed to mediate the fear of crime among the elderly, but shy older persons in our research report experiencing greater disruption of such relationships in old age. Not surprisingly, then, we find shy older adults to experience more broadly and intensely a fear of crime and personal victimization. Similarly, we find that shyness in our older sample correlates significantly with a standard index of emotionality, loading on fear and anxiety (Buss & Plomin, 1975).

Another interesting issue is one's attitude toward aging. Although there exists great variability, old age is indeed a period of decline and loss, and a time of continual adjustment and reintegration. A variety of the cognitive and emotional demands of adaptation characteristic of this period were outlined earlier in this chapter. We find that attitudes toward aging generally are positively related to self-estimates of current health, to anticipated income sufficiency for one's future needs, and to the level of confidence that one will continue to remain independent, whereas they are negatively related to the percentage of one's average day spent alone. However, a different pattern emerges when the correlates of one's attitudes toward aging are considered separately for shy versus nonshy older adults. In our research, attitudes among nonshy older adults, toward aging are for the most part associated with health and independence: positively with the quality of one's health habits and behavior, and with the quality of one's vision; and negatively with an index of required physical assistance in the activities of daily living (ADL), and with a form of the Beck Depression Scale (1967) that contains emotional and somatic items. Among shy subjects, however, attitudes toward aging appeared to be more people-oriented, reflecting, perhaps, a sensitivity to the practical implications of successful (or unsuccessful) social interaction in one's later years. Among shy subjects, attitudes toward aging were primarily related (positively) to the number of people with whom one interacted daily, and to frequency of participation in informal groupings/networks outside the home (e.g., clubs, church, social groups). Unfortunately, as our shy subjects grew older, they reported seeing fewer people each day. Finally, among shy subjects attitudes toward aging were related negatively to the frequency of seeing one's own family, a reflection, perhaps, of failure in interactions outside the family, or of growing dependence on family.

Another interesting issue in old age concerns one's pattern of responding to the inevitable declines in health, sensory capacity, and physical independence. For example, a critical indicator of one's at-risk status with respect to institutionalization is the extent to which one requires physical assistance in the routine activities of daily living (ADL). ADL items include such things as being able to climb stairs, bathe, prepare meals, and dress oneself. Among our nonshy older subjects, self-reports of increased dependency on others for physical assistance in ADL were related to most variables as might be expected. For example, more physically dependent people reported being in poorer health generally, and practicing less responsible or effective health behavior (exercise, diet, adherence to medication, etc.). They also reported spending more time per day alone. In addition, they were more likely to perceive their physical surroundings (home and neighborhood) as less safe (from accidents, crime, fire, etc.) and less predictable (things in their home do not work when needed). Also, they felt less safely in contact with family, friends, and medical services should they be needed. Not surprisingly then, they had lower scores on the Philadelphia Geriatric Morale Scale (Lawton, 1975), and higher scores on a depression inventory (after Beck, 1967). On the other hand, they exhibited an ability to accommodate reality, reporting less aversion to receiving support from others (e.g., living with their children, having a visiting nurse check on them regularly, accepting help with shopping or cooking, and accepting financial assistance from others). Indeed, they reported they were now living with a larger number of people. Shy persons on the other hand, were anormative with respect to increased dependence on the physical assistance of others. For them, none of the above relationships were significant. The importance of shyness was revealed, however, when receiving needed physical assistance meant having to approach and interact with others. One questionnaire dealt in part with one's interest in, and access to community outreach services (e.g., meals-on-wheels, dial-a-ride, and home health or care services) that make it possible for marginally healthy elderly to remain in their homes for as long as possible (deferring institutionalization). Subjects were asked to indicate the extent to which a variety of barriers might keep them from using such services if the need arose. Possible barriers included embarrassment about what others might think, fear of letting strangers into one's home, the possibility that service providers would not understand one's needs, and attitudes, such as "my family and friends wouldn't want me to do it." Among shy subjects, increased needs for physical assistance were associated with an increased likelihood that such barriers would keep them from using such services.

Response to vision loss among shy and nonshy subjects followed much the same pattern. Vision loss in the elderly generally implies decreased mobility, and increased social isolation, and is often associated with increased depression (Butler & Lewis, 1982). Again, among nonshy subjects (only) in our research vision loss was associated with more negative attitudes toward aging, reduced life satisfaction, reduced frequency of seeing friends, and increased anxiety and depression.

Finally, we were interested in how shyness might interact with age itself. In one sample a number of variables related to age differently in shy and nonshy groups. For example, among shy patients only, age was associated with greater reported declines in health in the last five years, and to the experience of less safe and supportive physical surroundings (home and neighborhood). Indeed, with increased age, among shy subjects only, there was an increase in reported criminal victimization (of self or neighbors). Also, among shy subjects only, age was related to reports of substantial disruption of one's personal relationships and networks due to such age-associated life events as widowhood, retirement, loss of income, and deaths of friends. They were also less likely to be currently married. Among nonshy subjects, however, increased age was associated with generally *increased* satisfaction with relationships with one's children and friendships, and with life satisfaction generally.

In another sample, a number of variables related to shyness differently among subjects classified as young-old (60–74) or old-old (75 and over). Gerontologists tend to view these two age-groups differently, because most of the young-old do not identify psychologically as old, and because substantial health and function declines usually do not occur until the mid-70s. In this sample, among the young-old, shyness was related to increased depression, but also to the perception of increased barriers to accessing community support networks for services that might help to defer institutionalization. Among the old-old, however, the implications of shyness were much more dramatic, and appeared to be less socially oriented. Among the old-old, shyness was associated with an increase in general health problems and limitations, with a need for greater physical assistance with the activities of daily living, with the experience of a less safe and supportive home and community environment, with less confidence in their ability to continue to survive for long (in terms of health, finances, and independence), and with greater loneliness.

SUMMARY

In closing there are four points I would like to emphasize from the preceding discussion. First, the implications of shyness may be more complex for older persons than for the young. This complexity may reflect changing interpersonal needs and opportunities for social interaction across the life span, but may also reflect relationships that have become more problematic and unpredictable.

Second, it seems useful to divide into two categories the circumstances in which shyness may affect older adults. In instrumental situations one must effectively interact with others to construct or maintain social support networks or to access needed resources. Here, shyness appears to operate as one of many relational competence variables (Hansson *et al.*, 1984), in this case making the interaction more difficult. Thus, as might be expected among younger populations also, shy elderly persons appeared to experience inhibition, reduced interaction, and feelings of uncontrollability and helplessness in important coping situations.

The influence of shyness on psychological adjustment and well-being more broadly defined, however, may well be mediated by the level of one's social integration. From a role-theoretical perspective, shyness may be relevant only to the extent that one is dependent on the social group for status or acceptance. There is some consensus that with normative, decreasing role involvement, the social environment of older adults becomes less threatening and evaluative; there are fewer demands from the social group to continue to rise to the occasion and to demonstrate competence and socially valued characteristics. It follows that the power of the social context to elicit shyness, and the extent to which shyness could interfere with interpersonal consequences or psychological well-being would be considerably reduced.

Third, our shyness findings are consistent with current notions about the qualitative difference between the young-old and the old-old. Among the young-old, our shyness findings reflect a continuing struggle with the evaluative nature of the social environment. Among the older, and more frail old-old, however, shyness may reflect a more generalized emotional response to failing health, and to increasing physical dependency and isolation.

Finally, shyness in our older samples was related consistently to a heightened responsivity to social support from important others. With increased social support, for example, shy unemployed subjects felt more in control and behaved accordingly. Such findings testify to the fundamental and enduring influence of personality in social interaction generally.

REFERENCES

Athay, M., & Darley, J. M. (1981). Toward an interaction centered theory of personality. In N. Cantor & J. F.Kihlstrom (Eds.), *Personality, cognition, and social interaction* (pp. 281–308). Hillsdale, NJ: Erlbaum.

Averill, J. R. (1980). A constructivist view of emotion. In R. Plutchik & H. Kellerman (Eds.), *Emotion: Theory, research, and experience.* New York: Academic Press.

Beck, A. T. (1967). *Depression: Causes and treatment.* Philadelphia: University of Pennsylvania Press.

Buss, A. H., & Plomin, R. (1975). *A temperament theory of personality development.* New York: Wiley.

Buss, T. F., & Redburn, F. S. (1983). *Mass unemployment: Plant closings and community mental health.* Beverly Hills: Sage.

Butler, R. N., & Lewis, M. I. (1982). *Aging and mental health: Positive psychological and biomedical approaches.* St. Louis: Mosby.

Cheek, J. M., & Buss, A. H. (1981). Shyness and sociability. *Journal of Personality and Social Psychology, 41,* 330–339.

Gottlieb, B. H. (1983). Social support as a focus for integrative research in psychology. *American Psychologist, 38,* March, 278–287.

Hansson, R. O., Rule, B., Briggs, S., & Thompson, C. (1984). *Shyness and coping among older unemployed adults.* Paper presented at the meeting of the American Psychological Association, Toronto, Canada.

Hansson, R. O., Jones, W. H., & Carpenter, B. N. (1984). Relational competence and social support. In P. Shaver (Ed.), *Review of personality and social psychology, vol. 5.* Beverly Hills, CA: Sage.

Hayes, J., & Nutman, P. (1981). *Understanding the unemployed.* London: Tavistock.

Herrington, L. H. (1983). Crime has a devastating, tragic impact on the nation's elderly. *Justice Assistance News,* 4(6), U.S. Dept. of Justice.

Hogan, R., Jones, W. H., & Cheek, J. M. (1985). Socioanalytic theory: An alternative to armadillo psychology. In B. Schlenker (Ed.). *Self and identity: Presentations of self in social life* (pp. 175–198). New York: McGraw-Hill.

Izard, C. E. (1978). On the ontogenesis of emotions and emotion-cognition relationships in infancy. In M. Lewis & L. A. Rosenblum (Eds.), *The development of affect.* New York: Plenum Press.

Johnson, C. L. (1983). Dyadic family relations and social support. *The Gerontologist, 23,* 377–383.

Jones, W. H., & Russell, D. (1982). The social reticence scale: An objective instrument to measure shyness. *Journal of Personality Assessment, 46,* 629–631.

Lawton, M. P. (1975). The Philadelphia geriatric morale scale: A revision. *Journal of Gerontology, 30,* 85–89.

Lawton, M. P. (1981). Community supports for the aged. *Journal of Social Issues, 37,* 102–115.

Lopata, H. Z. (1979). *Women as widows: Support systems.* New York: Elsevier.

Neugarten, B. L., & Hagestad, G. O. (1976). Age and the life course. In R. H. Binstock & E. Shanas (Eds.), *Handbook of aging and the social sciences,* (pp. 35–55). New York: Van Nostrand Reinhold.

Pfeiffer, E. (1977). Psychopathology and social pathology. In J. E. Birren & K. W. Schaie (Eds.), *Handbook of the psychology of aging* (pp. 650–671). New York: Van Nostrand Reinhold.

Rosenberg, M. (1965). *Society and the adolescent self-image.* Princeton, NJ: Princeton University Press.

Rosow, I. (1976). Status and role change through the life span. In R. H. Binstock & E. Shanas (Eds.), *Handbook of aging and the social sciences* (pp. 457–482). New York: Van Nostrand Reinhold.

Russell, D., Peplau, L. A., & Cutrona, C. E. (1980). The revised UCLA loneliness scale: Concurrent and discriminant validity. *Journal of Personality and Social Psychology, 39,* 472–480.

Seligman, M. E. P. (1975). *Helplessness: On depression, development and death.* San Francisco: Freeman.

Sheppard, H. L. (1976). Work and retirement. In R. H. Binstock & E. Shanas (Eds.), *Handbook of aging and the social sciences* (pp. 286–309). New York: Van Nostrand Reinhold.

Trieschmann, R. B. (1978). *The psychological, social, and vocational adjustment in spinal cord injury: A strategy for furture research (Final Report, RSA/13/59011-1)*. Los Angeles: Easter Seal Society for Crippled Children and Adults of Los Angeles County.

Yin, P. P. (1980). Fear of crime among the elderly: Some issues and suggestions. *Social Problems, 27,* 492–504.

III

The Experience of Shyness
Personal Aspects

Part III examines the construct of shyness as it fits into a comprehensive psychology of the person. Each of the four chapters explaines shyness using a conceptual perspective that originated independently of the construct of shyness, revealing its relevance for a diversity of psychological issues and phenomena.

In the first of these chapters, Crozier looks at shyness as a coherent and distinct construct within the universe of trait descriptors. He begins by locating shyness with respect to Eysenck's dimensions of extraversion-introversion and neuroticism. He then examines how shyness relates to sociability and other self-report and behavioral measures. In the remainder of his chapter, Crozier suggests some methods for refining the construct of shyness as a dimension of personality. He affirms the idea that there may well be several types of shyness (e.g., private versus public and early versus late developing), and he also reminds us that personality factors can best be examined in the context of the particular social situations in which they are elicited.

Izard and Hyson (Chapter 12) examine shyness as a dimension of emotion and as an emotional experience. Although their chapter concentrates specifically on the subjective-experiential aspects of shyness, the authors point out that emotions also have physiological and behavioral components and that it is therefore necessary to study shyness using multiple modes of measurement. In the major portion of their chapter, Izard and Hyson contrast shyness with a number of related emotional states, including guilt, shame, and fear. They present evidence that shyness is the least unpleasant of the negative emotions and, like all emotions, has adaptive value. Izard and Hyson also consider shyness from a developmental point of view. They propose a model of shyness emphasizing that (a) there is variation in emotional responsivity and expression across people; (b) this individuality is evident early in life; (c) patterns of emotionality are rooted in biological processes and molded by social interaction.

The third chapter in Part III looks at shyness from an entirely different perspective. Snyder and Smith discuss one of the strategies that an individual may use to cope with shyness. They begin by noting that shy people often violate conventional wisdom by reversing the fundamental attribution error: shy people tend to attribute their social incompetence to internal, personal attributes rather than external excuses. The authors then explain the processes that account for this self-denigration. In describing these self-presentational mechanisms, Snyder and Smith are careful to distinguish between how shyness originates and how it can be used strategically to one's own advantage. Thus, their self-handicapping approach emphasizes the maintenance and exaggeration of the behavioral and cognitive characteristics associated with shyness.

In the final chapter of Part III, Carver and Scheier briefly present a general model of how behavior is self-regulated. Their model assumes several feedback systems that work together to assure continuous self-reflective monitoring of one's efforts toward some goal or standard. In this scheme, shyness is seen as a tendency to disengage from or avoid social encounters because inadequate progress is being made in the direction of one's goals and because little hope exists for reducing the discrepancy between goals and the current situation. Thus, Carver and Scheier show how shyness could be accounted for within their system of information processing and cybernetic control, and they discuss the implications of their model for the treatment of shyness.

11

Individual Differences in Shyness

W. Ray Crozier

INTRODUCTION

A curious aspect of shyness has been the "shyness" of the construct itself in psychology. Until very recently the term has rarely appeared in textbooks of personality, the self-concept, or social psychology, and indeed this volume presents the first collection of papers on the subject. This might be thought to be curious for a number of reasons, not least of which is the apparently widespread occurrence of shyness, for example the high proportion of respondents in many countries who described themselves as shy in the Stanford surveys (Zimbardo, 1977). For a large number of these subjects shyness is a salient part of their social lives and a source of unhappiness, yet psychologists who have put considerable research effort into the study of interpersonal difficulties have neglected to incorporate this construct into their approach. Some further evidence for the salience of shyness is provided by Forgas (1976) who adopted a multidimensional scaling approach to judgments about everyday social situations and identified self-confidence in knowing how to behave as one of the principal dimensions underlying such judgments. Despite such findings the psychological study of social encounters has not yet paid sufficient attention to people's perceptions of, and confidence in, their social competence. It is not that shyness has only recently been identified or discussed by psychologists; for example, Lewinsky (1941) drew on clinical material to provide a description of shyness that matches quite closely the characteristics that are being fully discussed in this volume, and she indicates some problems that still preoccupy contemporary researchers.

A more plausible explanation might be that shyness is a popular term that is known in psychology by a more technical name, and certainly there is no shortage of those within this domain: audience sensitivity, communication apprehensiveness, embarrassability, nonassertiveness, reticence, self-consciousness, social neurosis, social skills deficits, social anxiety, and stage-fright. Yet none of these seems to capture the particular constellation of qualities

W. RAY CROZIER • School of Psychology, Lancashire Polytechnic, Preston, England PR1 2TQ.

that characterizes shyness: feelings of anxiousness and discomfort in particular social situations; anxiety resulting in silence and withdrawal from interaction; and the lack of overt behavior accompanied by self-consciousness and by heightened physiological arousal.

Alternatively, it might be that this plethora of terms and the variety of approaches that have been taken to questions of social anxiety and avoidance have obscured the concept. The relative neglect may be due to what Pilkonis and Zimbardo (1979) have called the "fuzziness" or lack of conceptual clarity of the term, and this fuzziness may only be reinforced by the large numbers of people who do describe themselves as shy, because the term may be a catch all for many anxieties. Hence one major goal of shyness research must be to establish the coherence of the construct and to mark it off from other constructs. There will be more than one route to this goal, but our approach has been to consider shyness in the context of major factor analytical studies of personality questionnaires, to ask whether these studies have isolated a Shyness factor whose items with highest loadings reflect the characteristics that less quantitative methods have identified with shyness. One must go further than that to examine the interrelationships among shyness factors and to see if these correlate with other factors in a pattern that is theoretically consistent. We would argue that such an approach is necessary to place shyness research on a firm foundation.

Factor analytical studies of personality measures have been closely associated with trait and type personality theories and these have been increasingly criticised in recent years. We will not present here any strong claims about such theories; it is sufficient to note that multivariate approaches have served two functions within the psychology of personality. First, it is a descriptive method, examining the patterns of relationships among, say, responses to questionnaires, to determine the structure of personality as it might be reflected in these. Second, it has helped to provide an explanation for behavior in that claims are made for fundamental types, traits, or dimensions of personality that reflect physiological differences among people and that produce characteristic patterns of responses; the personality theories of Cattell and Eysenck exemplify this approach. Our concern here is with the former goal, and with the scrutiny of evidence pertinent to the assumptions that if factor analytical studies have in some sense mapped out the personality sphere, and if shyness is an important personality characteristic, then it should be reflected in self-descriptions on questionnaires.

SHYNESS IN FACTOR ANALYTICAL STUDIES

A preliminary inspection of these studies would suggest that shyness has failed to emerge as a significant factor, and researchers have focused on two broad and uncorrelated types of temperaments: sociability (or extraversion or exvia) and emotionality (or neuroticism or anxiety). There is consensus on the interpretation of the sociability factor: people scoring high on sociability scales are motivated to affiliate with others and have interests that are social rather than solitary, whereas low scorers have little need to affiliate with others, prefer their own company, and have interests that are solitary rather than social. As this factor tends to be orthogonal to the anxiety or neuroticism factor, there is no necessary connection between reluctance to participate in social encounters and anxiety about participation, and hence a low score on the sociability dimension should not be equated with shyness. Yet, as Cheek and Buss (1981) have pointed out, there has often been an implicit assumption that shyness can be equated with low sociability, and shyness items are sometimes included in measures of sociability. For example, Eysenck (1953) has on occasion referred to shyness as a component in introversion, whereas the sociability subscale of the Eysenck Personality Inventory (EPI) included items that refer to shyness. Again, Comrey (1973) included his factored homogeneous item dimension of shyness on an extraversion–introversion dimension.

Eysenck and Eysenck (1969, p. 27) have argued against this practice and have made a distinction between introversion and shyness, contrasting introverted social shyness (the preference for one's own company but retaining the capacity to function effectively in social situations where necessary) with neurotic social shyness ("troubled with being self-conscious, experiencing feelings of loneliness, troubled with feelings of inferiority, and self-conscious with superiors, worrying over humiliating experiences . . . "). It is fear of social interaction rather than any lack of motivation for it that characterizes neurotic social shyness, and Eysenck and Eysenck (1969) see it as much closer to their Neuroticism factor than to introversion. They report two results to support this distinction. Eysenck (1956) carried out an item analysis of a number of scales from Guilford's personality inventory, including the Shyness scale (S), the Introversion scale (R), and the Neuroticism scale (C). Eysenck interpreted his results as implying the presence of two distinct shyness factors in the S scale, in that some S items correlated with R but not with C, whereas the remainder correlated with C and not with R. The second study (Eysenck & Eysenck, 1969) involved a series of factor analyses of EPI items that showed that sociability and shyness items were orthogonal and not negatively correlated. Again, this suggests that two distinct factors are involved.

The increasing attention that is currently being paid to shyness, and in particular the development of psychometric scales (e.g., Cheek & Buss, 1981; Jones & Russell, 1982; Morris, 1982) to supplement rating scales and yes/no answers to a question about being shy, have provided fresh information on the relationship between shyness and sociability. There is inevitably a certain ambiguity about this question, because the relationship can depend on which items are included or excluded from the particular personality scales examined, but nevertheless it is of some theoretical importance to know the factorial structure of the shyness domain. Jones and Russell (1982) reported a correlation of $-.54$ ($N = 88$) between their Social Reticence Scale and the Extraversion scale of the EPI, whereas Morris (1982) reported a range of correlations from $-.53$ to $-.57$ ($N = 65$ or 66) depending on the sex of subjects and the form of scale used, between his shyness measure and the EPI extraversion scale. Morris also reported that when only the items forming the Sociability factor of the EPI were considered (Eaves & Eysenck, 1975, have derived sociability and impulsivity subscales from the EPI), the correlation rose to $-.62$, whereas when shyness items were excluded from the subscale the correlation was reduced to $-.44$. A better test of the relationship would be to create factorially pure measures of shyness and sociability and to examine their correlation, and this was the strategy adopted by Cheek and Buss (1981). They constructed short shyness and sociability scales that avoided item similarity and that had satisfactory internal consistency. Factor analysis extracted two distinct factors, and all items loaded significantly on their appropriate factor and nonsignificantly on the inappropriate factor. The two scales correlated $-.30$ ($N = 912$). Cheek and Buss also examined behavioral measures for a sample of women, and found that shyness and sociability independently affected behavior in a social situation on measures such as time spent talking and self-manipulation. They detected significant interactions between shyness and sociability in that subjects in the subgroup who scored highest on both scales talked the least, spent the most time in self-manipulation, exhibited the most gaze aversion, and were judged as most tense, inhibited, and unfriendly.

We can feel confident about rejecting the two hypotheses that shyness and sociability are to be equated, and that they are independent; rather, there is a moderate correlation between them, moderate enough to warrant investigating them as separate variables. Crozier (1979) examined a number of factor analytical studies (see Table 1) and was able to conclude that (a) studies have frequently isolated factors similar in item content to Eysenck's Neurotic Shyness factor, where items with high loadings refer to tendencies to be troubled by shyness, to feel self-conscious, and to keep in the background on social occasions; and (b) these factors correlate with each other and with related factors in a theoretically consistent pattern. In particular, shyness shared features with introversion—quietness and keeping in the background on social occasions—and with anxiety—feelings of inadequacy and nervousness—and hence should be correlated with but separable from both. For example, Cattell's Threctia scale has significant loadings on both exvia ($-.50$) and anxiety ($.38$), the second-order factors that result from factor analysis of the correlations among source traits (Cattell, 1973). Comrey and Duffy (1968) carried out a factor analysis of the Cattell, Eysenck, and Comrey personality inventories, and extracted a Shyness factor that had its highest loadings on Cattell's Threctia, Eysenck's Extraversion, and Comrey's Shyness and Submission factors. Derogatis, Rickels, and Rock (1976) reported correlations of $.52$ and $.49$ between their Interpersonal Sensitivity measure and the introversion and anxiety scales of the MMPI. Ormerod and Billing (1982) report findings from four large-scale studies that factor analysed Cattell's High School Personality Questionnaire, showing that Threctia (H) has significant loadings on two extracted factors labelled as Classical Extraversion and Anxiety/Neuroticism. The loadings from their own study were $.69$ and $-.39$ respectively. Shyness is a replicable factor with significant but moderate correlations with both introversion and neuroticism.

A considerable amount of research has been stimulated by the development of self-consciousness scales by Fenigstein, Scheier, and Buss (1975). Their measure of tendencies to be self-conscious includes three subscales: Private Self-Consciousness, being attentive to one's thoughts and feelings; Public Self-Consciousness, the awareness of the self as a social object; and Social Anxiety,

TABLE 1. Shyness Factors in Factor Analytical Studies of Personality Scales

Author	Source	Factor name	Typical items refer to
Mosier (1937)	Items from Thurstone Neurotic Inventory (Thurstone & Thurstone, 1930)	Self-consciousness in intimate face-to-face situations	Being troubled with shyness Keeping in the Background on social occasions
Layman (1940)	Items from a number of personality scales	Social initiative	Making new friends easily Feeling embarrassed if have to enter a public assembly after everyone else has been seated
Cattell (1946)	Review of factor analytic studies	QPI: shyness	Being troubled with shyness Keeping in the background on social occasions Finding it difficult to make new acquaintances
Dixon, DeMonchaux, & Sandler (1957)	Items from Tavistock Self-Assessment Inventory	Social timidity	Feeling awkward with strangers Feeling nervous when speaking to someone in authority
Cattell (1965)	Development of 16PF	Threctia	Keeping in background on social occasions Embarrassed if focus of attention
Comrey (1965)	Items forming factored homogeneous item dimensions (FHIDs)	Shyness	Shyness, stagefright, lack of talkativeness
Derogatis, Lipman, & Covi (1973)	Self reported symptoms	Interpersonal sensitivity	Self-deprecation, feelings of unease and discomfort during interaction
Fenigstein et al. (1975)	Self-consciousness items	Social anxiety	Taking a long time to overcome shyness Finding it difficult to talk to strangers

Note: From "Shyness as a Dimension of Personality" by W. R. Crozier, 1979, British Journal of Social and Clinical Psychology, 18, 121–128. Copyright 1979 by the British Psychological Society. Reprinted by permission.

which seems to be a shyness factor in that items with highest loadings refer to difficulties in overcoming shyness and finding it difficult to talk to strangers. The intercorrelations among these three subscales are low, which seems to imply that although shyness seems to entail self-consciousness, the reverse does not necessarily hold, and one can be self-conscious without anxiety. Pilkonis (1977a) administered the Stanford Shyness Survey together with a number of scales, including the EPI and the self-consciousness measure, and found that self-rated shyness correlated .67 with Social Anxiety but only .19 with Public and .07 with Private Self-Consciousness. Cheek and Buss (1981) reported comparable correlations with their Shyness scale of .26 and .10 for the Public and Private scales. Jones and Russell (1982) report rather higher correlations of .36 and .30 respectively, but their Social Reticence scale explicitly includes items that refer to being self-conscious (this is borne out by their factor analysis of the scale), and hence similarity of item content has presumably contributed to these statistically significant, if moderate coefficients.

Psychometric studies present a coherent and reliable picture of relationships among shyness, sociability, and self-consciousness, and this is reinforced by a reanalysis of the matrix of intercorrelations presented by Pilkonis (1977a). Elementary linkage analysis (McQuitty, 1957) reveals three distinct clusters in these data: (a) shyness: Stanford Survey self-rating, Social Anxiety, EPI N scale; (b) self-consciousness: the Private and Public scales; and (c) sociability: EPI E scale and Sociability subscale; extraversion rating; Self-monitoring scale (Snyder, 1974).

Whereas these studies lend support to the construct validity of shyness, there is now also some evidence of its predictive validity, in terms of both behavioral correlates and descriptions of subjects' social encounters outside the laboratory. Studies have shown that shy subjects tend to maintain greater interpersonal distance in encounters with the opposite sex (Carducci & Webber, 1979); they tend to be slower to initiate conversations and to break silences, and to speak less frequently (Pilkonis, 1977b); they tend to spend less time speaking (Cheek & Buss, 1981; Pilkonis, 1977b); they tend to spend more time in self-manipulation (Cheek & Buss, 1981); they are judged by observers to be more anxious, tense, inhibited, unfriendly, and less attractive (Cheek & Buss, 1981; Jones & Russell, 1982); they tend not to be selected as a group leader (Jones & Russell, 1982); and they rate themselves as more inhibited and awkward (Cheek & Buss, 1981). Shy persons describe themselves as more lonely, and report a lower frequency of dating, fewer close friends, and fewer intimate friends of the opposite sex (Cheek & Busch, 1981; Jones & Russell, 1982; Jones, Freeman, & Goswick, 1981).

It seems to us that the reviewed studies do support the contention that shyness is a meaningful and coherent construct that can be marked off from other constructs, that psychometric studies of questionnaire items identify a shyness factor distinct from sociability, and that scores on this factor have behavioral correlates. Yet these findings do not provide an end in themselves, but serve to indicate the need for further research, and here we would highlight two directions that should be taken.

First, although there exists substantial evidence for individual differences along a dimension of shyness, a more fine grained analysis can provide empirical tests of the validity of the different kinds of shyness that have been proposed. For example, Pilkonis (1977a) postulated a distinction between public and private shyness which in a sense parallels the useful distinction between public and private self-consciousness (Scheier & Carver, 1983). Pilkonis reported that cluster analysis of subjects' ratings of their shyness problems identified two clusters, one emphasizing behavioral deficiencies and the other subjective discomfort and more private anxieties. To take a second example, Buss (1984, see also this volume) has proposed further dimensions: one relates to the relative salience of three components of shyness (behavioral, emotional, and cognitive reactions); another concerns a distinction between early and late appearing shyness. It is an empirical question whether these hypothesized structures have construct and predictive validity.

Second, the contribution of situations to shyness factors needs to be evaluated, and we note here two indications that there is considerable situational variance in shyness. Inspection of those items with highest loadings on extracted factors reveals frequent references to social encounters that reliably elicit shyness. Further evidence comes from the study of sex differences in shyness. Although shyness is sometimes held to be characteristic of a woman's personality and there are findings that it is a female personality stereotype (Bem, 1974; Stoppard & Kalin, 1978), there is in fact no compelling evidence that women are more shy than men; large-scale investigations by Zimbardo (1977), Cheek and Buss (1981) and Jones and Russell (1982) reported no sex differences. This would seem to conflict with those studies that do find that women are more shy than men (for example, this is reported for the Cattell 16PF factor Threctia by Saville, 1972, and Cattell, 1983). This apparent contradiction may be reconciled; we have data that imply that there are sex differences in sociability rather than in shyness (Crozier, 1984). But of greater significance to us here, it would appear that responses to shyness questionnaires reflect situational factors in that studies show that it is only a minority of items that refer to certain kinds of social encounters that produce sex differences. For example, although Hollandsworth and Wall (1977) found such differences on total scores of assertiveness scales, they reported that only a small number of items differentiated the sexes: males were more assertive with authority figures, when stating opinions, and in making complaints, whereas females were more assertive in expressing affection, in expressing anger towards parents, and in giving compliments. It would seem that differences in total scores may mask important situational factors, and that attention should be paid to situational determinants of shyness.

SITUATIONAL DETERMINANTS OF SHYNESS

Items with highest loadings on shyness factors refer to being shy (a) in the presence of authority figures, those whom respondents consider superior to themselves, or those whom they feel are evaluating them; (b) in novel situations, such as dealing with strangers or meeting someone for the first time; (c) when being required to take the initiative, such as expressing an opinion or taking the lead in an encounter with a member of the opposite sex; and (d) when in the presence of a number of others or in front of an audience. A similar pattern is apparent in other approaches, for example the Stanford Shyness Survey (Zimbardo, Pilkonis, & Norwood, 1974). In responses to the Survey the same kinds of situations elicited shyness and, conversely, although respondents described themselves as dispositionally shy, they claimed rarely to be shy in one-to-one same sex interactions or when interacting with parents, siblings, children, or friends. They also rated their shyness as varying to a large degree according to situations (Pilkonis & Zimbardo, 1979). Teglasi and Hoffman (1982) hypothesized that shy subjects would be characterised by self-defeating causal attributions and they reported that such attributions were situation specific. Shy subjects made more self-defeating attributions in response to situations that tend to elicit shyness (initiating new relationships with an individual or in a group), but they did not differ from the control group in response to situations that tend not to elicit shyness (task-oriented groups or close personal relationships).

It is clear from such studies that a considerable proportion of the variance in responses to social situations can be accounted for by differences in situations, and that making predictions about shyness will need to attend to these differences. It is clear too that classification of the situations that tend to elicit shyness will provide valuable information about the causes of shyness: explanations of individual differences may have to follow an account of what can produce shyness in anyone.

One approach to classification focuses on novelty as an elicitor of shyness. Darwin (1872, p. 329) wrote that

> shyness seems to depend on sensitiveness to the opinions of others . . . persons who are exceedingly shy are rarely shy in the presence of those with whom they are quite familiar and of whose good opinion and sympathy they are perfectly assured.

More recently Buss (1980) developed a model of shyness that regards novelty as an important eliciting factor. He argued that shyness, shame, embarrassment, and audience anxiety are distinct forms of social anxiety, and that although they share common features, such as acute self-consciousness and a desire to avoid the situation, they differ in both eliciting circumstances and reactions. According to Buss (1980, p. 187) "the most frequent and important situational cause of shyness appears to be novelty," and he distinguishes three kinds of novel situation: physical, such as moving to a new district or starting a new job; social, such as meeting strangers; and role novelty; "each time a new role is assumed, the novelty usually causes shyness ."

A second approach to classification emphasizes the evaluation of social performance. Lewinsky (1941) considered that the situations that were most likely to elicit shyness involved "showing your hand." Goffman (1972) has argued that social encounters assume that their participants have attained certain moral, mental, and physiognomic standards: "The individual is expected to possess certain attributes, capacities, and information which, taken together, fit together into a self that is at one coherently unified and appropriate for the occasion". Shyness results for participants when they believe, for whatever reason, that these standards are not met or these attributes not possessed. Goffman's account of shyness seems to emphasize two features: all social life involves the presentation of self; self-presentation coexists with evaluation of performance, not just the evaluation by others, but also self-monitoring. A similar approach to shyness is taken by Leary and Schlenker (1981), who conceptualize shyness as "anxiety resulting from the prospect or presence of interpersonal evaluation in real or imagined settings." (Crozier (1982) suggested that shyness-eliciting situations make the evaluation of performance salient in two ways; these situations place greater demands on performance, in that for example it is more difficult to know how to behave when meeting someone for the first time than when interacting with a friend; or else the outcome of negative evaluation would be more serious, as would be the case before an audience or in the presence of authority figures. A further cause of shyness that would seem to be related to the evaluation of performance is conspicuousness: Buss (1980) considered that feeling conspicuous could either be a function of situational factors, such as being the only woman in a room full of men, or the actions of others present, such as their paying excessive or insufficient attention.

Crozier (1979) proposed that a useful approach to classification would be to consider the kinds of fears about social situations that are commonly expressed, and to that end, the factorial structure of a series of Fear Survey Schedules was examined. These Schedules are questionnaires originally devised by Lang and Lazovik (1963) and Wolpe and Lang (1964) for clinical assessment purposes, and require respondents to rate how fearful or anxious they would be in a large number of situations. The same questionnaire items tend to be included in the different studies and hence it can be seen that although researchers might provide different labels for the two factors they are in fact highly similar from study to study. One factor seems to refer to fear of criticism or fear of negative evaluation (FNE), whereas the second factor has been labelled fear of lacking social competence (FLC) and has highest loadings on items that refer to fear of being with a member of the opposite sex or speaking before a large group. It should be noted that whereas the majority of investigations report this factorial structure, some, for example, Strahan (1974), combine the two into one social anxiety factor (see Crozier, 1979, for details of these studies). Crozier (1981) presented 26 items from the Fear Survey Schedule (Lang & Lazovik, 1963), including 8 FNE items, 8 FLC items, and 10 miscellaneous fears items, together with the short form of the Stanford Shyness Survey (Pilkonis, 1977a) to a sample of 98 college students. The presence of the two Social Fears factors in the fear survey items was confirmed by factor analysis with varimax rotation. Two regression analyses were carried out, the first with responses to the Yes/No question "Are you shy" as dependent variable, and the second with self-ratings of the level of shyness as dependent variable, with scores on the two Social Fears factors as predictors. Both analyses showed that fear of lacking social competence correlated significantly with shyness, but that fear of negative evaluation accounted for only a negligible proportion of the variance in shyness. Fears of looking foolish or of being criticized are widespread, and subjects who consider themselves to be shy seem to be no more prone to such fears than subjects who do not. Rather their fears are specifically about social encounters, and the items that make up the FLC factor refer to situations similar to those that are regularly cited in the shyness literature. Again we see that the shyness label seems to have quite specific social references and does not entail generalized fears of global anxiety, and this reinforces the findings of psychometric studies of personality.

The situational variance in shyness is of considerable theoretical importance and it needs to attract further research. Its importance rests not only in enabling us to avoid oversimplistic accounts of shyness but also in affording theoretical advances. Zimbardo, Pilkonis, and Norwood (1974) have taken account of their findings that both shy and nonshy respondents agree as to the eliciting conditions and experiences of shyness to propose the explanation that the two groups differ essentially in the attributions they make about the difficulties that certain kinds of situations pose to them both; those who label themselves shy attribute these difficulties to their own shortcomings whereas the nonshy attribute them to situational factors. This is an attractive and potentially valuable approach, but its basic premise does seem premature in the absence of studies that have systematically investigated shyness across a range of situations. To date, test items and behavioral assessments have not attempted any systematic sampling of situations or provided opportunities for a range of responses. For example, in the Stanford Surveys respondents indicated only whether certain specified reactions were characteristic of them when they were shy, so that there were no opportunities to report that they experienced greater intensity of reaction. In the absence of such investigations it remains unclear how situational and dispositional shyness are related.

We must also avoid simplified or mechanistic notions about social situations. Although experimenters seem able to contrive laboratory conditions (such as introducing the subject to a confederate of the opposite sex) that reliably elicit shyness, social encounters outside the laboratory can offer a more complex picture. As Leary and Schlenker (1981) have indicated, almost any social encounter can provide opportunities for the combined motivation to create a particular impression on others and lack of confidence in one's ability to do so that seems to produce shyness. We need to take into account the degree of *structure* in a social situation, as even novel situations can provide scripts that may be adequate to counteract tendencies towards shyness; for example, Pilkonis (1977b) reported less performance differences between shy and nonshy subjects when they made a rather formal prepared presentation than when they were in an informal one-to-one unstructured encounter. There is ample anecdotal evidence of highly successful actors who took up their profession because of their shyness and of people who are shy even with their closest family.

Finally, more systematic sampling of situations will require more representative samples of subjects, as an overreliance on college students or adolescents may give us a rather biased picture of shyness eliciting conditions. Such subjects are in a transitional period, often characterized by novelty, role changes, and concern over identity, and may be particularly prone to self-consciousness (e.g., Elkind, 1967). We lack research into the conditions which produce shyness among older people. One exception, a study that reported findings on self-confidence in social situations for different samples of subjects (Forgas, 1976), did show that the situations that caused problems were different for housewives and students.

SUMMARY

This chapter has drawn on factor analytical studies of personality to argue that there is evidence of consistent individual differences in shyness. A Shyness factor has regularly emerged in these studies that shares common features with anxiety and low sociability but that is distinct from these. The fears of shy people do not seem to extend beyond social situations, whereas it seems to be their fears about these rather than any lack of motivation to be sociable that leads to avoidance of interaction. A significant proportion of the variance in shyness is due to situational variance, and those situations that are novel or that imply the evaluation of an individual are most likely to elicit shyness.

REFERENCES

Bem, S. L. (1974). The measurement of psychological androgyny. *Journal of Consulting and Clinical Psychology, 42,* 155–162.

Buss, A. H. (1980). *Self-consciousness and social anxiety.* San Francisco: Freeman.

Buss, A. H. (1984). A conception of shyness. In J. A. Daly & J. C. McCroskey (Eds.), *Avoiding communication: Shyness, reticence, and communication apprehension.* London: Sage.

Carducci, B. J., & Webber, A. W. (1979). Shyness as a determinant of interpersonal distance. *Psychological Reports, 44,* 1075–1078.

Cattell, R. B. (1946). *Description and measurement of personality.* New York: World Book.

Cattell, R. B. (1965). *The scientific analysis of personality.* Harmondsworth: Penguin.

Cattell, R. B. (1973). *Personality and mood by questionnaire.* San Francisco: Jossey-Bass.

Cheek, J. M., & Busch, C. K. (1981). The influence of shyness on loneliness in a new situation. *Personality and Social Psychology Bulletin, 7,* 572–577.

Cheek, J. M., & Buss, A. H. (1981). Shyness and sociability. *Journal of Personality and Social Psychology, 41,* 330–339.

Comrey, A. L. (1965). Scales for measuring compulsion, hostility, neuroticism, and shyness. *Psychological Reports, 16,* 697–700.

Comrey, A. L. (1973). *A first course in factor analysis.* New York: Academic Press.

Comrey, A. L., & Duffy, K. E. (1968). Cattell & Eysenck factor scores related to Comrey personality factors. *Multivariate Behavioural Research, 3,* 379–392.

Crozier, W. R. (1979). Shyness as a dimension of personality. *British Journal of Social and Clinical Psychology, 18,* 121–128.

Crozier, W. R. (1981). Shyness and self-esteem. *British Journal of Social Psychology, 20,* 220–222.

Crozier, W. R. (1982). Explanations of social shyness. *Current Psychological Reviews, 2,* 47–60.

Crozier, W. R. (1984). *Sex differences in shyness?* Unpublished manuscript, Preston Polytechnic.

Darwin, C. (1872). *The expression of the emotions in man and animals*. 1965 Edition. Chicago, IL: Chicago University Press.

Derogatis, L. R., Lipman, R. S., & Covi, L. (1973). SCL-90: An outpatient psychiatric rating scale. *Psychopharmacological Bulletin, 9*, 13–27.

Derogatis, L. H., Rickles, K., & Rock, A. F. (1976). The SCL-90 and the MMPI: A step in the validation of a new self-report scale. *British Journal of Psychiatry, 128*, 280–289.

Dixon, J. J., DeMonchaux, C., & Sandler, J. (1957). Patterns of anxiety: An analysis of social anxieties. *British Journal of Medical Psychology, 30*, 107–112.

Eaves, L., & Eysenck, H. J. (1975). The nature of extraversion: A genetical analysis. *Journal of Personality and Social Psychology, 32*, 102–112.

Elkind, D. (1967). Egocentrism in adolescence. *Child Development, 38*, 1025–1034.

Eysenck, H. J. (1953). *The structure of human personality*, London: Methuen.

Eysenck, H. J. (1956). The questionnaire measurement of neuroticism and extraversion. *Revista Psicologia, 50*, 113–140.

Eysenck, H. J., & Eysenck, S. B. G. (1969). *Personality structure and measurement*. London: Routledge & Kegan Paul.

Fenigstein, A., Scheier, M. F., & Buss, A. H. (1975). Public and private self-consciousness: Assessment and theory. *Journal of Consulting and Clinical Psychology, 43*, 522–527.

Forgas, J. (1976). The perception of social episodes: Categorical and dimensional representations in two different cultural milieus. *Journal of Personality and Social Psychology, 34*, 199–209.

Goffman, E. (1972). *Interaction ritual*. Harmondsworth, England: Penguin.

Hollandsworth, J. G., & Wall, K. E. (1977). Sex differences in assertive behavior: An empirical investigation. *Journal of Counseling Psychology, 24*, 217–222.

Jones, W. H., & Russell, D. W. (1983). The Social Reticence Scale: An objective instrument to measure shyness. *Journal of Personality Assessment, 46*, 629–631.

Jones, W. H., Freemon, J. E., & Goswick, R. A. (1981). The persistence of loneliness: Self and other determinants. *Journal of Personality, 49*, 27–48.

Lang, P. J. & Lazovik, A. D. (1963). Experimental desensitization of a phobia. *Journal of Abnormal and Social Psychology, 66*, 519–525.

Layman, E. McC. (1940). An item analysis of the adjustment questionnaire. *Journal of Psychology, 10*, 87–106.

Leary, M. R., & Schlenker, B. R. (1981). The social psychology of shyness: A self-presentational model. In J. T. Tedeschi (Ed.), *Impression management theory and social psychological research* (pp. 335–358). New York: Academic Press.

Lewinsky, H. (1941). The nature of shyness. *British Journal of Psychology, 32*, 105–113.

Morris, C. G. (1982). *Assessment of shyness*. Unpublished manuscript, University of Michigan.

Mosier, C. I. (1937). A factor analysis of certain neurotic symptoms. *Psychometrika, 2*, 263–286.

McQuitty, L. L. (1957). Elementary linkage analysis for isolating orthogonal and oblique types and typal relevancies. *Educational and Psychological Measurement, 17*, 207–229.

Ormerod, M. B., & Billing, K. (1982). A six orthogonal factor model of adolescent personality derived from the HSPQ. *Personality and Individual Differences, 3*, 107–117.

Pilkonis, P. A. (1977a). Shyness, public and private, and its relationship to other measures of social behavior. *Journal of Personality, 45*, 585–595.

Pilkonis, P. A. (1977b). The behavioral consequences of shyness. *Journal of Personality, 45*, 596–611.

Pilkonis, P. A., & Zimbardo, P. G. (1979). The personal and social dynamics of shyness. In C. E. Izard (Ed.) *Emotions in Personality and Psychopathology* (pp. 133–160). New York: Plenum Press.

Saville, P. (1972). *The British standardization of the 16PF. Supplement of norms*. Windsor, Berkshire: NFER.

Scheier, M. F., & Carver, C. S. (1983). Two sides of the self: One for you and one for me. In J. Suls & S. Greenwald (Eds.), *Psychological perspectives on the self* (Vol. 2, pp. 123–157). Hillsdale, NJ: Erlbaum.

Snyder, M. (1974). Self-monitoring of expressive behavior. *Journal of Personality and Social Psychology, 30*, 526–537.

Stoppard, J. M., & Kalin, R. (1978). Can gender stereotypes and sex-role conceptions be distinguished? *British Journal of Social and Clinical Psychology, 17*, 211–217.

Strahan, R. (1974). Situational dimensions of nervousness. *Journal of Personality Assessment, 38,* 341–352.

Teglasi, H., & Hoffman, M. A. (1982). Causal attributions of shy subjects. *Journal of Research in Personality, 16,* 376–385.

Thurstone, L. L., & Thurstone, T. G. (1930). A neurotic inventory. *Journal of Social Psychology, 1,* 3–30.

Wolpe, J., & Lang, P. J. (1964). A fear survey schedule for use in behaviour therapy. *Behaviour Research and Therapy, 2,* 27–30.

Zimbardo, P. G. (1977). *Shyness: What it is and what to do about it.* Reading, MA: Addison-Wesley.

Zimbardo, P. G., Pilkonis, P. A., & Norwood, R. M. (1974). *The silent prison of shyness.* Office of Naval Research Technical Report Z-17, Stanford University.

12

Shyness as a Discrete Emotion

Carroll E. Izard and Marion C. Hyson

The publication of this volume is somewhat ironic. It exposes the concept of shyness to the merciless scrutiny of a large group of strangers—the very situation that shy individuals find most distressing. Whether this scrutiny uncovers new aspects of shyness, or results in its further retreat, may depend on our strategy in approaching this elusive construct. In this chapter, we propose that shyness may be cautiously but productively approached as a specific quality of emotion experience.

Recent work on human emotions has considerable potential for enlarging our understanding of shyness. First, we shall explain our concept of emotion and then outline five current emphases in emotions theory and research and discuss their implications for the study of shyness. These emphases are (a) the measurement of emotions, (b) the motivational and adaptive functions of the emotions, (c) identification of discrete emotions, (d) the process of emotional development, and (e) individual differences in patterns of emotion. In discussing these topics, our principal conceptual focus will be differential emotions theory (Izard, 1971, 1977; Izard & Malatesta, 1985), and research related to this theory. We will also include recent work on emotions from other laboratories and theoretical perspectives. Perhaps this focus will help to integrate existing work on shyness and related constructs; moreover, our approach may suggest some new questions to be pursued in future research on shyness.

Because the term "emotion" has been used even more variously than the term "shyness," let us explain at the outset what we mean by emotion and the emotions system. According to differential emotions theory (Izard, 1977), this system consists of a set of fundamental, discrete emotions (e.g., interest, anger, sadness, joy, shyness), each of which includes three components:

CARROLL E. IZARD • Department of Psychology, University of Delaware, Newark, DE 19716. MARION C. HYSON • Department of Individual and Family Studies, University of Delaware, Newark, DE 19716.
 Work for this paper was supported by NSF Grant BNS 811832.

(a) neurophysiological/biochemical substrates, (b) distinctive patterns of motor-expressive behavior, including facial expressions, and (c) a distinct subjective-experiential or feeling state.

The theoretical implications of distinguishing emotion as feeling (as in the "feeling of shyness") from cognition or cognitive processes have been presented in an earlier publication (Izard, 1984). In brief, it was argued that the emotion system precedes the cognitive system in ontogeny and that emotion feeling and emotion expression are the first foundations of personality and social relationships. The position of differential emotions theory in distinguishing the emotion system and the cognitive system is consistent with Zajonc's (1980) two-systems view of information processing.

Nevertheless, these systems are interrelated in many ways. Through the maturational and learning processes of development, emotions and cognition become highly coordinated and interactive systems. Emotions and cognition also become integrated in innumerable affective-cognitive structures that, after the acquisition of language, become a centrally important part of human motivation. However, even when emotion combines with cognition to form affective-cognitive structures, it is the emotion component of the structure that provides the motivational thrust, whereas the cognitive component is important in providing direction.

THE MEASUREMENT OF EMOTIONS

The study of emotions has grown from an amorphous area to one with considerable scientific rigor and methodological sophistication. Many of the measurement and assessment issues that are relevant to emotions in general also apply more specifically to the measurement of shyness. In terms of differential emotions theory, there are, as we have said, three components of emotion, the neurophysiological, the motor-expressive, and the subjective-experiential. These represent dimensions that can be assessed in different and complementary ways. A brief review of the kinds of measures that have been employed in the study of emotions may suggest some additional tools to use in further investigations of shyness.

On the neurophysiological level, attention has been paid to the distinctive patterns of autonomic activity associated with various emotion states. In infant research, for example, heart rate measures, electroencephalography (EEG), and electromyography (EMG) have been used in studies of responses to emotion-eliciting stimuli (Davidson & Fox, 1982; Langsdorf, Izard, Rayias, & Hembree, 1983). Some investigators have recognized the relevance of these kinds of measures for the study of shyness (Buss, 1979; Zimbardo, 1977) but further work is needed, using such measures to explore the psychophysiology of shyness and related emotions.

Emotion researchers have put considerable emphasis on facial expressions as indexes of discrete emotion states. Objective systems for coding these expressions (Ekman & Friesen, 1978; Izard, 1979; Izard & Dougherty, 1980) have been used in numerous cross-cultural and developmental studies. Unlike other emotion expressions, no specific facial muscle movements have been identified as unique to shyness or shame. Rather, the characteristic expression of shyness (and shame) is said to include a downward or averted gaze, together with a lowering of the head and sometimes blushing. Possibly this absence of facial movement is related to the particular motivational function of shyness. In shyness (and perhaps in shame and guilt) there is a desire to avoid emotion communication rather than to signal one's feelings. The effect of the "shy" pattern of nonverbal behavior is to decrease the possibility of face-to-face affective interchange.

In addition to facial expression, other aspects of nonverbal behavior have been studied in relation to discrete emotions (Gaensbauer, Connell & Schultz, 1983; Hyson & Izard, 1985; Lewis & Michalson, 1983). The hypothesis underlying this research is that different emotion states may motivate characteristic patterns of postural, locomotor, gestural, and visual behavior. Later in this chapter we will look at some of the nonverbal behaviors that have been observed in association with shyness.

Finally, a number of instruments have been developed to study discrete emotions on the subjective-experiential level. For example, Izard (1972) developed the Differential Emotions Scale (DES) as a means of studying the phenomenological component of the fundamental emotions of interest, joy, surprise, sadness, anger, disgust, contempt, shyness (originally termed shame/shyness), guilt, and fear. Numerous factor analytic investigations have provided support for the relative independence of these scales, though not all scales have emerged with the predicted item content in every factor analysis.

A repeated theme of emotions research in recent years is the use of multiple measures and levels of analysis. With some exceptions (e.g., Pilkonis, 1977b), studies of shyness have employed only one type of measure, usually a self-report instrument. Moreover, as Jones and Russell (1982) have noted, wide differences in these instruments have made comparisons of findings difficult. A combination of neurophysiological, behavioral-expressive, and subjective measures, used with consistency across subject populations and situations, would add considerably to our understanding of shyness.

THE MOTIVATIONAL AND ADAPTIVE FUNCTIONS OF THE EMOTIONS

The differential emotions theory just outlined and other recent work (Campos & Caplovitz, 1984; Sroufe, 1979) provide an adaptational perspective on emotions. Emotions, including negative emotions, such as anger or sadness— and shyness—are not viewed as inherently disturbing or problematic occurrences. In the tradition of Darwin (1872) and more recent ethological studies, we assume that emotions have evolved because they serve crucial functions in development.

What are the implications of this perspective for the study of shyness? It suggests that shyness, rather than being primarily a clinical syndrome, is a widespread, even universal emotion that has considerable adaptive value.

There is certainly ample evidence that shy feelings approach the status of a universal experience. Zimbardo, Pilkonis, & Norwood (1974) found that 99% of a sample of 800 young adults remembered having experienced feelings of shyness; 82% had been dispositionally shy at some point in their lives. If shyness is essentially pathological, then these are alarming data. But if one views shyness as an emotion with adaptive value, then the results are less distressing. Just as feelings of anger or sadness are normal and universal, and just as many people have experienced periods of irritability or "blue moods," shy feelings and "shy stages" may be part of normal emotional life.

It is true that numerous correlations have been found between self-reported shyness in adults and negative qualities such as loneliness, anxiety, depression, fearfulness, and neuroticism (Pilkonis, 1977a; Jones & Russell, 1982). But these maladaptive patterns of behavior have been linked to high levels of shyness rather than to the mild or moderate shyness experienced by the majority of people.

Further support for the essential normality of shyness is found in the responses of infants and young children to novel social situations (e.g., Amsterdam & Levitt, 1980; Bretherton & Ainsworth, 1974; Bronson, 1972; Greenberg & Marvin, 1982; Smith, 1974; Stern & Bender, 1974). The behaviors described in these studies are very similar to those described in the literature on adult shyness (e.g., gaze aversion, immobility, reserve, hesitant or absent vocalization, automanipulation). In contrast to the adult literature, however, in these studies shy behavior is regarded as normal and almost universal. The behavior patterns observed in these situations are commonly interpreted as a combination of affiliative and fearful/wary/cautious tendencies. Bronson (1972) and Sroufe (1979) have pointed out that this combination is highly appropriate for adaptation and survival, enabling the organism to expand the boundaries of its knowledge while avoiding possible dangers in the environment.

Certainly extreme shyness can be a problem and shy feelings are a source of pain for many people. But there is a good deal to be gained from viewing these clinical manifestations within a broader adaptive context.

THE IDENTIFICATION OF DISCRETE EMOTIONS

As others have noted (Buss, 1979; Mosher & White, 1981), our understanding of shyness would be greatly enhanced if we could be more precise in defining its characteristics in relation to other emotions, such as shame, guilt, anxiety, fear, and interest.

In contrast to various forms of the arousal-cognition model of emotion (Manstead & Wagner, 1981; Schachter & Singer, 1962), differential emotions theory holds that each fundamental emotion has unique neurochemical substrates, as well as unique behavioral-expressive and experiential components.

Using these three defining criteria, strong cases can be made for the distinctiveness or discreteness of a number of emotions, such as anger, fear, and interest. The evidence for shyness as a fundamental emotion is considerably less robust. In the following sections, we will first summarize the few attempts to define shyness as an emotion and then look at the theoretical and empirical relationships between shyness and several other emotions: guilt, shame, fear, and interest.

The Defining Characteristics of Shyness

On the phenomenological level, a few theorists have attempted to describe the emotion experience of shyness as distinct from shame or guilt, using terms such as shy, sheepish, and bashful (Izard, 1972). These adjectives imply a feeling of uneasiness or psychological discomfort in social situations. Mosher and White (1981) have suggested that a person feeling shy is oscillating between fear and interest and experiencing corresponding tendencies to avoid and to approach the social stimulus. This definition seems to capture some of the apparently conflicted phenomenology of shyness but is not wholly satisfactory, in that it relies on two other emotions and provides no unique descriptors. Nevertheless, if we consider shyness not as oscillation between fear and interest but as a unique feeling that shares common characteristics with interest and fear, we may begin to get a fix on this elusive phenomenon.

Shyness and Guilt. On the phenomenological level, shyness and guilt have a few commonalities: both are experienced as self-involved or self-focused emotions, and both may have a quality of avoidance of or withdrawal from social situations. However, the differences between these two emotions are more compelling than the similarities. Unlike shyness, guilt is generally the result of the violation of a standard. In guilt one typically feels responsible for physical or psychological harm to someone else. It is as though one feels the hurt one has imposed on the other. Thus from a motivational perspective guilt is a distressing feeling that may stimulate reparative behavior, even in toddlers (Zahn-Waxler, Radke-Yarrow, & King, 1979), whereas shyness appears to motivate socially ambivalent or avoidant behavior.

Research with the Differential Emotions Scale (DES) offers some evidence of the experiential distinctions between shyness and guilt. In numerous factor analytic studies, the Shyness scale, consisting of the items "shy," "embarrassed," and "sheepish," was regularly differentiated from the Guilt scale, consisting of the items "blameworthy," "repentant," and "guilty."

In another study, Izard (1972) asked subjects to recall various emotion-eliciting situations and then to complete the DES. This procedure resulted in a profile of emotions for each imagined situation. The profile in the shyness situation was quite distinct from that of the guilt situation. In the shyness situation the second highest mean in the emotion profile (after the shyness mean) was interest, whereas the second highest emotion in the guilt situation (after the guilt mean) was fear. The fear mean in the shyness situation was substantially lower than it was in the guilt situation profile. Thus these data, like those of

Mosher & White (1981), show that interest and fear are the most likely emotions to interact with shyness. Similarly, the most likely emotions to interact with guilt are fear and sadness. Sadness was not present in the shyness-situation profile. The guilt mean was very low in the shyness-situation profile and the shyness mean was very low in the guilt-situation profile.

Bartlett and Izard (1972) asked subjects to recall emotion-eliciting situations and then to rate their feelings on dimensions of pleasantness, self-assurance, impulsiveness, and tension. Despite the fact that the mean for tension was about the same in shyness and guilt, the pleasantness mean in shyness (7.3 on an 18-point scale) was significantly higher than it was in guilt (3.2). Further, shyness had a significantly higher pleasantness mean than any other negative emotion. These findings are consistent with the data of Izard (1972) and Mosher and White (1981) in showing that the discrete emotion of shyness as defined by these investigators is not experienced as completely negative. At the experiential level shyness apparently has a pleasantness dimension, but, of course, shyness has even stronger negative aspects, as suggested by the magnitude of the mean for tension (14.0), approximately the same as for guilt (13.4) and anger (14.4).

Shyness and Shame. The distinctions between shyness and shame are considerably fuzzier than those between shyness and guilt. Phenomenological descriptions of the shame experience (e.g., Lewis, 1971; Lynd, 1958; Tomkins, 1963) bear several resemblances to shyness, although these theorists have not specifically compared the two emotions. Certain themes run through all these descriptions of shame. Like shyness, the shame experience always involves the self, the concept of self or self-esteem. It involves a heightened awareness of self, or more particularly the aspect of self that is called into question in the shame-eliciting situation. In shame, one tends to perceive one's self as helpless, inept, emotionally hurt. Self-awareness and self-perceptions momentarily dominate consciousness, interrupting and impeding normal cognitive processes.

Still on the theoretical level, Buss (1979) makes some distinctions between the experiences of shame and shyness that are conceptually consistent with differential emotions theory. According to Buss, both of these constructs, along with embarrassment and audience anxiety, form a cluster that may be termed social anxiety. He theorizes that shyness may be distinguished from shame and embarrassment in several ways. Whereas shame is elicited by uncovering or disclosure, shyness is elicited by experiences of novelty or conspicuousness. Anxiety over being evaluated is more closely associated with shyness than with shame: generally, shyness is more future-oriented than shame, focusing on what might happen rather than on what is past. Parasympathetic reactions such as blushing are less commonly associated with shyness than with shame.

The empirical distinction between shame and shyness has been problematic. The item pool used in the early factor analytic studies of the differential Emotions Scale did not yield separate factors for shame and shyness. Therefore, early research with the DES employed one scale (Shame/Shyness), including the items "shy," "embarrassed," and "sheepish."

Recently, Mosher and White (1981) used a modification of the DES to investigate possible distinctions between shame and shyness. They argued correctly that, on the basis of the items contributing to it, the DES Shame/Shyness scale might be more appropriately named shyness. They developed a new, rationally constructed Shame scale by adding the three items "ashamed," "disgraced," and "humiliated." They administered the original DES plus their shame scale to 132 undergraduates as they recalled and visualized situations that elicited shame, shyness, embarrassment, guilt, anxiety, and depression. The subjects' DES profile in the shame-eliciting situation in comparison to that for the shyness situation had significantly higher means on shame, guilt, sadness, anger, disgust, and contempt. Further, the shame situation was experienced as more unpleasant than the shyness situation. This is consistent with Bartlett and Izard's (1972) finding that shyness was the least unpleasant of the negative emotions. Mosher and White also found that the rank order correlations of the DES profiles in the shame and shyness situations were inverse and nonsignificant, indicating that subjects had quite different perceptions of shame and shyness in terms of the situations eliciting them and as they are measured by the DES Shyness and Mosher-White Shame scale.

Shyness and Fear. Although most discussions have focused on distinctions between shyness, shame, and guilt, shyness has both logical and empirical associations with fear. Logically, it could be argued that shyness is a particular type of fear—that is, fear elicited by certain kinds of social situations. The autonomic activity associated with shyness, such as increased heart rate and elevated blood pressure (Buss, 1979), is similar to that identified with fear. Responses observed in self-reported shy people or in shyness-eliciting situations resemble the behaviors sometimes used to index mild to moderate fear in social settings (Lewis & Michalson, 1983). The "early appearing shyness" described by Buss (1979) is said to originate in fearful or wary responses to strangers. Subjects recalling shyness situations report substantial feelings of fear, combined with shyness and interest. As already noted, Mosher & White (1981) argued that shyness can be viewed as an oscillation between interest and fear. Clearly, fear is a more toxic emotion than shyness; it also seems less ambiguous in its motivational impact. "Pure" fear stimulates escape; shyness frequently seems to motivate both approach and avoidance tendencies.

Shyness and Interest. Finally, we might briefly consider the relationship between shyness and interest. Although shyness is a negative emotion, the DES studies of imagined shyness situations reviewed previously show a relatively high level of pleasantness and (specifically) of the positive emotion of interest, presumably social interest. At least among a normal population, then, feelings of shyness do not preclude attraction to others. In fact, one of the distinguishing qualities of shyness may be the conflict between positive and negative social feelings. As noted earlier, observational studies of children in novel social situations frequently show a mixture of social interest and social avoidance or withdrawal; Pilkonis (1977b) found that shy women engaged in more smiling and nodding than any other group, a finding that Pilkonis attributes to social anxiety but that can also be interpreted as an emotion blend of interest and shyness.

Shame, Shyness, and Guilt in Anxiety and Depression. Research with the DES IV, which includes a Shame scale and a Self-Directed Hostility scale, shows that the Shame, Shyness, and Guilt scales perform differently in hierarchical regressions with DES IV scores as predictors and indexes of depression or anxiety as criterion. With scores on the Beck Depression Inventory (BDI) (Beck, 1967) as criterion, guilt (but not shame or shyness) accounted for a significant amount of unique variance in depression in a sample of college students. In a similar hierarchical regression analysis for a sample of middle school children who took the State Trait Anxiety Inventory for Children (STAIC) (Spielberger, Edwards, Lushene, Montuori, & Platsek, 1973), both the Guilt and Shame scales (but not shyness) accounted for significant unique variance in anxiety. These data from studies of emotions scales as predictors of anxiety and depression provide further evidence for the distinctions among shame, shyness, and guilt at the experiential level and strengthen our view that mild to moderate shyness is not usually a pathological symptom.

TRACING THE DEVELOPMENT OF EMOTIONS

Increasingly, research in human emotions has turned to the early years of life. Our understanding of adult feelings can be greatly aided by tracing the developmental origins of emotion experiences and expressions. This generalization may be usefully applied to our study of shyness. In this section we will take up the questions of when normal shy feelings and shy-looking behavior may first appear, the relationship between these feelings and other developmental advances, and changes in those feelings over the life span.

There is considerable evidence that the fundamental human emotions are "wired in" (Malatesta & Izard, 1984). It makes adaptive sense for the human infant to have in its repertoire such clear-cut and powerful motivational conditions and communicative signals. This is not to say that when the 2-month-old baby "looks angry" she is experiencing an adult-like, cognitively mediated sense of outrage. But the basic motivational feeling state is there. More crucially, the emotion signal is there, clearly identified as anger by caretakers and objective coding systems, and the signal is responded to in a predictable fashion. The same may be true of "looking shy": developmentally, the appearance of shyness as an emotion precedes a full-blown set of cognitions and attitudes concerning social situations. Yet the signal itself (e.g., gaze aversion, lowering the head) may set in motion social interaction sequences that, over time, build complex connections between cognition and emotion.

When does the emotion of shyness first appear? Differential emotions theory posits that, although emotions can be identified very early in life, they do not emerge all at once. From an adaptational perspective, it may be especially important for the infant in the early months of life to signal physical distress and enjoyment, both of which engage the parents' full attention for different reasons. Other emotions, such as fear, emerge somewhat later, in synchrony with the child's growing repertoire of adaptive behaviors and cognitive skills.

As with other emotions, in looking for early manifestations of shyness we are forced to limit ourselves to observations of facial and other nonverbal behavior. On that basis, there is some evidence for shy behavior (i.e., avoidance of or discomfort in social situations) in the first year of life. However, terminology is a problem: early research often referred to "fear" of strangers rather than to "shyness." The research on infants' responses to strangers highlights a central problem in developmental investigations of emotion. Lacking the subject's own report, researchers have tended to attach a particular emotion label to a set of responses, on the basis of adult assumptions about children's probable feelings. Thus the belief that the 8-month-old would be afraid of new people led some investigators to label all negative reactions to strangers as "fear." Several pieces of evidence indicate that this label may be inaccurate. When the objective criteria of facial expression coding are used, the "fear face" has almost never been observed in these studies. Nor is crying a reliable index of fear: crying has been seen in association with facial expressions of anger, sadness, and physical distress as well as with fear. The behaviors most often observed in an experimental "stranger approach" situation might reasonably be regarded as early manifestations of shyness (gaze aversion, immobility, postural avoidance), often combining or alternating with affiliative behaviors, such as smiling, producing an appearance of coyness or bashfulness. This is at least superficially similar to the behavior pattern observed in somewhat older children (Greenberg & Marvin, 1982; Stern & Bender, 1974) and in "sociable-shy" adults (Cheek & Buss, 1981) or dispositionally shy women (Pilkonis, 1977b).

In the second year, further evidence of shy feelings appears, as well as rather clear indications of shame reactions. Both may be linked with the development of self-awareness and self-recognition and the internalization of standards for behavior. Discomfort at being the focus of attention (Amsterdam & Levitt, 1980; Kagan, 1982) has also been observed; again, this is similar to self-reported feelings of shy adults.

The developmental history of shy feelings beyond the first years of life has not yet been written. Within our theoretical framework, both emotion socialization and cognitive development would be expected to modify these early experiences of shyness. As with other emotions, on the experiential level feelings of shyness would become increasingly interwoven with thoughts, memories, and anticipations. On the expressive level, most people would probably become more adept at self-presentation and at concealing or miniaturizing their shyness expressions (Izard & Malatesta, 1985). In the normal adult, then, feelings of shyness may be expressed through subtle nonverbal cues as contrasted with the more direct messages of the toddler and preschool child.

One other developmental aspect of shyness needs at least a brief discussion. Shy feelings do not appear to develop in a simple linear fashion. Some periods of development (e.g., the last part of the first year, the middle of the second year, early adolescence) may predispose individuals to shyness, offering good possibilities for developmental research. In addition, several investigators have noted that individual children's tendencies toward shyness often disappear over time (Hinde, Easton, Meller, & Tamplin, 1982; Murphy, 1962). Longitudinal research with small samples may prove the best strategy for tracing these changes and the factors that influence them.

INDIVIDUAL DIFFERENCES IN PATTERNS OF EMOTION

Longitudinal studies of emotional development have begun to show early and stable individual differences in the expression of anger, sadness, and interest (Hyson & Izard, in press; Izard, Hembree, & Huebner, 1985) and in other patterns of emotion-relevant behavior (Arend, Gove, & Sroufe, 1979). These individual differences may also exist with respect to shyness.

Although some degree of shy behavior can be observed in most children in novel social situations, and although the vast majority of adults have experienced shy feelings, there are wide variations in the intensity and pervasiveness of those feelings. Indeed, much recent research on shyness has focused on these differences, comparing self-reported shy and nonshy adults on numerous personality and behavioral dimensions. (e.g., Cheek & Buss, 1981; Jones & Russell, 1982; Pilkonis & Zimbardo, 1979).

Our task in this section is to discuss the processes by which innate and universal emotions (e.g., shy feelings) become crystallized or organized into individual patterns of emotion, cognition, and behavior (e.g., dispositional shyness). This requires consideration of the relationship between nature and nurture in emotional development.

Once again, differential emotions theory and research offers a context in which to examine the more specific issue of dispositional shyness. From the earliest weeks of life, emotional individuality is apparent. Babies differ strikingly from one another in such emotion-related domains as irritability, soothability, lability of emotion expression, and intensity of engagement in affectively toned interchange (Brazelton, 1973; Hinde et al., 1982; Izard, et al., 1985). Are these early emotional differences the product of innate temperamental qualities or of early learning? The data suggest an interaction. Infants come into the world with unique, perhaps genetically influenced, affective predispositions or preferences (Buss & Plomin, 1975; Goldsmith, 1983). Buss (1979) has suggested that high emotionality (i.e., a tendency to become affectively aroused) may be a temperamental precursor of dispositional shyness. Thus some infants may avoid social involvement because it is overstimulating or unpleasantly arousing. Studies of interaction between mothers and young infants (Brazelton, Koslowski, & Main, 1974) seem to support this rationale: in face-to-face play, some babies who experience a strong buildup of tension modulate it through gaze aversion or "tuning out."

However, there is a considerable body of evidence to suggest that these innate emotion programs and related temperamental dispositions are modified by powerful early experiences of affect socialization. In the first 6 months, infants participate in repeated, face-to-face, affectively charged interchanges with parents. Strong contingent relationships have been found between mothers' and infants' facial expressions of emotion (Malatesta & Haviland, 1981). During these interchanges, mothers have been found not only to modify their own emotions but also to engage in selective imitation of their infant's expressions. Mothers imitate (and thereby reinforce) some expressions more than others. Moreover, Malatesta and Haviland's research showed that mothers and their infants had considerable similarity in the quality of their facial expressions, that is, the use of certain regions of the face or certain idiosyncratic facial muscle movements. From the first months of life, then, opportunities exist for the child to experience individual styles of interactive exchange that could encourage shyness. Exchanges with a parent having a highly intrusive, overpowering, or noncontingent style might result in avoidance or social withdrawal by the child; on the other hand, a very low-key mother might encourage shyness by modeling shyness or shy-like behavior, by failing to respond to the infant's strongly positive emotions, or by reinforcing shyness-related behavior in the child.

Moving beyond these early experiences, what later influences may help translate shy feelings into stable personality dispositions? In a recent cross-cultural study Babad, Alexander, & Babad (1983) found strong relationships between mothers' smiling tendencies and emotional demonstrativeness and their children's tendency to return the smile of a friendly stranger. The quality of a child's cumulative experiences with new adults (Bronson, 1978), the tendency of some parents and teachers to label a child as "shy," and the subsequent internalization of this label (Zimbardo, 1977) probably help to account for much of the variance in dispositional shyness.

Finally, we need to remember that individual continuities in patterns of emotion do not necessarily imply that these patterns are rigid or impervious to change. Hinde *et al.* (1982), for example, found that the behavior of temperamentally shy children varied considerably depending on the social situation. Pilkonis (1977a) found the same situational variability in a sample of self-reportedly shy college students. Studies of "slow to warm up" children (Thomas & Chess, 1977) show that although these children meet new social situations with reserve, over time they frequently become comfortable and outgoing.

CONCLUSION

Although the literature has defined relationships between shyness and a variety of personality factors, behavioral tendencies, attributional processes, and social interaction patterns, in this chapter we have argued that the most central fact about shyness is that it is an emotion. Within the context of differential emotions theory, shyness (like other emotions) has a strong organizational/motivational power, a coherent set of behavioral-expressive and experiential components, and a developmental history. Like other emotions, it is both universal and subject to wide individual variations that are influenced by genetic, environmental, and situational factors.

In future research, this perspective suggests several lines of investigation using a combination of physiological, behavioral-expressive, and self-report measures. First, more emphasis might be placed on studying experiences of shyness in normal populations. Under what circumstances do these feelings typically occur, what behaviors do they motivate, what (at least temporary) adaptive advantage is gained from them? Second, it seems important to be even more precise in distinguishing shyness from other related emotions. We have hypothesized in this chapter that shyness is a fundamental emotion and not simply a combination of other emotions or emotion–cognition interactions. However, as we have seen, the evidence is less robust than for some other emotions, especially in the physiological and behavioral-expressive domains. The development of new measures (Fox & Davidson, 1984; Izard, 1982) may offer answers to this question. Third, research efforts might profitably take a more developmental perspective; the chapters in this volume are a starting point in that effort. Finally, it might be helpful to look more closely at individual differences in shyness, moving beyond the shy/not shy dichotomy to investigate a broader range of differences, and to explore the genetic and environmental origins of those differences and their effects on behavior.

REFERENCES

Amsterdam, B. K., & Levitt, M. (1980). Consciousness of self and painful self-consciousness. *Psychoanalytic Study of the Child, 35*, 67–83.

Arend, R., Gove, F. L., & Sroufe, L. A. (1979). Continuity of individual adaptation from infancy to kindergarten. *Child Development, 50*, 950–959.

Babad, Y. E., Alexander, I. E., & Babad, E. Y. (1983). Returning the smile of the stranger: Developmental patterns and socialization factors. *Monographs of the Society for Research in Child Development, 48*(5), 203.

Bartlett, E. S., & Izard, C. E. (1972). A dimensional and discrete emotions investigation of the subjective experience of emotion. In C. E. Izard (Ed.), *Patterns of emotions: A new analysis of anxiety and depression* (pp. 129–173). New York: Academic Press.

Beck, A. T. (1967). *Depression*. New York: Harper & Row.

Brazelton, T. B. (1973). *Neonatal Behavioral Assessment Scale*. Clinics on Developmental Medicine, No. 50. Philadelphia, PA: Lippincott.

Brazelton, T. B., Koslowski, B., & Main, M. (1974). The origins of reciprocity: The early mother-infant interaction. In M. Lewis & L. A. Rosenblum (Eds.) *The effect of the infant on its caregiver* (pp. 49–76). New York: Wiley.

Bretherton, I., & Ainsworth, M. D.S. (1974). Responses of one-year-olds to a stranger in a strange situation. In M. Lewis & L. A. Rosenblum (Eds.) *The origins of fear* (pp. 131–164). New York: Wiley.

Bronson, G. W. (1972). Infants' reactions to unfamiliar persons and novel objects. *Monographs of the Society for Research in Child Development, 37* (3, Serial No. 148).

Bronson, G. W. (1978). Aversive reactions to strangers: A dual process interpretation. *Child Development, 49*, 495–499.

Buss, A. H. (1979). *Self-consciousness and social anxiety*. San Francisco: Freeman.

Buss, A. H., & Plomin, R. (1975). *A temperament theory of personality development*. New York: Wiley.

Campos, J. J., & Caplovitz, K. S. (1984). A new understanding of biological and cognitive influences on emotional development. In C. E. Izard, J. Kagan, and R. Zajonc (Eds.) *Emotion, cognition, & behavior*. New York: Cambridge University Press.

Cheek, J. M., & Buss, A. H. (1981). Shyness and sociability. *Journal of Personality and Social Psychology, 41*(2), 330–339.

Darwin, C. (1872). *The expression of the emotions in man and animals*. New York: Appleton.

Davidson, R. J., & Fox, N. A. (1982). Asymmetrical brain activity discriminates between positive and negative affective stimuli in human infants. *Science, 218*, 1235–1237.

Ekman, P., & Friesen, W. (1978). Manual for the facial affect coding system. Palo Alto, CA: Consulting Psychologist Press.

Fox, N., & Davidson, R. (1984). *The psychobiology of affective development*. Hillsdale, NJ: Erlbaum.

Gaensbauer, T. J., Connell, J. P. & Schultz, L. A. (1983). Emotion and attachment: Interrelationships in a structured laboratory paradigm. *Developmental Psychology, 19*, 815–831.

Goldsmith, H. H. (1983). Genetic influences on personality from infancy to adulthood. *Child Development, 54*, 331–355.

Greenberg, M. T., & Marvin, R. S. (1982). Reactions of preschool children to an adult stranger: A behavioral systems approach. *Child Development, 53*, 481–490.

Hinde, R. A., Easton, D. F., Meller, R. E., & Tamplin, A. M. (1982). Temperament and behavior. In R. Porter & G. M. Collins (Eds.) *Temperamental differences in infants and young children.* (Ciba Foundation Symposium no. 89). London: Pitman.

Hyson, M. C., & Izard, C. E. (1985). Emotion-behavior relationships during a brief separation. Paper presented at the biennial meeting of the Society for Research in Child Development, Toronto, Canada.

Hyson, M. C., & Izard, C. E. (in press). Continuities and changes in emotion expressions during brief separation at thirteen and eighteen months. *Developmental Psychology.*

Izard, C. E. (1971). *The face of emotion.* New York: Appleton-Century-Crofts.

Izard, C. E. (Ed.) (1972). *Patterns of emotions: A new analysis of anxiety and depression.* New York: Academic Press.

Izard, C. E. (1977). *Human emotions.* New York: Plenum Press.

Izard, C. E. (1979). *The maximally discriminative facial movement coding system (Max).* Newark, Delaware: University of Delaware, Instructional Resources Center.

Izard, C. E. (Ed.) (1982). *Measuring emotions in infants and children.* Cambridge: Cambridge University Press.

Izard, C. E. (1984). Emotion-cognition relationships and human development. In C. Izard, J. Kagan, & R. Zajonc (Eds.) *Emotions, cognition, & behavior* (pp. 17–37). New York: Cambridge University Press.

Izard, C. E., & Dougherty, L. M. (1980). *A system for identifying affect expressions by holistic judgements (Affex).* Newark, Delaware: University of Delaware, Instructional Resources Center.

Izard, C. E., & Malatesta, C. Z. (1985). Emotional development: A theoretical approach. Manuscript submitted for publication.

Izard, C. E., Hembree, E. A., & Huebner, R. R. (1985). *Continuities and changes in two to nineteen months old infants' facial expressions following acute pain.* Manuscript submitted for publication.

Jones, W. H., & Russell, D. (1982). The social reticence scale: An objective instrument to measure shyness. *Journal of Personality Assessment, 46*(6), 629–631.

Kagan, J. (1981). *The second year.* Cambridge: Harvard University Press.

Langsdorf, P., Izard, C., Rayias, M., & Hembree, E. (1983). Interest expression, visual fixation, and heart rate changes in 2- to 8-month-old infants. *Developmental Psychology, 19*,(3), 375–386.

Lewis, H. (1971). *Shame and guilt in neurosis.* New York: International Universities Press.

Lewis, M., & Michalson, L. (1983). *Children's emotions and moods: Developmental theory and measurement.* New York: Plenum Press.

Lynd, H. M. (1958). *On shame and the search for identity.* New York: Harcourt, Brace.

Malatesta, C. Z., & Haviland, J. M. (1982). Learning display rules: The socialization of emotion expressions in infancy. *Child Development, 53*, 991–1003.

Malatesta, C. Z., & Izard, C. E. (1984). The ontogenesis of human social signals: From biological imperative to symbol utilization. In N. Fox & R. J. Davidson (Eds.), *The psychobiology of affective development* (pp. 161–206). Hillsdale, NJ: Erlbaum.

Manstead, A. S. R., & Wagner, H. L. (1981). Arousal, cognition, and emotion: An appraisal of two-factor theory. *Current Psychological Reviews, 1*, 35–54.

Mosher, D. L., & White, B. B. (1981). On differentiating shame and shyness. *Motivation and Emotion, 5*(1), 61–74.

Murphy, L. (1962). *The widening world of childhood: Paths toward mastery.* New York: Basic Books.

Pilkonis, P. A. (1977a). Shyness, public and private, and its relationship to other measures of social behavior. *Journal of Personality, 45*(4), 585–595.

Pilkonis, P. A. (1977b). The behavioral consequences of shyness. *Journal of Personality, 45*(4), 596–611.

Pilkonis, P. A., & Zimbardo, P. G. (1979). The personal and social dynamics of shyness. In C. E. Izard (Ed.), *Emotions in personality and psychopathology* (pp. 133–160). New York: Plenum Press.

Schachter, S., & Singer, J. (1962). Cognitive, social and physiological determinants of emotional state. *Psychological Review, 69*(5), 379–399.

Smith, P. K. (1974). Social and situational determinants of fear in the playgroup. In M. Lewis & L. A. Rosenblum (Eds.), *The origins of fear* (pp. 107–129). New York: Wiley.

Spielberger, C. D., Edwards, C. D., Lushene, R. F., Montuori, J., & Platsek, D. (1973). *STAIC: Preliminary Manual*. Palo Alto, CA: Consulting Psychologists Press.

Sroufe, L. A. (1979). Socioemotional development. In J. D. Osofsky (Ed.) *Handbook of infant development*. New York: Wiley.

Stern, D. N., & Bender, E. P. (1974). An ethological study of children approaching a strange adult: Sex differences. In R. C. Friedman, R. M. Richart, & R. L. VandeWiele (Eds.) *Sex differences in behavior* (pp. 233–258). New York: Wiley.

Thomas, A., & Chess, S. (1977). *Temperament and development*. New York: Brunner/Mazel.

Tomkins, S. S. (1963). *Affect, imagery, consciousness (Vol. 2). The negative affects*. New York: Springer.

Zahn-Waxler, C., Radke-Yarrow, M., & King, R. (1979). Child rearing and children's prosocial initiations towards victims of distress. *Child Development, 50*, 319–330.

Zajonc, R. B. (1980). Feeling and thinking: Preferences need no inferences. *American Psychologist, 35*, 151–175.

Zimbardo, P. G. (1977). *Shyness: What it is, what to do about it*. Reading, MA: Addison-Wesley.

Zimbardo, P. G., Pilkonis, P. A., & Norwood, R. M. (1974). The silent prison of shyness. Office of Naval Research Technical Report No. Z-17. Stanford: CA: Stanford University.

13

On Being 'Shy like a Fox'
A Self-Handicapping Analysis

C. R. Snyder and Timothy W. Smith

INTRODUCTION

Several years ago one of the authors (CRS) was conducting a psychotherapy group with men and women who had a variety of difficulties involving social encounters. They reported feelings of nervousness and apprehensiveness in such social arenas as parties, meeting new people, being interviewed for employment, talking before groups, going on dates, and generally being the focus of attention. It was excruciating for these persons to even think about these situations, and much more so to talk about them. As the participants elaborated their problems, they also noted that they typically felt constrained in social situations and preferred to avoid them if possible. The sessions took on a "misery loves company" tone, in which people opened up and shared their feelings and behaviors related to interpersonal events. In those days (like now), the therapist found much merit in this consensus-raising discussion; it appeared to make people feel better, and perhaps paved the way for a lessening of the experiential social anxiety and associated shy behavior. This scene was shattered one evening, however, when a new group member suggested that some of the people seemed to be using their shyness as an excuse. The normally passive and reserved group members assailed the new person for the utter ridiculousness of this excuse notion. After emotional interchanges in this and subsequent sessions, a new perspective (for the therapist and the group) emerged: for a portion of the group members, the experience of shyness was serving as an excuse for their inability to cope with social situations. This revelation broadened the therapist's conceptualization of shyness to include the possibility that it, like other symptoms, may at times have a strategic, excuse-like component. The present chapter elaborates this view.

C. R. SNYDER • Department of Psychology, University of Kansas, Lawrence, KS 66045. TIMOTHY W. SMITH • Department of Psychology, University of Utah, Salt Lake City, UT 84112.

HISTORY OF THE STRATEGIC SIDE OF SYMPTOMS

To entertain the possibility of a strategic component to shyness, one must abandon a simple and commonplace idea of the shy person as being a totally passive victim of his or her "plight." Interestingly, there are many precedents for considering the strategic role of symptoms in general.

Symptoms as Safeguards and Defenses

Alfred Adler, some 70 years ago, boldly asserted that symptoms served as a purposeful, self-protective strategy. For example, in 1913 (p. 42), Adler wrote,

> The patient declares that he is unable to solve his task "on account of the symptoms, and only on account of these." He expects from others the solution to his problems, and the excuse from all demands, or, at least, the granting of "extenuating circumstances." When he has his extenuating alibi, he feels that his prestige is protected.

Thus, for Adler, symptoms were safeguards that protected the self-esteem from external threats to one's image (see Adler, 1929, 1931, 1936). Although Freud and Adler argued about this conceptualization of symptoms in the early 1900s, it should be noted that Freud eventually came to believe that all symptoms were defenses against instinctual drives. Later, Anna Freud (1948) acknowledged that symptoms were defenses against instinctual forces *and* external threats. Furthermore, the current conceptualization of defenses emphasizes their strategic role in diminishing the anxiety that is associated with external threats to the person. Defensive symptoms, in this vein, have obviously become very similar to Adler's safeguarding mechanisms.

Symptoms as Impression Management

In the 1950s and 1960s, several theorists and researchers began to explicitly suggest that people purposefully control their observable behavior so as to influence the impressions that they are making. This impression management concept represented a common assumption that was applied to normal and psychologically disturbed populations (e.g. Artiss, 1959; Goffman, 1959). Jay Haley (1963) warned psychotherapists to watch for the patient who uses his or her symptoms to lessen responsibility for behavior; moreover, in Eric Berne's widely-publicized book *Games People Play* (1964), the strategic games that were inherent in symptoms were vividly described.

In the latter part of the 1960 decade, two independent investigators provided empirical demonstrations of how psychiatric inpatients may strategically change their symptoms so as to garner personal benefits (e.g. Braginsky, Braginsky, & Ring, 1969; Fontana & Gessner, 1969; Fontana & Klein, 1968; Fontana, Klein, Lewis, & Levine, 1968). Although these empirical studies typically emphasize that the purpose of the symptom presentation is to garner concrete rewards (e.g. to allow the patient to retain the food and shelter of the hospital), we (Snyder & Smith, 1982) have argued elsewhere that there are potential psychological esteem benefits as well. By remaining in the hospital, for example, the patient holds onto a "safe" environment where the patient has some sense of control and competency. When the patient does feel a threat to esteem, he or she may be heard to utter "What do you expect out of me, I'm a chronic schizophrenic" (Fontana, personal communication, 1980). The symptom, in this latter vein, may be used to protect esteem both inside and outside the hospital.

Symptoms as Self-Handicaps

The most recent evolution in conceptual approaches to the strategic role of symptoms has been subsumed under the rubric of *self-handicapping*. This concept was introduced into the literature in 1978 by E. E. Jones and Steven Berglas (Berglas & Jones, 1978; Jones & Berglas, 1978). Self-handicapping is defined as a self-invoked impediment to performance in evaluative settings. In this sense, a self-handicap represents an excuse for a potentially negative personal outcome. Thus, the self-handicap enables the person to control and externalize the causal attribution related to a failure. Consider the following expanded definition:

> Self-handicapping may be understood as a process wherein a person, in response to an anticipated loss of self-esteem resulting from the possibility of inadequate performance in a domain where performance clearly implicates ability or competence, adopts characteristics or behaviors that superficially constitute admission of a problem, weakness, or deficit, but assist the individual in . . . controlling attributions (made by oneself or others) concerning performance so as to discount the self-relevant implications of poor performance . . . or maintaining existing environmental conditions that maximize positive self-relevant feedback and minimize negative self-relevant feedback. (Snyder & Smith, 1982, p. 107)

This self-handicapping concept obviously bears strong resemblances to Adler's safeguarding notion, and the impression management perspective of symptoms. Empirical evidence to date has documented the fact that people do adopt self-handicapping impediments in order to externalize potential failure. For example, self-handicapping has been shown in drug choices (Berglas & Jones, 1978; Kolditz & Arkin, 1982; Weidner, 1980), and alcohol consumption (Higgins & Harris, 1984; Tucker, Vuchinich, & Sobell, 1981) of students who anticipate esteem-threatening events. (These studies illustrate the common excuse of "It was the alcohol or drug that made me do it.") Likewise, persons have been shown to accentuate their history of traumatic life events as a self-handicap in anticipation of an evaluative task (DeGree & Snyder, 1985).

In order to extend the self-handicapping concept to the strategic reporting of symptoms, however, at least three issues are worthy of elaboration at this point. First, in the original conceptualization of self-handicapping, threats to personal esteem were "excused" by suggesting an external cause for the poor performance. With symptoms as a self-handicap, however, an internal source (the symptom) is the attributed cause. Although symptoms may be less stable and less centrally linked to esteem than dimensions such as attractiveness, intelligence, and ability, the "internal" attribution can nevertheless protect esteem (Snyder, Higgins, & Stucky, 1983); moreover, the fact that symptoms suggest a lack of personal control diminishes the responsibility for those symptoms (Averill, 1976; Averill, DeWitt, & Zimmer, 1978). Second, given the probability that symptoms may have developed for reasons not related to self-handicapping, the conceptualization of symptoms as self-handicaps emphasizes the subsequent maintenance and further development of symptoms. Third, symptoms can represent both stable individual differences and situationally elicited self-handicapping. The individual differences in symptomatic behavior are multiply determined, and appear across situations; further, those same symptomatic behaviors may vary as a function of their self-handicapping utility in an esteem-threatening situation. Symptoms thus appear as main effects across situations when considered from an individual differences perspective, but the *strategic* use of these symptoms as self-handicaps should appear as individual difference by situation interactions, that is, certain persons should be especially prone to exhibit their symptoms in certain situations. (This latter point will be illustrated in a subsequent section entitled "Shyness as a Self-Handicap: An Empirical Test.")

Two reported studies in our laboratory support the aforementioned hypothesis that seemingly internal symptoms may be reported in a manner that suggests self-handicapping. In the first study, high test-anxious persons reported more anxiety symptoms when anxiety was a viable explanation for poor performance on an intelligence test than when anxiety was not a viable explanation, and than when persons were in a nonevaluative situation; moreover, low test-anxious persons did not evidence this self-protective pattern of symptom reporting (Smith, Snyder, & Handelsman, 1982). In a conceptually similar study, hypochondriacal persons reported more current physical symptoms and more recent physical illnesses in an evaluative setting where poor health could serve as an alternative explanation for poor performance than in an evaluative setting where poor health was eliminated as an explanation and in a nonevaluative setting; further, the nonhypochondrical persons did now show this self-protective symptom-reporting pattern (Smith, Snyder, & Perkins, 1983). These latter studies are especially important in the present context because they suggest that two types of anxiety-related symptoms (test, and physical health) can be used as self-handicapping strategies. Such results obviously portend a purposeful manipulation of the reported anxiety symptoms by highly anxious persons facing evaluative arenas. It is a short leap to apply this theoretical and empirical analysis to *social* anxiety or shyness, and we turn to this in the next section.

THE SELF-PRESENTATION, SHYNESS, AND SELF-HANDICAPPING LINK

Self-Presentation and Shyness

Self-presentational views of people have captured the attention of recent theoretical and empirical work conducted by both social (see Baumeister, 1982; Schlenker, 1980; Schlenker, 1985, for reviews) and clinical psychologists (see Snyder, Higgins, & Stucky, 1983, for review). Self-presentational models share the assumption that persons are often motivated to create a favorable impression on an audience. When persons wish to present such a favorable image, but question their ability to achieve this outcome, a state of anxiety should result. This anxiety obviously has a social flavor when it is kindled in an interpersonal context. In this state of affairs in which persons simultaneously desire a positive outcome (i.e. to manage a good image) and doubt their ability to achieve it, Schlenker and Leary (1982) and Leary (1983) have suggested that the individual faces an intense self-assessment process in which a state of anxiety results.

Several aspects of this self-presentational model of shyness warrant amplification. The greater the extent to which the person is motivated to create a favorable impression, and the greater is the felt uncertainty that the person can achieve this favorable impression, then the level of shyness should also be commensurately higher (see Leary, 1983, p. 66). Thus, shyness reflects a multiplicative result of two factors; if either factor is not existent, then shyness should not result in this self-presentational model. Returning to the participants in the group therapy described at the beginning of this chapter, it should be noted that they were generally quite concerned with creating a good image of themselves *and* they questioned their ability to accomplish this goal in social encounters. They reported being anxious *and* constrained in social situations. These feelings and behaviors form the essence of *shyness* as employed in this chapter. The definition offered by Leary (1983, p. 23) is applicable here:

> The term "shy" should probably be reserved for the response *syndrome* characterized by both social anxiety and inhibited interpersonal behavior . . . Thus, a shy person is one who is anxious *and* inhibited in a social setting.

When Shyness Becomes Strategic

The previously described self-presentational model of shyness suggests that this state is a natural result of wanting to create a favorable image and doubting one's ability to achieve the positive image. Most anyone may occasionally face social circumstances where it is important to maintain a good image but difficult to do so. In this sense, the reader may imagine situations where he or she would manifest shyness. Further, there is a large percentage of persons who would be prone to exhibit this shyness across a multitude of social situations. So far, none of the shyness that we have described is necessarily strategic. However, consider the person who is frozen in a self-evaluative and uncomfortable state in which he or she is unable to create a favorable image. Feeling apprehensive and inhibited, our shy protagonist in this stressful saga may begin to *use* shyness as an excuse (Schlenker & Leary, 1982; Snyder & Smith, 1982). When a preferred approach for maintaining a positive image is not available, we suggest, people may at times adopt the very label—shyness—for the state that they are experiencing; in turn, this label of shyness may serve to preserve or maintain the person's image.*

---

*In the present analysis of shyness as a self-handicap, it should be emphasized that the shy person may *not* be fully aware of strategically employing the shyness. Indeed, the shyness often may have a self-deceptive aspect in which the person is not totally cognizant of this particular use of the symptom. A more complete discussion of the self-deceptive role of symptoms in general, and shyness in particular, is presented in Snyder (1985) and Snyder, Higgins, and Stucky (1983, pp. 56–68).

The idea that a person may embrace the shyness label may seem non-sensical at first, especially because shyness is considered to be a socially unde-sirable characteristic (Zimbardo, 1977) and people who wish to present a socially desirable impression are less prone to report shyness (Jones & Russell, 1982). Although in an ideal sense people may not want to experience shyness, in reality it is often the only option available to them. In fact, it may be far less pejorative to be labelled shy in comparison to such important labels as unintelligent, unat-tractive, etc. Additionally, given the considerable literature on the strategic use of psychological symptoms, it appears plausible to add shyness to the list of symptoms. Finally, it may be the case that shyness is especially applicable as a self-handicap because of its acknowledged debilitating influence on social per-formance; similarly, shyness is often viewed as a legitimate reason to avoid stressful social encounters.

SHYNESS AS A SELF-HANDICAP: AN EMPIRICAL TEST

Predictions

As described previously, the theory and research on the self-serving func-tion of symptoms leads to the speculation that shyness sometimes serves as a self-handicapping strategy. In a recent experiment in our laboratory (Snyder, Smith, Augelli, & Ingram, 1985), this general hypothesis was tested. It was predicted that socially anxious or shy persons would manifest their symptoms in a strategic fashion in response to a social-evaluative threat. Specifically, it was expected that shy subjects would report more symptoms in an evaluative setting where shyness could serve as an explanation for poor performance than would shy subjects in an evaluative setting where shyness was precluded as an excuse and in a nonevaluative setting (because there is no need for self-handicapping when a threat is not present). Additionally, it was reasoned that individuals who are not shy do not commonly use the symptoms of social anxiety strate-gically. As a result, no strategic pattern in the symptom reports of the nonshy person was expected. Finally, because the manifestations of shyness have been found to vary between genders (Glasgow & Arkowitz, 1975; Pilkonis, 1977), this factor was included in the design, although no specific predictions were made.

Design and Procedure

From an original pool of approximately 1,200 undergraduate students, high and low socially anxious males and females were selected from the top and bottom quintiles of a distribution of scores on the Social Avoidance and Distress Scale (SADS) (Watson & Friend, 1969). Subjects were randomly assigned, in blocks, to one of three experimental conditions: (a) evaluative threat/instruction that shyness has no effect on performance (i.e., the "no self-handicapping con-dition"); (b) evaluative threat/no instructions regarding the effects of shyness (i.e., the "self-handicapping condition"); or (c) a nonevaluative, no instructions control condition. Thus, the design was a 2 (high/low shyness) × 3 (conditions) × 2 (gender) factorial.

Approximately 16 subjects at a time reported for each experimental session. On arriving, they first filled out a state anxiety questionnaire. When this form was completed, the two evaluative conditions were distinguished from the control condition by telling the threat subjects that they were participating in a project to establish local norms for a widely used social intelligence test, the Illinois Social Intelligence Scale (ISIS) and would later receive feedback about their performance. The test was described as having two parts, a written test and a role-play component. The control condition subjects simply were told that they would be asked to fill out some additional forms. No mention was made of either role plays or evaluations of any sort. Subjects then filled out a second state anxiety questionnaire as a check on the threat manipulation. They then worked on an ambiguous paper-and-pencil task for 10 minutes, described as either the first half of the ISIS (evaluative conditions) or the first half of the additional forms (control condition). The task consisted of 20 items. In each item the subject was to guess the attitude of a hypothetical person based on the person's opinion on two related issues. Many of the items were ambiguous, making the task appear quite difficult in the evaluative conditions.

At the end of the first task, the two evaluative conditions were differentiated by additional instructions. Subjects in the "no self-handicapping" condition were told that one of the advantages of the ISIS, as compared to other tests of social intelligence, was that it is not affected by social anxiety. These subjects were further told that as a result, their score on the test was accurate regardless of their level of social anxiety. Finally, subjects were told that in order to document this fact further, they would be asked to fill out some questionnaires about their degree of shyness. In contrast, subjects in the self-handicapping and control conditions were simply asked to complete some additional questionnaires.

All subjects then filled out two measures of social anxiety symptoms. The first was a modified version of the SADS, where the usual true-false item format was changed to a 4-point Likert scale. This modification was intended to allow subjects to report finer degrees of shyness, thereby providing a more sensitive assessment of experimental effects. The second measure was a 6-item version of the Stanford Shyness Scale (SSS) (Zimbardo, personal communication, 1980), which correlated significantly with the SADS in the selection sample, r (1,207) = .70 p < .001. When subjects finished these two measures, they were debriefed, thanked, and excused from the experiment.

Results

In order to check the initial selection of high and low socially anxious subjects, the main effects on the modified SADS and SSS used during the experimental session were inspected. In both cases the expected high versus low social anxiety differences were highly significant. The high versus low socially anxious subjects in the control conditions were also compared separately in an effort to test expected group differences uninfluenced by threat or self-handicapping. Again, the expected differences were highly significant, indicating the successful selection of high versus low shyness groups. To check the effectiveness of the threat manipulation, an analysis of covariance of the state anxiety scores (adjusting for initial levels of state anxiety) contrasting the two evaluative conditions and the control condition was conducted. This expected difference was also highly significant, indicating that the threat manipulation was successful.

A 2 (shyness level) × 3 (conditions) × 2 (gender) ANOVA of the modified SADS scores revealed a significant ($p < .005$) 3-way interaction. Means for this interaction are presented in Table 1. For males alone, individual comparisons showed that there were no differences across experimental conditions for the low socially anxious males, but the high socially anxious males did exhibit the expected self-handicapping effects. That is, high socially anxious males in the evaluative threat/no instructions condition (i.e., the self-handicapping condition) reported more symptoms than did their high anxious counterparts in both the evaluative threat/shyness has no effect condition (i.e., no self-handicapping condition) and the nonevaluative/no instructions control condition.

When examining females separately, however, no significant differences across conditions for either the high or low socially anxious females were evident. It is clear, therefore, that the predicted strategic pattern of symptom reporting on the SADS was not found for socially anxious females.

A 3-way ANOVA of the SSS revealed the predicted 2-way, social anxiety level by conditions interaction ($p < .04$). Individual comparisons revealed the expected results for the high socially anxious subjects; those in the self-handicapping condition reported more shyness than those in the other two conditions.

Although the analysis of the SSS did not produce a significant 3-way interaction corresponding to that found in the case of the modified SADS, SSS scores

TABLE 1. Means for the Modified Social Avoidance and Distress Scale as a Function of Level of Trait Social Anxiety and Experimental Condition

Gender	Social anxiety group	Condition		
		Anxiety has no effect	No instructions	Nonevaluative
Males	High	61.6_b $n = 12$	74.9_a $n = 14$	67.1_b $n = 11$
	Low	46.0_c $n = 10$	41.9_{cd} $n = 12$	42.4_{cd} $n = 13$
Females	High	68.3_b $n = 11$	66.0_b $n = 12$	65.2_b $n = 11$
	Low	38.8_d $n = 14$	41.6_{cd} $n = 13$	37.8_d $n = 9$

Means not sharing a common subscript differ at $p < .05$ (two-tailed t).

were examined separately for each gender to determine if a parallel pattern had been obtained. These means are presented in Table 2. Individual comparisons of the means for high socially anxious females again revealed no evidence of self-handicapping. Comparisons among high socially anxious males, on the other hand, revealed the expected pattern reflecting self-handicapping. Thus, as in the case of the SADS, self-handicapping reflected in SSS scores was limited to shy males.

Interpretation

The pattern of results obtained by Snyder *et al.* (1985) support the hypothesis that, at least for males, symptoms of shyness can serve a self-protective, strategic function. The lack of such use by females, however, raises some interesting possibilities about gender differences in the function of shyness. It is unlikely that this gender differences is due to difference in overall *level* of shyness. With the exception of the condition reflecting self-handicapping, high socially anxious males and females were equally shy as measured by both the modified SADS and the SSS. Rather, the present gender effects may reflect differences in the manifestations of shyness and the ways in which shy males and females navigate social predicaments.

Relevant research (Pilkonis, 1977) reveals that shy males became more avoidant and withdrawn in response to a social-evaluative threat; in contrast, shy females were passively pleasing (i.e., smiling, nodding, etc.). Likewise, Glasgow and Arkowitz (1975) suggested that male low frequency daters (LFD) evidenced low self-evaluation, whereas their female counterparts were characterized by social skill deficits. Additional studies have also shown that shy males display negative self-evaluation (Cacioppo, Glass, & Merluzzi, 1979; Clark & Arkowitz, 1975), and that shy females display skill deficits but not the negative self-evaluation characteristics of their male counterparts (Greenwald, 1977).

TABLE 2. Means for the Stanford Shyness Scale Items as a Function of Level of Trait Social Anxiety and Experimental Condition

Gender	Social anxiety group	Anxiety has no effect	No instructions	Nonevaluative
Males	High	14.4_b $n = 12$	17.4_a $n = 14$	$15.3*_{ab}$ $n = 11$
	Low	11.4_c $n = 10$	10.0_{cd} $n = 12$	9.3_{cd} $n = 13$
Females	High	15.0_b $n = 11$	15.3_b $n = 12$	14.3_b $n = 9$
	Low	9.6_{cd} $n = 14$	8.9_{de} $n = 13$	6.7_e $n = 9$

Means not sharing a common subscript differ at $p < .05$ (two-tailed t).
*For high anxious males, the no instructions and nonevaluative conditions differ at $p < .08$ (two-tailed t).

These gender differences in the causes and correlates of shyness may account for the differential use of shyness as a self-handicapping strategy by males and females. Recall that the threat of negative self-evaluation is a precursor to the self-handicapping process. Shy males may be swift to evaluate social situations as potentially providing negative feedback. They may, as a result, respond with self-handicapping when their usual responses of withdrawal and avoidance (Pilknonis, 1977) are blocked (Schlenker & Leary, 1982). By comparison, shy females tend to respond to such situations with passive accommodation (Pilkonis, 1977). Schlenker and Leary (1982, proposition 6) have identified this response as one way of coping when the self-presentation goals of the shy person are threatened. This type of response by females also may be reinforced by prevailing norms assigning the major responsibility for active roles in social interaction to males (Berscheid & Walster, 1969).

It is unlikely that self-handicapping in general is limited to males, however, because two previous studies in our laboratory have demonstrated robust self-handicapping effects in the symptom reporting of test-anxious (Smith et al., 1982) and hypochondriacal (Smith, Snyder, & Perkins, 1983) females. Rather, the type of evaluative threat and the nature of available handicaps are likely to influence the degree of self-handicapping shown by male versus female subjects (Snyder & Smith, 1982). That is, sex roles may be related to the perception of threat, the selection of handicaps, and the individual difference dimensions associated with the tendency to employ self-handicapping. Though plausible, this account of the observed gender differences in the strategic use of shyness requires an experimental test before firm conclusions can be drawn. Nonetheless, beyond the issue of gender differences, the results of the Snyder et al. (1985) study extend previous research findings concerning both social anxiety and symptoms as self-handicapping strategies by demonstrating the strategic use of shyness.

SHYNESS: AUTHENTIC, BUT SOMETIMES AUGMENTED

The Authentic Base

The empirical findings and discussion just presented should not be taken to imply that shyness is "nothing but" a strategic ploy. Indeed, the contents of the rest of this volume represent a compelling demonstration of the multitude of factors contributing to the cause and maintenance of social anxiety. Shyness has clear genetic (Plomin & Daniels, this volume), developmental (Cheek, Carpentieri, Smith, Rierdan, & Koff, this volume; Kagan & Reznick, this volume), cognitive (Carver & Scheier, this volume; Smith, Ingram, & Brehm, 1983), and social components (Arkin & Lake, this volume; Jones & Carpenter, this volume). The results of the Snyder et al. (1985) study provide indirect evidence of the relative contribution of self-handicapping to shyness levels. The self-handicapping effects were comparatively small, situation-specific variations in symptom reports (i.e., shyness by conditions interactions). Larger, cross-situational effects were observed between high and low shy groups (i.e., shyness level main effects). Thus, there is no doubt that there are several authentic factors beyond self-handicapping that contribute to shyness.

The Augmentation

Given the overdetermined nature of shyness, the strategic component is evident nonetheless. The shy individual is sometimes more than the passive victim of this menu of contributions to the problem. Indeed, the shy person's problem may be more than just a problem. The present analysis would suggest that shyness can be a problem that also, in part, is a solution. It reflects, but also provides a partial answer to, awkward social predicaments. Thus, it is tempting to revise the old saying, "Sly like a fox," to "Shy like a fox." This revision would capture one more facet of the nature of shyness.

REFERENCES

Adler, A. (1913). Individual Psychologische Behandlung der Neurosen. In D. Sarason (Ed.), *Jahres-kures für ärztliche Fortbildung*. Munich: Lehmann, 1913.

Adler, A. (1929). *Problems of neuroses: A book of case-histories*. London: Kegan Paul, Trench, Truebner.

Adler, A. (1931). *What life should mean to you*. Boston: Little, Brown.

Adler, A. (1936). The neurotic's picture of the world. *International Journal of Individual Psychology, 2*, 3–13.

Artiss, K. (1959). *The symptom as communication in schizophrenia*. New York: Grune & Stratton.

Averill, J. R. (1976). Emotion and anxiety: Sociocultural, biological, and psychological determinants. In M. Zuckerman & C. D. Spielberger (Eds.), *Emotion and anxiety: New concepts, methods and applications* (pp. 87–130). New York: Erlbaum-Wiley.

Averill, J. R., DeWitt, G. W., & Zimmer, M. (1978). The self-attribution of emotion as a function of success and failure. *Journal of Personality, 46*, 323–347.

Baumeister, R. F. (1982). A self-presentational view of social phenomena. *Psychological Bulletin, 91*, 3–26.

Berglas, S., & Jones, E. E. (1978). Drug choice as a self-handicapping strategy in response to non-contingent success. *Journal of Personality and Social Psychology, 36*, 405–417.

Berne, E. (1964). *Games people play*. New York: Grove Press.

Berscheid, E., & Walster, E. H. (1969). *Interpersonal attraction*. Reading, MA: Addison-Wesley.

Braginsky, B., Braginsky, D., & Ring, K. (1969). *Methods of madness: The mental hospital as a last resort*. New York: Holt, Rinehart, & Winston.

Cacioppo, J. T., Glass, C. R., & Merluzzi, T. V. (1979). Self-statements and self-evaluation: A cognitive response analysis of heterosocial anxiety. *Cognitive Therapy and Research, 3*, 249–262.

Clark, J.V., & Arkowitz, H. (1975). Social anxiety and self-evaluation of interpersonal performance. *Psychological Reports, 36*, 211–221.

DeGree, C. E., & Snyder, C. R. (1985). Adler's psychology (of use) today: Personal history of traumatic life events as a self-handicapping strategy. *Journal of Personality and Social Psychology, 48*, 1512–1519.

Fontana, A. F., & Gessner, T. (1969). Patients' goals and the manifestation of psychopathology. *Journal of Consulting and Clinical Psychology, 33*, 247–253.

Fontana, A. F., & Klein, E. B. (1968). Self-presentation and the schizophrenic "deficit." *Journal of Consulting and Clinical Psychology, 32*, 250–256.

Fontana, A. F., Klein, E. B., Lewis, E., & Levine, L. (1968). Presentation of self in mental illness. *Journal of Consulting and Clinical Psychology, 32*, 110–119.

Freud, A. (1948). *The ego and the mechanisms of defense*. London: Hogarth Press.

Glasgow, R., & Arkowitz, H. (1975). The behavioral assessment of male and female social competence in dyadic heterosexual interactions. *Behavior Therapy, 6,* 488–498.

Goffman, E. (1959). *The presentation of self in everyday life.* New York: Doubleday.

Greenwald, D. P. (1977). The behavioral assessment of differences in social anxiety in female college students. *Behavior Therapy, 8,* 925–937.

Haley, J. (1963). *Strategies of psychotherapy.* New York: Grune & Stratton.

Higgins, R. L., & Harris, R. N. (1984).*Strategic alcohol consumption: Drinking to maintain a positive image.* Unpublished manuscript, University of Kansas.

Jones, E. E., & Berglas, S. (1978). Control of attributions about the self through self-handicapping strategies: The appeal of alcohol and the role of underachievement. *Personality and Social Psychology Bulletin, 4,* 200–206.

Jones, W. H., & Russell, D. (1982). The social reticence scale: An objective instrument to measure shyness. *Journal of Personality Assessment, 46,* 629–631.

Kolditz, T. A., & Arkin, R. M. (1982). An impression management interpretation of self-handicapping. *Journal of Personality and Social Psychology, 43,* 492–502.

Leary, M. R. (1983). *Understanding social anxiety: Social, personality, and clinical perspectives.* Beverly Hills, CA: Sage.

Pilkonis, P. A. (1977). The behavioral consequences of shyness. *Journal of Personality, 45,* 596–611.

Schlenker, B. R. (1980). *Impression management: The self-concept, social identity, and interpersonal relations.* Monterey, CA: Brooks/Cole.

Schlenker, B. R. (Ed.) (1985). *Self and identity: Presentations of self in social life.* New York: McGraw-Hill.

Schlenker, B. R., & Leary, M. R. (1982). Social anxiety and self-presentation: A conceptualization and model. *Psychological Bulletin, 92,* 641–669.

Smith, T. W., Snyder, C. R., & Handelsman, M. W. (1982). On the self-serving function of an academic wooden leg: Test anxiety as a self-handicapping strategy. *Journal of Personality and Social Psychology, 42,* 314–321.

Smith, T. W., Ingram, R. E., & Brehm, S. S. (1983). Social anxiety, anxious self-preoccupation, and recall of self-relevant information. *Journal of Personality and Social Psychology, 44,* 1276–1283.

Smith, T. W., Snyder, C. R., & Perkins, S. (1983). The self-serving function of hypochondriacal complaints: Physical symptoms as self-handicapping strategies. *Journal of Personality and Social Psychology, 44,* 787–797.

Snyder, C. R. (1985). Collaborative companions: The relationship of self-deception and excuse-making. In M. W. Martin (Ed.), *Self-deception and self-understanding: Essays in philosophy and psychology,* (pp. 35–51). Lawrence, KS: University Press of Kansas.

Snyder, C. R., & Smith, T. W. (1982). Symptoms as self-handicapping strategies: On the virtues of old wine in a new bottle. In G. Weary and H. L. Mirels (Eds.), *Integration of clinical and social psychology* (pp. 104–127). New York: Oxford University Press.

Snyder, C. R., Higgins, R. L., & Stucky, R. J. (1983). *Excuses: Masquerades in search of grace.* New York: Wiley-Interscience.

Snyder, C. R., Smith, T. W., Augelli, R., & Ingram, R. E. (1985). On the self-serving function of social anxiety: Shyness as a self-handicapping strategy. *Journal of Personality and Social Psychology, 48,* 970–980.

Tucker, J. A., Vuchinich, R. E., & Sobell, M. B. (1981). Alcohol consumption as a self handicapping strategy. *Journal of Abnormal Psychology, 90,* 220–230.

Watson, D., & Friend, R. (1969). Measurement of social-evaluative anxiety. *Journal of Consulting and Clinical Psychology, 43,* 448–457.

Weidner, G. (1980). Self-handicapping following learned helplessness and Type A coronary-prone behavior pattern. *Journal of Psychosomatic Research, 24,* 319–325.

Zimbardo, P. G. (1977). Shyness: *What it is and what to do about it.* Reading, MA: Addison-Wesley.

14

Analyzing Shyness

A Specific Application of Broader Self-Regulatory Principles

Charles S. Carver and Michael F. Scheier

We have been interested in processes by which people carry out their intentions successfully, and processes by which those efforts are disrupted. Unlike most theorists represented in this volume, we do not focus specifically on shyness as the primary object of our analysis. Our viewpoint is broader, an attempt to point out principles common to many different circumstances in behavioral self-regulation, principles that may account for patterns of successful and disrupted functioning across a wide range of domains.

As it happens, one domain we have studied in some detail is responses to anxiety and frustration. More specifically, we have examined certain influences on people's attempts to cope with such experiences. We believe that a careful examination of these influences allows us to say something important about the nature of shyness and social anxiety. Indeed, we suggest that the general approach taken here is a useful integrating framework for analyzing the situational antecedents, phenomenology, behavioral consequences, and treatment of shyness and social anxiety. Attempting to make this case is the purpose of this chapter.

PRINCIPLES OF SELF-REGULATION

We have come to assume that human behavior is guided by the operation of feedback systems within the person. These systems incorporate the same functional elements as are found in control systems such as thermostats, guided

CHARLES S. CARVER • Department of Psychology, University of Miami, Coral Gables, FL 33124. MICHAEL F. SCHEIER • Department of Psychology, Carnegie-Mellon University, Pittsburgh, PA 15213. Portions of the research described in this chapter, and preparation of the chapter itself, were facilitated by grants BNS 81–07236, BNS 84–14601, BNS 84–06235, and BNS 80–21859 from the National Science Foundation.

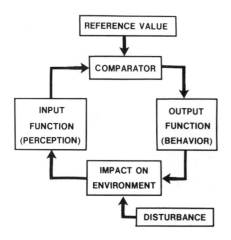

FIGURE 1. Outline of a discrepancy reducing feed-back loop, the basic unit of cybernetic control.

missiles, and computers (see also MacKay, 1966; Powers, 1973; Wiener, 1948). The component functions implicit in this view include the following. People sense or examine their present actions, qualities, or states, a function that is labelled in Figure 1 as "input function." These perceptions are then compared against salient reference values or standards. This function takes place at the point in Figure 1 marked "comparator." If the two values are discrepant, the person attempts to bring the one into line with the other by making a change—changing what one is doing, or attempting to change the personal qualities that one is manifesting. This attempt to change is represented in Figure 1 by what is labelled "output function."

This approach assumes a continuous (or repeated) self-reflective monitoring of the effects of one's actions, assessing how closely the perceived outcomes of the actions match the reference values to which they are intended to conform. The function of a feedback system—taken as a whole—is to minimize any sensed discrepancies between these two values.

Our emphasis has been upon the general notion that human self-regulation displays the characteristics of feedback control, but another aspect of what we just said is also important. Comparator (Figure 1) is a generic name for a component processor whose function it is to make comparisons. In talking about behavior, this function is what occurs when people self-reflectively check on the correspondence between what they are doing and what they are trying to do.

The modifier "self-reflectively" is particularly important here. We have suggested (e.g., Carver & Scheier, 1981, 1982a, 1983) an equivalence between this component function and what often occurs when attention is focused inward to the self when some standard has been made salient for behavior.* As one reflects on oneself, the standard and one's present actions become subjectively

---

*Self-directed attention can have other effects in other circumstances. For example, self-focus tends to make people more aware of existing internal states such as emotions (Carver, Blaney, & Scheier, 1979a; Scheier & Carver, 1977), and can similarly render people less susceptible to external suggestions concerning those internal states (Gibbons, Carver, Scheier, & Hormuth, 1979; Scheier, Carver, & Gibbons, 1979). Further consideration of such effects is beyond the scope of this chapter, however.

more salient. At this point, we believe, the comparator function of a feedback system is becoming engaged. Comparisons are made, and behavior is altered so as to more closely approximate the standard. In this fashion, we believe, self-awareness serves as an important mediator of consciously controlled behavior.

Self-Focus and the Comparator Function

Two lines of evidence support these assertions. One bears on the component function engaged in at the comparator: the comparison between present state and reference value. Recent research indicates that high levels of self-focus lead directly to such a function (Scheier & Carver, 1983a). More specifically, self-focus promotes efforts to seek out concrete information that would allow one to make a mental comparison at a more abstract level between actual performance and situationally salient performance standards.

As an illustration, test norms provide information that allows people to assess the adequacy of their performance on the test (cf. Trope, 1975). Seeking out norms thus may be seen as an attempt to engage in a comparison between one's own test behavior and some meaningful reference value. Persons who are highly self-attentive seek out such normative information more than do less self-attentive persons (Scheier & Carver, 1983a). These findings thus appear to indicate that self-directed attention (in this sort of situation) promotes a function very much like that of the comparator in Figure 1.

The second line of evidence bears on the overall function of the feedback system as a whole—that is, reducing discrepancies. There is a large accumulation of research demonstrating that self-attention does promote closer behavioral correspondence to salient reference values. These effects have been demonstrated in diverse behavioral contexts, ranging from copying a prose passage (Wicklund & Duval, 1971), to the use of the equity norm in resource allocation (Greenberg, 1980). In each of these cases—and in many more—self-focused attention enhanced conformity to whatever had been made salient as a behavioral standard in that situation.

At this point let us say a word about how self-attention is varied in this research. In some cases people are made more aware of themselves at given points in the experimental session by confronting such devices as mirrors or TV cameras. In other cases chronic differences in the tendency to be aware of oneself are measured (Fenigstein, Scheier, & Buss, 1975; Scheier & Carver, in press). Both techniques—experimental manipulation and personality disposition—have been subjected to a good deal of validity testing, with both standing up quite well in that regard (see Carver & Scheier, 1981, Chapter 3, for detailed discussion).

We should note, in this context, a distinction commonly made between private self-aspects and public or social self-aspects (Fenigstein et al., 1975; Scheier & Carver, 1983b). We suggest, along with others (e.g., Schlenker & Leary, 1982), that the public self is the more directly related of the two to an analysis of phenomena such as shyness and social anxiety. This is, if these phenomena concern self-presentational or social goals—as we believe they do—then it is monitoring of the social side of the self that may be most important to understanding behaviors relevant to those goals.

THEORETICAL ELABORATIONS

Focusing one's attention on the self, briefly or for longer periods, once or perhaps repeatedly, appears to promote conformity to salient reference values. But we must make two additional qualifications or elaborations on this statement. One of them produces complexities that are somewhat peripheral to the focus of this chapter, though not entirely unrelated to it. The other is critically important for an adequate examination of shyness.

Hierarchical Organization

We we talk about monitoring action, we really mean that people monitor some *quality* of their action. How is the whole behavior done correctly on the basis of such a circumscribed kind of check? We have tentatively adopted the line of reasoning suggested by Powers (1973) in this regard, who has pointed out that feedback systems can be organized hierarchically. Recall the single loop from Figure 1. Powers holds that the reference value of a low-level feedback loop is provided as the behavioral output of an overriding or superordinate loop (see Figure 2). Various systems then monitor input at the level of abstraction appropriate to their own functioning.

This kind of organization can be multileveled. It can be used to account for self-regulation from what might be thought of as the superordinate reference value of one's idealized self, on downward through concrete action strategies, on downward to the level of muscle tensions. If self-regulation is active at the very highest level of control—if, for example, something has caused you to wonder whether you are currently living up to your idealized self-image—behavior is simultaneously regulated on downward through the hierarchy (relatively automatically, at lower levels) in the effort to ensure discrepancy reduction at that highest level (see Carver & Scheier, 1981, for greater detail). Figure 2 portrays (in part) a momentary slice of the behavior of a person who is involved in such an attempt to minimize discrepancies concerning a self-image.

Our description here is necessarily abbreviated, and we have omitted discussion of many important issues. For example, attention often is directed to levels far lower than the superordinate ideal self that is shown at the top of this figure. When this occurs, self-regulation utilizes only reference values at that level and lower. For more detail concerning the broader implications of such hierarchial models, see more complete discussions elsewhere (Carver & Scheier, 1982a, 1983).

Interruption and Disengagement

Thus far we have a basis for thinking about successful, effective behavior, but we have not yet brought up the fact that people sometimes have trouble attaining the goals they have undertaken. Sometimes actions do not reduce the discrepancies to which they are directed. Any analysis of behavior needs a way to talk about how people respond to blockages or failures.

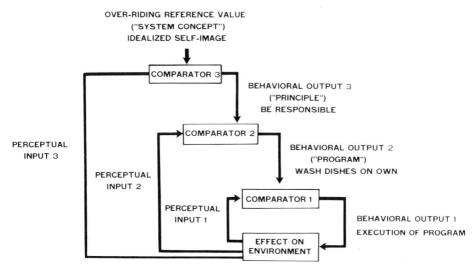

FIGURE 2. A three-level hierarchy of feedback systems, in which the output of a superordinate level consists of the setting of reference values at the next lower level. The levels illustrated here are those at the top of the hierarchy postulated by Powers (1973). This illustration captures an instant in the behavior of a young man who is actively attempting to match his present self to his idealized self, by following the principle of responsibility, which is presently being realized in terms of the programmatic activity of washing the dishes unbidden (see Carver & Scheier, 1981a, or Powers, 1973, for greater detail concerning this hierarchical organizational principle.)

We assume that self-regulatory efforts mediated by self-focus generally proceed uninterrupted until and unless cues begin to appear that difficulties are in the way, that discrepancy reduction is not taking place despite these efforts. But if anxiety wells up, or frustration is encountered in the course of one's efforts, the person may stop for a moment—interrupt the attempt—and consider, if only for a moment, how likely the desired outcome is to occur (cf. Simon, 1967). This assessment presumably makes use of information concerning the present situation, one's preceding actions, and the relative effectiveness with which those actions have moved one toward the goal that is focal in one's phenomenological field.

We view expectancy assessment as producing a sort of psychological watershed, leading to one of two categories of behavioral response (see Figure 3). If expectancies are sufficiently favorable, efforts are renewed. If expectancies are sufficiently unfavorable (having thereby passed the watershed point), there is a tendency to disengage from further efforts (cf. Klinger, 1975; Kukla, 1972). Serious doubts produce abandonment of the goal altogether. The subjective probability at which efforts give way to disengagement presumably varies with the subjective importance of the behavioral dimension. Regardless of where the watershed occurs, we believe that both renewed efforts and disengagement are exaggerated by subsequent self-focus.

The disengagement function often is adaptive (Janoff-Bulman & Brickman, 1982) in allowing people quite sensibly either to defer or to abandon goals because of impediments making goal attainment impossible. There are times, however,

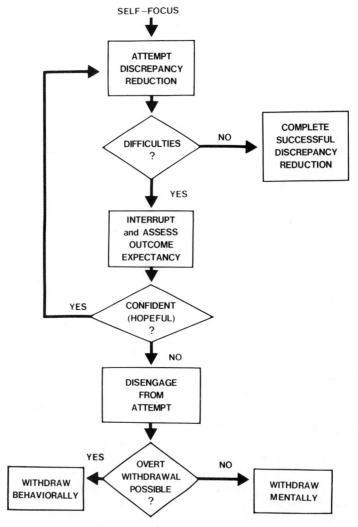

FIGURE 3. Postulated sequence following from self-directed attention when a behavioral reference value is salient, including the possibilities of interruption (leading to expectancy assessment) and disengagement (if expectancies are sufficiently unfavorable), which may be either overt or covert (adapted from Carver et al., 1979a).

when it is less adaptive—times when it leads to ineffective coping with the ordinary difficulties of life. We believe that shyness is a manifestation of this disengagement function in which there is ineffective coping.

Evidence supportive of the watershed aspect of this model comes from a fairly wide range of sources (e.g., Carver, Blaney, & Scheier, 1979a, 1979b; Carver & Scheier, 1982b). Perhaps the clearest experimental test was a study in which we looked at how task-directed efforts were influenced by self-focus and expectancies concerning discrepancy reduction (Carver et al., 1979b). Large discrepancies on the behavioral dimension were created among all subjects by causing them to fail on an initial task. An experimental manipulation was then introduced in which we varied expectations of being able to reduce this discrepancy by doing well at a second, ostensibly closely related task.

The second task was actually a measure of persistence or continued efforts in the face of frustration. The result, as expected, was an interaction between the experimentally manipulated expectancies and experimentally manipulated self-focus. High levels of self-attention caused an *increase* in the persistence of the hopeful subjects. And high self-attention caused a *decrease* in the persistence of the doubtful subjects. Very recent research (Carver, Antoni, & Scheier, 1985) even extends this interactive principle to the seeking of information concerning one's present state.

Disengagement: Additional Issues

It is the disengagement portion of this model that is of the greatest interest here. In order to make our position quite clear, we should specify several additional assumptions that we make in thinking about disengagement. These assumptions stem from the fact that it is not always easy for people to withdraw from discrepancy-reduction attempts. There are many circumstances in which one would *like* to withdraw physically from the attempt to match behavior to a reference value, but the social context does not sanction it (or in some cases the physical setting does not permit it). We assume that under these conditions the disengagement impulse is likely to be expressed psychologically or mentally, rather than overtly (see Figure 3).

In the kinds of situations receiving the greatest research attention thus far, mental disengagement has meant disengagement of effort or attention from an experimental task (usually an achievement task). This, in turn, is operationalized via some index of off-task thinking (Diener & Dweck, 1978), or a litle more indirectly as a decrement in task performance.

Mental disengagement is sometimes a very useful strategy for people, but the strategy can not always be carried out completely, or for long periods of time. It is important to consider more fully what happens when people experience this impulse to disengage and cannot give it full expression. Recall that we see the impetus to disengage as stemming from doubts about being able to reduce discrepancies between salient goals and one's present behavior. Unfortunately, the standards or goals in question are sometimes important, even central to one's life. It is possible to refuse to attend to those values—to disengage from them in one's thoughts as well as one's efforts. But the freedom to do so is not absolute. Without a rather drastic reorganization of one's value system (or of the pattern of one's life activities), it is impossible to avoid for very long a reconfronting of psychological dimensions that are important. If difficulties in discrepancy reduction recur, one thereupon reconfronts the doubts that prompted the disengagement impulse in the first place.

Here we reencounter the notion of hierarchical organization, and the potential importance and usefulness of that notion. Given a hierarchical structure of values, a failure to reduce discrepancies at a low level often has serious implications regarding discrepancy reduction at a higher level. Indeed, a disengagement from efforts at the lower level may be seen as creating discrepancy *enlargement* at that higher level. The logic of hierarchical organization thus suggests that programmatic activities acquire their importance in large part via this relation to higher order goals.

Add to this picture one final assumption, alluded to earlier but not made explicit: that the process yielding the watershed among behavioral responses also results in the experience of affect. Favorable expectancies (even if discrepancy reduction in the action loop has a very long way to go) give rise to positive affect—confidence, hope, sometimes even elation (cf. Stotland, 1969). Unfavorable expectancies give rise to negative affect—doubt, or when more extreme, depression or despair. In cases where expectancy assessment was prompted initially by negative affect (i.e., by rising anxiety), the anguish is simply multiplied by salient doubts about being able to cope.

SHYNESS

How does this general model apply to the specific experiences labelled shyness or social anxiety? Consider for a moment the breadth and variety of goals and standards that guide human behavior. It may be most intuitive to think of the existence of standards in terms of instrumental tasks or activities, but this obviously is not the only class of activities to which the concept applies. More specifically, a great deal of human behavior is prompted by the desire to create and maintain particular kinds of self-presentations (see, e.g., Schlenker, 1985). This is a motive that is widely accepted as a fundamental part of our nature as social beings. Creating appropriate impressions of ourselves in the minds of others leads to social acceptance, contributing to a broader sense of personal adequacy. The attempt to create desired impressions cannot occur in an informational vacuum, however. It is guided by reference values. In this respect self-presentational goals are no different in principle from any other kind of goals.

Expectancies Concerning Self-Presentation

What, then, of shyness? Shyness would seem to represent a case in which people have serious doubts about being able to create and maintain desired self-presentations (see, e.g., Schlenker & Leary, 1982; Smith & Sarason, 1975). These doubts may be specific to self-presentations of one particular type, or impressions to be created in one particular class of situations (e.g., public speaking), or they may be more general. We believe that these doubts are fundamental and critical to the experiences called shyness or social anxiety. The doubts are critical because of the predictable set of consequences that we see as following from them. Given this assumption about the existence of such doubts, our assertions about shyness directly parallel the more general arguments outlined in the preceding section.

We assume that many social interactions are stressful and difficult for most people. Speaking one's mind in front of a group of strangers, meeting people for the first time, knowing that one must make a favorable impression on someone in a job interview—these are all circumstances that typically generate nervousness, not just for "shy" people but for *most* people. Different people respond to this nervousness, however, in different ways. Our approach to self-regulation holds that people respond to rising tension by interrupting their task efforts, and momentarily considering their chances of attaining the desired goals—in this case, self-presentational goals. People who are not shy presumably have relatively favorable expectancies of being successful in their self-presentations. Thus they respond to such interruptions by returning to the self-presentation attempt (cf. Figure 3).

People who doubt their abilities to create successful self-presentations, on the other hand, are more likely to respond in other ways to these momentary interruptions of their efforts. Unfavorable outcome expectancies lead to an impulse to disengage from the attempt to match the salient standard. This disengagement impulse usually cannot be expressed overtly if the person is in the midst of social interaction. Thus its expression is usually less direct—a mental disengagement or dissociation from the ongoing events.

The setting of social interaction is usually such that even these limited disengagements cannot be sustained for too long. The person eventually reconfronts the self-presentational goal. Commonly enough, this is followed by another interruption and expectancy assessment. This, in turn, reminds the person once again of the doubts that prompted the disengagement impulse in the first place, evoking the impulse once again. If the interaction setting has important implications for the person's broader self-worth, even the impulse to disengage is itself painful, because it enlarges a discrepancy with respect to that higher order standard. The final consequence of such a cycle is a phenomenology of negatively toned self-related cognition, a wholly aversive experience that the person may feel helpless to escape.*

This description is consistent with the observation that socially anxious persons often display verbal, paraverbal, and nonverbal signs of discomfort while engaged in social interaction (e.g., Carducci & Weber, 1979; Conville, 1974; Daly, 1978; Mandel & Shrauger, 1980). And it fits with the idea that such persons anticipate lack of acceptance by others, to the point where they may misread others' responses to them as more negative than they really are (cf. Curran, Wallander, & Fischetti, 1980; Smith & Sarason, 1975).

Our analysis focuses on processes that occur in the midst of social interaction. But similar processes implicitly can occur when the person anticipates social interaction. Anticipation may occasion thoughts of self-doubt (Cacioppo, Glass, & Merluzzi, 1979), and the consequences of this self-doubt may unfold

*Perceptive readers will note a distinct similarity between this portrayal and descriptions of the phenomenology of test anxiety (e.g., Wine, 1982). We have, in fact, analyzed the processes of test anxiety elsewhere in terms of precisely the same general theoretical statement (see Carver & Scheier, 1984; Carver, Peterson, Follansbee, & Scheier, 1983).

even before the interaction takes place. In the extreme case, a person who anticipates poor outcomes may simply avoid any situations in which those poor outcomes are anticipated. Theoretically, such behavior would reflect a disengagement of goal-directed effort at an extremely early stage in the behavioral sequence. Interestingly enough, avoidance of social encounters is often taken as the very defining characteristic of shyness.

Shyness, Expectancies, and Self-Focus

This model of the dynamics of social anxiety has been supported in at least two studies. The prediction in each case was that behavior would diverge as a function of subjects' expectations of being able to create desired impressions in a social interaction. Subjects with positive expectancies were predicted to behave more adaptively than subjects with negative expectancies, who should act in ways that seem to reflect avoidance or disengagement. In line with the broader theoretical statement presented earlier in the chapter, it was also predicted that this divergence of behavioral responses would be greatest among persons whose attention was highly self-directed.

One of these studies focused on the quality of self-presentations made by men to women (Burgio, Merluzzi, & Pryor, in press). Subjects were chosen as moderately high in social anxiety, but as differing from each other in their expectancies. Some expressed confidence about being able to create a good impression in a brief telephone interaction, others reported doubts about being able to do so. Each subject later phoned an undergraduate (who was expecting the call) to get acquainted. They were to talk for 4–5 minutes, just as they ordinarily would interact with someone they were getting to know. Half the subjects did this while in front of a TV camera (high self-focus). For the rest there was no camera present (low self-focus).

The woman was actually a confederate, instructed to be moderately positive to all the subjects, and to try to form an impression of how friendly, responsive, and socially skilled they were. The results were very much in line with the analysis developed throughout this chapter. As predicted, self-focus interacted with expectancy level in determining the confederate's impressions of the subjects. Subjects with favorable expectancies were seen as friendlier and more skilled than were subjects with less favorable expectancies—but only if they had been highly self-focused while making the phone call. Subjects who were less self-focused were seen as intermediate on these indices, regardless of their confidence level.

A more recent study has examined what goes through people's minds while anticipating a similar kind of interaction. Subjects in this research (Scheier et al., 1985) were either relatively high or relatively low in social anxiety. Thus, they presumably differed from each other in their level of confidence about being able to make a desired impression. Independent of level of social anxiety, some subjects were dispositionally high in the tendency to focus on their social self-aspects, others were lower in this disposition.

Upon arriving at the laboratory, subjects were told that they would have a discussion with an opposite-sexed peer for several minutes, to form first impressions. Both before and after this discussion, they would be completing questionnaires. The experimenter then left the subject alone (on a ruse), and returned with the ostensible prediscussion questionnaire. This was actually a thought-listing measure (taken from previous research by Cacioppo *et al.*, 1979), used to assess "contents of consciousness" during a given interval. Subjects were told to write down everything that had come into their minds after being left by the experimenter. These records were scored in a variety of ways, including an assessment of the frequency of positive and negative self-related thoughts.

As predicted, and consistent with the Burgio *et al.* data, self-attention interacted with expectancy level as predictors of self-reported contents of consciousness. Subjects low in social anxiety reported fewer negative self-related thoughts and more positive self-related thoughts than did subjects high in social anxiety. But these differences were reliable only among those who were relatively high in the disposition to be self-focused.

Taken together, the results of these two studies provide important preliminary support for the line of reasoning advanced earlier in the chapter. The Scheier *et al.* study suggests that the anticipation of a social encounter causes people to examine their expectations of being able to create good impressions, leading to a phenomenology of self-derogation among doubtful subjects, but something more like self-exhortation among confident subjects. The Burgio *et al.* study suggests that these differences in expectancy have important implications for people's actual acts of self-presentation.

Obviously, more work must be done before this analysis can be regarded as definitive. Nevertheless, these initial results are quite encouraging. Also encouraging is the high degree of conceptual similarity between the findings of these studies and results of previous research in other behavioral domains. Whether the studies focused on responses to anxiety (Carver *et al.*, 1979a) or responses to frustration (Carver *et al.*, 1979b) the data typically form an interactive pattern similar to those described above. This has also been true whether expectancy differences have been operationalized in terms of experimental manipulations or in terms of individual differences of various types. This convergence suggests that the concepts under discussion have considerable breadth of applicability.

CLOSING COMMENT

Our focus in the preceding section was on the dynamics of the moment-to-moment experience of shyness or social anxiety. We should note briefly that our approach also has implications for how such problems are to be alleviated. In general, our suggestions would appear to be consistent with the kinds of strategies that are discussed in Part VI of this volume.

More specifically, our analysis of the structure of self-regulation suggests two points at which problems are created. The first is the existence of doubts about being able to create adequate self-portrayals. One very straightforward way to approach the problem of shyness thus would be to provide opportunities for the person to engage in activities that would serve to raise those expectations. In some cases this may require the acquisition of needed social skills. In other cases, it may mean fostering the discovery that present expectations are unrealistic. In either case, an improvement in expectancies should lead to a greater likelihood of sustained efforts.

A second way of circumventing the difficulties associated with shyness or social anxiety is to try to stifle the tendency to interrupt behavior in order to assess expectancies. If the person avoids engaging in this process, any doubts that exist will be less salient, and will intrude less on self-regulation. In simple terms, it may be important to attend less to the assessment of how things are going, or whether bad outcomes are going to result, and attend more to the concrete aspects of acting.

REFERENCES

Burgio, K. L., Merluzzi, T. V., & Pryor, J. B. (in press). The effects of performance expectancy and self-focused attention on social interaction. *Journal of Personality and Social Psychology*.

Cacioppo, J. T., Glass, C. R., & Merluzzi, T. V. (1979). Self-statements and self-evaluations: A cognitive-response analysis of heterosocial anxiety. *Cognitive Therapy and Research, 3,* 249–263.

Carducci, B. J., & Webber, A. W. (1979). Shyness as a determinant of interpersonal distance. *Psychological Reports, 44,* 1075–1078.

Carver, C. S., & Scheier, M. F. (1981). *Attention and self-regulation: A control-theory approach to human behavior*. New York: Springer-Verlag.

Carver, C. S., & Scheier, M. F. (1982a). Control theory: A useful conceptual framework for personality-social, clinical, and health psychology. *Psychological Bulletin, 92,* 111–135.

Carver, C. S., & Scheier, M. F. (1982b). Outcome expectancy, locus of attribution for expectancy, and self-directed attention as determinants of evaluations and performance. *Journal of Experimental Social Psychology, 18,* 184–200.

Carver, C. S., & Scheier, M. F. (1983). A control-theory model of normal behavior, and implications for problems in self-management. In P. C. Kendall (Ed.), *Advances in cognitive-behavioral research and therapy* (Vol. 2, pp. 127–194). New York: Academic Press.

Carver, C. S., & Scheier, M. F. (1984). Self-focused attention in test anxiety: A general theory applied to a specific phenomenon. In H. van der Ploeg, R. Schwarzer, & C. D. Spielberger (Eds.), *Advances in test anxiety research* (Vol. 3, pp. 3–20). Hillsdale, NJ: Erlbaum.

Carver, C. S., Blaney, P. H., & Scheier, M. F. (1979a). Focus of attention, chronic expectancy, and responses to a feared stimulus. *Journal of Personality and Social Psychology, 37,* 1186–1195.

Carver, C. S., Blaney, P. H., & Scheier, M. F. (1979b). Reassertion and giving up: The interactive role of self-directed attention and outcome expectancy. *Journal of Personality and Social Psychology, 37,* 1859–1870.

Carver, C. S., Peterson, L. M., Follansbee, D. J., & Scheier, M. F. (1983). Effects of self-directed attention on performance and persistence among persons high and low in test anxiety. *Cognitive Therapy and Research, 7,* 333–354.

Carver, C. S., Antoni, M., & Scheier, M. F. (1985). Self-consciousness and self-assessment. *Journal of Personality and Social Psychology, 48,* 117–124.

Conville, R. L. (1974). Linguistic nonimmediacy and communicators' anxiety. *Psychological Reports, 35,* 1107–1114.

Curran, J. P., Wallander, J. L., & Fischetti, M. (1980). The importance of behavioral and cognitive factors in heterosexual-social anxiety. *Journal of Personality, 48,* 285–292.

Daly, S. (1978). Behavioral correlates of social anxiety. *British Journal of Social and Clinical Psychology, 17,* 117–120.

Diener, C. I., & Dweck, C. S. (1978). An analysis of learned helplessness: Continuous changes in performance, strategy, and achievement cognitions following failure. *Journal of Personality and Social Psychology, 36*, 451–462.

Fenigstein, A., Scheier, M. F., & Buss, A. H. (1975). Public and private self-consciousness: Assessment and theory. *Journal of Consulting and Clinical Psychology, 43*, 522–527.

Gibbons, F. X., Carver, C. S., Scheier, M. F., & Hormuth, S. E. (1979). Self-focused attention and the placebo effect: Fooling some of the people some of the time. *Journal of Experimental Social Psychology, 15*, 263–274.

Greenberg, J. (1980). Attentional focus and locus of performance causality as determinants of equity behavior. *Journal of Personality and Social Psychology, 38*, 579–585.

Janoff-Bulman, R., & Brickman, P. (1982). Expectations and what people learn from failure. In N. T. Feather (Ed.), *Expectations and actions: Expectancy-value models in psychology* (pp. 207–237). Hillsdale, NJ: Erlbaum.

Klinger, E. (1975). Consequences of commitment to and disengagement from incentives. *Psychological Review, 82*, 1–25.

Kukla, A. (1972). Foundations of an attributional theory of performance. *Psychological Review, 79*, 454–470.

MacKay, D. M. (1966). Cerebral organization and the conscious control of action. In J. C. Eccles (Ed.), *Brain and conscious experience* (pp. 422–445). Berlin: Springer-Verlag.

Mandel, N. M., & Shrauger, J. S. (1980). The effects of self-evaluative statements on heterosocial approach in shy and nonshy males. *Cognitive Therapy and Research, 4*, 369–381.

Peters, R. S. (1970). The education of emotions. In M. B. Arnold (Ed.), *Feelings and emotions: The Loyola Symposium.* New York: Academic Press.

Powers, W. T. (1973). *Behavior: The control of perception.* Chicago: Aldine.

Scheier, M. F., & Carver, C. S. (1977). Self-focused attention and the experience of emotion: Attraction, repulsion, elation, and depression. *Journal of Personality and Social Psychology, 35*, 625–636.

Scheier, M. F., & Carver, C. S. (1983a). Self-directed attention and the comparison of self with standards. *Journal of Experimental Social Psychology, 19*, 205–222.

Scheier, M. F., & Carver, C. S. (1983b). Two sides of the self: One for you and one for me. In J. Suls & A. G. Greenwald (Eds.), *Psychological perspectives on the self* (Vol. 2, pp. 123–157). Hillsdale, NJ: Erlbaum.

Scheier, M. F., & Carver, C. S. (in press). The Self-Consciousness Scale: A revised version for use with general populations. *Journal of Applied Social Psychology.*

Scheier, M. F., Carver, C. S., & Gibbons, F. X. (1979). Self-directed attention, awareness of bodily states, and suggestibility. *Journal of Personality and Social Psychology, 37*, 1576–1588.

Scheier, M. F., Carver, C. S., & Colding, D. (1985). *Self-evaluative thoughts while awaiting a social interaction: Effects of social anxiety and dispositional public self-consciousness.* Manuscript in preparation.

Schlenker, B. R. (Ed.) (1985). *The self in social life.* New York: McGraw-Hill.

Schlenker, B. R., & Leary, M. R. (1982). Social anxiety and self-presentation: A conceptualization and model. *Psychological Bulletin, 92*, 641–669.

Simon, H. A. (1967). Motivational and emotional controls of cognition. *Psychological Review, 74*, 29–39.

Smith, R. E., & Sarason, I. G. (1975). Social anxiety and the evaluation of negative interpersonal feedback. *Journal of Consulting and Clinical Psychology, 43*, 429.

Stotland, E. (1969). *The psychology of hope.* San Francisco: Jossey Bass.

Trope, Y. (1975). Seeking information about one's own ability as a determinant of choice among tasks. *Journal of Personality and Social Psychology, 32*, 1004–1013.

Wicklund, R. A., & Duval, S. (1971). Opinion change and performance facilitation as a result of objective self-awareness. *Journal of Experimental Social Psychology, 7*, 319–342.

Wiener, N. (1948). *Cybernetics: Control and communication in the animal and the machine.* Cambridge, MA: M. I. T. Press.

Wine, J. D. (1982). Evaluation anxiety: A cognitive-attentional construct. In H. W. Krohne & L. C. Laux (Eds.), *Achievement, stress, and anxiety* (pp. 207–219). Washington, DC: Hemisphere.

IV

The Experience of Shyness
Social Aspects

Part IV of the volume considers shyness in the context of social interaction and social perception. The first chapter picks up where Part III ended, with an analysis of the self-presentational strategies associated with shyness. The second and third chapters turn from how shy people want to be regarded to how others in fact regard them. The final chapter explores the issue of whether shyness can best be predicted and understood from the perspective of trait characteristics, situational factors, or the statistical interactions among these and related factors.

The last two chapters in the previous section (i.e., the chapters by Snyder and Smith and by Carver and Scheier) both drew on the concept of self-presentation in their explanations of shyness. In Chapter 15, Arkin, Lake, and Baumgardner outline another self-presentational approach to shyness. They begin by defining the concept of self-presentation and by specifying some of the assumptions of their viewpoint. They then distinguish between self-presentational styles that are acquisitive or aggressive and those that are protective or defensive. The authors suggest that shy individuals are capable of adopting both styles, but that typically they opt for the protective stance that prevents them from capitalizing on some social opportunities and fosters neglect from others. Arkin et al. consider the consequences—positive and negative—of the "playing it safe" strategy and in so doing explicate the nature of the relationship between shyness and self-presentation.

The essay by Gough and Thorne (Chapter 16) describes data dealing with how observers rate individuals who label themselves as shy. The authors identify adjectives on the Adjective Check List that are characteristic of shy people but that differ in terms of their social desirability. They group these items into scales with positive, negative, or balanced connotations and then compare these shyness scales with a number of self-report personality inventories, including the California Personality Inventory, the Minnesota Multiphasic Personality Inventory, and the Myers-Briggs Type Indicator. The bulk of the chapter, however, describes the relationships among the three measures of shyness and ratings by others. The authors draw on a varied data base in which the observers differ in terms of amount of training (naive versus professional), intimacy of the relationship (interviewer versus friend or spouse), and amount of information available (observations within a single setting versus a long and shared relational history).

Jones and Carpenter (Chapter 17) consider available evidence regarding the connections between shyness as a dispositional characteristic and indexes of social behavior as well as measures of the quality and quantity of interpersonal relationships. They review literature demonstrating substantial and stable correlations between self-reported shyness and various indicators of interpersonal behavior, perceptions of shyness and social self-awareness. Furthermore, they present new evidence that shyness is linked to satisfaction with one's relationships, with qualitative and quantitative aspects of one's social support network, and with interpersonal dimensions considered to be important in the development and maintenance of friendships. However, Jones and Carpenter caution against the assumption that shy persons are totally without friends and companions and suggest that the implications of shyness may be greatest at the initial stages of a developing relationship and for less intimate relationships.

The final chapter in Part IV (Chapter 18) presents evidence bearing on the situations that are often associated with feeling shy. Russell, Cutrona, and Jones discuss the development of an instrument that measures the capacity of various situations frequently encountered by college students to elicit feelings of shyness. In addition, they examine the situational versus dispositional contributions to the experience of shyness. Hypothetical and diary methodologies are used to apportion the amount of variance in shyness-related responses attributable to situations, persons or traits, modes of responding (e.g., behavioral responses, cognitive responses, etc.) and trait variability. From these studies, Russell et al. conclude that the main effects for dispositional and situational shyness account for substantial and comparable proportions of variance. Consequently, they also emphasize the need for simultaneously examining personality and external factors in studies examining the experience of shyness.

15

Shyness and Self-Presentation

Robert M. Arkin, Elizabeth A. Lake, and Ann H. Baumgardner

"Safe . . . safe . . . I only wanted to be liked."—Leonard Zelig
(From the Woody Allen movie *Zelig*)

Research on self-presentation and impression management has grown immensely in scope and sophistication during the past two decades. Standing on the shoulders of such astute observers of social behavior as Erving Goffman (e.g., 1959) and Edward E. Jones (e.g., 1964), social psychologists have begun sampling the panorama of fascinating and theoretically compelling behaviors that fall into this category of social influence tactic; one can hardly scan a journal in social psychology without seeing some insightful account or intriguing demonstration of the ways people behave to create impressions on others. Moreover, theory has not lagged behind. Taxonomies, models, and analyses of the motivational bases of self-presentation have been offered (e.g., Arkin, 1981; Arkin & Baumgardner, 1985; Baumeister, 1982; Hogan, 1982; Jones & Pittman, 1982) and lengthy reviews of the process and collections of perspectives on the problem have come fast and furious as well (e.g., Schlenker, 1982; Tedeschi, 1981).

Interest in self-presentation has been sparked from time to time by various individual difference approaches. In the early 1970s, there was a flurry of activity among a group of social and personality psychologists studying the "Machiavellian" personality (Christie & Geis, 1970). Named after Niccolo Machiavelli, the 16th century advisor to the Prince of Florence (who recommended unchecked manipulation and deceit for political gain), the person scoring high on the "Mach Scale" was found to demonstrate awe-inspiring manipulative skill (Christie & Geis, 1970). Earlier, in the 1960s, the influential Marlowe-Crowne Social Desirability Scale was written (Crowne & Marlowe, 1964). People scoring high in social desirability needs (i.e., need for approval) conform more than others, suppress overt hostility toward those who insult them, and show a wide range

ROBERT M. ARKIN and ELIZABETH A. LAKE • Department of Psychology, University of Missouri at Columbia, Columbia, MO 65211.   ANN H. BAUMGARDNER • Department of Psychology, Virginia Polytechnic Institute and State University, Blacksburg, VA, 24061.

of other socially desirable behaviors (Crowne & Marlowe, 1964). Most recently, in the 1970s, a scale was developed (Snyder, 1974) to distinguish the skilled impression manager (the "high self-monitoring" individual) from the person who relies solely on internal dispositions, rather than self-presentation cues, to determine how to behave (the "low self-monitoring" individual). Research using the scale shows that the high self-monitoring individual has

> the flexibility and adaptiveness to cope quickly and effectively with a diversity of social
> roles . . . (she) can choose with skill and grace the self-presentation and social behavior
> appropriate to each of a wide variety of social situations. (Snyder, 1981, p. 102)

Notably, each of these approaches has focused expressly on the successful, facile, smooth, and graceful among us. It is natural to consider the polar opposite to the skill of the Machiavellian or the High Self-Monitor as the person unconcerned with social influence, or driven to practice morality and live by the dictates of internal dispositions alone. However, by focusing on the painfully shy individual, whom we have all met at one time or another, another polar opposite to the skilled impression manager or facile Machiavellian seems readily apparent. Conventionally, the shy individual is characterized as wanting to make a favorable impression on others, but as failing in this endeavor more often than not. It seems as much could be learned about self-presentation by studying this sort of individual as by analyzing the behavior of the effective impression manager.

The purpose of this chapter is to examine the role played by shyness in the arena of self-presentation. Surprisingly, although shyness seems an obvious place to look for individual differences in self-presentation styles, research has only begun to focus on the merging of these two literatures. We begin with a definition of self-presentation, describe the theoretical link between shyness and self-presentation, and then review the evidence for presentational differences between shy persons and their nonshy counterparts. In closing, we provide a discussion of the motivational basis of the shy person's self-presentational style.

THE THEORETICAL LINK BETWEEN SHYNESS
AND SELF-PRESENTATION

Defining Self-Presentation

Although it does not seem necessary to spend time and space defining shyness or social anxiety (see appropriate chapters in this volume), it does seem useful to define self-presentation briefly. The term *self-presentation* refers to the process by which individuals attempt to establish an identity by controlling the images of self available to others. The existence of self-presentation is the "inevitable consequence of social perception" (Snyder, 1977); people are acutely aware that others form impressions of them, and make use of these impressions to guide the course and outcome of social interaction. Thus, the tendency to convey a definition of the situation and of oneself to others is a natural extension of the human capacity to view social interaction from perspectives other than one's own egocentric point of view (cf. Schneider, 1981).

The particular image an actor is likely to convey depends on the specific interests, or goals, the presenter has in that social interaction (cf. Weary & Arkin, 1981). The goals are many and varied, of course (cf. Goffman, 1959, p. 3). To achieve certain audience reactions, quite diverse presentations of self may be in order (e.g., Hogan, 1982; Jones & Pittman, 1982). However, a unifying theme has emerged despite the apparent diversity of interaction goals sought through self-presentation; usually, people prefer to present themselves in socially desirable ways (in order to engender social approval, sustain the interaction, and maximize the likelihood that others will help meet their social and material needs). In short, it is clearly in an individual's "interests to control the conduct of others, especially their responsive treatment of him" (Goffman, 1959, p. 3), and one common way to obtain such control is to garner social approval whenever and wherever possible.

Shyness: An Exception to the Rule

Two approaches to linking self-presentation and shyness have been proposed. These approaches are complementary, in that one is focused on self-presentation as an antecedent of social anxiety (Schlenker & Leary, 1982) and the other is concerned with shyness as an antecedent to presentation of self (Arkin, 1981). Together, these two approaches imply that shyness is an exception to the rule that people usually try to behave in socially desirable ways and win the approval of significant others. We shall begin by discussing the model that explicitly addresses shyness as a precursor to stylistic differences in self-presentation, and turn later to a broader analysis of the relationship between self-presentation and social anxiety.

There is some social risk inherent in all interpersonal relations. Failure, embarrassment, rejection, and losses in social status loom as potential outcomes of social relations right alongside the joys and pleasure of relating to others. The terms "acquisitive self-presentation" and "protective self-presentation" were coined to capture individual differences in reactions to this risk (Arkin, 1981). Acquisitive self-presentation refers to those instances in which an individual approaches and embraces this risk, treating the presentation of self as a challenge, by presenting an image of self that is the most favorable possible. The term acquisitive self-presentation would also seem to handle the individual who is blissfully unself-conscious about his or her presentation of self. By contrast, the term "protective self-presentation" characterizes social conservatism. The individual who attempts to create an impression that is merely "safe" is engaged in protective self-presentation.

The word "safe," which appears in the quote at the outset of this chapter, seems particularly apt because of the unique motive system thought to underlie protective self-presentation. Whereas the traditional motive to achieve social approval was seen as underlying acquisitive self-presentation, the motive to avoid social disapproval was posed as the motivational basis of the protective self-presentation style. Specifically, it was proposed that all people from time to time, and some people chronically approach social situations intending merely to avoid social disapproval rather than seek approval, and that people accomplish this proactively—by choosing, modifying, or creating social contexts so that social disapproval is unlikely to occur.

An intriguing example is the innocuous impression resulting from the "reticence syndrome," in which individuals are highly reluctant to interact with others actively and freely unless prodded to do so (Jones & Russell, 1982; Phillips & Metzger, 1973). As Zimbardo (1977) puts it, the individual sometimes acts "like a very conservative investor in a risky, volatile economic market. Expectations of what might be gained is outweighed by anticipation of what could be lost by getting involved" (p. 40).

It was proposed that the shy individual is the prototypical sort of person inclined to adopt such a conservative social orientation (Arkin, 1981). In proposing this link between shyness and disapproval concerns, self-doubts and shaky self-confidence were given a prominent role to play. Doubts about social competence are intimately linked with doubts about self-worth in general. Indeed, there are almost always inverse relationships between measures of shyness and measures of general self-esteem (e.g., Cheek & Buss, 1981; Zimbardo, 1977). Further, theory (e.g., Coopersmith, 1967) and research (e.g., Manis, 1955) have traditionally placed self-evaluation at the mercy of social evaluation (and, thus, social competence). Minimally, doubts about social competence should contribute to a subjective probability of engendering disapproval; this should at least raise doubts about general self-worth. Conversely, it seems axiomatic that low (or uncertain) self-esteem should raise doubts about social competence, and thus produce concerns about engendering disapproval.

THE EMPIRICAL LINK BETWEEN SHYNESS AND SELF-PRESENTATION

Only a small amount of research has directly examined the self-presentations of shy individuals; much basic work on this interesting topic remains to be done, and the reader may well generate some fascinating questions that seem to beg for an answer. Nevertheless, a substantial number of studies shed some indirect light on this relationship, and a few seem to illuminate the issue directly.

Avoidance and Withdrawal

Affiliating with others is one of the very most basic of all human tendencies (cf. Geen, Beatty, & Arkin, 1984, p. 312). You may be alone as you read this chapter, but if you think for a moment about your daily activities, you will find that you typically have a remarkable array of experiences in the company of others. One of the most profound observations about human behavior is contained in Aristotle's remark in his *Politics*: "man is by nature a social animal."

However, the disaffiliative tendencies of persons high in social anxiety have been noted many times. Shy people will often disaffiliate completely by avoiding social encounters, or by leaving encounters quickly. For instance, students who score high on inventories of shyness and social anxiety date less frequently than those who score lower (e.g., Curran, 1977). Similarly, socially anxious persons often express a preference to work alone rather than with others (McGovern, 1976).

But the most interesting of such studies hint that shy persons migrate to the fringes of social interaction, where they are better able to regulate its course and therefore its outcome. Dykman and Reis (1979) found that students scoring high in feelings of vulnerability and inadequacy tended to occupy seats near the rear and far sides of the classroom. From this vantage point, they could remain withdrawn and safe when uncertain, yet remain able to enter into the flow of classroom activity whenever they felt more competent.

Once engaged in social interaction, shy individuals appear unwilling to initiate and structure conversation. Several studies have shown that shy people speak for a smaller percentage of time, take longer to respond to others' conversational sallies, contribute more to conversational dysfluencies (i.e., allow uncomfortable silences to occur unbroken), and tend not to interrupt (e.g., Natale, Entin, & Jaffe, 1979) relative to their nonshy counterparts. Instead of speaking, shy individuals can be safe and avoid the social limelight by engaging in "back-channel responses," such as murmuring "un-huh," smiling, nodding, or otherwise appearing attentive (Natale et al., 1979). It has been suggested that shy persons will "bide their time" in this innocuous way, and remain removed from the ebb and flow of social interaction. Only when they have figured out a safe conversational territory will they enter the interaction as a full, perhaps even dominant, participant (cf. Efran & Korn, 1969). However, this interesting idea has not yet been tested.

One recent study directly implicates fear of disapproval in social avoidance and withdrawal, though it was not expressly focused on shyness. Bernstein, Stephenson, Snyder, and Wicklund (1983) found that men were far more willing to approach an attractive woman if their approach could occur under the guise of a motive other than a desire to be with the woman. Specifically, the men chose to watch the same movie as the attractive woman watched, and thus sit next to her, only when it appeared they had joined her because they preferred the movie she had chosen over another film presented elsewhere. When the two movie options were the same, most of the men sat away from the attractive confederate. Interestingly, a follow-up study indicated that the only men willing to approach the woman in the same-movie condition, where no cover for affiliating was available, were those rated as physically attractive—who were presumably self-confident.

Attitude Neutrality and Conformity

Ordinarily, people are perceived most favorably when they appear knowledgeable, authoritative, expert, and well informed. One way to accomplish this favorable presentation of self is to have attitudes about things that are strong, though not dogmatic, well supported by facts, and that are at least somewhat unique from the humdrum views of the majority, or the average person (Jellison & Arkin, 1977; Myers, 1978).

Yet, one study has shown that shy individuals do not follow this strategy. Turner (1977) found that shy individuals moderated their judgments (that is, they endorsed neutral attitudinal positions) when they expected to be confronted by someone who supposedly held a strong, and perhaps different, opinion from their own. By doing this, the shy individuals seized a part of the attitude scale that was safe: by appearing to have no attitude at all, one can avoid appearing to have the wrong attitude. A person who has no attitude can be persuaded, but cannot be attacked and embarrassed. By remaining neutral at the outset of a social encounter shy persons can avoid disapproval for the moment, and can later adopt the position advocated by others and gain approval for being similar, or through allowing the other to enjoy the rewards of being persuasive (Cialdini & Mirels, 1978).

There is evidence that individuals highly concerned about disapproval do use conformity as an impression management strategy. For instance, Santee and Maslach (1982) found that individuals scoring low on a measure of self-esteem or high on a measure of social anxiety conformed much more than their counterparts. By contrast, their opposite numbers were much more likely to offer novel responses, reflecting a willingness to draw attention to themselves and to acquisitively seek the approval of others.

In a related way, Arkin and Schuman (1983) found that shy individuals wrote less in defense of a decision (relative to nonshy individuals) when the experimental situation was rigged so that they could only lose social approval they had gained earlier (i.e., their essays might produce disapproval). Interestingly, when subjects could only gain social approval (i.e., their essays could only produce approval), shy individuals wrote more than their nonshy counterparts! On another measure, shy persons took longer to get started writing a defense of a decision (i.e., were more cautious and hesitant) when they were facing the prospect of disapproval, but were even quicker getting started than their nonshy counterparts when they could only gain approval.

These findings provide direct evidence for the link between fear of disapproval and protective self-presentation. When fear of disapproval was experimentally eliminated, shy persons were even more acquisitive in their presentation of self than were their nonshy counterparts. This also implies that shy persons exceed their nonshy counterparts in both fears of disapproval and in desires for approval, an issue we will take up later.

Self-Attribution and Self-Handicapping

The most direct way to establish a particular identity is to describe oneself to others. One sort of self-description that has received a great deal of research attention is self-attribution for successful and unsuccessful task performance (cf.

Arkin, Cooper, & Kolditz, 1980). It has been demonstrated time and again that individuals make greater self-attributions for their positive-outcome behaviors than for their negative-outcome behaviors. By taking credit for good acts and denying blame for bad ones, an individual is able to sustain or enhance his or her public image (cf. Weary & Arkin, 1981).

However, socially anxious individuals report far more modest attributions (attributing greater causality to themselves for failure than for success), especially when they anticipate close scrutiny of their attributions and behavior (Arkin, Appleman, & Burger, 1980). By contrast, persons low in social anxiety report more personally flattering attributions of responsibility under these very same conditions. In the same way that attitudinal neutrality is safe, modesty in attributions of responsibility is the most easily defensible presentation of self.

Although modesty in one's attributions is safe and defensible, it has the disadvantage of being an unfavorable presentation of self—especially in the case of failure. A more favorable presentation of self could be achieved by asserting the presence of a persuasive external excuse for poor performance (Snyder, Higgins, & Stucky, 1983). Naturally, shy individuals should be reluctant to claim such an excuse, unless the excuse is patently obvious to observers and would clearly interfere with successful performance.

Jones and Berglas (1978) recently proposed a subtle behavioral strategem called "self-handicapping." In self-handicapping an individual seeks out or creates a handicap (an external, inhibitory factor that interferes with performance), and thereby obscures the link between performance and evaluation (at least in the case of failure). Thus, the handicap should mitigate the impact of the failure experience because the failure cannot be viewed as a clear reflection of low ability. This type of behavior provides a perfect solution to the dilemma of the shy individual. Indeed, the presence of a persuasive handicap should free the shy individual to pursue acquisitive types of self-presentation, because failure would no longer compromise one's public image.

Two sets of findings support the idea that handicapping is a close cousin to protective self-presentation. First, there is mounting evidence that self-handicapping is found predominantly among individuals who harbor self-doubts and are plagued with concerns over social disapproval (Arkin & Baumgardner, 1985). Second, there is some evidence that shy persons do indeed stop worrying about failure, adopt an acquisitive self-presentation style, and perform much better in social relations when (ironically) there is a clear external reason why they should be unsuccessful! For instance, Leary (1984) found that socially anxious individuals, exposed to a distracting noise that would supposedly interfere with an ability to interact with others, were less anxious and actually performed better during a social interaction than their counterparts not exposed to the handicap. Indeed, in the loud-noise condition, meant to be analogous to a noisy party or nightclub with a loud band, high and low social anxiety individuals described themselves equally positively on a self-presentation questionnaire; however, in the soft-noise condition, high social anxiety individuals were much more modest in their self-descriptions than their low social anxiety counterparts.

THE MOTIVATIONAL BASIS OF PROTECTIVE
SELF-PRESENTATION: THE ROLES OF STATE AND
TRAIT SOCIAL ANXIETY

In introducing research on the link between shyness and self-presentation, we placed the basis of the protective self-presentational style at the doorstep of self-doubts and an uncertain sense of self-worth. Having reviewed the evidence, we are now in a position to expand our analysis to encompass both the antecedents of such self-doubts and consequences of the protective presentation style. In between, we will discuss briefly the motivational basis of the protective presentation style and address the role played by social anxiety in our approach.

Etiology

The etiology of the tendency to engage in self-critical ideation, and thus the etiology of the protective self-presentation style, is perhaps the most fascinating aspect of the entire topic. Several authors have written the ideal prescription for producing chronic anxious uncertainty in an individual and, thus, an overriding concern with the question of self-worth. The socialization conditions that might foster such a concern likely rest with the reinforcement history of the child, most particularly in early family relationships.

For instance, a child punished (labeled inadequate) when the child's bahavior does not live up to high parental standards, and unrewarded when it does, may easily acquire an abiding "fear of failure" (Canavan-Gumpert, 1977; Teevan & McGhee, 1972). Similarly, consistent rejection, or anticipated rejection, coupled with reinforcement of the child for dependency (Weinstein, 1968, p. 772), may produce anxiety and focus the child's attention on disapproval avoidance rather than approval seeking. This attention to potential losses as opposed to potential gains has been shown to engender an increasingly conservative and hesitant response style (Canavan-Gumpert, 1977).

In another scenario, one's reinforcement history could be insufficiently contingent. The individual who has suffered a chaotic or capricious reinforcement history may have difficulty discerning what rewards have been for, and may therefore view "ill-gotten gains" as precarious and likely to be unattainable in the future. Even if abundant, the rewards are uninformative concerning one's competence. This set of circumstances would also place one's sense of self-worth at risk.

Self-Enhancement and Self-Doubt

When evidence for the protective self-presentation style was first reviewed (Arkin, 1981), it was concluded that acquisitive self-presentation and protective self-presentation, and the need for approval versus the motive to avoid disapproval, were quite separate processes. Our review of the evidence at this point suggests another view. At least among shy individuals, it appears that the motive to seek approval and the motive to avoid disapproval co-occur, and indeed may be intimately related. The shyness experience may be viewed most accurately as conflicting feelings of a need for self-enhancement, and an overwhelming sense of self-doubt.

To summarize, it has been found that shy individuals are delighted at receiving positive interpersonal evaluations, yet they harbor doubt about the accuracy of such feedback and the insight of their benefactor (Lake & Arkin, 1984); this work suggests the simultaneous occurrence of self-enhancement and self-doubts in shy persons. Second, it has been suggested (Efran & Korn, 1969), though not yet demonstrated, that shy persons withdraw to the fringes of social interaction. There, they can better regulate the ebb and flow of social interaction by waiting for opportunities to garner social approval (acquisitively) without the threat of embarrassment or loss. It has also been demonstrated that shy persons are quite likely to adopt a neutral, safe attitudinal position (Turner, 1977), and that they are also likely to engage in conformity; moreover, shy persons may carry out these processes sequentially, being protective first (by being neutral) and acquisitive later (by letting the other persuade them). It has been demonstrated that shy persons who can only lose social approval will behave quite protectively (they reveal less about their rationale for taking a position, and are hesitant in doing so), but that shy persons who believed they could only gain approval behaved quite acquisitively (Arkin & Schumann, 1983). Finally, the presence of a persuasive handicap appears to free the shy individual from fears of disapproval, and permits him or her to adopt an acquisitive self-presentation style (Leary, 1984).

Together, this list of findings suggests that shy individuals are quite concerned with achieving social approval as well as with avoiding social disapproval. Indeed, the evidence suggests that they subscribe to both of these two motive systems more than their nonshy counterparts.

Nevertheless, it also seems that shy individuals differ from their not-so-shy counterparts in that they must fulfill the requirements of the motive to avoid disapproval before turning to the job of seeking approval. The energetic and active acquisitive self-presentation of socially anxious individuals when they feel safe (e.g., Arkin & Schumann, 1983; Leary, 1984) occurs only when features of the context suggest that disapproval is unlikely to ensue. The model of the self-presentation process presented in Figure 1 illustrates this point. People who are reward oriented generate little concern over disapproval; however, the cost-oriented shy individual must be very sensitive to situational factors that make disapproval likely or unlikely. The cost-oriented shy person must always debate the choice between a protective and an acquisitive self-presentation style.

It may be that shy individuals tend to see most situations as potentially costly (i.e., disapproval is likely), and that this accounts for the diverse and abundant findings that shy people spoil their social image through such conservative and protective tactics as modesty, conformity, social withdrawal, social reticence, attitudinal neutrality, and occasionally alcohol and drug abuse. If so, then shy persons may actually receive less social reinforcement from others than their nonshy peers, rendering social approval all the more powerful for them. It is tempting, therefore, to suppose that the energetic acquisitive self-presentation

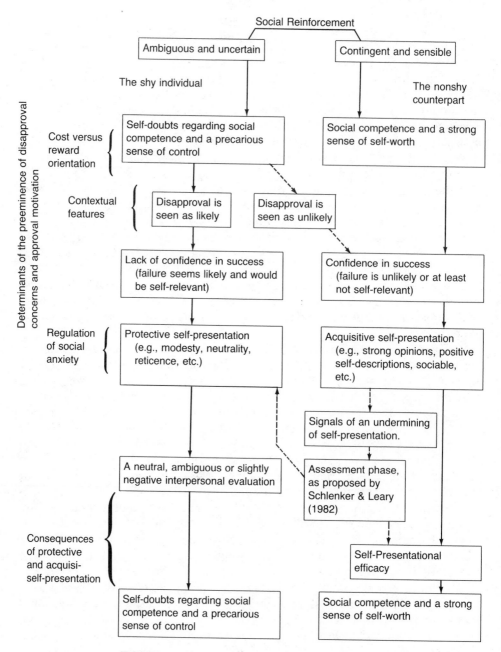

FIGURE 1. A model of shyness and self-presentation.

of the shy individual—when it occurs—results from their suppression of acquisitive tendencies under most other circumstances.

The Regulation of State Social Anxiety

Schlenker and Leary (1982) proposed that social anxiety arises when a person is motivated to make a particular impression on an audience, but doubts that it is possible to do so. Specifically, a person should feel very insecure interpersonally (and therefore, feel socially anxious) when that person (a) wishes to create some impression but is uncertain how to accomplish this goal (b) believes oneself to lack the capacity to produce the desired impression, or (c) feels that some event will transpire to repudiate the presentation of self, and thus cause embarrassment and a failed self-presentation. In short, when a person desires to create a particular impression but perceives that an unsatisfactory evaluative reaction from a subjectively important audience is likely, social anxiety should result.

Naturally, an individual must assess the likelihood of achieving a preferred self-presentation, or social anxiety should never occur. Schlenker and Leary (1982) therefore proposed that an assessment process is triggered whenever a self-presentational goal is important to the individual, and when some signal indicates that the social performance underway may be undermined. If the assessment process indicates that the desired image will be achieved, then the initial presentation of self is reinaugurated. However, if the assessment process indicates that the desired image is not likely to be achieved, then withdrawal from the social situation is likely. If the individual is unable to withdraw from the social situation, however, he or she must "make the best of a bad situation" (p. 658). To cope with such a predicament, the individual will adopt a cautious, innocuous, or noncommittal presentation (Schlenker & Leary, 1982).

In short, Schlenker and Leary (1982) proposed protective self-presentation as a way to deal with disapproval avoidance, and keep feelings of social anxiety in check, but they introduced the switch from acquisitive motives to protective motives later in the self-presentation sequence. Further, they tended to focus on the average, nonshy individual's decision to switch from an acquisitive pattern to a protective pattern. The assessment phase proposed by Schlenker and Leary (1982) is illustrated in the bottom right-hand side of the model of the self-presentation process illustrated in Figure 1.

The self-presentation-styles approach emphasizes that the shy individual is chronically engaged in an assessment process, and therefore opts for the protective style from the outset of interpersonal relations. The shy individual readily sees disapproval as likely, and keeping feelings of social anxiety in check is therefore of paramount importance. Nevertheless, the two approaches are identical in asserting that protective self-presentation is designed to minimize feelings of social anxiety.

Rather than beg the question, it seems useful to discuss briefly why people—especially shy ones—should be so motivated to avert feelings of social anxiety. Anxiety, of course, is a cognitive and affective response associated with apprehension about an impending negative outcome that appears unavoidable. Clearly, the negative outcome that social anxiety signals is forthcoming is disapproval. Thus, the essential question is why social disapproval is so compelling an experience that some people will go to such extremes to avoid it.

For the shy individual, disapproval must be a most compelling experience because it would confirm self-doubts and damage an already precarious sense of self-worth. Because disapproval would diminish one's feelings of competence and self-worth, confirming the shy person's worst fears, it would also diminish the shy individual's sense of efficacy (Bandura, 1977) and perhaps have a paralyzing impact on the individual's future behavior. To behave in ways that maximize pleasure and minimize pain, one must have some measure of personal control over one's own actions and the environment. Perhaps more importantly, one must *believe* in one's own efficacy; if one does not, the likelihood of initiating potentially rewarding actions and continuing such actions to their completion may be diminished (e.g., Bandura, 1977). In the extreme, this may even lead to the sort of inaction associated with learned helplessness.

Ironically, then, protective self-presentation may be a strategy for maintaining a sense of personal control. By engaging in the relatively safe strategy of avoiding disapproval, rather than seeking approval, the individual can avoid the sort of crippling self-attributional pattern that would be paralyzing and inevitably lead to retreat and total passivity. In other words, self-doubts are prevented from becoming certain disabilities; by avoiding disapproval, the individual's fragile sense of personal worth can be protected for the moment. The protective self-presentation style, then, can serve to forestall the debilitating effects of failure that result from a clear and indisputable attribution to lack of ability, and prevent the individual from the paralytic and painful results of having to give up hope and retreat entirely from the company of others. In short, for the shy individual, uncertainty is far preferable to certanty.

Consequences of Protective Self-Presentation

Shy individuals who adopt a protective stance are unable to gain valuable social information. In an effort to protect a precarious sense of self-worth, and to avoid confirmation of self-doubts, these individuals structure interpersonal encounters so that others are in a position to provide little, or at best ambiguous, evaluative feedback. The shy individual who "plays it safe" may not receive disapproval, but is not likely to be highly regarded either. As shown in the bottom of Figure 1, a vicious cycle ensues: to protect themselves from confirmation of self-doubts, shy persons avoid social evaluation, and this contributes to the uncertainty that fed their doubts about self-worth to begin with.

Although shy persons may desire approbation even more than others, they rarely attempt to gain it. However, on the exceptional occasion when they seek positive evaluation acquisitively, shy individuals appear to do so with more effort and vigor than their nonshy counterparts. This effort may, ironically, sap the power of any positive evaluation received to increase feelings of self-worth; approval that is achieved through great efforts may be discounted as self-relevant (e.g., Arkin & Baumgardner, 1985; Jones & Pittman, 1982), and is unlikely to be incorporated into one's self-concept. This would also contribute to the vicious cycle just described.

SUMMARY

Shyness appears to be a clear exception to the rule that people usually attempt to garner social approval. It was suggested that the shy person is preoccupied with avoiding social disapproval and, more often than not, adopts a protective self-presentation style (withdraws from social interaction, adopts neutral or conforming attitudes, is modest in attributions, and self-handicaps) to self-regulate feelings of social anxiety. However, the evidence reviewed also implied that when the shy person is highly confident that one has nothing to lose in a social setting, an acquisitive self-presentation style may be adopted. By adopting a protective self-presentation whenever failure is possible, and an acquisitive self-presentation only when success is guaranteed, the shy individual has little opportunity to diagnose true self-worth. As a consequence, the self-doubts and precarious sense of self-worth that characterize the shy individual are sustained.

To be "safe," yet be liked, was the desire of Woody Allen's character Leonard Zelig. Zelig, "The Human Chameleon," was obsessed with himself—with his misfortune, his nothingness. The character eventually faded, and then disappeared entirely. This appears to be the challenge, and perhaps often the fate, the shy individual faces as well.

REFERENCES

Arkin, R. M. (1981). Self-presentation styles. In J. T. Tedeschi (Ed.), *Impression management theory and social psychological research* (pp. 311–333). New York: Academic Press.

Arkin, R. M., & Schumann, D. (1983). *Self-presentational styles: The roles of cost orientation and shyness.* Paper presented at the American Psychological Association, Anaheim, CA.

Arkin, R. M., & Baumgardner, A. H. (1985). Self handicapping. In J. H. Harvey & G. Weary (Eds.), *Basic issues in attribution theory and research* (pp. 169–202). New York: Academic Press.

Arkin, R. M., Appelman, A. J., & Burger, J. M. (1980). Social anxiety, self-presentation, and the self-serving bias in causal attribution. *Journal of Personality and Social Psychology, 38,* 23–35.

Arkin, R. M., Cooper, H. M., & Kolditz, T. (1980). A statistical review of the literature concerning the self-serving attribution bias in interpersonal influence situations. *Journal of Personality, 48,* 435–448.

Bandura, A. (1977). Self-efficacy: Toward a unifying theory of behavioral change. *Psychological Review, 84,* 191–215.

Baumeister, R. F. (1982). A self-presentational view of social phenomena. *Psychological Bulletin, 91,* 3–26.

Bernstein, W. M., Stephenson, B. O., Snyder, M. L., & Wicklund, R. A. (1983). Causal ambiguity and heterosexual affliation. *Journal of Experimental Social Psychology, 19,* 78–92.

Canavan-Gumpert, D. (1977). Generating reward and cost orientations through praise and criticism. *Journal of Personality and Social Psychology, 35,* 501–513.

Cheek, J. M., & Buss, A. H. (1981). Shyness and sociability. *Journal of Personality and Social Psychology, 41,* 330–339.

Christie, R., & Geis, F. L. (1970). *Studies in Machiavellianism.* New York: Academic Press.

Cialdini, R. B., & Mirels, H. L. (1976). Sense of personal control and attributions about yielding and resisting persuasion targets. *Journal of Personality and Social Psychology, 33,* 395–402.

Coopersmith, S. (1967). *The antecedents of self-esteem.* San Francisco: Freeman.

Crowne, D. T., & Marlowe, D. (1964). *The approval motive.* New York: Wiley.

Curran, J. (1977). Skills training as an approach to the treatment of heterosexual-social anxiety: A review. *Psychological Bulletin, 84,* 140–157.

Dykman, B., & Reis, H. T. (1979). Personality correlates of classroom seating position. *Journal of Educational Psychology, 71,* 346–354.

Efran, J. S., & Korn, P. R. (1969). Measurement of social caution: Self-appraisal, role playing, and discussion behavior. *Journal of Consulting and Clinical Psychology, 33,* 78–83.

Geen, R. G., Beatty, W. W., & Arkin, R. M. (1984). *Human motivation: Physiological, behavioral, and social approaches.* Boston: Allyn & Bacon.

Goffman, E. (1959). *The presentation of self in everyday life.* Garden City, NY: Doubleday Anchor.

Hogan, R. (1982). A socioanalytic theory of personality. In M. Page & R. Dienstbier (Eds.), *Nebraska symposium on motivation* (pp. 55–89). Lincoln: University of Nebraska Press.

Jellison, J. M., & Arkin, R. M. (1977). Social comparison of abilities: A self-presentation approach to decision making in groups. In J. M. Suls & R. L. Miller (Eds.), *Social comparison processes: Theoretical and empirical perspectives* (pp. 235–257). Washington, DC: Hemisphere.

Jones, E. E. (1964). *Ingratiation.* New York: Appleton-Century-Crofts.

Jones, E. E., & Berglas, S. (1978). Control of attributions about the self through self-handicapping strategies: The appeal of alcohol and the role of underachievement. *Personality and Social Psychology Bulletin, 4,* 200–206.

Jones, E. E., & Pittman, T. S. (1982). Toward a general theory of strategic self-presentation. In J. Suls (Ed.), *Psychology perspectives on the self* (pp. 231–262). Hillsdale, NJ: Erlbaum.

Jones, W. H., & Russell, D. (1982). The social reticence scale: An objective instrument to measure shyness. *Journal of Personality Assessment, 46,* 629–631.

Lake, E. A., & Arkin, R. M. (1984). *Reactions to objective and subjective interpersonal evaluation: The influence of social anxiety.* Manuscript submitted for publication.

Leary, M. R. (1984). *Social anxiety and interpersonal concerns: Testing a self-presentational explanation.* Unpublished manuscript, University of Texas, Austin.

Manis, M. (1955). Social interaction and the self-concept. *Journal of Abnormal and Social Psychology, 51,* 362–370.

McGovern, L. P. (1976). Dispositional social anxiety and helping behavior under three conditions of threat. *Journal of Personality, 44,* 84–97.

Myers, D. G. (1978). Polarizing effects of social comparison. *Journal of Experimental Social Psychology, 14,* 554–563.

Natale, M., Entin, E. & Jaffee, J. (1979). Vocal interruptions in dyadic communications as a function of speech and social anxiety. *Journal of Personality and Social Psychology, 37,* 865–878.

Phillips, G. M., & Metzger, N. J. (1973). The reticence syndrome: Some theoretical considerations about etiology and treatment. *Speech Monographs, 40,* 15–24.

Santee, R. T., & Maslach, C. (1982). To agree or not to agree: Personal dissent amid social pressure to conform. *Journal of Personality and Social Psychology, 42,* 690–700.

Schlenker, B. (1982). *Impression management: The self-concept, social identity, and interpersonal relations* (pp. 193–247). Monterey, CA: Brooks/Cole.

Schlenker, B. R., & Leary, M. R. (1982). Social anxiety and self-presentation: A conceptualization and model. *Psychological Bulletin, 92,* 641–669.

Schneider, D. J. (1981). Tactical self-presentation: Toward a broader conception. In J. T. Tedeschi (Ed.), *Impression management theory and social psychological research* (pp. 23–40). New York: Academic Press.

Snyder, C. R., Higgins, R. L., & Stuckey, R. J. (1983). *Excuses: Masquerades in search of grace.* New York: Wiley.

Snyder, M. (1974). The self-monitoring of expressive behavior. *Journal of Personality and Social Psychology, 30,* 526–537.

Snyder, M. (1977). Impression management: The self in social interaction. In L. S. Wrightsman & K. Deaux (Eds.), *Social psychology in the eighties* (pp. 90–121). Monterey, CA: Brooks/Cole.

Snyder, M. (1981). On the influence of individuals in situations. In N. Cantor & J. F. Kihlstrom (Eds.), *Personality, cognition, and social interaction.* Hillsdale, NJ: Erlbaum.

Tedeschi, J. T., Ed. (1981). *Impression management theory and social psychological research.* New York: Academic Press.

Teevan, R. C., & McGhee, P. E. (1972). Childhood development of fear of failure motivation. *Journal of Personality and Social Psychology, 21,* 345–348.

Turner, R. G. (1977). Self-consciousness and anticipatory belief change. *Personality and Social Psychology Bulletin, 3,* 438–441.

Weary, G., & Arkin, R. (1981). Attributional self-presentation. In J. H. Harvey, W. Ickes, & R. F. Kidd (Eds.), *New direction in attributional research* (Vol. 3, pp. 223–246). New York: Erlbaum.

Weinstein, E. (1968). The development of interpersonal competence. In D. Goslin (Ed.), *Handbook of socialization theory and research* (pp. 753–775). Chicago: Rand-McNally.

Zimbardo, P. G. (1977). *Shyness.* Menlo Park, CA: Addison Wesley.

16

Positive, Negative, and Balanced Shyness

Self-Definitions and the Reactions of Others

Harrison G. Gough and Avril Thorne

Prior research has shown shyness to be related to concern about evaluations or possible evaluations by others (Schlenker & Leary, 1982; Zimbardo, 1977), discomfort and inhibition in the presence of others (Cheek & Buss, 1981), diffidence about entering into social interaction (Pilkonis, 1977), and exaggerated self-scrutiny and self-appraisal (Fenigstein, Scheier, & Buss, 1975; Leary, 1982). Small wonder that shyness is typically viewed as a problem or deficit to be overcome (Zimbardo & Radl, 1981), and as a barrier preventing individuals from demonstrating their true worth in dealings with others (Leary & Schlenker, 1981). Even from this very brief formulation, it seems clear that research investigations of shyness may profitably address two themes, (a) assessment of the inner or self-view of oneself as shy, and (b) analyses of reactions of others to determine whether such responses have the negative tone feared and expected by the shy person.

Our work in an assessment center makes study of others' reactions to shy persons an attractive possibility. Typically, in programs at the Institute of Personality Assessment and Research, 10 persons at a time are asked to come for periods of from one to three days, during which they are observed by staff members in individual interviews, informal discussions, games, meals, and standardized settings. Panels of five or six staff members complete Q-sort (Block, 1961) descriptions of each assessee, and panels of 10 staff members complete adjectival (Gough, 1960) descriptions. In addition, the entire assessment staff, usually totalling 15 to 20 persons, contributes trait ratings of all of the individuals being studied. These procedures give rise to numerous observational reactions that may then be linked to any designated self-reported characteristic, such as

HARRISON G. GOUGH • Institute of Personality Assessment, University of California, Berkeley, Berkeley, CA 94720. **AVRIL THORNE** • Department of Psychology, Wellesley College, Wellesley, MA, 02181.

a view of oneself as shy. Persons taking part in the assessments are also administered a comprehensive battery of objective and self-report tests. The observers, of course, have no access to or knowledge of assessees' scores on the tests at the time that their Q-sort, adjectival, and trait ratings are submitted. The assessment sample chosen for the present study consisted of 169 university students (83 male, 86 female) seen between 1978 and 1982.

During the mid-1970s, we also carried out a number of projects with married couples, or persons having enduring and long-lasting cross-sex relationships (see Gough, 1979). Altogether, 236 couples were seen. Each partner took the self-report form of the Adjective Check List (ACL) (Gough & Heilbrun, 1983) and also completed an ACL to describe his or her spouse or partner. These adjectival descriptions by intimates can be used to expand on the picture of persons as furnished by the assessment staff.

In a third series of studies in the early 1970s, the ACL was given to 194 men who were members of five fraternities at the University of California, and to 192 women who were members of the same number of sororities. Within each living group, three persons were selected at random to contribute ACL descriptions of each member. Adjectives felt to be very descriptive were checked twice, those believed to be moderately descriptive once, and those judged to be nondescriptive were given a -1 rating. Summing over the three observers thus gave rise to a scale ranging from -3 to $+6$ for each item. To permit compositing of the total sample, the item totals were converted to standard scores for each fraternity or sorority separately. These computations led to a set of 300 adjectival ratings for each person, with both within-sample and overall means of 50 for each item and standard deviations of 10. These data from the male and female housemates carried information on the views of peers. In toto, then, we have at our disposal descriptions of individuals furnished by assessment staff members, by intimates, and by peers.

The task that we set for ourselves in this chapter was to see how views of oneself as shy would be related to the descriptions and reactions of others. Because of the availability of a comprehensive battery of psychological test data for the assessed sample, we could also examine the relationships of our measures of shyness to other scales and indexes. The theoretical model to be applied in determining the meaning of our shyness scales is called "conceptual analysis" (Gough, 1965). Essentially, the model calls for specifications of the mode of construction of the measure, inspection of its content, linkage to well-known and benchmark variables, and finally, elaboration of the interpersonal and sociodiagnostic implications that give a functional picture of the measure's contextual consequences.

DEVELOPMENT OF ACL SCALES FOR SHYNESS

Self-descriptive ACL protocols were on hand for all of the samples mentioned in the preceding section, and could therefore be used for the construction and scoring of a scale or scales for shyness. The ACL seems to be an appropriate vehicle for the assessment because it includes a broad range of common language descriptors, a number of which seem indicative or contraindicative of feelings of shyness.

To identify adjectives that would be diagnostic of shyness, we asked 16 colleagues to rate each of the 300 adjectives according to its descriptiveness of the self-perceptions of a shy person. Shyness was defined as bashfulness, hesitancy, or reticence in social situations, based on a view of self as shy. Each adjective was rated on a 5-step scale, going from $+2$ for adjectives highly indicative of the self-concept of a shy person down to -2 for adjectives strongly contraindicative. The intercorrelation matrix for the eight female judges showed an estimated interjudge reliability of .90, and the matrix for the eight male judges generated an identical coefficient. The correlation between the male and female composited item ratings was .92, which when corrected by the Spearman-Brown formula indicates an overall reliability of .96 for the total panel of raters.

For computation of item statistics, the ratings were converted from the $+2$, $+1$, 0, -1, and -2 scale to equivalent values of 5-4-3-2-1. The prototypical adjective, as might be expected, was "shy", with means for both panels of 5.00 and sigmas of zero. The five items with the next highest ratings were reserved (mean = 4.87), quiet (4.75), inhibited (4.69), timid (4.44), and sensitive (4.31). The six items with lowest mean ratings, hence most contraindicative of shyness, were outgoing (1.37), talkative (1.37), uninhibited (1.44), bossy (1.50), aggressive (1.56), and loud (1.62).

A scrutiny of the most differentiating items made us aware of something that we had intuitively expected, namely that among the indicative items were both favorable and unfavorable qualities, and that positive and negative elements were also present among the most differentiating contraindicative terms. Anyone who has listened to the public radio broadcasts of Garrison Keillor's "A Prairie Home Companion" will know that tucked into the shy person's self-view as one lacking in social skills, imperturbability, and other prepossessing qualities may also be found feelings of superior self-worth and merit. In a gentle spoof of the usual put-downs of shy people, Keillor (1983, p. 218) remarked

> To us in the shy movement, however, shyness is not a disability or disease to be "overcome." It is simply the way we are. And in our own quiet way we are secretly proud of it. It isn't something we shout about at public rallies and marches. It is Shy Pride.*

The point here is that there may well be different isomorphs of shyness, some of which will carry strong titers of anxiety, fear, and timidity, but others of which will stress qualities of discretion, tact, and self-control. Also, the not-so-shy may be described as self-confident, outgoing, and spontaneous, but they (or some of them) may also be described as bumptious, self-seeking, and exhibitionistic.

Our resolution of this issue was a decision to construct three self-report ACL scales for shyness. Each contained items judged prototypic of the self-concept of a shy person, but the social desirability levels of the items differed. One scale, called Shy-positive, was composed of 11 relatively favorable indicators of shyness and 11 relatively unfavorable indicators of nonshyness. The second scale, called Shy-negative, contained 11 rather unfavorable indicators and 11

---

*From "A Shy Rites Poem—Why Not Pretty Soon?" in *Happy To Be Here* (p. 121) by Garrison Keillor, 1982, New York: Atheneum. Copyright 1982 by Garrison Keillor. Reprinted by permission.

rather favorable contraindicative items. The third, called Shy-balanced, was made up of items in which the desirability levels of the shy and not-shy subsets were equated.

The index of favorability for each item was drawn from the ACL manual (Gough & Heilbrun, 1983), which reports mean ratings on a 7-step scale of desirability by male and female college students. Mean desirability ratings for the item "shy" should perhaps first be noted. Its mean desirability rating by males was 3.47, and by females 3.74. Both values are just below the midpoint on the 7-step scale for desirability. In the normative sample of over 5,000 males, 28% checked "shy," and 37% of the over 4,000 women in the normative sample did likewise. These endorsement rates may be compared to the finding of Zimbardo, Pilkonis, and Norwood (1974) that 40% of university students are willing to refer to themselves as shy.

"Reserved" was the second strongest indicator of shyness. Its mean desirability ratings were 4.08 for men and 4.11 for women, and its endorsement rateswere 41% and 39% respectively. Individuals with a favorable view of their own shyness might well check this item, whereas someone with a more diffident or self-critical view might omit it.

In contrast, consider the item "fearful." This item was rated sixth highest as an indicator of shyness. However, its mean rating of desirability was 2.42 by males and 2.84 by females. It is also a low-endorsement item; "fearful" was checked by 9% of the men and 16% of the women in the normative sample. Thus, although "fearful" is associated with a self-view of shyness, it is not very often checked and probably would not be checked by people who viewed their shyness as a commendable status.

By paying attention to the joint occurrences of the ratings for shyness and desirability, items were selected for the three scales as follows:

1. *Shy-positive*
   Indicative items (count one point for each adjective checkpoint)

cautious	quiet	serious
discreet	reserved	shy
mild	self-controlled	tactful
modest	sensitive	

   Contraindicative items (subtract one point for each adjective checked)

argumentative	bossy	obnoxious
arrogant	egotistical	quarrelsome
blustery	loud	show-off
boastful	noisy	

2. *Shy-negative*
   Indicative items

anxious	meek	silent
awkward	nervous	timid
fearful	retiring	withdrawn
inhibited	shy	

   Contraindicative items

aggressive	outgoing	spontaneous
assertive	outspoken	talkative
daring	self-confident	uninhibited
forceful	sociable	

3. *Shy-balanced*
Indicative items

cautious	quiet	shy
inhibited	reserved	silent
mild	retiring	timid
modest	sensitive	

Contraindicative items

aggressive	loud	show-off
assertive	outgoing	talkative
bossy	outspoken	uninhibited
daring	self-confident	

Inspection of the item content easily reveals the different emphases each scale places on social desirability. In Shy-positive, the shy cluster of items defines a person who is modest, not invasive, is attentive to the wishes of others, and admirably self-regulated. The adjectives in the contraindicative cluster emphasize undesirable qualities, such as arrogance, pretension, and swagger.

Shy-negative, as its name connotes, includes qualities such as anxiety, inhibition, timidity, and diffidence. The adjectives defining nonshyness emphasize favorable themes such as spontaneity, self-confidence, and enterprise. As will be seen later, Shy-negative is closer to current conceptions of shyness than are Shy-positive and Shy-balanced.

Shy-balanced attempts to blend the favorable and unfavorable facets of shyness into an integrated whole that neither stigmatizes the shy person, nor attempts to conceal the self-evident problems that such individuals face in their dealings with others. For example, inhibition is included in the indicative cluster, but so is modesty. In the contraindicative listing are found both self-confidence and aggression. Shy-balanced proposes a relatively unbiased, nonpejorative assessment of the syndrome of shyness.

Statistical data on the ratings of shyness and social desirability for the three scales are given in Table 1. For Shy-positive, both males and females rated the indicative or shy items as significantly ($p < .01$) more diagnostic of shyness than the contraindicative, or not-shy items. The mean desirability ratings of the shy items were significantly higher than those for the not-shy items.

The Shy-negative indicative items were rated as significantly ($p < .01$) more diagnostic of shyness by both panels than were the not-shy items. Mean ratings of social desirability, on the other hand, were significantly higher for the not-shy than for the shy items.

Finally, the Shy-balanced indicative items were rated as significantly ($p < .01$) more diagnostic of shyness than were the contraindicative items. However, the differences in rated social desirability for the two subsets of items were minimal and far short of statistical significance.

SCALE RELIABILITIES AND INTERCORRELATIONS

Because each scale contained 11 positively and 11 negatively weighted items, a simple tally of responses could produce scores ranging from a low of -11 to a high of $+11$. To avoid problems of negative numbers, a constant of

TABLE 1. Shyness and Desirability Ratings for Indicative and Contraindicative Items
of each ACL Shyness Scale

| | Shyness ratings by | | | | Desirability ratings by | | | |
| | Males | | Females | | Males | | Females | |
Scale	Mean	SD	Mean	SD	Mean	SD	Mean	SD
Shy-positive								
Indicative items	4.06	.60	4.09	.56	4.64	.61	4.85	.65
Contraindicative	2.03	.42	1.89	.29	2.47	.46	2.28	.61
t-test	8.76*		11.03*		8.98*		9.12*	
Shy-negative								
Indicative items	4.21	.37	4.25	.44	2.96	.39	3.02	.40
Contraindicative	1.69	.28	1.71	.37	4.68	.46	4.84	.64
t-test	17.17*		13.97*		−9.02*		−7.63*	
Shy-balanced								
Indicative items	4.36	.45	4.31	.49	3.88	.76	3.97	.84
Contraindicative	1.59	.28	1.59	.24	4.01	1.15	4.06	1.25
t-test	16.53*		15.76*		−0.30		−0.19	

Note: Each scale contains 11 indicative and 11 contraindicative items.
*$p < .01$.

20 was added to each scale; this modified the possible range of each scale to a
low of 9 and a high of 31.

The first question concerns the internal consistency or reliability of each
set of items. For the 472 persons in the sample of couples, the alpha reliability
coefficients were .68 for Shy-positive, .68 for Shy-negative, and .70 for Shy-
balanced. For the 169 assessed college students, the corresponding coefficients
were .77, .81, and .83. For the 386 fraternity and sorority members, reliabilities
were .71, .73, and .76. All of these coefficients are in the range usually found
for self-report measures and were deemed acceptable.

A second query concerns the intercorrelations among the scales. Although
each has its own emphasis, all three are directed at the same basic concept and
should therefore be positively correlated. For the couples, the correlations were
.22 between Shy-positive and Shy-negative, .66 between Shy-positive and Shy-
balanced, and .80 between Shy-negative and Shy-balanced. The same three
correlations for the 169 assessed students were .50, .80, and .86. For the 386
students in the living groups, scale intercorrelations were .38, .74, and .82. In
all cases, the lowest correlations, as expected, were between Shy-positive and
Shy-negative. Shy-balanced, which in a sense splits the difference between the
other two scales, was strongly related to both. It should be noted, however,
that Shy-positive and Shy-balanced have 10 items in common, and that Shy-
negative and Shy-balanced share 13 items; minimum correlations must therefore
be .50 and .59. Shy-positive and Shy-negative have only one item in common
("shy").

A third question pertains to the correlations of the three scales with the
total number of items checked on the ACL, and with the standard scores on the
remaining 36 scales of the instrument. Calculations of these relationships were
carried out only for the sample of 169 assessed students. Correlations with the

TABLE 2. Average Scores on Three ACL Shyness Scales for Samples Indicated

Scale and sample	Males		Females		
	Mean	SD	Mean	SD	t
Shy-positive					
Couples	22.61	3.39	23.66	3.23	−3.42**
Assessed students	23.84	4.12	23.87	3.78	−0.05
Student living groups	23.08	3.64	23.64	3.37	−1.58
Shy-negative					
Couples	18.23	3.39	18.94	3.57	−2.21*
Assessed students	19.14	4.39	18.19	4.40	1.42
Student living groups	18.67	3.46	18.38	3.75	0.80
Shy-balanced					
Couples	20.13	3.50	20.59	3.77	−1.39
Assessed students	21.27	4.69	20.33	4.68	1.30
Student living groups	20.53	3.86	20.62	4.05	−0.25

Note: For males, $N = 236$ spouses, 83 assessed students, and 194 students in living groups; corresponding N's for females are 236, 86, and 192.
*$p < .05$, **$p < .01$.

number of items checked were .07 for Shy-positive, −.13 for Shy-negative, and −.11 for Shy-balanced. These coefficients are all small enough to permit use of the unstandardized scores on the three shyness scales, without need to make adjustments for the total number of items checked.

The highest correlations among the other 36 ACL scales were for Exhibition (Heilbrun, 1959), with coefficients of −.81 for Shy-positive, −.81 for Shy-negative, and −.93 for Shy-balanced, and for Free Child (Williams & Williams, 1980) with corresponding coefficients of −.84, −.83, and −.82. These findings suggest that high scorers on all three scales for shyness will not behave in such a way as to elicit the attention of others (Exhibition), nor will they act in a freely expressive, impulse-dominated manner (Free Child).

Table 2 gives means and standard deviations on the shyness scales for males and females in each sample. On both Shy-positive and Shy-negative, the women from the sample of couples had significantly ($p \leq .05$) higher scores than the men, although the magnitudes of the differences were very small. Sex differences were not apparent for either of the two samples of students. Grand means for all 513 males and 514 females on Shy-balanced (the most comprehensive of the three scales) were 20.47 and 20.56, respectively. The difference between these two values was not significant.

CORRELATIONS WITH OTHER MEASURES

Table 3 presents correlations of the three scales for shyness with the scales of the California Psychological Inventory (CPI) (Gough, 1957), the MMPI (Hathaway & McKinley, 1943), the Myers-Briggs Type Indicator (MBTI) (Myers, 1962), and various measures of cognitive functioning and academic achievement.

TABLE 3. Correlations of the Three Shyness Scales with Other Personality and Cognitive Measures

Scale	Shy-positive	Shy-negative	Shy-balanced
California Psychological Inventory			
Dominance	−.28**	−.52**	−.45**
Capacity for status	−.20**	−.36**	−.34**
Sociability	−.26**	;−.59**	−.48**
Social presence	−.37**	−.58**	−.51**
Self-acceptance	−.26**	−.54**	−.47**
Well-being	−.07	−.25**	−.14
Responsibility	.16*	.11	.14
Socialization	.20**	.06	.16*
Self-control	.23**	.19*	.24**
Tolerance	−.06	−.09	−.09
Good impression	.06	−.13	−.03
Communality	.18*	.02	.12
Achievement via conformance	.11	−.11	−.01
Achievement via independence	.08	.14	.11
Intellectual efficiency	−.12	−.24**	−.18*
Psychological-mindedness	−.08	−.14	−.11
Flexibility	−.02	.04	.04
Femininity	.11	.13	.10
Empathy (Hogan, 1969)	−.15*	−.40**	−.35**
Shyness (Cheek & Zonderman, 1983)	.26**	.57**	.45**
MMPI scales			
L (Lie)	.11	.04	.07
F (infrequency)	−.02	.15*	.05
K (correction)	−.04	−.15*	−.13
Hs (hypochondriasis) + .5K	.04	.10	.03
D (depression)	.14	.46**	.30**
Hy (hysteria)	−.06	.04	−.07
Pd (psychopathic deviate) + .4K	−.12	.10	−.05
Mf (femininity)	.04	.25**	.12
Pa (paranoia)	.03	.13	.05
Pt (psychasthenia) + K	.06	.39**	.20**
Sc (schizophrenia) + K	.01	.21**	.09
Ma (hypomania) + .2K	−.26**	−.41**	−.40**
Si (social introversion)	.31**	.64**	.53**
A (anxiety) (Welsh, 1956)	.15*	.43**	.30**
R (repression) (Welsh, 1956)	.19*	.30**	.25**
ES (ego strength) (Barron, 1953)	−.14	−.31**	−.22**
SD (social desirability) (Edwards, 1957)	−.12	−.40**	−.26**
Myers-Briggs Type Indicator scales			
Introversion (vs. Extraversion)	.33**	.57**	.54**
Intuiting (vs. Sensing)	−.14	−.10	−.15*
Feeling (vs. Thinking)	.16*	.18*	.14
Perceiving (vs. Judging)	−.12	−.15*	−.17*
Scholastic Aptitude Test			
Verbal	.00	.06	−.03
Mathematical	.01	.07	−.06
General Vocabulary Test	.03	.11	.01
Crutchfield Embedded Figures	.01	.04	.02
High school grade point average	−.06	−.03	−.04
College grade point average	.01	−.04	−.06

Note: N = 169 (83 males, 86 females).
$*p < .05$, $**p < .01$.

Included in the list of CPI scales is a new measure of shyness developed by Cheek and Zonderman (1983). The scale consists of 11 items, 10 scored for a "true" response and one for a "false." Examples are, "It is hard for me to start a conversation with strangers," "I get very tense and anxious when I think other people are disapproving of me," and "I usually feel nervous and ill-at-ease at a formal dance or party," scored for "true," and "I have no dread of going into a room where other people have already gathered and are talking," scored for "false." Cheek and Zonderman reported an alpha reliability coefficient of .89 for this scale, and a correlation of .84 with the widely used 9-item Cheek and Buss (1981) scale for shyness, in a sample of 114 persons. The new 11-item CPI scale for shyness may therefore be taken as representative of current measures. In our sample of 169 students, the Cheek and Zonderman scale correlated significantly ($p < .01$) with all three ACL measures of shyness. However, as expected, the largest coefficient ($r = .57$) was with Shy-negative, and the smallest ($r = .26$) was with Shy-positive. The correlation between the CPI shyness scale and the Shy-balanced scale was .45.

Perusal of the correlations between the standard CPI scales and the ACL shyness scales indicates that relationships are largely confined to the first cluster of scales on the CPI, those assessing social poise, assurance, and self-confidence. In all instances, higher scores on the shyness scales are associated with lower scores on these CPI scales. Hogan's (1969) scale for empathy, which factorially is linked to the first CPI cluster, also showed significant ($p < .01$) negative correlations with the ACL measures. The only CPI scale with significant ($p \leqslant .05$) positive relationships to all three ACL measures was Self-Control. In general, the correlations with CPI measures are somewhat stronger for Shy-negative and Shy-balanced than for Shy-positive.

The MMPI scales also tend to correlate more strongly with Shy-negative and Shy-balanced than with Shy-positive. For instance, D (depression) was insignificantly associated with Shy-positive, but had correlations of .46 with Shy-negative and .30 with Shy-balanced. The MMPI scales most strongly related to each of the three shyness measures are Si (social introversion) and K-corrected Ma (hypomania). Persons scoring higher on the ACL shyness scales tended to score higher on Si and lower on Ma.

The special MMPI scales cited in Table 3 provide information about general aspects of adjustment. The three shyness measures were significantly and positively related to both of Welsh's (1956) factor scales (A, or anxiety; and R, or repression). Barron's (1953) scale for ego strength was negatively related to Shy-negative and Shy-balanced, as was Edwards' (1957) scale for social desirability. In regard to Edwards' scale, it should be noted that its correlations with MMPI and other scales for adjustment are typically much higher than the three coefficients reported in Table 3.

The major tie between the ACL shyness measures and the scales of the Myers-Briggs Type Indicator was with the continuous scale for Introversion versus Extraversion. Persons who give MBTI responses indicative of introversion tend to obtain higher scores on the three ACL shyness measures.

The remaining measures in Table 3 provide information relative to intellectual and cognitive qualities and performances. In every instance, the correlations are statistically insignificant and in fact converge on zero. This generalization holds for the two measures of scholastic aptitude, for an experimental test of general vocabulary, for the Crutchfield nonverbal test of analytic functioning (Crutchfield, Woodworth, & Albrecht, 1958), and for both self-reported high school and college academic performance.

In summary, the findings in Table 3 indicate that differential standing on the three ACL measures of shyness is unassociated with verbal, quantitative, and analytic ability, does not relate to either better or poorer academic performance, nor to psychopathology in general. Specific areas of concern and self-doubt, however, are implicated, such as lack of social presence, feelings of anxiety, and a tendency toward overcontrol and repression. Strong links were demonstrated between the ACL scales and all measures of introversion (MMPI Si and MBTI Introversion), and sociability (CPI). Qualitative differences among the three shyness scales were not readily discernible, but in general all relationships were more strongly defined for Shy-negative and Shy-balanced than for Shy-positive. Shy-positive, because of its generally weak relations to standard personality measures, appears to be somewhat of an anomaly.

REACTIONS OF OTHERS

The responses of observers were examined from three perspectives: impersonal, as embodied in descriptions and ratings by assessment staff members; intimate, as recorded in the reactions of spouses or partners; and interpersonal, as contained in the reactions of peers. For the most part, we report findings holding equally for both males and females. However, where differences appear to be important, findings are reported separately for each sex.

ASSESSMENT STAFF

Group Discussion Ratings

One of the procedures in the assessments was a leaderless group discussion, in which the 10 persons under scrutiny on any day were asked to spend approximately an hour discussing a topic, such as what students want in a college education, and what are the major social and economic problems facing the world today. The 10 to 15 staff members observing these discussions ranked the 10 participants on several criteria, including the extent and quality of participation and the manifestation of critical or negative responses to the comments of others. Interjudge reliabilities were typically high, almost always at .90 or above. The evaluations for each group of 10 were standardized so that the subgroups could be combined for overall analyses. Extent of participation in these sessions correlated $-.26$ with Shy-positive, $-.21$ with Shy-negative, and $-.32$ with Shy-balanced; all three coefficients are significant beyond the .01 level of confidence. Corresponding correlations for quality of participation were

− .26, − .30, and − .38, and for criticality − .28, − .22, and − .34. Students with higher scores on the three ACL scales tend not to enter into informal discussions readily, tend not to make highly rated comments when they do, and refrain from criticizing or negatively evaluating the remarks made by others. Their behavior in open discussions, in other words, is about what one would expect from persons with a self-view of shyness.

Personal Qualities and Traits

The assessment staff also rated each assessee on a series of personal qualities and traits, drawing on impressions formed over the entire day. These ratings also had high ($r > .90$) interjudge reliabilities. Several of these are relevant to the concept of shyness, and are shown in Table 4. Staff ratings of dominance and extraversion showed the strongest relationships to shyness scores for the total sample, in all cases correlating negatively at the $p < .001$ level. A variable of concern to shy persons, likability, was also rated. This rating was not significantly correlated with Shy-positive for the total sample, but did manifest significant correlations with Shy-negative ($r = -.22$) and Shy-balanced ($r = -.23$).

Likability was also one of the few ratings that showed a difference for males and females. For all three shyness scales, the negative implications for likability of higher scores on shyness were distinctly stronger for men than for women. For instance, Shy-positive correlated − .21 with likability of male assessees, whereas for the female assessees the coefficient was only − .05. A similar sex-linked reaction was found for the rating of personal soundness. For male assessees, ratings of soundness correlated − .26 with Shy-positive, − .43 for Shy-negative, and − .35 for Shy-balanced; the same three correlations for female assessees were − .05, − .25, and − .25. Shyness, as indexed by the three ACL scales, appears to define a syndrome more negatively evaluated in men than in women.

Ratings of cognitive abilities, as opposed to likability and adjustment, tended to show a reversal of these sex differences. For males, ratings of intellectual competence correlated − .15, − .08, and − .19 with Shy-positive, Shy-negative, and Shy-balanced. For females, the correlations were − .27, − .20, and − .33. Correlations with ratings of need for achievement showed a similar trend. Thus, men who viewed themselves as shy were generally seen as less likable and less adjusted than shy women, whereas the reverse tended to be the case for inferences about cognitive abilities. It should be noted that the link between shyness and lower intellectual competence inferred by assessors was not supported by correlations with cognitive performance measures, such as grades and achievement test scores.

Adjective Check List

Staff ACL descriptions provide a more elaborated portrait than do ratings of what observers are likely to say about persons scoring high or low on the shyness scales. Ten staff members independently described each assessee on

TABLE 4. Correlations between Staff Trait Ratings and ACL Shyness Scales

	Shy-positive			Shy-negative			Shy-balanced		
Rating	Total	M	F	Total	M	F	Total	M	F
Dominance	−.34**	−.27*	−.42**	−.37**	−.37**	−.38**	−.45**	−.37**	−.54**
Extraversion	−.28**	−.22*	−.34**	−.34**	−.34**	−.35**	−.38**	−.30**	−.45**
Intellectual Competence	−.21**	−.15	−.27*	−.14	−.08	−.20	−.26**	−.19	−.33**
Likability	−.14	−.21	−.05	−.22**	−.29**	−.15	−.23**	−.28**	−.18
Need Achievement	−.18*	−.09	−.26*	−.25**	−.23*	−.26*	−.28**	−.20	−.36**
Personal Soundness	−.16*	−.26*	−.05	−.33**	−.43**	−.25*	−.30**	−.35**	−.25*

Note: N = 169 for total sample, 83 males and 86 females.
*p < .05, **p < .01.

the ACL. By summing the number of observers checking an item, a composite score ranging from 0 to 10 was generated for each of the 300 adjectives. The 300 adjectives were then correlated with the three self-report shyness scales, separately by sex and for the total sample of 169 students. The number of significant correlations for each panel of analyses far exceeded chance levels, averaging in this case 130 out of 300 correlations. To cite all of the adjectival descriptions producing significant ($p < .05$) correlations would defeat the purpose of the analysis, which is to bring into visibility only the most salient and informative implications. For this reason, only the 10 staff descriptions with largest positive and 10 with largest negative correlations in the total sample will be given. In nearly every instance, these items were correlated at the .01 level of significance, and in all cases at or beyond the .05 level. Also, each item had a nonzero correlation in the same direction for males and females considered separately; in most cases, these separate correlations were also significant at or beyond the .05 level.

As an example of the method employed, consider the adjective "withdrawn." It had the largest positive correlation with Shy-positive in the total sample ($r = .43$) and it was also positively correlated among the males alone ($r = .53$) and the females alone ($r = .31$). Thus, withdrawal is a characteristic one can expect observers to attribute to someone scoring high on Shy-positive. Of course, a correlation of .43 is far from 1.00, so the association is not perfect. A better and more reliable picture of how observers will react can be formed by examining all 10 of the strongest descriptors, and then thinking of them as defining a gestalt or mode of reaction rather than as single words that either will or will not be checked.

The 10 adjectives with largest positive correlations, and hence descriptive of high scorers on Shy-positive, were withdrawn, quiet, reserved, shy, timid, meek, mild, cautious, modest, and inhibited. The 10 adjectives with largest negative correlations, and hence descriptive of persons with low scores, were assertive, dominant, aggressive, resourceful, confident, robust, outgoing, active, outspoken, and energetic.

For Shy-negative, the 10 descriptions with largest positive correlations were withdrawn, shy, meek, anxious, fearful, nervous, weak, awkward, quiet, and silent. The 10 descriptions with largest negative correlations were confident, self-confident, strong, energetic, assertive, healthy, resourceful, determined, outgoing, and active. The word *shy* is associated with both measures. However, note that the image of shyness conveyed by the Shy-negative scale contains undesirable elements, such as nervous, anxious, and weak, that are not present in that associated with Shy-positive.

For Shy-balanced, the 10 strongest descriptors of high scorers were shy, withdrawn, meek, quiet, timid, fearful, silent, mild, dependent, and reserved. The most salient descriptors of low scorers were confident, assertive, energetic, resourceful, self-confident, strong, dominant, outgoing, active, and initiative. The correlation between Shy-balanced and the item "shy" was .45 for the total sample, .41 for males alone, and .50 for females alone.

California Q-Set

Five assessment staff observers each contributed a 100 item-California Q-set (Block, 1961) description of a designated assessee. The composite for five judges was then determined, and the items rearrayed in Q-sort form with numerical values assigned according to the relative salience of each descriptor. This procedure produced consensual descriptions on each of the 100 items for each student. The items were then correlated with the three ACL scales for shyness, in the total sample and separately by sex. In order to emphasize the strongest Q-descriptive implications of the scales, only the 5 items with largest positive and 5 with largest negative correlations have been selected for listing. In all instances, these items correlated at or beyond the .01 level of confidence in the total sample, and had nonzero correlations in the same direction for each sex separately.

The 5 items having largest positive correlations with Shy-positive were, "Is emotionally bland; has flattened affect," "Keeps people at a distance; avoids close interpersonal relationships," "Is vulnerable to real or fancied threat, generally fearful," "Gives up and withdraws where possible in the face of frustration and adversity," and "Reluctant to commit self to any definite course of action; tends to delay or avoid action."

The 5 items having largest negative correlations with Shy-positive were, "Interested in members of the opposite sex," "Behaves in an assertive fashion," "Is self-dramatizing, histrionic," "Is a talkative individual," and "Expresses hostile feelings directly."

For Shy-negative, the 5 most salient descriptors of high scorers were, "Concerned with own adequacy as a person, either at conscious or unconscious levels," "Is basically anxious," "Is self-defeating," "Feels a lack of personal meaning in life," and "Is vulnerable to real or fancied threat, generally fearful." The 5 items most descriptive of low scorers were, "Is turned to for advice and reassurance," "Behaves in an assertive fashion," "Is subjectively unaware of self-concern; feels satisfied with self," "Has social poise and presence; appears socially at ease," and "Emphasizes being with others; gregarious."

For Shy-balanced, the 5 items most strongly associated with high scores were, "Gives up and withdraws where possible in the face of frustration and adversity," "Concerned with own adequacy as a person, either at conscious or unconscious levels," "Is vulnerable to real or fancied threat; generally fearful," "Is basically anxious," and "Is self-defeating." The 5 items with largest negative correlations were, "Behaves in an assertive fashion," "Is a talkative individual," "Has social poise and presence; appears socially at ease," "Expresses hostile feelings directly," and "Is turned to for advice and reassurance."

In the assessment setting, all three shyness scales array people in ways that lead observers to give rather similar descriptions of those with higher and lower scores. High scorers are seen as shy, withdrawn, and meek, and low scorers as confident, resourceful, and outgoing. Q-sort descriptions calling attention to psychological vulnerability and concern with personal adequacy tend to be assigned to persons with high scores, and attributions of social poise and assertiveness to those with low scores. In general, the correlations leading to the selection of these descriptors were larger for the Shy-balanced scale than for the other two scales.

PEER DESCRIPTIONS

In the samples of 194 fraternity and 192 sorority members, the descriptive information came from the Adjective Check List characterizations discussed earlier. The standardized scores on each of the 300 items were correlated with scores on the three scales for shyness for the total sample of 386 students and for the males and females separately. The 10 items having largest positive and 10 having largest negative correlations in the total sample, and nonzero correlations in the same direction for each sex separately, have been selected for citation.

The 10 adjectives with largest positive correlations for Shy-positive were calm, mild, reserved, moderate, cautious, quiet, withdrawn, shy, silent, and gentle. The 10 adjectives with largest negative correlations were loud, noisy, mischievous, show-off, talkative, impulsive, realistic, sarcastic, aggressive, and boastful.

For Shy-negative, the 10 most positively correlated items were shy, quiet, withdrawn, reserved, silent, timid, cautious, meek, retiring, and mild. The 10 with largest negative correlations were outgoing, aggressive, sociable, talkative, confident, adventurous, active, daring, energetic, and forceful.

For Shy-balanced, the 10 items with largest positive correlations were quiet, reserved, shy, withdrawn, silent, cautious, mild, meek, retiring, and timid. The 10 with largest negative correlations were outgoing, talkative, aggressive, noisy, show-off, boastful, loud, outspoken, sociable, and quick.

In the analyses of peer reactions, differences seem detectable among the three scales. The picture of high scorers on Shy-positive is on the whole favorable, whereas that of low scorers tends to be unfavorable. Shy-negative defines the low scorer (the not shy person) in relatively favorable terms. Thus, in the peer setting, the tone of the characterizations one will get for shyness will depend on the manner in which the phenomenology is assessed. If qualities of reserve, sensitivity, and prudence are emphasized, the shy person will tend to make a good impression. If qualities of timidity, anxiety, and self-doubt are stressed, the low scorer or nonshy person will be more favorably described. Probably the least biased appraisal is given by the Shy-balanced scale, which prompts attention to both favorable and unfavorable qualities at each pole. Also, in identifying the most significant correlates we noted that their magnitudes were generally larger for Shy-balanced than for the other two scales.

SPOUSE DESCRIPTIONS

Adjective Check List

The next cluster of descriptive data came from the adjectival descriptions that spouses or partners made of each other. These ACL protocols were scored on a 0–1 basis, depending on whether an item had been checked or not. The 300 adjectives were correlated with the three shyness scales in the total sample of 472 persons, and separately for each sex. The 10 items with largest positive and 10 with largest negative correlations in the total sample were chosen for each scale, with the proviso that nonzero correlations in the same direction were obtained for each sex separately. In interpreting these correlations, note that the scores of the men on the scale were correlated with the descriptions that their wives or partners made of them; likewise for the women, whose scores on the scales were correlated with descriptions of them given by their husbands or partners.

For Shy-positive, the 10 items with the largest positive correlations were reserved, modest, sincere, cautious, dignified, mannerly, organized, precise, calm, and patient. The 10 items with largest negative correlations were loud, aggressive, boastful, blustery, disorderly, self-centered, argumentative, impulsive, distractible, and noisy. This is perhaps the most favorable portrait so far encountered of the shy person, and perhaps the least favorable of the not-shy person. It suggests that when shyness is defined in a relatively favorable way, intimates and presumably those who know the individual well will attribute rather desirable characteristics to those who are shy.

For Shy-negative, the 10 items with largest positive correlations were shy, inhibited, quiet, reserved, mild, moderate, calm, conventional, meek, and modest. The 10 items with largest negative correlations were assertive, outgoing, aggressive, ambitious, talkative, forceful, enthusiastic, self-confident, confident, and pleasure seeking. Note that even in the Shy-negative formulation, spouses do not attribute very undesirable qualities such as nervousness, anxiety, and timidity to their partners. And the unfavorable qualities attributed to low scorers on Shy-positive, such as arrogance and impulsivity, give way to attributions of positive social initiative.

For Shy-balanced, the 10 items with largest positive correlations were reserved, quiet, mild, calm, shy, patient, inhibited, submissive, modest, and meek. The 10 items with largest negative correlations were aggressive, talkative, loud, outgoing, forceful, assertive, headstrong, restless, demanding, and energetic. This set of reactions includes favorable and unfavorable components on each side. Spouses with higher scores are seen as patient and modest, but also as inhibited and submissive. Spouses with lower scores are seen as outgoing and energetic, but also as headstrong and demanding.

Interpersonal Q-Sort

A final source of information comes from an experimental 50-item interpersonal Q-sort administered to 200 of the 236 couples. Each person described his or her spouse or partner by means of the 50 items. Then, the 50 items were correlated with the three shyness scales in the total sample of 400 individuals, and in the two subsamples of 200 persons of each sex. In order to highlight the most prominent implications of this analysis, only the 4 items with largest positive and 4 with largest negative correlations with each scale have been chosen for citation. In all instances, the correlations were significant at or beyond the .01 level in the total sample, and had nonzero correlations in the same direction for both sexes separately.

The 4 items with largest positive correlations with Shy-positive were "A conscientious and serious-minded person," "Submissive; gives in easily; lacking in self-confidence," "Well-organized, capable, patient, and industrious; values achievement," and "Patient and self-controlled; restrained and self-contained in behavior." The 4 items with largest negative correlations were "Active and robust in manner; hard-headed and forthright in judgment," "Enterprising and outgoing; enjoys social participation," "Critical and outspoken; disparages other people and their ideas," and "Impulsive and uninhibited; easily angered and irritated." Here again, when shyness is indexed in a rather favorable way, persons scoring low on the scale are attributed unattractive or undesirable qualities by persons who know them well.

Also, once again, for Shy-negative the desirability implications are reversed. Persons with higher scores are less favorably described, whereas those with lower scores receive more favorable evaluations. The 4 items with largest positive correlations with Shy-negative were "Easily embarrassed; feels inferior and inadequate," "Awkward and ill-at-ease socially; shy and inhibited with others," "Submissive; gives in easily; lacking in self-confidence," and "Unambitious; commonplace and conventional in thinking and behavior." The 4 items with largest negative correlations were "Enterprising and outgoing; enjoys social participation," "Is forceful and self-assured in manner," "Is an effective leader; able to elicit the response and cooperation of others," and "Independent, intelligent, and self-reliant; values achievement."

For Shy-balanced, the 4 items with largest positive correlations were, "Submissive; gives in easily; lacking in self-confidence," "Awkward and ill-at-ease socially; shy and inhibited with others," "Gentle, considerate, and tactful in dealing with others; appreciative and helpful," and "Tolerant, permissive, and benevolent; considerate and charitable." The 4 items with largest negative correlations were, "Enterprising and outgoing; enjoys social participation," "Is forceful and self-assured in manner," "Quick and alert in manner; likes the new and different; impatient with and critical of delay or hesitation," and "Active and robust in manner; hard-headed and forthright in judgement." Again, a mixture of desirable and undesirable self-views of shyness elicits a like mixture in perceptions by those who know the person well.

INTERVIEWERS' FIRST IMPRESSIONS

Each of the 472 individuals in the sample of couples was administered a life history interview, at the conclusion of which the interviewer completed a 99-item interviewer's check list calling for physical description, characterization of social manner and response to the interview, and some cautious inferences about family dynamics and childhood experiences. These 99 items were correlated with the three ACL shyness scales in the total sample, and also in each subsample of 236 persons, using dummy weights of 0 for unchecked items and 1 for those that had been checked.

In order to accentuate the major themes from the analysis, only the 6 largest positive and 6 largest negative covariants have been chosen for listing in each summary. As before, these items are significantly correlated with the scales in the total sample and have nonzero correlations in the same direction for each sex alone.

The 6 items with largest positive correlations with Shy-positive were, "Has many worries and anxieties," "Thin, appears weak and frail," "Cooked, sewed, etc., with mother," "Poised and overtly cooperative, but nevertheless evasive," "Has strong religious beliefs," and "Family maintained definite traditions, for example, certain foods at holidays, trips at certain times, family sayings, etc." The 6 items with largest negative correlations were, "Made considerable use of hands while talking," "Was relaxed and at ease during the interview," "Witty and animated, an interesting conversationalist," "Seemed to enjoy being interviewed," "Has an alert, 'open' face," and "Father absent from home much of the time."

For Shy-negative, the 6 items with largest positive correlations were, "Has many worries and anxieties," "Is unsure of self, doubts own ability," "Thin, appears weak and frail," "Diverts gaze; seldom looked directly at the interviewer," "Slow rate of movement," and "Reticent and taciturn." The 6 items with largest negative correlations were, "Unusually self-confident; feels able to meet nearly any situation," "Witty and animated, an interesting conversationalist," "Has an alert, 'open' face," "Attractive, good-looking," "Made considerable use of hands in talking," and "Animated facial expressiveness."

For Shy-balanced, the 6 items with largest positive correlations were, "Has many worries and anxieties," "Thin, appears weak and frail," "Diverts gaze; seldom looked directly at the interviewer," "Slow rate of movement," "Reticent and taciturn," and "Defensive and guarded in manner." The 6 items with largest negative correlations were, "Unusually self-confident; feels able to meet nearly any situation," "Witty and animated, an interesting conversationalist," "Made considerable use of hands in talking," "Animated facial expressiveness," "Has an alert, 'open' face," and "Quick tempo of movement."

For all three shyness scales, the strongest initial reaction of observers to high-scorers was the impression that they had many worries and anxieties. Another was that they appeared thin and frail. For Shy-negative and Shy-balanced, the high scorers were described as diverting their gaze and not looking directly at the interviewer. Low scorers on all three scales were described as witty and animated, and as having an alert, "open" face. Although these relationships are only weakly defined (with correlations typically falling between $+.15$ and $+.30$), they are consonant with what one would expect of shy and less shy persons in an initial contact.

DISCUSSION

Our analyses have centered primarily on the question of how others react to people who are shy. Do friends, intimates, and professional observers respond differently to persons who view themselves as shy or as not shy? One of the critical factors affecting answers to this question is the method by which shyness is appraised. If the assessment of shyness is based primarily on self-reported fears, anxieties, doubts concerning personal worth, and irresolution in dealing with others, then observers will tend to attribute qualities of weakness, timidity, and anergy to shy persons. If the self-description stresses more positive characteristics, such as patience, forbearance, and self-control, shy persons will be seen as possessing certain favorable qualities such as equanimity, modesty, and self-restraint, along with key indicators of shyness, such as taciturnity and caution. If a balanced measure is employed, one including positive and negative features of the self-concept, then the reactions of others will reflect this fact and contain both favorable and unfavorable elements in appropriate configuration.

When we examined our three scales (Shy-positive, Shy-negative, and Shy-balanced) in reference to a measure strongly linked to indexes often used in research on shyness, similarity was strongest for Shy-negative. This at least raises the possibility that the long list of undesirable qualities usually attributed to shyness may stem, in part, from a negative bias in the assessment of shyness. No one seems to have used a scale such as our Shy-positive measure, that emphasizes the admirable features of shyness versus the invasive, unattractive aspects of its opposite. Inasmuch as Shy-positive merely shifts bias from the negative to the positive pole, the absence of such study is perhaps inconsequential. The least biased and most comprehensive understanding of shyness should come from the use of a scale such as our Shy-balanced measure, in which social desirability ratings of indicative and contraindicative components are equated.

A second factor affecting the responses of observers is their relationship to the persons being described. Our analyses considered the reactions of same-sex peers, opposite-sex spouses or partners, and staff members taking part in research programs at a personality assessment center. Although all three samples described high scorers on Shy-Balanced as shy, reserved, quiet, mild, and meek, the integrated gestalts of persons with higher or lower scores were somewhat different across these samples of observers. Peers seemed to adopt a more evaluational set than did the other two samples, describing, for example, nonshy persons as noisy and boastful. Spouses saw favorable qualities in their shy mates, such as patience and modesty, that were less salient in peers' and professionals' perceptions of the individuals that they described.

A third factor affecting responses to shyness concerns the degree or depth of acquaintance. This factor, of course, is not independent of the groupings just reported for staff observers, peers, and spouses. That is, it seems reasonable to postulate that the range of information, time spent together, and variety of experience are minimal for the research staff and maximal for the spouses. Thus, observers with not a great deal on which to base their descriptions will tend to see high scorers on Shy-balanced as dependent and fearful, and low scorers as confident, resourceful, and strong. The least favorable reactions to shy persons came from assessment staff who formed their impressions solely on the basis of an interview. High scorers on all three shyness scales impressed interviewers as worrying, anxious, weak, frail, and reticent. Nonshy persons, on the other hand, were invariably seen as animated, expressive, and alert. Intimates, in contrast, become aware of less obvious qualities, such as the patience of the shy person and the restlessness of the nonshy.

The final topic we would like to take up in this discussion is the extent to which the shy person's worries about being negatively evaluated can be confirmed. Information relevant to this issue came from staff ratings of such qualities as dominance, intellectual competence, personal soundness, and likability, and from indexes such as the MMPI, achievement test scores, and college grades. Staff ratings of dominance and extraversion were significantly and negatively correlated with all three shyness scales. This finding would come as no surprise to shy persons, nor would it constitute a blow to their self-esteem. The self-concept of being shy seems to entail the notion of ranking low on interpersonal dispositions such as dominance and extraversion.

But what about intellectual competence? Shyness does not appear to carry any essential implications for below average standing on this attribute, and indeed there are folk notions of the abstracted, unsociable genius that suggest an association between detachment and intelligence. Nonetheless, in the assessments, staff members tended to give high scorers on Shy-negative and Shy-balanced low ratings on intellectual competence. In contrast, correlations between all three shyness scales and scores on the Scholastic Aptitude Test were near zero, indicating that staff observers undervalued the intellectual competence of shy persons.

A similar devaluing of shy persons is seen in the ratings of need achievement when compared with actual achievement as indexed by self-reported high school and college grades. Staff ratings of need achievement were negatively correlated with Shy-balanced scores in the total sample of assessed students, whereas correlations between Shy-balanced and grades in high school and college were near zero.

Ratings and indexes of personal soundness may also be examined. Staff ratings of personal soundness correlated − .30 with Shy-balanced, a coefficient of the same magnitude found for the Welsh first-factor scale on the MMPI. If Welsh's measure is accepted as an index of general or overall adjustment, as seems reasonable, then the correlation between Shy-balanced and the rating of soundness is appropriate. However, near-zero correlations were found between Shy-balanced and MMPI scales indicative of specific kinds of maladjustment, for instance, schizophrenia, paranoia, hypochondriasis, hysteria, and psychopathy. The relationships between our Shy-balanced scale and indexes of psychopathology are thus not overwhelming or massive. In this regard, it should be noted that an important follow-up study of shy and withdrawn children seen 16 to 27 years later as adults found little if any long-term residuals or subsequent disturbance (Morris, Soroker, & Burruss, 1954).

A final comment about negative evaluations of shyness concerns ratings of likability. The worry of shy persons that others, in this case initial acquaintances, will not like them very well was, unfortunately, confirmed for the total sample and for males, and partially confirmed for females.

If we now attempt to draw together all of the major strands from the present study, the following conclusions appear to be warranted: (a) in assessing the self-concept of shyness, a scale balanced for the social desirability of indicative and contraindicative features is superior to one stressing either more favorable or less favorable facets; (b) shy persons will be perceived and described differently by respondents whose associations with the shy are in different contexts; (c) on first acquaintance or at first encounter, observers are more influenced by the fact of shyness and its related behavioral manifestations than by underlying qualities and subtle differences among shy persons; varieties of shyness are more apparent to longer-term acquaintances, who respond more in kind to the shy person's self-evaluation of shyness; and (d) the worries of shy persons that they will tend to be less well-liked on initial acquaintance than nonshy or not so shy persons, and that certain of their favorable qualities may be undervalued, are justified.

REFERENCES

Barron, F. (1953). An ego-strength scale which predicts response to psychotherapy. *Journal of Consulting Psychology, 17*, 327–333.

Block, J. (1961). *The Q-sort method in personality assessment and psychiatric research.* Springfield, IL: Charles C Thomas.

Cheek, J. M., & Buss, A. H. (1981). Shyness and sociability. *Journal of Personality and Social Psychology, 41*, 330–339.

Cheek, J. M., & Zonderman, A. B. (1983, August). Shyness as a personality temperament. In J. M. Cheek (Chair), *Progress in research on shyness*. Symposium conducted at the meeting of the American Psychological Association, Anaheim, CA.

Crutchfield, R. S., Woodworth, D. G., & Albrecht, R. E. (1958). Perceptual performance and the effective person. *Personnel Laboratories Report*. (WADC-TN-58-60, ASTIA Document No. 131039). Lackland Air Force Base, TX.

Edwards, A. L. (1957). *The social desirability variable in personality assessment and research*. New York: Dryden.

Fenigstein, A., Scheier, M. F., & Buss, A. H. (1975). Public and private self-consciousness: Assessment and theory. *Journal of Consulting and Clinical Psychology, 43*, 522–527.

Gough, H. G. (1957). *Manual for the California Psychological Inventory*. Palo Alto, CA: Consulting Psychologists Press.

Gough, H. G. (1960). The Adjective Check List as a personality assessment research technique. *Psychological Reports, 6*, 107–122.

Gough, H. G. (1965). Conceptual analysis of psychological test scores and other diagnostic variables. *Journal of Abnormal Psychology, 70*, 294–302.

Gough, H. G. (1979). Some factors related to men's stated willingness to use a male contraceptive pill. *Journal of Sex Research, 15*, 27–37.

Gough, H. G., & Heilbrun, A. B., Jr. (1983). *The Adjective Check List manual—1983 edition*. Palo Alto, CA: Consulting Psychologists Press.

Hathaway, S. R., & McKinley, J. C. (1943). *The Minnesota Multiphasic Personality Schedule*. Minneapolis: University of Minnesota Press.

Heilbrun, A. B., Jr. (1959). Validation of a need scaling technique for the Adjective Check List. *Journal of Consulting Psychology, 23*, 347–351.

Hogan, R. (1969). Development of an empathy scale. *Journal of Consulting and Clinical Psychology, 33*, 307–316.

Keillor, G. (1982) *Happy to be here*. New York: Atheneum.

Leary, M. R. (1982). Social anxiety. In L. Wheeler (Ed.), *Review of personality and social psychology* (Vol. 3, pp. 97–120). Beverly Hills, CA: Sage.

Leary, M. R., & Schlenker, B. R. (1981). The social psychology of shyness: A self-presentational model. In J. T. Tedeschi (Ed.), *Impression management theory and social psychological research* (pp. 335–358). New York: Academic Press.

Morris, D. P., Soroker, E., & Burruss, G. (1954). Follow-up studies of shy, withdrawn children. I. Evaluation of later adjustment. *American Journal of Orthopsychiatry, 24*, 743–754.

Myers, I. B. (1962). *The Myers-Briggs Type Indicator: Manual*. Palo Alto, CA: Consulting Psychologists Press.

Pilkonis, P. A. (1977). The behavioral consequences of shyness. *Journal of Personality, 45*, 596–611.

Schlenker, B. R., & Leary, M. R. (1982). Social anxiety and self-presentation: A conceptualization and model. *Psychological Bulletin, 92*, 641–669.

Welsh, G. S. (1956). Factor dimensions A and R. In G. S. Welsh & W. G. Dahlstrom (Eds.), *Basic readings on the MMPI in psychology and medicine* (pp. 264–281). Minneapolis: University of Minnesota Press.

Williams, K. B., & Williams, J. E. (1980). The assessment of transactional analysis ego states via the Adjective Check List. *Journal of Personality Assessment, 44*, 120–129.

Zimbardo, P. G. (1977). *Shyness: What it is and what to do about it*. New York: Jove.

Zimbardo, P. G., & Radl, S. L. (1981). *A description and theory of shyness*. New York: McGraw-Hill.

Zimbardo, P. G., Pilkonis, P. A., & Norwood, R. M. (1974). *The silent prison of shyness* (ONR Tech. Rep. Z-17). Stanford, CA: Stanford University.

17

Shyness, Social Behavior, and Relationships

Warren H. Jones and Bruce N. Carpenter

Beyond the distress that the shy person experiences in social situations, one is tempted to ask what difference shyness makes. It is one thing to assert that shyness is related to self-reports of anxiety, self-esteem, fearfulness, etc., and quite another to demonstrate its relevance to overt social behavior or its impact on the development or continuation of important and ongoing personal relationships. Shyness is often conceptualized as a dimension of personality, and in that regard it is important to note that the concept of personality is used in two distinct ways in psychology: personality refers to (a) internal psychological structures and dynamics (e.g., individual differences, traits, expectations, beliefs, etc.); and (b) the reputation an individual acquires within the context of a social group. Some personality psychologists have recently emphasized not only the need to examine the linkages between these two conceptualizations, but also that the primary purpose of investigating personality in the former sense is to explain personality in the latter sense (e.g., Hogan, 1983). Similarly, the focus of this chapter is to examine research relating shyness (conceived as a relatively stable dimension of personality) to social behavior, relationships, and the reactions of others.

We begin by proposing relevant research questions for investigating the relationship between shyness and interpersonal outcomes. Next, we briefly discuss the literature and our own studies regarding shyness and contact with strangers in laboratory settings. We then examine in some detail our recent work on shyness and ongoing relationships. Finally, we summarize and briefly discuss our major points.

WARREN H. JONES and BRUCE N. CARPENTER • Department of Psychology, University of Tulsa, Tulsa, OK 74104.

RESEARCH ISSUES

Virtually all persons, including those who are intensely shy, are regularly involved in a wide variety of relationships. These differ on a number of dimensions, including, for example, intimacy, duration, amount of contact, and goals. The nature of a relationship is critical for understanding the interpersonal phenomena that emerge in its context and is therefore important also for understanding the connections between shyness and its social consequences. For example, shyness may be more important for initial interactions than for social behavior with good friends. As a consequence, in this chapter we will distinguish between studies involving strangers versus those involving friends.

The central issue with which we are concerned is whether shyness affects interpersonal behavior and, if so, whether differences in interpersonal style in turn influence the number, quality, or types of personal relationships available to shy individuals. More specifically, do shy as compared to not shy persons behave differently in the presence of others? If such differences exist, how are shy versus not shy persons perceived? Do shy persons expect to be perceived differently by others, and is their awareness of how they are being perceived accurate?

The above questions are, of course, pertinent to interactions both between strangers and friends. However, examining shyness with regard to ongoing and meaningful relationships raises additional questions of relevance. For example, to what extent does shyness inhibit the development or continuation of mutually satisfying relationships? Are shy persons satisfied with their relationships and if not, what do they believe is lacking? To what extent does shyness affect the way a person perceives and evaluates others, including friends? Does shyness have implications for how a friend feels about and reacts to the relationship with a shy person? And finally, is shyness related to the characteristics of the friends with whom one is involved?

SHYNESS AND INTERACTIONS WITH STRANGERS

Shy persons report feeling clumsy and inadequate in social situations. Various measures of shyness have been found to correlate with doubts regarding one's social facility (Crozier, 1979), and shyness is strongly correlated with other dimensions that have been themselves related to deficient and problematic social behaviors, such as social anxiety, public self-consciousness, loneliness, low assertiveness, communication apprehension, and introversion (e.g., Cheek & Busch, 1981; Jones, Freemon, & Goswick, 1981; Jones & Russell, 1982).

Behavioral Differences

There is evidence, although most of it is indirect, that shy persons simply avoid or fail to take advantage of social opportunities, and that they are less intimate and less involved in the interactions they do have. For example, shy as compared to not shy college students report lower dating frequencies, less participation in social and extracurricular activities, and less self-disclosure and affection for others (Jones & Russell, 1982; Jones & Briggs, 1984).

More direct assessments suggest that shyness involves relatively less effective verbal and nonverbal behaviors. For example, studies involving videotaped monologues and dyadic conversations indicate that high as compared to low shyness college students initiate fewer conversations, talk less, smile less, give less eye contact, and look into the camera less (e.g., Cheek & Buss, 1981; Daly, 1978; Mandel & Shrauger, 1980; Pilkonis, 1977). These studies have also demonstrated that shy as compared to not shy participants show fewer facial expressions and slower speech latencies. Kupke, Hobbs, & Cheney (1979) found that self-identified shy men engaged in greater self-focused attention (e.g., asking fewer questions, talking more about oneself) in dyadic conversations with female partners than did not shy men. Thus, research suggests that shy persons do report less interpersonal contact and do act differently; specifically, the conversational and interpersonal behaviors associated with shyness appear to involve less frequent, more passive, and also less responsive interactions with others.

Perception of Shyness by Others

Zimbardo (1977) reported that shy people fear that their reticence is misperceived by others as disinterest in interacting or as snobbishness. Consequently, the perception of shyness involves three important questions: (a) is shyness detectable by others; (b) is it perceived as positive or negative; and (c) do observers attribute additional qualities or motives to shy behavior? Pilkonis (1977) reported that shy as compared to not shy college students were rated by observers as more shy and less relaxed, but also as less assertive and less friendly. Similarly, the shyness scores of the female participants in the dyads studied by Cheek and Buss (1981) correlated with ratings for shy, tense, inhibited, and unfriendly. Also, in a study of videotaped monologues, we found that a target's shyness scores were significantly correlated with judges' ratings of shyness and anxiety and inversely correlated with ratings of poise and talent (Jones, Cavert, & Indart, 1983). Thus, observers tend to see shy persons as shy, but also as unfriendly and lacking in talent. Furthermore, it is reasonable to suppose that to the extent that observers assume that the shy person's reticence derives from disinterest in interaction, or worse, from a sense of superiority, the probability that a lasting relationship will develop is correspondingly diminished.

Social Awareness of Shy Persons

Another issue of relevance to the role of shyness in initial interactions with strangers concerns the facility with which shy persons process social feedback, and hence the degree to which they are aware of their interpersonal impact on others. In one study examining this issue (Jones & Briggs, 1984), we assessed shyness with the Social Reticence Scale (SRS) (Jones & Russell, 1982) and involved participants in various activities among groups of strangers. At the completion of the activities, participants were asked to rate themselves and their fellow group members on several interpersonal dimensions (e.g., friendly, talkative, warm, etc.), all of which might be considered positive. Furthermore, ratings were made from each of three perspectives: (a) self-ratings; (b) reflected self-ratings, that is, how the participants expected to be rated by their group; and (c) ratings of the other members of the group. The ratings of others may also be combined so as to create a fourth perspective, namely, ratings by the group.

These data were analyzed in two ways. First, shyness scores were correlated with ratings from each of the perspectives. We found that, for the most part, shyness was inversely correlated with self- and reflected self-ratings (i.e., high shyness was associated with rating oneself and expecting to be rated as less friendly, less warm, etc.). Also, shyness was significantly correlated with rating others more negatively (e.g., as less friendly), and with more negative ratings received by one's group.

For the second set of analyses, participants were divided at the median of shyness scores into high and low shyness groups. Within these groups, we correlated rating dimensions across perspectives (e.g., the self-rating for warm was correlated with mean rating by others for warm). Our analyses indicated that both groups expected to be rated more or less in accordance with the self-view. Also, high shyness participants tended to rate their partners similarly to their self-ratings whereas low shyness participants did not. Most important were the correlations between expected and actual ratings. Among low shyness participants, the average correlation between these two perspectives was .45, whereas for the high shyness group, the average correlation was .01. Thus, participants high in shyness were less accurate in predicting how the other participants viewed them. On the assumption that accurate feedback is necessary for the performance of any skilled activity (including social skills), these data would seem to imply that shy persons are at a definite disadvantage in their initial interactions with strangers. Moreover, we have replicated these findings using heterosexual dyads, as opposed to groups, suggesting not only stability of these results, but generalizability to other social situations as well.

SHYNESS AND RELATIONSHIPS

For the most part, the previously discussed studies involved brief interactions among strangers. By contrast, more intimate, long-term relationships are clearly much more significant in our everyday lives. Unfortunately, empirical data concerning such relationships is less plentiful. Therefore, we will discuss some of our own ongoing work in this area. As will be seen, some of these studies address the same questions we attempted to answer above concerning interactions with strangers. But they also extend our understanding of the social impact of shyness to the development and maintenance of mutually satisfying relationships.

Previous data suggests that shy persons behave less effectively with strangers and specifically in ways that would seem to reduce the likelihood that a mutually satisfying relationship will develop from any given interaction. On the other hand, it is reasonable to assume that for all but the most extreme cases, shy persons have some friends, although perhaps fewer such relationships than not shy persons. Within the context of ongoing relationships, the central issue becomes, does shyness influence the number, quality, or type of such relationships?

Satisfaction with Relationships

In order to examine the connections between shyness and existing relationships, we initially studied two samples of college students (total $N = 159$). Both groups completed the SRS as the measure of shyness. They also completed the Revised UCLA Loneliness Scale (Russell, Peplau, & Cutrona, 1980) and either the Social Provisions Scale (Russell, Cutrona, Rose, & Yurko, 1984) or the Differential Loneliness Scale (Schmidt & Sermat, 1983). The Revised UCLA scale yields a single, global index of loneliness and has been widely used in recent research. The Social Provisions Scale measures the extent to which respondents report being satisfied with their current relationships with respect to each of six relational provisions: guidance, reassurance of worth, integration, attachment, nurturance, and reliable alliance. Theoretically, satisfaction of these provisions across one's social network is necessary to avoid a sense of loneliness, although different provisions may be satisfied by different types of relationships. The Differential Loneliness Scale assesses loneliness in each of four types of relationships: romantic/sexual, family, friendship, and community or group.

Shyness scores for the Social Reticence Scale were correlated with each variable for men and women separately and combined as shown in Table 1. As indicated, for men shyness scores were significantly correlated with global loneliness as measured by the UCLA scale and with loneliness for each type of relationship measured by the Differential Loneliness Scale (particularly for friendship and community/group relationships). Also, shyness scores were inversely correlated with each provision of the Social Provisions Scale, with the

TABLE 1. Correlations Between SRS II and Measures of Relational Satisfaction

Variable	Combined	Males	Females
UCLA Loneliness	.59***	.68***	.41***
Differential loneliness			
Romantic/sexual	.31***	.41***	.29**
Friendship	.51***	.69***	.47***
Family	.33***	.31*	.40***
Community/group	.53***	.54***	.54***
Social provisions			
Guidance	−.23**	−.14	−.26**
Reassurance of worth	−.38***	−.35**	−.40***
Integration	−.46***	−.42**	−.47***
Attachment	−.28***	−.34**	−.25**
Nurturance	−.08	−.29*	.04
Reliable alliance	−.45***	−.44***	−.45***

$*p < .10$, $**p < .05$, $***p < .01$.

exception of guidance. For female respondents, shyness correlated significantly with global loneliness, with loneliness in each type of relationship (with community/group and friendship correlations again being strongest), and with all of the social provisions except nurturance. Thus, the patterns for men and women are quite similar, and suggest that shy persons feel that their available relationships fail to meet their needs and hence are dissatisfying.

Social Support

Another approach to assessing relationships that has received considerable attention is that of social support, defined as emotional and/or material support received from one's social network (e.g., family, friends, coworkers, etc.). In order to assess the possible role of shyness in social support we administered the SRS and several measures of social support to a sample of college students ($N = 326$).

Shyness scores were correlated with social support measures, including one adapted from Hirsch (1980), the Social Rewards Scale (Briggs & Buss, 1984), the Social Support Scale (Sarason, Sarason, Hacker, & Basham, 1983), and the Inventory of Socially Supportive Behaviors (ISSB)(Berrera, Sandler, & Ramsey, 1981). Results (see Table 2) indicated that shyness was inversely related to the proportion of the social network who are friends, but directly correlated with the proportion of significant others who are family members and whom the respondents have known for more than 5 years. Also, shyness was negatively correlated with the proportion of significant others one can confide in, turn to for help, with whom one is satisfied, and so on. Results with the Social Rewards Scale indicated that shy persons see a lower proportion of their friends as sympathetic and understanding, lively, affectionate, attentive, encouraging, and similar. The ISSB measures the perception of how frequently others offer support. Shy individuals tended to see others as offering them support less often. With regard to the Social Support Questionnaire, shy persons tended to list fewer persons they could count on for support, and tended to indicate that they were less satisfied with the support that they received.

In another study, we compared shyness and a measure of social support among beginning college students during their first week of classes and again 2 months later. During the initial assessment shyness was significantly and inversely related to the number of current friends, satisfaction with friends, number of campus activities, size of the social network, and the proportion of individuals in the social network in which one can confide. A direct correlation was observed between shyness and the proportion of the social network classified as members of one's family. These results were primarily, although not exclusively, due to students who were attending college in locations other than their hometown.

In addition, we found that initial shyness inversely predicted subsequent (i.e., 2 months later) percentage of new friends, number of current friends, number of campus activities, and the density of the social network (i.e., proportion of the members of the network who are acquainted with one another).

TABLE 2. Correlations of Shyness with Social Support Measures

Measure	Combined	Males	Females
Hirsch			
Attends same university	−.07	−.05	−.10
Family	.24***	.14	.29***
Sibling	.19***	.20*	.19**
Friend	−.16**	−.17	−.16*
Coworker	.00	.06	−.04
Parent	.17**	.10	.21**
Romantic involvement	−.07	−.18	−.01
Can confide in	−.26***	−.17	−.30***
Can turn to for help	−.14*	−.13	−.14
Important to person	−.22***	−.12	−.27***
Satisfied with relationship	−.16**	−.10	−.18*
Known over 5 years	.14*	.19*	.13
Social Rewards			
Shows sympathy and concern	−.11	−.11	−.10
Invigorating and lively	−.18**	−.20*	−.16*
Shows affection and liking	−.13*	−.09	−.14
Listens, is interested	−.14*	−.17	−.11
Encourages, compliments	−.15**	−.14	−.15*
Shares similiarities	−.22***	−.26**	−.20**
	−.21***	−.21	−.20*
ISSBN			
Social Support Questionnaire			
Quantity of support	−.18**	−.16	−.19*
Satisfaction with support	−.33***	−.17	−.40***

*$p < .05$, **$p < .01$, ***$p < .001$.

Again, these relationships were largely accounted for by out-of-town students. It is evident, then, that shyness is related to the acquisition of social support over time in new situations, and this appears to be particularly so for individuals for whom the situation is most unfamiliar and farthest removed from preexistent social support networks.

Thus, shyness is related to both the size and structure of one's social network and to the perception of receiving support from others. At least among college students, shy individuals report that they have a smaller network, that their network is more likely to be made up of family members, and that they receive less support from their social network. Furthermore, shyness appears to be more strongly related to the subjective perception of being supported and feeling satisfied with support than to the objective size and structure variables of support networks. In our data the statistical relationships were somewhat stronger for females than for males. The reasons for this are unclear, although one might speculate that this is due to the greater cultural emphasis on relationships and interpersonal sensitivity for women. The magnitude of the findings across most measures is reliable, but small. This is as would be expected in that the evaluation of relationships probably involves many factors, most notably the individuals who comprise the network and the interactions involved.

Shyness in Friendships

Dimensions of Friendship. As we have suggested, shy persons are not without friends and companions. Instead, our previous data suggests that shy persons have smaller friendship and social support networks and that they are less satisfied with their relationships. In addition, our data suggests that shy persons lack some, although perhaps not all, of the various kinds of interpersonal rewards or functions that relationships afford.

In order to explore further this pattern of findings we conducted a preliminary study on shyness and dimensions of friendship. College students ($N =$ 161) who had previously completed the SRS were given a questionnaire listing 20 dimensions or qualities of a friend (e.g., "easy to talk to," "gives good advice," "sensitive to my feelings"). Participants were instructed to indicate whether they had a male and/or a female friend who met their needs with respect to that dimension. Furthermore, the instructions indicated that a given friend should be listed only once in conjunction with the one item that was most pertinent to that friend. This procedure allowed us to assess two features of the friendships of shy persons: (a) the size of the friendship network, and (b) the qualities or dimensions of friendships not satisfied by the shy person's current network of friends.

In our initial analysis we correlated the number of friends listed with the participants' shyness scores. As may be seen in Table 3, among female participants shyness was inversely correlated with the number of dimensions for which both a male and a female friend were listed, and with the total number of female friends. Also, shyness was directly related to the number of dimensions for which neither a male nor a female friend were listed. Among male participants, shyness was positively correlated with the number of dimensions for which no friend was listed and inversely correlated with the total of male friends. Interestingly, then, shyness appeared to be particularly related to the relative lack of same sex friends who satisfy the friendship dimensions of the questionnaire.

TABLE 3. Correlations between SRS and Number of Friendship Needs Met

Dimensions for which a friend was listed	Combined	Males	Females
Both a male and a female listed	$-.16^{**}$	$-.12$	$-.20^{*}$
Neither a male or a female listed	$.25^{***}$	$.31^{***}$	$.20^{**}$
Total number of males listed	$-.15^{**}$	$-.26^{**}$	$-.07$
Total number of females listed	$-.23^{***}$	$-.14$	$-.30^{***}$

$^{*}p < .10$, $^{**}p < .05$, $^{***}p < .01$.

In addition, for each item we compared differences in shyness scores between participants indicating that they had a friend (of either gender) who satisfied each dimension versus those indicating no friend. Among female respondents shyness was significantly greater for participants lacking a friend who, "does what I want to do," "loves me," "could tell anything to him/her," "depends on me," and "is loyal to me." For men, the items for which shyness scores differed significantly were, "bolsters my ego," "loves me," "best friend," and "could tell anything to him/her." Taken together, these results would seem to suggest that shy—as compared to not shy—college students feel that they lack intimacy and esteem in their friendships.

Friendship Ratings. As indicated previously, most studies involving ratings of shy persons have involved ratings of strangers following a brief exposure to the target's dyadic behavior or monologue. In a recent study, (cf. Jones & Briggs, 1984) we compared shyness scores with average ratings of college students by friends and family members who had known the targets for varying periods of time. As with the ratings of strangers, shyness on the part of targets was inversely correlated with ratings such as friendly, talkative, extraverted, and outgoing. Also, shyness was inversely correlated with sociable, leadership, and likes people. On the other hand, the target's shyness was positively correlated with abiding by rules, conscientiousness, and dependability. This suggests that shyness is a factor in evaluations by longer term friends and relatives, as well as by strangers, and that within the context of such relationships the rating dimensions associated with shyness are not all socially undesirable.

To further assess the relationship between shyness and dimensions of friendships we constructed a new measure, the Dimensions of Friendship Rating Scale (DFRS). The initial pool of items for this scale consisted of adjectives and phrases actually used by college students to describe their friends. Statistical and logical procedures reduced the large initial pool to a final set of 40 descriptors, on which respondents are asked to rate a specific friend on a 5-point scale. Factor analysis of the items has yielded meaningful factors for each of four data sets, males and females each rating same and opposite sexed friends.

A sample of 111 male and 227 female college students rated their best same and opposite sex friends, using the DFRS. In addition, participants completed the SRS and answered questions about the length of the friendships. Shyness was related to the length of the same sex friendships for males, and marginally so to the length of opposite sex friendships for females, with shy persons reporting longer friendships. Regarding the dimensions of friendship, our most consistent finding was that shyness of the rater was inversely correlated with the consideration and courteousness of the friend being rated. Also, whereas the correlations between shyness and the rating factors were all relatively small (r's from −.15 to −.31), they were negative in each case. Because the characteristics rated might all be considered positive, this indicated that shy individuals tended to rate their friends more negatively. However, it cannot be determined from this data set whether this is due to a more critical attitude or to selection of friends who are actually lower in these attributes.

In another study college students were asked to bring their best friend with them to the testing session. Each member of the 49 pairs completed self-report measures, including the SRS, as well as rated their friend on the DRFS. A portion of the results from this study are given in Table 4. First note that the shyness scores of friendship partners were unrelated. Also, whereas the usual finding of shyness being strongly related to self-esteem is present, one's shyness was not related to the self-esteem of one's partner. As expected, there was a very strong relationship between shyness and self-reported relational competence (e.g., assertiveness, masculinity, esteem, lack of social anxiety). In contrast, partners of shy individuals did not tend to rate themselves lower on relational competence. Thus, it seems that shy college students are not necessarily prone to develop friendships with others who are shy, low in self-esteem, or low in relational competence, in spite of the shy person's apparent deficits in these areas. Table 4 also indicates that for opposite partnerships, the involvement tended to be romantic more often for shy than for not shy males.

The findings of the previous study, that shy individuals tend to rate their friends negatively on several factors of the DFRS, were essentially replicated in this study of friendship pairs. However, we found even stronger correlations between the DFRS ratings and the shyness of the person being rated. For example, male participants rated shy male friends as less fun to be with, r (12) = $-.56$, $p < .06$, whereas they tended to rate shy female friends as less likable, r (17) = $-.55$, $p < .05$, sensitive and sympathetic, r (17) = $-.45$, $p < .07$, and physically attractive, r (17) = $-.42$, $p < .10$. Women participants rated shy male friends as less warm, r (17) = $-.55$, $p < .05$, similar, r (17) = $-.45$, $p < .07$, and likable, r (17) = $-.64$, $p < .01$, whereas they rated shy female friends as less happy, r (52) = $-.30$, $p < .05$, affectionate, r (52) = $-.28$, $p < .05$, and easy to talk to, r (52) = $-.32$, $p < .05$. As expected, then, shy individuals were rated more negatively, even though the individuals rating them were good friends.

TABLE 4. Correlations of Shyness with Characteristics of Self and of Friend

	Combined	Same sex friends		Opposite sex friends	
		Male	Female	Male	Female
n	98	12	52	17	17
Shyness of Friend	.02	$-.41$	.00	.10	.10
Self-esteem of Self	$-.58**$	$-.14$	$-.66**$	$-.78**$	$-.23$
Self-esteem of Friend	.00	.06	.03	$-.12$	$-.10$
Relational Competence of Self	$-.83**$	$-.95**$	$-.83**$	$-.87**$	$-.80**$
Relational Competence of Friend	$-.07$	.55	$-.04$	$-.12$	$-.30$
Romantic Involvement	.38*	—	—	.60*	.18

*$p < .05$, **$p < .001$.

SUMMARY AND DISCUSSION

To summarize, previous research indicates that shy persons have—or take advantage of—fewer social opportunities than do others; that they behave differently in the company of strangers and specifically that they demonstrate reticence, withdrawal, and less responsiveness in interpersonal behaviors; and that they are judged by others as shy, but also as unfriendly, lacking in talent, and other negative attributes. Many of these findings are undoubtedly due to the inhibitory effects of anxiety experienced in unfamiliar and unstructured social settings. In addition, our research has begun to suggest that the ineffective interpersonal behaviors associated with shyness may also result from (or be compounded by) the shy persons' relatively poor appreciation for how one is coming across to others. Thus, although many specific issues with respect to the interpersonal consequences of shyness await clarification through further research, at this point it is reasonable to conclude that shyness as a feature of one's personality implies fewer, less effective, and perhaps dysfunctional styles of interacting with others, particularly strangers.

Although less data is available with which to assess the role of shyness in ongoing relationships, some general conclusions are warranted here as well. First, shy as compared to not shy persons report less satisfaction with the relationships they do have and greater loneliness, especially with respect to less intimate relationships (e.g., friendships). Second, social support analyses indicated that shy persons report smaller social networks that tend to contain a larger proportion of family members as opposed to friends. Assuming that shy and not shy persons do not differ with respect to family size, the latter result may simply derive from the tendency on the part of shy respondents to report fewer friendships. Also, our social support data again suggested less satisfaction with current relationships among shy as compared to not shy persons. On the other hand, there were indications that shy persons retain their friends for a longer period of time than do others and additional evidence that shy persons are perceived more positively by their friends at least with respect to some rating dimensions.

Third, we found evidence to suggest that initial shyness predicts subsequent indicators of social support in the specific social context of a college environment. As would be expected, these findings were strongest for shy students who by virtue of attending college away from home were most in need of social skill and confidence to make friends in a new situation. Fourth, we found that shyness was associated with the tendency to describe even one's friends more negatively, and conversely the friends of shy participants rated them as less likable and less affectionate. Finally, although shy persons apparently have friends who are not themselves shy, low in self-esteem nor socially incompetent, shy persons nevertheless report that they lack certain qualities in their friendships such as loyalty, intimacy, and pleasurable companionship.

These results do not suggest that dispositionally shy persons are without friends, nor indeed without some of the fundamental rewards of friendship. In addition, it is not yet clear what psychological mechanisms account for the various findings we have discussed. On the other hand, these results would clearly seem to implicate dispositional shyness in relatively problematic interpersonal styles and relationships. From a theoretical perspective, then, shyness may be seen as a contributor to important social consequences, such as the acceptance and status that one achieves within a social group. From a practical point of view, these results suggest the need to develop intervention strategies that not only alleviate anxiety but also that enable shy persons to engage more fully in a wider and more satisfying array of relationships.

REFERENCES

Berrera, M. Jr., Sandler, I. N., & Ramsay, T. B. (1981). Preliminary development of a scale of social support: Studies on college students. *American Journal of Community Psychology, 9,* 435–447.

Briggs, S. R., & Buss, A. H. (1984). *The Social Rewards Scale.* Unpublished manuscript, University of Texas.

Cheek, J. M., & Busch, C. M. (1981). The influence of shyness on loneliness in a new situation. *Personality and Social Psychology Bulletin, 7,* 572–577.

Cheek, J. M., & Buss, A. H. (1981). Shyness and sociability. *Journal of Personality and Social Psychology, 41,* 330–339.

Crozier, R. (1979). Shyness as a dimension of personality. *British Journal of Social and Clinical Psychology, 18,* 121–128.

Daly, S. (1978). Behavioral correlates of social anxiety. *British Journal of Social and Clinical Psychology, 17,* 117–120.

Hirsch, B. J. (1980). Natural support systems and coping with major life changes. *American Journal of Community Psychology, 8,* 159–172.

Hogan, R. (1983). A socioanalytic theory of personality. In M. M. Page (Ed.). *Nebraska Symposium on Motivation 1982* (pp. 55–90). Lincoln: University of Nebraska Press.

Jones, W. H., & Briggs, S. R. (1984). The self-other discrepancy in social shyness. In R. Schwarzer (Ed.). *The self in anxiety, stress and depression* (pp. 93–107). Amsterdam: North Holland.

Jones, W. H., & Russell, D. (1982). The social reticence scale: An objective instrument to measure shyness. *Journal of Personality Assessment, 46,* 629–631.

Jones, W. H., Freemon, J. E., & Goswick, R. A. (1981). The persistence of loneliness: Self and other determinants. *Journal of Personality, 49,* 27–48.

Jones, W. H., Cavert, C., & Indart, M. (1983, August). *Impressions of shyness.* Paper presented at the annual meeting of the American Psychological Association, Anaheim, CA.

Kupke, T. E., Hobbs, S. A., & Cheney, T. H. (1979). Selection of heterosocial skills: 1. Criterion-related validity. *Behavior Therapy, 10,* 327–335.

Mandel, N. M., & Shrauger, J. S. (1980). The effects of self-evaluative statements of heterosocial approach in shy and nonshy males. *Cognitive Therapy and Research, 4,* 369–381.

Pilkonis, P. A. (1977). The behavioral consequences of shyness. *Journal of Personality, 45,* 596–611.

Russell, D., Cutrona, C. E., Rose, J., & Yurko, K. (1984). Social and emotional loneliness: An examination of Weiss' typology of loneliness. *Journal of Personality and Social Psychology, 46,* 1313–1321.

Russell, D., Peplau, L. A., & Cutrona, C. E. (1980). The revised UCLA loneliness scale: Concurrent and discriminant validity evidence. *Journal of Personality and Social Psychology, 39,* 472–480.

Sarason, B. R., Sarason, I. G., Hacker, T. A., & Basham, R. B. (1985). Concomitants of social support; Social skills, physical attractiveness, and gender. *Journal of Personality and Social Psychology, 49,* 469–480.

Schmidt, N., & Sermat, V. (1983). Measuring loneliness in different relationships. *Journal of Personality and Social Psychology, 44,* 1038–1047.

Zimbardo, P. G. (1977). *Shyness.* Reading, MA: Addison-Wesley.

18

A Trait-Situational Analysis of Shyness

Dan Russell, Carolyn E. Cutrona, and Warren H. Jones

Few researchers would disagree that the feeling of shyness derives from the interplay of both situational and individual factors. However, situations that lead to shyness have not been extensively researched and consequently are not well understood. As a result, situational factors typically have not been included in theoretical statements about shyness. In order to do so, two issues need to be resolved. First, what kinds of situations lead to the experience of shyness? Second, how do such situations combine with internal psychological factors (e.g., personality) to produce shyness? We have been conducting research relevant to these two issues, and will focus in some detail on the question of how best to predict shyness-related experiences from individual difference and situational variables.

SHYNESS SITUATIONS

Although very little research regarding situational factors in shyness is available, the literature does contain some clues as to the kinds of situations that might be involved. For example, Buss (1980) theorized that the immediate experience of shyness—as opposed to dispositional shyness—is elicited by three factors: novelty, the presence of others, and the actions of others. Buss argued that shyness may occur in conjunction with the novelty of unfamiliar physical surroundings (attending classes at a new school), social novelty (meeting strangers), and role novelty (assuming a new position within an organization).

DAN RUSSELL • Graduate Program in Hospital and Health Administration, College of Medicine, University of Iowa, Iowa City, IA 52242. CAROLYN E. CUTRONA • Department of Psychology, University of Iowa, Iowa City, IA 52242. WARREN H. JONES • Department of Psychology, University of Tulsa, Tulsa, OK 74104.

The presence of others, according to Buss, elicits shyness by virtue of formality (a wedding ceremony), high status (meeting important or famous people), and conspicuousness (being the only person who thought it was a costume party). Finally, shyness may be the result of certain actions on the part of others, including excessive attention (being stared at), insufficient attention (being ignored by your spouse at a party), and intrusiveness (being asked personal questions in public). Buss suggested that the combination of formality and meeting a stranger of high status lead to particularly intense shyness.

Some confirmation of these speculations is available in a survey of college students reported by Zimbardo (1977). Among those situations sampled, the most powerful in terms of eliciting shyness involved being the focus of attention in a large group (e.g., giving a speech), which 73% of the respondents said made them feel shy. Other common situational causes of shyness included large groups (68%), being of lower status (56%), novel situations (55%), and evaluative situations (52%). In addition, Zimbardo found that shyness in response to other people was greatest for strangers (70%), followed by the opposite sex (64%), and authorities (55%). On the other hand, these data make clear that most people do not feel shy in all social situations. For example, the shyness endorsement rates were considerably lower for being with friends (11%), children (10%), parents (8%), and in one-to-one same sex interactions (14%).

MEASURING SHYNESS SITUATIONS

In order to determine more specifically the kinds of situations that contribute to the experience of shyness, we developed the Shyness Situations Measure (SSM) (Jones, Russell, & Cutrona, 1985). We began by asking a group of 56 college students to describe briefly the situations that result in their feeling shy. These descriptions were grouped according to thematic content and are presented in Table 1 along with the proportion of the sample that listed each of the themes. Table 1 provides some additional confirmation of Buss's (1980) conceptualization regarding the situational elicitors of shyness in that virtually all of the descriptions, particularly those most frequently cited, involved either novelty (e.g., strangers, new situations) or other people (e.g., authority figures, impressive people). On the other hand, relatively fewer themes suggested actions of others as primary elicitors of shyness.

From these descriptions, an initial set of 110 shyness-eliciting situations was developed. Brief depictions of these situations were presented to an independent sample of over 500 students who were asked to rate, on a 7-point scale, the extent to which each situation would make them feel shy. The mean and standard deviation of these ratings were computed for each situation. A final set of 30 items was selected, which consisted of situations that (a) represented the full range of shyness-eliciting values, that is, mean shyness ratings, and (b) demonstrated high interrater agreement, that is, small standard deviations. A sample of these situations and their shyness-eliciting values are presented in Table 2.

TABLE 1. Shyness Situation Themes

Theme	Examples	Percentage
Strangers	With a group of strangers	78.6
Authority figures	Talking with a professor	78.6
Public performances	Giving a speech	46.4
Meeting people/introductions	Meeting a date's parents	39.3
Embarrassments	Saying something stupid, tripping	37.5
Heterosexual risks	Asking for a date, blind dates	33.9
Social functions	Parties	32.1
Heterosexual situations	Dates, being with opposite sex	26.8
New situations	New job, new school	25.0
Evaluations	Oral exams, interviews	23.2
Impressive people	High status, attractive others	19.6
Undesirable people	Loud, intoxicated others	19.6
Discussions/opinions	Class discussions	19.6
New activities	Skiing for the first time	16.1
Crowds/public places	Crowded restaurants	16.1
Nudity/exposure	Wearing a bikini, seen nude	16.1
Misbehavior	Late to class, telling a lie	16.1
Public praise	Awards	16.1
Emotional confrontations	Arguing with friends	16.1
Intimate interactions	Saying "I love you"	14.3

Subsequent analyses have indicated that the SSM is quite reliable. A test–retest correlation of .89 was obtained for ratings of the situations over a 2-week period. Average shyness ratings for the situations also appear to be consistent across samples. For example, the correlation between mean shyness ratings for each of the 30 situations was .93 for two independent groups of college students.

Validity for the SSM has been established in several ways. For example, we found a significant correlation between the shyness ratings of one sample

TABLE 2. Shyness Situations Measure Sample Items

Items	Shyness-eliciting values
Eating in restaurants	1.93
Asking directions	2.43
With successful people	2.82
Talking to a professor	3.19
Emotional confrontations	3.57
At a party with strangers	3.99
First day on a new job	4.44
Being asked personal questions in public	4.70

and the proportion of students from a separate sample who indicated that they had felt shy in each situation, $r (28) = .73$, $p < .01$. In another study, we asked students to indicate which of the situations they had actually experienced during the past two weeks. We then correlated the sum of the shyness-eliciting values (obtained from previous samples) for the situations experienced by each student with measures of emotional arousal on the assumption that exposure to such situations would be associated with feeling more shy and upset. Our results indicated that students exposed to more intense shyness situations also reported being more shy (*r*s varied from .51 to .61 on 5 measures of shyness, all $p < .001$); as well as more self-conscious, $r (134) = .30$, $p < .001$, more fearful, $r (132) = .45$, $p < .001$, less relaxed, $r (128) = -.28$, $p < .002$, less friendly, $r (131) = -.22$, $p < .02$, and less sociable, $r (120) = -.36$, $p < .001$.

To summarize, our initial studies indicated that we were successful in constructing a measure of the shyness-eliciting potential of relevant social situations. Subsequently, the SSM was used in our trait versus situational analyses of the experience of shyness.

TRAIT AND SITUATIONAL DETERMINANTS OF SHYNESS

One focus of our research has involved the relative importance of individual differences (i.e., dispositional shyness) versus situational characteristics in determining the experience of shyness. Second, we have tested whether trait shyness interacts statistically with the shyness-eliciting value of the situation in predicting participants' responses to social situations. Third, we have looked at the issue of cross-situational consistency in shyness by comparing persons who report being consistent or inconsistent in their experience of shyness. Finally, we have examined these issues in response to both hypothetical and actual social situations.

Trait–Situation Interactions

In one study a sample of 136 college students completed the Social Reticence Scale (Jones & Russell, 1982)—as a measure of trait shyness—and several weeks later were randomly assigned to one of the 30 shyness-eliciting situations. The students were asked to indicate how they would feel in that situation by completing the Multiple Affect Adjective Checklist (MAACL) (Zuckerman & Lubin, 1965), which yields measures of anxiety, depression, and hostility.

To analyze these data, students and situations were divided into high, moderate, and low groups based on trait-shyness scores and shyness-situation scores, respectively. A series of 3 × 3 ANOVAs were then performed on each dependent variable. Our results indicated significant main effects for anxiety, depression, and hostility for both dispositional shyness and the shyness-eliciting value of the situation. As expected, higher dispositional shyness and higher shyness-eliciting values were both associated with greater anxiety, hostility, and depression. However, only very weak evidence of trait by situation interactions were found, accounting for from 0% to 4% of the variance in the dependent variables as contrasted with the 3% to 21% of the variance accounted for by trait shyness and 10% to 15% by the shyness-eliciting value of the situation.

These findings suggest that trait and situational characteristics were more or less equally important in predicting the affective arousal associated with the experience of shyness. As part of the same study, participants responded to each of the 30 situations by indicating the degree to which it would make them feel shy, resulting in a within-subjects design. Results were analyzed as previously discussed, with a very similar pattern of findings emerging. Thus, scores on the SRS and the SSM were significant predictors of both emotional arousal and the self-report of shyness. However, in contrast with the popular notion in psychology that most of the variance in behavior is accounted for by the interaction between persons and situations (cf. Bem & Funder, 1978; Ekehammer, 1974), little evidence for the predictive utility of interactions between these two factors was found.

Why might this unexpected finding have occurred? Further analyses of these and other data we have collected (Jones et al., 1985) suggest that trait–situation interaction effects may be an artifact of the methodology used in some previous studies. That is, when persons or situations are treated as unordered, discrete entities (i.e., when measures of trait and/or situational characteristics are not incorporated into the analyses), large interaction effects among these factors in predicting shyness-related responses are found. By contrast, when differences between persons and situations in terms of shyness are assessed and used in prediction, then simply additive effects of traits and situations on shyness-related responses are found.

In another study a third variable, modes of responding, was added to the design described above. Students who had previously completed the SRS were presented with one of the items of the SSM and asked to anticipate their reaction with respect to five modes of shyness-related responding: (a) subjective feelings of shyness; (b) cognitive reactions; (c) emotional arousal; (d) overt behavioral changes; and (e) somatic complaints. Again, our results indicated that although substantial main effects were present for dispositional shyness, shyness situations, and modes of responding, the statistical interactions among these variables were modest in the proportion of variance accounted for and, for the most part, nonsignificant.

Cross-Situational Consistency in Shyness

In a widely cited article, Bem and Allen (1974) suggested that personality research should proceed ideographically by assessing the relevance of personality dimensions for specific individuals. Rather than assuming that trait dimensions are important predictors of the behavior of all persons, Bem and Allen advocated identifying individuals who are cross-situationally consistent on the trait being studied and omitting individuals whose behavior is not consistent. In an empirical demonstration of this proposition, they found that for consistent subjects, self-ratings of friendliness were more predictive of five independent measures of friendliness than was true for inconsistent participants.

In a recent study, we examined how self-perceptions of consistency affected the relationship between individual differences, situational characteristics, and shyness. Two issues were addressed. First, would self-perceptions of cross-situational consistency be related to participant's responses across the situations on the SSM? Assuming that such self-perceptions are accurate, we would expect consistent individuals to report less variation in shyness across situations than persons who indicate that they are variable in shyness. Second, would the impact of traits and situations on shyness-related responses be different for individuals who indicate they are cross-situationally consistent? Based on the findings of Bem and Allen (1974), we would expect trait shyness to be a better predictor of shyness-related responses for consistent subjects in contrast to variable subjects, whereas we would expect characteristics of the situation to be a better predictor of shyness-related responses for variable subjects in contrast to consistent subjects.

College students ($N = 120$) who had previously completed the SRS participated in the study. The students were asked to indicate on a 7-point scale the extent to which they were consistent or variable across situations in their feelings of shyness. The students were then asked to respond to each of the 30 situations on the SSM by indicating the extent to which they would feel shy in that situation. Finally, students were randomly assigned to one of the 30 shyness situations, and asked to indicate how they would feel in that situation by completing the MAACL.

Students were divided into consistent and variable groups by omitting individuals who chose the middle alternative on the 7-point scale, resulting in 44 and 33 students in the consistent and variable groups, respectively. Based on responses to all 30 of the situations, analyses indicated that the consistent group reported less variation in their responses across situations than the variable group. For example, the average intersituation correlation in shyness for the consistent group was .50, whereas the comparable average correlation for the variable group was .27. These and other differences between the two groups were highly significant, indicating that self-perceptions of cross-situational consistency did correspond with the responses by students to the 30 shyness situations.

To examine how individual differences and situational characteristics impact on the affective responses of consistent and variable subjects to the shyness situations, a series of multiple regression analyses were conducted separately for the two groups of students. These analyses are presented in Table 3. Responses on the MAACL were regressed on scores from the SRS, the SSM, and a product term formed by multiplying the trait and situation scores. These predictor variables were entered into the regression equations in the order listed.

Considering the results for the consistent group first, trait shyness was found to be a strong predictor of anxiety and depression scores. However, the shyness-eliciting value of the situation was also found to predict how these students responded to the situations, accounting for from 24% to 28% of the variance in the mood measures. Thus, the responses of these consistent

TABLE 3. Trait-Situation Results for Consistent and Variable Subjects

Group	Variable	Predictor	F	R^2
Consistent				
	Anxiety	Trait	41.67***	.41
		Situation	11.67**	.28
		Interaction	<1.	.00
	Depression	Trait	6.37*	.12
		Situation	15.33**	.28
		Interaction	1.04	.02
	Hostility	Trait	2.15	.05
		Situation	10.27**	.24
		Interaction	<1.	.00
Variable				
	Anxiety	Trait	6.11	.12
		Situation	6.06*	.12
		Interaction	<1.	.00
	Depression	Trait	2.47	.05
		Situation	5.96*	.12
		Interaction	<1.	.01
	Hostility	Trait	<1.	.00
		Situation	5.90*	.12
		Interaction	1.63	.03

*$p < .05$, **$p < .01$, ***$p < .001$.

individuals were predictable from both individual differences and situational characteristics.

As expected, the responses of the variable students were only weakly related to trait shyness, and the nature of the situation was a significant predictor of mood for these subjects. However, in contrast to expectations, these students were less responsive to situational characteristics than the consistent students. The responses of these variable students appeared in general to be less predictable than was the case for the consistent students. Finally, for both groups none of the trait by situation interaction effects were statistically significant, replicating our previous results.

To summarize, self-perceptions of cross-situational consistency in shyness do appear to be related to how individuals respond to different social situations. However, our ability to predict the responses of cross-situationally consistent individuals to social situations is not limited solely to trait characteristics. These individuals also appear to be more responsive than variable subjects to variations in the shyness-eliciting value of the situation. As a result, their behavior is generally more predictable from a knowledge of either trait or situational characteristics than is true for variable individuals.

The previous studies have provided important data concerning trait and situational determinants of shyness. However, all of these studies used hypothetical situations in which participants imagined how they would feel or respond. By contrast, our final study involved naturally occurring social situations.

Determinants of Shyness in Actual Social Situations

Our final study (Jones, Russell, & Cutrona, 1985) afforded the opportunity to replicate our earlier findings concerning trait and situational determinants of shyness in a more realistic context. In addition, we were able to examine whether trait shyness determines exposure to shyness-eliciting situations. Several authors have suggested that trait–situation interactions occur due to differential selection of situations by persons who are high and low on a given trait dimension (e.g., Diener, Larsen, & Emmons, 1984). So, for example, individuals who are high in trait shyness may tend to avoid social situations that are high in shyness-eliciting values, whereas individuals who are low in trait shyness may participate in a more representative cross-section of naturally occurring social situations.

During class periods, college students completed the SRS and the item regarding cross-situational consistency in shyness just described. Subsequently, an unselected group of 26 students participated in what appeared to be a separate investigation. Students were asked to keep a record of their social interactions over a 14-day period, recording information on the 5 most important interactions which occurred each day. For the purposes of this study, a social interaction was defined as an encounter with another person that (a) was longer than 5 minutes, and (b) involved verbal or nonverbal exchanges. Examples of social interactions that met these criteria included talking to a classmate or on the telephone, whereas writing a letter or listening to a lecture did not meet these criteria.

For each interaction reported, students were asked to indicate their response to the interaction on several 7-point rating scales. Specifically, the students indicated how shy, self-conscious, and anxious they felt during the interaction. The students also indicated how good they felt about themselves during the interaction and how satisfied they were with their behavior. Finally, participants rated the appropriateness and awkwardness of their behavior from the perspective of an outside observer. After rating each interaction on these dimensions, students indicated which of the shyness-eliciting situations from the SSM applied to the interaction. Students were able to check any of the characteristics that they felt were relevant.

Prior to analyzing these data, it was necessary to assign a shyness-eliciting value to each interaction reported. Students typically indicated that a number of the SSM items applied to the interaction. Thus, we computed a shyness-eliciting score for each interaction by averaging the shyness-eliciting values of the applicable SSM items.

Participants reported from 19 to 70 social interactions over the 14-day period ($M = 53.5$, s.d. $= 12.72$). The first issue that was addressed in our analyses concerned possible relationships between individual differences in shyness and characteristics of the social interactions reported. SRS scores were correlated with the number of social situations, average shyness-eliciting scores, and variation in the shyness-eliciting scores for the interactions reported. None of these correlations were significant, indicating that trait shyness was not related to either the number or nature of the social interactions. We also correlated ratings of cross-situational consistency in shyness with these measures. Students who indicated that they varied from situation to situation in their shyness also participated in interactions that were more variable in shyness-eliciting value, r (24) = .35, p < 05. Thus, the variability in shyness reported by these students may have simply reflected the types of social interactions they experienced.

Due to the nature of these data, it was not possible to simultaneously examine trait and situational determinants of shyness-related experiences in one overall analysis. Instead, the effects of individual differences and situational characteristics on these responses were examined separately. Our first analysis examined the relationship between scores on the SRS and the average responses of students to the social situations. The results of these analyses are presented in Table 4. As may be seen, trait shyness scores were associated with most of the shyness-related responses. Due to the small sample size for these analyses (N = 26), however, several of these correlations only approached statistical significance.

A second set of analyses examined the correlation between the shyness-eliciting values for each situation and the shyness-related responses, computed separately for each student. Table 5 presents several summary statistics regarding these correlations. The average correlation for each response measure was computed by first normalizing the correlations with Fisher's r-to-z transformation, computing an average value, and then transforming that z-value to a correlation. These average values ranged from .17 to .26 in magnitude, indicating weak but consistent relationships between characteristics of the situation and the response measures. The range of these correlations for each student is also presented in Table 5. As can be seen, there was a great deal of variability in the magnitude of these correlations between subjects. Finally, the percentage of the 26 correlations between the situations measure and each response measure that were statistically significant (p < .05) is indicated in Table 5. These percentages ranged from 23% to 50%, and were consistently higher than the 5% that would be expected to be significant by chance.

As a test of statistical interactions between individual differences and situational characteristics, we divided the students into high and low trait-shyness

TABLE 4. Correlations between Social Reticence Scores and the Response Measures

Response measure	Correlation
Shy	.46***
Self-conscious	.24
Anxious	.04
Good about self	− .43**
Satisfied with behavior	− .30*
Appropriateness of behavior	− .32*
Awkwardness	.32*

df = 24.
*p < .10, **p < .05, ***p < .01.

TABLE 5. Correlations between the Shyness-Evoking Potential of the Situation and the Response Measures

Measure	Average r	Range	% Significant[a]
Shy	.174	−.19 to .54	42%
Self-conscious	.254	−.12 to .49	50%
Anxious	.222	−.02 to .70	35%
Good about behavior	−.187	−.43 to .15	23%
Satisfied with behavior	−.199	−.46 to .15	42%
Appropriateness of behavior	−.170	−.49 to .07	23%
Awkwardness	.211	−.03 to .55	50%

[a]These figures represent the percentage of the 26 correlations (one for each subject) that were significant, $p < .05$.

groups based on a median split of scores on the SRS. Average correlations between the shyness-eliciting values of the interpersonal interactions and the response measures were then computed for each of these two groups (using a Fisher transformation), and a t test was then computed comparing these average correlations. None of the comparisons were statistically significant, indicating that, consistent with our earlier findings, trait–situation interactions were not present in these data.

To summarize, the findings from this last study generally replicated our earlier findings. Both individual differences and situational factors were found to predict how students responded to social situations that occurred in their everyday experiences. Once again, no evidence of trait–situation interactions in determining responses to the situations was found. Trait shyness was also unrelated to characteristics of the social situations experienced by the person.

SUMMARY AND DISCUSSION

The results of these studies indicate that the immediate experience of shyness is determined by properties of the person and by properties of the situation. In general, trait and situational factors appear to be more or less equally important in producing shyness, when both factors are assessed in a systematic and comparable fashion.

In contrast to the general acceptance of the interactionist perspective by personality and social psychologists, we failed to find any evidence of statistical interactions between individual differences and situational factors in determining shyness. Additional results presented by Jones and Russell (1984) indicate that previous findings of person–situation interactions may have been an artifact of the methodology used to test for these effects. In addition, our results regarding cross-situational consistency in shyness indicated some utility in assessing self-perceived consistency. However, in contrast to expectations, highly variable subjects were not more responsive to characteristics of the situation. Instead, our results suggest that consistent subjects are generally more predictable in their shyness-related responses, both from dispositional and situational measures.

Concerning the experience of shyness, we believe that our approach yields important information. Our findings indicate that a strictly trait or situational approach to the psychological state of shyness is limited in that the experience of shyness is clearly a function of both the person and the situation. Future research needs to address how a person becomes dispositionally shy, and intervention methods are needed to modify those features of personality that interfere with social functioning. Similarly, further research on the contribution of social situations to shyness is also necessary. Our data indicate that the shyness-eliciting potential of social settings is predictive of the experience of shyness. To understand how situational factors elicit shyness, we need to examine what properties or characteristics of social situations are associated with low and high shyness scores on the SSM. Ultimately, a more complete model of shyness may be developed from these beginnings, which specify how characteristics of the person and the situation act together to produce the experience of shyness.

REFERENCES

Bem, D. J., & Allen, A. (1974). On predicting some of the people some of the time: The search for cross-situational consistencies in behavior. *Psychological Review, 81,* 505–520.

Bem, D. J., & Funder, D. C. (1978). Predicting more of the people more of the time: Assessing the personality of situations. *Psychological Review, 85,* 485–501.

Buss, A. H. (1980). *Self-consciousness and social anxiety.* San Francisco: Freeman.

Diener, E., Larsen, R. H., & Emmons, R. A. (1984). Person × situation interactions: Choice of situations and congruence response models. *Journal of Personality and Social Psychology, 47,* 580–592.

Ekehammer, B. (1974). Interactions in personality from a historical perspective. *Psychological Review, 81,* 1026–1048.

Jones, W. H., & Russell, D. (1982). The Social Reticence Scale: An objective instrument to measure shyness. *Journal of Personality Assessment, 46,* 629–631.

Jones, W. H., Russell, D., & Cutrona, C. E. (1985). *A personality congrument analysis of situations.* Unpublished manuscript, Department of Psychology, University of Tulsa.

Zimbardo, P. G. (1977). *Shyness.* Reading, MA: Addison-Wesley.

Zuckerman, M., & Lubin, B. (1965). *Multiple Affect Adjective Checklist.* San Diego, CA: Educational & Industrial Testing Service.

V
Related Constructs

Part V of the volume focuses on four constructs that are closely related to shyness: anxiety, introversion, communication apprehension, and embarrassment. Each of the chapters briefly summarizes the literature on one of these related constructs, and then describes its similarities and differences with respect to shyness. The first two chapters involve broad constructs that tend to subsume the more focused concept of shyness (anxiety and introversion), whereas the last two chapters deal with constructs at about the same level of specificity as shyness (communication apprehension and embarrassment).

In the first chapter of this section, Sarason and Sarason point out that shyness is similar to other forms of anxiety, and they suggest that the literature on evaluation (or test) anxiety might provide certain insights into the nature of shyness. Their discussion focuses primarily on cognitive components of anxiety, such as self-preoccupation and cognitive distortions, and they summarize evidence showing that individuals high in test anxiety differ from those low in test anxiety in terms of their thoughts during a preperformance waiting period, their attentional focus during an evaluation, and their attributions for success or failure. However, the Sarasons also acknowledge that anxiety involves behavioral and physiological components as well as cognitive aspects, and they conclude by proposing more complex instruments for the measurement of both test anxiety and social anxiety.

Extraversion-introversion has long been thought to be one of the central dimensions of personality. In Chapter 20, Geen provides a brief overview of this construct, focusing specifically on Eysenck's influential theory and the research it has generated. Geen first describes the basic dimension, linking it to individual differences in excitation and inhibition that are physiologically based and genetically predisposed. He then reviews the evidence for this proposal, summarizing research in which varying levels of stimulation differentially influence introverts and extraverts in terms of arousal, affect, and task performance. Geen further examines how sociability and impulsivity might contribute independently to these findings, and concludes by discussing the relationship between extraversion-introversion and the concept of shyness.

The third concept in this section concerns communication apprehension, a construct that has generated considerable research in the field of communication. McCroskey and Beatty carefully define communication apprehension as a subjective, affective experience and shyness as a behavioral tendency. They further distinguish trait-like communication anxiety from forms that are increasingly dependent on specific situations or people, and from general anxiety. McCroskey and Beatty suggest that trait-like communication anxiety serves as a predisposition to interpret arousal that occurs while communicating as fear. They also argue that self-report measures provide the only valid measures of communication apprehension and that behavioral and physiological indexes must be evaluated with respect to such self-reports. Finally, McCroskey and Beatty outline how communication apprehension might develop, and they propose possible treatment strategies.

In the last chapter of this section (Chapter 22), Miller summarizes the theoretical approaches to and the research on embarrassment. He begins by describing the various circumstances that can elicit embarrassment, and he reviews several schemes for their classification. Miller then outlines several theoretical accounts of embarrassment that emphasize, respectively, its interactional nature, the socialization processes involved, and individual differences in embarrassability. After reviewing the empirical research on embarrassment, Miller attempts to integrate these findings and the various theoretical approaches into a single account. Finally, he compares embarrassment and shyness and suggests some ways in which they are similar.

19

Anxiety and Interfering Thoughts
Their Effect on Social Interaction

Irwin G. Sarason and Barbara R. Sarason

The shy person, when placed in certain social situations, displays symptoms similar to those observed in varying degrees among people who can be characterized as anxiety prone as well as those who have clinically definable anxiety syndromes. Shy people, like most anxiety-prone individuals, are not anxious all the time and do not even experience anxiety in all social situations. In familiar social situations involving nondemanding friends and family members, shy people are likely to seem at ease, participate easily in the group and even take social initiatives. However, when they find themselves with unfamiliar companions or in settings where they believe that their social behavior will be evaluated, shy people become inhibited and anxious. At these times the shy individual is likely to be preoccupied with thoughts of personal inadequacy and with the desire to withdraw from the social interaction (Jones & Russell, 1982).

Because of the similarities between the responses of the anxious person and the individual who is shy, it seems likely that some of the findings from the literature on evaluational anxiety may be of value both in studying shyness and in understanding the meaning of the concept more completely. One of the generalizations that has emerged from research on evaluational anxiety, or as it is often known, test anxiety, is that it is not really a unitary concept. Single sentence definitions of anxiety often acknowledge its various aspects by referring to the individual's apprehension, experience of an unpleasant emotional state, and physiological reactivity. More important than acknowledging this variety of characteristics, however, is the realization that they may not be very highly intercorrelated and consequently, thinking of anxiety as a unitary concept could be misleading to a significant degree. A more complex but preferable approach might be to focus on the components of anxiety and the correlations that might or might not exist among them (Lang, 1969, 1979; Rachman, 1978). At any given

IRWIN G. SARASON and BARBARA R. SARASON • Department of Psychology, University of Washington, Seattle, WA 98195.

time, people can be characterized by their observable behavior (e.g., social with-drawal), their thoughts (e.g., worries), and their bodily reactions (e.g., heart rate). For a given individual, these components might or might not be correlated. Because we know little about the degree of synchrony or desynchrony that may exist among these anxiety components for particular aspects of life, this approach could be of considerable value in increasing reliability or anxiety measurement and in understanding the relationships among anxiety components and also in devising a selection of appropriate dependent measures, such as performance, sense of well-being, and the reactions of others to a target person as a social object. In this article, we will review some findings from the anxiety literature and explore the possibility that they have a bearing on the phenomenon of shyness.

Although we have noted both the need to interrelate the behavioral, cog-nitive, and physiological components of anxiety and also the need to consider their separate effects on a variety of behaviors, we shall limit ourselves mainly to aspects of better specification of the cognitive component, both because it has been intensively studied and because it seems highly relevant to the behavior constituting shyness.

THE COGNITIVE COMPONENT OF ANXIETY

The cognitive component of anxiety includes personal beliefs, construals, assumptions, and expectations about how the world works and one's role in the world. Cognitive theorists view human beings as information processors who respond to the environment based on the data they receive, how they interpret that data and their available problem-solving strategies. How infor-mation is acted on is the result of the interaction between the individual's per-sonal characteristics and environmental events. Personal factors to consider include residues of earlier life experiences; self-assessment of personal skills, talents, and inadequacies; and coping skills. The environment provides a variety of opportunities, constraints, and demands for some action. The joint contri-butions of personal resources and personal interpretations and the situational requirements determine overt behavior.

Although all people think about their personal capabilities in relation to the task at hand, anxious individuals seem to become overly preoccupied with these self-evaluative thoughts. Thoughts such as "I don't know what to do now" can be self-defeating if the person in fact has the wherewithal to handle the situation. One type of cognition that may be particularly relevant to anxiety in social situations consists of perceptions and thoughts about one's physical attri-butes. Many socially anxious people worry, often quite unrealistically, about what they see as unappealing or even revolting features of their appearance. These worries, of course, may or may not be based on reality. Anxious self-preoccupation may arouse emotions that interfere with the perception and appraisal of events and of the reactions of others. This is likely to produce errors and uncertainties in interpersonal behavior. The anxious person may at the same time notice too much and too little and is prone to distort and misinterpret available cues.

COGNITIVE ASSESSMENT

Finding out about style and content of thought is of obvious relevance to the cognitive approach to anxiety. Cognitive assessment is needed to provide information about thoughts that precede, accompany, and follow anxiety-provoking events. It also can provide information about the effects of treatment procedures intended to modify behavior and how someone thinks about a problem.

Efforts to assess the thoughts and ideas that pass through people's minds is a relatively new development. Cognitive assessment can be carried out in a variety of ways (Kendall & Korgeski, 1979). Questionnaires have been developed to sample thoughts, for example, after an upsetting event has taken place. "Beepers" have been used as signals to subjects to record their current thoughts at certain specific points in time (Klinger, Barta, & Maxeiner, 1981). There are also questionnaires to assess the directions people give themselves while working on a task and their personal theories about why things happen as they do. All of these procedures have been used in research on the cognitive component of anxiety. However, they are limited because of the possible confounding of self-presentational styles with the cognitions reported by subjects.

In some cases, distortion of cognitions is created by subjects' defensiveness and their need to present themselves in a particular light, either favorable or unfavorable. In other cases, subjects may not be able to provide accurate accounts of their cognitions because many of these may be habitual responses, as if the individual were on "automatic pilot." Despite the limitations of self-reports, the data they provide are valuable as indicators of individual difference variables and as dependent variables that may reflect clinical treatments, experimental manipulations, or events of everyday life.

In addition to measures of thought in particular situations, researchers have also worked to measure an individual's habitual cognitive patterns. An example of this kind of cognitive assessment is provided by Krantz and Hammen's (1979) study of distortions in thinking that play roles in depression. Their work grew out of research and theory suggesting that depression-prone individuals tend to commit certain errors in thinking which stimulate feelings of depression. Krantz and Hammen developed a questionnaire consisting of several stories that dealt with interpersonal relationships and themes concerning activities and the achievement of goals. For each story, the subjects answered questions pertaining to the central character's feelings, thoughts, and expectations. The answers were scored for various types of distorted thinking, such as the tendency to draw a general conclusion either from a single incident, or from no evidence whatever, and failure to attend to relevant aspects of a situation.

On the basis of the subjects' interpretations of the central character, Krantz and Hammen were able to show that those who were depressed were more likely to make certain types of thinking errors than were nondepressed subjects.

Their findings, together with those of other researchers, suggest that persons with depressive tendencies are particularly prone to accept more responsibility in difficult situations than they should, feel more self-blame, and expect the worst to happen.

Cognitive distortion is also found in problems that come to the attention of clinicians. There is evidence that couples who experience marital disorder have more maritally related irrational beliefs than do better adjusted couples (Eidelson & Epstein, 1982). There is also evidence that groups differing in anxiety symptoms differ in their irrational beliefs and dysfunctional cognitive styles, with high anxiety being associated with high levels of irrational beliefs. Furthermore, cognitively oriented therapy is associated with positive changes in these characteristics. For example, Smith (1983) showed that clients who received rational-emotive therapy had significant pre- to posttherapy decrements in irrational beliefs and desires (e.g., "I want everyone to like me"). In addition there were decrements in emotional distress.

Like the study of depressed persons and clinically anxious individuals, investigations of the cognitive behavior of individuals differing in test anxiety have also shown cognitive distortion. Such studies have consistently revealed that those high in test anxiety spend more time during the testing situation occupied with thoughts not relevant to task completion. These may be worries about performance, negative thoughts about ability, or off-task thoughts. In order to understand this anxiety-associated cognitive behavior better, two more specific instruments have been developed to assess cognitive content in evaluational situations: the Thought Occurrence Questionnaire (TOQ) (Sarason, 1984) and the Cognitive Interference Questionnaire (CIQ) (Sarason & Stoops, 1978). These questionnaires, the former a trait measure and the latter a state or situational measure, require subjects to endorse statements regarding their typical or situational thought content in test-like situations. The TOQ has 4 factor analytically derived subscales related to task-relevant negative thoughts, task-irrelevant affective thoughts, time-irrelevant thoughts and escape thoughts. The CIQ has 3 parts relating to thoughts about the task, thoughts not about the task, and general mind wandering. Although these subscales are relatively highly correlated within and between the two instruments, they vary differentially in predictable ways as the characteristics of evaluational tasks and task instructions are manipulated (Keefe, Schmaling, Sarason, Sarason, & Hayes, 1984).

The variety of techniques and measures described here have given some insight into cognitive patterns both related to individual personality characteristics or cognitive styles and also to situational demands. All these approaches may be useful in assessing what people are thinking about in particular types of situations over time.

TEST ANXIETY

Test anxiety is a personal and social problem for several reasons, not the least of which is the ubiquitousness of test taking. Like shyness, it is not simply an unpleasant experience for the affected individual but it also plays a role in

personal phenomenology and influences performance and personal development. Some aspects of the test anxiety reflect the personal salience of situations
in which people perform tasks and their work is evaluated. A relationship between
assessed test anxiety and performance could come about either because (a) persons
low in ability become anxious about the need to confront situations that produce
failure or relatively poor performance or (b) anxiety somehow prevents full use
of personal wherewithal. Although each of these directions of influence makes
sense, perhaps the more challenging one is the second, because it is completely
expectable that failure situations are aversive and likely to lead to hopelessness,
helplessness, and feelings of inefficacy.

Evidence of a negative correlation between test anxiety and performance
in evaluative situations has led to research concerning the processes that may
be involved. Experimental evidence has added to knowledge about the dele-
terious influence of high levels of test anxiety on information processing and
performance. There is considerable evidence that the performance of highly test
anxious individuals on complex tasks is deleteriously affected by evaluational
stressors (Sarason, 1972a, 1972b, 1975). The less complex, less demanding the
task, the weaker this effect is. An example of an evaluational stressor used in
laboratory studies is achievement-orienting instructions that either inform subjects that some kind of evaluation of their performance will be made or provide
some other rationale for the importance of performing well.

Cognitive Behavior during a Preperformance Waiting Period

A study focused on the cognitive time-filling techniques of anxious individuals (Sarason & Stoops, 1978) illustrates the experimental approach to test
anxiety. The investigation was aimed at providing information about the way
individuals differing in anxiety fill time or what they think about when there is
not a strong situational demand for their attention. The study comprised a series
of three experiments concerning subjective judgments of the passage of time.
After being given either achievement-orienting or neutral instructions, subjects
waited for an undesignated period of time before performing an intellective task.
It was predicted that, in the presence of achievement-oriented cues, time would
pass more slowly for high than for middle and low on the Test Anxiety Scale
(TAS) scorers. When these cues were not present no significant difference in
estimates of time duration among groups differing in test anxiety was expected.
The effects of an achievement orientation were expected to be as noticeable
while the individual was waiting to perform as during performance itself. Most
important, in the context of the present discussion, was the prediction that the
number of negative thoughts reported by the subjects during the waiting period
would be a function both of the presence or absence of the evaluational stressor
and also of the subjects' self-described high or low test anxiety.

The results showed that individuals for whom tests were worrisome experiences (high TAS subjects) tended to overestimate, to a greater degree than did
other subjects, both the duration of the performance evaluation period and the
time spent waiting for the evaluation to take place. Sarason and Stoops also

found that when emphasis was placed on the evaluational implications of performance, highly test-anxious subjects performed at significantly lower levels than did low or middle scorers. Furthermore, highly test-anxious subjects under the achievement-orienting condition experienced levels of cognitive interference that were significantly higher than those of subjects in other conditions, including highly test-anxious subjects who performed under neutral conditions.

Attributional Style and Test Anxiety

The available evidence suggests that there usually is more to a proclivity to test anxiety than simply a history of failure experiences. Every teacher can think of bright, successful students who, contrary to what one would expect, spend inordinate amounts of time worrying about whether they can meet the next academic challenge they must face. Test-anxious people process their objective successes and failures in distinctive ways and their anxiety is related importantly to how they, and significant others in their lives, view test-taking experiences.

An important factor related to performance is attributional style or the way in which responsibility for outcome is typically assessed. In a recent experiment, Turk and Sarason (1983) studied the performance of subjects differing in test anxiety, as a function of a prior success or failure experience and the subject's assignment of responsibility for the performance level achieved. Half of the subjects began the experiment by working on either insoluble or easy anagrams. For each difficulty level, the subjects were given either achievement-orienting or neutral instructions. All subjects were asked to check "passed" on their test if they solved three of the five anagrams and "failed" if they solved fewer than three problems. (All the subjects who worked on the easy anagrams "passed.") They then filled out a questionnaire that dealt with causal attributions. The questionnaire asked the subjects about the extent to which they interpreted their anagrams performance as being due to ability, effort, luck, and task difficulty. Attributions were made on a Likert-type scale of 7 points. In the next phase of the experiment all subjects worked on a series of moderately difficult anagrams.

Following the failure condition, the high test-anxious group performed at a lower level than did all other groups in the experiment. This is consistent with previous work on test anxiety. Following the success condition, the high test-anxious group performed at a higher level than did all other groups. When the subjects were categorized on the basis of their causal attributions, subjects who made internal attributions on the failure task (e.g. "I'm not good at solving problems.") had poorer subsequent performance on the anagrams regardless of their anxiety score. Following the success condition, the best performing group consisted of high test-anxious subjects who made internal attributions (e.g. "I'm an intelligent person."). This study illustrates the need to know more about the effects of success as well as failure experiences for subjects differing in test anxiety and in attributional style. Positive attributions might be particularly effective with highly test anxious people because they counter the worrying and preoccupation that is characteristic of anxiety.

In a study that addressed this question of the interaction and attributional style, Goldberg (1983) correlated test anxiety, assessed using the total score of the Reactions to Tests (to be described shortly), with the Attributional Styles Questionnaire (ASQ) (Peterson *et al.*, in press) which yields scores for causal attributions regarding both good and bad (desirable and undesirable) events. She found that highly test-anxious subjects tend to attribute successful task performance to external factors (e.g., "It was an easy test.") and unsuccessful performance to internal factors ("I don't have good aptitude."). She also found that test anxiety is positively correlated with scores on the Fear of Negative Evaluation Scale (Watson & Friend, 1969). Thus, highly anxious individuals worry about what other people think of them and attribute bad outcomes to "personal helplessness," while low test anxious individuals tend to attribute their successes to personal competence and their failures to external factors. In other words, attributions to long-lasting pervasive causes rather than temporary situational factors are reversed for success and failure in the two groups.

Attentional Focus in Text Anxiety

These differences in attributional style that seem to characterize high and low anxious subjects may be related to different types of cognitive activity and different foci of attention that occur prior to and during the evaluational session. There is now considerable evidence that highly test-anxious subjects in situations that pose test-like challenges perform at relatively low levels and experience relatively high levels of task-irrelevant thoughts (such as self-deprecating attributions). The evidence also indicates that for the most part individuals at different test-anxiety levels show either smaller or no differences in performance and cognitive interference in nontest situations. This type of evidence led Wine (1971, 1982) to an attentional interpretation of test anxiety, according to which people at high and low levels of test anxiety differ in the types of thoughts to which their attention is directed in the face of an evaluative stressor. Consistent with this interpretation are the results of Ganzer's (1968) experiment that showed that, while performing on an intellective task, high test-anxious subjects made many more irrelevant comments than did low test-anxiety scorers. A high percentage of these comments were self-deprecatory. Various researchers have found that high are more likely than low test-anxious people to be preoccupied with and blame themselves for their performance level, feel less confident in making perceptual judgments, and set lower levels of aspiration for themselves (Sarason, 1980).

The Components of Anxiety

There is a sizable body of evidence consistent with the idea that proneness to self-preoccupation, and more specifically worry over evaluation, is a powerful component of what is referred to as test anxiety. If, as several studies suggest, the most active ingredient of test anxiety is self-preoccupation, there are some important and practical implications for assessment. Although general and test anxiety are usually defined as complex states that include cognitive, emotional, behavioral, and bodily components, most anxiety measures reflect this inclusive definition by yielding only one global score. Wine (1982) has recently pointed out that it is not immediately obvious how to identify the active or most active ingredients in this complex and has suggested that test anxiety might fruitfully be reconceptualized primarily in terms of cognitive and attentional processes aroused in evaluational settings.

In order to assess separately several components of a person's reactions to test situations, an instrument, Reactions to Tests (RTT), has recently been created (Sarason, 1984). It consists of four factor analytically derived scales:

- Tension or Emotionality ("I feel distressed and uneasy before tests").
- Worry ("During tests, I wonder how the other people are doing").
- Test-Irrelevant Thought ("Irrelevant bits of information pop into my head during a test").
- Bodily Reactions ("My heart beats faster when the test begins").

Although these scales are positively intercorrelated, these correlations are low enough to justify comparisons among them concerning their predictive value.

In preliminary studies, the RTT was related to performance on a difficult digit-symbol task under evaluative conditions. The Worry scale was more consistently related to performance and postperformance reports of cognitive interference than were the other scales. The Tension scale approached the Worry scale as a predictor of performance.

In another study using a proofreading task the Worry scale was highly related to on- and off-task negative thoughts. The Test-Irrelevant Thought scale was related, as might be expected, most highly to off-task thoughts; however, individuals scoring high on this scale also showed a relatively high degree of negative task-related thoughts and reported that their minds wandered during the proofreading. The Tension scale was related only to negative thoughts about the task. The Bodily Reactions scale was not related to any of the cognitive interference measures.

The RTT has also been related to physiological measures obtained during a test-taking situation (Burchfield, Sarason, Sarason, & Beaton, 1982) Interestingly, the Bodily Reactions scale was unrelated to the physiological change measures used (GSR, EMG, and finger tip temperature). Both the Tension and Worry scales were significantly correlated with GSR and finger tip temperature changes during performance.

SOCIAL ANXIETY, SHYNESS, AND THEIR COMPONENTS

Just as the componential approach seems to hold promise of a better understanding of evaluational anxiety, the same approach may prove useful in the study of social anxiety and shyness. Although these two concepts are among the most widely used in analyses of social behavior, unfortunately they refer to such a wide variety of phenomena that their referents are often difficult to identify. For example, social anxiety can be specific or general. Some people experience it prior to, during, or after their social interactions, whereas others experience it in particular situations. For some people, social anxiety and shyness are highly correlated, whereas for others there seems to be only a slight relationship. Although most shy people show anxiety and social inhibition in interpersonal situations, others may display timidity or introversion without apparent personal discomfort (Leary, 1983). Thus, two important problems present themselves: (a) How general or trait-like are the tendencies toward social anxiety and shyness? (b) What are the components of reactions to social situations and what is their interrelationship? A third question also needs an answer: (c) How do moderator variables (either within the individual or in the environment) influence social behavior and the experience of social anxiety and shyness?

These questions are being approached by us and by others in a variety of ways. Because the component analysis of test anxiety seemed promising, we are using a similar approach to social behavior. The Reactions to Tests described earlier consists of four 10-item scales: (Tension or Emotionality, Worry, Test-Irrelevant Thought, and Bodily Reactions) that grew out of factor analytic studies. The RTT items were rewritten to refer to social rather than testing situations. The new instrument, called Reactions to Social Situations (RSS), was administered to a large group of college students, and factor analyzed. Essentially the same four factors found for the RTT emerged in the factor analysis of the RSS. However, the RSS tension and worry factors were less pure than the comparable RTT factors. The correlation between the RTT and RSS total scores over several samples is of the order of .50.

When the RSS was correlated with three other individual difference indexes, several significant relationships were found. One of these indexes was the Social Competence Questionnaire (Com Q), a 10-item scale designed to tap the degree of comfort in social situations (Sarason, Sarason, Hacker, & Basham, 1985). Each Com Q item is rated by the subject on a 4-point rating scale from "not at all like me" to "a great deal like me." Table 1 presents the Com Q's items. Whereas there were significant negative correlations between all four RSS scales and the Com Q for both sexes, those involving the RSS Tension scale were the highest

TABLE 1. Items Included in the Social Competence Questionnaire (COMQ)[a]

1. Start a conversation with someone I don't know well, but would like to get to know better
2. Be confident in my ability to make friends, even in a situation where I know few people
3. Be able to mix well in a group
4. Feel uncomfortable looking at other people directly
5. Have trouble keeping a conversation going when I'm just getting to know someone
6. Find it hard to let a person know that I want to become closer friends with him/her
7. Enjoy social gatherings just to be with people
8. Have problems getting other people to notice me
9. Feel confident of my social behavior
10. Seek out social encounters because I enjoy being with other people

[a]Each item is marked on a four point scale ranging from "not at all like me" to "a great deal like me."

(rs = $-.67$ and $-.63$ for males and females, respectively.) The comparable Worry scale correlations were $-.45$ and $-.49$. Thus, self-reported tension or emotionality and worry on the RSS is reflected in lower levels of self-described social competence.

The RSS scores were also correlated with the two scales of the Social Support Questionnaire (SSQ) (Sarason, Levine, Basham, and Sarason, 1983). The SSQ has two scores: the Number score measures the number of persons that the individual perceives to be available if support were needed, the Satisfaction score measures how satisfactory the available support is perceived to be. Just as was the case with the Com Q, the Tension scale correlated the most negatively of the four RSS scales with the SSQ Number score (rs = $-.30$ and $-.29$ for males and females, respectively) and with the Satisfaction score (rs = $-.35$ and $-.33$ for males and females, respectively).

The third individual difference measure with which the RSS was correlated was a specially constructed, slightly shortened version of the Thought Occurrence Questionnaire (TOQ) mentioned earlier in this chapter. The TOQ asks subjects to rate the frequency with which task-irrelevant thoughts generally occur while they work on various types of tasks. The 5-point rating scale extends from "Never" to "Very often." Examples of TOQ items are, "I think about how poorly I am doing"; "I think about what someone will think of me"; "I think about how hard it is."

The correlation of the RSS score (summing over its 40 items) with the TOQ was .44 for males and .53 for females. Every item on the TOQ was correlated significantly and positively with the RSS's score reflecting the tendency to experience task-irrelevant thoughts in social situations. It may well be that task-irrelevant thinking plays as detrimental role in social behavior as it does in test-taking situations. Twenty-two of the 28 items in this shortened version of the TOQ correlated significantly with the RSS Tension Scale. Twenty-four of the correlations with the RSS Worry scale were significant.

These findings using the RSS are only small first steps in specifying the relationships among dimensions of social behavior and personality and cognitive characteristics. They are presented here because it is possible that a multidimensional approach to social behavior will provide an empirically based vocabulary that reduces some of the semantic disagreements surrounding such terms as shyness and social anxiety.

CONCLUSIONS

The literature on anxiety is giving increasing recognition to its multidimensionality. The three dimensions that have been studied in some depth—the behavioral, cognitive, and physiological—may not be highly correlated. The Reactions to Tests was designed to provide an instrument that goes beyond one global index for evaluational anxiety. The Reactions to Social Situations was designed to serve a similar function for a study of an individual's response to interpersonal contacts. Although more research into the dimensions and correlates of test and social anxiety is clearly needed, the available data suggests that more complex assessment instruments may play an important role in specifying the nature of complex concepts such as anxiety and shyness. Research thus far suggests that the cognitive dimensions of worry and task-irrelevant thinking that seem to be so important in test anxiety function similarly with regard to social anxiety.

REFERENCES

Burchfield, S., Sarason I. G., Sarason, B. R. & Beaton, R. (1982). *Test anxiety and physiological responding*. (Unpublished manuscript), University of Washington.

Eidelson, R. J., & Epstein, N. (1982). Cognition and relationship maladjustment: Development of a measure of dysfunctional relationship beliefs. *Journal of Consulting and Clinical Psychology, 50*, 715–720.

Ganzer, V. J. (1968). The effects of audience pressure and test anxiety on learning and retention in a serial learning situation. *Journal of Personality and Social Psychology, 8*, 194–199.

Goldberg, S. A. (1983). *Cognitive correlates of test anxiety: Examination of the relationship among test anxiety, fear of negative evaluation, social anxiety, and attributional style*. Providence, R.I. Unpublished honors thesis, Brown University.

Jones, W. H., & Russell, D. (1982). The social reticence scale: An objective instrument to measure shyness. *Journal of Personality Assessment, 46*, 629–631.

Keefe, D. E., Schmaling, K. B., Sarason, I. G., Sarason, B. R., & Hayes, B. E. (1984, April). *Cognitive interference, cognitive failure and the effects of stress*. Paper presented at the meeting of the Western Psychological Association, Los Angeles, CA.

Kendall, P. C., & Korgeski, G. P. (1979). Assessment and cognitive-behavioral interventions. *Cognitive Therapy and Research, 3*, 1–21.

Klinger, E., Barta, S. G., & Maxeiner, M. E. (1981). Current concerns: Assessing therapeutically relevant motivation. In P. C. Kendall & S. D. Hollon (Eds.) *Assessment strategies for cognitive-behavioral interventions* (pp. 97–120). New York: Academic Press.

Krantz, S., & Hammen, C. (1979). Assessment of cognitive bias in depression. *Journal of Abnormal Psychology, 88*, 611–619.

Lang, P. J. (1969). The mechanics of desensitization and the laboratory study of fear. In C. M. Franks (Ed.), *Behavior therapy: Appraisal and status* (pp. 270–301). New York: McGraw-Hill.

Lang, P. J. (1979). A bio-informational theory of emotional imagery. *Psychophysiology, 16*, 129–133.

Leary, M. R. (1983). Social anxiety. *Understanding social anxiety: social, personality, and clinical perspective*. Beverly Hills, CA: Sage.

Peterson, C., Semmel, A., von Baeyer, C., Abramson, L., Metalsky, G., & Seligman, M. E. P. (1982). The Attributional Style Questionnaire. *Cognitive Therapy and Research, 6*, 287–300.

Rachman, S. J. (1978). *Fear and courage*. San Francisco: Freeman.

Sarason, B. R., Sarason, I. G., Hacker, T. A., & Basham, R. B. (1985). Concomitants of social support, social skills, physical attractiveness and gender. *Journal of Personality and Social Psychology, 49*, 469–480.

Sarason, I. G. (1972a). Experimental approaches to test anxiety: Attention and the uses of information. In C. D. Spielberger (Ed.), *Anxiety: Current trends in theory and research* (Vol. 2, pp. 383–403). New York: Academic Press.

Sarason, I. G. (1972b). Test anxiety and the model who fails. *Journal of Personality and Social Psychology, 22*, 410–423.

Sarason, I. G. (1975). Test anxiety, attention and the general problem of anxiety. In C. D. Spielberger & I. G. Sarason (Eds), *Stress and anxiety*, (Vol. 1, pp. 165–187). Washington, DC: Hemisphere.

Sarason, I. G. (1980). *Test anxiety: Theory, research and applications*. Hillsdale, NJ: Erlbaum.

Sarason, I. G. (1984). Stress, anxiety and cognitive interference: Reactions to tests. *Journal of Personality and Social Psychology. 26,* 929–938.

Sarason, I. G. & Stoops, R. (1978). Test anxiety and the passage of time. *Journal of Consulting and Clinical Psychology, 46,* 102–109.

Sarason, I. G., Levine, H. M., Basham, R. B., Sarason, B. R. (1983). Assessing social support: The Social Support Questionnaire. *Journal of Personality and Social Psychology, 44,* 127–139.

Smith, T. W. (1983). Change in irrational beliefs and the outcome of rational-emotive psychotherapy. *Journal of Consulting and Clinical Psychology, 51,* 156–157.

Turk, S. & Sarason, I. G. (1983). *Test anxiety, success-failure, and causal attribution.* Unpublished manuscript. Seattle, WA: University of Washington.

Watson, D., & Friend, R. (1969). Measurement of social-evaluative anxiety. *Journal of Consulting and Clinical Psychology, 33,* 448–457.

Wine, J. D. (1971). Test anxiety and direction of attention. *Psychological Bulletin, 76,* 92–104.

Wine, J. D. (1982). Evaluation anxiety: A cognitive-attentional construct. In H. W. Krohne & L. Laux (Eds.), *Achievement, stress and anxiety* (pp. 207–219). New York: Hemisphere.

20

Physiological, Affective, and Behavioral Implications of Extraversion-Introversion

Russell G. Geen

THE STRUCTURE OF EXTRAVERSION-INTROVERSION

The concept of extraversion-introversion has a long history. As Eysenck (1981) has noted in a recent historical overview, the idea is implicit in the earliest views of character types. The four temperaments of Galen (and later Kant)—long a staple item in introductory psychology textbooks—can be shown to fit into the four quadrants of a two-factor space defined by two broad orthogonal dimensions. Wundt defined the latter as changeability and emotionality. The Dutch psychologist Gerardus Heymans and his associates later described eight basic character types arranged along three dimensions—changeability, emotionality, and activity. (See Figure 1.) Even later, Spearman became the first to demonstrate the factors now called extraversion-introversion and neuroticism (Spearman's "w" and "c," respectively). Other historical contributions to the development of the notion of extraversion-introversion were made by Jung, who linked the two types to two different neurotic disorders, and Kretschmer, who indicated a relationships between introversion and hereditary constitutional factors.

The most thoroughgoing approach to the construct of extraversion-introversion in recent times has been that of Eysenck, who has proposed a theoretical basis for the construct and also reported extensive data supporting the theory. Eysenck arrived at his theory as a result of factor analysis of information on the traits, symptoms, and life histories of several hundred hospitalized patients in a military hospital (Eysenck, 1947). The theory in its latest form includes three orthogonal factors labelled Extraversion-Introversion, Neuroticism, and Psychoticism. In this review we will not be concerned with Psychoticism, nor with Neuroticism (N) except insofar as it affects the Extraversion-Introversion

RUSSELL G. GEEN • Department of Psychology, University of Missouri at Columbia, Columbia, MO 65211.

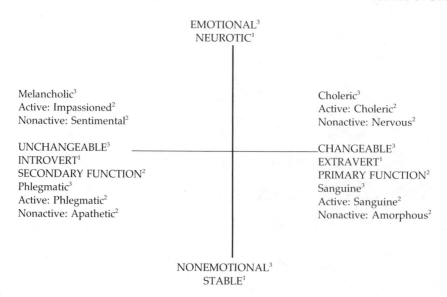

EMOTIONAL[3]
NEUROTIC[1]

Melancholic[3]
Active: Impassioned[2]
Nonactive: Sentimental[2]

UNCHANGEABLE[3]
INTROVERT[1]
SECONDARY FUNCTION[2]
Phlegmatic[3]
Active: Phlegmatic[2]
Nonactive: Apathetic[2]

Choleric[3]
Active: Choleric[2]
Nonactive: Nervous[2]

CHANGEABLE[3]
EXTRAVERT[1]
PRIMARY FUNCTION[2]
Sanguine[3]
Active: Sanguine[2]
Nonactive: Amorphous[2]

NONEMOTIONAL[3]
STABLE[1]

FIGURE 1. Scheme of common personality traits along hypothesized dimensions of changeability and stability (see text for explanation). Superscripts refer to: [1]dimensions of E-I and N (Eysenck, 1967); [2]dimensions and types of Heymans (from Roback, 1927); and [3]types of Galen on dimensions of Wundt (from Eysenck, 1981).

(E-I) variable. In general, the E-I dimension is comparable to the dimension of Changeability-Unchangeability in Figure 1, and the N dimension to the Emotional-Nonemotional.

Assessment of the variables described by the theory has been by means of a number of paper-and-pencil, self-report inventories. Most of the older studies in the literature involved the use of the Maudsley Personality Inventory, a 48-item questionnaire containing subscales for E-I and N (Eysenck, 1962). This instrument was supplanted by the Eysenck Personality Inventory (Eysenck & Eysenck, 1968), a 57-item test containing, in addition to the E-I and N subscales, a lie (L) scale for the detection of dissimulation. The most recently developed instrument is the Eysenck Personality Questionnaire (Eysenck & Eysenck, 1977), a test of 90 items that contains subscales for E-I, N, L, and Psychoticism (P). As a means of measuring E-I and N it is comparable to the earlier Eysenck Personality Inventory.

THE PHYSIOLOGY OF EXTRAVERSION-INTROVERSION

The Theoretical Model

Physiology. The key concepts in Eysenck's theory of the physiological basis of extraversion-introversion are *excitation* and *inhibition*. Inhibition is considered to be an active process that opposes excitation, not merely a passive loss of excitatory potential. Eysenck thus defines inhibition in terms similar to those used by Hull. The fundamental relationship between extraversion-introversion and physiology rests on two sets of variables: (a) the speed with which excitation is generated in the central nervous system, the speed with which it is dissipated, and the relative strength of excitatory processes thus produced; and (b) the strength, speed of generation, and rapidity of dissipation of inhibition. Extraverts generate relatively weak excitatory potentials slowly and dissipate them rapidly; they also generate strong inhibitory potentials rapidly and dissipate them slowly. Introverts do the opposite in each case.

Individual differences in excitation and inhibition reflect differential thresholds for arousal in the ascending reticular activating system (ARAS), a bundle of neurons in the midbrain that ultimately activates the cells of the cortex (Eysenck, 1967). The ARAS conveys both specific sensory information to sensory regions of the cortex and nonspecific impulses that raise the general activation level of the entire cortical surface. It is, in turn, dampened and inhibited by impulses descending from the cortex. The introvert is therefore a person characterized by high levels of excitation at the reticular level whereas the extravert is one characterized by high levels of descending cortical inhibition.

Activation of the ARAS may be initiated by either external stimuli like loud noises and bright lights or internal emotional events. The dimension of neuroticism is important in this respect. The difference between neurotic and stable personalities reflects different levels of activity in another part of the brain, the limbic system. Neurotics are characterized by high levels of limbic activity. Because of known links between the limbic structures and the ARAS, activity in the former can trigger activation in the latter. This connection accounts for the general findings of a weak, but positive, correlation between extraversion-introversion and neuroticism. Because neurotics are more likely than normals to manifest activity in the limbic system they are therefore also more likely to initiate reticular activation. Thus the most highly aroused type of personality in Eysenck's system is the neurotic introvert (McLaughlin & Eysenck, 1967; Schwartz, 1975).

Heritability. Further evidence of the physiological basis of extraversion-introversion comes from studies showing a heritability component in the variable. One such study was a major investigation by Eaves and Eysenck (1975) in which 837 pairs of adult twins responded to a scale measuring the sociability and impulsivity components of extraversion-introversion. The data showed that both environmental and genetic factors contributed to the variation and covariation of sociability and impulsiveness, with the genetical correlation between the two estimated to be .42 and the environmental correlation .66; furthermore, adding sociability to impulsivity to obtain a single measure of extraversion yielded the best single means of discriminating between individuals in regard to their scores on the impulsiveness and sociability subscales. Overall, approximately 40% of the variation in sociability, impulsiveness, and the combinations of the two could be attributed to genetic factors.

Research Evidence

EEG. Effects of individual differences in extraversion-introversion on cortical alpha have been the subject of two major reviews by Gale (1973; 1981), who has emphatically concluded that "no adequate test has yet been made of the theory" (p. 186). Research on the problem has been beset by both conceptual and methodological problems. Although numerous studies have been reported over the years, none has stated precisely the situational conditions under which introverts show greater EEG activity than extraverts, or vice versa. The reader is referred to Gale's excellent reviews for details.

Habituation of the Electrodermal Orienting Response. Eysenck's postulation of greater arousability in introverts than in extraverts also leads to the expectation that introverts habituate to repeated stimuli more slowly than extraverts. As was the case with EEG measures, however, evidence pertaining to extravert-introvert differences in orienting response (OR) habituation is equivocal and dependent on consideration of experimental treatments (e.g., Coles, Gale, & Kline, 1971; Crider & Lunn, 1971; Stelmack, Bourgeois, Chien, & Pickard, 1979). Inspection of findings on the magnitude of initial orienting responses to habituation stimuli likewise shows the importance of differences in stimulus intensity. The results of a series of reports by Smith and his colleagues present a complex picture from which a curvilinear relationship of initial response strength to stimulus intensity appears to emerge (Smith & Wigglesworth, 1978; Smith, Wilson, & Rypma, 1981; Wigglesworth & Smith, 1976). Thus arousal and stimulus intensity may be related in the form of an inverted U with introverts peaking at lower intensity levels than extraverts (Figure 2).

Stimulation and Arousal: The Inverted U. Findings suggesting the functions shown in Figure 2 have come from a number of studies involving behavioral and physiological measures. Both Revelle, Amaral, and Turriffe (1976) and Gilliland (1980) showed that a combination of time pressure and ingestion of caffeine caused the performance of introverts on a test of verbal ability to decline in quality, whereas the same treatment brought about improvement in the performance of extraverts. More direct evidence of the curvilinear relationship is found in several psychophysiological studies. Smith and his associates (Smith, Rypma, & Wilson, 1981; Smith, Wilson, & Jones, 1983) have shown that administration of caffeine causes the skin conductance level in response to a tone to

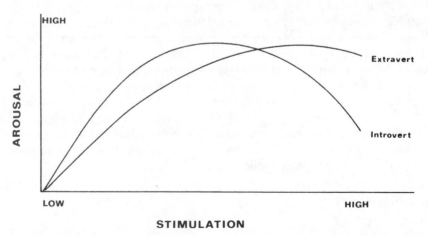

FIGURE 2. Hypothesized relationship between stimulation and arousal.

be lower for introverts than for extraverts, a reversal of the ordering of the two groups found under conditions of less stimulation. Fowles, Roberts, and Nagel (1977) have shown that when the delivery of arousing noise is preceded by a difficult task, introverts show maximum conductance levels in response to noise of intermediate intensity, suggesting that the combination of intense noise and a difficult task pushes introverts beyond the point of maximum arousal.

Extraversion and Motor Control. To date, most of the interest in the physiological significance of extraversion-introversion has been directed toward the study of sensory stimulation, as noted in the preceding section. Recently, however, there has been a growing interest in extravert-introvert differences in motor performance (e.g., Brebner, 1983; Brebner & Cooper, 1974), much of it arising from research on the relationship between extraversion and impulsivity (e.g., Barratt, 1983). Stelmack and Plouffe (1983) have reviewed evidence indicating that extraverts may, in addition to being generally less sensitive to sensory stimulation that introverts, also be more likely to emit brief but strong bursts of motor activity. These bursts tend to facilitate performance on tasks requiring gross motor action, but to have a debilitating effect on tasks requiring motor control or inhibition. Stelmack and Plouffe recommend a renewed interest in the distinction between sensory and motor nerves, which might provide a useful model for future studies of extravert-introvert differences.

EXTRAVERSION-INTROVERSION AND BEHAVIOR

Extraversion and Affect

When we turn to the behavioral side of differences between extraverts and introverts we encounter another inverted U involved with the level of stimulation. The amount and quality of affect experienced in response to a stimulus varies with the stimulus intensity level according to the theoretical functions described in Figure 3. As stimulus intensity is increased above absolute threshold, positive affect is generated up to a point, beyond which further increases in stimulation lead to progressive experience of negative affect. According to the theory of extraversion-introversion, introverts reach the maximum state of positive affect at a lower stimulation level than extraverts. A number of findings corroborate this general model. For example, extraverts have been shown to tolerate higher levels of noise (Elliott, 1971) and pain (Schalling, 1971) than introverts, whereas introverts show greater tolerance for prolonged sensory deprivation (Petrie, Collins, & Solomon, 1960).

It must be understood that the functions relating stimulation to arousal (Figure 2) and to affect (Figure 3), although both are curvilinear, do not describe the same process. Evidence from a recent study by Geen (1984) indicates that the stimulus intensity associated with maximum positive affect is lower than that associated with maximum arousal. In this experiment, some introverts and some extraverts chose the intensity of noise with which they would be stimulated during a task. Other subjects of both types were assigned noise at levels either

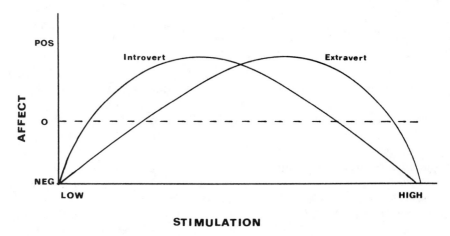

FIGURE 3. Hypothesized relationship between stimulation and positive, neutral, and negative affect.

higher than the highest chosen level or lower than the lowest chosen level. As Figure 4 shows, extraverts chose noise levels higher than those selected by introverts. The two levels thus chosen operationally define the optimal stimulus levels for maximum positive affect in the two groups. When noise of intensity higher than those was administered, which would presumably produce a decrease in positive affect, both introverts and extraverts continued to manifest increased arousal.

Extraversion and Stimulus Seeking

One direct corollary of the model shown in Figure 3 is that introverts and extraverts will be motivated to attain the maximum level of positive affect by seeking out a stimulation level appropriate to the respective personality type. Thus, given a free choice of stimulus levels, extraverts should prefer higher levels than introverts. Although few investigators have approached this problem directly, the prediction is supported by some evidence. Studies have shown that extraverts actively seek stimulation when it is made available (Brebner & Cooper, 1978), whereas introverts avoid it (Davies, Hockey, & Taylor, 1969). The study by Geen (1984) noted above showed that when extraverts and introverts were free to choose the levels of intensity of ambient noise, extraverts chose noise at a mean intensity level of 70 dB whereas the mean intensity chosen by introverts was 54 dB.

The extravert's desire for levels of stimulation higher than those considered optimal by the introvert has some interesting implications for more complex behavior. Extraverts tend also to score higher than introverts on Zuckerman's Sensation Seeking Scale (SSS), (Zuckerman, 1971) and on the SSS subscales for Disinhibition and Thrill and Adventure Seeking (S. Eysenck & Zuckerman, 1978). The first of these subscales measures desire for excitement through the adoption of a "fast" lifestyle involving parties, drinking, and sexual variety. The second measures a desire to participate in outdoor activities involving speed and danger.

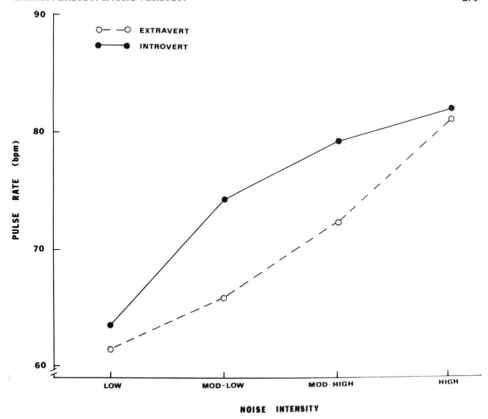

FIGURE 4. Arousal (operationalized as pulse rate) as a function of stimulus (noise) intensity in extraverts and introverts. *Note*: Mod-Low is mean stimulus intensity chosen by introverts; Mod-High is mean stimulus intensity chosen by extraverts; Low is mean lowest intensity chosen by introverts; High is mean highest intensity chosen by extraverts. From "Preferred Stimulation Levels in Introverts and Extraverts: Effects on Arousal and Performance" by R. G. Geen, 1984, *Journal of Personality and Social Psychology, 46*, 1303–1312. Copyright 1984 by the American Psychological Association. Reprinted by permission.

A study by Maddi, Hoover, and Kobasa (1982) shows a negative correlation between extraversion and alienation, a concept that includes feelings of powerlessness, a disposition not to become involved in activities, and the tendency to regard the changing events of life as a threat rather than a challenge. Maddi and his associates also found that extraverts engage in more exploratory behavior in a novel situation than do introverts. The overall picture derived from data such as these is of the extravert as a more active, engaged person who experiences strong stimulation as pleasant and of the introvert who experiences it as less pleasant or even aversive, and hence avoids it.

Impulsivity and Sociability

Certain critics of Eysenck's theory have argued that extraversion-introversion is not a unitary construct, but instead a combination of unrelated factors of sociability and impulsivity (Carrigan, 1960; Guilford, 1975). In response, Eysenck and Eysenck (1977) have cited evidence that the impulsivity and sociability dimensions are indeed correlated and that this covariation is shown to be influenced by the genetic factors in the variable (Eaves & Eysenck, 1975). In general, a fairly impressive amount of support for the correlation between impulsivity and sociability can be marshalled. However, the results of a factor analytic study reported by Barratt and Patton (1983) cloud the issue somewhat; their data indicate that whereas sociability and impulsivity are highly related in women, they are orthogonal in men.

Part of the problem may be that impulsivity is probably not a unitary construct. Eysenck and Eysenck (1977) have suggested that the term can be defined in either a narrow sense to describe only a tendency toward rash and uncontrolled acts or in a more broad sense to describe such other behaviors as risk taking, lack of rational planning, and overall activity level. The Eysencks in fact isolated four subfactors of impulsivity broadly defined; those they labelled narrow impulsivity, risk taking, nonplanning, and liveliness. Of these four, narrow impulsivity and nonplanning were not found to correlate with extraversion-introversion, whereas risk taking and liveliness were positively correlated with E-I. A subsequent study (Eysenck, 1983) has shown that the risk taking and nonplanning subfactors are positively correlated with scores on Zuckerman's Sensation Seeking Scale, with risk taking showing the highest overall correlation. Narrow impulsivity and liveliness tend to be positively, but weakly, correlated with sensation seeking.

Of the two subfactors of extraversion-introversion, impulsivity appears to be the one associated with observed behavioral and arousal differences. Farley and Farley (1970) found that the impulsivity subscale correlated with sensation seeking more than the sociability subscale, and Zuckerman (1974) likewise concluded that the link between sensation seeking and extraversion is accounted for by impulsivity. Impulsivity has also been shown to be correlated with inability to tolerate boredom (Schalling, Edman, & Asberg, 1983).

Experimental evidence tends to bear out this conclusion. Revelle, Humphreys, Simon, and Gilliland (1980) found that whereas extraversion and caffeine interacted to influence performance on complex cognitive performance tasks in an inconsistent way, impulsivity and caffeine interacted consistently when time of day was taken into account. When testing was carried out in the morning, low impulsives were hindered in their performance by caffeine ingestion, but high impulsives were helped. This finding agrees with that of Revelle *et al.* (1976) just cited. The pattern of effects was reversed when testing was done in the evening, however. Even with this additional factor of diurnal rhythm complicating the picture, it is clear the impulsivity component of extraversion-introversion is what underlies the arousal and behavioral effects. In an interesting field experiment, Campbell (1983) has reported similar findings. Students in a college library who preferred studying in noisy, somewhat crowded, and generally stimulating areas were found to score higher in both extraversion and impulsivity, but not sociability, than students preferring to study in more quiet surroundings. In addition, impulsivity was a better predictor than sociability of preferred noise level and, interestingly, perceived importance of and preferred level of socializing opportunities. Sociability was more highly correlated with preferred level of crowdedness.

Extraversion and Vigilance

The experimental procedure of vigilance requires a subject to maintain close attention to a stimulus display for a prolonged period, usually in isolation. The task involves detecting and reporting brief and infrequent signals occurring against a background of random auditory or visual stimulation. The vigilance situation is usually monotonous and the overall level of ambient stimulation is low. Because introverts generally find low stimulation to be more pleasant than extraverts, and also because of the introvert's superior sensitivity to stimuli near the sensory threshold (Smith, 1968), introverts should, according to the theory, perform better on vigilance tasks than extraverts.

Several measures of vigilance performance are reported in the literature on the subject. The simplest is hit rate, that is, the number of signals accurately reported. Although there is some evidence that introverts detect more signals than extraverts (Bakan, 1959; Gange, Geen, & Harkins, 1979; Harkins & Geen, 1975), such findings alone do not necessarily indicate better sensitivity to signals in introverts. They may show only that introverts have a higher overall response rate on both signal and nonsignal trials. More convincing are studies that show that extraverts decrease in hit rate as the vigilance period goes on (Bakan, Belton, & Toth, 1963; Davies & Hockey, 1966; Keister & McLaughlin, 1972). Prolonged understimulation might be expected to cause extraverts increasing discomfort and motivation to seek stimulation. This could lead to daydreaming, random movement, or progressive agitation; any of these reactions could be detrimental to sustained attention. Thus, the data on both absolute hit rate and decrements in rate over time tend to support the conclusion that introverts are more sensitive to signals than extraverts.

Another way of determining whether introverts are really more sensitive than extraverts or merely more prone to emit a high response rate is by analysis of the false-alarm rate, that is, the number of times the subject reports a signal when none was in fact given. Studies that have included such an analysis tend to agree by showing that extraverts are more likely to show a higher rate of false alarms than introverts (Harkins & Geen, 1975; Krupski, Raskin, Bakan, 1969; Tune, 1966). Thus, the higher hit rate for introverts is probably not due to a higher overall response rate, because the latter would probably also produce a higher rate of false alarms. It is the extraverts, not the introverts, that set a liberal criterion for reporting signals. Harkins and Geen (1975) carried out an analysis of data from a visual vigilance experiment based on signal-detection theory and found that introverts had higher mean scores for d' (an indicator of sensitivity to signals) and for *beta* (an indicator of conservatism in reporting signals). Harkins and Geen concluded that the extravert's tendency to set a liberal criterion for responding and hence to make more false alarms was due to the greater impulsivity of extraverts. It appears, therefore, that the greater need for stimulation in extraverts lies at the roots of both their inferiority in detecting signals and in their tendencies to report signals when none are given.

A few studies have investigated the effects of raising the level of ambient stimulation on vigilance performance. If the superiority of introverts is due to their ability to function better than extraverts under unstimulating conditions, then the addition of other situational stimuli could be expected to reduce that superiority (cf. Davies *et al.*, 1969; Keister & McLaughlin, 1972).

A reversal of the normal difference between introverts and extraverts at high levels of stimulation has been shown in a study of visual vigilance by Geen, McCown, and Broyles (1985). Introverted and extraverted subjects were instructed to report occurrences of brief and infrequent visual signals while being stimulated with random noise at an intensity of either 65 dB or 85 dB. The data were analyzed according to signal-detection theory. Introverts were found to show less sensitivity to signals (d') when 85 dB noise was given than when the noise was of the lower intensity, whereas extraverts given the louder noise performed with somewhat greater sensitivity than when less intense noise was given. Geen *et al.* argued that the combination of the stressful task, instructions that created a strong ego-involvement, and a relatively intense noise stimulated introverts to such an extent that their arousal levels were on the declining portion of the curve shown in Figure 2. Extraverts, by contrast, under equivalent conditions were still below the stimulation level associated with maximal arousal.

Extraversion, Shyness, and Social Anxiety

The picture of extraverts that emerges even from this brief and inexhaustive review is that of people who are highly sociable, disposed to be active, somewhat impulsive, and motivated to seek stimulation from their environments. Extraversion would therefore appear to be the antithesis of shyness. Although no really systematic and extended research has been done on the subject, studies that relate extraversion to shyness and social anxiety come to that conclusion. In a comprehensive review of intercorrelations between extraversion-introversion and a number of other trait variables, Morris (1979) has shown that E-I is not correlated with either locus of control or field dependence, but is correlated with repression-sensitization. Introverts generally have been shown to be sensitizers and extraverts to be repressors (Cohen & Oziel, 1972; Dana & Cocking, 1969), a finding that Morris interprets as meaning that extraverts are relatively less attentive than introverts to internal stimuli that might inhibit behavior. Thus "the lack of restraint and lack of social inhibition of the extravert may be as much a matter of choosing not to attend to . . . internal stimuli as a matter of not having learned them" (p. 79). Morris also suggests an interaction with neuroticism, such that sensitizers might be characterized as neurotic introverts and repressors as stable extraverts, but concedes that we have little evidence bearing on such a hypothesis.*

*The possibility of a complex relationship among E-I, Neuroticism, and shyness is indicated by some unpublished data obtained by Cheek (personal communication). Cheek found that shyness, as measured by the Cheek-Buss Shyness Scale (Cheek & Buss, 1981) correlated negatively with extraversion for both males ($r = -.31$) and females ($r = -.28$) and positively with neuroticism for males ($r = .29$) and females ($r = .47$). The shy person is therefore likely to be a neurotic introvert.

Perhaps the clearest evidence to date of a relationship between extraversion-introversion and variables related to shyness and social anxiety comes from a study by Pilkonis (1977) in which 263 persons were asked to indicate whether they perceived themselves to be shy. Subjects were also given the Eysenck Personality Inventory (EPI), the Self-Consciousness (SC) Scale of Fenigstein, Scheier, & Buss (1975), and Snyder's (1974) Self-Monitoring Scale (S-M). The SC Scale yields scores for public self-consciousness, which is concern for oneself as an object of social attention, private self-consciousness, which indicates sensitivity to private thoughts and feelings, and social anxiety, which is distress in social situations. The S-M Scale indicates the degree to which a person uses cues emanating from other people versus those arising from a personal system of standards in choosing behaviors for self-presentation. Ratings of shyness were found to be negatively correlated with extraversion as measured by the EPI ($r = -.43$) and by an E-I scale specifically designed to measure the degree to which thoughts and attention are directed toward or away from the self ($r = -.38$). Several other correlations of interest to the present review emerged: EPI extraversion correlated positively with self-monitoring (showing sensitivity to behavioral cues emanating from other people), and negatively with social anxiety. EPI sociability showed similar correlations with self-monitoring and social anxiety, whereas neuroticism was correlated positively with public self-consciousness, private self-consciousness, and social anxiety.

SUMMARY

1. Extraversion-introversion is a higher order factor of personality that is derived from correlations among lower order traits. It defines the endpoints on a continuum associated with overall activity or excitability. This continuum, described by different names over the years, constitutes one of the basic dimensions in personality as it has been discussed in history.

2. Extraversion-introversion is grounded in individual differences in excitatory and inhibitory activity in the central nervous system. In general, extraverts tend toward generation of inhibitory potentials and introverts toward generation of excitatory potentials. The basis for this difference is the threshold for activation in the ascending reticular activating system, with introverts showing a lower threshold than extraverts.

3. Introverts and extraverts both reveal an inverted U function relating stimulation level to arousal, with introverts reaching the peak in arousal at a lower level of stimulation than extraverts. Thus, introverts show greater arousal than extraverts at low-to-moderate levels of stimulation, but are less aroused at higher levels.

4. The level of stimulation associated with maximum positive affect is lower for introverts than for extraverts. Extraverts seek stimulation more than introverts. Extraverts and introverts therefore differ in tolerance for sensory deprivation, in ability to withstand pain and excessive noise, and in performance in tasks demanding sustained attention.

5. Extraversion is negatively related to shyness and social anxiety, and positively to impulsivity and sociability. In general, therefore, introverts are more likely to be shy than extraverts. One reason for this may be the introvert's need to avoid overstimulation in social settings.

REFERENCES

Bakan, P. (1959). Extraversion-introversion and improvement in an auditory vigilance task. *British Journal of Psychology, 50* 325–332.

Bakan, P., Belton, J., & Toth J. (1963). Extraversion-introversion and decrement in an auditory vigilance task. In D. N. Buckner & J. J. McGrath (Eds.), *Vigilance: A symposium.* (pp. 22–28). New York: McGraw-Hill.

Barratt, E. S. (1983). The biological basis of impulsiveness: The significance of timing and rhythm disorders. *Personality and Individual Differences, 4,* 387–391.

Barratt, E. S., & Patton, J. H. (19830. Impulsivity: Cognitive, behavioral, and psychophysiological correlates. In M. Zuckerman (Ed.) Biological bases of sensation seeking, impulsivity, and anxiety (pp. 77–116). Hillsdale, N.J.: Erlbaum.

Brebner, J. (1983). A model of extraversion. *Australian Journal of Psychology, 35,* 349–359.

Brebner, J., & Cooper, C. (1974). The effect of a low rate of regular signals upon the reaction times of introverts and extraverts. *Journal of Research in Personality, 8,* 263–276.

Brebner, J., & Cooper, C. (1978). Stimulus- or response-induced excitation: A comparison of the behavior of introverts and extraverts. *Journal of Research in Personality, 12,* 306–311.

Campbell, J. B. (1983). Differential relationships of extraversion, impulsivity, and sociability to study habits. *Journal of Research in Personality, 17,* 308–314.

Carrigan, P. M. (1960). Extraversion–introversion as a dimension of personality: A reappraisal. *Psychological Bulletin, 57,* 329–360.

Cheek, J. M., & Buss, A. H. (1981). Shyness and sociability. *Journal of Personality and Social Psychology, 41,* 330–339.

Cohen, R. H., & Oziel, L. J. (1972). Repression-sensitization and stress effects on Maudsley Personality Inventory scores. *Psychological Reports, 30,* 837–838.

Coles, M. G. H., Gale, A., & Kline, P. (1971). Personality and habituation of the orienting reaction: Tonic and response measures of electrodermal activity. *Psychophysiology, 8,* 54–63.

Crider, A., & Lunn, R. (1971). Electrodermal lability as a personality dimension. *Journal of Experimental Research in Personality, 5,* 145–150.

Dana, R. H., & Cocking, R. R. (1969). Repression–sensitization and Maudsley Personality Inventory scores: Response sets and stress effects. *British Journal of Social and Clinical Psychology, 8,* 263–269.

Davies, D. R., & Hockey, G. R. J. (1966). The effects of noise and doubling the signal frequency on individual differences in visual vigilance performance. *British Journal of Psychology, 57,* 381–389.

Davies, D. R., Hockey, G. R. J., & Taylor, A. (1969). Varied auditory stimulation, temperament differences and vigilance performance. *British Journal of Psychology, 60,* 453–457.

Eaves, L., & Eysenck, H. J. (1975). The nature of extraversion: A genetical analysis. *Journal of Personality and Social Psychology, 32,* 102–112.

Elliott, C. D. (1971). Noise tolerance and extraversion in children. *British Journal of Psychology, 62,* 375–380.

Eysenck, H. J. (1947). *The dimensions of human personality.* London: Routledge & Kegan Paul.

Eysenck, H. J. (1962). *The manual of the Maudsley Personality Inventory.* San Diego: Educational and Industrial Testing Service.

Eysenck, H. J. (1967). *The biological basis of personality.* Springfield, IL: Thomas.

Eysenck, H. J. (1970). *The structure of human personality.* London: Methuen.

Eysenck, H. J. (1981). General features of the model. In H. J. Eysenck (Ed.), *A model of personality*. (pp. 1–37). New York: Springer-Verlag.

Eysenck, H. J. (1983). A biometrical-genetical analysis of impulsive and sensation-seeking behavior. In M. Zuckerman (Ed.), *Biological bases of sensation seeking, impulsivity, and anxiety*. (pp. 1–27). Hillsdale, NJ: L. Erlbaum Associates.

Eysenck, H. J. & Eysenck, S. B. G. (1968). *The manual of the Eysenck Personality Inventory*. San Diego, Educational and Industrial Testing Service.

Eysenck, S. B. G., & Eysenck, H. J. (1977). The place of impulsiveness in a dimensional system of personality description. *British Journal of Social and Clinical Psychology, 16*, 57–68.

Eysenck, S., & Zuckerman, M. (1978). The relationship between sensation-seeking and Eysenck's dimensions of personality. *British Journal of Psychology, 69*, 483–487.

Farley, F. H., & Farley, S. V. (1970). Impulsiveness, sociability, and the preference for varied experience. *Perceptual and Motor Skills, 31*, 47–50.

Fenigstein, A., Scheier, M. F., & Buss, A. H. (1975). Public and private self-consciousness: Assessment and theory. *Journal of Consulting and Clinical Psychology, 43*, 522–527.

Fowles, D. C., Roberts, R., & Nagel, K. (1977). The influence of introversion/extraversion on the skin conductance response to stress and stimulus intensity. *Journal of Research in Personality, 11*, 129–146.

Gale, A. (1973). The psychophysiology of individual differences: Studies of extraversion-introversion and the EEG. In P. Kline (Ed.), *New approaches in psychological measurement*. (pp. 211–256). London: Wiley.

Gale, A. (1981). EEG studies of extraversion-introversion: What's the next step? In R. Lynn (Ed.), *Dimensions of personality: Papers in honour of H. J. Eysenck*. (pp. 181–207). Oxford: Pergamon.

Gange, J. J., Geen, R. G., & Harkins, S. G. (1979). Autonomic differences between extraverts and introverts during vigilance. *Psychophysiology, 16*, 392–397.

Geen, R. G. (1984). Preferred stimulation levels in introverts and extraverts: Effects on arousal and performance. *Journal of Personality and Social Psychology, 46*, 1303–1312.

Geen, R. G., McCown, E. J., & Broyles, J. W. (1985). Effects of noise on sensitivity of introverts and extraverts to signals in a vigilance task. Unpublished manuscript. *Personality and Individual Differences, 6*, 237–241.

Gilliland, K. (1980). The interactive effect of introversion-extraversion with caffeine induced arousal on verbal performance. *Journal of Research in Personality, 14*, 482–492.

Guilford, J. P. (1975). Factors and factors of personality. *Psychological Bulletin, 82*, 802–814.

Harkins, S. G., & Geen, R. G. (1975). Discriminability and criterion differences between extraverts and introverts during vigilance. *Journal of Research in Personality, 9*, 335–340.

Keister, M. E., & McLaughlin, R. J. (1972). Vigilance performance related to extraversion-introversion and caffeine. *Journal of Experimental Research in Personality, 6*, 5–11.

Krupski, A., Raskin, D., & Bakan, P. (1971). Physiological and personality correlates of commission errors in an auditory vigilance task. *Psychophysiology, 8*, 304–311.

Maddi, S. R., Hoover, M., & Kobasa, S. C. (1982). Alienation and exploratory behavior. *Journal of Personality and Social Psychology, 42*, 884–890.

McLaughlin, R. J., & Eysenck, H. J. (1967). Extraversion, neuroticism, and paired-associates learning. *Journal of Experimental Research in Personality, 2*, 128–132.

Morris, L. W. (1979). *Extraversion and introversion*. Washington, D.C.: Hemisphere.

Petrie, A., Collins, W., & Solomon, F. (1960). The tolerance for pain and sensory deprivation. *American Journal of Psychology, 73*, 80–90.

Pilkonis, P. A. (1977). Shyness, public and private, and its relationship to other measures of social behavior. *Journal of Personality, 45*, 585–595.

Revelle, W. Amaral, P., & Turriff, S. (1976). Introversion/extraversion, time stress, and caffeine: Effect on verbal performance. *Science, 192*, 149–150.

Revelle, W., Humphreys, M. W., Simon, L., & Gilliland, K. (1980). The interactive effect of personality, time of day, and caffeine: A test of the arousal model. *Journal of Experimental Psychology: General, 109*, 1–31.

Roback, A. A. (1927). *The psychology of character*. London: Paul.

Schalling, D. (1971). Tolerance for experimentally induced pain as related to personality. *Scandinavian Journal of Psychology, 12*, 271–281.

Schalling, D., Edman, G., & Asberg, M. (1983). Impulsive cognitive style and inability to tolerate boredom: Psychobiological studies of temperamental vulnerability. In M. Zuckerman (Ed.), *Biological bases of sensation seeking, impulsivity, and anxiety*. Hillsdale, NJ: L. Erlbaum Associates.

Schwartz, S. (1975). Individual differences in cognition: Some relationships between personality and memory. *Journal of Research in Personality, 9,* 217–225.

Smith, B. D., & Wigglesworth, M. J. (1978). Extroversion and neuroticism in orienting reflex dishabituation. *Journal of Research in Personality, 12,* 284–296.

Smith, B. D., Rypma, C. B., & Wilson, R. J. (1981). Dishabituation and spontaneous recovery of the electrodermal orienting response: Effects of extraversion, impulsivity, sociability, and caffeine. *Journal of Research in Personality, 15,* 233–240.

Smith, B. D., Wilson, R. J., & Jones, B. E. (1983). Extraversion and multiple levels of caffeine-incited arousal: Effects on overhabituation and dishabituation. *Psychophysiology, 20,* 29–34.

Smith, B. D., Wilson, R., & Rypma, C. B. (1981). Overhabituation and dishabituation: Effects of extraversion and amount of training. *Journal of Research in Personality, 15,* 475–487.

Smith, S. L. (1968). Extraversion and sensory threshold. *Psychophysiology, 5,* 293–299.

Snyder, M. (1974). Self-monitoring of expressive behavior. *Journal of Personality and Social Psychology, 30,* 526–537.

Stelmack, R. M., & Plouffe, L. (1983). Introversion–extroversion: The Bell–Magendie Law revisited. *Personality and Individual Differences, 4,* 421–427.

Stelmack, R. M., Bourgeois, R., Chien, J. Y. C., & Pickard, C. (1979). Extraversion and the OR habituation rate to visual stimuli. *Journal of Research in Personality, 13,* 49–58.

Tune, G. S. (1966). Errors of commission as a function of age and temperament in a type of vigilance task. *Quarterly Journal of Experimental Psychology, 18,* 358–361.

Wigglesworth, M. J., & Smith, B. D. (1976). Habituation and dishabituation of the electrodermal orienting reflex in relation to extraversion and neuroticism. *Journal of Research in Personality, 10,* 437–445.

Zuckerman, M. (1971). Dimensions of sensation seeking. *Journal of Consulting and Clinical Psychology, 36,* 45–52.

Zuckerman, M. (1974). The sensation seeking motive. In B. A. Maher (Ed.), *Progress in experimental personality research* (Vol. 7, pp. 80–148). New York: Academic Press.

21

Oral Communication Apprehension

James C. McCroskey and Michael J.Beatty

Communication apprehension (CA) is a broadly based anxiety related to oral communication (McCroskey, 1970). More specifically, CA is "an individual's level of fear or anxiety associated with either real or anticipated communication with another person or persons" (McCroskey, 1982b; 1984).

For the purposes of this volume it is critical that we distinguish between CA and shyness as we employ these constructs. Shyness is the predisposition to withdraw from or avoid communication with other people. Hence, CA is a subjective, affective experience whereas shyness is a behavioral tendency that may result from CA or other causes. The distinction we draw is similar to that drawn by Leary (1983a; 1983c) between social anxiety and social-communicative behavior.

The distinction we draw may be made clearer by examining the most recent version of the Personal Report of Communication Apprehension (PRCA-24, Table 1) and the McCroskey Shyness Scale (Table 2). The PRCA (McCroskey, 1970b; 1978; 1982a) is the most widely used operationalization of CA. The McCroskey Shyness Scale (McCroskey, Andersen, Richmond, & Wheeless, 1981) was specifically designed to measure shyness as conceptualized here. Readers are cautioned that "shyness" measures exist that do not measure shyness as we employ that construct. For example, the scale reported by Cheek and Buss (1981) from our view is simply a partial measure of CA, one which focuses on CA in interpersonal communication.

Although CA and shyness are presumed to be related (that is, CA may lead to withdrawal and/or avoidance), they are not presumed to be isomorphic. A number of research studies employing the operatalizations reported in tables 1 and 2 have obtained correlations between .57 and.63 (McCroskey & Richmond, 1982a; 1984). Higher correlations were not expected since shyness is presumed to result from a variety of causes with CA being but one of those causes.

JAMES C. McCROSKEY and MICHAEL J. BEATTY • Department of Speech Communication, West Virginia University, Morgantown, WV 26506.

TABLE 1. Personal Report of Communication Apprehension (PRCA-24)*

Directions: This instrument is composed of 24 statements concerning your feelings about communication with other people. Please indicate in the space provided the degree to which each statement applies to you by marking whether you (1) Strongly Agree, (2) Agree, (3) Are Undecided, (4) Disagree, (5) Strongly Disagree with each statement. There are no right or wrong answers. Many of the statements are similar to other statements. Do not be concerned about this. Work quickly, just record your first impression.

_____ 1. I dislike participating in group discussions.

_____ 2. Generally, I am comfortable while participating in a group discussion.

_____ 3. I am tense and nervous while participating in group discussions.

_____ 4. I like to get involved in group discussion.

_____ 5. Engaging in a group discussion with new people makes me tense and nervous.

_____ 6. I am calm and relaxed while participating in group discussions.

_____ 7. Generally, I am nervous when I have to participate in a meeting.

_____ 8. Usually I am calm and relaxed while participating in meetings.

_____ 9. I am very calm and relaxed when I am called upon to express an opinion at a meeting.

_____ 10. I am afraid to express myself at meetings.

_____ 11. Communicating at meetings usually makes me uncomfortable.

_____ 12. I am very relaxed when answering questions at a meeting.

_____ 13. While participating in a conversation with a new acquaintance, I feel very nervous.

_____ 14. I have no fear of speaking up in conversations.

_____ 15. Ordinarily I am very tense and nervous in conversations.

_____ 16. Ordinarily I am very calm and relaxed in conversations.

_____ 17. While conversing with a new acquaintance, I feel very relaxed.

_____ 18. I'm afraid to speak up in conversations.

_____ 19. I have no fear of giving a speech.

_____ 20. Certain parts of my body feel very tense and rigid while giving a speech.

_____ 21. I feel relaxed while giving a speech.

_____ 22. My thoughts become confused and jumbled when I am giving a speech.

_____ 23. I face the prospect of giving a speech with confidence.

_____ 24. While giving a speech I get so nervous, I forget facts I really know.

Scoring:

Group	$= 18 - (1) + (2) - (3) + (4) - (5) + (6)$
Meeting	$= 18 - (7) + (8) + (9) - (10) - (11) + (12)$
Dyadic	$= 18 - (13) + (14) - (15) + (16) + (17) - (18)$
Public	$= 18 + (19) - (20) + (22) + (23) - (24)$
Overall CA	$=$ Group + Meeting + Dyadic + Public

*Norms based on 29,478 college students: PRCA-24 ($X = 16.4$, $SD = 15.3$); Group ($X = 15.4$, $SD = 4.8$), Meeting ($X = 16.4$, $SD = 4.8$); Dyadic ($X = 14.5$, $SD = 4.2$); Public ($X = 19.3$, $SD = 5.1$). Alpha reliabilities have ranged from .92 to .97 for the total score.

CONCEPTUALIZATIONS OF CA

CA is viewed from both trait and state perspectives (Spielberger, 1966). That is, CA exists as a trait-like predisposition toward communication and as a state-like response to a given communication situation. Most of the early research

TABLE 2. McCroskey Shyness Scale*

Directions: The following fourteen statements refer to talking with other people. If the statement describes you very well, circle "YES." If it somewhat describes you, circle "yes." If you are not sure whether it describes you or not, or if you do not understand the statement, circle "?." If the statement is a poor description of you, circle "no." If the statement is a very poor description of you, circle "NO." There are no right or wrong answers. Work quickly; record your first impression.

YES yes ? no NO 1. I am a shy person.
YES yes ? no NO 2. Other people think I talk a lot.
YES yes ? no NO 3. I am a very talkative person.
YES yes ? no NO 4. Other people think I am shy.
YES yes ? no NO 5. I talk a lot.
YES yes ? no NO 6. I tend to be very quiet in class.
YES yes ? no NO 7. I don't talk much.
YES yes ? no NO 8. I talk more than most people.
YES yes ? no NO 9. I am a quiet person.
YES yes ? no NO 10. I talk more in a small group (3–6 people) than other people do.
YES yes ? no NO 11. Most people talk more than I do.
YES yes ? no NO 12. Other people think I am very quiet.
YES yes ? no NO 13. I talk more in class than most people do.
YES yes ? no NO 14. Most people are more shy than I am.

SCORING: YES = 1, yes = 2, ? = 3, no = 4, NO = 5.

Score your responses as follows:
1. Add the scores for items 1, 4, 6, 7, 9, 11, and 12.
2. Add the scores for items 2, 3, 5, 8, 10, 13, and 14.
3. Complete the following formula: Shyness = 42 − (total from step 1) + (total from step 2).

*Norms based on 3845 college students: $X = 39.88$, $SD = 10.86$. Alpha reliabilities have ranged from .89 to .93.

in this area was directed toward the trait-orientation (McCroskey, 1977). More recent research has looked at CA from both a trait and a state perspective (Behnke & Beatty, 1981; McCroskey & Beatty, 1984; Richmond, 1978). Conceptualizations of CA have not, however, been restricted to pure trait or pure state. Rather, CA has been viewed in four ways that are presumably distributed between pure trait and pure state. These are referred to as trait-like, generalized context, person–group, and situational CA.

Trait-like CA

Trait-like CA is viewed as a relatively enduring, personality-type orientation toward oral communication across a wide variety of contexts. The PRCA-24 is the primary operationalization of this type of CA. It is assumed that scores for an individual on this type of measure will be highly similar across an extended period of time, barring an intervention program designed to alter the CA level or a demand characteristic introduced into the CA measurement. High internal and test–retest reliabilities of the PRCA instrument are suggestive of the existence of such a phenomenon and of the appropriateness of the PRCA instrument as an operational index of it. More importantly, recent research indicates that the PRCA is a good index of CA concerning communication contexts not represented by the items on the measure, such as situations demanding assertiveness (Beatty, Plax, Kearney, & McCroskey, 1984).

Generalized-Context CA

Generalized-context CA is viewed as a relatively enduring, personality-type orientation toward communication in a given type of communication context. A wide variety of measures have been advanced that presumably tap this type of CA. Whereas the trait-like view of CA assumes apprehension about communication in one communication context is substantially correlated with apprehension in other contexts (and research has strongly supported that assumption), the generalized-context view does not require that assumption. Constructs such as "stage fright" and "audience anxiety" are representative of this approach.

Some of the available measures of this type of CA include the Personal Report of Confidence as a Speaker (Gilkinson, 1942; Paul, 1966), the Personal Report of Public Speaking Apprehension (McCroskey, 1970), the Interaction Anxiousness and Audience Anxiousness scales (Leary, 1983a), the Shyness Scale (Cheek & Buss, 1981), and the Audience Anxiety scale (Buss, 1980). Recently, McCroskey and Richmond (1982b) isolated four common communication contexts and provided instruments to measure each. The contexts addressed were the same four measured in the PRCA-24; public speaking, speaking in meetings, speaking in small groups, and speaking in dyads. The subscores on the PRCA-24 (see Table 1) provide estimates of CA in each of these generalized contexts.

As was the case with trait-like CA, it is assumed that measures of generalized-context CA will generate scores for individuals that will be relatively consistent across time unless contaminated by intervention or measurement error. Trait-like measures are assumed to be at least moderately correlated with scores on generalized-context measures.

Person–Group CA

Person-group CA is viewed as a relatively enduring orientation toward communication with a given person or group of people. It is not viewed as personality based, but rather as a response to situational constraints generated by the other person or group.

Although presumed to be relatively enduring, this type of CA would be expected to change as a function of changed behavior on the part of the other person or group. Although people with high trait-like CA or high generalized-context CA would be expected to experience high CA with more persons and groups, knowledge of the levels of either of these should not be expected to be predictive of CA experienced with a given individual or group. In short, this type of CA is presumed to be more a function of the situational constraints introduced by the other person or group than by the personality of the individual. Length of acquaintance should be a major consideration here. Whereas in early stages of acquaintance the personality orientations should be somewhat predictive, in later stages the situational constraints should be expected to overpower these orientations (Richmond, 1978).

Few attempts to measure this type of CA have appeared in the literature. However, the state anxiety measure developed by Spielberger (1966), particularly as modified for this purpose by Richmond (1978), appears to be an excellent tool. It can be adapted readily for use with any person or group in any communication context.

Situational CA

Situational CA is viewed as a transitory orientation toward communication with a given person or group of people. It is not viewed as personality based, but rather as a response to the situational constraints generated by the other person or group. The level of this type of CA should be expected to fluctuate widely as a function of changed constraints introduced by the other person or group. Although people with high trait-like CA or high generalized-situation CA would be expected to experience high CA in more individual situations than would other people, knowledge of the levels of either of these should not be expected to be highly predictive of CA experienced by an individual in any given situation. On the other hand, the level of person–group CA should be expected to be moderately highly related to situational CA. Person–group CA primarily is a function of the prior history of the individual with the given person or group. Such a history can be assumed to produce expectations that would influence the level of CA in the given situation involving communication with that person or group.

Measurement of situational CA has received little attention in the previous research. However, the Spielberger (1966) instrument as modified by Richmond (1978) appears to be a very satisfactory tool for this purpose.

Relationship between Trait-like and State CA

In its original conceptualization, CA was viewed exclusively as a predisposer of communication state anxiety. The possibility that state CA feeds back to affect trait-like CA was not considered. With respect to the dispositional nature of trait-like CA, studies have demonstrated the ability of the PRCA to predict self-reported communication state anxiety (Beatty & Behnke, 1980; Behnke & Beatty, 1981). Thus, the assumption that trait-like CA predisposes state CA has been supported.

Recent research has produced evidence suggesting that state CA may temporarily affect trait-like CA (Beatty, Behnke, & McCallum, 1978). It has been shown that anxiety experienced during a communication task that differs from that predicted by a person's level of trait-like CA alters that person's level in the direction of the discrepancy (Beatty & Behnke, 1980). There is also evidence that indicates that trait-like CA may be viewed as the accumulation of state CA experiences (McCroskey & Beatty, 1984). Although it appears that trait-like and state CA affect one another, the exact nature of this dynamic process remains unclear.

CA and General Anxiety

Zuckerman (1976) proposed that trait-like constructs could be viewed as either general or specific. General anxiety refers to the predisposition to experience anxiety in a broad range of situations, such as taking tests, being exposed to snakes, flying, or being confined to small spaces. Because CA focuses exclusively on communication-related situations, the construct is considered a *specific trait*.

Although specific-trait theorists argue that a narrower focus is more useful than a general one in predicting state anxiety reactions, research based on the specific-trait paradigm has produced equivocal findings. At times, specific-trait measures are better predictors than general anxiety measures (e.g., Hodges & Spielberger, 1966; Mellstrom, Zuckerman, & Cicala, 1974), whereas at other times general anxiety measures are at least as predictive as specific measures (e.g., Rappaport, 1979).

With regard to CA, the current theory, which has been supported thus far by research, is that measures of general anxiety may be as predictive as CA measures in communication situations with which the subject has had little or no experience. Because performances in such situations represent novel experiences for the subjects, their general level of anxiety proneness may provide as good (and possibly sometimes better) prediction of the magnitude of state anxiety they will experience in the situations. However, measures of CA should more accurately predict state anxiety for subjects who have some prior exposure to the situation. Thus, the assumption is that the stability and predictiveness of trait-like CA depends on the amount of information and experience subjects have relating to the specific communication contexts assessed by the measure.

Although related (usually around $r = .30$), trait-like CA and general anxiety are viewed as conceptually and empirically distinct constructs. CA is not viewed as a subset of a more general anxiousness. Instead, CA is conceptualized as a contributing factor, rather than an effect, in the development of both general anxiety and social anxiety. There is research in progress in which PRCA scores and general anxiety scores were collected at four separate times during a semester-long introductory communication course. The analysis of the panel data indicates that changes in PRCA scores are followed by similar changes in general anxiousness. However, changes in general anxiousness have no such effect on PRCA scores. These findings are consistent with the results obtained when structural equations are used to analyze the data. Moreover, the absence of significant autocorrelation of the PRCA residuals suggests that CA is not an artifact of some unobserved disturbance variable. Thus, it is improbable that the observed CA–general anxiety relationship is a spurious one. Although this line of research is in its early stages, the preliminary findings suggest that CA is unique but partially related to general anxiety.

Trait-like CA and Physiological Arousal

The body of literature concerning the relationship between trait-like CA and physiological activation is scant. Available research, for the most part, shows no meaningful relationship (Beatty, 1984). However, several studies have reported significant moderate relationships between heart rate and state CA scores (Behnke & Beatty, 1981; Behnke & Carlile, 1971).

Schachter and Singer (1962) proposed a paradigm explaining the role of physiological arousal in emotional response that appears to explain why heart rate correlates with state CA yet is uncorrelated with trait-like CA. They suggested that "an emotional state may be considered a function of a state of physiological arousal and of a cognition appropriate to the state of arousal" (p. 380). The existence of physiological arousal engenders pressure to understand and label the drive state. How a person labels this condition depends on past cues "as interpreted by past experience" (p. 380). According to this theory, neither physiological arousal nor cognitive perception alone would account for the emotions experienced during communication. Emotional responses during specific communication experiences are viewed as contingent on the presence of physiological activation along with an interpretation of the arousal as being caused by the communication situation. For example, people who perceive themselves to be high in CA would interpret increased heart rate during communication as fear or anxiety, whereas confident people low in CA might interpret the arousal as excitement. Theoretically then, trait-like CA serves as the predisposition to interpret arousal during communication as anxiety or fear.

Viewed in this context, trait-like CA does not cause, nor is it caused by, increased activation such as heart rate. There is evidence supporting this Schacterian paradigm of CA. Using PRCA scores and elevations in heart rate as predictors, Behnke and Beatty (1981) accounted for 79.6% of the variance in state CA related to public speaking. Each of the predictors accounted for approximately 40% of the variance, and the two predictors were not significantly correlated with each other.

In sum, it is argued that cognitive, trait-like CA predisposes the individual to evaluate whether or not a particular emotion is experienced in a given communication situation. However, it is the feedback in the form of physiological arousal that determines the magnitude of the emotional response. Consequently, an individual perceives tremendous fear related to communication because that individual has high trait-like CA *and* experiences elevated heart rate and/or other physiological activation during a communication encounter. A cycle in which the perception is assimilated into the predisposition is created, thereby reinforcing the person's level of trait-like CA. Thus trait-like CA, physiological arousal, and state CA are entwined in a complex system of attitudes and responses.

EFFECTS OF CA

The effects of CA, particularly trait-like CA, have been the focus of extensive research. High CA has been found to be negatively associated with desirable outcomes in interpersonal relationships, in the work environment, and in the educational environment. This research has been summarized extensively elsewhere (Daly & Stafford, 1984; McCroskey, 1977; Richmond, 1984), so we will not repeat those efforts here. However, we do wish to note that much of that research has not examined the direct effects of CA. Rather, it has focused on the effects of shyness or communication disruption produced by CA. Consequently, CA should be viewed as an indirect, rather than a direct, causal factor in the negative outcomes commonly found in this body of research. To explain the theoretical relationship between varying levels of CA and varying communication outcomes, we will look at both the internal and the external impact of CA.

Internal Impact of CA

CA is a subjective, affective response of an individual to communication. Thus, although CA is not unrelated to communication behavior, the experience of CA is strictly internal to the individual. The only effect of CA that is predicted to be universal across both individuals and types of CA is an internally experienced feeling of discomfort. The higher the CA, the greater the internal discomfort.

The implications of conceptualizing CA as strictly an internally experienced phenomenon must be emphasized. Because CA is experienced only internally, the only potentially valid indicant of CA is the individual's report of that experience. Thus, self-reports of individuals, whether obtained by paper-and-pencil measures or careful interviews, provide the only potentially valid measures of CA. Measures of physiological activation and observations of behavior can provide, at best, only indirect evidence of CA and, thus, are inherently inferior approaches to measuring CA. Such measures must be validated against self-report measures, not the reverse. To the extent such measures are not related to self-report measures, they must be judged invalid. Currently available data indicate that such physiological measures (Beatty, 1984; Behnke & Beatty, 1981) vary in validity from moderate to low as do available observer rating instruments (McCroskey & Richmond, 1982a, 1984; Mulac & Wiemann, 1984).

External Impact of CA

There is no behavior that is predicted to be a universal product of varying levels of CA. Nevertheless, there are some externally observable behaviors that are more likely to occur as the level of CA increases. However, when examining behavioral manifestations of CA, we must keep in mind the distinctions among the types of CA discussed above. Trait-like CA, for example, will be manifested in behavior in a given situation only as it interacts with the constraints of that situation. A person with high trait-like CA may behave in a manner no different from anyone else in a quiet conversation with a good friend. Similarly, a person with low trait-like CA may behave in a manner no different from anyone else if called to a meeting to be reprimanded by a supervisor. The behavioral manifestations of high CA we will note below, therefore, presuppose that CA actually is present to a sufficient degree in a given situation to trigger the behavior. The link is most direct for the most situational type of CA. For trait-like CA the link is most tenuous. The behavioral prediction should only be assumed to be correct when considering aggregate behavioral observations of the individual across time and across contexts.

Three patterns of behavioral response to high CA may be predicted to be generally applicable and one pattern can be described as sometimes present, but as an atypical response pattern. The three typical patterns are communication avoidance, communication withdrawal, and communication disruption. The atypical pattern is excessive communication. Let us consider each.

When people are confronted with a circumstance that they anticipate will make them uncomfortable, and they have a choice of whether or not to confront it, they may either decide to confront it and make the best of it or to avoid it and thus avoid the discomfort. Some refer to this as the choice between "fight and flight." Research in the area of CA indicates the latter choice should be expected in most instances (Beatty, Springhorn, & Kruger, 1976). In order to avoid having to experience high CA, people may select occupations that involve low communication responsibilities, may pick housing units that reduce incidental contact with other people, may choose seats in classrooms or in meetings that are less conspicuous, and may avoid social settings. At the lowest level, if a person makes us uncomfortable, we may simply avoid being around that person. Avoidance, then, is a common behavioral response to high CA.

Avoidance of communication is not always possible. One can find oneself in a situation that generates a high level of CA with no advance warning. Under such circumstances, withdrawal from communication is the behavioral pattern to be expected. This withdrawal may be complete, that is, absolute silence, or partial, resulting in talking only as much as absolutely required. In a public speaking setting, this response may be represented by the very short speech. In a meeting, class, or small group discussion, it may be represented by talking only when called upon. In a dyadic interaction, it may be represented by only answering questions or supplying agreeing responses with no initiation of discussion.

Communication disruption is the third typical behavioral pattern associated with high CA. The person may not be fluent in verbal presentation or exhibit unnatural or inappropriate verbal or nonverbal behaviors. Equally as likely are poor choices of communicative strategies, sometimes reflected in the after-the-fact "I wish I had (had not) said . . . " phenomenon. It is important to note, however, that such behaviors may be produced by inadequate communication skills as well as by high CA. Thus, inferring CA from observations of such behavior is not always appropriate.

Overcommunication is a response to high CA that is not common but is the pattern exhibited by a small minority. This behavior represents overcompensation. It may reflect the fight rather than the flight reaction, the attempt to succeed in spite of the felt discomfort. The person who elects to take a public speaking course in spite of having extreme stage fright is a classic example. Less easily recognizable is the individual with high CA who attempts to dominate social situations. Most of the time people who employ this behavior option are seen as poor communicators but are not recognized as having high CA; in fact they may be seen as people with very low CA.

To this point we have looked at the typical behaviors of people with high CA levels. We might assume that the behaviors of people with low CA would be the exact reverse. That assumption might not always be correct. Although people with low CA should be expected to seek opportunities to communicate rather than avoid them, and to dominate interactions in which they are a member rather than withdraw from them, people with low CA may also have disrupted communication and overcommunicate. The disruptions may stem from pushing too hard rather than from tension, but the behaviors may not always be distinctly different to the observer. Similarly, the person who overcommunicates engages in very similar behavior whether the behavior stems from high or low CA. Although future research may permit us to train observers who can distinguish disrupted communication resulting from high CA from that resulting from low CA and possibly distinguish between overcommunication behaviors stemming from the two causes, these behaviors are, and probably will remain, indistinguishable to the average person in the communication situation.

To summarize, the primary impact of CA is internal to the individual. In attempting to avoid or reduce the internal discomfort produced by CA, individuals may engage in a variety of behavioral choices that will lead to either reduced communication (avoidance or withdrawal) or less effective communication (disruption, overcommunication), or both. It is these choices that lead to communication behaviors which, in turn, lead to the variety of negative outcomes that research has found to be associated with high CA.

Development of CA

Although there is considerable speculation concerning how trait-like CA is acquired, few studies have focussed on CA development. Recent writers have acknowledged that there may be a hereditary contribution. This conclusion is based on the work of social biologists who have established that traits such as sociability can be observed in infants shortly after birth (see McCroskey, 1984). However, because none of this work has involved measurement of CA itself, the question of a hereditary contribution remains open.

Although it is possible that heredity contributes to CA development, most writers allege that reinforcement patterns in a person's environment, particularly during childhood, constitute the dominant causal factors. One view is that a child who is reinforced for communicating will communicate more whereas a child who is punished for communicating will communicate less. In the latter case, CA increases as a result of an approach-avoidance conflict. On the one hand, the child desires to engage in a normal human urge, communication. On the other hand, the child wishes to avoid punishment. There is evidence that suggests that children who are reinforced for communicating by parents and teachers tend to be low in CA (Daly & Friedrich, 1981). Similarly, there is evidence that children who are punished for communication by parents or teachers develop more self-deprecating attitudes about communication (Beatty, Plax, & Payne, 1984; Plax, Beatty, & Payne, 1984).

A second view of the reinforcement paradigm is that inconsistent reward and punishment for communicating produces trait-like CA. According to this perspective, anxiety about communication develops because the child is unable to predict when reward or punishment will follow behavior. Thus, the child is unable to control the environment and is, in a sense, helpless in it. In the Beatty, Plax, and Payne (1984) and the Plax *et al.* (1984) studies, a considerable proportion of subjects who expressed completely negative attitudes about communication reported childhoods in which rewards and punishments for communication were inconsistent. Thus, there appears to be some support for each of the reinforcement views of CA development.

Modeling of significant others frequently appears as an explanation for CA development. Modeling theory suggests that children (and to some extent adults) observe the communication behavior of others in their environment and attempt to emulate it. Theoretically, if the child observes the model being reinforced for the behavior or the child is rewarded directly for imitating the model, the behavior will continue. If these contingencies are not perceived by the child, modeling is unlikely. Although there has been little CA research focusing on the impact of modeling, the existing research has been unable to detect a modeling effect (Beatty, Plax, & Kearney, 1984). We believe that modeling may serve as a useful theory for partially explaining the development of shyness, but its applicability to CA appears to be minimal.

Finally, CA is sometimes discussed as being a function of inadequate development of important communication skills. However, such an explanation fails to account for numerous cases of show business personalities, such as Johnny Carson and Richard Burton, who clearly demonstrate more than adequate communication skills and yet report being extremely apprehensive in some interpersonal settings and prior to public performances. It is possible that it is the perception of inadequate communication skills, rather than the actual skill level, which contributes to CA. We have videotaped numerous highly apprehensive individuals in communication settings where they have exhibited excellent skills. However, their judgment of their skills was negative, even when confronted directly by videotaped evidence to the contrary. In contrast, we have observed numerous individuals who exhibit very poor communication skills but report little or no CA. Thus, although we do not wish to completely rule out a link between skills and CA, the available evidence does not point to any substantial relationship between the two.

In sum, there is considerable speculation but little solid research concerning the factors that influence the development of trait-like CA. Obviously, it is impractical and probably unethical to manipulate many of these factors in children's environments and observe directly the effects on CA. However, research is needed, even if the developmental process can be studied only cross-sectionally or indirectly, if we hope to gain needed insight into CA development.

TREATMENT OF CA

From the earliest days of research involving CA, treatment has been a major concern (McCroskey, 1972; McCroskey, Ralph, & Barick, 1970). The focus has always been on those individuals with high levels of CA, although more recently we have noted some concern for a possible need to help those with extremely low CA as well (McCroskey, 1984).

Treatment approaches have focused on the behavior therapies of systematic desensitization (Friedrich & Goss, 1984; McCroskey, 1972; McCroskey, Ralph, & Barrick, 1970) and cognitive restructuring (Fremouw, 1984; Fremouw & Zitter, 1978; Glowgower, Fremouw, & McCroskey, 1978; Meichenbaum, 1977). These methods have been found to be highly effective for reducing trait-like and generalized-context CA, both on an absolute scale and in comparison to other treatment methods.

Because CA is not conceptualized as a skills-based problem, it should not be surprising to find that skills training approaches have proven much less satisfactory for overcoming CA than behavior therapy approaches (McCroskey, Richmond, Berger, & Baldwin, 1983). Formal communication courses, with or without specific skills training components, have been found to be generally ineffective (although not harmful) in reducing CA. For some individuals with high trait-like CA, however, skills training produces a negative impact.

The choice of treatment, then, is between systematic desensitization and cognitive restructuring. There is little empirical data on which such a choice can be based. Both are effective, and both seem to be about equally effective. Theoretically, because systematic desensitization involves conditioning relaxation responses to stimuli that before treatment produced high arousal, subjects who experience unusually high arousal from communication encounters might profit most from this treatment. On the other hand, subjects who experience only normal arousal but cognitively interpret that arousal as high anxiety might benefit more from cognitive restructuring. In practice, however, both methods appear to both reduce arousal and improve the cognitive response to arousal. Hence, the choice between the two methods may be of little consequence. For a person with little or no clinical background, systematic desensitization is much easier to learn to implement. This may explain its much wider acceptance on the part of professionals in the communication field.

As we noted previously, CA is not seen as developing primarily as a function of low communication skills. That is not to say that CA is not aggravated by low skills in any context or that no person with high CA also has low skills. Thus, although skills training is not generally effective in substantially reducing trait-like CA, it may have an important role to play in the overall improvement of an individual's communication behavior.

It is not uncommon for individuals to lack sufficient skills for certain communication contexts, such as public speaking, interviewing, or dating. We believe that skills training is called for under such circumstances. The individuals may also be apprehensive about communicating in those contexts, but we should not count on the skills training to overcome that apprehension. People with high CA have been found to derogate their own skill level. Even when their skill is enhanced, many maintain their CA and do not believe their skill has improved to a satisfactory level. Thus, we believe that when there is a problem of CA and a problem of skills, the problem of CA should be addressed first. A reduction of the CA problem should be expected to enhance and to expedite the training to overcome the skills problem.

REFERENCES

Beatty, M. J. (1984). Physiological measurement. In J. A. Daly & J. C. McCroskey (Eds.), *Avoiding communication: Shyness, reticence, and communication apprehension* (pp. 95–105). Beverly Hills, CA: Sage.

Beatty, M. J., & Behnke, R. R. (1980). An assimilation theory perspective of communication apprehension. *Human Communication Research, 6,* 319–325.

Beatty, M. J., Springhorn, R. G., & Kruger, M. W. (1976). Toward the development of cognitively experienced speech anxiety scales. *Central States Speech Journal, 27,* 181–186.

Beatty, M. J., Behnke, R. R., & McCallum, K. (1978). Situation determinants of communication apprehension. *Communication Monographs, 45,* 186–191.

Beatty, M. J., Plax, T. G., Kearney, P. (November, 1984). *Reinforcement vs. modeling theory in the development of communication apprehension.* Paper presented at the Annual Meeting of the Speech Communication Association, Chicago, IL.

Beatty, M. J., Plax, T. G., Kearney, P., & McCroskey, J. C. (November, 1984). *Communication apprehension and assertiveness: A test of cross-situational consistency.* Paper presented at the convention of the Speech Communication Association, Chicago, IL.

Beatty, M. J., Plax, T. G., & Payne, S. K. (1984). Self-appraisal as a function of recollected parental appraisal. *Psychological Reports, 54,* 269–270.

Behnke, R. R., & Beatty, M. J. (1981). A cognitive-physiological model of speech anxiety. *Communication Monographs, 48,* 158–163.

Behnke, R. R., & Carlile, L. W. (1971). Heart rate as an index of speech anxiety. *Speech Monographs, 38,* 65–69.

Buss, A. H. (1980). *Self-consciousness and social anxiety.* San Francisco: Freeman.

Cheek, J. M., & Buss, A. H. (1981). Shyness and sociability. *Journal of Personality and Social Psychology, 41,* 330–339.

Daly, J. A., & Stafford, L. (1984). Correlates and consequences of social-communicative anxiety. In J. A. Daly & J. C. McCroskey (Eds), *Avoiding communication: Shyness, reticence, and communication apprehension* (pp. 125–143). Beverly Hills, CA: Sage.

Daly, J. A., & Friedrich, G. (1981). The development of communication apprehension: A retrospective analysis and contributing correlates. *Communication Quarterly, 29,* 243–255.

Fremouw, W. J. (1984). Cognitive-behavioral therapies for modification of communication apprehension. In J. A. Daly & J. C. McCroskey (Eds.), *Avoiding communication: Shyness, reticence, and communication apprehension* (pp. 209–215). Beverly Hills, CA: Sage.

Fremouw, W. J., & Zitter, R. E. (1978). A comparison of skills training and cognitive restructuring-relaxation for the treatment of speech anxiety. *Behavior Therapy, 9,* 248–259.

Friedrich, G., & Goss, B. (1984). Systematic desensitization. In J. A. Daly and J. C. McCroskey (Eds.), *Avoiding communication: Shyness, reticence, and communication apprehension* (pp. 173–187). Beverly Hills, CA: Sage.

Gilkinson, H. (1942). Social fears as reported by students in college speech classes. *Speech Monographs,* 9, 141–160.

Glowgower, F. D., Fremouw, W. J., & McCroskey, J. C. (1978). A component analysis of cognitive restructuring. *Cognitive Therapy and Research, 2,* 209–223.

Hodges, W. F., & Spielberger, C. D. (1966). The effects of threat of shock on heart rate for subjects of differ in manifest anxiety and fear of shock. *Psychophysiology, 2,* 287–294.

Leary, M. R. (1983a). The conceptual distinctions are important: Another look at communication apprehension and related constructs. *Human Communication Research, 10,* 305–312.

Leary, M. R. (1983b). Social anxiousness: The construct and its measurement. *Journal of Personality Assessment, 47,* 66–75.

Leary, M. R. (1983c). *Understanding social anxiety: Social, personality, and clinical perspectives.* Beverly Hills, CA: Sage.

McCroskey, J. C. (1970). Measures of communication-bound anxiety. *Speech Monographs, 37,* 269–277.

McCroskey, J. C. (1972). The implementation of a large-scale program of systematic desensitization for communication apprehension. *Speech Teacher, 21,* 255–264.

McCroskey, J. C. (1977). Oral communication apprehension: A summary of recent theory and research. *Human Communication Research, 4,* 78–96.

McCroskey, J. C. (1978). Validity of the PRCA as an index of oral communication apprehension. *Communication Monographs, 45,* 192–203.

McCroskey, J. C. (1982a). *An introduction to rhetorical communication* (4th ed., chap. 2). Englewood Cliffs, NJ: Prentice-Hall.

McCroskey, J. C. (1982b). Oral communication apprehension: A reconceptualization. In M. Burgoon (Ed.), *Communication Yearbook 6* (pp. 136–170). Beverly Hills, CA: Sage.

McCroskey, J. C. (1984). The communication apprehension perspective. In J. A. Daly & J. C. McCroskey (Eds.), *Avoiding communication: Shyness, reticence, and communication apprehension* (pp. 13–338). Beverly Hills, CA: Sage.

McCroskey, J. C., & Beatty, J. C. (1984). Communication apprehension and accumulated communication state anxiety experiences. *Communication Monographs, 51,* 79–84.

McCroskey, J. C., & Richmond, V. P. (1982a). Communication apprehension and shyness: Conceptual and operational distinctions. *Central States Speech Journal, 33,* 458–468.

McCroskey, J. C., & Richmond, V. P. (1982b). *The quiet ones: Communication apprehension and shyness* (2nd ed.). Dubuque, IA: Gorsuch-Scarisbrick.

McCroskey, J. C., & Richmond, V. P. (1984). *Self-reported and observed communication apprehension and shyness.* Unpublished paper, West Virginia University.

McCroskey, J. C., Ralph, D. C., & Barrick, J. E. (1970). The effect of systematic desensitization on speech anxiety. *Speech Teacher, 19,* 32–36.

McCroskey, J. C., Andersen, J. F., Richmond, V. P., & Wheeless, L. R. (1981). Communication apprehension of elementary and secondary students and their teachers. *Communication Education, 30,* 122–132.

McCroskey, J. C., Richmond, V. P., Berger, B. A., & Baldwin, H. J. (1983). How to make a good thing worse: A comparison of approaches to helping students overcome communication apprehension. *Communication: The Journal of the Communication Association of the Pacific, 12*(1), 213–220.

Meichenbaum, D. (1977). *Cognitive behavior modification.* New York: Plenum Press.

Mellstrom, M., Zuckerman, M., & Cicala, G. A. (1974). Anxiety: General versus specific trait anxiety measures in predicting fear of snakes. *Psychological Reports, 35,* 317–318.

Mulac, A., & Wiemann, J. M. (1984). Observer-perceived communicator Anxiety. In J. A. Daly & J. C. McCroskey (Eds.), *Avoiding communication: Shyness, reticence, and communication apprehension* (pp. 107–121). Beverly Hills, CA: Sage.

Paul, G. L. (1966). *Insight versus desensitization in psychotherapy.* Stanford, CA: Stanford University Press.

Plax, T. G., Beatty, M. J., & Payne, S. K. (1984). Influence of recollections of teachers' and peers' evaluations on students' self-appraisals. *Psychological Reports, 54,* 472–474.

Rappaport, E. (1979). General and situation specific traits and states: New approaches to assessment of anxiety and other constructs. In M. Zuckerman & C. D. Spielberger (Eds.), *Emotions and anxiety: New concepts, methods, and applications* (pp. 133–174). New York: Wiley.

Richmond, V. P. (1978). The relationship between trait and state communication apprehension and interpersonal perception during acquaintance stages. *Human Communication Research, 4,* 338–349.

Richmond, V. P. (1984). Implications of quietness: Some facts and speculations. In J. A. Daly & J. C. McCroskey (Eds.), *Avoiding communication: Shyness, reticence, and communication apprehension* (pp. 145–155). Beverly Hills, CA: Sage.

Schachter, S., & Singer, J. F. (1962). Cognitive, social and physiological determinants of emotional state. *Psychological Review, 69,* 379–399.

Spielberger, C. D. (1966). *Anxiety and behavior.* New York: Academic Press.

Zuckerman, M. (1976). General and situation specific traits and states: New approaches to assessment of anxiety and other constructs. In M. Zuckerman, & C. D. Speilberger (Eds.), *Emotions and anxiety: New concepts, methods, and applications* (pp. 133–174). New York: Wiley.

22

Embarrassment
Causes and Consequences

Rowland S. Miller

Does there exist anyone who has never been embarrassed? Is there someone who has never felt the chagrin and abashment of the inadvertent social miscue? If so, such a person must be very uncommon; there may well be differences among us in our susceptibility to embarrassment, but the state seems so inextricably tied to our socialization and interaction that to be entirely immune to it would be rare indeed. This chapter will explore the nature and origins of this pervasive—and usually discomfiting—experience, cataloging the occasions in which it occurs, describing different rationales for its existence, reviewing the empirical literature, and generally speculating here and there. First, however, a descriptive analysis: What is it?

B. F. Skinner reports that he was once embarrassed when he bit into an apparent delicacy in a dim corner of a Chinese restaurant, remarked on its light and crispy coating, and only then realized he was chewing the shell of a hardboiled egg (Morley, 1983)! Momentarily, at least, he probably felt mortified, abashed, awkward. He may have had an acute feeling of being exposed (Buss, 1980), and he may have blushed, trembled, fumbled, or stuttered (Modigliani, 1968). He may have felt ungraceful and clumsy, with nothing to say, unable to meet the gaze of another person (Sattler, 1965). Indeed, he probably felt uncomfortable emotions that were a "regrettable deviation from the normal state" (Goffman, 1967, p. 97).

Embarrassment, then, is generally described as an aversive state of momentary chagrin, and from these descriptions, several themes emerge. First, it is a state of emotional *arousal*, a change from the resting state; in fact, Buck and Parke (1972) report that embarrassment is characterized by an increase in skin conductance and a decrease in heart rate. Second, an embarrassed person suffers a sense of *exposure* and conspicuousness; one is acutely aware that one's actions

ROWLAND S. MILLER • Department of Psychology, Sam Houston State University, Huntsville, TX 77341.

may be being evaluated by others. And third, there is usually a resulting feeling of deficiency or *abashment*, as if one had failed to comport oneself properly.

Altogether, embarrassment seems best avoided, but that begs the question of *why* it occurs. We will survey several possibilities, but as background to that discussion, let us next investigate the situations in which embarrassment occurs.

EMBARRASSING CIRCUMSTANCES

Many of the early empirical studies of embarrassment were devoted to a compilation of events associated with the state. Three major classification schemes emerged from the 1960s, and each of them provided something of value. The first and most general of these was proffered by Gross and Stone (1964) who suggested that disruption of any of three essential elements of interaction would cause embarrassment. For instance, embarrassment could result when one's *identity* is threatened; this could occur when (a) one's identity is undocumented, as when one realizes, having eaten at a restaurant, that one has left one's wallet at home; (b) one misplaces an identity, misnaming another person; or (c) one misplays an identity, allowing other incompatible roles to intrude on the role one is attempting to play.

Embarrassment was also said to result from a loss of *poise*, the control of one's self and situation. This could occur if one loses command of one's (a) territory, as when one inadvertently invades another's dressing area; (b) equipment, as when one's car stalls in the middle of a busy intersection; (c) clothes, as when one rips one's pants; or (d) body, as when one is audibly flatulent.

Finally, when a person's *confidence* in assumptions about others is shaken, the disconfirmation of expectations could cause embarrassment. Gross and Stone suggested that we thus develop performance norms that allow others flexibility in their roles so that we can minimize the number of embarrassing surprises that can result from others' behavior.

Weinberg (1968) extended Gross and Stone's (1964) formulation, accepting their tripartite scheme but suggesting that two basic dimensions underlie any embarrassing loss of identity, poise, or confidence. For Weinberg, the intended or unintended nature of one's act and the accuracy of one's definition of the situation were independent dimensions that together describe four elementary instances of embarrassment.

The first form of embarrassment involves situations in which one's intentional behavior is defined post facto as inappropriate to the social situation. These are *faux pas*, as when one arrives at a party decidedly underdressed; actor David Niven once dressed in clown's makeup for a Halloween party that turned out to be black tie—and was never invited back (Morley, 1983). A second form of embarrassment may occur when one's expectations are correct, but they are breached by an unintended act. Such events are *accidents*; one may share others' conceptions of appropriate behavior but still disrupt the situation by an unmeant act, such as spilling coffee in one's lap. Embarrassment may also result when one's incorrect definition of the situation leads to an unintended act. This third form of embarrassment is characterized by *mistakes*, as when a person incorrectly believes that his zipper is zipped and walks around all day with it open. Finally, even situations in which one's act is intended and one's definition of the situation is correct may cause embarrassment, although Weinberg suggests that such embarrassment is evoked only by one's "internal audience," not by reactions of others. This may occur when one must perform *duties* that may be personally embarrassing but that do not engender public disrepute, such as a young girl submitting to her first gynecological examination.

Altogether, then, Gross and Stone (1964) grounded embarrassment squarely in the realm of interpersonal interaction, describing how disruptions of self-definition or self-control could cause us chagrin if witnessed by others. More-over, they and Weinberg (1968) elaborated that embarrassment was generally unforeseen, resulting from the unanticipated actions of others or from the unin-tended and uninformed errors of ourselves. Sattler (1965) added other illumi-nating information, suggesting that we could either be actors in, or merely observers of, those events that caused us embarrassment.

After collecting 3,000 instances of recalled embarrassment from over 300 subjects, Sattler found that they were best organized by sorting them into one of three main groups, situations in which the embarrassed person is (a) an agent in, (b) the recipient of, or (c) an observer of an embarrassing act. When the person (P) is an *agent*, the person's own actions prove embarrassing to the person; one may, for instance, dress inappropriately, forget a name, be clumsy, or, importantly, place another person in an awkward position, as when refusing one a date. By contrast, when P is a *recipient*, another person (O) with whom P is interacting does something which embarrasses P; O may criticize, praise, or tease P, invade P's privacy, or expose P's lack of knowledge or ability. Finally, one may be a mere *observer* of another's actions but be embarrassed by them nonetheless. This may occur either because O does something that reflects on P, as a child's improprieties reflect on his parents, or because P is simply embar-rassed for O—when O is in embarrassing circumstances—even though O's actions are in no way connected with P.

This last, observer category of embarrassing situations is often overlooked, and we will remind the reader of it later on. For now, let us note that, with the exception of Weinberg's duties and Sattler's observer status, all the early authors agreed that embarrassment occurs publicly in situations in which we believe untoward or undesirable information about us is made known to onlookers, whether by the actions of ourselves or others. In fact, Arnold Buss (1980) has recently summarized the surveys of the 1960s by suggesting that there are five events that most often cause embarrassment. The first three of these were iden-tified by Sattler (1965): *impropriety*, improper dress or dirty talk; *lack of competence*; a failure of social graces and poise; and *conspicuousness*, being singled out for attention by others. To these Buss added: *breaches of privacy*, the invasion of physical or personal space, or the unwanted leakage of emotion, and, interest-ingly, *overpraise*, receiving more acclaim than one deserves. (Being regarded too highly by onlookers apparently results in more blushing and giggling than is caused by conspicuousness alone, L. Buss, 1978.) Thus, embarrassment occurs in a variety of circumstances, none of which, it seems, are desirable. Why do these situations cause us discomfort? Is embarrassment inescapable?

THEORETICAL RATIONALES

Embarrassment has long been of interest, and scholars have addressed it from several different perspectives. More than a century ago, Charles Darwin (1873/1965) noted the "desire for concealment" and nonverbal agitation of embarrassment and saw it as a biological response to interpersonal events: "It is not the simple act of reflecting on our own appearance, but the thinking what others think of us, which excites a blush" (p. 325). Freud and his followers generally considered embarrassment an intrapsychic defense against exaggerated desires to exhibit oneself to others (e.g., Dann, 1977) with blushing a "sign of unsuccessful repression which paradoxically leads the person to become even more conspicuous" (Sattler, 1966, p. 120). Existentialists like Sartre (1956) spoke of the sense of exposure and potential discomfort that could result from the presence of others, suggesting that "myself-as object," one's recognition of one's appearance to others, is "an uneasiness, a lived wrenching away from the ecstatic unity of the for-itself" (p. 251).

Whatever the theoretical perspective employed, however, a person's relations with others are implicated in the experience of embarrassment (Sattler, 1966). Accordingly, we will examine more closely social psychological explanations for the existence of embarrassment. There are three of these.

Erving Goffman's (1959, 1967) interactional approach suggests that during an interaction people present themselves to others by claiming a particular face that describes them and is appropriate to the situation. *Face* refers to the desirability of the social image that the person is trying to maintain, and it depends on all the expressive information available about that person at any given time—information that the person is attempting to control. One tries to establish and maintain a single consistent face throughout a given interaction, choosing a face to which one is entitled, and skirting issues and aspects of interaction that could endanger it. This is done so that interactants may generally know what to expect from each other; the goals of all participants are to avoid disruption and to maintain smooth, predictable interaction.

However, despite the good intentions of those concerned, all interactions do not proceed smoothly; any of the mishaps described earlier may endanger the face of a participant, disrupting the interaction, and abruptly forcing the person to be concerned with the restoration of face. Embarrassment may be the result. For Goffman, then, embarrassment occurs when unfulfilled expectations discredit one's claims to an acceptable face, that is, when the "facts at hand threaten or discredit the assumptions a participant finds he has projected about his identity" (1967, p. 107). The person is found not to be the person he or she had seemed, others' beliefs about the person are shaken, and the entire interaction is awkwardly incapacitated.

Goffman's approach is purely interactional. A crucial aspect, for instance, is the individual's concern for the impression projected to the present audience, those "others felt to be there at the time" (1967, p. 98). Thus, Goffman considers embarrassment to be situationally specific; if one's audience changes, an embarrassing incident should be forgotten.

Arnold Buss would likely disagree. He suggests that embarrassment depends not so much on the intrinsic aversiveness of maladroit interaction as on the thorough socialization that teaches us that certain social transgressions result in punishment. Buss' (1980) socialization approach emphasizes that embarrassment is a consequence of our Western enculturation—we are taught which social behaviors are acceptable, and which are not, "mainly through punishment and correction of behavior" (p. 243). When children lose their self-control during toilet training, for instance, they may be teased, ridiculed, or laughed at by their peers; such treatment creates the awkward discomfort of embarrassment. Thereafter, children are subject to forceful lessons that breaches in privacy, modesty, and manners will also be met with disdain. A fear of these situations is created, and susceptibility to embarrassment results.

An important developmental sequence is involved here. For embarrassment to occur, a child must be able to imagine how he or she is appearing to others; some degree of public self-consciousness (Buss, 1980) must have developed, allowing one to realize that others are viewing one as clumsy or foolish. Thus, we must not only learn appropriate behavior in order to be embarrassed, we must develop a social self, and this takes some years. Very young children should not be embarrassable. For Buss, then, embarrassment does not depend on the structure and pattern of interaction. As long as others are judged to be aware of a person's actions (and given an appropriate level of development), embarrassment, a learned response to incidents associated with social ridicule, is possible. And once formed, embarrassment is not easily forgotten—the strong emotional response likely persists for a time, influencing later behavior.

However, Buss would also argue that embarrassment is not inescapable. Indeed, "change the way children are socialized, and embarrassment would be sharply reduced" (1980, p. 233). This may already be true in other countries (Buss cites modern China as a possible example) and suggests the likelihood of important individual differences in susceptibility to embarrassment. Some of us may be more embarrassable than others. Buss notes, for example, that any disposition that would predispose a person to feel conspicuous, improper, invaded, or exposed would probably increase that person's tendency to become embarrassed. Thus, high public self-consciousness, a lack of social skills, excessive modesty, or a high need for privacy might make a person more embarrassable.

Such variations in *embarrassability* have actually been studied by Andre Modigliani (1968). This third approach to the study of embarrassment is derived in part from Goffman's work. Modigliani suggests that when an interaction goes awry, the person whose face is threatened may believe that others now find him or her less worthy, and that this damaging belief causes an actual drop in situational self-esteem that is part of embarrassment. Those people who have both a high sensitivity to the evaluations of others and a tendency to believe that those evaluations are more negative than they really are, says Modigliani, are likely to be particularly susceptible to embarrassment. In testing these hypotheses, Modigliani developed an Embarrassability Scale that consists of 26 items, each describing a potentially embarrassing situation; respondents are asked to rate how embarrassed they would be in each situation. The Scale supported the characterization of the highly embarrassable person as one who is both sensitive and pessimistic, but, unfortunately, it has not been used since. No normative data exists, and the Scale has only been administered to men. There is much to learn about individual differences in embarrassment.

Still, an examination of the content of the Embarrassability Scale is interesting. Factor analysis indicated that it contains five distinct classes of embarrassing situations:

> (1) Situations in which a person discredits his own self-presentation through some inadvertent foolishness or impropriety (e.g., tripping and falling in a public place); (2) situations in which a person finds himself unable to respond adequately to an unexpected event which threatens to impede the smooth flow of interaction (e.g., having attention drawn suddenly to some physical stigma of a co-actor); (3) situations in which a person loses control over his self-presentation through being the center of attention without having any well defined role (e.g., being the focal point of "Happy Birthday to You"); (4) situations involving empathic embarrassment wherein a person observes another individual who is in a seemingly embarrassing predicament (e.g., watching an ineffectual comedian on an amateur show); (5) situations in which an individual is involved in an incident having inappropriate sexual connotations (e.g., walking into a bathroom occupied by a person of the opposite sex). (Modigliani, 1968, p. 319)*

Situations like these exemplify embarrassing circumstances and serve to summarize our discussion thus far. They encompass the intended/unintended and accuracy dimensions of Weinberg (1968) and the agent, recipient, and observer categories of Sattler (1965); indeed, four of them are readily identifiable as Buss' (1980) impropriety (factor 1), lack of competence (2), conspicuousness (3), and breaches of privacy (5). They contain instances of disrupted interaction and of predictable social sanction. Again, however, there is a mention of an observer-oriented "empathic embarrassment" which is, as yet, largely unexplained. Moreover, with a survey of perspectives and precipitating factors now complete, we must also ask about the consequences of embarrassment. What are the effects of embarrassment? What is "empathic embarrassment"?

EXPERIMENTAL STUDIES

Early experimental investigations of embarrassment were prompted by Goffman's (1967) assumptions that embarrassment is situationally specific, that interactants are motivated to avoid it, and that, once it occurs, deliberate efforts

---

*From "Embarrassment and Embarrassability" by Andre Modigliani, 1968, *Sociometry*, p. 319. Copyright by the American Sociological Association. Reprinted by permission.

to bolster one's image and regain lost face—called "facework"—are often needed to recover from it. For instance, Brown (1970) and Brown and Garland (1971; Garland & Brown, 1972) conducted a number of studies that showed that subjects are likely to forego tangible profits in order to avoid making public an embarrassing event. In Brown (1970), subjects performed an embarrassing or nonembarrassing task—either sucking on a rubber pacifier or touching with their hands a small rubber figure—and then chose between (a) maximizing the money paid them by describing their actions to some of their classmates, or (b) accepting smaller payoffs to avoid public exposure. Embarrassed subjects sacrificed more money and retained more privacy than did unembarrassed subjects, especially when their audience was unaware of their costs for doing so. Moreover, a second experiment showed that embarrassed subjects sacrifice more money when confronted with an audience that is described as evaluative than when confronted with a nonevaluative audience. As Brown concluded, people apparently tend to engage in "costly face-saving behavior"—in this case, the avoidance of public exposure—after a potentially embarrassing incident.

Brown and Garland (1971) extended Brown's work, conducting two studies that again investigated the sacrifice of monetary rewards in order to preserve face. In both studies subjects received a computerized evaluation of their singing ability which judged them as either competent or incompetent, and were then asked to sing before an audience; the longer they sang, the greater their cash reward. The first study showed that incompetent subjects—who reported greater embarrassment—sang for a shorter time than did competent subjects. The second study, which manipulated the degree of acquaintanceship existing between incompetent singers and their audience, found that embarrassment avoidance was greater—subjects sang for a shorter time—before close friends than before acquaintances or strangers. Friendship did not seem to reduce the motive to protect one's face. A similar subsequent study by Garland and Brown (1972) demonstrated that women tended to avoid embarrassment to a greater extent than men and that avoidance was greater before a judgmental expert audience, one supposedly composed of "excellent" singers, than before an inexpert audience. Thus, Brown and Garland's work tends to confirm one of Goffman's primary hypotheses, that embarrassment is an aversive state that one will avoid if possible, even at cost to oneself.

The aversion of embarrassment apparently pervades our social lives, influencing many important behaviors. For example, Herold (1981) has found that the more embarrassment young women associated with the prospect of visiting a physician or pharmacy to obtain contraception, the less likely they were to be actually using contraception during sexual intercourse. Similarly, Foss and Crenshaw (1978) have shown that when helping another person involves a risk of embarrassment, subjects are less likely to help. In their study, men were much less likely than women to pick up a box of tampons that a hapless female had dropped, but there was no such sex difference (and men were much more helpful) when the fumbled object was an innocuous box of envelopes. In fact, adults may also be unlikely to risk embarrassment by asking for help. Druian and DePaulo (1977) found that, even when they needed aid on a spelling test, adults were reluctant to ask a competent child for help; they had fewer qualms about seeking aid from another adult.

Thus, people will go to considerable lengths to avoid embarrassment. How do they behave when it has already occurred? Goffman asserts that embarrassed people are motivated to redeem their public images through facework, somehow accounting for the incident and trying to reestablish their desirability. Several studies concur. For instance, Brown (1968) found that subjects who had been exploited by an opponent in a bargaining game, and then embarrassed by an evaluation from their audience that told them they looked foolish and weak, were much more likely than unembarrassed subjects (who had been told they looked good for playing fair) to sacrifice monetary reward in order to retaliate against their opponents. Having been humiliated, the subjects apparently ignored their own best interests in order to reassert their strength for their audiences.

Similarly, Modigliani (1971) found that embarrassed subjects who had publicly failed their portion of a group task made more image-enhancing statements to their fellow group members than did unembarrassed subjects; they tended to minimize their failures, derogate the task, excuse their performances, describe other abilities, or defensively change the subject. Thus, embarrassment usually seems to involve some attempt by an individual to restore one's deficient image, assuring those present that one is not generally as awkward or incapable as one may have momentarily appeared.

However, another of Goffman's assumptions holds that such actions by embarrassed people are ordinarily directed only at the audience that witnesses the embarrassing incident; one's subsequent interactions with other people should be unaffected. Apsler (1975) tested this assumption, examining (unlike Brown, 1968, and Modigliani, 1971) the behavior of embarrassed subjects toward others who were unaware of the embarrassing incident, and his results provide little support for Goffman's position. Apsler embarrassed half of his subjects by having them perform tasks that made them appear foolish—for example, laughing for 30 seconds as if they had just heard a joke, and imitating a 5-year-old having a temper tantrum—in front of a peer observer/confederate. Other subjects performed unembarrassing tasks, such as counting silently to 50. Then, either the observer or another confederate who ostensibly was completely unaware of the embarrassing performances privately asked the subject for help with a class project. Embarrassed subjects complied more than did unembarrassed subjects, regardless of the source of the request, and embarrassed subjects agreed to help an observer and a nonobserver of their embarrassment equally. The results undermine Goffman's assumption that embarrassment is situationally specific, suggesting instead that embarrassment creates a general discomfort or concern for face that embarrassed individuals then attempt to relieve, regardless of audience. Apsler's embarrassed subjects seemed to seek the image-enhancing experience of helping someone, anyone, whether the person had witnessed their embarrassment or not.

What of the audience that witnesses another's embarrassment? Goffman's approach suggests that *all* interactants share the burden of surviving an embarrassing incident; everyone present is expected to take remedial steps to patch up the interaction, bypassing the disruption and helping the embarrassed participant regain his composure. Importantly, the vital first step in this repair procedure may be the person's demonstration and acknowledgement that he or she *is* embarrassed. Semin and Manstead (1982) suggest that a display of embarrassment is an essential part of interaction ritual in which people communicate that they recognize that they have broken the norms of social conduct, and they are sorry. In short, "an actor who shows signs of feeling embarrassed . . . is in effect providing a non-verbal apology for his/her behavior" (p. 369). Armstrong (1974) makes a similar point.

Thus, given similar behavior, a person who becomes embarrassed following some social miscue may actually elicit more friendly aid and more liking from an audience than a person who reacts with aplomb. Indeed, when subjects watched a shopper accidentally knock down a tall stack of toilet paper in a grocery store, they liked the shopper more when he reacted with embarrassment than when he remained totally calm (Semin & Manstead, 1982). Moreover, Levin and Arluke (1982) have even shown that a student who becomes embarrassed in front of a class (and then regains composure) is likely to receive more volunteer help from peers than one who does nothing embarrassing at all.

Others who are present, then, may well react to, and become involved in, a person's embarrassment. Paradoxically, to help the person, they may laugh. Observational studies by Coser (1960) and Oleson and Whittaker (1966) have found that an audience often responds to a person's embarrassment with laughter, and this response may help rather than hinder the interaction. Laughter demonstrates that the incident is one to be taken lightly, not a serious matter that will demand future attention. (Imagine, by contrast, doing something embarrassing and having the onlookers react with a cool, disapproving, stony silence.) Laughter "combines criticism with support, acceptance with rejection" (Coser, p. 91), informing the person that one *should* be embarrassed but that the consequences will not be severe. Thus, it yields "a type of correction for the person even as the individual and situation are saved" (Oleson & Whittaker, p. 388), and, "importantly, it allows the onward flow of interaction" (p. 388). Thus, Goffman's assumptions again seem reasonable; audiences do often seem to humourously accept a person's improprieties, glossing over incidents so that interaction can continue. (Embarrassed individuals may themselves benefit from reacting with humor to their plight—audiences like embarrassed people who laugh more than those who do not, Edelmann, 1982,—but the use of humor is uncorrelated with embarrassment in naturalistic situations, Fink & Walker, 1977).

Still, audiences do not always respond lightly to another's embarrassment, and herein lies another reason why they may so readily aid the other in overcoming the other's distress: they may be affected by empathic embarrassment. Onlookers can be greatly affected by the embarrassing predicaments of even total strangers. In Miller (1979), I had subjects watch from behind a one-way mirror as another subject with whom they had just interacted (a) cooperatively, (b) competitively, or (c) not at all, performed Apsler's (1975) embarrassing tasks. The observers were instructed either to watch the actor's movements dispassionately or to concentrate on the actor's feelings, and they looked on as, for example, the actor sang the "Star-Spangled Banner" and danced to recorded disco music for 60 seconds. The actors were embarrassed by all of this, of course, but *so were the observers*, particularly when they were asked to empathize with the actors, and even when the actors were strangers with whom they had not interacted. The observers' skin potentials were recorded as they watched, and afterwards they were asked to describe their own feelings during the observation period. They reported a variety of feelings, including sympathy and sorriness, that were stronger than those of control observers who had watched an actor perform unembarrassing tasks, but none of these other feelings were as strongly correlated with their increased physiological reactions as their self-reports of embarrassment. It appeared that the emotional arousal that accompanied their observation of embarrassed others was more clearly related to the state of awkward fluster described as embarrassment than to anything else, and that this reaction was not dependent on prior interaction. Hence, empathic embarrassment: embarrassment felt for another even though one's own face is in no way endangered.

Goffman (1967) admits that this can occur; he agrees, for instance, that "when an individual finds himself in a situation which ought to make him blush, others present usually will blush with him" (p. 100) even if he fails to blush on his own account. Nevertheless, the existence of empathic embarrassment suggests that too narrow a focus on the give-and-take of interaction can obscure some of the power of this social phenomenon. During debriefing, several of my subjects spontaneously admitted that it sometimes pained them to watch "I Love Lucy" on television; Lucy would get herself into such predicaments they could barely stand it, and they would change channels! These reactions are clearly independent of the awkward uncertainty that accompanies disrupted interaction. Instead, as Buss would suggest, it appears that we are well trained to dread embarrassing circumstances whenever, and to whomever, they occur. No interaction is necessary; simply being aware of another's embarrassment can cause us similar chagrin.

These effects of embarrassment are particularly important because embarrassment is so readily recognizable. A series of studies by Edelmann and Hampson (1979, 1981a, 1981b) has shown that there are specific nonverbal behaviors that usually accompany embarrassment. People generally display a decrease in eye contact and an increase in smiling, body motion, and speech disturbances when they are embarrassed. Moreover, other people are likely to correctly recognize those reactions as embarrassment if they can see the person's entire body. Edelmann and Hampson (1981b) found that embarrassment could be mistaken for amusement if only the face were visible, but the addition of body cues—especially from the hands and lower legs where gestures and postural shifting would be visible—made embarrassment distinct. The combination of apparent amusement with downcast eyes and nervous hands and legs indicated something amiss.

We have seen, then, that Goffman's assumptions about embarrassment are generally correct, though he errs in tying embarrassment too closely to the flow of specific interactions. Buss' argument, too, has specific merit in that there does seem to be a developmental pattern to the emergence of embarrassment. Buss, Iscoe, and Buss (1979) asked parents of children aged 3 to 12 to recall and report any signs of embarrassment that had occurred recently in their children, and they found that in preschool children embarrassment was rare. However, embarrassment was seen in 59% of the 5-year-olds, and in greater numbers thereafter, marking a discrete change in the children's behavior. The data are open to various sources of error, but their pattern is reasonable; thus, Buss *et al.* suggest that "at roughly 5 years of age children have the social perspective-taking ability and other cognitive achievements necessary for the appearance of a social self" (p. 230) and that "embarrassment begins for most children" (p. 229) at age 5.

From a psychoanalytic perspective, Amsterdam and Levitt (1980) would place the emergence of embarrassment even earlier, at age 2 when the child can recognize himself in a mirror and is beginning to be punished for genital behavior. Nevertheless, developmentalists agree that a certain level of maturation is necessary in order for embarrassment to occur, and that it is the teaching we receive concerning appropriate and inappropriate behavior that underlies its origin. Moreover, age-related variations in embarrassment may continue. For instance, Horowitz (1962) asked high school and college students to recall past embarrassments and found that the years of early adolescence, ages 11 to 15, were usually fertile ground for embarrassing predicaments. Longitudinal studies tracing the development of self-concept, social skills, and embarrassment could be most interesting, but these, and the needed individual difference studies, have not been done.

Finally, let us note that as an emotional response embarrassment does have a physiological basis. Buck and Parke (1972) have distinguished it from the bodily response to fear; Buss (1980) suggests that it is controlled by the parasympathetic nervous system; and Devinsky, Hafler, and Victor (1982) argue that the capacity for embarrassment is localized in the prefrontal cortex; their examination of patients with lesions in the frontal lobes suggests that one's embarrassability is impaired when that area is damaged.

We have found, then, that embarrassment is an aversive state of both physiological and psychological arousal that is avoided if possible; it is characterized by facework directed toward any available audience. Other people who are present may be affected by an embarrassing episode, becoming involved in a person's efforts to overcome embarrassment and, perhaps, becoming embarrassed themselves. Embarrassment is recognizable as a specific constellation of nonverbal behavior, but it is not present at birth; it apparently takes some time for a young person to learn what social behavior is inappropriate, and to care what others may be thinking of her. There may be important individual differences in embarrassability.

INTEGRATION AND SPECULATION

Can we integrate the perspectives of Goffman (1967), Buss (1980), and Modigliani (1968)? That would be desirable, as it appears that an understanding of embarrassment must incorporate the emphases of all three. It is very likely that, as Buss suggests, our upbringing predisposes us to embarrassment; better studies of Modigliani's embarrassability disposition will almost certainly show that this is true. However, it is also true that once we learn that social transgressions will be punished and the rules of encounter are internalized, embarrassment is most often realized as a result of interaction.

The presence of other people is key to embarrassment, and when embarrassment occurs, face-to-face interaction is likely to increase the awkwardness of the event, making escape and relief more difficult. Any prior relationship with the witnesses of one's embarrassment may also enhance one's distress; subjects try harder to avoid embarrassment in front of friends than in front of strangers (Brown & Garland, 1971), and people rate the embarrassment of friends and relatives more negatively than that of strangers (Sattler, 1963). Nevertheless, it is clear that embarrassment is possible in the absence of interaction. People do generally assume that when they violate a social rule they will be evaluated negatively by any witnesses, whether or not they have interacted (Semin & Manstead, 1981). Moreover, the embarrassment of actors who knew merely that someone was watching behind a one-way mirror, and the empathic embarrassment of those observers themselves (Miller, 1979), argue that the experience of embarrassment is not dependent solely on disrupted interaction.

Let us suggest, therefore, that the cause of embarrassment is broader than Goffman's primary focus. A loss of face is involved, but the distress created may depend more on our long histories of punishment for public transgression than on the intrinsic awkwardness of fumbled interaction. Still, Goffman's stress on the social context of embarrassment is invaluable. Interaction likely heightens embarrassment when it occurs, but more importantly, Goffman reminds us that embarrassment is an interpersonal event. It can affect everyone present, having inescapable impact on the social situations in which it occurs (and the maintenance of any ongoing interactions).

Our survey of embarrassment is nearly complete, but a few intriguing questions remain. First, is embarrassment always aversive? We have defined it so, but, admittedly, different levels of distress will result from different predicaments. To a certain extent, the pain of embarrassment will be context specific; some of our actions are embarrassing before a given audience but not before others. Thus, the situation helps define whether or not a particular event is embarrassing, and we may occasionally begin to become embarrassed only to realize that our present audience does not define our actions negatively; such "embarrassments" will be only minimally aversive, if at all.

However, even genuine embarrassment may sometimes provide us a mixture of punishment and reward. As an instructor, I occasionally embarrass myself before a class to the degree that student laughter results. The event *feels* embarrassing, but even as I blush I may be grateful for its occurrence; it may be endearing me to my students, improving our rapport. Thus, pratfalls can have their benefits (Aronson, Willerman, & Floyd, 1966), and even embarrassment can have its instrumental rewards (cf. Levin & Arluke, 1982). Still, it should be noted that, even though my audience is learning something about me that is inconsistent with my projected identity, the embarrassment is increasing my desirability, not minimizing it, and it is not unacceptable to me to be seen as fallible. Perhaps we should say that, although all embarrassments (particularly overpraise, for example) may not be wholly aversive, those that involve an unwanted, actual loss of face invariably are. We would be unlikely to find a case of strong embarrassment that is not entirely uncomfortable.

Is there such a thing as "private embarrassment" that does not involve actual exposure before other people? Recall that Weinberg (1968) suggests that "duties" can cause an internal, private form of embarrassment even when others would not judge one's behavior to be deficient. Goffman (1967) allows that other people need not actually be present—embarrassment can occur in the "imagined presence of others" (p. 93)—but he argues that an embarrassed person must believe that others are aware of his behavior. Does embarrassment exist when a person knows that he or she is the only one aware of the embarrassing circumstances?

The only experimental evidence concerning this question is equivocal. Modigliani (1971) measured what he believed to be private embarrassment in subjects who had privately failed their portion of a group task and found that their level of reported embarrassment was intermediate to—and significantly different from—that of embarrassed subjects who had failed publicly and that of unembarrassed subjects who had privately succeeded. The private failure subjects reported less embarrassment than did those who had publicly bungled their assignments, but more embarrassment than did those who had not failed at all. Thus, at first glance, Modigliani's results suggest the existence of a mild form of embarrassment that exists even in the absence of an audience. However, the private failure subjects expected that some of their subsequent performances would be public, and their expectation of an audience's scrutiny may have led to an anticipatory embarrassment that was not truly private at all. Still, it is noteworthy that no actual loss of face occurred to produce the subject's discomfort. Instead, their mild embarrassment seemed to result from some cognitive process; as Modigliani suggests, "private-failure subjects allowed their sense of self-deficiency to produce an imagined sense of social disapproval" (p. 22).

This explicit recognition of the role of cognition in embarrassment and the possibility that an audience is not necessary for embarrassment to occur are both intriguing and intuitively plausible. Consider, for instance, this plight of a writer to the popular advisor-columnist, Abigail Van Buren (1978, p. 83), who complained that the noisy love life of a next-door neighbor could be easily heard through the thin walls of her apartment: "I am not an eavesdropper. What he does is his own business, but how do I keep his private life from ruining my sleep and embarrassing me and my guests?" She noted that she was reluctant to tell him that she could overhear his amorous actions, but wondered, "is there some way I can let him know that he is disturbing me and embarrassing me?" In such a situation, when guests are present and her neighbor's actions intrude upon her territory and the decorum she is trying to maintain, the writer's loss of poise causes her to be publicly embarrassed. However, she is probably also embarrassed in some manner even when she is alone and her neighbor's maneuvers are intrusively apparent; though no audience is present, the very fact that the situation would be embarrassing to all participants if the neighbor knew he had been or was being overheard may be enough to induce a private form of embarrassment in the writer. Indeed, many situations involve an "if they only knew" quality in which one anxiously attempts to keep from one's audience's notice some past or present deficiency that would surely be embarrassing if brought to their attention, and the fear of discovery in such situations is a discomfort akin to embarrassment, if not embarrassment itself. Even Darwin (1873/1965) suggested that blushing was possible in private "when we reflect what others would have thought of us had they known of the act" (p. 335). In addition, Schlenker (1980) argues that "social predicaments do exist in 'private' . . . all that is required is *an imagined audience that prompts attention to the self as a social object*" (p. 130). It may be proper to suggest that, whether or not we label it "private embarrassment," private events do often involve a fear of embarrassment that closely relate them to public embarrassments.

EMBARRASSMENT AND SHYNESS

The preceding discussion puts us in position to elucidate the relation between embarrassment and shyness. Leary (1982), in his integrative description of the social anxieties, suggests that shyness refers to that discomfort that comes with a person's expectation that he will not be able to satisfactorily manage his face, whereas embarrassment refers to the discomfort that occurs after something has already happened to discredit his face. Shyness speaks of a person's dread that the person will blow it, embarrassment of the knowledge that the person has already blown it. In addition, Buss (1980), though he argues that "we might as well compare apples with pears" (p. 213), cites situational causes of shyness—conspicuousness, others' intrusiveness, novel environments (in which *faux pas* and mistakes are much more likely)—that can also precipitate embarrassment. Finally, we have reasoned that a private fear of embarrassment may create a state that is not unlike public embarrassment itself. Are the pessimistic expectations of shyness much different in their effects than the unfortunate realities of embarrassing circumstances?

We may be able to answer that question by examining the reactions of people who know that they will soon be embarrassed. Fish, Karabenick, and Heath (1978), for example, informed some of their subjects that they would soon be asked to do something potentially embarrassing—sucking on infantile objects—

either while alone or in the presence of observers. However, before the task, they were given a choice of waiting their turn with others or alone. Subjects expecting embarrassment preferred isolation, not affiliation, and this preference was stronger the closer the surveillance they expected to receive during the tasks. The preferences of these subjects were quite different from those of other participants who were threatened with fear-arousing tasks; fear produced a desire to affiliate. Thus, Fish *et al*. noted, "Some types of misery (embarrassment) do not prefer *any* type of company" (p. 264).

Similarly, when Miller and Miller (1983) warned subjects that they would soon perform Apsler's (1975) embarrassing tasks before an observer, they found that the subjects were more pessimistic than those faced with unembarrassing tasks. The subjects were unhappy about the threat of embarrassment, ill at ease and unenthusiastic, and they described themselves less positively than those not facing embarrassment. In short, they acted shy.

We can argue, then, that embarrassment blends into shyness when subjects are faced with the certain expectation of a predicament that has not yet occurred. A continuum of certainty may underlie any distinction between the two: if shyness is based on a fear that something will go wrong in social situations, private embarrassment may refer to the belief that something *has* gone wrong that others do not yet know about, whereas embarrassment refers to the belief that others do know of one's predicament. There may be other important links between embarrassment and shyness; the chronically shy may also be more embarrassable, and they may be more likely to blunder into embarrassing circumstances. Clearly, there are many intriguing questions waiting to be answered.

REFERENCES

Amsterdam, B. K., & Levitt, M. (1980). Consciousness of self and painful self-consciousness. *Psychoanalytic Study of the Child, 35,* 67–83.

Apsler, R. (1975). Effects of embarrassment on behavior toward others. *Journal of Personality and Social Psychology, 32,* 145–153.

Armstrong, W. D. (1974). The social functions of embarrassment. *Dissertation Abstracts International, 35,* 2479B.

Aronson, E., Willerman, B., & Floyd, J. (1966). The effect of a pratfall on increasing interpersonal attractiveness. *Psychonomic Science, 4,* 227–228.

Brown, B. R. (1968). The effects of need to maintain face on interpersonal bargaining. *Journal of Experimental Social Psychology, 4,* 107–122.

Brown, B. R. (1970). Face-saving following experimentally-induced embarrassment. *Journal of Experimental Social Psychology, 6,* 225–271.

Brown, B. R., & Garland, H. (1971). The effects of incompetency, audience acquaintanceship, and anticipated evaluative feedback on face-saving behavior. *Journal of Experimental Social Psychology, 7,* 490–502.

Buck, R., & Parke, R. D. (1972). Behavioral and physiological response to the presence of a friendly or neutral person in two types of stressful situations. *Journal of Personality and Social Psychology, 24,* 143–153.

Buss, A. H. (1980). *Self-consciousness and social anxiety*. San Francisco: Freeman.

Buss, A. H., Iscoe, I., & Buss, E. H. (1979). The development of embarrassment. *Journal of Psychology, 103,* 227–230.

Buss, L. (1978). *Does overpraise cause embarrassment?* Unpublished manuscript, University of Texas, Austin.

Coser, R. (1960). Laughter among colleagues: A study of the social functions of humor among the staff of a mental hospital. *Psychiatry, 23,* 81–95.

Dann, O. T. (1977). A case study of embarrassment. *Journal of the American Psychoanalytic Association, 25,* 453–470.

Darwin, C. R. (1965). *The expression of the emotions in man and animals.* Chicago: University of Chicago Press. (Originally published 1873.)

Devinsky, O., Hafler, D. A., & Victor, J. (1982). Embarrassment as the aura of a complex partial seizure. *Neurology, 32,* 1284–1285.

Druian, P. R., & DePaulo, B. M. (1977). Asking a child for help. *Social Behavior and Personality, 5,* 33–39.

Edelmann, R. J. (1982). The effect of embarrassed reactions upon others. *Australian Journal of Psychology, 34,* 359–367.

Edelmann, R. J., & Hampson, S. E. (1979). Changes in non-verbal behavior during embarrassment. *British Journal of Social and Clinical Psychology, 18,* 385–390.

Edelmann, R. J., & Hampson, S. E. (1981a). Embarrassment in dyadic interaction. *Social Behavior and Personality, 9,* 171–177.

Edelmann, R. J., & Hampson, S. E. (1981b). The recognition of embarrassment. *Personality and Social Psychology Bulletin, 7,* 109–116.

Fink, E. L., & Walker, B. A. (1977). Humorous responses to embarrassment. *Psychological Reports, 40,* 475–485.

Fish, B., Karabenick, S., & Heath, M. (1978). The effects of observation on emotional arousal and affiliation. *Journal of Experimental Social Psychology, 14,* 256–265.

Foss, R. D., & Crenshaw, N. C. (1978). Risk of embarrassment and helping. *Social Behavior and Personality, 6,* 243–245.

Garland, H., & Brown, B. R. (1972). Face-saving as affected by subjects' sex, audiences' sex, and audience expertise. *Sociometry, 35,* 280–289.

Goffman, E. (1959). *The presentation of self in everyday life.* Garden City, NY: Doubleday.

Goffman, E. (1967). *Interaction ritual.* Garden City, NY: Doubleday.

Gross, E., & Stone, G. P. (1964). Embarrassment and the analysis of role requirements. *American Journal of Sociology, 70,* 1–15.

Herold, E. S. (1981). Contraceptive embarrassment and contraceptive behavior among single young women. *Journal of Youth and Adolescence, 10,* 233–242.

Horowitz, E. (1962). Reported embarrassment memories of elementary school, high school, and college students. *Journal of Social Psychology, 56,* 317–325.

Leary, M. R. (1982). Social anxiety. In L. Wheeler (Ed.), *Review of personality and social psychology* (Vol. 3, pp. 97–120). Beverly Hills, CA: Sage.

Levin, J., & Arluke, A. (1982). Embarrassment and helping behavior. *Psychological Reports, 51,* 999–1002.

Miller, G. A., & Miller, R. S. (1983). *Reactions to the threat of embarrassment.* Paper presented at the 29th Annual Meeting of the Southwestern Psychological Association, San Antonio, TX.

Miller, R. S. (1979). *Empathic embarrassment: Reactions to the embarrassment of another.* Paper presented at the 87th Annual Meeting of the American Psychological Association, New York.

Modigliani, A. (1968). Embarrassment and embarrassability. *Sociometry, 31,* 313–326.

Modigliani, A. (1971). Embarrassment, facework, and eye contact: Testing a theory of embarrassment. *Journal of Personality and Social Psychology, 17,* 15–24.

Morley, R. (1983). *Pardon me, but you're eating my doily.* New York: St. Martin's Press.

Oleson, V. L., & Whittaker, E. W. (1966). Adjudication of student awareness in professional socialization: The language of laughter and silences. *Sociological Quarterly, 7,* 381–396.

Sartre, J. P. (1958). *Being and nothingness.* New York: Citadel Press.

Sattler, J. M. (1963). The relative meaning of embarrassment. *Psychological Reports, 12,* 263–269.

Sattler, J. M. (1965). A theoretical, developmental, and clinical investigation of embarrassment. *Genetic Psychology Monographs, 71,* 19–59.

Sattler, J. M. (1966). Embarrassment and blushing: A theoretical review. *Journal of Social Psychology, 69*, 177–133.

Schlenker, B. R. (1980). *Impression management: The self-concept, social identity, and interpersonal relations.* Monterey, CA: Brooks/Cole.

Semin, G. R., & Manstead, A. S. R. (1981). The beholder beheld: A study in social emotionality. *European Journal of Social Psychology, 11*, 253–265.

Semin, G. R., & Manstead, A. S. R. (1982). The social implications of embarrassment displays and restitution behavior. *European Journal of Social Psychology, 12*, 367–377.

Van Buren, A. (1978, February 17). Untitled. *Gainesville Sun*, p. 8B.

Weinberg, M. S. (1968). Embarrassment: Its variable and invariable aspects. *Social Forces, 46*, 382–388.

VI
Therapeutic Interventions

Part VI deals with approaches to the treatment of shyness. Clinicians have only recently turned their attention to the treatment of shyness specifically and, as a consequence, much of the discussion in this section draws on treatment strategies originally designed for other forms of "social phobia." No one intervention technique has emerged as the treatment of choice for shyness, and the chapters in this section reflect the range of options currently available.

Glass and Shea (Chapter 23) advocate a cognitive approach to the treatment of shyness. They argue that shyness is due to negative and irrational beliefs about oneself. When anxious, shy individuals overestimate the potential threat of the situation, and they underestimate their ability to handle the problem. According to Glass and Shea, this process is in part mediated internally by what individuals say to themselves and is manifested externally in what individuals say about themselves. Glass and Shea argue further that by changing the way shy people think, one can change also the way shy people feel. Thus, their treatment program teaches shy clients how to identify, test, and discard irrational beliefs in favor of more effective assessments of their social lives.

The second chapter in Part VI acts as a counterweight to the first. Haemmerlie and Montgomery suggest that shy clients improve when they experience social success. They argue that attitudes, feelings, and cognitions follow the lead of behavior and that rewarding interactions generate positive affect and self-confidence. They recommend, therefore, a biased interaction technique in which shy clients participate in multiple interactions that have been structured unobtrusively to ensure a positive experience. This approach deliberately minimizes the role of the therapist. Three studies are described that suggest that the biased interaction technique is effective, produces long-lasting results, and is perceived as a pleasant experience. Haemmerlie and Montgomery acknowledge the contribution of Bem's theory of self-perception to their approach, and they point out that several additional types of intervention also incorporate an in vivo experience that may account, at least in part, for the success of such approaches.

Alden and Cappe begin their chapter by examining the social-skills approach to the treatment of shyness. Simply stated, this approach assumes that shy people lack the ability and confidence necessary to successfully engage in mutually satisfying social interactions. As in the previous chapter, Alden and Cappe emphasize the importance of the in vivo experience in understanding the success of the social-skills approach, but they also consider what is meant by effective social skills. Often the terms refers to micro-behaviors, such as the amount of eye contact and duration of speech, but Alden and Cappe argue for the need to assess process skills such as the flow of interaction and the synchronicity of behavior between the participants. In particular, they suggest that good social skills involve attending to one's interaction partner. Alden and Cappe also describe a training process in which participants are encouraged to become active listeners and empathic responders, to respect others' rights, and to reciprocate the intimacy of self-disclosure. Finally, they report the results of a study that examines whether such training contributes significantly beyond the effects of a gradual exposure procedure alone.

In the next chapter of this section (Chapter 26), Phillips provides a synopsis of the assumptions and principles underlying rhetoritherapy. As the name implies, this treatment approach focuses explicitly on the art of speaking effectively, and improvement in verbal skills is the sole criterion of success. Phillips rejects the idea that reticence is something that needs to be cured, asserting instead that the problem of shyness is one of social ineptness. Phillips then outlines the process by which speaking incompetence can be corrected, and describes the lessons to be mastered and the role of the trainer in rhetoritherapy.

The last chapter in Part VI and the final chapter of the book deals with two broad issues in the treatment of shyness. Pilkonis first considers whether it is more appropriate to treat shy clients individually or in groups. He argues that group sessions offer a number of advantages but also notes that shy people seem to prefer an informal, "drop-in" group approach rather than structured weekly sessions. The second issue Pilkonis examines has to do with the length of treatment. In discussing the merits of short- and long-term strategies, he argues that decisions must be made with regard to the needs of a particular client. Although short-term intervention will suffice for most, extended and individual counseling is sometimes necessary to overcome private forms of shyness. Pilkonis concludes his chapter by suggesting that shyness may sometimes be but one manifestation of inadequate attachment, and in such instances may therefore prove to be only one feature of a deeper psychological disorder.

23

Cognitive Therapy for Shyness and Social Anxiety

Carol R. Glass and Cheryl A. Shea

INTRODUCTION

In a review of the recent literature, Pilkonis (1984) reported that 15% to 20% of the general adult population may experience distressing social anxiety. Shyness has been linked with depression, occupational difficulty, sexual dysfunction, and assertiveness deficits (Zimbardo, 1977). Thus, it is clear that shyness and social anxiety are important and clinically relevant problems.

In the present chapter, we will focus on cognitive interventions for interaction anxieties, including shyness and heterosocial anxiety, and will use the terms *shyness* and *social anxiety* interchangeably. Treatments for nonassertion, which frequently deal only with stating opinions and/or refusing requests, will not be included. After a discussion of the cognitive factors involved in shyness, we will devote the major portion of this chapter to a summary of clinical techniques employed in cognitive therapy for social anxiety, and will also review the empirical support for its effectiveness.

COGNITIVE FACTORS IN SHYNESS AND SOCIAL ANXIETY

In recent years, more and more excitement has been generated over cognitive approaches to psychological problems. Pivotal works by Beck (1976), Ellis (1962), Mahoney (1974), and Meichenbaum (1977) have offered an alternative to traditional psychoanalytic and behavioral models of emotional disorders. Instead of viewing shyness and social anxiety as related to unconscious psychological

CAROL R. GLASS and CHERYL A. SHEA • Department of Psychology, Catholic University, Washington, DC 20064.

315

factors, or to prior conditioning or skills deficits, a cognitive perspective has emerged that suggests that negative self-evaluations, faulty attributions, distorted thinking, unrealistic expectations, irrational beliefs, and a negative "internal dialogue" of thoughts and images play an important role.

According to Beck (1976; Beck & Emery, 1979), the crucial distorted thoughts of the anxious client center around the anticipation of danger and harm, involving an overestimation of the probability of harm and what might happen, and an underestimation of his or her ability to cope. In the case of social anxiety, this danger could be psychological rather than physical in nature, involving anticipated rejection, failure, disapproval, or embarrassment. Beck and Emery (1979) discuss a number of distorted thoughts and cognitive concerns of the socially anxious individual: (a) other people have a low opinion of me; (b) other people can easily see I'm anxious, are put off by it, and see me as weak and inferior; (c) other people don't become anxious in similar social situations; (d) my social skills are inadequate and deficient; (e) people will reject me; and (f) other people's approval of me is crucial to my sense of worth.

This last concern is also one of the 10 "irrational beliefs" postulated by Albert Ellis (1962) to lead to feelings of extreme emotional upset. Ellis (1963) has specifically suggested that shyness stems from the fear that it would be awful to be rejected and that this would prove one's worthlessness. A second irrational belief (Ellis, 1962) that may be important in shyness concerns having to be thoroughly competent, achieving, and adequate in all respects. If the shy individual also feels lacking in social skills, such a belief could lead to avoidance of social situations.

In what sense, then, is shyness a problem of distorted thinking rather than one of deficient skills? Our own experience working with the adults who volunteered for our Shyness Program research over the past three years (Arnkoff, Glass, McKain, Shea, & Greenberg, 1984; Glass & Furlong, 1984) is that only 10%–20% could be called "painfully shy" in that they seemed not to know what to do in conversations, were quiet and anxious in the group setting, and tended to have few friends. Therapists reported that these individuals seemed to benefit from social skills training. For the majority of participants, however, shyness seemed more of a self-confidence issue, involving highly negative self-evaluations and expectations such as "I won't do well" or "I can't do this." It was thus a real eye-opener for them to observe other participants in their group, who appeared comfortable and skilled, yet who voiced many of the same poor self-images and negative thoughts as themselves. As one participant reported at the end of our program, "It was just the way I was thinking about myself, I could do it all along."

Research has clearly demonstrated that maladaptive cognitions are linked to feelings of shyness and social anxiety (i.e., Glass, Merluzzi, Biever, & Larsen, 1982; Goldfried & Sobocinski, 1975). For example, one of the participants in our Shyness Program research gave the following response on a thought-listing measure (Cacioppo, Glass, & Merluzzi, 1979) administered just before the pretreatment assessment conversation with two strangers:

I am scared—nervous and anxious—What in the world will I say—I will look and act like an idiot—How will I begin—How long will I have to talk—Will the people I am talking to laugh at me—Maybe I should walk out—I hope I don't stutter—Am I weird for feeling this way?

It follows, then, that treatments could be designed to focus specifically on changing such negative self-evaluations. In the next section, we will briefly describe the theory and techniques of cognitive therapy interventions. This will serve as an introduction to a more specific look at cognitive therapy for socially anxious clients.

COGNITIVE THERAPY FOR INTERPERSONAL ANXIETY

Introduction to Cognitive Therapy

The cognitive therapies share the viewpoint that problematic cognitive processes underlie maladaptive behavior and emotional disorders; the way people evaluate and/or label situations or events can affect, if not determine, their emotional reactions (Ellis, 1962; Goldfried, 1979). One type of cognitive therapy, cognitive restructuring, is the most frequently used cognitive intervention for social anxiety. Although there are minor differences in techniques, rational-emotive therapy (RET) (Ellis, 1962), systematic rational restructuring (Goldfried, Decenteceo, and Weinberg, 1974), self-statement modification (Meichenbaum, 1977) and cognitive therapy (Beck, 1976) have a common goal.

In general, cognitive therapists help clients understand that irrational beliefs, expectations, and negative thoughts or self-statements mediate their maladaptive affective reactions. Therapists focus directly on modifying clients' distorted, self-defeating cognitions and replacing them with more adaptive ways of thinking (Goldfried, 1979), in order to produce cognitive, behavioral, and affective change. Treatment is generally brief, problem oriented, time limited, and directive, and is based on a collaborative effort between the therapist and client (Beck & Emery, 1979). However, as Arnkoff (1981) points out, cognitive therapy need not be restricted to cognitive techniques. Because the cognitive viewpoint is more characteristic of cognitive therapy than in any particular technique, behavioral or gestalt methods can, for example, be part of cognitive therapy if such procedures are conceptualized in a cognitive way.

Cognitive Intervention Strategies

In conjunction with our Shyness Program research, we have run almost a dozen group treatments that were either exclusively cognitive in nature or that involved a combination of cognitive restructuring and social skills training. Our program, like most other examples of cognitive therapy for social anxiety in the literature, was carried out in group format.

In this section, we will present a synthesis of cognitive therapy procedures and methods, drawing when possible on examples from our own program. We will discuss methods for helping clients (a) adopt the cognitive rationale; (b) recognize the irrationality of certain beliefs; (c) become aware of their own thoughts and beliefs; (d) learn to dispute and challenge these negative, unrealistic self-statements and irrational beliefs; (e) begin to analyze faulty logic; and (f) develop facilitative coping self-statements and more rational interpretations or beliefs.

In beginning a cognitive therapy intervention, it is crucial at first to present a rationale for treatment and help clients arrive at a shared understanding of this rationale. This common cognitive conceptualization generally involves the notion that feelings of shyness stem from the ways we think about, evaluate, and interpret social situations, and our fears of negative consequences of initiating social interactions (Gormally, Varvil-Weld, Raphael, & Sipps, 1981; Kanter & Goldfried, 1979).

In our treatment groups, we used an approach similar to Meichenbaum's (1972) in his cognitive therapy for test anxiety. As clients began to share and discuss the duration and extent of their social anxiety and situations in which they felt uncomfortable, the group leader pulled for information on their expectations and what they were saying to themselves about their behavior in these situations. The therapist then suggested that perhaps there was some relationship between the anxiety clients felt in these situations and the kinds of thoughts they had, using illustrations from the previous discussion. If clients could discover these negative self-statements and the beliefs that underlie these thoughts, they could then learn to change the way they think and therefore change the way they feel.

Goldfried (Goldfried & Davison, 1976) illustrates this rationale by describing two individuals who are going to the same party, where one is nervous and worried and one is confident and relaxed. After presenting examples of the thoughts or self-statements each of these people might be making, and allowing group members to discuss how each person is probably feeling and why, the therapist makes the point that what we tell ourselves influences the way we feel.

Before beginning to look at the client's own thoughts, Goldfried (Goldfried & Davison, 1976) recommends discussion of various irrational attitudes, such as the need to be loved or the need for perfection described by Ellis. The distinction is made between insisting that these should or must occur, versus the more rational interpretation that it would be nice to be approved of or to do well. For example, the therapist can play devil's advocate and pretend to hold the attitude that he or she must be liked and approved of by everybody. Group members are encouraged to argue against this point of view, thus convincing themselves of the unrealistic nature of such beliefs.

One way of then helping clients to become aware of their own negative self-statements and beliefs in social situations is to have them observe their thoughts in actual situations outside of therapy, monitoring the nature of the situation and their actions, level of anxiety, and what they were thinking about at the time. Group leaders can get participants to discuss these self-statements and how their internal dialogue may have contributed to their level of anxiety and choice of action.

Becoming aware of negative thoughts can also be practiced in the group setting. The therapist can present a common situation, such as "You've just walked into a room full of people at a party." Clients are then asked to imagine the situation as vividly as possible. They can then discuss what they are saying to themselves in this situation, and share their thoughts out loud with other group members. Gaining awareness of the self-defeating nature of this internal dialogue may be especially helpful.

Once clients become adept at using their anxiety as a cue to identify their maladaptive thoughts, they can proceed to modify these negative self-statements, beliefs, and expectations. Gormally *et al.* (1981) followed the lead of Kanter and Goldfried (1979): clients were asked to imagine each scene in a hierarchy of problematic social situations and write down their level of anxiety and irrational thoughts, followed by a more rational reevaluation and subsequent level of anxiety. After each situation, group members shared what coping thoughts they had generated and were reinforced by the therapist for their efforts at more rational reevaluation.

Cognitive modeling can also be a very useful technique at this point. Glass, Gottman, and Shmurak (1976) utilized audiotapes consisting of coping models in 11 empirically derived problematic social situations. After the situation description, the model verbalized a sequence of self-talk. This self-talk began with negative self-statements, but the model became aware of these self-defeating thoughts, confronted them, and replaced them with positive self-talk. Finally, the model gave himself reinforcing self-statements, a pat on the back for his attempts to cope.

But how do clients learn how to dispute and challenge their thoughts in order to replace them with more rational appraisals? Here we are really talking about two separate processes: one dealing with undermining the maladaptive cognitions, and the other with substituting more positive self-statements.

One of the most powerful techniques for disputing thoughts is to analyze the faulty logic that may be operating. "What is the evidence?" is thus a key question for clients to ask themselves. "Does the evidence support my conclusion? What is the actual probability that such catastrophic consequences will occur? How likely is it that I never make a good impression or that others can always tell that I'm nervous? Am I really totally responsible for the outcome in this situation?"

Beck and Emery (1979) suggest a focus on "decentering," having clients challenge their belief that they are in fact the center of attention and that others are acutely aware of their anxiety or shyness. "What are concrete criteria to determine when I am the focus of attention?" This task requires that clients actually begin to observe other people's reactions, which shifts their preoccupation away from their own internal reactions. As clients come to realize how infrequent and limited their own observations of others are, they may see that the same may be true for other people's observations of them. Feedback from group members may also be helpful in illustrating the incongruity between self-appraisals and actual performance.

Trower, O'Mahoney, and Dryden (1982) suggest that clients keep a diary of their social behavior, gathering evidence to contradict their negative thinking patterns. Thus, homework outside the sessions serves as a chance for clients to test hypotheses, and gather evidence to test whether their catastrophic predictions actually occur.

Another useful method in disputing negative cognitions is what Beck calls "decatastrophizing" (Beck & Emery, 1979). "Even if the worst possible outcome occurs, how bad would that really be? How would it be so terrible?" This "what if" technique helps clients to face the ultimate negative consequences, and see that they are building up certain social situations to be much more significant than they actually are.

Once negative thoughts and beliefs are challenged, tested, and disputed, clients can substitute more positive self-statements. Together, group members can generate a number of coping thoughts that can be employed in actual social situations. Throughout this discussion of different kinds of coping self-statements, it is important to stress the individual nature of positive thoughts. Those that work well for one person may not fit for another individual. The only way to know for sure whether particular thoughts are beneficial is to try them out in real life. During the session, role plays can be used to set up typical situations such as "sitting next to an attractive stranger on a long plane ride" or "talking to someone at a party you want to get to know better." Thus, clients practice disputing negative cognitions and countering them with positive thoughts in a safe setting with the support of the group leader and other group members.

Combining Cognitive and Behavioral Approaches

Cognitive therapy alone may not be equally effective for all clients, especially those with social skill deficits. Although reducing anxiety and avoidance in social situations using a cognitive approach may lead to more frequent interactions and thus a chance to learn new social skills, perhaps some clients would benefit from a more direct approach, teaching them *what to do* in various social situations.

Along with Diane Arnkoff, Tom McKain, and Jim Greenberg, in our second Shyness Program study we have looked more closely at combined cognitive-behavioral interventions with shy adults. We conducted three eight-session groups that began with social skills training and then moved on to cognitive restructuring, as well as three groups conducted with the opposite order of treatments: cognitive restructuring first followed by social skills training. An outline of the latter program is presented in Table 1. There were no significant differences in outcome for clients, and group leaders (who ran one group of each order) had positive comments in support of the choice of either treatment order. Of course, there is another alternative to the treatment orders we used, and that is to combine a focus on skills and cognitions within each and every session. It is

TABLE 1. An 8-week Cognitive-Behavioral Group for Shy Adults

Week 1: Get to know other group members, share reasons for coming to program, experience of shyness in daily life as well as during role-play assessment, discuss cognitive-behavioral rationale for program. Task assignment—Make a record of your thoughts during the week in at least one social situation each day.

Week 2: Discuss homework, importance of negative self-statements and underlying unrealistic beliefs in contributing to social anxiety, analysis of thoughts and beliefs in specific situations. Task assignment—Monitor social situations, your negative thoughts and beliefs, how you felt in each situation.

Week 3: Discuss homework, develop coping self-statements and learn to dispute maladaptive beliefs, practice becoming aware of and challenging negative cognitions in specific situations. Task assignment—Record social situations, negative thoughts and beliefs, how you felt, and positive thoughts and beliefs you substituted for the negative ones. List best coping thoughts.

Week 4: Discuss homework, focus on awareness of and countering catastrophic expectations, dealing with feeling overwhelmed, additional practice and review of cognitive restructuring. Task assignment—Choose a situation that is moderately difficult and practice cognitive coping.

Week 5: Discuss homework, review social skills rationale, teach act-react, answer-ask, and attend-understand guidelines for initiating and maintaining conversations (Watkins, 1972), modeling and practice. Task assignment—Practice starting a conversation and keeping it going with a friend, and with an acquaintance or stranger.

Week 6: Discuss homework, review previous conversation guidelines, teach elaborate-associate rule, discuss how to plan and initiate activities, modeling and practice. Task assignment—Become aware of thoughts that make it hard for you to initiate activities and challenge them, then plan and initiate an activity with each of two persons you'd like to get to know better, one man and one woman.

Week 7: Discuss homework, distinguish assertion from aggression and nonassertion, discuss why people act nonassertively and benefits of acting assertively, modeling and practice to identify personal rights and carry out more assertive ways of responding. Task assignment—Become aware of cognitions that hinder you in being more assertive and practice coping with them. Then attempt to respond more assertively in at least one situation during the week.

Week 8: Discuss homework, review of skills and coping strategies, group members share changes experienced, feelings about ending, what can continue to do on own after program, etc.

also possible to add relaxation training or in vivo exposure sessions to the treatment package.

Consideration of individual differences among clients may be an important focus if we are to decide how best to combine treatment approaches. Perhaps we need to look at each client's cognitive and social skill deficits prior to therapy, as well as at what Glass and Arnkoff (1982) have called the client's predispositions for various methods. One such predisposition might be clients' comfort and familiarity with procedures that are similar to those we use in therapy. Some individuals would be highly introspective, regularly examining thoughts and feelings, whereas others would find this new. Others may already be adept at observing others as models, providing self-reinforcement, and believe that "practice makes perfect." Additional predispositions include clients' expectancies and goals for what will go on in therapy, and their own implicit theory of why they are shy. We might, then, want to match those persons with a more cognitive predisposition to an intervention that would begin with cognitive techniques making use of the client's preferred style, and then in later stages help the client to work in uncomfortable or unfamiliar behavioral modes to learn new competencies. The opposite would be true for the client with a predisposition towards more of a behavioral approach. This design was the basis for our second Shyness Program outcome study (Arnkoff et al., 1984).

RESULTS OF CLINICAL OUTCOME RESEARCH

Reviews of the literature examining the use of cognitive therapies in the treatment of anxiety, particularly cognitive restructuring or self-statement modification approaches, have found them to be effective interventions (Goldfried, 1979; Mahoney & Arnkoff, 1978). In this final section, we will present a comprehensive review of the therapy-outcome literature for cognitive therapy of social anxiety and shyness. On the whole, outcome studies have established that this type of intervention contributes significantly to behavioral, cognitive, and affective change.

Comparative Group Investigations

In one of the first cognitive therapy outcome studies, Glass et al. (1976) found that self-statement modification, social skills training, and a combined treatment all increased social skills in practiced role-play situations, but heterosocially anxious college men who had received the cognitive component demonstrated significantly better performance on untrained situations. Because the cognitive self-statement modification group also made significantly more phone calls during assessment and made better impressions on the women called, cognitive therapy was useful for achieving generalization to new situations.

Gormally et al. (1981) used a similar design, and found cognitive counseling, skills training, and a cognitive/behavioral combination to be equally effective for minimally dating college men in producing changes on measures of social behavior, dating, self-confidence, maladaptive thoughts, and irrational beliefs. Cognitive counseling produced the greatest changes on a measure of negative expectancies. Tiegerman and Kassinove (1977) conducted a similar study with socially anxious student volunteers. Although the cognitive-rational therapy was most effective in increasing assertive behavior, only the assertiveness training and combined treatment proved helpful in reducing social anxiety.

In a slightly different type of approach, Schlever and Gutsch (1983) investigated the effects of self-administered cognitive therapy (bibliotherapy) for socially anxious college students. Both cognitive and attention-placebo groups showed equivalent reductions in shyness, state and trait anxiety, and maladaptive thoughts compared to no-contact controls.

Finally, our initial Shyness Program outcome study (Glass & Furlong, 1984) found no differences among social skills, cognitive restructuring, problem solving, traditional group therapy, and a waiting-list control group on self-report, cognitive, and behavioral measures. All five groups showed significant change, suggesting that our extensive pretherapy assessment may have had a sensitizing effect on the highly motivated control subjects, leading them to change on their own.

Although these five studies compared noncognitive and cognitive interventions, they do not tell us who benefited more from each approach. The next six studies all included client variables in their design, in order to address this question.

Comparative Group Studies and Client Variables

One of the earliest studies comparing cognitive therapy with other approaches for treating interpersonal anxiety classified subjects according to personality type as introverts or extroverts (DiLoreto, 1971). DiLoreto found that RET, systematic desensitization, and client-centered therapy differed significantly from both attention-placebo and no-contact controls on behavioral and self-report measures of general and interpersonal anxiety, although the client-centered group failed to indicate a significant decrease in self-reported interpersonal anxiety. RET was more effective in reducing interpersonal anxiety with introverts than was client-centered therapy, and client-centered therapy was more effective than RET for extroverts.

Kanter and Goldfried (1979) took another client characteristic, high or moderate level of social anxiety, into account in their treatment study with socially anxious community residents. Contrary to prediction, no interaction was obtained between anxiety level and the efficacy of different treatments. Compared to waiting-list controls, systematic rational restructuring, self-control desensitization, and a combination treatment were all effective in reducing anxiety. Rational restructuring was significantly more effective in reducing self-report measures of state and trait anxiety and irrational beliefs than was systematic desensitization, and resulted in greater generalization of anxiety reduction to nonsocial situations.

With a cognitive client variable, Malkiewich and Merluzzi (1981) examined the efficacy of matching clients with high or low conceptual level (CL) to treatment orientations with different amounts of structure. Although the results did not support the matching model, cognitive restructuring and systematic desensitization were more effective than the waiting-list control group in reducing anxiety, increasing social skill, and decreasing negative thoughts, and rational restructuring was significantly more effective than systematic desensitization.

Using the client variables of autonomic perception and physiological reactivity, Shahar and Merbaum (1981) had few matching predictions supported. Overall, both strategies were effective in reducing self-reported anxiety and in improving social behavior. Rational restructuring showed a tendency to be more effective than self-control desensitization on some measures and significant improvements were noted from pretest to posttest for all subjects who received rational restructuring.

Elder, Edelstein, and Fremouw (1981) found more positive matching results, suggesting that response acquisition (social skills training) was equally effective in reducing anxiety for both high and low socially anxious clients, whereas cognitive restructuring was extremely effective for high anxious subjects and only minimally effective for those lower in social anxiety. Although both treatments produced social skills enhancement and social-anxiety reductions, response-acquisition procedures were more effective than cognitive restructuring.

In our second Shyness Program outcome study (Arnkoff et al., 1984), we examined the interaction between clients' predispositions and the order in which they received a combined cognitive-behavioral intervention. Virtually all of the measures showed a significant improvement from pretest to posttest and follow-up. Predisposition measures were related as expected to other pretreatment measures, providing initial evidence for the validity of the predisposition assessment. However, as in many of the studies cited in this section, the matching hypothesis was not supported: subjects initially assigned to treatments that reflected their predispositions for therapy showed no greater improvement than subjects initially assigned to unfamiliar treatment strategies.

Treatment Packages including Cognitive Therapy

Cognitive therapy has been included in a number of treatment packages for social anxiety reduction, but many investigations have not examined the magnitude of its contribution. For example, Heimberg, Becker, Goldfinger, and Vermilyea (1983) administered cognitive restructuring for socially phobic clients immediately after behavioral performance in anxiety-provoking situations, a program that resulted in large and significant reductions in anxiety.

Stravynski, Marks, and Yule (1982) examined the contribution of the cognitive component with a sample of socially anxious outpatients. They found that both social skills training and a combination social skills plus cognitive modification condition were equally effective in reducing social anxiety and increasing social skill, suggesting that the addition of cognitive modification did not enhance outcome.

Contrary to Stravynski et al.'s (1982) findings, Pipes (1982) found that shy male students achieved significantly greater reductions in social anxiety and increases in self-esteem with a combination treatment (anxiety management training and response practice) than with a response practice condition alone or no treatment. Interestingly, the shy women in the study appeared to profit less from the combined strategy than did male subjects.

Summary

Cognitive therapy, particularly cognitive restructuring strategies, has been shown to be effective in reducing social anxiety and shyness. Unfortunately, many of the studies testing cognitive approaches have not included cognitive assessment in their designs. In the future, this serious shortcoming must be corrected if we are to explain treatment outcomes in terms of cognitive change (Glass & Merluzzi, 1981). Individualized cognitive assessment might also be helpful in achieving treatment goals by facilitating the development of individualized coping strategies and positive self-statements.

It is striking that only two studies used therapy clients as subjects. Although four others used adults who volunteered for programs to reduce their shyness or social anxiety, the great majority of outcome research on cognitive therapy for social anxiety has relied on college student subjects. Thus, the generalizability of positive findings remains in question.

Finally, the results of the investigations that examined client variables and their relationship to outcome have been inconsistent. Although introversion-extroversion interacted with type of treatment, conceptual level, client predispositions, and autonomic perception/reactivity did not. Conflicting findings were obtained for initial level of social anxiety as a matching variable. It is clear that further research is needed to determine which client variables affect the outcome of cognitive therapy. Although no consistent superiority of a cognitive approach over a behavioral strategy in reducing social anxiety has been demonstrated, perhaps further investigations of client variables and client–treatment matching will show that these interventions are differentially effective for different individuals.

CONCLUSION

The present chapter has reviewed cognitive factors, clinical techniques, and outcome research related to the cognitive treatment of social anxiety and shyness. A growing number of clinicians and researchers are finding evidence that clients' experiences of shyness are highly related to their maladaptive ways of perceiving and thinking about social situations.

Although the outcome literature suggests that cognitive therapy alone may be effective for certain clients, still others may benefit from a more eclectic combination of cognitive and noncognitive approaches. Additional clinical exploration and research validation is crucial if we are to achieve optimal understanding of how best to combine therapeutic procedures. We must also not lose sight of the importance of individual differences. Thus, Paul's (1967) famous statement of the outcome question that directs us to look at "*What* treatment, by *whom*, is effective for *this* individual with *that* specific problem, and under *which* set of circumstances" (p. 111), is just as important today in our consideration of cognitive therapy for shyness as it was 18 years ago.

ACKNOWLEDGMENTS

The authors wish to extend their thanks to Diane Arnkoff for her helpful comments on a previous draft of this chapter.

REFERENCES

Arnkoff, D. B. (1981). Flexibility in practicing cognitive therapy. In G. Emery, S. D. Hollon, & R. C. Bedrosian (Eds.), *New directions in cognitive therapy* (pp. 203–223). New York: Guilford Press.
Arnkoff, D. B., Glass, C. R., McKain, T., Shea, C. A., & Greenberg, J. M. (1984, August). Client predispositions to respond to cognitive and social skills treatments for shyness. In J. M. Cheek

(Chair), *Shyness: Personality development, social behavior, and treatment approaches*. Symposium conducted at the meeting of the American Psychological Association, Toronto.

Beck, A. T. (1976). *Cognitive therapy and the emotional disorders*. New York: International Universities Press.

Beck, A. T., & Emery, G. (1979). *Cognitive therapy of anxiety and phobic disorders*. Philadelphia: Center for Cognitive Therapy.

Cacioppo, J. T., Glass, C. R., & Merluzzi, T. V. (1979). Self-statements and self-evaluations: A cognitive response analysis of heterosocial anxiety. *Cognitive Therapy and Research, 3*, 249–262.

DiLoreto, A. O. (1971). *Comparative psychotherapy*. Chicago: Aldine.

Elder, J. P., Edelstein, B. A., & Fremouw, W. J. (1981). Client by treatment interactions in response acquisition and cognitive restructuring approaches. *Cognitive Therapy and Research, 5*, 203–210.

Ellis, A. (1962). *Reason and emotion in psychotherapy*. New York: Lyle Stuart.

Ellis, A. (1963). *Sex and the single man*. New York: Lyle Stuart.

Glass, C. R., & Arnkoff, D. B. (1982). Think cognitively: Selected issues in cognitive assessment and therapy. In P. C. Kendall (Ed.), *Advances in cognitive-behavioral research and therapy* (Vol. 1, pp. 35–71). New York: Academic Press.

Glass, C. R., & Furlong, M.R. (1984, August). A comparison of behavioral, cognitive, and traditional group therapy approaches for shyness. In J. M. Cheek (Chair), *Shyness: Personality development, social behavior, and treatment approaches*. Symposium conducted at the meeting of the American Psychological Association, Toronto.

Glass, C. R., & Merluzzi, T. V. (1981). Cognitive assessment of social-evaluative anxiety. In T. V. Merluzzi, C. R. Glass, & M. Genest (Eds.), *Cognitive assessment* (pp. 388–438). New York: Guilford Press.

Glass, C. R., Gottman, J. M., & Shmurak, S. H. (1976). Response acquisition and cognitive self-statement modification approaches to dating skills training. *Journal of Counseling Psychology, 23*, 520–526.

Glass, C. R., Merluzzi, T. V., Biever, J. L., & Larsen, K. H. (1982). Cognitive assessment of social anxiety: Development and validation of a self-statement questionnaire. *Cognitive Therapy and Research, 6*, 37–55.

Goldfried, M. R. (1979). Anxiety reduction through cognitive-behavioral intervention. In P. C. Kendall & S. D. Hollon (Eds.), *Cognitive-behavioral interventions: Theory, research, and procedures* (pp. 117–152). New York: Academic Press.

Goldfried, M. R., & Davison, G. C. (1976). *Clinical behavior therapy*. New York: Holt, Rinehart, & Winston.

Goldfried, M. R., & Sobocinski, D. (1975). Effect of irrational beliefs on emotional arousal. *Journal of Consulting and Clinical Psychology, 43*, 504–510.

Goldfried, M. R., Decenteceo, E. T., & Weinberg, L. (1974). Systematic rational restructuring as a self-control technique. *Behavior Therapy, 5*, 247–254.

Gormally, J., Varvil-Weld, D., Raphael, R., & Sipps, G. (1981) Treatment of socially anxious college men using cognitive counseling and skills training. *Journal of Counseling Psychology, 28*, 147–157.

Heimberg, R. G., Becker, R. E., Goldfinger, K., & Vermilyea, J. A. (1983, December). *Cognitive-behavioral treatment of social phobia*. Paper presented at the meeting of the Association for Advancement of Behavior Therapy, Washington, DC.

Kanter, N. J., & Goldfried, M. R. (1979). Relative effectiveness of rational restructuring and self-control desensitization for the reduction of interpersonal anxiety. *Behavior Therapy, 10*, 472–490.

Mahoney, M. (1974). *Cognition and behavior modification*. Cambridge, MA: Ballinger.

Mahoney, M. J., & Arnkoff, D. B. (1978). Cognitive and self-control therapies. In S. L. Garfield & A. E. Bergin (Eds.), *Handbook of psychotherapy and behavior change* (2nd ed., pp. 689–722). New York: John Wiley & Sons.

Malkiewich, L. E., & Merluzzi, T. V. (1980). Rational restructuring vs. desensitization with clients of diverse conceptual level: A test of a client-treatment matching model. *Journal of Counseling Psychology, 27*, 453–461.

Meichenbaum, D. H. (1972). Cognitive modification of test anxious college students. *Journal of Consulting and Clinical Psychology, 39*, 370–380.

Meichenbaum, D. H. (1977). *Cognitive-behavior modification*. New York: Plenum Press.

Paul, G. L. (1967). Strategy of outcome research in psychotherapy. *Journal of Consulting Psychology, 31*, 109–118.

Pilkonis, P. A. (1984). Avoidant and schizoid personality disorders. In H. Adams & P. Sutker (Eds.), *Comprehensive handbook of psychopathology*. New York: Plenum Press.

Pipes, R. B. (1982). Social anxiety and isolation in college students: A comparison of two treatments. *Journal of College Student Personnel, 23*, 502–508.

Schlever, S. R., & Gutch, K. U. (1983). The effects of self-administered cognitive therapy on social-evaluative anxiety. *Journal of Clinical Psychology, 39*, 658–666.

Shahar, A., & Merbaum, M. (1981). The interaction between subject characteristics and self-control procedures in the treatment of interpersonal anxiety. *Cognitive Therapy and Research, 5*, 221–224.

Stravynski, A., Marks, I., & Yule, W. (1982). Social skills problems in neurotic outpatients: Social skills training with and without cognitive modification. *Archives of General Psychiatry, 39*, 1378–1385.

Tiegerman, S., & Kassinove, H. (1977). Effects of assertive training and cognitive components of rational therapy on assertive behaviors and interpersonal anxiety. *Psychological Reports, 40*, 535–542.

Trower, P., O'Mahoney, J. F., & Dryden, W. (1982). Cognitive aspects of social failure: Some implications for social skills training. *British Journal of Guidance and Counselling, 10*, 176–184.

Watkins, B. R. (1972). The development and evaluation of a transductive learning technique for the treatment of social incompetence (Doctoral dissertation, University of Oregon, 1972). *Dissertation Abstracts International, 33*, 2861B.

Zimbardo, P. G. (1977). *Shyness: What it is, what to do about it*. Reading, MA: Addison-Wesley.

24

Self-Perception Theory and the Treatment of Shyness

Frances M. Haemmerlie and Robert L. Montgomery

INTRODUCTION

For many people, the feeling of uncertainty, apprehension, and awkwardness in interpersonal situations is a common problem. Surveys indicate that at least 90% of Americans report feeling shy occasionally; and 50% indicate that shyness sometimes constitutes a significant problem for them (Zimbardo, 1977). Although a variety of theoretical approaches have been employed to date to help individuals overcome this problem, (Curran, 1977; Leary, 1983), Bem's (1972), self-perception theory, a potentially important perspective, has received little attention. In fact, except for an earlier review paper by Kopel and Arkowitz (1975) and a series of studies (Haemmerlie, 1983; Haemmerlie & Montgomery, 1982; Haemmerlie & Montgomery, in press) by the present authors, this approach has received hardly any attention at all in the therapy or treatment literature.

According to Bem (1967, 1972), people come to know their emotions, attitudes, and other internal states by inferring them from observations of their own behavior. Bem's theory views the person as forming attitudes, cognitions, and emotional responses in much the same way an external observer might infer that person's attitudes. One knows what one believes or feels based on how one behaves. Of particular interest to us, from a therapeutic standpoint, was that instead of assuming a reduction in fear results in an increase in approach behavior and a decrease in avoidance behavior, as a more traditional model might do, self-perception theory instead suggests the opposite. An increase in approach behavior and/or a decrease in avoidance behavior might cause a decrease in perceived anxiety. Moreover, whereas a more traditional approach might

FRANCES M. HAEMMERLIE and ROBERT L. MONTGOMERY • Department of Psychology, University of Missouri at Rolla, Rolla, MO 65401.

assume that an individual does not engage in social interactions because of a lack of requisite skills or because of a negative attitude or emotional state, self-perception theory suggests that individuals may perceive that they are shy (i.e., do not have social skills and/or have a negative attitude or emotional state) because they do not engage in social interactions. In general, in the absence of strong environmental or physiological cues that elicit a particular behavior, the behavior itself provides compelling information on which to base inferences concerning internal states. Although Bem's theory is now considered to be an attribution theory by most social psychologists (Harvey & Weary, 1981; Shaw & Costanzo, 1982), as originally conceived it was developed from the radical behaviorism of B. F. Skinner.

In the present chapter, we will describe how we came to develop a clinical approach based on this theoretical framework, the results of some empirical studies demonstrating its effectiveness, and a comparison of this approach to others in the social and clinical psychology literatures. Finally, we will discuss some of the positive features associated with the treatment, its possible limitations, and directions that future research in this area might take.

DEVELOPMENT OF THE TECHNIQUE

Clinical Observation

Initial interest in applying self-perception theory to the problem of shyness occurred after one of the authors, a clinical psychologist, had worked with several college students who were trying to overcome it. Their fear of meeting and talking to members of the opposite sex had been described as both a humiliating experience and as one that had made life miserable for them. Yet, after spending 10 to 15 sessions with many of these clients, and using a variety of traditional clinical treatment methods (e.g., rational restructuring, rational emotive therapy, desensitization, behavior rehearsal, and supportive therapy), not much behavioral change seemed to occur. Instead, it appeared largely that only the clients' adeptness for providing labels for their condition (e.g., a conditioned avoidance response, an irrational belief, a lack of positive regard) had changed. In some of these cases, however, practice homework assignments had also been given between therapy sessions that required clients to engage in different social interactions in the real world. Moreover, after having had only a few of these successful homework experiences (especially with members of the opposite sex), an abrupt change for the better usually occurred, and the client would indicate that therapy was no longer needed, because, miraculously, the client had been cured.

With this somewhat humbling clinical experience in mind, the treatment of choice became rather obvious. If these clients were typical, the most direct way for resolving shyness problems might simply be one of having them talk to several strangers under pleasant, carefully prearranged conditions rather than spending hours in talk therapy, behavior rehearsal, and/or desensitization exercises. Moreover, direct observation and control over whatever it was that might be occurring during the homework assignments would also be feasible.

Theoretical Approach

Although self-perception theory had not been previously employed within the context of therapy, it appeared to represent a promising, easy to implement intervention that would be parsimonious with, and explain the essential features of the prearranged, positive homework procedure. A treatment for shyness based on self-perception theory would simply involve arranging a series of purposefully biased social interactions in which the individuals would appear to themselves to have performed competently as a function of their own behavior and ability and not as a function of environmental constraints. The interactions should appear to be natural rather than contrived, and the behaviors of the other persons interacting with the subjects would need to be spontaneous and unrehearsed. Furthermore, intrusion from a therapist should be minimized. Otherwise, the positive behaviors exhibited by subjects in these interactions would likely be attributed to environmental constraints (characteristics of the treatment, the setting, or the therapist) or to the person with whom they were interacting, rather than to themselves. To the extent that nonobvious, purposefully biased environmental factors conspired to cause their behavior, but did not appear to do so, these subjects should see themselves as fairly adept in social interactions following the treatment and as not having the problem of shyness. Finally, this treatment would provide a simple, easily administered intervention for shyness, that would not involve large amounts of professional time.

EMPIRICAL STUDIES

Procedure

To test these observations and ideas, three studies were conducted (Haemmerlie, 1983; Haemmerlie & Montgomery, 1982; 1984). In each an unobtrusively biased interaction technique was used to help shy college students. Overall, the guiding principles were that the positively biased interactions would appear natural rather than contrived. The behavior of the interaction assistants, although positively biased, would be spontaneous and unrehearsed, and minimal intrusion from a therapist would occur. Compared to subjects in a waiting-list control group, we expected that those receiving the biased interactions treatment would change in their degree of self-perceived shyness. Moreover, when in the presence of a target college student of the opposite sex, performance would be enhanced, and anxiety, as assessed by a variety of measures, would be reduced. Finally, we expected that this change would be fairly permanent.

Actual treatment procedures used in the three studies involved subjects receiving two sessions of treatment given one day apart. During each, an individual engaged in a series of 6, 10–12 minute positively biased social interactions with an opposite sexed confederate. An undergraduate male, introduced simply as a research assistant, administered and monitored the sessions. The research assistant told clients that the sessions would involve a series of brief interactions with individuals who were students "much like themselves" at the university. He then took subjects individually to different rooms and seated them at a table across from an opposite sexed interaction assistant who was already seated. After instructing both to carry on a conversation, the research assistant left the room and did not return again until near the end of the conversation period. After each interaction period, subjects were rotated into other rooms with other interaction assistants such that by the end of the treatment session, all had interacted once with each of the interaction assistants available during a particular treatment session.

The interaction assistants were opposite sexed peers enrolled in psychology courses and received extra credit for their role in these studies. They had been initially screened on the basis of being a typical college undergraduate and on the basis of their ability to carry on a pleasant conversation. None were told about the full purpose of the research in any of these studies. To do so, we thought, would cause them to behave in a less spontaneous manner. Approximately 15 minutes before the first session began, the interaction assistants reported to the experiment and were told by the research assistant that they would be acting as facilitators in several 10–12 minute social interactions with other students whom they had not met before. They were instructed to simply carry on a pleasant conversation as they might with anyone they had just met and with whom they would be interested in having a brief conversation. Additionally, they were told to initiate conversation topics and to be as friendly and natural as possible. Further, they were *not* to discuss sex, make or accept dates, and in general to not be negative in any way to the subjects.

Results of Research

In the first study (Haemmerlie & Montgomery, 1982), heterosocially anxious, low-frequency-dating male subjects were not even aware that their anxiety was being treated. Instead they believed themselves to be in a psychology experiment investigating the nature of dyadic interaction processes. A significant reduction in heterosocial anxiety did occur, however, and on a variety of measures, including Rehm & Marston's (1968) Situation Questionnaire, Watson & Friend's (1969) Fear of Negative Evaluation and Social Avoidance and Distress Scales, the State Anxiety Inventory of Speilberger, Gorsuch, & Lushene (1970); the number of conversation initiations by a subject in a conversation period; and the number of personal statements uttered by a subject in a conversation period. Moreover, a follow-up six months later indicated that following the intervention a significant increase in dating frequency had occurred and that the reduced levels of anxiety were fairly permanent.

In the second study (Haemmerlie, 1983), the subjects were heterosocially anxious females and expectancy of treatment outcome was manipulated. Again, the intervention (this time with male assistants) produced significant changes on a variety of measures (i.e., the Situation Questionnaire and State Anxiety Inventory, the percent of conversational silences in a conversation period, and ratings by interaction assistants of the subjects' anxiety level). In addition, the treatment technique was not susceptible to expectancy of therapeutic outcome.

In a third study (Haemmerlie & Montgomery, 1984), with heterosocially anxious males as subjects, expectancy of treatment outcome was manipulated and the efficacy of the treatment was compared to an imaginal exposure treatment condition. Again, the treatment based on self-perception theory effectively reduced anxiety on a number of measures (e.g., the Situation Questionnaire and State Anxiety Inventory; digit span backwards, a behavioral task; and pulse, a physiological measure) and the expectancy manipulation had no effect on the self-perception treatment. In the imaginal exposure treatment, on the other hand, expectancy of outcome did have a significant effect, and the treatment had little impact when subjects did not believe that it would help them.

Conclusions and Implications

What conclusions and observations can be drawn from these three studies? First, the treatment was highly effective with males and females on a variety of measures. Secondly, a 6-month follow-up in the first study indicated that the effect was fairly permanent. Third, the treatment did not appear to be susceptible to expectancy of treatment outcome effects and it was clearly superior to an imaginal exposure treatment technique. Fourth, in all three studies, subjects found the treatment of interest to be highly enjoyable. None of the subjects expressed suspicion that the interaction assistants had been prompted to be positive towards them. Moreover, even when told of this aspect of the experiment at a later time, it seemed of little interest to them. What seemed instead to be of interest was that they had enjoyed the interactions and felt good about having done well in them. Moreover, many spontaneously expressed an interest in participating in future projects of this nature that might be available. Several also indicated an interest (though disallowed) in possible future interactions with particular interaction assistants whom they had met in the various sessions.

Consistent with Bem's theory, these studies suggested that the number of visible external constraints could be a very important ingredient not only with this particular treatment, but also in many other therapeutic interventions. Furthermore, the effect of visible external constraints might be in the direction opposite to that believed to exist by many therapists. Most startling in these three studies, at least from the perspective of the subject, was that a reduction of anxiety occurred in the absence of a therapist or a truly obvious therapeutic agent. Instead, agents of change were the subject's own behavior as elicited by a group of minimally trained undergraduates in a setting resembling real life. The implications of this were twofold. First, a powerful intervention technique was provided when subjects focused on the successful performance of behaviors related to their specific individual problem area. As suggested by Heider (1958), the behavior engulfed the perceiver's view of the social context in which it occurred. Second, the interesting possibility was raised that when an individual's focus was on the individual's own performance or behavior, maximally effective results could be obtained if the therapeutic aspects of the treatment package and setting were downplayed. Otherwise, as suggested by Bandura (1977) and Meichenbaum (1977), and consistent with Bem's (1972) theory, success experiences might be attributed to the therapist, the setting or the treatment package, and this in turn could lessen the overall effectiveness of the intervention.

COMPARISON WITH OTHER APPROACHES AND TECHNIQUES

Although easy to implement and elegantly simple in the number of theoretical assumptions needed to explain its effectiveness, the biased interaction technique is also consistent with several other theoretical and treatment frameworks in social and clinical psychology.

Social Psychological Literature

Sherif and Asch Research. First, the biased interaction treatment technique captures many of the features found in the classic autokinetic studies of Sherif (1935) and the line judging task of Asch (1952). Although these two social influence paradigms have frequently been lumped together, in reality they differ (Pollis & Montgomery, 1966) from one another on a number of dimensions, including the underlying phenomena studied in each, the permanancy of the effect obtained, and the degree of ambiguity surrounding the task in which subjects are engaged. Whereas the biased interactions technique resembled the Asch study with regard to a person being influenced by a "rigged" majority, it more closely resembled Sherif's paradigm with regard to the permanancy of the effect obtained and the degree of ambiguity present (i.e., a conversation with an opposite sexed stranger and little in the way of a script or guidelines to follow). Consistent with our procedures and both of these research literatures, we would expect clients to be most heavily influenced when there are several assistants (up to 10 or 12), when they are unanimous, and when each reacts positively to a client and in a consistent manner. Moreover, stronger effects would be expected by having the assistants interact with each client, separately, rather than all at once (Wilder, 1978).

Importance of a Vivid Event. Although sharing differences, the Sherif and Asch paradigms resemble one another in that both represent a fairly vivid event for their participants. In general, vivid events have been shown (Nisbett & Ross, 1980) to have a powerful impact on memory, the way we process future information, and on how we perceive ourselves and the behavior of others.

Consider yourself in the role of one of our subjects. Generally, you have felt awkward and ill at ease around members of the opposite sex. Surprisingly, however, you meet six in a row, in two sessions on separate days. Further, your interaction with each one goes quite well. Would that not be an event of peculiar significance to you? Further, if an experimenter then attempted to debrief you with regard to what actually transpired, do you think that you would be influenced much by this discrediting information? Consistent with the research of Jennings, Lepper, and Ross (1981) and Ross, Lepper, and Hubbard (1975), which demonstrate that it is extremely difficult to debrief subjects of inferences arrived at on the basis of direct experience, our subjects continued believing that their outcomes were due in large measure to their own behavior.

Other Research and Theory in Social Psychology. The biased interaction technique, and the results found when using it, are also consistent with other aspects of human behavior studied by social psychologists. As noted by Fazio and Zanna (1981), years of research relating to both the self-perception and cognitive dissonance (Festinger, 1957) literatures show that although an attitude-to-behavior link may not be very strong, a behavior-to-attitude link is. Active experience provides a far more powerful experiential referent that does passive acceptance (or many hours of talk therapy). Research studies by Ross and his colleagues (Jennings *et al.*, 1981; Lord, Ross, & Lepper, 1979), moreover, have shown that once established, an erroneous belief (and we assume that a fear of interacting with members of the opposite sex is such a belief) is difficult to disconfirm, discredit, or rid oneself of. Further, research by Fazio, Effrein, and Falender (1981), and Snyder and Swann (1978), suggests how such beliefs can be strengthened and maintained even more by means of a "self-fulfilling prophecy" process that occurs during social interaction with others. In spite of this, however, and also consistent with the research of Ross and his colleagues, our research results indicated that this past history of erroneous beliefs could be broken up by providing these individuals with appropriate disabusing or invalidating vivid events (Nisbett & Ross, 1980); that they easily forgot their previous erroneous beliefs (Bem & McConnell, 1970); and that during a debriefing they continued to deny a real influence (Nisbett & Wilson, 1977) on their behavior.

From an attribution theory perspective, these events were arranged such that it was difficult for subjects to infer that their success was due to constraints coming from the environment. A high degree of choice in the behaviors in which subjects engaged was perceived; and they could not infer that their success was due to the dispositional characteristics of any single interaction assistant. Instead of only one partner, each subject interacted with 10 or 12 assistants. Thus, the subjects' environments were purposefully manipulated in such a way that each was left largely with the possibility of only themselves to blame or hold responsible for their success.

Clinical Treatment Literature

In general, although social and clinical psychologists often look at similar problems, for example shyness, there is a large difference in emphasis or focus in each area. Clinical psychologists, in general, and behavior therapists in particular, have focused on getting a behavioral change. Social psychologists since the advent of cognitive dissonance theory, at least (Festinger, 1957), have generally focused on an individual's reaction to himself or herself after a behavioral change has been managed. Thus, although the self-perception technique bears some resemblance to other clinical methods in matters of procedure, with regard to emphasis and underlying process variables being studied, it represents a departure from most previous treatments. Four clinical psychology approaches will be examined that procedurally resemble the self-perception technique: flooding or exposure, social-skills training or behavioral rehearsal, practice techniques, and cognitive therapies.

Flooding or Exposure. Flooding or exposure is the oldest of these behavioral techniques. Its roots lie in the acquisition and extinction of avoidance responses in animals (Solomon, Kamin, & Wynn, 1953) and its primary theoretical underpinning is the extinction of conditioned anxiety. More recently, it has been used with humans (Boulougouris & Marks, 1969; Malleson, 1959) to reduce fear and anxiety. Procedurally, the technique involves forced exposure of a fearful individual to realistic, anxiety-provoking stimuli while not permitting the client to avoid these stimuli. It differs from desensitization, a more commonly used conditioned anxiety technique, by not including a systematic, graded hierarchy of stimuli, and by not having the client engage in an explicit competing activity, such as relaxation (Davison & Wilson, 1972). Although it can be conducted imaginally, superior results have generally been obtained when *in vivo* procedures are used by exposing clients to real-life feared objects (Emmelkamp & Wessels, 1975). Perhaps the most salient feature concerning flooding is the exposure aspect—a component common to nearly all behavioral therapeutic interventions. A number of clinicians, in fact, assert that the exposure factor is the single most active ingredient common to all behavioral therapy treatments (Boyd & Levis, 1983; Mavissakalian & Michelson, 1983).

Exposure or flooding has been demonstrated to be effective in treating a number of human emotional and behavioral problems, including phobias (Mavissakalian & Michelson, 1983), obsessive-compulsive disorders (Meyer, Robertson, & Tatlow, 1975), and social withdrawal in children (Kandel, Ayllon, & Rosenbaum, 1977). Whereas there is no doubt that flooding works, one wonders whether it does so because of the extinction of conditioned anxiety, or an avoidance response, or for other reasons. Self-perception theory suggests that to the extent an individual emits successful behavior during the exposure procedure, any improvement achieved may also be due to the fact that a client's self-perceptions were also concomitantly altered.

Social Skills Training. Social skills training represents a second related clinical approach for treating social anxiety problems. This approach assumes that shy individuals lack sufficient or appropriate social skills and it includes a variety of specific techniques such as modeling, behavior rehearsal, shaping, and *in vivo* practice (Curran, 1979) to change this state of affairs. The primary change strategy shared by all such techniques is behavior rehearsal, a procedure in which a client practices new skills and receives feedback in simulated situations (Galassi & Galassi, 1979).

Leary (1983) has suggested that this general skills deficit approach may not explain all instances of shyness, however, because not all individuals with social anxiety possess a skills deficit. Moreover, there are also others who lack such skills but who do not report feeling particularly apprehensive or anxious. Even so, Jones, Hobbs, & Hockenbury (1982) have demonstrated that lonely college students display a particular conversational skill deficit (i.e., giving appropriate partner attention), and that when subjects are subsequently trained to improve this skill, a significant reduction in loneliness occurs. Other studies have also demonstrated that social skills training procedures can improve friendship patterns among socially isolated children (Oden & Asher, 1977), enhance social skills in schizophrenic patients (Finch & Wallace, 1977), and reduce anxiety and/ or change the behavior of minimal daters (Twentyman & Zimering, 1979). These techniques differ from flooding and the self-perception technique in that they require a client to overtly practice responses with a model who, in turn, provides the subject with direct, positive and negative feedback concerning the effectiveness of his or her behavior. Additionally, these training techniques are normally carried out with a therapist or other subjects in obviously simulated situations that are under the direct supervision of the therapist (Galassi & Galassi, 1979; Twentyman & Zimering, 1979).

A general comparison of social skills training and the self-perception theory technique shows some overlap in that they both provide an *in vivo* exposure experience. Yet, social skills training differs from the self-perception therapy in that it includes additional corrective feedback procedures—an aspect that the self-perception theory technique avoids in attempting to create a natural, unstructured conversation session in the absence of a therapist or therapeutic agent. In the realm of conjecture, given that we found a reduction in shyness in the absence of the manipulation of any skill variables, it is possible that the success of these behavior change therapies may not be simply due to reinforcement, punishment, or extinction of behavior as is often claimed, but are also confounded by the fact that the client successfully emits the target behavior in the first place. Thus, improvement might come more from the client having simply observed that he is capable of mastering the behavior deemed appropriate than from the actual acquisition of skills. This line of reasoning, of course, is similar to Bandura's (1977) notion of self-efficacy.

Real Life Practice Techniques. A third therapy approach, and procedurally most similar to the self-perception technique, is the real life practice method that has been used to help minimal daters. Theoretically, these techniques have been generally classified as conditioned-anxiety reduction techniques (Arkowitz, 1977; Galassi & Galassi, 1979). In the first of these studies, Martinson and Zerface (1970) reduced anxiety and increased dating frequency by having college males simply arrange interactions with volunteer females and instructing them to discuss their problems and personal concerns. Similarly, dating anxiety reduction and/or improvement in dating behavior have also been reported by Christensen & Arkowitz (1974) and Christensen, Arkowitz, & Anderson (1975). These latter procedures differ from the Martin and Zerface technique, however, in that they were clearly described to subjects as practice dates and not as peer counseling situations.

These real life practice techniques resemble the self-perception technique in that they both include *in vivo* exposure and practice in natural social situations. Moreover, they do not involve a therapist being present during actual treatment sessions. They differ from the self-perception approach, however, in that the subject arranges the interactions and in the fact that the length and nature of the social experiences are not carefully monitored. Consequently, it is difficult to know exactly the cause of these successful results. To us, self-perception theory would be an equally viable, if not an even more parsimonious explanation of the results found in these studies.

Cognitive Therapies. The last clinical approach to be reviewed that has been used to treat individuals with shyness problems is the cognitive approach. This perspective includes a variety of specific therapy techniques that resemble each other in that they help shy individuals change their cognitions or beliefs about themselves or their social worlds (Leary, 1983). A substantial body of research and clinical evidence has grown out of this approach that generally supports its value in helping people with social problems. For example by changing clients' self-statements, Glass, Gottman, & Shmurak (1976) were able to improve their dating skills. Kramer (1975) used a cognitive restructuring technique to increase the frequency of subject heterosocial interactions and reduce their heterosocial anxiety.

Whereas the self-perception technique resembles the cognitive approach in its attempt to change an individual's self-perceptions related to shyness, it differs from most of these procedures in that it attempts to change cognitions indirectly, by first changing behavior. With most cognitive approaches the emphasis is on changing behavior by first changing cognition. Thus, the self-perception technique is not a cognitive/behavioral approach as much as it is a behavioral/cognitive approach. Additionally, in contrast to most cognitive approaches, an emphasis is on maximizing naturalness and positive outcomes in a therapy situation and deemphasizing the therapist's role or role of the therapy in the change process.

SUMMARY AND CONCLUSIONS

The self-perception approach to helping shy individuals overcome their problem has a number of positive features associated with it. First, it is a relatively inexpensive and easy to administer technique that can be given to a large number of individuals at one time. It does not involve a large amount of therapist time or skill and can be easily administered and monitored by a minimally trained undergraduate assistant. Furthermore, it appears to be a relatively short-term treatment procedure. Lastly, it is consistent with a great deal of previous research in experimental and applied social psychology and appears to include a number of the components found in several of the clinical procedures that have been previously demonstrated to be effective. In fact, from the perspective of self-perception theory, a single explanation might be advanced as to why most all the procedures surveyed appear to work. Perhaps the technique used is not nearly as important as providing any procedure that systematically helps people to initiate successful behavior in situations that were previously avoided. Stated more boldly, it is quite likely that nothing succeeds like success, and the perception of that success, in an area where one has previously been unsuccessful.

On the negative side, in some circumstances it may be hard to arrange realistic, natural interactions and to unobtrusively positively bias them. Although we ourselves were initially concerned about how the interaction assistants might perform, it turned out that, in fact, as we had hoped, a minimum amount of prompting was quite effective in getting them to emit the appropriate positive behaviors that in turn elicited positive, effective interaction behaviors from the subjects. Nevertheless, the careful selection of a research/therapy assistant and the interaction assistants could be an important factor in the effectiveness of the procedure.

Another problem is that, theoretically, the actual mechanism(s) of change in this technique are difficult to tease out. In this regard, it seems to the authors that it may be problematic to isolate empirically the *in vivo* exposure, practice, and self-observation components of this procedure given that all occur simultaneously in live, behaving, cognitively intact humans. However, the role of such components as unobtrusiveness (or external vs. internal constraints present), nature and frequency of positive responses from the interaction assistants, and role of other cognitive variables (e.g., fear of negative evaluation, self-presentational efficacy, and irrational beliefs) would be more amenable to experimental manipulation, and research on these factors could provide a more exact accounting of the active ingredients involved in this and other techniques.

To arrange any treatment for a client without the client's knowledge might also violate the legal and ethical principles of the client's right to give informed consent and the right to refuse treatment (see Schwitzgebel & Schwitzgebel, 1980). Although such deception may occasionally be permissable by researchers, for practitioners it is not, even when doing so might increase the effectiveness of a particular treatment. Fortunately, it appears that even with fairly strong discrediting information during a debriefing session, clients still tend to see themselves as having been the primary cause for their successful outcome. Even so, and although obligated to explain fully the nature of an arranged experience procedure, our research also suggests that it might be in the client's best interest for the therapist to downplay the extent to which the interactions are biased and to minimize as much as possible the therapist's role, or the role of the technique itself, in producing changes in the client's behavior. For in general, and contrary to conventional wisdom, to the extent a therapist attempts to maximize these placebo and/or nonspecific treatment factors, the therapist could also be lowering the client's chances for achieving long lasting changes.

A final caution concerning the use of the self-perception technique pertains to the type of subject that may profit from it. Our subjects (i.e., male and female college students, who indicated shyness in interactions with the opposite sex) appeared to be highly motivated to reduce their shyness. Indeed, even before we began these studies, previous research had indicated that shyness in situations involving members of the opposite sex was of primary concern among college students (Arkowitz, Hinton, Perl, & Himadi, 1978). Other types of subjects, especially more disturbed clients (e.g., some schizophrenic or antisocial personality disorders), might not possess sufficient motivation to benefit from this approach. Additionally, the technique might work only with those who already have fairly well developed social skills. Most of the university students that we studied were sophisticated enough to engage in at least a rudimentary social conversation, and it is not known if this procedure would benefit subjects who do not possess such skills. This should not pose an insurmountable problem for self-perception theory itself, however, with its original bent toward Skinner's behaviorism, because once an individual acquired such skills (perhaps through some operant training technique), that individual's effectiveness could be enhanced even further through factors identical to the ones described in the current series of studies.

In conclusion, though the generalizability of this approach to treating shyness in certain subject populations (e.g., the psychiatrically disturbed) may be limited, its potential value should not be prematurely dismissed with regard to most populations. Consistent with both clinicians and social psychologists (Curran, 1977; Galassi & Galassi, 1979; Leary, 1983), the authors believe that the critical task is not one of finding a single theory or treatment that will solve all human problems. Instead the task is one of first assessing a particular client's needs and then matching treatment procedures to meet those needs. As such, the self-perception theory technique appears to represent a promising addition to the range of several beneficial interventions for helping individuals overcome shyness.

REFERENCES

Arkowitz, H. (1977). Measurement and mofidication of minimal dating behavior, In M. Hersen, R. M. Eisler, & P. M. Miller (Eds.), *Progress in behavior modification* (Vol. 5, pp. 1–62). New York: Academic Press.

Arkowitz, H., Hinton, R., Perl, J., & Himadi, W. (1978). Treatment strategies for dating anxiety in college men based on real-life practice. *The Counseling Psychologist, 7,* 41–46.

Asch, S. E. (1952). *Social Psychology.* Englewood Cliffs, NJ: Prentice-Hall.

Bandura, A. (1977). Self-efficacy: Toward a Unifying theory of behavioral change. *Psychological Review, 84,* 191–215.

Bem, D. J. (1967). Self-perception: An alternative interpretation of cognitive dissonance phenomena. *Psychological Review, 74,* 183–200.

Bem, D. J. (1972). Self-perception theory. In L. Berkowitz (Ed.), *Advances in experimental social psychology* (Vol. 6, pp. 183–200). New York: Academic Press.

Bem, D. J., & McConnell, H. K. (1970). Testing the self-perception explanation of dissonance phenomena: On the salience of premanipulation attitudes. *Journal of Personality and Social Psychology, 14,* 23–31.

Boulougouris, J. C., & Marks, I. M. (1969). Implosion (flooding): A new treatment for phobias. *British Medical Journal, 2,* 721–723.

Boyd, T. L., & Levis, D. J. (1983). Exposure is a necessary condition for fear-reduction: A reply to de Silva and Rachman. *Behavior Research and Therapy, 21,* 145–150.

Christiansen, A., & Arkowtiz, H. (1974). Preliminary report on practice dating and feedback as a treatment for college dating problems. *Journal of Counseling Psychology, 21,* 92–95.

Christiansen, A., Arkowitz, H., & Anderson, J. (1975). Practice dating as a treatment for college dating inhibitions. *Behavior Research and Therapy, 13,* 321–331.

Curran, J. P. (1977). Skills training as an approach to the treatment of heterosexual-social anxiety. *Psychological Bulletin, 84,* 140–157.

Curran, J. P. (1979). Social skills: Methodological issues and future directions. In A. S. Bellack & M. Hersen (Eds.), *Research and practice in social skills training* (pp. 319–354). New York: Plenum Press.

Davison, G. C., & Wilson, G. T. (1972). Critique of "Densensitization: Social and cognitive factors underlying the effectiveness of Wolpe's procedure." *Psychology Bulletin, 78,* 28–31.

Emmelkamp, P. M. G., & Wessels, H. (1975). Flooding in imagination vs. flooding *in vivo*: A comparison with agoraphobics. *Behavior Research and Therapy, 13,* 7–15.

Fazio, R. H., & Zanna, M. P. (1981). Direct experience and attitude-behavior consistency. In L. Berkowitz (Ed.), *Advances in experimental social psychology* (Vol. 13, pp. 161–202). New York: Academic Press.

Fazio, R. H., Effrein, E. E.,& Falender, V. J. (1981). Self-perception following social interaction. *Journal of Personality and Social Psychology, 41,* 232–242.

Festinger, L. *A theory of cognitive dissonance.* (1957). Stanford, CA: Stanford University Press.

Finch, B. E., & Wallace, C. J. (1977). Successful interpersonal skills training with schizophrenic inpatients. *Journal of Consulting and Clinical Psychology, 45,* 855–890.

Galassi, J. P., & Galassi, M. D. (1979). Modification of heterosocial skills deficits. In A. S. Bellack & M. Hersen (Eds.), *Research and practice in social skills training* (pp. 131–138). New York: Plenum Press.

Glass, C. R., Gottman, J. M., & Shmurak, S. (1976). Response acquisition and cognitive self-statement modification approaches to dating-skills training. *Journal of Counseling Psychology, 23,* 520–526.

Haemmerlie, F. M. (1983). Heterosocial anxiety in college females: A biased interactions treatment. *Behavior Modification, 7,* 611–623.

Haemmerlie, F. M., & Montgomery, R. L. (1982). Self-perception theory and unobtrusively biased interactions: A treatment for heterosocial anxiety. *Journal of Counseling Psychology, 29,* 362–370.

Haemmerlie, R. M., & Montgomery, R. L. (1984). Purposefully biased interactions: Reducing heterosocial anxiety through self-perception theory. *Journal of Personality and Social Psychology, 47,* 900–908.

Harvey, J. H., & Weary, G. (1981). *Perspectives on attributional processes.* Dubuque, IA: William C. Brown.

Heider, F. (1958). *The psychology of interpersonal relations.* New York: Wiley.

Jennings, D. L., Lepper, M. R., & Ross, L. (1981). Persistence of impressions of personal persuasiveness: Perseverance of erroneous self-assessments outside the debriefing paradigm. *Personality and Social Psychology Bulletin, 7,* 257–263.

Jones, W. H., Hobbs, S. A., & Hockenbury, D. (1982). Loneliness and social skills deficits. *Journal of Personality and Social Psychology, 42,* 682–689.

Kandel, H. J., Ayllon, T., & Rosenbaum, M. S. (1977). Flooding or systematic exposure in the treatment of extreme social withdrawal in children. *Journal of Behavior Therapy and Experimental Psychiatry, 8,* 75–81.

Kopel, S., & Arkowitz, H. (1975). The role of attribution and self-perception in behavior change: Implications for behavior therapy. *Genetic Psychology Monographs, 92,* 175–212.

Kramer, S. R. (1975). *Effectiveness of behavior rehearsal and practice dating to increase heterosexual social interaction.* Doctoral dissertation, University of Texas, *Dissertation Abstracts International, 36,* 913B-914B. (University Microfilms No. 75–16, 693).

Leary, M. R. (1983). *Understanding social anxiety: Social, personality, and clinical perspectives.* Beverly Hills, CA: Sage Publications.

Lord, C. G., Ross, L., & Lepper, M. R. (1979). Biased assimilation and attitude polarization: The effects of prior theories on subsequently considered evidence. *Journal of Personality and Social Psychology, 37*, 2098–2109.

Malleson, N. (1959). Panic and phobia. *Lancet, 1*, 225–227.

Martinson, W. D., & Zerface, J. P. (1970). Comparison of individual counseling and a social program with nondaters. *Journal of Counseling Psychology, 17*, 36–40.

Mavissakalian, M. & Michelson, L. (1983). Self-directed *in vivo* exposure in behavioral and phar- macological treatments of agoraphobia. *Behavior Therapy, 14*, 506–519.

Meichenbaum, D. H. (1977). *Cognitive behavior modification*. New York: Plenum Press.

Meyer, V., Robertson, J., & Tatlow, A. (1975). Home treatment of an obsessive-compulsive disorder by response prevention. *Journal of Behavior Therapy and Experimental Psychiatry, 6*, 37–38.

Nisbett, R. E., & Ross, L. (1980). *Human Inference: Strategies and shortcomings of social judgment*. Englewood Cliffs, NJ: Prentice-Hall.

Nisbett, R. E., & Wilson, T. D. (1977). Telling more than we know: Verbal reports on the mental process. *Psychological Review, 84*, 231–259.

Oden, S., & Asher, S. R. (1977). Coaching children in social skills for friendship making. *Child Development, 48*, 495–506.

Pollis, N. P., & Montgomery, R. L. (1966). Conformity and resistance to compliance. *Journal of Psychology, 63*, 35–41.

Rehm, L. P., & Marston, A. R. (1968). Reduction of social anxiety through modification of self- reinforcement. *Journal of Consulting and Clinical Psychology, 32*, 565–574.

Ross, L., Lepper, M. R., & Hubbard, M. (1975). Perseverance in self-perception and social perception: Biased attributional processes in the debriefing paradigm. *Journal of Personality and Social Psychology, 32*, 880–892.

Schwitzgebel, R. L., & Schwitzgebel, R. K. (1980). *Law and Psychological practice*. New York: Wiley.

Shaw, M. E., & Costanzo, P. R. (1972). *Theories of social psychology*. New York: McGraw Hill.

Sherif, M. (1935). A study of some social factors in perception. *Archives of Psychology, 27*(187).

Snyder, M., & Swann, W. B. (1978). Behavioral confirmation in social interaction. From social perception to social reality. *Journal of Experimental Social Psychology, 14*, 148–162.

Solomon, R. L., Kamin, L. J., & Wynn, L. C. (1953). Traumatic avoidance learning: The outcomes of several extinction procedures with dogs. *Journal of Abnormal and Social Psychology, 48*, 291– 302.

Spielberger, C. D., Gorsuch, R. L., & Lushene, R. E. (1970). *The State-Trait Anxiety Inventory (STAI) test manual for Form X*. Palo Alto, CA: Consulting Psychologists Press.

Twentyman, C. T. & Zimering, R. T. (1979). Behavioral training of social skills: A critical review. In M. Hersen, R. M. Eisler, & P. M. Miller (Eds.), *Progress in behavior modification* (Vol. 7). New York: Academic Press.

Watson, D. & Friend, R. (1969). Measurement of social-evaluative anxiety. *Journal of Consulting and Clinical Psychology, 33*, 448–457.

Wilder, D. A. (1978). Perceiving persons as a group: Effects on attributions of causality and beliefs. *Social Psychology, 41*, 13–23.

Zimbardo, P. G. (1977). *Shyness: What it is and what to do about it*. Reading, MA: Addison-Wesley.

25

Interpersonal Process Training for Shy Clients

Lynn Alden and Robin Cappe

Shy clients often report a sense of painful self-consciousness. To take some examples:

> Karen, a shy 32-year-old housewife, described her fear at a neighborhood party by stating: "I felt that everyone was looking at me, and that I was doing all the wrong things." Eventually, she left the party without talking to anyone.

> Rob, a 24-year-old student, says: "When I'm with a woman, I wonder what she thinks of me, whether I'm a loser, or what. And then I start watching myself and think how stupid I am." Rob has never been able to ask a woman out and fears he will remain alone for the rest of his life.

These individuals, and other shy people like them, appear to be preoccupied with the acceptability of their behavior to others. This leads to an ongoing process of self-observation and evaluation, generally with negative conclusions. The shy people we have seen in treatment seem to be continually assessing themselves, asking: "Do I measure up to what is wanted?" It is not surprising that this self-focused attention and negative self-evaluation increases anxiety and behavioral inhibition.

After several years of clinical experience, we became interested in whether this anxiety-generating self-consciousness could be modified by providing shy persons with social strategies that require that they redirect their attention to the person with whom they are interacting. This chapter will summarize our clinical and research experiences to date.

The chapter will begin with a consideration of the treatment literature. We wish to highlight unanswered questions about the mechanism underlying treatment effectiveness. In particular, we will first contrast two major explanations of treatment change: the skills-augmentation position, which suggests that

LYNN ALDEN and ROBIN CAPPE • Department of Psychology, University of British Columbia, Vancouver, BC, Canada V6T, 1W5.

improvement occurs because the client learns new behavioral skills, and the counterconditioning position, which argues that shyness is due to anxiety and that improvement occurs when this anxiety is in some way neutralized. Second, we will analyze the skills-training strategies described in the clinical literature and make suggestions for modification based on recent research evidence. Third, we will consider personality and social psychology research on attentional focus, extending the results of laboratory studies to the context of treatment. Next, we will describe the development of a treatment strategy designed specifically to reduce self-consciousness and to redirect the shy client's attention away from his or her self-observation and evaluation. Process issues that arise during treatment will be discussed. Finally, a preliminary investigation of the effectiveness of this treatment regimen will be described.

EXPLANATIONS OF TREATMENT EFFECTS

Many treatment programs for shyness, social anxiety, and other forms of social dysfunction are based on a skills-deficit hypothesis. The dysfunctional individual is assumed to lack the behavioral skills necessary to cope with social situations. Numerous studies show that skills training procedures produce improvements in self-reported and laboratory assessed discomfort and skill in nonassertive individuals (e.g., Eisler, Hersen, & Miller, 1974), heterosocially anxious college males (e.g., Twentyman & McFall, 1975), and socially inadequate psychiatric patients (e.g., Edelstein & Eisler, 1976; Goldsmith & McFall, 1975). However, the mechanism underlying such treatment effects has not been clearly established.

If social dysfunction stems from a skill deficit, one would expect treatments involving skill training to produce greater improvement than alternatives such as systematic desensitization or *in vivo* exposure. Though relatively few studies have examined this issue, those that have found skills training to be no more effective than treatments based on the concept of counterconditioning. For example, Marzillier, Lambert, and Kellett (1976) found systematic desensitization to be as effective as skill training with socially inadequate psychiatric patients; Royce and Arkowitz (1978) concluded that practice interactions with others were as effective as skill training in changing the self-perceptions and social activity of socially isolated college students; Kazdin and Mascitelli (1982) demonstrated that *in vivo* homework assignments were a powerful aspect of treatment for nonassertiveness, and that such assignments contributed more to behavior change than did either covert or overt rehearsal.

Whereas the common finding of no differences between treatment strategies can be attributed to the presence of shared nonspecific treatment factors or to the choice of measures of improvement, this research also raises the question of whether the active treatment ingredient is exposure to the fear-provoking social situation rather than skill augmentation. Indeed, because the counterconditioning techniques just mentioned specifically did not include skill-training procedures, whereas the skill training generally involved *in vivo* exposure in the form of rehearsal during sessions and homework between sessions, the scales tip slightly toward a graduated-exposure explanation of change.

If social dysfunction is primarily due to skill deficits one would expect functional and dysfunctional populations to differ significantly on measures of behavioral skill. Unfortunately, the results of research addressing this issue are inconsistent. Some researchers find behavioral differences between subjects high and low in social anxiety (e.g., O'Banion & Arkowitz, 1978), whereas others do not (Clark & Arkowitz, 1975; Borkovec, Stone, O'Brien, & Kaloupek, 1974). Although several studies demonstrate behavioral deficits in nonassertive psychiatric inpatients (e.g., Eisler, Miller, & Hersen, 1973), several studies of nonassertive university students did not find such deficits (Alden & Cappe, 1981; Schwartz & Gottman, 1977). Research results from studies of heterosocially anxious males are also inconsistent (Greenwald, 1977; Twentyman & McFall, 1975; Wessberg, Mariotto, Conger, Farrell, & Conger, 1979). The strongest support for the skills-deficit position comes from studies of psychiatric inpatients. However, such individuals generally suffer from thought disorder or serious personality disturbance and are also likely to be receiving medication and other treatment. The results of these investigations may not generalize to the outpatient populations usually studied in shyness and loneliness research. Although inconsistencies in research results may be due to population factors or to the analogue nature of the roleplaying often used to assess social competence (Bellack, Hersen, & Turner, 1978; Bellack, Hersen, & Lamparski, 1979), the data do not provide the strong support for the skills-deficit position adherents would wish.

Another factor to consider is that the differences noted between functional and dysfunctional groups usually involve behaviors, such as eye contact, smiles, or conversational pauses, that are not so much skills, in the sense of complex chains of responses to be learned, as behavioral expressions of anxiety. For example, many of the behaviors studied are similar to those included in the Timed Behavioral Checklist, a behavioral measure of anxiety (Paul, 1966). Thus, it is not clear if behavioral differences are due to skill deficits or to conditioned anxiety.

Suggestions for Modification of Skills Training Procedures

Whereas treatment-outcome studies and behavioral comparisons of functional and dysfunctional populations do not provide strong support for skill-deficit formulations, recent research suggests that skills training procedures require modification. When one examines skill training from a clinical perspective, several shortcomings emerge.

First, most published studies assess or teach the behaviors just described, eye contact, voice volume, etc., behaviors described by Trower (1980) as component skills, that is, specific behaviors performed without conscious monitoring. Trower and others emphasize that social interaction is a fluid ongoing process requiring monitoring of the other person's behavior and synchronization of one's own behavior with one's partner. Trower suggests that skills training has neglected this second factor. In support of this line of thinking, Trower (1980) reported data suggesting that socially incompetent psychiatric patients are less responsive to changes in the other person's behavior than are socially more competent patients. Similarly, Fischetti, Curran, & Wessberg (1977) found that dysfunctional males timed their response to others differently, and perhaps less successfully, then skilled males. Both studies suggest that socially dysfunctional individuals either do not monitor the other's behavior as well as socially skilled individuals or do not understand how or when to respond so as to maintain the smooth flow of the interaction.

Second, the behaviors commonly taught might also be called discrete, or molecular, in that they involve but one or two aspects of an individual's social behavior or one or two social situations. The shy, dysfunctional individual is not provided with a global strategy for approaching interactions.

The third concern with skills training, as presented in the published literature, is a more philosophical one. The literature often conveys the notion that social interactions are performances in which the client should be careful to display "appropriate" behaviors. In fact, the process of developing intimate, supportive relationships, which is our true clinical goal, is generally believed to involve factors like sensitivity to others, mutual self-disclosure, and respect. Although clinicians instinctively include such elements in treatment, such factors have not been extensively addressed in the social-skills literature.

Finally, during skills training the client is generally asked to make specific changes in his behavior and to monitor and to evaluate those changes, a process that directs the client's attention to the client's own performance. However, as discussed previously, self-focused attention and evaluation may be precisely the shy individual's problem. It may be that treatment techniques that involve self-focused attention contribute to, or, at least, are not the most effective means of alleviating, the dysfunctional individual's disruptive self-focus. Research conducted by Jones and his colleagues provide support for the disruptive role of self-focused attention in lonely university students. Goswick and Jones (1980) found that lonely students reported attending more to their own reactions during social interactions than to those of the other person. A second study concluded that lonely individuals displayed significantly fewer behaviors indicating partner attention than did nonlonely individuals (Jones, Hobbs, & Hockenbury, 1982).

The picture of the shy person that emerges is that of an individual, anxious and self-focused, who is somewhat insensitive to or unaware of the nuances of the other person's behavior. Skill training procedures might be more effective if they modified this pattern. Direct support for this notion is provided in a laboratory study by Jones et al. (1982) who asked lonely students to increase the frequency of other-directed behaviors. He found that this resulted in reductions in self-reported loneliness and positive changes in self-perceptions. Other research indicates that engaging in other-directed behaviors makes an individual more attractive to others (Kupke, Hobbs, & Cheny, 1979). The shy person, whose self-directed attention disrupts such behaviors, may appear less interesting to possible social contacts, and hence the shy person may receive negative social feedback.

THE ROLE OF SELF-FOCUSED ATTENTION

The effects of self-focused attention have been the source of numerous investigations in personality and social psychology research. Much of this research is based on Duval and Wicklund's (1972) theory of attentional focus, which states: attention can be directed either toward or away from the self. Self-focused attention (increased self-awareness) leads to self-appraisal. If this appraisal process reveals a discrepancy between one's behavior and one's standards or goals, the individual experiences discomfort and attempts to withdraw from the situation, or failing that, attempts to reduce the discrepancy by changing behavior. Although this original theory explained how self-focused attention could impair performance, it failed to explain several studies suggesting that self-focused attention could also facilitate performance (e.g., Liebling & Shaver, 1973; Wicklund & Duval, 1971). Carver, Peterson, Follansbee, and Scheier (1983) reconciled these findings with the original theory by suggesting that the self-appraisal process could lead either to positive conclusions ("I will be successful") or negative conclusions ("I will fail"). According to these writers, if the self-appraisal process resulted in positive expectancies the individual would persist in his task-related efforts. If, however, self-appraisal resulted in negative self-evaluation and expectancies, the individual would display the discomfort and withdrawal described above. In light of this formulation it is interesting to note that socially dysfunctional individuals report negative social expectancies (Eisler, Fredericksen, & Peterson, 1978; Fieldler & Beach, 1978) and self-evaluations (Alden & Cappe, 1981; Clark & Arkowitz, 1975).

Research indicates that attentional focus plays a role in disorders related to social dysfunction. For example, in evaluation situations, the test-anxious have been observed to engage in self-critical thinking (Meichenbaum, 1972) and to neglect or misinterpret task-relevant cues (Geen, 1976; West, Lee, & Anderson, 1969). Several writers suggest that this self-critical thinking is produced by self-focused attention and impairs performance by distracting from task-relevant cues (Meichenbaum, 1977; Sarason, 1975; Wine, 1980, 1982). In a recent study, Carver et al. (1983) demonstrated that increasing self-focused attention impaired the performance of test anxious subjects and reduced their task persistence relative to nonanxious controls. Other research suggests that manipulations that direct the attention of test-anxious subjects to the task at hand produce improvements in performance (Sarason, 1973, 1975).

Self-focused attention has also been implicated in low self-esteem. Shrauger (1972) found that high and low self-esteem subjects reacted differently to self-focusing stimuli: low self-esteem subjects displayed greater impairment when observed by an audience than did high self-esteem subjects. Brockner and Hulton (1978) also concluded that increased self-awareness impaired the performance of low self-esteem subjects relative to high self-esteem subjects. In addition, they manipulated attentional focus by instructing subjects to focus completely on the task. Under these task-focused conditions low self-esteem subjects actually made fewer errors than did high self-esteem subjects.

Taken together, these studies underscore the importance of attentional focus in anxiety-producing situations. Further, they suggest that increasing task-focused attention may be beneficial for anxious and low self-esteem individuals. Extending this reasoning to social dysfunction, one might expect that situations that increase the shy individual's self-consciousness would result in critical self-evaluation and discomfort that would disrupt performance. Shifting the shy person's attentional focus to the other person in the interaction might offset this process, reduce anxiety, and improve social performance. These conclusions are consistent with Trower's emphasis on process skills and Jones' research on other-directed behaviors.

TREATMENT DEVELOPMENT

We wanted to develop a treatment strategy that would accomplish the four goals suggested by the research literature: (a) increase the shy client's social monitoring skills, that is, encourage the client to track the ongoing interaction so that they can synchronize their behavior with that of their partner; (b) provide the client with a global strategy for developing intimate relationships, (c) provide the shy person with a social philosophy that recognizes the importance of factors such as respect and sensitivity, as opposed to a performance-oriented ("Am I performing well enough?") stance; and (d) enable the client to center attention on task-relevant information, that is, the other person, thereby modifying the client's preoccupation with self-focused evaluation.

A review of the clinical literature suggested that these issues were addressed in the human relations training (HRT) literature (Carkhuff, 1969; Rogers, 1951). Although HRT was originally developed as a training process for mental health professionals, the concepts and techniques are readily modified to apply to social interactions between friends, rather than a counseling situation. Key HRT skills, like active listening and empathic responding, require an individual to monitor the other person's behavior and to engage in other-directed responses. It also seemed likely that involving the client in such activities might direct the client's attentional focus away from self-evaluation and toward more task-relevant matters. The behaviors described in human relations training, such as active listening, empathic responding, communicating respect, and self-disclosure, can be combined to provide the client with a global strategy for initiating social interactions and transforming superficial social encounters into more intimate relationships. It was hoped that the humanistic philosophy surrounding HRT, which emphasizes that human interactions should be characterized by sensitivity, respect, and concern for another's feelings, would reduce the anxiety created by the shy individual's often performance-oriented view of human interactions.

Four human relations skills were selected to form the basis of the treatment regimen and were modified to apply to social interactions between friends rather than counselor and patient: (a) Active listening. Clients were taught both psychological attending, that is, carefully listening to the other's underlying message, and physical attending, that is, nonverbal and verbal behaviors that encourage the other person to continue; (b) Empathic responding. Clients were taught to recognize the other person's feelings and to communicate this understanding to that person; (c) Communicating respect for the other's opinions. Respect was defined as identifying the other person's opinions and communicating acceptance of, though not necessarily agreement with, that position. Respect was included as a means of teaching shy individuals how to express their own opinions and needs without ignoring those of the other person. This skill, as modified in this program, was similar to skills taught in assertiveness training; (d) Self-disclosure. Clients were taught to identify the level of disclosure, or intimacy, of the other's conversation and to match this level, or to become more self-disclosive to increase the intimacy of the interaction. Self-disclosure was included because we felt it provided shy individuals with a strategy for actively participating in the interaction, rather than serving only to facilitate the other person's conversation. In addition, some research indicates that socially dysfunctional individuals are deficient at matching their level of self-disclosure to the interpersonal context (Solano & Batten, 1979). Four skills seemed a reasonable number to include in the time-limited treatment programs generally offered for shyness.

Clinical Procedures

Group Format. We generally treat shy clients in groups of 8–10 individuals. The group format allows shy individuals the opportunity to discuss their shyness with others with similar problems and provides a chance to practice interacting with others in a relatively safe context. This group size also appears to be the maximum number of individuals many of our shy clients can tolerate without being incapacitated by anxiety. Even with groups of eight, some shy individuals withdrew rather than face the prospect of interacting with so many people. Some clients requested groups of four or less.

Intake. All clients are initially seen for a lengthy intake interview. In addition to our developing an understanding for the individual, this interview allows us to inform prospective clients about various aspects of treatment and to clarify their role in the treatment group. At this time clients are told that to improve they must take the risk of talking in the group, practicing their problem situations, and making an attempt to complete *in vivo* social exercises. Many shy clients we have seen require this extra push to benefit from time-limited treatment regimens.

The intake interview is also used to screen for the presence of depression and suicidal ideation. It is our clinical experience that 40% of individuals seeking treatment for shyness have significant levels of depression. Perhaps 5% of these have moderate to serious thoughts of suicide. This combination of depression and shyness deserves serious clinical and research consideration. At this point, however, we refer such clients to treatment agencies prepared to treat the depressive component and to carefully monitor suicidal tendencies. Clients with other serious problems, for example, alcohol abuse or thought disorder, are also referred elsewhere for treatments that focus primarily on these conditions. Such problems, even if complicated by shyness, generally require treatment procedures in addition to those included in time-limited shyness programs. As shyness and social avoidance are found in a number of psychiatric conditions, a careful screening is necessary to ensure clients receive optimum treatment for their specific condition. It is worth noting that researchers have not always been careful to screen clinical subjects carefully either.

Introduction and Group Process Factors. The group sessions begin with a general discussion of how clients feel about coming for treatment, how they view themselves, and how they view their shyness. This introductory discussion functions as an icebreaker that allows clients to participate somewhat more freely in the discussions that follow. However, any therapist working with shy individuals should be prepared for the general tension and periods of awkward silence that occur in such groups. Tolerance of anxiety and silence are necessary prerequisites for therapists. Commenting on hesitation and identifying the group's fears do aid in overcoming these periods. However, the therapist can expect five or so sessions predominated by awkwardness and can anticipate periods of anxious silence throughout treatment. Common therapist maladaptive responses include such things as talking too much, continuing on with skills training, or other structured techniques, while trying to ignore the group process (no doubt hoping problems will disappear), and infantalizing the client by assuming responsibility for presenting the client's thoughts or making treatment decisions (e.g., what homework assignment the client should attempt the next week). Therapists must be alert to their own tendencies to do all the work in the group. A useful rule of thumb is that if the therapist feels exhausted after treatment, a group-process issue is probably being ignored. It is our experience that if process issues are ignored, clients cease doing *in vivo* assignments, begin to miss sessions, and are unusually quiet when they do attend.

Rationale. Over the initial sessions the group is presented with a treatment rationale similar to the following:

> Your social anxiety causes you to become self-conscious and self-focused. This self-consciousness produces self-evaluation and criticism that increase your fear. Even more, focusing attention on yourself distracts you from the person with whom you're interacting and disrupts the interaction. The key to relating to others is to attend to their feelings and reactions. Attending to the other person will also reduce your anxiety and help you feel better.

Treatment Regimen. The treatment program, which we labeled interpersonal process training, is best conceptualized as a combination of graduated-exposure and skills-training procedures. The structured aspects of treatment can be broken into four steps. First, clients are taught relaxation training (as in Paul, 1966). Second, clients assess the social situations that are problematic for them and organize them into a hierarchy in terms of the level of fear each situation produces. Typically, we strive to identify several situations at each level of difficulty. Shyness is less ammenable to graduated-exposure procedures than many fears because social situations are often at least partially under the control of others. Hence, clients cannot reliably approach a specific situation when they choose (e.g., talking with the boss). Identifying several problematic situations of approximately the same level of difficulty provides the client with options for *in vivo* encounters during a given week and increases the chances that practice will occur. It also increases the number of situations the client encounters.

Third, the interaction skills are presented following a typical skill-training format. The skills are first introduced and discussed. The therapist demonstrates how each skill might be useful in various situations. Clients then practice their own problematic social situations, beginning with the least difficult, and attempt to adapt the social strategies to their particular situation.

Finally, each week clients select several social situations to encounter *in vivo*. Clients report back to the group providing details about how they adapted the human relations skills to their situation and the results obtained. Feedback and support are provided.

It should be noted that this brief description of the more structured techniques involved in treatment does not include all the other therapeutic procedures that enter into any effective therapy program. Although an elaboration of such elements go beyond the limits of this chapter, the reader is reminded that providing techniques alone is insufficient if the basic elements of therapy are missing.

TREATMENT EVALUATION

The final segment of this chapter will briefly describe the results of a preliminary evaluation study comparing the interpersonal process training program just described to a graduated-exposure treatment regimen and a waiting-list control. A detailed description of the research can be found in Cappe and Alden (1985).

Subject Recruitment. As noted earlier, social anxiety and inhibition accompany a number of psychological conditions. Therefore, clinicians and researchers must conduct careful screening to ensure collecting a homogeneous population of shy individuals. In this research prospective clients were solicited through a newspaper article discussing shyness and describing the research to be conducted. Applicants participated in a lengthy screening interview. Clients were excluded if they scored above 19 on the Beck Depression Inventory (Beck, 1967), had a history of inpatient hospitalization, displayed any signs of substance abuse or other psychiatric disorders, or were currently facing a major life crisis. Our intent was to select a group of adults for whom shyness was the major life problem, uncomplicated by other psychiatric conditions or severe life stress.

The subjects selected displayed at least moderate life impairment stemming from shyness. The majority were not married, and over 50% had never had a date. A number had changed jobs to avoid having to interact with people. Several had dropped out of university because of social fears. These individuals were extremely shy and in clinical appearance were quite similar to what has been called avoidant personality disorder.

Treatment. In all, 54 clients were accepted and randomly assigned to the three conditions. The interpersonal process (IP) regimen has already been described. The graduated exposure (GE) regimen consisted of all the elements in the IP condition with the exception of the skills training procedures. The waiting list control (WL) subjects completed pre- and postassessment only. Treatment consisted of 10 weekly 2-hour group sessions conducted by cotherapists. Treatment effectiveness was evaluated with a variety of measures in two contexts: client daily social encounters and social behavior during a laboratory interaction.

Results. Our primary concern was whether clients changed their daily social functioning following treatment. Subjects who received treatment improved more than the untreated controls. More central to the current discussion is the fact that IP clients reported significantly more changes in their daily social activities than did GE clients. Following treatment, IP clients reported participating more frequently in social activities, participating in more diverse social activities, and feeling more comfort in and satisfaction with their social encounters than did GE clients. In addition, three months following treatment completion treated clients participated in a 1-hour interview that focused in greater detail on changes in the client's social life. During this interview, clients were asked whether any specific social changes had occurred as a result of treatment. These clinically significant life changes included events such as joining a club, giving a party, inviting a colleague to dinner, asking someone for a date, in short, any social change considered by the client to be a significant life event. Whereas 45% of GE subjects reported making a significant life change following treatment, 82% of the IP subjects reported such changes. A test of independent proportions revealed this difference to be statistically significant. These results suggest that the addition of training in process and other-focused skills produced greater change in the daily social functioning of shy individuals than did graduated-exposure procedures alone.

No significant differences were observed between the two groups during the laboratory interaction, neither on self-report nor observer's ratings of subject comfort and skill. It is interesting that the presence of changes in daily social functioning were not accompanied by changes in the laboratory interaction. However, the laboratory interaction consisted of a brief (10 minute) interaction with an experimental collaborator. The subject was provided with specific instructions to "get to know this person. Draw them out. Find out about them." A number of recent studies suggest that, when placed in a structured analogue situation, socially anxious individuals are capable of functional social behavior (e.g., Vitkus & Horowitz, 1985). It was our impression that the majority of these shy individuals handled the preassessment interaction reasonably well. Another explanation of these results is that the interpersonal process training did not so much modify the shy person's behavioral skills as increase that person's social initiation behaviors. The shy person, though no more skillful, may have been able to approach previously feared situations in real life.

The discrepancy between data collected from daily interactions and from the laboratory points back to the question asked at the beginning of this chapter: What is the mechanism responsible for treatment improvement? These data offer little support for the notion that these shy clients gained behavioral skill. Neither self-ratings (in the laboratory or in the community) nor observers' ratings of the laboratory interaction suggested that the IP clients were more skilled following treatment. At first glance, there is some evidence to support the notion that the shy individuals' conditioned social anxiety was reduced through graduated exposure to feared situations. IP clients did report feeling more comfortable in their daily interactions. However, counterconditioning alone does not explain why clients provided with human relations skills improved more than graduated-exposure clients.

Our own hypothesis was that the interpersonal process training would shift the shy person's attentional focus, thereby reducing anxiety and disinhibiting social behavior. We assessed change in attentional focus in two ways. First, therapists were asked to rate self- and other-focused verbal and nonverbal behaviors. Ratings were made in treatment sessions two and eight. The rating procedure followed those of Jones *et al.* (1982). Data analyses revealed that therapists rated IP clients as displaying significantly increased other-focused verbal and nonverbal behavior relative to graduated exposure clients. However, these ratings are problematic in that therapists were, of course, aware of the treatment received by clients, and this may have biased their ratings. Also, because IP clients were instructed in treatment to use certain types of responses (active listening, empathic reflection), the increase in other-focused behavior may have been due to situational demand factors. There is no guarantee the other-focused behaviors generalized to nontreatment social settings.

Ratings of self-focused and other-focused behaviors were also made by trained raters who watched videotapes of the laboratory interactions. These raters found no differences between IP and GE clients. However, given the lack of differences in social behaviors in this structured laboratory setting, shifts in attentional focus would not be predicted from our hypothesis.

Overall, then, there is some evidence to support a shift in attentional focus in IP clients. However, the procedural complications described previously necessitate a very cautious interpretation of the significance of this data.

In terms of attentional focus, two additional questions should be investigated. First, are changes in self- and other-focused *behaviors* accompanied by changes in subjective attentional focus? Perhaps shy persons can increase their other-focused behaviors while maintaining a subjective attentional focus on themselves ("How well am I performing these other-directed behaviors?"). We need to assess the client's subjective sense of focus in addition to surface behaviors. Second, do IP clients display other-focused attention in their daily social interactions, as well as in the treatment setting? Measures of attentional focus during ongoing interactions are required. Answers to these two questions would allow clinicians and researchers to judge more clearly the role of attentional focus as a mediator of client improvement.

In summary, this research data suggested that training in interpersonal process skills did produce changes in the social fuctioning of shy individuals, as least as compared to this graduated exposure procedure. However, some questions remain to be answered about the extent to which these improvements were due to changes in attentional focus.

SUMMARY

In this chapter, we attempted to describe the empirical and theoretical literature suggesting that focus of attention plays a role in shyness. The development of a treatment program designed to alter self-focused attention and evaluation were presented, and preliminary research results evaluating the treatment regimen were briefly outlined. Our clinical and research experience to date suggest that further consideration of the role of attentional focus will be valuable.

REFERENCES

Alden, L., & Cappe, R. (1981). Nonassertiveness: Skill deficit or selective self-evaluation? *Behavior Therapy*, 107–114.

Alden, L., & Safran, J. (1978). Irrational beliefs and nonassertive behavior. *Cognitive Research and Therapy*, 4, 356–364.

Beck, A. T. (1967). *Depression: Clinical, experimental and theoretical aspects*. New York: Harper & Row.

Bellack, A. A., Hersen, M., & Turner, S. (1978). Roleplay tests for assessing social skills: Are they valid? *Behavior Therapy*, 9, 448–461.

Bellack, A. S., Hersen, M., & Lamparski, D. (1979). Roleplay tests for assessing social skills: Are they valid? Are they useful? *Journal of Consulting and Clinical Psychology*, 47, 335–342.

Borkovec, T. D., Stone, N. M., O'Brien, G. T., & Kaloupek, D. G. (1974). Evaluation of a clinically relevant target behavior for analog outcome research. *Behavior Therapy*, 5, 503–513.

Brockner, J., & Hulton, A. M. (1978). How to reverse the vicious cycle of low self-esteem: The importance of attentional focus. *Journal of Experimental Social Psychology*, 564–578.

Cappe, R., & Alden, L. (1985). *Process skill training and graduated exposure as treatment options for extremely shy clients*. Manuscript submitted for publication.

Carkhuff, R. (1969). *Helping and human relations. Vol. I and II*. New York: Holt, Rinehart & Winston.

Carver, C. S., Peterson, M., Follansbee, D. J., & Scheier, M. F. (1983). Effects of self-directed attention on performance and persistence among persons high and low in test anxiety. *Cognitive Therapy and Research*, 7, 333–354.

Clark, J., & Arkowitz, H. (1975). Social anxiety and self-evaluation of interpersonal performance. *Psychological Reports*, 36, 211–221.

Duval, S., & Wicklund, R. A. (1972). *A theory of objective self-awareness*. New York: Academic Press.

Edelstein, B. A., & Eisler, R. M. (1976). Effects of modeling with instructions and feedback on the behavioral components of social skills. *Behavior Therapy*, 7, 382–289.

Eisler, R. M., Frederiksen, L. W., & Peterson, G. L. (1978). The relationship of cognitive variables to the expression of assertiveness. *Behavior Therapy*, 9, 419–427.

Eisler, R. M., Hersen, M., & Miller, P. M. (1974). Shaping components of assertive behavior with instructions and feedback. *American Journal of Psychiatry*, 131, 1344–1347.

Eisler, R. M., Miller, P. M., & Hersen, M. (1973). Components of assertive behavior. *Journal of Clinical Psychology*, 28, 295–299.

Fiedler, D., & Beach, L. R. (1978). On the decision to be assertive. *Journal of Consulting and Clinical Psychology*, 46, 537–546.

Fischetti, M., Curran, J., & Wessberg, H. (1977). Sense of timing: A skill deficit in heterosexual socially anxious males. *Behavior Modification*, 1, 179–195.

Fried, E. (1980). *The courage to change: From insight to self-innovation*. New York: Brunner/Mazel.

Geen, R. G. (1976). Test anxiety, observation, and range of cue utilization. *British Journal of Social and Clinical Psychology*, 15, 253–259.

Goldfried, M. R. (Ed.). (1982). *Converging themes in psychotherapy*. New York: Springer.

Goldsmith, J. B., & McFall, R. M. (1975). Development and evaluation of an interpersonal and skill-training program for psychiatric inpatients. *Journal of Abnormal Psychology*, 84, 51–58.

Goswick, R. A., & Jones, W. H. (1981). Loneliness, self-concept, and adjustment. *The Journal of Psychology*, 107, 237–240.

Greenwald, D. P. (1977). The behavioral assessment of differences in social skill and social anxiety in female college students. *Behavior Therapy*, 8, 925–938.

Jones, W. H., Hobbs, S. A., & Hockenbury, D. (1982). Loneliness and social skill deficits. *Journal of Personality and Social Psychology*, 42, 682–689.

Kazdin, A. E., & Mascitelli, S. (1982). Covert and overt rehearsal and homework practice in developing assertiveness. *Journal of Consulting and Clinical Psychology*, 50, 250–258.

Kupke, T. E., Hobbs, S. A., & Cheny, T. H. (1979). Selection of heterosocial skills: I. Criterion-related validity. *Behavior Therapy*, 10, 326–335.

Liebling, B. A., & Shaver, P. (1973). Evaluation, self-awareness, and task performance. *Journal of Experimental Social Psychology*, 9, 298–306.

Marks, I. M. (1969). *Fears and phobias*. New York: Academic Press.

Marzillier, J. S., Lambert, C., & Kellett, J. (1976). A controlled evaluation of systematic desensitization and social skills training for socially inadequate psychiatric patients. *Behavior Research and Therapy*, 14, 225–238.

Meichenbaum, D., 1972, Cognitive modification of test anxious college students. *Journal of Consulting and Clinical Psychology*, 39, 370–380.

Meichenbaum, D. H. (1977). *Cognitive-behavior modification*. New York: Plenum Press.

O'Banion, K., & Arkowitz, H. (1977). Social anxiety and selective memory for affective information about the self. *Social Behavior and Personality*, 5, 321–328.

Paul, G. (1966). *Insight versus desensitization in psychotherapy*. Stanford, CA: Stanford University Press.

Rogers, C. R. (1951). *Client-centered therapy*. Boston: Houghton Mifflin.

Royce, W. S., & Arkowitz, H. (1978). Multimodal evaluation of practice interactions as treatment for social isolation. *Journal of Consulting and Clinical Psychology*, 46, 239–245.

Sarason, I. G. (1973). Test anxiety and cognitive modeling. *Journal of Personality and Social Psychology*, 28, 58–61.

Sarason, I. G. (1975). Anxiety and self-preoccupation. In I. G. Sarason & C. D. Spielberger (Eds.), *Stress and anxiety*. New York: Wiley.

Schwartz, R. M., & Gottman, J. M. (1976). Toward a task analysis of assertive behavior. *Journal of Consulting and Clinical Psychology*, 44, 910–920.

Shrauger, J. S. (1972). Self-esteem and reactions to being observed by others. *Journal of Personality and Social Psychology*, 23, 192–200.

Solano, C. H., & Batton, P. G. (1979). *Loneliness and objective self-disclosure in an acquaintanceship exercise*. Unpublished manuscript, Wake Forest University.

Trower, P. (1980). Situational analysis of the components and processes of behavior of socially skilled and unskilled patients. *Journal of Consulting and Clinical Psychology*, 48, 327–339.

Twentyman, C. T., & McFall, R. M. (1975). Behavioral training of social skills in shy males. *Journal of Consulting and Clinical Psychology*, 43, 384–395.

Vitkus, J., & Horowitz, L. M. (1985). *Situational inhibition of social skills*. Paper presented at the Western Psychological Association Annual Convention.

Watson, D., & Friend, R. (1969). Measurement of social-evaluative anxiety. *Journal of Consulting and Clinical Psychology*, 33, 448–457.

Wessberg, H. W., Mariotto, M. J., Conger, A. J., Farrell, A. D., & Conger, J. D. (1979). Ecological validity of role plays for assessing heterosocial anxiety and skill of male college students. *Journal of Consulting and Clinical Psychology*, 47, 525–535.

West, C. K., Lee, J. F., & Anderson, T. H. (1979). The influence of test anxiety in the selection of relevant from irrelevant information. *Journal of Educational Research*, 63, 51–52.

Wicklund, R. A., & Duval, S. (1971). Opinion change and performance facilitation as a result of objective self-awareness. *Journal of Experimental Social Psychology*, 7, 319–342.

Wine, J. D. (1980). Cognitive-attentional theory of test anxiety. In I. G. Sarason (Ed.), *Text anxiety: Theory, research, and application*. Hillsdale, NJ: Erlbaum.

Wine, J. D. (1982). Evaluation anxiety: A cognitive-attentional construct. In H. W. Krohne & L. C. Laux (Eds.), *Achievement, stress, and anxiety*. Washington, DC: Hemisphere.

26

Rhetoritherapy

The Principles of Rhetoric in Training Shy People in Speech Effectiveness

Gerald M. Phillips

INTRODUCTION

The data for this chapter are drawn largely from the files of 19 years of operation of the Pennsylvania State University Reticence Program and formal research done with program participants. All training in the program is done with a common format referred to as "rhetoritherapy," consisting of approximately 40 hours of training: 5 hours in lecture, 15 hours in small groups, 20 hours of practicum, plus about 10 hours individual counseling/instruction. Efforts have been made, with little success, to apply systematic desensitization, sensitivity training, and private support counseling. The fundamentals of the program have crystallized in recent years in a combination of cognitive restructuring, consisting mainly of learning basic rhetorical principles (Thonssen & Baird, 1948) and skills training based on a combination of traditional speech performance instruction and instruction in communication competencies (Phillips, 1984; Phillips, Butt, & Metzger, 1975).

For an overview of reticence, its relationship to shyness, and the various forms in which it is considered in the speech communication discipline, see the two symposium issues of *Communication Education* (Phillips, 1980, 1982).

Rhetoritherapy originated with Muir (1964), who identified a type of person who appeared to be speech defective but did not fit any diagnostic category. She referred to the problem as "reticence" and noted that it was characterized by reduced speech output. The earliest definitions of reticence referred to it as

GERALD M. PHILLIPS • Department of Speech Communication, Pennsylvania State University, University Park, PA 16802.

a pathology (Phillips, 1968). The condition was later defined as an absence of skill at social speaking sometimes connected with anxiety, sometimes not (Phillips, 1977).

The term *reticent* is relatively neutral. Recent investigations classify reticence as a self-perceived condition not necessarily discernible by others (Kelly, 1982b; Kelly, Phillips, & McKinney, 1982). In short, there are a great many socially ineffective speakers. Some see themselves as inept and wish assistance. They may or may not be apprehensive about it. Others do not perceive their own inadequacy. A few are not even aware of the importance of skillful communication and still others are apprehensive but are also high quality performers. Rhetoritherapy is a system of training directed at volunteers who see themselves as inept at performing specific social tasks *and* who wish to become more effective. Their internal emotional states are not relevant to the process of training.

The characteristic sign of reticence is avoidance of particular social situations in which the individual feels most inept. Some social situations can be avoided conveniently. Others, like job interviews and public presentations, cannot be avoided. Rhetoritherapy is directed at helping individuals achieve competency in the social situations they are most likely to encounter. It is not directed at unusual and particular kinds of social circumstances.

Rhetoritherapy makes no assumptions about emotional states. Trainers are prepared to apply systematic desensitization for mildly apprehensive trainees in order to facilitate training. Trainees who appear to have serious emotional problems are referred to appropriate professionals. However, their performance training can proceed even when they are in therapy.

The decision to be reticent is made in the interest of personal economy. Reticent people tend to avoid situations in which they do not think they can do well. Training enables them to expand the number of situations in which they can participate. The reticent person may have good reason to feel incompetent. But, incompetent or not, it is virtually impossible to perform competently if one does not believe it possible. The reticent person believes there is more to gain by silence than by speech.

BELIEFS ASSOCIATES WITH RETICENCE

There is a huge self-help industry directed at people who wish to acquire or improve communication (or social relations) skills. Dale Carnegie, Toastmasters, est, sensitivity training, and encounter groups are all directed at people who wish to become more effective with others. Most of these therapies regard people who are unskilled socially as emotionally distressed. Personal therapy is an important part of instruction; the goal of therapeutic social skills training is to make people feel better about themselves. Dale Carnegie and Toastmasters also work on skills acquisition. It is counterproductive, however, to help low-skill communicators feel better about themselves without facilitating skills acquisition. Positive feelings wither quickly in the face of failure. Thus, the sterling record amassed by Dale Carnegie and Toastmasters over the years is mainly a tribute to quality performance training. Amateur therapy, however, is always questionable, and the best therapy directed at the wrong outcome is wasteful. It is the main assumption of rhetoritherapy that training ought to be directed at what the trainee needs and wants. By appealing only to those who understand their need for performance skills acquisition, rhetoritherapy avoids drawing trainees who are primarily concerned with solving personal and emotional problems.

Reticent people tend to define themselves, however, by belief in a set of myths about their condition. Although the signs of the problem can range from simple silence to vocal hesitancies and social gaucheness, virtually all of the reticent people who have participated in our program have expressed the following beliefs.

- Effective speakers are born not made. Most reticent speakers believe speech skill is hereditary and thus there is no point to training. Though envious of skillful speakers, they excuse their own deficiencies on the grounds they "just don't have it." Reticents sometimes fantasize defeating skillful speakers in some kind of embarrassing encounter.
- To learn to speak skillfully is unethical because it is "manipulation." Reticent speakers believe that effective speech consists of a set of proper phrases and expressions that "cause" behavior in others. They excuse themselves from trying on the grounds that learning to be effective would be "manipulative." They are largely unfamiliar with the personal aspects of rhetorical systems and tend to take a behavioral stance on persuasiveness.
- Speech is not important. Most people talk too much. Reticents wave off social speech and small talk as a silly waste of time. They believe social success is the result of *vibes* and believe in some kind of magical process that brings people together. They are generally reluctant to experiment with social conversation, small talk, and phatic communion on the grounds they are silly and foolish, a waste of time.
- I can speak whenever I want to. But I am a good listener and I don't want to speak very often. This tautology is the most frequent excuse for nonparticipation. Evasions often take elaborate forms. For example, "It is unfair for job interviewers to base their decisions on the way people speak. They should consider only competency." Reticents avoid speaking at public meetings because "people already have their minds made up." Reticent students tend to select courses based on lecture and exam on the grounds that discussion courses are "Mickey Mouse." The role of "good listener" is important to them, since "too many people are talking, anyway."
- Better to remain silent and let people think you are a fool than to speak and prove it to them. Reticent speakers have an anti-Copernican view of the universe. They believe other people watch them carefully and judge them harshly. Thus they are very sensitive to what they think will be the consequences of their inept participation.

- Whatever is wrong with me can be cured. Reticents believe that whatever is wrong with them is pathological and can be treated. They see their ineptitude at speaking as a defect. When they come for assistance, they expect formulary treatment and tend to resist the kind of experiential learning required to acquire skill at rhetorical speech. People with communication problems often seek psychotherapy or counseling. It is no accident that so many psychiatric diagnoses are made of speech components (withdrawn, flat affect, lack of expression, interpersonal difficulties, quavering voice, vocal tremors, vocal hesitations, etc.) But often therapists can find nothing treatable. Kleinsasser's (1968) investigations into effects of desensitization on actual speaking ability are very important. He discovered neither treatment nor placebo had much effect on speaking ability whatever it may have done to feelings, but those subjects who simply sat around and practiced talking with others while they waited for therapy seemed to experience the most improvement. Though reticent speakers are attracted by sensitivity training, assertiveness training, and est, there is little evidence that any of these systems improve skill at social communication, although they may release blocked skills in those few who are already competent.
- Reticent speakers do not understand the role of speech in democratic society. They do not seem to understand the process that underlies problem solving, social affiliation, and conflict resolution. They tend, rather, to seek revealed truth. Many are attracted to organizations led by charismatics. They make heroes of celebrities and set unattainable goals for themselves. Rhetoritherapy trainers often find themselves the objects of heavy transference. That is why it is so important to focus training on performance and heuristics of carryover and to avoid personal engagement with trainees.

ROLE OF THE MEDICAL MODEL

It is often hard for clinical psychologists to understand rhetoritherapy because they are orthogenetically oriented. Clinical treatment implies symptoms having an etiology amenable to a remedy. Disorders can be named, objectivized and treatments studied through "double blind" investigations. The implication in clinical treatment is that "symptoms" can be examined and named. Rhetoritherapy, on the other hand, is criticism oriented, that is, it is based on the principle that any skill or art can be improved through understanding, guided performance, and informed criticism.

Rhetoritherapy rejects the medical model as a basis for the retraining of reticent speakers (Phillips, 1979). The term *rhetoritherapy* is paradoxical, for it literally refers to "treatment of rhetoric." The concept "treatment" implies generalization. A conclusion must be drawn about all cases and the treatment must be consistent in each case. Because rhetoric is defined by Aristotle as "the art of finding in the given case, all the available means of persuasion," there can be no generalization about rhetoric. In fact, improvement of rhetoric proceeds through application of a set of heuristics, referred to as *topoi*, literally questions or suggestions that can be asked about the given case in order to guide individual choice.

Neither reticence nor shyness have literal symptoms that can be generalized, and there are no "treatments of record." Although efforts have been made to measure shyness through paper-and-pencil tests and to measure anxiety through various physiological devices, neither method measures social communication performance. As a matter of fact, quality of performance at social communication is a judgment call. There are no measurable or even socially accepted standards. Each person defines success his or her own way, based on personal goals. (Phillips, 1984).

A treatment that must be tailored to the given case is not a treatment at all. It is a learning program. In essence, rhetoritherapy is based on an individualized speech skills training program for each individual *regardless of the individual's physical or mental condition*. Neurotic speakers can benefit from rhetoritherapy; cerebral palsy victims can benefit from rhetoritherapy. The question to be answered is: What training method will facilitate maximum improvement in speech effectiveness based on specifically defined performance goals (Mager, 1972)? It is important to avoid the terms therapy or treatment. Rhetoric and treatment are oxymoronic. The role of therapy in rhetori*therapy* is no therapy at all. Why, then, do we employ the term? Answer: because our society is so heavily oriented to psychological *treatment* that it is virtually impossible to call attention to a training method without suggesting that it is "therapeutic."

It is sometimes necessary to modify the trainee's point of view in order to motivate commitment to training. This is not done through cognitive restructuring, however, but by simple *quid pro quo* persuasion. "You will receive payoffs if you learn the following . . . " (Phillips, 1981).

THE CONSEQUENCES OF RETICENT BEHAVIOR

When reticent speakers decide to improve it is largely because they have begun to recognize the connection between their personal distress and the acquisition of skill at performance of social speech. Reticent people complain of *loneliness*, separation from others, inability to make regular human contacts and to sustain desired relationships; of *boredom*, a state of ennui characterized by a sameness in activities usually conducted apart from others; and of *ineffectuality*, inability to influence social events (Phillips & Wood, 1983). When they understand that at least part of their problem is not psychological but relevant to communication performance, they become legitimate candidates for rhetoritherapy. Because reticence is not a psychological problem (although some reticent people have psychological problems), attempting to remedy it with psychological measures would be inefficient. Having an emotional problem does not exempt people from participating socially with others, however. One normally does not excuse inept social performance by claiming diminished responsibility through reduced mental and emotional facility. Regardless of one's internal state, one must go on with life.

Actually, it would be inefficient to treat reticence and shyness through psychotherapy even if the former were psychological problems: there are few psychotherapists who have the time and skill to handle reticent people and there are so many reticent people that if psychotherapy were the only treatment, only a very few could ever improve. Most important, it is impossible to learn public performance in private. Thus, rhetoritherapy must be conducted in simulated life conditions (as in a classroom) and it must be formally applied to the trainee's personal experience.

All of this notwithstanding, reticence is a highly emotional state. McCroskey (1970) noted that apprehension about speaking often interferes with training and must be removed before effective training can begin. It is not possible to train an unwilling trainee. Thus, reticent individuals hampered by anxiety do not usually come forward for help. They remain anxious and their communication problem is intensified. Hyde (1980) described the phenomenology of anxiety as it affects people with communication problems. He made it clear that it would take a great deal of therapy to remove the anxiety, and furthermore, even when the individual was relaxed, there would still be no necessary improvement in communication skill.

Peer support is important in convincing reticents they are doing well. Reticent speakers often associate with people who interpret their limited communication output as subservience. Once reticent speakers begin to perform adequately they may threaten dominant associates. At this point it is crucial to avoid giving a medical flavor to reticence. Trainers are admonished to "describe, not name." Thus, a trainee does not try to overcome "shyness," rather the trainee seeks to accomplish specific goals like shaking hands with three new people at the party and learning one thing about each of them. When troubles begin outside the training group, reticent speakers can be taught to describe what they see and apply goal-setting solutions similar to those used in class. Names applied by outsiders are epithets, nothing more, to a person trained to concentrate only on empirical information. In short, if they were never sick, they cannot become well, nor can they be penalized for their sickness. Phrasing personal problems in the form of palpable goals provides trainees with a verifiable method of estimating progress. Retrained reticents must often find new associates once their skills improve, for their old friends preferred them in their state of reduced competence. By changing social milieus they avoid exploitation and facilitate productive interpersonal exchanges with others.

IDENTIFICATION OF CANDIDATES FOR RHETORITHERAPY

Psychological screening and testing procedures are not appropriate for identifying candidates for rhetoritherapy. The most reliable method is self-report and observation by experts (Sours, 1979). Problems most commonly reported by volunteers are:

- Inability to ask and answer questions at work or in school
- Inability to present connected discourse in public
- Inability to make social conversation and small talk
- Inability to develop friends and intimates
- Inability to interact with the opposite sex
- Inability to participate in group activities
- Inability to talk with authority figures or prestigious people.

Reticent people are not inept or fearful in all situations. Virtually all can identify some situations in which they felt competent. (Many, like stutterers, felt effective with small children and animals.) A major problem in training is to resolve an apparent paradox: there are techniques effective in all situations, but each situation requires individualized adaptation. Individualized solutions, however, are the guiding principles of classical rhetoric. Reticent speakers will often request formulas or particular techniques for situations in which they feel incompetent. Moreover, they will often display their incompetence while being interviewed prior to admission to the program. Many will give signs that could be interpreted as nervousness, but there is no consistent set of signs. Interviewers sometimes note blotching, perspiring, averted gaze, vocalized pauses, excessively soft or tremulous voice, trembling or clammy hands, and fidgeting during interviews. It is interesting to note, however, that instructors in public speaking classrooms notice the same phenomena among people who claim to feel quite competent.

About half will talk about "butterflies in the stomach," "feeling ill or "nauseous,' " "pounding heart," "weak knees," "headache," "dry mouth," and similar symptoms but these are not unusual. Many highly competent performers will report these same signs prior to performance. The effects of adrenalin flow are various and hard to predict, but there does not seem to be any consistent connection between symptoms and personal reports of incompetence or observations of it. A number of the self-defined reticents actually appear quite composed. Kelly (1982a) demonstrated that, at least in performing simple social tasks, observers cannot detect the difference between self-identified reticents and those not so classified.

There are five main patterns of response reticents display once training begins. First, they resist participating. First sessions are markedly silent. Trainees file in and sit separated from one another. If the light is off, no one will turn it on. Most will avoid looking at the trainer in order to avoid being asked to respond to questions. Rhetoritherapy trainers must learn techniques of involving trainees. This is most effectively done by direct questioning and pressure to make conversation. Reticents are accustomed to having others initiate contact. When you have a room full of reticents, they are soon motivated to initiate on their own.

A second pattern is expression of a "self-fulfilling prophecy" of ineptitude. Many reticents have great ability to snatch defeat from the jaws of victory. They are upset when things go well and sometimes appear to try to fail in order to sustain the idea they have about themselves. Often they will try to deny success. This important resistance is overcome by careful structuring of activity so that any response can be regarded as successful. A characteristic of early sessions following initial performances is considerable persuasive activity by trainers designed to convince individuals that they met standards for competent performance.

A third pattern is programmatic activity. Some reticents habitually and consistently use phrases, clichés, monosyllabic responses, and trivialities. They struggle to get conversation centered on topics with which they are familiar. By mastering a few social routines, they excuse themselves from broadening their repertoire. Trainers deal with this problem by broadening programming, that is, providing trainees with heuristic performance systems that cannot be used without consideration of the individual case.

Fourth, reticent people are very edgy about criticism. They often regard critical remarks as personal attacks. Trainers are cautioned not to criticize any-thing for which a remedy cannot be offered, because any comment that does not appear completely instructional can be taken as a criticism of person. It is for this reason that it is important to avoid talk about personal feelings that cannot be altered by performance assignments. By concentrating on activity that individuals can willfully control, reticents can be distracted from concern about their feelings.

Finally, some perseverate nervous mannerisms. They seem to be soliciting reassurance and pity. Trainers are advised to offer a dollop of sympathy to everyone. They are told to avoid unconditional positive regard, however. By pointing to accomplishments and using remaining problems as a basis for goal setting, trainees are prevented from using their symptoms to avoid further training. If a person continues to say "and uh, like, y'know" the trainer will work out performance assignments designed to eliminate the mannerism.

It has not been possible to find specific and consistent causes of reticent behavior. Obvious causes like embarrassment, social ridicule, poor parental model, excessive school discipline, marginality, and lack of training have all been implicated, but these problems afflict normal speakers as well. There is nothing that happens to reticents that does not happen to nonreticents. This leads to the conjecture that the problem lies in the perception of events. Reticents tend to be narcissistic. They excuse themselves from participation and place the responsibility on others. They expect special attention. They often appear to be gentle, unassuming, silent, and respectful, just what teacher ordered. However, in a society that places a high premium on skillful social interaction, their with-drawal places unfair burdens on others.

They are often naive about how business gets done in the world. They prefer to ascribe success to luck or "knowing someone" rather than to personal effort. The idea that communication is a responsible citizen's method of problem solving is fundamental to rhetoric. It is easy enough to wave off reticent per-sonalities with the diagnosis of low self-esteem. They do not participate because they feel badly about themselves. But it is hard to see how self-esteem can be raised without providing some empirical confirmation of competence. Treatment systems (sensitivity training, for example) that try to raise self-esteem through psychological means are deceitful in the sense that they try to con people into believing things about themselves that are not true. Reticent people deserve to have low self-esteem because they are not competent and they are not doing anything about it. When they start training, they earn consideration and attention. As they become more competent, they evoke more compliments, accomplish more goals and qualify for more positive evaluations. Thus, rhetoritherapy focuses on acquiring skills and the conviction that one is skillful.

FUNDAMENTAL ASSUMPTIONS OF RHETORITHERAPY

It is axiomatic to rhetoritherapy that altered emotional states have no necessary effect on social performance. Reticent speakers must acquire skill and *know* they have acquired it. Some claim they are more apprehensive after their successful performance because doing it well once confers responsibility to do it well on subsequent occasions. The idea is to make apprehension and tension work for the speaker. The trainer must use techniques of a good theater director or football coach. Active participating is encouraged. Trainees are taught to prepare their presentations by the use of "structures," in which they literally build diagrams of their presentations (Phillips & Zolten, 1976). They are given frequent group assignments or sent to the library or community to ask for information. These assignments are more than busy work, for they involve the student in many kinds of communication situations without thinking about them as such. There is something different about interviewing a person to get information for an assignment than talking to a stranger. Even the act of reporting back becomes a real, rather than simulated, social experience. The trainee must analyze, plan, and prepare; the trainee must then perform, experience critique, and restructure the decision making process for subsequent experiences.

The fundamental pedagogical procedure is drawn from the work of Robert Mager (1972). His assumptions were (a) it is easier to teach behavior than attitude, (b) people can learn behavior best by observing successful behavior and imitating it, (c) attention to action distracts learners from interfering emotions. Learning by imitation of successful behavior is also instrumental in rhetorical training. Goal setting does not apply to the behavior of the listener. It is not valid to set a goal, for example, "to make friends" for this implies something about the listener's actions which the speaker cannot control directly. Goals are set for only for the speaker's behaviors which can be controlled directly, for example:

- I want to ask three questions of the boss tomorrow.
- I want to sustain a 10-minute conversation with Fred at the party.
- I want to ask the operator to get my father person-to-person.
- I want to deliver a 10-minute lecture on "dog grooming".

Goals are set within the framework of the classical rhetorical canons: *inventio, dispositio, elocutio, pronuntiatio,* and *memoria* (Thonssen & Baird, 1948) Trainees learn skills of analyzing audiences and situations, gathering materials, generating speech and conversation ideas, organizing ideas, selecting words and forming sentences and phrases, formal delivery techniques, self-monitoring, and methods of retaining repertoires of performance behaviors.

Trainees must also understand that planning and rehearsal are legitimate. Many tend to believe rehearsal is equivalent to manipulation. The idea that social communicators use repertoires of talk, much of which is carried from situation to situation, is alien to them. The work of James Winans (1938) is used to impress trainees with the idea that "public speech is enlarged conversation." This justifies preparation of social discourse. The trainer must then, of course, distinguish between types of preparation, making it clear that formal composition and outlining are practical for formal speaking, but informal, social situations are best handled by a repertoire of conversational options.

Trainees are also urged not to take full responsibility for failure in social encounters. They must be convinced that no one has an obligation to listen (only to be polite) and that they have the burden of getting and holding attention. On the other hand, they must believe it is sometimes impossible to get attention. People have the right to be preoccupied, concerned with their own thoughts and when this is the case, nothing a speaker can do will be successful.

Finally, trainers continually assault the medical model. Reticent speakers seem to prefer to be sick rather than stupid. If reticence is an illness, then sufferers are entitled to special privilege and some healer must come along and "cure" them. It is hard for anyone to admit ineptitude; particularly hard for people whose ineptitude has been its own defense. Throughout training, reticence trainees will attempt to get referred to someone who can solve their problem. Although trainers must be attentive for cues of acute emotional distress that require consultation with a professional, they must be careful to ignore cries for special privilege because of ineptitude.

KEY RHETORICAL CONCEPTS

Trainees must master six rhetorical propositions to profit from rhetoritherapy. Rhetoric is a considerate process in which a speaker offers a listener a good reason to cooperate. It is not a demand, it is an exchange. The six propositions will make this clear.

1. Rhetorical Situation. A speaker speaks in a situation that includes listeners and their goals and purposes and a set of norms that regulate interaction. A speaker examines a situation to discover an *exigence* for speaking (Bitzer, 1968). That is, the speaker seeks what might be modified by talking. Once the object of talk is discovered, the speaker analyzes persons and norms in order to shape the content of talk. It is from this analysis that the speaker generates personal performance goals. Notice that consideration of audience and social norms *precede* goal setting. This sort of analysis keeps speakers focused on listeners rather than their personal social concerns.

2. Rhetorical Sensitivity. Skilled speakers are adaptable, able to adjust their responses to responses of others. Rhetorical sensitivity is the counterpart of narcissism (Hart & Burks, 1972). What the speaker wants is immaterial unless and until it is associated with what the listener needs. Rhetorical sensitivity is the operational counterpart of the "internal radar" mentioned by David Riesman (1950). Constant attention to listeners helps speakers expand their understanding of nonverbal responses by listeners.

3. Audience Analysis and Adaptation. Audience analysis and adaptation are foundations of instruction in public speaking. Consideration of audience leads facilitates decisions about what should be said, in what words, and in what ways. There are sets of topics (*topoi*) available to guide speakers through this analysis (Wilson & Arnold, 1983). There are also techniques of organization based on information acquired by systematic examination of listeners' behavior patterns and needs. (Phillips & Zolten, 1976) These principles of the public platform must be adapted to social speech.

4. Dual Perspective. The best way to understand an audience is to understand yourself. Dual perspective implies that speakers can project their own needs and emotions onto the audience (Phillips, Butt, & Metzger, 1975). Whatever offends the speaker is likely to offend the audience. Dual perspective facilitates acquisition of a capacity of *negative spontaneity* (Murray, Phillips, & Truby, 1969), that is, knowing how to injure the listener and consciously rejecting it as an option.

5. Nonverbal Punctuation and Emphasis. Speakers are expected to display energy and concern about their topic. Careful use of voice, gesture, and body helps speakers gain and sustain attention. The process of management of vocal and physical expression is gained through skill at oral reading in which readers try to get the message to the audience so that attention is on the message as opposed to the speaker (medium) (Hopf, 1970).

6. Development of Repertoires and Alternate Plans. Concern for audience is displayed by preparations of alternate plans. Speakers must be aware of the fact that they can "win," "lose," or "get by" and be prepared to adjust to each outcome. By rehearsing alternative plans in advance speakers can set themselves for the uncertainty of the audience situation.

PRINCIPLES OF PEDAGOGY

The basic propositions are taught through lecture, reading, and criticism where appropriate. Careful criticism can support efforts to improve. The purpose of criticism is to make trainees aware of how they can manage their own performance in order to motivate listeners. Trainees are helped to understand their own performance behavior via feedback from role-play partners.

Trainees choose their activities; they literally prepare their own menu. Regular college students are required to give a 10-minute speech in order to satisfy a university requirement. In adult training units it is optional. Students may also choose learning programs in asking and answering questions in class or on the job, participating in classroom groups or on committees, managing job interviews, basic conversational strategies and skills, and special training packages in developing relationships, shopping, using the phone, improving family communication, and participating in organizations.

The practicality of goal selection is very important. Trainers urge trainees to concentrate on situations they face on a *daily* basis. It is much easier to observe improvement if newly acquired skills are practiced regularly. Getting the trainee to be aware that improvement has taken place is often as important as the improvement itself. The real issue in apprehension is commitment. People will not start a car unless convinced they can drive. The reticent speaker who has acquired a new skill must be convinced that skill will work in a real setting before the speaker will take the social risk.

Trainees work out a list of goals to accomplish in consultation with their trainer. They select the simplest goal with which to start, and then progress to the most difficult. Usually four or five goals can be accomplished in a 10-week training session. It is very important that the trainer make sure the trainee accomplishes the first goal in an unambiguous way in order to motivate commitment to the more difficult goals. The goalsetting conference often takes on the appearance of a contract negotiation for this reason. Trainees prepare a written plan for their personal action to accomplish their goal, check the plan with the trainer, rehearse their part of the plan, set a time and place to put it into operation, execute the plan, and report back on it. The written plan includes identification of audience and situation as well as a set of optional responses for at least three possible conditions of audience response. The trainer commits to conference time, pledges advice about possible techniques, and is available to provide encouragement and reinforcement.

The lecture series covers the six main propositions plus orientation to techniques for accomplishing the goals most frequently selected. Private instruction on techniques is provided for those selecting unusual goals. A lecture is 30 minutes in length, usually followed by formal exercises in which trainees apply the substance of the lecture to their own performance. Lectures are supplemented by reading assignments which review lecture material. It is important to maintain the flavor of the classroom regardless of the setting for the training. Students in classrooms focus on tasks and activities rather than on personal feelings.

How Speech Can Be Used to Modify Social Situations. (One Lecture). This lecture is used to introduce the course and motivate the first major assignment, the "Self as Communicator" paper, in which the trainees describe personal strengths and weaknesses and identify social situations in which communication skill is important for them. The lecturer reviews and demonstrates (live and film) effective formats for simple communication situations, like asking and answering questions, social speaking, speaking in task groups, interviewing, and public speaking. Special reference is made to career applications (or company concerns if the program is run in conjunction with a business enterprise).

What People Are Required to Do in order to Be Reasonably Effective Speakers. (Three Lectures). This series deals with making judgments of adequacy, competency, and skill (Phillips, 1984) so trainees can identify behaviors associated with analysis, preparation, performance, and evaluation of communication performance. Its purpose is to help students set goals in behavior terms and associate their behavior with audience responses. Trainees are advised to think in terms of *quid pro quo* and discover "sayables" that will convince listeners the speaker is concerned with their needs and wants. These questions are the basis of a residual message, the kernel of understanding the speaker wants to remain with the listener. Reticent speakers are often not aware of the limitations of the communication process. They want to say everything on their minds and are frustrated when they find listeners can only accommodate to a few simple ideas.

How to Set Goals. (Two Lectures and Private Consultation). This presentation is based on Mager's *Goal Analysis* (1972) as modified in *Help for Shy People* (Phillips, 1981). Trainees follow a prepared form to prepare personal goals. The first goal analysis produces an agenda for a trainer/trainee conference to agree on a contract about goals to be accomplished, the order in which they will be accomplished, and standards for satisfactory accomplishment.

How to Organize Ideas. (Two Lectures). Trainees are taught to outline through the structural method, literally to draw visual diagrams of the message to be communicated and prepare flow charts for discussion and conversation (Standard Agenda) (Phillips *et al.*, 1979). Mental and physical involvement in preparation keeps attention focused on the task and off emotions. Trainees are taught to spot-organize impromptu presentations by simulating social engagements. Support procedures for public performance (note preparation and mnemonic systems) are taught to facilitate retention of information.

How to Prepare, Rehearse, and Present. (Two Lectures). The extemporaneous mode is emphasized. Trainees are cautioned not to memorize, but to prepare. Those concerned are taught script-reading and media-related techniques. Trainees are grouped by common goals for rehearsal, role playing, and peer assistance with preparation. Trainees are offered extensive vocal training, including oral reading and platform movement. The purpose of this training is to acquaint trainees with possibilities of vocal range and body movement. Video and audio are only used for those seeking direct microphone or camera training. It has been our experience that nothing more uniformly ensures increased apprehension than the prospect of viewing or hearing oneself while being criticized.

No trainee is permitted to perform any goals without a prior rehearsal either before a group of peers or the instructor. The idea is convince the trainee that he or she is capable of a polished performance the quality of which is not in doubt. The formality of rehearsal in a classroom setting reinforces the performance (as opposed to emotional) aspects of goal accomplishment.

How to Interpret Listener Response. (One Lecture). The word *feedback* is not used by rhetoritherapy trainers. Feedback connotes cybernetic regularity. Trainees learn the ambiguity and unpredictability of the audience situation. They are taught to examine and interpret responses that vary from person to person. Part of required debrief consists of trainees describing what their listeners did in response to the communication. This assignment helps objectivize the task and distract trainees from their tendency to narcissism. It also helps trainees make achieve directness through eye contact and natural movement, neither of which are considered *per se*. Based on this information, students are asked to report on what they did and how their listeners responded to each effort to accomplish a communication goal.

ASSIGNMENTS AND ACTIVITIES IN SEQUENCE

Training follows a common format regardless of setting.

Self-as-Communicator Paper. Trainees write a report on their strengths and weaknesses as communicators. This is used as an agenda for trainer conferences to learn goal setting and set a sequence of goals to accomplish.

Social Skills Experiences. Training sessions include a structured social experience in which trainees meet each other, meet strangers, guests, etc., and learn to make small talk and get simple information from conversation partners. These experiences culminate in a simulated cocktail party at which trainees are asked to meet three new people and learn two things about each. Trainees then report back to the group. This provides an experience in public presentation that can be used as a basis for training for an actual public speaking experience.

Specialized Skill Interest Groups. Trainees are grouped with others seeking similar goals for rehearsal and role play. Some groups are "Making Dates," "Committees," "Reciting and Reporting," "Asking and Answering Questions in Class and on the Job," "Interviews with Advisors and Supervisors," "Handling Job Interviews," "Cooperating with Physicians and Therapists," "Presentational Speaking," "How to Use Visuals." Peer groups provide consensual validation, peer consultation, and colleagues useful in role playing. Trainees are encouraged to attempt spontaneous socialization (let's have a cup of coffee and discuss our common tasks on the way home). These sessions often lead to budding friendships. Special advisory sessions are held on building friendship and maintaining relationships.

Interviewing Techniques. Shy college students are fearful about job interviews. Shy employees are apprehensive about evaluation interviews. A kit of standard questions is provided. Trainees learn to prepare 15- to 30-second responses to questions most frequently asked. Where possible, help is solicited from the business community for an evening of simulated interviewing. Trainees are also helped to prepare resumes.

Public Speaking Training. Speech-making activities are simulated in groups but trainees are then urged to speak in front of some live group. Civic Clubs and Toastmasters have been very cooperative in providing audiences. Emphasis in speaking training is largely on preparation and delivery technique. Trainers give no criticism for which a performance remedy cannot be provided. All criticism is offered in private. Respect is given to all topics: trainees learn to attend to performance business rather than fear rejoinder. Public question periods are often simulated so students can get the feel of a public response.

SUMMARY OF HEURISTICS

Additional experiences are devised to meet particular trainee goals. Training emphasizes performance skills. Trainers note behavior changes and are able to advise trainees on the growth of performance repertoires. The idea is to convince them to work on actions. Heuristics based on the classical principles of rhetorical preparation are provided to facilitate preparation for situations not covered in training sessions. The emphasis of heuristics is on carryover.

- What actions on my part may modify information, attitudes, or behavior in listeners? On what evidence do I make this judgment?
- What goals shall I set for my own behavior?
- What listener needs will my performance meet?
- What ideas shall I present and in what order?
- All communication must be carefully organize.
- What must I do with voice, face, and body?
- What is the best, worst, and most likely response I can get and what are my alternatives in each case?
- What is the minimum level of acceptable performance? What constitutes a good job?

The most important heuristic question is, How can I discriminate between the desirable and the doable. Why people often want to do the impossible. Effective communication, however, is a function of doing the doable. Helping trainees understand what is reasonable to expect helps them overcome their frustration at not being able to do a perfect job of communicating.

EVALUATION OF PROGRAM SUCCESS

Two evaluations are used. Trainees are asked, at the end of the course, to produce a final self-as-communicator paper in which they describe and evaluate *behavior* changes they experienced as a result of training. Before and after comparisons are made (Domenig, 1978). Trainees identify their own improvements and isolate continuing problems. A final interview with the trainer is used to provide a set of goals for accomplishment and to corroborate gains, where justified.

Follow-ups are conducted at 1-, 3-, 5-, and 7-year intervals. A random sample of former students is phoned and asked the following questions:

1. Do you remember taking the course? Do you remember the instructor's name (94% do).
2. Can you name two or more things you learned to do in the course. (90% name at least two, 75% name four or more.)
3. Can you tell us how you used something you learned in the course within the last two weeks. (85% can.)

Interviewers confirm an average of two-plus performance gains per student. Follow-up surveys indicate that about 85% retain these skills as long as 5 years after training (Oerkvitz, 1975, 1976).

Occasional longitudinal studies are done following particular trainees for a year after completion of training (Metzger, 1974). These studies are particularly useful in obtaining information about the effect of training on emotions and attitudes. Although there is no strong evidence that training removes prior apprehension, 90% of former trainees report that apprehension disappears once performance starts, and therefore does not impede performance. Many still report ambivalence about participation in social situations, but virtually all report they are able to deal with unavoidable situations, and about half report voluntary participation.

RHETORITHERAPY: A SUMMARY

Rhetoritherapy is a training program demonstrably effective in helping shy people to acquire communication skills. It has some effect on reducing performance apprehension and raising self-esteem as it relates to performance. Acquiring skill seems to enable trainees to become involved in necessary communication situations. Although it does not make them eloquent or charming, it helps them get essential communication tasks done reasonably effectively.

No egregious promises are made. No miracle cures have been reported. The idea of rhetoritherapy is to get small gains from everyone and to provide trainees with heuristics they can use in subsequent situations after training is over. In that sense it is a viable model of classical rhetorical training. Because it is not psychologically based, no effort is made to provide counseling. Cooperative arrangements are made with professionals to handle trainee's psychoemotional needs. However, because most feelings of inadequacy stem from lack of skill, awareness of improvement of technique is often sufficient to overcome self-defeating feelings.

Rhetoritherapy is based on pedagogical principles of classical rhetoric. It purposely avoids a clinical flavor, rejects the medical model, and uses tested methods of performance training applied to tension-evoking social/communication situations. In the final analysis, reticence or shyness is seen as an eminently practical problem experienced by a great many people. Many reticents do not recognize a need to do anything about it. Those who do seek retraining often do so reluctantly and struggle against surrendering their defensive behavior. Reticence cannot be regarded as a psychological problem *per se* because communication incompetence clearly exists in both neurotic and nonneurotic people. Focus on skills acquisition instills confidence in performance ability. Effective participation tends to ameliorate some counterproductive feelings about the self without the necessity of dealing with psychoemotional content. This should not be construed as objection to psychological counseling, but merely as argument on behalf of the premise that some psychological objectives can be accomplished indirectly through direct performance training.

Speech is the way humans communicate their personality, solve their problems, organize their societies, and achieve intimacy. Hardly anyone is free from tension in speaking. The difference between effectiveness and ineptitude lies in skillful performance. Most people can be trained. About 5 years ago, a local psychiatrist sent one of his patients to the Reticence Program. The patient was a delusional schizophrenic who mumbled incoherently to refrigerators and answered nonexistent telephone calls in an inaudible voice. The psychiatrist asked us to try to teach his patient to speak more clearly. The result of training was a schizophrenic who gave instructions to an imaginary person trapped in a refrigerator in very clear and coherent terms. Ability to understand what the patient was saying helped the therapy materially. The patient is still schizophrenic and still occasionally delusional, but he is able to live in the community, take care of his basic needs, and work on a part-time job.

This is the mandate of rhetoritherapy: *everyone can be helped a little*. There are, after all, a great many helpers in the world, none of whom has a total cure. If we all do our thing in an atmosphere of mutual respect our clients will accrue a material advantage.

REFERENCES

Bitzer, L. F. (1968). The rhetorical situation. *Philosophy and Rhetoric*. I, 1, 165–168.

Domenig, K. (1978). *An examination of self-reports of reticent and non-reticent students before and after instruction*. Master's thesis, The Pennsylvania State University.

Hart, R., & Burks, D. M. (1972). Rhetorical sensitivity and social interaction. *Speech Monographs*. 39, 2, 75–91.

Hopf, T. S. (1970). Reticence and the oral interpretation teacher. *Speech Teacher*. 19, 4, 268–271.

Hyde, M. J. (1980). The experience of anxiety: a phenomenological investigation. *Quarterly Journal of Speech*. 66, 2, 140–154.

Kelly, L. (1982a). *Observers' comparisons of the interpersonal communication skills of students who self-selected a special speech course and students who self-selected a regular speech course*. (Doctoral dissertation, Pennsylvania State University.

Kelly, L. (1982b). A rose by any other name is still a rose: A comparative analysis of reticence, communication apprehension, unwillingness to communicate and shyness. *Human Communication Research*. 8, 2, 99–113.

Kelly, L., Phillips, G. M., & McKinney, B. (1982) Reprise: farewell reticence, goodbye apprehension! Building a practical nosology of speech communication problems. *Communication Education*. 31, 3, 211–222.

Kleinsasser, D. (1968). *The reduction of performance anxiety as a function of desensitization, pre-therapy vicarious learning, and vicarious learning alone*. Doctoral dissertation, Pennsylvania State University.

Mager, R. (1972). *Goal analysis*. Belmont, CA: Fearon.

McCroskey, J. C. (1970). Measures of communication-bound anxiety. *Speech Monographs*. 37, 267–277.

Metzger, N. J. (1974). *The effects of a rhetorical method of instruction on a selected population of reticent students*. Doctoral dissertation, Pennsylvania State University.

Muir, F. (1964). *Case studies of selected examples of reticence and fluency*. Master's thesis, Washington State University.

Murray, E., Phillips, G. M., & Truby, J. D. (1969). *Speech: Science-Art*. New York: Bobbs, Merrill.

Oerkvitz, S. (1975). *Reports of continuing effects of instruction in a specially designed speech course for reticent students*. Master's thesis, Pennsylvania State University.

Oerkvitz, S. (1976). Continuing effects of a rhetorical method of instruction for reticent students. *Communication*. 4, 2, 104–114.

Phillips, G. M. (1968). Reticence: pathology of the normal speaker. *Speech Monographs*. 35, 1, 39–49.

Phillips, G. M. (1977). Rhetoritherapy vs. the medical model: dealing with reticence. *Communication Education*. 26, 1, 34–43.

Phillips, G. M. (Ed.). (1980). The practical teacher's symposium on shyness, communication apprehension, reticence and a variety of other common problems. *Communication Education*. 29, 3, 213–263.

Phillips, G. M. (1981). *Help for shy people*. Englewood Cliffs, NJ: Prentice-Hall.

Phillips, G. M. (Ed.). ((1982). Symposium. *Communication Education*. 31,3.

Phillips, G. M. (1984). A competent view of "competence." *Communication Education*, 33, 1, 25–36.

Phillips, G. M., Butt, D., & Metzger, N. J. (1974). *Communication in Education*. New York: Holt, Rinehart, & Winston.

Phillips, G. M., & Sokoloff, K. A. (1979). An end to anxiety: Treating speech problems with rhetoritherapy. *Journal of Communication Disorders*. 12, 3, 385–397.

Phillips, G. M., Pedersen, D. J., & Wood, J. T. (1979). *Group discussion: A practical guide for participants and leader*. Boston, MA: Houghton Mifflin.

Phillips, G. M., & Wood, J. T. (1983). *Communication and human relationships*. New York: Macmillan.

Phillips, G. M., & Zolten, J. J. (1976). *Structuring speech*. Indianapolis, IN: Bobbs-Merrill.

Riesman, D. (1950). *The lonely crowd*. New York: Doubleday Anchor.

Sours, D. (1979). *Comparison of judgments by placement interviewers and instructors about the severity of reticence in students enrolled in a special option of a basic speech course*. Master's thesis, Pennsylvania State University.

Thonssen, L., & Baird, A. C. (1948). *Speech criticism: The development of standards for rhetorical appraisal*. New York: Ronald Press.

Wilson, J. & Arnold, C. (1983). *Public speaking as a liberal art* (5th ed.). Boston, MA: Allyn & Bacon.

Winans, James. (1938). *Speech making*. New York: D. Appleton.

27

Short-Term Group Psychotherapy for Shyness

Paul A. Pilkonis

INTRODUCTION

It is ironic that shyness, intrinsically an interpersonal problem, has been treated most frequently with individual therapies. Depending on the underlying model of shyness, the therapies have varied, but they can be characterized broadly as fitting into one of three groups: (a) relaxation and desensitization therapies aimed at alleviating anxiety and disinhibiting behaviors that are a part of the patient's repertoire but that the patient is unable to perform easily; (b) behavioral therapies designed to enhance social skills that are not yet within the patient's capability; and (c) cognitive therapies aimed at restructuring the patient's negative self-image and expectancies in social situations. The typical paradigm has been to develop and implement such therapies in individual treatments. When group work has been done, it is usually employed for reasons of efficiency (i.e., it is more cost-effective to teach several individuals together rather than separately).

The present chapter will review the evidence (admittedly limited) on the comparative effectiveness of individual versus group approaches in the treatment of shyness, discuss some of the potential advantages of a group format, and describe a model of short-term group psychotherapy that incorporates cognitive, behavioral, and traditional group-process features. A final section will consider the possibility that genotypic difficulties in attachment may have different phenotypic expressions. These phenotypes can include compulsive self-reliance, compulsive care giving, emotional detachment, and overt social anxiety (Bowlby, 1977). Such a view suggests that similar treatments may be effective for all these subgroups and that there may be some advantages to treating together patients with different phenotypes. Shy people are often benefited by the realization that others who appear to be self-sufficient or well-adjusted,

PAUL A. PILKONIS • Department of Psychiatry, University of Pittsburgh School of Medicine, 3811 O'Hara Street, Pittsburgh, PA 15213.

perhaps too much so, can also be subject to interpersonal anxieties, fears of rejection, and defensiveness about relationships.

GROUP VERSUS INDIVIDUAL TREATMENT OF SHYNESS

Contrary to clinical expectations, it is frequently difficult to demonstrate strong comparative outcome differences between psychotherapies (Luborsky, Singer, & Luborsky, 1975; Shapiro & Shapiro, 1982). At the same time, there is good evidence that active treatments (either individual or group) are more beneficial than no treatment or placebo and control treatments (Andrews & Harvey, 1981; Landman & Dawes, 1982; Smith, Glass, & Miller, 1980). As a result, researchers are currently asking more differentiated questions: What specific kinds of treatments are most effective with what specific patient groups in achieving which goals?

The literature on shyness is consistent with the broader psychotherapy-outcome literature in all these aspects. Different individual therapies have been found to be effective in the treatment of shyness, social anxiety, interpersonal difficulties, and lack of assertiveness (see Arkowitz, 1977; Curran, 1977; Marzillier, 1978; and Twentyman & Zimering, 1979, for relevant reviews). Twentyman and Zimering (1979) point out that "studies in the literature are nearly equally divided in presenting treatment individually or in groups" and that conclusions applicable to individual treatments also apply to group interventions; therefore, they assert that "little evidence is present to support the use of one treatment approach over another" (p. 343). Within the literature on group treatments of shyness and social-skills problems, there are suggestions that more orthodox treatments (either behavioral or cognitive) are more effective than certain alternative treatments, such as sensitivity groups, consciousness raising groups, and bibliotherapy groups (Monti et al., 1979; Monti, Curran, Corriveau, Delancey, & Hagerman, 1980; Wolfe & Fodor, 1977). However, among orthodox group treatments themselves, the similarities in results tend to outweigh the differences.

Linehan, Walker, Bronheim, Haynes, and Yevzeroff (1979) have done one of the few direct comparisons of individual versus group training, focusing on the specific problem of assertiveness. Their results supported the position that both active treatments are preferable to no treatment, but they found no substantive differences between them. They pointed out that their study was limited to a small sample of women who received highly structured treatments in both modalities, allowing for minimal individualized work and limiting any emergent group process.

Pilkonis, Imber, Lewis, and Rubinsky (1984) have reported on a psycho-therapy-outcome study comparing individual, group, and conjoint therapy that sheds some light on the present issue. Although their patient sample was not preselected for problems with shyness, most patients cited various interpersonal difficulties among the reasons bringing them to treatment. Pilkonis et al. found that for patients with more chronic presenting problems, the interpersonal therapies (both group and conjoint treatment) were more beneficial than individual therapy on interpersonal-outcome measures. These measures included the Social Avoidance and Distress Scale (Watson & Friend, 1969), a measure commonly used in studies of shyness and social anxiety, and the Locus of Control of Interpersonal Relationships Scale (Lewis, Cheney, & Dawes, 1977).

Hargreaves, Showstack, Flohr, Brady, and Harris (1974) have reported a finding that is also relevant here. They did not provide treatment-outcome data but did describe the initial acceptability of treatment assignments and the perceived helpfulness of therapy following an initial appointment. Shy patients tended to prefer individual therapy or a daily drop-in group rather than a more traditional group with weekly appointments. Patients for whom shyness was less of a problem preferred both of the more usual modalities (individual therapy or a weekly therapy group) over the contact-on-demand group. There has been some discussion in the clinical literature (e.g., Imber, Lewis, & Loiselle, 1979) about the potential value of short-term or contact-on-demand groups for managing extended waiting lists or educating patients about the usual processes occurring in group therapy, and it is interesting to speculate that such techniques may have particular applicability to shy patients. Such approaches may provide shy individuals with greater control over the timing and amount of exposure to a feared interpersonal situation, and such control may enhance their ultimate willingness to persist in a group.

CLINICAL CONSIDERATIONS SUPPORTING THE USE OF GROUP PSYCHOTHERAPY

Although the empirical evidence is limited, there are persuasive clinical arguments on behalf of the use of group psychotherapy in the treatment of shyness. Krueger (1979) contends that group therapy is the treatment of choice for ego-syntonic, interpersonal problems like shyness, and there are several reasons to endorse his position. First, the *in vivo* desensitization provided by a group experience is likely to be more potent than imaginal or covert techniques. The extinction promoted by an initially anxiety-arousing and then progressively more comfortable group can be dramatic. In this same vein, some researchers (Royce & Arkowitz, 1978) have argued that even behavioral treatments aimed at skill acquisition (e.g., practice dating) operate most powerfully by providing opportunities for *in vivo* desensitization, opportunities inherent in group therapy.

Second, group therapy creates a richer and more complex social environment than individual treatments. Although participants may all regard themselves as shy, members of a group will include men and women with different life experiences, social styles, and ethnic and social class backgrounds, thereby providing a variety of models and feedback to each individual. The use of cotherapists (usually one male and one female—see following) also provides more flexibility and a wider range of therapist behavior from which patients may potentially benefit. This richer social environment is more likely to promote generalization than are most short-term individual treatments, which often do not include components aimed at generalization beyond the treatment setting. The group itself is a social situation that is similar to many interpersonal encounters outside treatment, and therefore it may enhance the consolidation of new behavior in extra-therapeutic settings.

Third, the consensual validation that can occur in a group often creates more powerful contingencies for shaping behavior than those available in individual treatment. Resistant patients often find it easier to disqualify a single therapist (e.g., "my therapist is different from me," "my therapist doesn't really understand me") than to ignore consistent feedback from a group with diverse members, most or all of whom agree on some troublesome aspect of the patient's behavior.

Fourth, one of the dangers of individual treatment with shy patients is the inordinate dependency that such patients sometimes develop in a one-to-one relationship. Such a relationship can be beneficial during the course of treatment, but it often leaves patients vulnerable following termination when the therapist is no longer available on a regular basis. The use of group psychotherapy is helpful in minimizing the overly intense attachment that shy persons may develop in individual work (and that cannot be successfully resolved without longer term individual therapy).

Finally, group psychotherapy can be more efficient in terms of time and effort. A typical group of six to eight members, led by two cotherapists, represents a more cost-effective solution than individual therapy to the problem of providing accessible and adequate care for what all investigators agree is a prevalent problem. Of course, the advocates of individual therapy for shyness can marshal alternative arguments about the advantage of that mode (e.g., the greater tailoring of treatment to specific personal needs, the enhanced respect for the patient's privacy, and the avoidance of negative modeling provided by group members), but we contend that group psychotherapy is the treatment of choice for shyness.

SELECTION CRITERIA

Having made a case for the use of short-term group psychotherapy in treating shyness, it is still necessary to use considerable judgment in identifying those patients who will benefit from short-term therapy (as opposed to longer treatment, either individual or group) and those patients who present as shy but for whom shyness is only the tip of the psychological iceberg. Numerous criteria have been proposed for the use of short-term psychotherapy in general (Malan, 1976; Mann, 1973; Sifneos, 1972), but the three most important are the presence of a focal, target complaint; some understanding of the psychological nature of the problem; and adequate motivation to work toward psychological changes.

To be suitable for brief treatment, a patient's shyness should be focused on interpersonal anxieties and be relatively circumscribed around this theme.

The shyness should not simply be one of a number of neurotic problems or a convenient label for the generalized anxiety that some psychotherapy patients describe. In addition, the overall severity of the patient's problems should be moderate. The shyness should be part of a reasonably intact personality with some positive history of interpersonal and occupational functioning rather than one bit of evidence for a more severe disorder that may include little or no history of interpersonal attachments, severely flawed self-esteem, chronic dysphoria, substance abuse problems, or other signs of more basic "characterological" problems. For such personality disorders, treatment is more likely to be long term and to demand more intensive involvement on the part of the therapist, who will be required to help the patient manage a wide range of intra- and interpersonal difficulties. In these cases, individual therapy may be a prerequisite for group work (cf., Malan, Balfour, Hood, & Shooter, 1976) in order to bring the patient to a level of adaptation and functioning more suited to the give-and-take and frustrations of group therapy.

Although we regard short-term group psychotherapy as the treatment of choice for shyness, it is still important to be aware of the different needs of publicly versus privately shy patients (Pilkonis, 1977). Although most shy people present with a mix of physiological, affective, cognitive, and behavioral complaints, there are differences in the extent to which they emphasize behavioral avoidance and interpersonal awkwardness (public shyness) versus concerns about excessive arousal and fears of negative evaluation (private shyness). Excessive arousal and behavioral inhibitions can be adequately addressed with a standard group experience. However, there are some privately shy patients with an adequate behavioral repertoire that they can perform with moderate levels of arousal who still insist on their interpersonal failings because of private images, schema, and self-evaluations that can be notoriously resistant to behavioral evidence and interpersonal feedback. Such patients require a rather careful analysis of the meanings they attach to their interpersonal behavior (Yardley, 1979), and in some cases, individual treatment may be preferable for this purpose. Our group model (see below) includes attention to cognitive restructuring, but for highly resistant or self-conscious persons, there may be a need for individual interventions to avoid sidetracking a group with excessively idiosyncratic concerns.

STRUCTURING THE PSYCHOTHERAPY GROUP

A group will usually meet for 14 weekly sessions lasting about 1½ hours each. The first session is used for introductory purposes and the last session for termination and a review of treatment. The middle 12 sessions are organized as a series of six 2-week units addressing specific content areas on which the members of the group have agreed to work. Because shyness has both public and private components, we attempt to influence each. The first week of every unit is ordinarily focused on cognitive issues and restructuring. Patients are asked to read relevant materials prior to the session as a way of prompting discussion, providing a common starting point, and exploring some of the implicit and maladaptive assumptions that frequently underlie shyness. During the session, they are encouraged to share ideas, expectations, and beliefs about the situations in which they experience the greatest difficulty. Such discussion also plays the role of promoting cohesion among the group members and providing opportunities for feedback and support.

The second week of each unit is devoted more explicitly to behavioral change. The session is aimed at identifying specific, anxiety-arousing situations; role-playing them; and using both live and videotaped feedback to evaluate performance and generate new behavioral alternatives. Interaction among group members is also processed when appropriate in order to provide greater here-and-now awareness of dysfunctional patterns that have become habitual and are manifested in the group. Outside the group, members are asked to keep diaries of social encounters, both successful and unsuccessful, and to set interpersonal tasks to perform.

Videotape is an especially useful adjunct in short-term group therapy. It can be used in two ways: first, to provide specific and immediate feedback on those behavioral tasks that are role-played in the group; and second, as a complete record of the group where facilities allow the sessions to be taped on an ongoing basis. Even excessively shy people are often fascinated by the opportunity to see themselves on videotape. Videotape can be a valuable tool for correcting distortions in recall and for exploring discrepancies between one's private experience and one's public behavior. Although most members will express some initial discomfort with the idea of being taped, desensitization to the presence of cameras and the notion of being recorded is often quite rapid—once the group process begins, it is usually sufficiently engrossing to command the attention that may have initially been focused on the equipment associated with taping.

One potential drawback to taping is the boomerang effect it elicits in some patients, who use the visual record to insist that they are as inept as they had always believed and to interpret quite acceptable behavior as more evidence of their inadequacy. Such negative biases, however, often provide valuable material for the group process itself. If there is some consensus that the behavior in question is not as deficient as the patient proposes, it frequently becomes difficult for that patient to persist to the same extent in such self-deprecatory beliefs.

Topics selected by group members for exploration typically include problems in establishing intimate relationships, loneliness and a lack of a sense of belonging, difficulties in interacting with authority figures, a lack of general assertiveness, the development of conversational skills, strategies for meeting people and establishing new relationships, and the management of loss and rejection. Patients are also encouraged to diagnose deficiencies in their social networks using a conceptual framework developed by Weiss (1974) for describing the "provisions of social relationships." Rather than simply regarding relationships in general as helpful, Weiss has attempted to define the specific kinds of support that a gratifying social network can provide. Weiss has organized his ideas around the themes of primary emotional attachment and general social integration (which he regards as independent). For example, it is possible to have a group of friends and acquaintances that seems lacking because it does not contain a confidant with whom one is intimate, and conversely, one may have an important one-to-one relationship but still be lonely for a broader set of companions and a sense of community.

The six specific provisions that Weiss has described are:

1. Primary emotional attachment, most often provided in our society by an intimate, cross-sex relationship;
2. Social integration, fostered by a network of associations among people who share common concerns and interests and a feeling of "belonging" (whether at work, in the community, or within an extended family);
3. Opportunities for nurturance, provided obviously in raising children but also available in other care-giving situations;
4. Reassurance of worth, bestowed by relationships which acknowledge one's competence, either at work or at home;
5. A sense of reliable alliance, provided by relationships with some history and continuity and containing the promise of future help regardless of their current level of intimacy; and
6. The obtaining of guidance, available from authoritative sources who can be depended on to provide assistance and direction (e.g., physicians, attorneys, clergymen, therapists). The use of such a conceptual framework encourages group members to be more thoughtful about the kinds of relationships they currently lack and leads naturally to developing strategies for supplementing areas in which they are deficient.

A general goal of treatment is to provide patients with a problem-solving approach to interpersonal difficulties. The matter-of-factness of such an approach is often useful in lessening dysfunctional levels of arousal, limiting catastrophic thinking, and promoting more objective appraisal of social problems and the coping responses appropriate to them (cf. Weick, 1984). In accomplishing this task, an important tone to establish is that of flexibility and adaptation. In our experience, this atmosphere is often most apparent in groups where, although an early agenda has been established, there is some movement away from the constraints of the initial structure. Such structure is valuable in getting the ball rolling and ordinarily requires that the group leaders play a fairly directive role in organizing the work of the group. However, it is usually a favorable prognostic sign when members become more assertive regarding their own needs and expectations for the group. At such times, the six units originally defined by the group may be altered in midstream, with newly emerging issues replacing the earlier ones defined or with an emphasis on only one or two themes that seem most important to the group members. Related to the phenomenon of changing the initial agenda is a second alteration, that of focusing increasingly on the here-and-now process of the group, rather than relying more exclusively on second-hand reports of difficulties outside the group. Speaking to the group process itself is often quite threatening initially to group members. Nevertheless, it is often most beneficial in the long term because it involves addressing some of the most affectively laden material available to the group and eliminates the distance characterizing discussion of incidents outside the group.

Socializing by members of the group apart from sessions is a topic that requires explicit discussion during the life of most groups. At first, it can provide interpersonal opportunities that would otherwise be lacking and may become a helpful way of undertaking homework assignments (Falloon, Lindley, McDonald, & Marks, 1977). However, because the group is intended to be a short-term one, this model of engaging in new relationships can often be misleading and interfere with the more difficult task of establishing new relationships with people who are not already drawn together by some imperative, such as therapy. There are also dangers involved in patients becoming attached to each other in the role of playing therapist rather than because of more genuine mutual interests and values. Our own tendency has been to discourage socializing outside the group, pointing out that therapy is not intended ultimately to provide a pool of potential friends. Rather, therapy is aimed at helping patients to come to terms with previously existing relationships and to teach them strategies of establishing new relationships that will outlive the initial attraction that is commonly felt toward group members.

The use of cotherapists, one male and one female, is often helpful in the treatment of shyness. Having both a male and female leader provides examples of more diverse, modeled behaviors than the use of a single leader (of either sex) or of two leaders of the same sex. With a combined male and female membership, it also allows all members the possibility of identifying with a positive role model of the same sex. In addition, the use of opposite-sex coleaders sometimes creates interesting opportunities for eliciting patients' thoughts about the degree and style of intimacy that exists between the leaders. Such thoughts provide valuable information about the images that patients have of idealized good relationships. It is often important that such schemata be made explicit because shy people frequently have unrealistic and glowing images of the social worlds that other people inhabit, along with equally unrealistic but negative views of their own interpersonal encounters.

CHRONIC DIFFICULTIES IN ATTACHMENT

Shyness, especially public shyness, is relatively easy to recognize. Shy people appear to be nervous in social situations, they are often reluctant to speak or make eye contact, and they frequently succeed in making those around them anxious also. In addition, they are usually willing to report that they are unhappy with themselves and their social presentations. Such overt social anxiety is unambiguous, but it may be just one possible manifestation of a consistent difficulty in forming interpersonal attachments.

Bowlby (1969, 1973, 1977, 1980) is the best known proponent of attachment theory and its implications for psychopathology. His portrait of "anxiously attached" individuals bears a strong resemblance to our everyday stereotypes of shy people. Shy people are insecure about relationships with others, inhibited in attempting to establish them, and often excessively dependent and clinging once a bond is formed. They have serious doubts about the stability of any relationship, anticipating that rejection and loss are inevitable. They assume that they are worth little in the eyes of others. Bowlby has described the kinds of "pathogenic parenting" that such persons have sometimes received and that promotes fears of loss, separation, and abandonment.

Bowlby's thinking is of interest in the present context because he points out that anxious attachment (e.g., shyness) is only one of the possible manifestations of chronic difficulty in attachment. Other patterns include:

1. Compulsive self-reliance. Such persons appear to be quite self-sufficient, perhaps excessively so, but this self-reliance serves defensive purposes. These are individuals who are

> deeply distrustful of close relationships and terrified of allowing themselves to rely on anyone else, in some cases in order to avoid the pain of being rejected and in others to avoid being subjected to pressure to become someone else's caretaker. (Bowlby, 1977, p. 207)

In the latter case, a review of childhood experience often reveals a person forced into the role of "parental child," a role that reverses the usual attachment relationship by requiring that the child nurture the parent rather than vice versa.

2. Compulsive care giving. Some individuals can become attached only in the role of caring for others. Again, this may have been a pattern fostered in their own families of origin, but having become a winning game it then generalizes to all relationships. Such persons actively foster dependency in others (or seek out dependent partners). Such behavior defends against the possibility of abandonment, but it also creates resentment at times about the amount that one is doing for others while receiving so little in return (the "martyr complex"). Ironically, when the opportunity to be cared for does appear, such persons often refuse to acknowledge or to satisfy their own dependency needs.

3. Emotional detachment. Some people are unable to establish any satisfying emotional exchange with others. They frequently appear to be unmoved by affect (either positive or negative) that others regard as important. If their behavior is self-centered, manipulative, or exploitative (with a notable absence of remorse or concern for others), they are likely to be labeled "sociopathic." In other cases, when such persons appear to be aloof, remote, and withdrawn, they are more likely to be called "schizoid."

If one accepts that such different phenotypes are the expression of a similar genotypic disturbance, then several consequences follow. First, in assessing shyness, it is also necessary to determine the extent to which these other tendencies also exist, as a measure of the breadth and severity of attachment problems. Second, shy people are often attracted to those who appear, at first, to be socially confident and self-reliant or those who promise to take care of them in some way. Such relationships can be painful and disappointing when the original perception of the partner changes. One often leaves such relationships wondering what happened—"he seemed so different at first, but then when I got to know him better. . . . " An understanding of the nature of compulsive self-reliance and compulsive care giving makes it possible to appreciate that one's partner may also have been struggling with problems of intimacy and attachment and that neither person had the emotional resources to allow the relationship to grow. Third, to the extent that all these patterns are similar etiologically and dynamically, one can predict that they will respond to the same treatments. Although we have only anecdotal evidence in this regard, it is plausible that a particularly effective psychotherapy group might consist not only of shy people, but also of patients with other chronic difficulties in attachment. Such a group would allow all participants to recognize the covert similarities that underlie their apparent differences.

REFERENCES

Andrews, G., & Harvey, R. (1981). Does psychotherapy benefit neurotic patients? *Archives of General Psychiatry, 38,* 1203–1208.

Arkowitz, H. (1977). The measurement and modification of minimal dating behavior. In M. Hersen, R. M. Eisler, & P. M. Miller (Eds.), *Progress in behavior modification, Vol. 5* (pp. 1–61). New York: Academic Press.

Bowlby, J. (1969). *Attachment and loss, Vol. 1: Attachment.* New York: Basic Books.

Bowlby, J. (1973). *Attachment and loss, Vol. 2: Separation: Anxiety and anger.* New York: Basic Books.

Bowlby, J. (1977). The making and breaking of affectional bonds: I. Aetiology and psychopathology in the light of attachment theory. *British Journal of Psychiatry, 130,* 201–210.

Bowlby, J. (1980). *Attachment and loss, Vol. 3: Loss: Sadness and depression.* New York: Basic Books.

Curran, J. P. (1977). Skills training as an approach to the treatment of heterosexual-social anxiety: A review. *Psychological Bulletin, 84,* 140–157.

Falloon, I. R. H., Lindley, P., McDonald, R., & Marks, I. M. (1977). Social skills training of outpatient groups: A controlled study of rehearsal and homework. *British Journal of Psychiatry, 131,* 599–609.

Hargreaves, W. A., Showstack, J., Flohr, A., Brady, C., & Harris, S. (1974). Treatment acceptance following intake assignment to individual therapy, group therapy, or contact group. *Archives of General Psychiatry, 31,* 343–349.

Imber, S. D., Lewis, P. M., & Loiselle, R. H. (1979). Uses and abuses of the brief intervention group. *International Journal of Group Psychotherapy, 29,* 39–49.

Krueger, D. W. (1979). Clinical considerations in the prescription of group, brief, long-term, and couples psychotherapy. *Psychiatric Quarterly, 51,* 92–105.

Landman, J. T., & Dawes, R. M. (1982). Psychotherapy outcome. *American Psychologist, 37,* 504–516.

Lewis, P., Cheney, T., & Dawes, A. S. (1977). Locus of control of interpersonal relationships questionnaire. *Psychological Reports, 41,* 507–510.

Linehan, M. M., Walker, R. O., Bronheim, S., Haynes, K. F., & Yevzeroff, H. (1979). Group versus individual assertion training. *Journal of Consulting and Clinical Psychology, 47,* 1000–1002.

Luborsky, L., Singer, B., & Luborsky, L. (1975). Comparative studies of psychotherapies: Is it true that "everyone has won and all must have prizes"? *Archives of General Psychiatry, 32,* 995–1008.

Malan, D. (1976). *The frontier of brief psychotherapy.* New York: Plenum Press.

Malan, D. H., Balfour, F. H. G., Hood, V. G., & Shooter, A. M. N. (1976). Group psychotherapy: A long-term follow-up study. *Archives of General Psychiatry, 33,* 1303–1315.

Mann, J. (1973). *Time-limited psychotherapy.* Cambridge, MA: Harvard University Press.

Marzillier, J. S. Outcome studies of skills training: A review. In P. E. Trower, B. M. Bryant, & M. Argyle (Eds.), *Social skills and mental health* (pp. 103–130). Pittsburgh, PA: University of Pittsburgh Press.

Monti, P. M., Fink, E., Norman, W., Curran, J., Hayes, S., & Caldwell, A. (1979). Effect of social skills training groups and social skills bibliotherapy with psychiatric patients. *Journal of Consulting and Clinical Psychology, 47,* 189–191.

Monti, P. M., Curran, J. P., Corriveau, D. P., Delancey, A. L., & Hagerman, S. M. (1980). Effects of social skills training groups and sensitivity training groups with psychiatric patients. *Journal of Consulting and Clinical Psychology, 48,* 241–248.

Pilkonis, P. A. (1977). Shyness, public and private, and its relationship to other measures of social behavior. *Journal of Personality, 45,* 585–595.

Pilkonis, P.A., Imber, S. D., Lewis, P., & Rubinsky, P. (1984). A comparative outcome study of individual, group, and conjoint psychotherapy. *Archives of General Psychiatry, 41,* 431–437.

Royce, W. S., & Arkowitz, H. (1978). Multimodal evaluation of practice interactions as treatment for social isolation. *Journal of Consulting and Clinical Psychology, 46,* 239–245.

Shapiro, D. A., & Shapiro, D. (1982). Meta-analysis of comparative therapy outcome studies: A replication and refinement. *Psychological Bulletin, 92,* 581–604.

Sifneos, P. (1972). *Short-term psychotherapy and emotional crisis.* Cambridge, MA: Harvard University Press.

Smith, M. L., Glass, G. V., & Miller, T. I. (1980). *The benefits of psychotherapy.* Baltimore: The Johns Hopkins University Press.

Twentyman, C.T., & Zimering, R. T. Behavioral training of social skills: A critical review. In M. Hersen, R. M. Eisler, & P. M. Miller (Eds.), *Progress in behavior modification, Vol. 7* (pp. 319–400). New York: Academic Press.

Watson, D., & Friend, R. (1969). Measurement of social-evaluative anxiety. *Journal of Consulting and Clinical Psychology, 33,* 448–457.

Weick, K. E. (1984). Small wins: Redefining the scale of social problems. *American Psychologist, 39,* 40–49.

Weiss, R. S. (1974). The provisions of social relationships. In Z. Rubin (Ed.), *Doing unto others* (pp. 17–26). Englewood Cliffs, NJ: Prentice-Hall.

Wolfe, J. L., & Fodor, I. G. (1977). Modifying assertive behavior in women: A comparison of three approaches. *Behavior Therapy, 8,* 567–574.

Yardley, K. M. (1979). Social skills training—A critique. *British Journal of Medical Psychology, 52,* 55–62.

Author Index

Subject Index